Evolutionary Epistemology, Rationality, and the Sociology of Knowledge

Evolutionary Epistemology, Rationality, and the Sociology ══════ of Knowledge ══════

Edited by
Gerard Radnitzky and W. W. Bartley, III

With contributions by
Sir Karl Popper, Donald T. Campbell, W. W. Bartley, III,
Günter Wächtershäuser, Rosaria Egidi, Gerhard Vollmer,
John F. Post, John Watkins, Gerard Radnitzky,
Peter Munz, and Antony Flew

Open  Court

La Salle, Illinois

First printing 1987.
Second printing 1988.

Printed and bound in the United States of America.

Library of Congress Cataloging-in-Publication Data

Evolutionary epistemology, rationality, and the
    sociology of knowledge.

    Includes bibliographies and index.
    1. Knowledge, Theory of.   2. Knowledge, Sociology of.
3. Evolution–Philosophy.   4. Biology–Philosophy
5. Physics–Philosophy.   I. Radnitzky, Gerard.
II. Bartley, William Warren, 1934–   .   III. Popper,
Karl Raimund, Sir, 1902–   .
BD161.E86   121   86-23589
ISBN 0-8126-9038-9
ISBN 0-8126-9039-7 (pbk.)

To Hans Albert

Contents

Introduction
By the Editors

1. This Volume and Its Origins

This volume presents some important developments in the theories of knowledge and rationality, and shows their close connection with biological theory and method, and – in particular – with the theory of evolution. It also explores some of the extensive ramifications of these developments for traditional, and most current, epistemology and philosophy of physics, and also for the sociology of knowledge.

The volume has, for the most part, gradually grown from a series of conversations and meetings, as well as extensive correspondence, among those who have contributed to it. In a sense, our discussions about evolutionary epistemology and the theory of rationality began two decades ago, but the initial talks that shaped most of this particular volume probably occurred at the Austrian College, in Alpbach, Tyrol, in the late summer of August 1982, when Popper, Wächtershäuser, Radnitzky, Bartley, and our friend Hans Albert, the scientific director of the Alpbach conference (to whom this volume is dedicated), met for discussion almost every afternoon in the great lounge of the Böglerhof Hotel, together with some other friends and colleagues such as Junichi Aomi and Angelo Petroni. Our discussions were sparked by an address on evolutionary theory and epistemology with which Popper had opened the first plenary session at Alpbach that year. In the following months, some of us had further opportunities to meet and debate these problems. Radnitzky, Egidi, Vollmer, and Bartley attended the symposium on evolutionary epistemology at the Seventh Wittgenstein Symposium, in Kirchberg; Wächtershäuser, Campbell, Vollmer, Munz, Post, Watkins, Radnitzky, Flew, and Bartley met in New York City in November 1982, at the convocation of the Open Society and Its Friends, a meeting devoted largely to evolutionary epistemology. Bartley, Egidi, Vollmer, Munz, Post, Watkins, Radnitzky, and Flew met again a few days later in Philadelphia at the International Conference on the Unity of the Sciences, where there were sessions both on evolutionary epistemology and on theory of rationality. Some of us – Popper, Bartley, Radnitzky, Watkins – met at a conference in Turin sponsored by Angelo Petroni and his colleagues at the Institute for Methodology and Philosophy of Science in January 1983; Bartley, Radnitzky, Vollmer, and Popper were in Vienna in May of 1983 for the conference celebrating Popper's 80th birthday; Popper, Munz, and Wächtershäuser were in Alpbach again in August 1984; and Popper, Campbell, Radnitzky, and Bartley met again in November 1984 at a conference on Popper's philosophy sponsored by the University of Madrid. Meanwhile there were many other smaller meetings among the various participants. And the final work on the volume was done, again in Alpbach, in August 1985, by Bartley, Radnitzky, and Wächtershäuser.

Eleven of the chapters in this volume – or drafts or sections of them, in one form or another – were first presented in one or more of these meetings. To these we have added six earlier essays – Popper's Darwin Lecture, two of Donald Campbell's pioneering essays in evolutionary epistemology, Popper's reply to Campbell, and two of John Post's early essays on problems of self-reference in critical rationalism – to provide background and context for the book as a whole. We wish to thank the various sponsors of these conferences, as well as the other participants, for the opportunities they gave us to meet and to develop our ideas. These meetings provided some of the first international platforms for the presentation and examination of evolutionary epistemology, as well as the first public debate on alleged semantic paradoxes within the theory of rationality.

2. *This Volume and Its Parts*

Part of the excitement of our discussions lay in our increasing appreciation of the interconnections among three areas that are usually treated quite separately, and which are now the focus of the three parts of this volume.

The first such area is evolutionary epistemology itself. Evolutionary epistemology – which stands in sharp contrast to most traditional approaches – treats knowledge and knowledge-processes as objective evolutionary products, to be compared and contrasted with other such products. Although charted in the nineteenth century, it was neglected for decades, but has now been revived and developed in differing but closely overlapping ways by Sir Karl Popper, Konrad Lorenz, F. A. Hayek, and Donald T. Campbell.

Evolutionary epistemology is not a mere application of evolutionary theory to the theory of knowledge, but has led to an investigation of the situational logic underlying the evolutionary process. In a remarkable case of congruence, the situational logic underlying evolutionary processes proves to coincide fundamentally with the nonjustificational account of criticism and rationality. This means that, whereas nonjustificational accounts of rationality and the growth of knowledge are Darwinian, most traditional and contemporary accounts of rationality and knowledge remain Lamarckian. This is a startling result, with grave implications for epistemology as it is usually taught and investigated.

This is only one of numerous connections between the three parts of the volume – Part I being devoted to evolutionary epistemology, or theory of knowledge; and Parts II and III being devoted to the theory of rationality and the sociology of knowledge. In fact, the theories of knowledge and rationality are connected in this discussion in a variety of ways. Historically, they have been connected, as it were, mainly through alleged conflicts between them. Thus an apparent conflict between knowledge and rationality may appear when it is found – as by Hume, Kant, and many other epistemologists – that according to one's theory of rationality, knowledge is impossible; or that according to one's theory of knowledge, rationality is impossible. Such conflicts are in turn sometimes occasioned by the existence of a conflict within the theory of rationality itself – a conflict that appears when it is discovered that, according to one's theory of rationality, rationality is impossible.

Just such allegations of multiple conflict are the center of attention in Parts II and III of the book, both of which explore the limits of rationality. Part II examines the claim that the nonjustificational approach – which is argued in Part I to underlie natural selection, and which has also been used to rebut relativist and sceptical challenges to reason – is nonetheless intrinsically paradoxical. In Part III, a second, related claim – which stems from determinism and reductionism – is considered. According to this claim, associated with the sociology and psychology of knowledge, the *apparent* products of reason are in fact only expressions of the natural circumstances – whether social, physiological, psychosexual, economic, or otherwise – of the societies or individuals whence they spring. This alleged limitation on rationality is, in turn, closely linked to the first, in that deterministic explanations are often used to account, relativistically, for conflicting "ultimate" ideological presuppositions in different groups. The contributors to Part III attempt to identify some of the basic philosophical and scientific objections to such attempts to use the theory of human reason to explain human reason away. In particular, they use some of the results of evolutionary epistemology to rebut contemporary sociology and psychology of knowledge.

The book as a whole is an example of the continuing attempt to attain a theory of knowledge and a theory of rationality that are in basic harmony.

Stanford, California, and Trier, West Germany
April 1986

Part I

Evolutionary Epistemology

Philosophy of Biology versus Philosophy of Physics

By W. W. Bartley, III

> *He who understands a baboon would do more toward metaphysics than Locke.*
> — *Charles Darwin*

1. *Philosophy of Biology* versus *Philosophy of Physics*

Not long ago I witnessed a remarkable interchange between Sir Karl Popper and the cosmologist and physicist John Archibald Wheeler. Popper and Wheeler were meeting with a dozen other philosophers and scientists at Schloss Kronberg, the Victorian castle built by Kaiser Wilhelm's mother outside Frankfurt during the closing years of the nineteenth century. The group was gathered in the late afternoon at an enormous round table in the Grand Salon, and Wheeler had just delivered a brilliant exposition of his interpretation of quantum mechanics. Popper turned to him and quietly said: "What you say is contradicted by biology." It was a dramatic moment. A hush fell around the table. The physicists present appeared to be taken aback. And then the biologists, including Sir Peter Medawar, the Nobel prizewinner who was chairing the meeting, broke into a delighted applause. It was as if someone had finally said what they had been thinking.[1]

No one present meant to suggest that the reported facts of physics and biology were in conflict – nor even that physical and biological *theory* conflicted. Rather, it was meant that Wheeler's *interpretation* (or philosophy) of physics was incompatible with fact and interpretation in the life sciences. Behind Popper's remark, unstated on this occasion yet lending it bite, was yet another contention: *that the interpretation of physics that had been presented did not apply to physics either.*

2. *Philosophy of Physics* versus *Biology*

Philosophy of science in the twentieth century has until recently been dominated both by physics and by a particular interpretation of physics.

---

1. The papers and conversations of this conference have now been published, in somewhat edited form. See Peter Medawar and Julian Shelley, eds., *Structure in Science and Art* (Amsterdam-Oxford-Princeton: Excerpta Medica, 1980).

Some biologists have noticed and complained about this. Thus, in a splendid short essay, Ernst Mayr wryly remarked:

> I have some five or six volumes on my book shelves which include the misleading words "philosophy of science" in their title. In actual fact each of these volumes is a philosophy of physics, many physicist-philosophers naively assuming that what applies to physics will apply to any branch of science. Unfortunately, many of the generalizations made in such philosophies of physics are irrelevant when applied to biology. More important, many of the generalizations derived from the physical sciences, and made the basis for a philosophy of science, are simply not true for biological phenomena. Finally, many phenomena and findings of the biological sciences have no equivalent in the physical sciences and are therefore omitted from philosophies of science that are based on physics.[2]

But it is the domination of all discussion, in physics, biology, and elsewhere, by a particular *interpretation* of science that causes most difficulties.[3] This aspect of the problem Mayr failed to pick up: while he notes that the philosophical accounts of physics *do not apply to, are irrelevant to, are not true of, and have no equivalent in* biology, he does not see, or at any rate does not say, that biological theory and fact *conflict with* these philosophical interpretations of science stemming from physics. It is this stronger claim that is implicit in Popper's challenge to Wheeler, and which is also the contention of this chapter. To be explicit, there are two separate and conflicting philosophical interpretations of science, and – lying behind them – two separate cosmologies. One dominates in physics and in philosophy of physics; the other is more common in biology and philosophy of biology. Both interpretations claim to apply to all of science.

3. Leading Themes of the Dominant Philosophy of Physics

What is this interpretation of science that dominates physics? And what are the facts and theories, and what the interpretation, of biology that conflict with it?

To answer these questions fully would take more space than the compass of this chapter permits. For the philosophical interpretation commonly associated with physics is not a single clearly defined perspective, but arises in hundreds of variations. Its main components are leading or recurring *themes* woven into as many individual philosophies as there are philosophers of physics; and which

2. Ernst Mayr, "Discussion: Footnotes on the Philosophy of Biology", *Philosophy of Science* 36, 1949, pp. 197–202. See also Gerhard Vollmer, in his report of Rupert Riedl in *Allgemeine Zeitschrift für Philosophie*, 1982.

3. Note that I indicate here that this interpretation of physics is *also* widely accepted *within* biology, by biologists. As one example, out of very many, see Theodosius Dobzhansky, "Chance and Creativity in Evolution", in F. J. Ayala and T. Dobzhansky, eds., *Studies in the Philosophy of Biology: Reduction and Related Problems* (Berkeley: University of California Press, 1974), pp. 307–38. In this essay Dobzhansky presupposes a subjective interpretation of probability and a metaphysical determinism which conflict with the Popperian framework on which, I believe, a sound evolutionary epistemology must be built. See K. R. Popper, *Quantum Theory and the Schism in Physics*, vol. III of his *Postscript to the Logic of Scientific Discovery*.

themes may indeed, individually, vanish altogether in some variations. Nonetheless, these persistent themes do lend it a great measure of unity.

Some of these leading themes are phenomenalism, operationalism, reductionism, instrumentalism, determinism, inductivism, positivism, justificationism, and the subjectivist interpretation of the calculus of probability.

As hinted earlier, when I suggest that these themes are dominant within the philosophy of physics, I do not intend to imply that they are even correct within physics. Quite the contrary, I reject each of the "isms" I have named, disputing their role in physics just as much as in biology. Like Popper and other evolutionary epistemologists, I am realist, indeterminist, deductivist, anti-instrumentalist, anti-positivist, and anti-justificationist, and also advocate objective interpretations of probability.

I shall not rehearse here the old arguments on all these themes, but rather will focus on a single one of them, phenomenalism, and will indicate how deeply it is opposed by the experience of the life sciences – in fact, theory, and interpretation. To make my case I shall highlight the contrast between the phenomenalist or presentationalist interpretation, as represented for example by Ernst Mach and those whom he has influenced, and, on the other hand, the position of the evolutionary epistemologists as represented by Popper, Hayek, Campbell, and Lorenz.

4. Mach's Philosophy of Physics: Presentationalism

The interpretation at issue – having to do with the subject matter and purpose, the scope and limitations, the justification and degree of certainty, of the sciences – is rooted in eighteenth-century British empiricism, especially in the thought of Bishop Berkeley and David Hume. But it reached its classic and most influential statement in the work of the great Austrian physicist Ernst Mach (1838–1916).

To understand Machian philosophy of physics one must set aside one's commonsense notions. Indeed, Machian philosophy can be seen as a sophisticated *critique of common sense*. Thus Gregory Bateson begins his lecture on "Pathologies of Epistemology" as follows:

> Let me ask you for a show of hands. How many of you will agree that *you see me?* I see a number of hands – so I guess insanity loves company. Of course, you don't "really" see *me*. What you "see" is a bunch of pieces of information . . . which you synthesize into a picture image . . . It's that simple.[4]

4. Gregory Bateson, *Steps to an Ecology of Mind* (New York: Ballantine Books, 1972), p. 478. Elsewhere in his work Bateson often seems to be a representationalist (see below). Presentationalism (see below) has so clouded these issues, and has so deeply influenced all discussion of them, that it is often hard to tell what a particular writer's position *really* is, since it oscillates in a characteristic way. See John. T. Blackmore's enlightening essay: "On the Inverted Use of the Terms 'Realism' and 'Idealism' Among Scientists and Historians of Science", *British Journal for the Philosophy of Science* 30, 1979, pp. 125–34. See also Blackmore's discussion of the inverted use of these terms by Helmholtz and Schlick in *Annals of Science* 35, 1978, pp. 427–31. Compare Popper, *Objective Knowledge* (London: Oxford University Press, 1972), pp. 64–5.

Machian philosophy, like most of the schools of thought that it has influenced, such as logical positivism, enjoys talk and examples like this. It is *presentationalist*, as opposed to *representationalist*, to borrow William Hamilton's useful terms, recently revived by John Blackmore.[5]

Representationalism, the opposing, commonsense position which Bateson appears to criticize in our example, and which is rejected outright by Machian philosophy, is also the position of many of the founders of the western scientific tradition – including Galileo, Boyle, and Newton. As Newton wrote: "In philosophical disquisitions we ought to abstract from our senses and consider things themselves, distinct from what are only sensible measures of them."[6] Such representationalism, focusing on things themselves rather than on appearances, maintains that the members of Bateson's audience – at least those that had vision – *did* see Bateson (at least if he was there). Representationalism maintains that the *subject matter* of science (and of seeing) is the external world *as it is*, independently of human (or animal) perceptions and descriptions of it. The *aim* of science, for a representationalist, is to attain increasingly accurate accounts of this world in language. To accomplish this, one *uses* sense perceptions as aids; and these sense perceptions or sensations are themselves only more or less accurate symbolic representations of external reality formed through the interaction between that external reality and organs of sense. One sees external reality, more or less accurately, with the aid of imperfect sense impressions. If one needs eyeglasses, they are to see Bateson more accurately by correcting one's retinal image of Bateson. This is not to deny that there may be sensations without benefit of external reality: but when this happens one is not seeing; one is hallucinating, or experiencing an optical illusion or some such. Nor is this to deny that there may be many aspects of reality which are quite beyond the capacities of our perceptual apparatus to register, let alone to represent.

Presentationalism or phenomenalism rejects all this. Presentationalist critiques of representationalism are in no sense new, in no sense dependent on the findings of contemporary physics. They existed long before Mach, and even before Berkeley and Hume. One famous early statement of it came from Galileo's adversary, Robert Cardinal Bellarmino, who contested Galileo's representationalist interpretation of Copernican astronomy. The role of science – and of Copernican astronomy – Bellarmino maintained, was "to give a better account of the *appearances*".[7] It was the role of the Church, not of science, to pronounce on the real

5. See Blackmore, "On the Inverted Use of the Terms 'Realism' and 'Idealism' among Scientists and Historians of Science", *op. cit.*; see also his *Ernst Mach: His Work, Life, and Influence* (Berkeley: University of California Press, 1972). On Mach see Popper, "A Note on Berkeley as Precursor of Mach and Einstein", in *Conjectures and Refutations*, pp. 166–74; John Myhill, "Berkeley's 'De Motu': An Anticipation of Mach", *University of California Publications in Philosophy* 29, 1957, pp. 141–57; see also Gerard Hinrich, "The Logical Positivism of *De Motu*", *Review of Metaphysics* 3, 1950. See also Joseph Agassi, "Sensationalism", in *Science in Flux* (Boston: D. Reidel, 1975), pp. 92–126, and his "The Future of Berkeley's Instrumentalism", *International Studies in Philosophy* 8, 1975, pp. 167–78.
6. Isaac Newton, "Absolute and Relative Space, Time, and Motion", *Philosophy of Science*, ed., Arthur Danto and Sidney Morgenbesser, eds. (Cleveland: Meridian Books, 1964), p. 325.
7. See *Le Opere di Galileo Galilei, XII* (Firenze: Barbera, 1902), Item 1110*, pp. 171–72.

nature of the world. The role of science should be only to provide *instruments* to link together, in a simpler or more efficient way, the appearances, the presentations of our senses. Science should not attempt to go beyond presentations to penetrate the nature of reality: it should *confine* itself to the apparent.

Such a view of science has been widely rejected, in Galileo's time and after, as a self-serving proposal on the part of the Roman Catholic Church – as a way for it to insulate its own doctrine about reality against challenge from science. Similar objections were raised against the presentationalist stands of the Anglican Bishop Berkeley (in the eighteenth century) and of the Roman Catholic physicist Pierre Duhem (in the twentieth century). Although he thought of himself as a kind of Buddhist, no such ulterior motive can be readily ascribed to Ernst Mach: he was strongly anti-clerical, and he did not for a moment suppose that some other discipline – such as religion or metaphysics – gave access to a real world beyond sense perception. The restrictions that he placed on science, and on knowing, were made not for religious but for epistemological reasons. "Colors, space, tones, etc. These are the only realities", Mach had written in his daybook.[8] In his book *The Analysis of Sensations*, he only slightly qualified this pronouncement, writing: "colors, sounds, spaces, times, . . . are provisionally the ultimate elements, whose given connexion it is our business to investigate. It is precisely in this that the exploration of reality consists."[9] For Ernst Mach sense perception was all there was for anyone: "Nature", he said, "is composed of sensations". *To be was to be perceived.*

In sum, presentationalists see the subject matter of science not as an external reality independent of sensation. The subject matter of science is our sensory perceptions. The collectivity of these sensations is renamed "nature" (thus rendering the account idealist in fact – whatever it may happen to be called[10]). The aim of science is seen not as the description and explanation of that independent external reality but as the efficient computation of perceptions.

5. *Presuppositions of Presentationalism*

What explains the appeal of presentationalism to contemporary physicists and philosophers of physics?[11] Part of its appeal no doubt consists just in the fact that, being contrary to common sense, it enjoys the possibility of being sophisticated. Thus one acquires philosophical depth by noticing that everything in the world is surface. There is, moreover, an apparent spareness and austerity in the ostentatious superficiality of this philosophy.

8. See H. Dingler, *Die Grundgedanken der Machschen Philosophie*, p. 98.
9. Ernst Mach, *The Analysis of Sensations* (New York: Dover, 1959), pp. 29-30.
10. See Blackmore: "On the Inverted Use . . . ", *op. cit.*
11. I shall not discuss here the many possible irrational sources of such a philosophy. In some cases, however, this might be a profitable pursuit. Thus Blackmore suggests that Mach's phenomenalism, his restriction of science to the ordering and assimilating of sense experiences, may be related to his reported difficulties, beginning in childhood, with visual perspective, and with shading in paintings.

More seriously, one would have to discuss two matters in any adequate explanation of the hold that presentationalism exerts on contemporary physics and philosophy of physics. The first would be the history of twentieth-century physics, particularly of quantum physics, and I shall turn to this very briefly in the next two sections.[12]

A second force holding presentationalism in place is the logical effect of certain philosophical and methodological assumptions. Presentationalist philosophers find themselves trapped in a web woven of such assumptions. Preoccupied with the avoidance of error, they suppose that, in order to avoid error, they must make no utterances that cannot be justified by – i.e., derived from – the evidence available. Yet sense perception seems to be the only available evidence; and sense perception is insufficiently strong, logically, to justify any claim about the existence of the external world, or about the laws and entities of science, such as atoms and forces.[13] The claim that there is an external world *in addition* to the evidence is a claim going *beyond* the evidence. Hence, claims about such realms are unjustifiable. Worse, many presentationalists argue that they are intrinsically faulty: they are not genuine but pseudo-claims; they are indeed *meaningless*. For a word to have meaning, they say, it must stand for an idea: that is, for a perception or for a memory of a perception. Since there can be no perception of any reality *beyond* perception, there can be no idea of it, and hence no meaningful language "about" it. The quotation marks just used mark the scope and limitations of science as understood by presentationalists. Thus Mach denied the existence of any external world, and the existence of atoms,[14] forces, and mass. Later he denied Einstein's special theory of relativity, in which Einstein had contended that the velocity of light in a vacuum is independent of other phenomena, contrary to Mach's dictum that all sensations are dependent on all other sensations.[15]

Crucial to the presentationalist argument are, then, two things: the desire to give a firm foundation or justification to the tenets of science, and the construal

12. See also my "The Philosophy of Karl Popper. Part II: Consciousness and Physics", *Philosophia*, Israel 7, 3-4, July 1978, pp. 675-716; and Popper's *Quantum Theory and the Schism in Physics*.

13. See my *The Retreat to Commitment*, 2nd edition, revised and enlarged (La Salle and London: Open Court, 1984), Appendix 2.

14. Except for a brief period at the beginning of his career: see Erwin N. Hiebert's account, "The Genesis of Mach's Early Views on Atomism", p. 79; and Hiebert's article on Mach in the *Dictionary of Scientific Biography*, p. 596. See Mach's own comments on this early period in his *Die Geschichte und Wurzel des Satzes von der Erhaltung der Energie* (Leipzig, 1909), pp. 68-88; and *Space and Geometry in the Light of Physiological, Psychological and Physical Inquiry* (Open Court, 1906), pp. 138-39. See also Wolfram Swoboda's review of Blackmore in *Studies in History and Philosophy of Science* 5, 1974, pp. 187-201, esp. p. 191.

15. The issues between Mach and Einstein are now often interpreted in Mach's favor by presentationalist relativity theorists of the present day. See C. W. Misner, K. S. Thorne, and J. A. Wheeler, *Gravitation* (San Francisco: W. H. Freeman, 1973), esp. pp. 543-49; and R. H. Dicke: "Mach's Principle", in John R. Klauder, ed., *Magic Without Magic: John Archibald Wheeler*, (San Francisco: W. H. Freeman and Co., 1972), pp. 297-308; R. H. Dicke: *The Theoretical Significance of Experimental Relativity* (London: Gordon and Breach, 1964), esp. pp. vii-viii.

of sense experience as the incorrigible source of all knowledge. (An incorrigible or certain source – i.e., a source that does not need to be justified – appears to be needed, since otherwise there could be no justification in terms of it: to the extent that the source can be challenged, the foundation is infirm.) The doctrine about "meaningfulness" is also commonly associated with presentationalism, although probably not essential to it.

One way to escape the presentationalist trap is to give up the aim of justifying one's knowledge. This possibility is the focus of discussion in the second part of this book.[16] Another way – also correct – is to abandon the claim that sense observation is the source of all knowledge. Presentationalists considered and rejected the second route; they did not even consider the first. Instead, they gave up the external world and its furniture, as well as the descriptive import of the laws of science. Thus they restrict the attention of science to sense presentations, and must construe scientific laws, so-called, as non-descriptive instruments for connecting such phenomena: for generating sense observations from sense observations.

6. The Scientific Background to Presentationalism: Philosophy of Physics versus Physics

It was chiefly this network of epistemological, logical, and methodological argument that led Mach and others into presentationalism. But some important scientific discussion also contributed. From 1860 until the 1910s, coinciding with the main part of Mach's scientific career, atomic theory was steadily gaining support within the sciences, and the story of its rise is intimately connected with presentationalism. After the virtual rediscovery, in 1860, of the old law that Avogadro (1776–1856) had published in 1811 (that equal volumes of gas contain equal numbers of molecules under the same conditions of pressure and temperature) many physicists attempted to explain thermodynamics in terms of atomic theory. One of the greatest to work in this area was Ludwig Boltzmann (1844–1906), Professor of Physics in the University of Vienna.

Mach and his students relentlessly opposed atomic theory and mechanistic explanation as metaphysical. They centered their attack on Boltzmann's work, exploiting one difficulty after another to win him to their cause. There was for instance a serious problem connected with entropy. The second law of thermodynamics asserts the existence of irreversible processes. Thus differences of density, temperature, and average velocity disappear, but do not arise, by themselves: entropy always increases. Yet it was difficult for atomic theory to explain processes

16. Just such a route was first suggested in my *The Retreat to Commitment*, in my "Rationality versus the Theory of Rationality", in Mario Bunge, ed., *The Critical Approach to Science and Philosophy*, (New York: The Free Press, 1964), and in my "The Philosophy of Karl Popper: Part III: Rationality, Criticism and Logic", *Philosophia* 11, 1–2, February 1982, pp. 121–221; see also Part II below.

of this sort: for in classical mechanics all motion is reversible.[17] Hence physicists such as Loschmidt could argue that heat and entropy simply *could not* involve *mechanical* motion of atoms and molecules. Boltzmann's work, by contrast (like Maxwell's in Britain), was directed to *explaining* entropy statistically in terms of atomic theory.

Mach and his students dismissed such efforts as arising from pseudo-problems and metaphysical excursions beyond the phenomena, arguing instead for a phenomenalist account of thermodynamics in which atoms and molecules do not appear. For a time, particularly during the 1890s, many scientists accepted phenomenalist thermodynamics. It seemed to have the merit of explaining the difficulties of atomism while providing an alternative in which such "metaphysical" entities as matter, substance, atom, and molecule do not figure.

The battle between these two approaches was fierce and rude. On the one hand, Robert Mayer claimed that Boltzmann's work was "of a piece with the efforts of the alchemists". On the other, the American philosopher C. S. Peirce ridiculed Mach's scientific work.[18] Warning of Mach's "very inaccurate reasoning", Peirce accused him of "making fact bend to theory", and charged that "Mach's sensationalism appears upon most important points quite at odds with the conclusions of science".

The issue was not decided until 1905, when scientific experiment went against Mach's views. At that time, with Einstein's work on Brownian movement, the physical import of atomic theory was corroborated.[19] Brownian movement, discovered by the English botanist Robert Brown in 1827, is the incessant irregular or "zigzag" motion of small particles in liquid suspension. As interpreted by Einstein, this became a visible demonstration of bombardment of the particles by the molecules of the liquid; the visible motion was exactly as would be predicted in the kinetic theory of gases. Einstein himself remarked that Brownian movement, in providing evidence of molecular action, falsified *the phenomenalist* ("phenomenological") *version* of the second law of thermodynamics propagated by Mach and his students. But Boltzmann also lost this battle. His own brilliant probabilistic derivation of the second law of thermodynamics from the kinetic

17. Many issues connected with this controversy remain unsettled. See Popper's series of papers relating to the matter: "Irreversibility: or Entropy since 1905", *British Journal for the Philosophy of Science* 8, 1957–58, pp. 151–55; "The Arrow of Time", *Nature*, 17 March 1956, p. 538; "Irreversibility and Mechanics", *Nature*, 18 August 1956, pp. 381–82; "Irreversible Processes in Physical Theory", *Nature*, 22 June 1957, pp. 1296–97; "Irreversible Processes in Physical Theory", *Nature*, 8 February 1958, pp. 402–403; "Time's Arrow and Entropy", *Nature*, 17 July 1965, pp. 233–234; "Time's Arrow and Feeding on Negentropy", *Nature*, 21 January 1967, p. 320; "Structural Information and the Arrow of Time", *Nature*, 15 April 1967, p. 32.

18. C. S. Peirce: *Collected Papers* (Cambridge: Harvard University Press, 1960), vol. II, p. 48, referring to Mach's *Die Mechanik*, Chapter 2, vi, 6 and 9. See also Peirce's unsigned review of *Die Mechanik* in *The Nation* 57, 1893.

19. See Einstein in *Annalen der Physik* 17, 1905, pp. 549–60; and 19, pp. 371–381. Published in translation in R. Fürth, ed., *Investigations on the Theory of the Brownian Movement* (London: Methuen, 1926).

theory, his "H-Theorem", was refuted by Zermelo, using a proof by Poincaré.[20]
The whole matter is further clouded in that Boltzmann, in his later years, under
pressure from Mach, compromised his representationalism and introduced subjective elements, particularly regarding time, into his scientific work.

Some Machians were sufficiently impressed by Einstein's interpretations of
Brownian movement to accept atomism. Mach himself brushed such objections
aside, and also emphatically rejected Einstein's relativity theory. He also virtually disregarded two other important blows to his position. The first came from
Max Planck who, beginning in 1908, launched a frontal attack on Mach's views,
blaming him and his presentationalist followers for the backwardness of physics.[21]
A second reversal came from the work of the psychologist and representationalist
philosopher at Würzburg, Oswald Külpe (1862–1915), the teacher of Koffka,
Köhler, and Bühler, the founders of Gestalt psychology. Whereas Mach and his
followers contended that sensations were certain and incorrigible, and that all
thought could be reduced to sensory, imaginal elements, Külpe showed that all
claims about sensations are fallible, and demonstrated the existence of "imageless
thought", thoughts that occur without any sensory or imaginal content.[22] So important were Külpe's arguments that John T. Blackmore, the biographer of Mach,
has written, "had they been sufficiently publicized, Külpe's criticisms might well
have mortally wounded if not Mach's philosophy at least his influence and much
of his reputation. . . . If there were 'imageless thoughts', . . . then Mach's onto-

20. See Popper's discussion in *Unended Quest* (La Salle: Open Court, 1976), pp. 156–62.

21. Max Planck, "Die Einheit des physikalischen Weltbildes", *Physikalische Zeitschrift* 10, 1909,
pp. 62–75; "Zur Machschen Theorie der physikalischen Erkenntnis: Eine Erwiderung", *Vierteljahr-
schrift für Wissenschaftliche Philosophie* 34, 1910, pp. 497–507; "Naturwissenschaft und reale Aussen-
welt", *Die Naturwissenschaften* 28, 1940, p. 779. The idea that Mach's influence seriously hindered
scientific progress has been challenged by a number of persons: see Thomas S. Kuhn: "The Halt
and the Blind: Philosophy and History of Science", *British Journal for the Philosophy of Science* 31,
1980, pp. 181–92; and Noretta Koertge's review of Gerald Holton's *The Scientific Imagination: Case
Studies*, in *The British Journal for the Philosophy of Science*, *op. cit.*, pp. 193–95. Blackmore has replied
in an unpublished manuscript: "A Reply to Kuhn and Koertge on the Influence of Mach's Positivism", which he has kindly allowed me to read.

22. On Gestalt psychology, imageless thought, and its impact on philosophy, see my "Theory
of Language and Philosophy of Science as Instruments of Educational Reform: Wittgenstein and Popper
as Austrian Schoolteachers", in *Methodological and Historical Essays in the Natural and Social Sciences*,
ed. R. S. Cohen and Marx Wartofsky (Boston: D. Reidel, 1974); and my *Wittgenstein*, new edition,
revised and enlarged (La Salle and London: Open Court, 1985). See also Richard Gregory's discussion in "The Confounded Eye", p. 52. As Walter B. Weimer has pointed out to me, it is possible
for presentationalism to form a reply to Külpe's argument – contending for instance that "thoughts"
are unreliable components of the mind, and that a "pure core" must be sought in experience, possibly even by phenomenological methods. The idea that there exists a pure core to experience, out
of which the world can be built, is of course like many other "purely existential statements"– e.g.,
"There exists a fountain of youth", or "There exists a philosopher's stone". These are unfalsifiable
metaphysical statements; but while the latter have played a constructive role in the history of exploration and of chemistry, the former seems to have no value other than as a dogma of primitive empiricist methodologies. On such metaphysical statements see J. W. N. Watkins, "Confirmable and Influential
Metaphysics", *Mind* 1958, pp. 345–47; and K. R. Popper, *Realism and the Aim of Science*. See also
Walter B. Weimer and David S. Palermo, "Paradigms and Normal Science in Psychology", *Science
Studies* 3, 1973, p. 241.

logical phenomenalism, monism, and psycho-physical parallelism were undermined."[23]

7. Presentationalism: Metaphysics Masquerading as Anti-Metaphysical Science

One might have expected presentationalism to collapse, shorn of scientific support both in physics and in psychology. Obsolete in physics, it was now attacked not only by Planck but also by Einstein, who had initially supported Mach. Einstein's considered view of the matter, which was not widely known, was stated only many years later, when he refused P. A. Schilpp's invitation to contribute to the volume celebrating the work of the presentationalist positivist philosopher Rudolf Carnap. Einstein wrote:

> I cannot accede to your request. For I have dealt with this slippery material only whenever my own problems made it absolutely necessary. . . . I would not be able to do justice to this swarm of incessantly twittering positivistic birdies. . . . *Entre nous* I think that the positivistic nag, which originally appeared so frisky, after the refinements which it had of necessity to undergo, has become a somewhat miserable skeleton and has become addicted to a fairly dried-up petty-foggery. In its youthful days it nourished itself on the weakness of its opponents. Now it has become respectable and finds itself in the difficult position of having to make a go of its existence under its own power, the poor thing.[24]

After 1905, if not before, Machian presentationalism was a *metaphysical* theory – metaphysical precisely in the sense that Mach himself had decried. Yet, despite the opposition of Planck, Einstein, and others, it now became not only "respectable" but more influential than ever. A now discredited "paradigm", it nonetheless continued to promote its old research program, became the dominant twentieth-century *philosophy* of physics, and no doubt was the governing interpretation in most of those textbooks of which Ernst Mayr complained.

This was done with the aid of some of the most important philosophers of the twentieth century – whose doctrines of justification and the authority of sense experience ultimately prevented them from settling on any alternative. Bertrand Russell in his middle period of "logical atomism", Ludwig Wittgenstein, A. J. Ayer, C. I. Lewis, and Rudolf Carnap, to name only a few, adopted presentationalist philosophies, at least for a time. The logical positivists, including Carnap, who formed their famous group around Moritz Schlick in Vienna – the "Vienna Circle" – named themselves the "Ernst Mach Society", even though not all were presentationalists. And with the mass exodus of philosophers of science from Austria and from Hitler's Germany immediately before the Second World War,

---

23. Blackmore, *op. cit.*, pp. 229–30.
24. Albert Einstein, letter to P. A. Schilpp, quoted by the latter in his "The Abdication of Philosophy", *Kant Studien* 51, 1959–60, pp. 490–91. Compare Einstein's letter to M. Besso of 13 May 1917, where Einstein refers to positivism and phenomenalism as "Mach's little horse".

phenomenalist, presentationalist philosophy of science – under various names: operationalism, positivism, instrumentalism, and so on – spread around the world, firmly establishing itself in the universities of the English-speaking countries, where it remains dominant today.[25]

It was not philosophers alone, however, who were responsible for the survival of presentationalism. For it was taken up by physicists themselves, and incorporated into twentieth-century microphysics – incorporated so deeply that it has become exceptionally difficult to disentangle the physics from the philosophy. There are three main routes on which phenomenalism and presentationalism have re-entered physics. There is, first, the so-called Copenhagen interpretation of quantum mechanics (as represented by Niels Bohr, Werner Heisenberg, and Wolfgang Pauli), including the doctrines of wave-particle duality and of the intrusion of the observer into physical results, and the resultant dissolution of the subject-object distinction. It is impossible simultaneously to *measure* both the position and the momentum of a particle; hence it is concluded by those who take this approach that it is meaningless to talk of the particle's simultaneously *having* both position and momentum. That is, it is meaningless to talk of existence independent of observation; and for all the same presentationalist reasons advanced by Mach. Secondly, there is the "subjectivist theory of entropy", as found in the work of Leo Szilard, according to which the entropy of a system increases with decrease in our information about it, and vice versa. Finally, there is the subjective theory of time, according to which the arrow of time is a subjective illusion. These three routes (all of which I believe to be wrong), and the re-entrenchment of presentationalism within physics, I have discussed elsewhere.[26]

8. The Challenge of Evolutionary Epistemology

This philosophy of science – which I have been calling presentationalism, and which I have, somewhat arbitrarily, attributed chiefly to Mach, although he was not the only important figure to develop it – is under a new and strong challenge

25. The passion with which some other philosophers have, however, repudiated this philosophy is, however, illustrated by Blackmore in his "On the Inverted Use . . . ", pp. 130–31: "few things are more ironic than for a self-styled 'empiricist' openly to repudiate philosophy, when he himself has unconsciously adopted the philosophical views of Comte, Mill, Mach, or Carnap and unconsciously repudiated the scientific *practice* of anti-positivists such as Lavoisier and Dalton in chemistry, Lyell and Darwin in biology, and Galileo, Newton, Planck, and Einstein in physics who *all* assumed the reality of a physical world *beyond* sensory appearances and who thought that the primary task of science was to understand that trans-empirical world (i.e., 'elements' and 'atoms' were not observable, geological and biological history are not observable, the real motion of the planets is not observable, and the absolute speed of light in a vacuum is a constant whether observable or not). In other words, 'anti-philosophical' empiricists are commonly the victims of the most *anti-scientific* of all philosophies, namely the positivism and subjective idealism of Berkeley and Hume, *who aimed above all else to restrict the scope and importance of science . . .* "

26. See my article on "Consciousness and Physics", as referred to in footnote 12 above. See also Popper's *Postscript*, whose volumes listed in the following section, and are available from (London: Hutchinson, 1982/3; Totowa: Rowman and Littlefield, 1982/3).

today, a two-pronged attack from both physics and biology.

It is challenged, first of all, as wholly inadequate to physics. This challenge comes chiefly from Popper. Although Popper's critique dates from the early thirties, it has continued to be ramified and developed, and reached its climax in 1982 and 1983 with the publication in three volumes of his *magnum opus*, the *Postscript to the Logic of Scientific Discovery* – that is, with *Quantum Theory and the Schism in Physics*; *The Open Universe*; and *Realism and the Aim of Science*. Another challenge comes from biologists and philosophers of biology, and has come to be known as "evolutionary epistemology". Here too, the challengers are led by Popper.

What is the bite behind the new approach?

Popper has found in biology and evolutionary theory, and particularly in the comparative study of animal and human cognition, a new argument for objectivism and realism – an argument against presentationalism and for representationalism. This new argument is strategically important in providing him with a line of defense for realism independent of his controversial critique of the subjectivist Copenhagen interpretation of quantum mechanics. (It may be mentioned in parenthesis that this new argument is also important to Popper in another way. While neither subjectivism nor idealism is an issue in contemporary biology, evolutionary theory has in the past been used to support relativism and historicism, and contributed to the strength of these positions in the nineteenth century. Thus Popper's new biologically based argument for objectivism and realism also relates to, and furthers, his longstanding battle against relativism and historicism.)

9. The Development of Popper's Thought

Popper's leading role as a philosopher of biology may seem surprising to those who know him chiefly as a philosopher of physics; for biology was hardly mentioned in his early work. To be sure, biology dominates his later work. It is the leading theme of his *Objective Knowledge: An Evolutionary Approach* (1972), and of *The Self and Its Brain* (1977), and also plays a major role in his intellectual autobiography, *Unended Quest* (1974). As I write this (1986), he has just developed an important new account of "active Darwinism". Moreover, his interest in biology and in evolutionary theory is of long standing. I recall one day in the spring of 1959, as we were walking through Hyde Park together, when he discussed, in the most animated and delightful way, the issues between Darwin and Lamarck, and the treatment Samuel Butler gave to evolution in *Erewhon*. It was, so he told me, a subject that had excited him since he was a youth.

Popper's *public* discussion of biology is, however, comparatively recent. It can be dated exactly to the afternoon of Tuesday, November 15, 1960. On that day, the members of his seminar had assembled as usual around the long table in the old seminar room on the fourth floor of the old building of the London School of Economics (now long dismantled to make way for the expansion of the Senior

Common Room). When Popper appeared, he announced that he would abandon the usual format and would read a new paper of his own. That paper, which spoke of "three worlds" and of biology, and gave qualified support to Hegel's theory of objective mind, took the members of the seminar off guard. The discussion that followed was more bewildered than heated; and Popper, usually the most persistent of men, did not pursue the matter that term. No member of his seminar could have predicted that they had just heard the first note in a new development in his thought. None of them had, themselves, more than marginal interest in biology. None of them – if asked to give a sketch of his ideas and development – would have mentioned biology. And Popper himself, in his early autobiographical sketches (for *British Philosophy in Mid-Century* and elsewhere), made virtually no mention of biology or its philosophy.

In the years since then, Popper has continued to develop his ideas on biology, drawing in large strokes, and has thereby generalized and unified his entire philosophy. Although the fundamental components of his philosophy of physics – developed in the twenties and thirties – have not been much affected by his turn to biology, their presentation has been transformed; they are explained and in minor ways corrected. Prior to 1960 the development of Popper's thought could have been presented in an incremental way: his new foundations for logic and his work in indeterminism in physics, his contributions to probability theory, all could be presented as elaborations of his early work on induction and demarcation. The new work in philosophy of biology, however, is more than incremental: it unifies the whole.

The way in which biology integrates his thought can be seen in his new formulation of the chief problem of epistemology: *"The main task of the theory of knowledge is to understand it as continuous with animal knowledge; and to understand also its discontinuity – if any – from animal knowledge."* [27]

This formulation contrasts with earlier statements by Popper. In *The Logic of Scientific Discovery* (p. 15), he had written: "The central problem of epistemology has always been and still is the problem of the growth of knowledge." Later in the same work (p. 51), he wrote that the "main problem of philosophy is the critical analysis of the appeal to the authority of experience". And in *Conjectures and Refutations*, he described the solution to the problem of demarcation between science and non-science as "the key to most of the fundamental problems of the philosophy of science" (p. 42).

Although Popper from time to time mentioned or alluded to animal knowledge in his earlier work, he did not give animal cognition an important, let alone the central, place among the problems of epistemology. Now it is in the forefront: epistemology is chiefly concerned with the continuities and discontinuities of human and animal knowledge; indeed it is to become a science of comparative cognitive apparatuses. Whereas in *The Logic of Scientific Discovery* (p.

27. K. R. Popper: "Replies to My Critics", in P. A. Schilpp, ed., *The Philosophy of Karl Popper* (La Salle: Open Court, 1974), p. 1061; and Chapter IV below.

15) Popper had maintained that the most effective way to study the growth of knowledge was to study the growth of the most advanced form of knowledge, physics, he now also turns to prehuman forms of knowledge and to evolution for examples of such growth.

These two forms of knowledge are, however, useful to the epistemologist in similar ways. Both scientific knowledge, as recorded in theories, and the biologically based cognitive structures of animals can be studied *objectively* as products. Both are objective structures, the first being an exosomatic development, the second being endosomatic. And both, so Popper maintains, are produced by the same Darwinian mechanism: the highest creative thought, just like animal adaptation, is the product of blind variation and selective retention – trial and error. The same process governs both biological emergence and the growth of knowledge in science. Scorning traditional approaches to knowledge that focus on the subjective interior experience of the cognizer or "knowing subject" – his beliefs and perceptions – Popper turns to the objective products of the cognitive process, viewing cognitive structures and scientific theories alike as knowledge achievements.[28]

Just as, for the earlier Popper, the philosopher compared the content of competing theories and estimated their "verisimilitude", for the later Popper the philosopher examines the entire range of cognitive structures found in the animal kingdom to compare the "fit" between organic system and environment. Thus Popper significantly generalizes his earlier approach: not only is our experience theory-impregnated; it is structure-impregnated as well.

10. The Evolutionary Epistemologists

Popper is joined in the development of evolutionary epistemology by two powerful supporters and collaborators: Konrad Lorenz, the Nobel prizewinning philosopher and ethologist, and Donald T. Campbell, the American psychologist. It is ironic that Popper and Lorenz should be joined in this particular way. Yet unresolved quarrels of yesterday have a way of re-emerging, and one such quarrel that is relevant to our discussion has reappeared through Popper's and Lorenz's contribution to evolutionary epistemology. Popper and Lorenz, who were boyhood friends in Altenberg, near Vienna, also were both students of the philosopher-psychologist Karl Bühler, who was, in turn, a disciple of Oswald Külpe, Mach's powerful and neglected antagonist. Not only is the issue between Mach and Külpe finally joined in the work of Popper and Lorenz; Popper also acclaims Boltzmann's work (although not his H-theorem), saying that he agrees

---

28. An extended use of the word "knowledge" is no doubt involved here. As Campbell sees it, what is meant is that "any process providing a stored program for organismic adaptation in external environments is included as a knowledge process, and any gain in the adequacy of such a program is regarded as a gain in knowledge". See Chapter III below.

with Boltzmann "more closely than with any other philosopher".[29] The connections, clearly, are manifold.

Evolutionary epistemology results from pursuing the ramifications of Popper's understanding of the fundamental task of epistemology. This task is, as Popper and his associates conceive it, to clarify and investigate the process by which knowledge grows. In this context, "knowledge" refers to the objective products of certain evolutionary processes, ranging from the endosomatic cognitive structures of men and animals to the most abstract scientific theories. The resulting epistemology – drawing from logic, methodology and physics, from psychology, and from physiology – amounts to a systematic development of, and vindication of, representationalism.

The logical and methodological arguments are due chiefly to Popper, as are those that are drawn from physics. The biological and physiological support and interpretation come in part from Popper, but also from Lorenz[30] and from such biologists as Sir John Eccles, Sir Peter Medawar, Ernst Mayr, and Jacques Monod.[31] The psychological work can be traced back to Külpe and Bühler, and is continued in the work of F. A. von Hayek (the Nobel-prizewinning economist, and an old friend and associate of Popper's, who is the author of an important but neglected work in psychology: *The Sensory Order*), as well as by Campbell.[32] Campbell has made a fuller, more consistent, and more adequate statement of the position than

29. Popper, *Unended Quest*, p. 156.

30. See Konrad Lorenz, *Behind the Mirror* (New York: Harcourt Brace Jovanovich, 1973); "Gestalt Perception as a Source of Scientific Knowledge", in *Studies in Animal and Human Behaviour* (London: Methuen & Co., Ltd., 1971), vol. II, pp. 281–322; also available in L. von Bertalanffy and A. Rapoport, eds., *General Systems, Yearbook of the Society for General Systems Research* 7, 1962, pp. 37–56, and in "Gestaltwahrnehmung als Quelle wissenschaftlicher Erkenntnis", *Zeitschrift für experimentelle und angewandte Psychologie* 6, 1959, pp. 118–65; Kant's Doctrine of the A Priori in the Light of Contemporary Biology" in L. von Bertalanffy and A. Rapoport, eds., *General Systems* 7, 1962, pp. 23–35; also available as "Kants Lehre vom apriorischen im Lichte gegenwärtiger Biologie", *Blätter für Deutsche Philosophie* 15, 1941, pp. 94–125. See also J. C. Eccles, *Facing Reality* (New York: Springer Verlag, 1970); *The Self and Its Brain* (with K. R. Popper) (New York: Springer Verlag, 1977); Jacques Monod, *Chance and Necessity* (New York: Alfred A. Knopf, Inc., 1971); and Ernst Mayr, *Evolution and the Diversity of Life* (Cambridge: Harvard University Press, 1976). Note Monod's chapter 3, where it is argued that an analogue of representation is at work already on the microscopic chemical level in the stereospecific powers of recognition or discrimination of molecules.

31. See also Gerhard Vollmer, *Evolutionäre Erkenntnistheorie* (Stuttgart: S. Hirzel Verlag, 1981); Rupert Riedl, *Order in Living Organisms* (New York: John Wiley & Sons, 1978); *Biologie der Erkenntnis* (Berlin: Paul Parey, 1981); Franz M. Wuketits, *Biologie und Kausalität* (Berlin: Paul Parey, 1981).

32. F. A. von Hayek, *The Sensory Order* (Chicago: University of Chicago Press, 1952); Donald T. Campbell, "Perception as Substitute Trial and Error", *Psychological Review* 63, 5, 1956, pp. 330–42; "Methodological Suggestions for a Comparative Psychology of Knowledge Processes", *Inquiry* 2, 3, Autumn 1959, pp. 152–82; Chapters II and III below; and "Descriptive Epistemology: Psychological, Sociological, and Evolutionary", William James Lectures, Harvard, 1977, Preliminary Draft; October, 1978, mimeographed.

any other person. And it is he who has given it the name of "evolutionary episte-mology".[33]

In the following, I shall sketch the bare outlines of the view. In particular, I shall attempt to reconstruct a part of the argument that emerges from the work of Popper, Campbell, and Lorenz.

But I shall not limit myself to their presentation or examples, and shall elicit a point of view supported by their discussion and directly applicable to the issue of presentationalism versus representationalism. Although I support their approach, I shall also, occasionally, indicate points of disagreement with them. And there are also, of course, many such points of disagreement among them despite the underlying unity of their approach.

Before turning to this task, some further ironies of our approach are worth mentioning. It is not customary to present Darwinian philosophy of biology as an alternative to presentationalism. Indeed, the representationalist implications of Darwin's work were ignored in the contest between Mach and Boltzmann. Both acclaimed Darwin's work, and Mach stated that the "external aim" of science was to serve biological survival. But Mach elaborated such remarks rather little; and as late as 1916 he was endorsing Lamarck's theory of the inheritance of acquired characteristics. And Boltzmann, who did apply Darwinian results appropriately in his critique of the Kantian categories, nonetheless never turned Darwinian principles to the critique of Mach's views.[34] Indeed, there is a rather poignant irony in opposing the Machian position by arguments drawn from biology. For Mach himself, through his work in physiology, was deeply interested in biology, and

---

33. Although it is not my task here to trace the intellectual lineage of evolutionary epistemology or to assign priorities, the contribution that Campbell has made must be especially noted. Popper, whom Campbell credits with the chief development of the approach, has called Campbell's chief essay on the matter ("Evolutionary Epistemology", Chapter II of this volume) a treatise of prodigious learning: "There is scarcely anything in the whole of modern epistemology to compare with it", he reports (see Chapter IV below). Popper also describes this paper as a reliable guide to his own thinking, and as showing "the greatest agreement with my epistemology and . . . an astonishing anticipation of some things which I had not yet published when he wrote the paper". The paper referred to is based on a much neglected earlier essay: "Blind Variation and Selective Retention in Creative Thought as in Other Knowledge Processes", 1960, *op. cit.*, reprinted here as Chapter III. Although Campbell's "Evolutionary Epistemology" is presented in a modest historical and descriptive style, it is densely packed with information. It is also valuable because of the new level of abstraction which it attains. Popper also reaches a new level of abstraction as a result of his interchange with Campbell on these matters — and also from his encounter with some related work by Konrad Lorenz to which Campbell drew his attention. Although Campbell says that Popper is the modern founder and leading advocate of this approach, Popper had not previously put the problem in so full a context. The work by Campbell cited enables one to see the power of an approach along Popper's lines; it opens some problems only touched by Popper; and it illuminates a broad area of the history of philosophy.

34. Ludwig Boltzmann, *Populäre Schriften* (Leipzig: Ambrosius Barth Verlag, 1905), chapter 22, esp. pp. 394–402. See also Mach, "Einige vergleichende Tier- und Menschenpsychologische Skizzen", in *Naturwissenschaftliche Wochenschrift* 15, 1916, pp. 241–47. Mach's preference for Lamarck is not surprising. Darwinism stands in the same relation to Lamarckism as does deductivism to inductivism and criticism to justification. Machian theory of inductive learning and verification is Lamarckian, in that it stresses induction (the passive receipt of sense impressions) from the environment, rather than selection by the environment. See Popper, *Unended Quest, op. cit.*, pp. 45, 86, and 167–68.

wrote that "the foundations of science as a whole, and of physics in general, await their next greatest elucidations from the side of biology, and especially from the analysis of sensations".[35] I quite agree with Mach, but I will use the results of contemporary biology, and of the "analysis of sensations" to be found in evolutionary epistemology, to undermine Mach's philosophy of physics.

11. Presentationalism is Lamarckian

I do not know why there has been so little appreciation that Darwinian evolutionary mechanisms and western epistemologies could be compared – let alone that they conflict radically. I suppose that this has to do with the difficulty people still have in grasping how utterly naturalistic Darwin's approach to life is, and how relatively unimportant, and how very late, is the role man plays in the evolutionary drama. Thus the older epistemologies – in which the subjective experience of man is paramount – continue to go unchallenged.

Whatever the explanation, *both Darwinian evolutionary theory and western epistemology are accounts of the growth of knowledge; and evolution is itself a knowledge process.* Evolution is a process in which information regarding the environment is literally incorporated, incarnated, in surviving organisms through the process of adaptation. Adaptation *is*, for Darwinians, an increment of knowledge. This idea can be illustrated not only with examples of animals, whose "knowledge" is more like our fairly conventional images of knowing, but also by plants.[36] For instance, the New England fruit tree has evolved a kind of "temporal map", genetically transmitted, in terms of which imperfect clues concerning seasonal change govern its budding, leafing, and fruiting. This species of tree has developed the capacity to adapt to passing changes in its environment, this capacity expressing itself in what amounts to primitive rules for behavior.[37] Another, more dramatic example comes from the migratory capacities of birds. Night warblers reared in captivity are able to orient to the star patterns in the night sky. Such warblers, after having been flown in closed boxes from Germany to southwest Africa, immediately are able to orient when they encounter their new night-sky environment. Such birds then appear to have evolved some sort of "spatial map", a genetically determined ability to read star patterns and steer by them – and also to have some sort of time sense, since the star patterns shift continually with the earth's rotation. The bird appears to have a "built-in" analogue of planetarium, sextant, chronometer, and altimeter, by the aid of which it is able to read and compensate for the movements of the stars around the North Star, or the Southern Cross, rather in the way in which a trained navigator does this.[38]

35. See the preface to Mach's *Beiträge zur Analyse der Empfindungen* (1886, rev. ed., 1900), p. v; see English translation: *The Analysis of Sensations and the Relation of the Physical to the Psychical* (New York: Dover, 1959), pp. xxxv–xxxvi.
36. See note 28 above.
37. See Campbell, "Descriptive Epistemology", Lecture 2.
38. See Donald R. Griffin, *Bird Migration* (New York: Anchor Books, 1964), and R. M. Lockley, *Animal Migration* (London: Pan Books, 1967).

Evolutionary epistemologists contend, simply, that (exosomatic) scientific knowledge, as encoded in theories, grows and develops according to the same method as (and is indeed adaptationally continuous with) the embedded (endosomatic) incarnate knowledge shown in our examples, and in other organisms, including man. In the second case there is an increasing fit or adaptation between the organism and its environment when its stored templates model stable features of the environment. In the first case there is an increasing fit or adaptation between theory and fact. (Such theory *grows and develops* according to the same method; of course it is *transmitted* somewhat differently.)

The way in which this "teleonomy" or "fit" is achieved in organisms is now well known, as a result not only of Darwinian theory and Mendelian genetics, but also of the stunning breakthroughs in the understanding of the workings of DNA and RNA. There is blind variation[39], which may be attained through gene mutation or random recombinations of the genetic material, and which also may be attained by variation in behavior leading to the selection by the organism of a new niche. This is followed by duplication or invariant reproduction, and by natural selection.

Human knowledge appears to develop similarly. The highest creative thought, like animal adaptation, is the product of blind variation and selective retention.[40] Growth of knowledge is achieved through variation and selective retention – or, to use Popper's phrase, through conjecture and refutation. Science is, on this account, *utterly unjustified and unjustifiable.*[41] It is a shot in the dark, a bold guess going far beyond all evidence. The question of its justification is irrelevant: it is as irrelevant as any question about whether a particular mutation is justified. The issue, rather, is of the viability of the mutation – or of the new theory. This question is resolved through exposing it to the pressures of natural selection – or attempted criticism and refutation. Survival in this process does not justify the survivor either: a species that survived for thousands of years may nonetheless become extinct. A theory that survived for generations may eventually be refuted – as was Newton's. There is *no* justification – *ever*. The process that began with unjustified variations ends in unjustified survivors.

Sense observations, the building blocks of the presentationalists, play a different role: they are not the elements or justifiers of theories. Rather, they trim the sails of thought. They are only among the *winnowers* of theories: scientific theory is winnowed, selected, through confrontation with observation. Sense observation is not the source of knowledge, yet plays an important role in criticizing and shaping it – in selecting it.[42]

39. See Campbell's discussion of the differences between "blind" and "random" variation in Chapters II and III below.
40. *Ibid.*
41. See Donald T. Campbell, "Unjustified Variation and Selective Retention in Scientific Discovery", in F. J. Ayala and T. Dobzhansky, eds., *Studies in the Philosophy of Biology, op. cit.*, pp. 159–61.
42. Moreover, the related presentationalist fear of "occult" theories and concepts that describe invisible structural properties is inappropriate here: on this account scientific theories do describe invisible properties; yet they are *testable* by observation; hence they are scientific and not occult.

It is important to notice that the two assumptions mentioned earlier (in section 5), as imprisoning presentationalists and other traditional epistemologists in their positions, are here abandoned: the assumption that claims must be justified; and that sense observations are the source of all knowledge. The implications for conventional epistemologies are profound. Indeed, to express the situation in biological terms, almost all traditional epistemologies are *Lamarckian* in their accounts of the growth of knowledge. This is conspicuously true of presentationalism, almost all adherents to which maintain an inductivist, justificationalist account of knowledge growth, according to which knowledge is constructed out of sensations (as building blocks or elements) by a relatively passive process of combination, accumulation, repetition, and induction. This is a process of learning by *instruction*, rather than adaption and *selection* by the environment.[43] This means that it is impossible to give a presentationalist reconstruction of these matters that is compatible with the findings of contemporary biological science.

12. Sensation Is Not Authoritative

Evolution is, then, not a process whose products are predictable from, or justifiable by, any combination of elements. But suppose it were. Even if evolution *did* occur in such a way, it would be absurd – from an evolutionary, biological, perspective – to hope to build (or induce) the world or science out of *human* sensations as elements.

To do so is arbitrarily to grant a special authority to sensation *at its present stage* of evolutionary development. In fact, human sensations are a latecomer in the history of the world: there was a time when there were no sensations at all, and then a later time when the only sensations were of a quality inferior to the best available today. There is no reason to suppose that this process has stopped, or that it has, at any stage, produced in any organism (human or otherwise) sensations or sensation-generating cognitive structures which are in any way finished, complete, perfect, authoritative.

This can be shown readily even on the level of individual human experience, without going into the logic of the matter, deeply investigating human cognitive structures, or attempting a comparative study of cognitive structures in different species. Human sensation is well known to be unreliable: that sensations are in any way authoritative is contradicted not only by scientific investigation, physiological studies of the brain and sense organs, optical illusion, and such like, but also by ordinary experience, from which we know that our sensations are often both crude and educable. A good example is wine tasting: the connoisseur knows what to look for and how to describe both what he searches for and what he experiences. His sensations are, as a result of cultivation, made *more* authoritative. Or, to take a related personal example: I remember some twenty-five years ago having a severe pain in my back, reporting it to my doctor, being X-rayed. I had described it as being a diffuse pain in my back concentrated in the area of my

43. See Popper, *Objective Knowledge*, pp. 97, 144, 149, 271, 245, 268–72, 279, 284.

kidneys. The doctor diagnosed it as being due to poor posture and gave me a lecture on the nerves, musculature, and fascia of the back, using a vivid chart of the human body to illustrate his argument. *As he talked*, as I absorbed information, *the pain sensation changed permanently*: I no longer had a "diffuse pain in the back concentrated in the area of the kidneys". I now had a very definite pain following certain muscle and nerve lines – incidentally nowhere near my kidneys. In short, an increase in information helped me *to sense* more accurately.[44] Similar experiences are known to anyone who has practiced autogenic or "relaxation" exercises on various parts of his body, or who has practiced yoga. Sensations are, then, anything but authoritative: they are themselves interpretations. They can be educated and refined. In this process they *become* more authoritative in the sense that they are better tested and educated but not in the sense that they are ever beyond error: any wine connoisseur or yoga practitioner knows better than that.

In sum, there is a clear conflict with Mach's insistence that all sensations are immediately given and are certain – "as if their character were independent of the way in which they were identified, or misidentified".[45] Such a theory, such an "epistemology which takes our sense perceptions as 'given', as the 'data' from which our theories have to be constructed", is "pre-Darwinian". As Popper puts it, it fails "to take account of the fact that the alleged data are in fact adaptive reactions, and therefore interpretations which incorporate theories and prejudices. . . . there can be no pure perception, no pure datum . . . Sense organs incorporate the equivalent of primitive and uncritically accepted theories, which are less widely tested than scientific theories."[46]

13. The Evolution of Sensation: Campbell versus Wächtershäuser

Thus far we have concentrated chiefly on the individual experience of human sensation. This first step already undermines any plausibility that presentationalism might have, yet it still moves within the province chosen by presentationalism: human sensation. The next two steps (to which the next two sections will be devoted) – an examination of the evolution of sensation, and a comparative look at cognitive structures in non-human organisms – are generally neglected by presentationalists. Most presentationalism, that is, is anthropomorphic in practice. Yet it is only by taking these further steps that we move fully into evolutionary epistemology, for, as Popper puts it: "The main task of the theory of knowledge is to

44. For Mach this is a contradiction in terms. As he writes (*Analysis of Sensations*, p. 10n), "*the senses represent things neither wrongly nor correctly*" (italics are Mach's).

45. Blackmore, *Ernst Mach*, p. 66. See Mach, *The Analysis of Sensations*, p. 10. For Mach it appears that sensations were not subject to what later was called the "uncertainty principle", that is, that sensations alone were independent of being perceived.

46. *Objective Knowledge*, pp. 145–46, also pp. 36–37. See also Roger James, "Conditioning is a Myth", in *World Medicine*, 18 May 1977.

understand it as continuous with animal knowledge; and to understand also its discontinuity – if any – from animal knowledge."[47] Cognitive structures in animals provide yet further independent and complementary witnesses to the reality of the world.

Let us begin at what, for a presentationalist, would have to be the beginning: with the origin of sensation. To approach this question, it is helpful to consider an important aspect of the eco-niche inhabited by human and other organisms which is usually neglected by epistemologists: the electromagnetic spectrum.

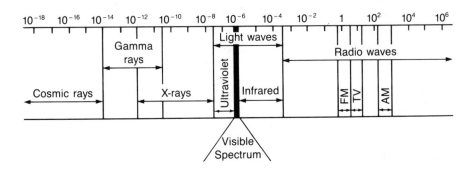

The entire spectrum is wide: ranging in wavelength from less than one billionth of a meter to more than a thousand meters. But the *visible* spectrum is but a tiny slice of the entire energy band: we can see – and most animal vision also occurs – only in that small section between approximately 400 and 700 nanometers. Man has no direct access to information carried within the larger part of the spectrum. Our senses do not immediately respond in this realm. Cosmic rays, gamma rays, X-rays, radio waves: we live in an electromagnetic sea, as it were, and nonetheless these waves do not register unassisted on our eyes, or any other sense organs. Our sensory apparatus in effect filters out all except a narrow band of light waves. Prior to the discovery of this spectrum, and prior to the invention of means to tap, channel, and register X-rays, radio waves, and such like, the realms of existence and knowledge now opened by them were beyond human ken.

Why do our sense organs not tap these other realms directly? This turns out to be a most productive question. I once thought that there was a simple answer to it,[48] but recent discoveries have made the question more complicated although still readily understandable. Let us begin with the older explanation, which is due to Campbell – and then see how the new explanation, due to Günter Wächters-

47. Popper, Chapter IV below, p. xx.
48. See Campbell's "Evolutionary Epistemology", Chapter II below.

häuser, corrects it and alters the situation. (See Chapters II, III, and V below, and also the Appendix to Chapter VI.)

Campbell's hypothesis is that light waves happen to be able to be *exploited* by simple organisms in a way that other wave bands cannot. *Vision has arisen as the opportunistic exploitation of a coincidence*: the coincidence of impenetrability with opaqueness. Generally speaking, things which *cannot be seen through* within the narrow band of light waves also *cannot be moved through*. Thus air and water are both transparent and penetrable to moving organisms. An ability to exploit this coincidence – as by a mutant light-sensitive cell – would give an organism an obvious survival advantage.

This coincidence is not always present, and when it is not, its cue value obviously disappears. Take clear ice and fog. The first is clear but may not be penetrable; the second, penetrable but not clear. Campbell calls such cases "paradoxical". On other wave lengths, there are different coincidences, and hence different cues. Such other coincidences of the electromagnetic spectrum can sometimes now be exploited, as in radar and sonar, in order to cope with such obstacles to vision and movement as night and fog.

Campbell's discovery of the significance of this coincidence is of fundamental importance, one of the deepest insights into the evolution of vision and of all those knowledge processes connected to vision. Günter Wächtershäuser has, however, recently challenged Campbell's simple account – and has done so with a beautiful and original account of his own. This is published for the first time in Chapter V below.[49]

Wächtershäuser begins with Campbell's problem: Why is it that, from the whole electromagnetic spectrum, animals use for orientation – for what we now call vision – only the tiny radiation segment between 400 and 700 nanometers? But he gives a different answer.

---

49. My report of Wächtershäuser's work in this chapter is derived from his "Light and Life: On the Nutritional Origins of Perception and Reason", read at the AAAS Annual Meeting, New York, May 27, 1984, and from personal conversations. He has also allowed me to read his manuscripts: "Remarks on the Difference Between the Positions of Popper and Lorenz on Evolutionary Epistemology", "Remarks on 'Biology and Evolutionary Epistemology' by W. W. Bartley", and "Patent Law, Genetic Engineering and World 3", the last of which was read at the Convocation of the Open Society and Its Friends, New York City, November 22–24, 1982. My quotations are taken from the AAAS paper and from his "Remarks on 'Biology and Evolutionary Epistemology' . . . ". Donald Campbell has very kindly informed me that he accepts, provisionally, Wächtershäuser's criticism. (*Note added in proof*) An interesting experiment that relates to Wächtershäuser's work has now been reported by Professor Pill-Soon Song, of Texas Tech University. As reported in the *Times-Picayune*, New Orleans, p. A-6, on 27 June 1985, and in *The Stanford Daily*, 28 June 1985, and at the American Society for Photobiology meeting in New Orleans on June 27, Song has discovered a one-celled organism that uses light for food – the first animal definitely known to do so. The organism in which Song found evidence of photosynthesis (hitherto generally thought confined to plants and bacteria) is a blue-green, trumpet-shaped protozoan called *Stentor coeruleus*, "a creature about as long as a thread is wide that looks like a speck of dust in water to the naked eye". Song's discovery was, he reports, made eighteen months previously, and its announcement delayed while he and his colleagues were testing their discovery.

Starting from the familiar primordial "broth" of organic compounds in which micro-organismic life is thought first to have originated about four billion years ago, Wächtershäuser adopts Popper's program of "situational logic" – that is, to reconstruct events in terms of sequences of problems and solutions. Suppose, Wächtershäuser suggests, that, as micro-organisms developed within it, the broth itself began to be used up. At this point, to escape the threat of starvation, some mutant micro-organism was able to "invent" photosynthesis – a process in which light, perhaps additionally to the "broth", could serve as food. "In this earliest encounter with life", as he puts it, "light functioned solely as food". And not, that is, for orientation around impenetrable objects.

But what does all this have to do with our original question: that is, why was only that tiny radiation segment between 400 and 700 nanometers utilized in the evolution of vision? The question is very well taken; and also, with Wächtershäuser's account, readily answered. For in this account, this *same* tiny radiation segment, between 400 and 700 nanometers, once again plays a crucial role, here, however, as a source of food rather than, at least initially, as a means of vision. And in this new example, the question may be repeated: why was the organism "interested" only in this very same range for food? The question is readily answered.

For as it turns out, another peculiar coincidence occurs here. For the most part, oxygenic photosynthesis uses only those segments of the electromagnetic spectrum which are now used for visible light. That is, there is a close overlap between those wavelengths employed for photosynthesis and those now used for vision.

This is a coincidence, but no accident, for the range within which photosynthesis is possible is *forced*, as Wächtershäuser explains, by the laws of photochemistry. I shall not go into these laws here (but see his own account in Chapter V below), but will only mention that, due to them, it would be virtually impossible for other areas of the electromagnetic spectrum to serve as food: for in its other ranges, absorption of the radiation in question either would hardly lead to oxygenic photosynthesis (only light up to 700 nanometers has enough energy to fuel the necessary photochemical reaction); or – most important – it would lead to intolerable chemical destruction of organic molecules (as does ultraviolet radiation below about 400 nanometers: e.g., the destructive effects of ultraviolet light on essential biomolecules such as proteins and DNA). That is, radiation in other ranges would, in general, be either non-nourishing or poisonous. Hence only that narrow non-lethal segment now used for vision would qualify as a viable and exploitable source, through photosynthesis, for nourishment.

For the early photosynthesizers, a new, secondary, problem now emerged – yet one that was to be crucial to the development of vision from photosynthesis. Lighting conditions fluctuate locally. How was the organism to locate and remain in a place of optimum radiation? The solution was to adapt the already developed apparatus for photosynthesis – for feeding from light – to the new, additional function of detecting light in order to control movement: i.e., *photocontrolled locomo-*

tion. It is now that vision begins, gradually and primitively, to be developed, and it is also now that the association between light and movement becomes crucial – *restricted from the start* to that narrow but nutritive and nonpoisonous range (400-700 billionths of a meter) with which we began our meditation. Thus, not surprisingly, we find that the receptor pigments for photosynthesis and the receptor pigments for photocontrolled locomotion respond only to this "edible" light.

(Even prior to locomotion, however, the photosynthesis metabolism may have been utilized for certain kinds of more primitive control. As Wächtershäuser has informally suggested:

> Some organisms utilize light to control the metabolic machinery for photosynthesis. In the presence of light, the photosynthesis is turned on; and in its absence, it is turned off: maintaining the photosynthesis machinery in the dark would be a waste. This shows how the detection of light by chromophores could have been beneficial to an organism long before locomotion.)

The fruitful survival-serving combination of photosynthesis with photocontrolled locomotion lasted long, biologically speaking. But eventually protozoa emerged from algae, the capacity for photosynthesis itself was abandoned, and the protozoa fed on free-swimming algae and bacteria.

Which only created a new problem situation. How now, asks Wächtershäuser, was this new food to be found? He suggests that it was tracked down by means of a photocontrolled locomotion in which the protozoa used a similar control program as their prey. The necessary photosensitive machinery was either retained from earlier plant days or secondarily acquired from plants by ingestion.

In some cases plants are, literally, used as *eyes*. Thus he reports:

> As for the protozoa, . . . Paramecium bursaria utilizes for its photomovement the endosymbiotic green alga Chlorella as a light receptor. Here a tiny plant organism serves literally as the eye of an animal.

The last point is important. For all animals seem to require for their eyes protein-bonded vitamin A aldehyde as a light-sensitive pigment; yet they cannot produce this themselves, but must ingest it with their food. Its source, then, is bacteria and plants which use its precursor (carotene) as a pigment for photosynthesis.

Primitive locomotion and light are, then, of course connected. But at these early stages the detection of bodies impenetrable to locomotion is involved only very indirectly, is hardly primary, and at this level would serve little function. There is a long way to go before Campbell's coincidence between transparency and penetrability comes into play.

But Wächtershäuser, who admires Campbell's work, does not want to deny that vision, as it evolved, would also benefit the development of a collision-preventing control of locomotion. Quite the contrary. But he rejects Campbell's idea that its primary use, origin, and chief evolutionary function must have been to steer around (or towards) impenetrable bodies. Those more advanced forms of vision that serve to detect bodies impenetrable to locomotion already presuppose a keen sense of light direction. And such a sense of direction, requiring lenses, was only acquired recently, biologically speaking, by such creatures as vertebrates, molluscs, and insects, long after the basic photochemistry of vision had developed.

Campbell has tentatively accepted Wächtershäuser's account. Yet it seems to me that the insights of Campbell and Wächtershäuser can readily be integrated here, simply by acknowledging that *vision, as we know it, appears to be the outgrowth of the opportunistic exploitation of several important coincidences.* There is the fact that "edible" radiation ranges between 400 and 700 nanometers, plus the fact that this range falls into (it need not be coextensive with it) the range in which occurs the exploitable coincidence between the transparent and that which is penetrable to locomotion. The first is in effect the precondition for the second. Evolution indeed favors the survival of organisms that can exploit such multiple coincidences that can, as it were, build on one another. Photosynthesis paved the way for, provided the opportunity for, vision.

Thus Wächtershäuser's account leaves intact most of the facts on which Campbell's further argument rested, and then goes on powerfully to supplement them.[50] For there *are* important coincidences of transparency and penetrability, and the possibilities of exploiting them have considerable ramifications for the development of cognitive structures during more advanced stages of evolution – after the basic photochemistry of vision has developed.

Campbell himself had pointed out that *direct* exploratory movement that did not exploit any coincidence between penetrability and transparency doubtless came first, and has epistemological priority. The use of light as food (photosynthesis), and the resulting search for light, and for higher light intensities, can be accommodated easily here.

Or to take Campbell's own example, one may consider an organism that enjoys exploratory movement and virtually nothing else: the slipper animalcule (paramecium). To survive, it must find a nourishing and nonpoisonous ecological niche. It solves this problem not through anything that might well be called cognition, but through random variation of movement into various parts of its environment. This starts when hunger begins, and ends when the organism is sated or has been killed in its search. Its exploration is direct, and its existence is relatively dangerous. Its main presupposition about the nature of the world, the

---

50. Wächtershäuser does, however, make several critical remarks which pertain to the facts themselves. 1). Since life began in water, diffuse light would have sufficed for photosynthesis; and in such a context, neither turbid water nor the fog that may lie above it are "paradoxical" in Campbell's sense. Moreover, the sort of clear transparency needed to judge the shape, size, and distance of impenetrable bodies often does not occur in water, wherein light is scattered from many sources. Hence such judgement of shape, etc. (e.g., to move around objects) could hardly be basic to the exploitation of light. 2). There is, moreover, rather less coincidence between penetrability to locomotion and transparency to visible light than originally contended: some bodies impenetrable to locomotion are also not transparent to ultraviolet and infrared; whereas, on the other hand, water and air are also transparent for ultraviolet and near infrared light.

presupposition undergirding its activity, and rendering it adaptive, is that the discontinuity to be experienced in nature is greater spatially than temporally: that is, change relevant to nourishment appears more rapidly if one moves around than if one stands still. A simple philosophy, but one evidently adequate to the life of the paramecium. Light of course may play a role here, and it *will* play a role in cases where photocontrolled locomotion is involved; but it is not light in the service of representation of impenetrable objects.

Campbell's account becomes applicable in the later course of human and animal evolution, after numerous organs, structures, and activities have been added to the repertory of many organisms. These additions expand their exploratory capacities far beyond those of organisms limited to random movement alone, and also beyond those limited to orientation towards light; and they also expand the aim of their search far beyond the quest for consumable light or for objects that consume light. These additions include habit, instinct, thought supported by visual and other forms of memory, social organization, language, science.

These additions tend, Campbell emphasizes, to be both *vicarious* and *indirect*, and thus contrast with direct search for food by random movement. It is Campbell who has stressed the importance of vicariousness and indirectness; and such vicariousness and indirectness seems to be prerequisite to – and to mark the step to – higher cognition. Take radar as an analogy. Radar is used, by a ship, for instance, as a *substitute* for movement, i.e., going and looking directly. Instead of exploring its environment directly, with all the attending risks, the ship sends out radar and perhaps also sonar. The radar beam is emitted blindly[51] and is selectively reflected from objects, their opaqueness to the wave band vicariously representing their impenetrability. Trial and error is thus removed from full movement on the part of the organism and is vicariously invested in the radar beam. Similarly with vision, wherein an environment far beyond the range of probing touch can be represented vicariously in the image in the visual cortex. This image may be utilized in a vicarious trial and error search or consideration of potential movements, and itself works as an error-eliminating control over movement. Successful movements in thought may be put into *overt* movement.

Vision may be supported by *memory*. The environment may be searched vicariously through examining representations held in memory, the memory substituting not only for the external state of affairs but also for a new direct look at the external state of affairs. Such memories will also work to diminish the importance of any circumstances which may momentarily make it difficult to examine the external state of affairs directly. Thus a good memory of the harbor diminishes the importance of fog in the harbor this morning.

Similarly for social exploration. Social forms of animal life are found subsequent to solitary forms. Within a social organization, an individual member may – as a scout, say – have his own trial and error exploration substituted for explora-

51. See note 39 above.

tion on the part of the group. The scout here is the vicar, or substitute, for the group. The "ontological" assumption here is also fairly definite: it is assumed that the scout is exploring *the same world* as that in which his group is living, and that that common world is moderately stable – sufficiently so for the experience of the scout to hold, vicariously, for the group.

Language also functions vicariously, and immensely increases the usefulness of the scout, enabling the results of his search to be relayed to the group without either movement or visual representation. Underlying, but not constituting, language is the discovery that things and actions may be represented by words and other symbols. Science, art, tradition, and culture extend and objectify this process. To explain how they work, Popper has presented an account of "Objective Mind" (see Chapters IV and VI below). He refers to the physical universe as *World 1*, and to the world of subjective conscious experience as *World 2*. He uses the term *World 3* to refer to the realm of objective mind, that is, to such things as the *logical contents* of books, libraries, computer memories, the logical structure of arguments, the objective problem situation at any time in a particular science. This third realm is, he contends, a "natural product of the human animal, comparable to a spider's web".[52] This world is autonomous and objective, and exists independently of being realized in the subjective conscious (World 2) experience of any human individual. The objective contents of World 3 objects are, then, potentialities.[53]

Those aspects of the contents of World 3 that are intended to represent the physical world (World 1) may be consulted vicariously in lieu of consulting World 1 directly. Indeed a double vicariousness and indirectness comes into play. World 2 experience can serve both as a vicarious representation of World 1 and as a vicarious representative of World 3, which may in turn be a vicarious representation of World 1. World 2 experience can conduct an exploration of World 3 in lieu of conducting an exploration of World 1. And World 2 experience can explore World 1 in order to test World 3. In the latter case, available experimental evidence, sense observation, is a crucial part of those eco-niches to which theories adapt. As Campbell puts it: "At this level there is a substitute exploration of a substitute representation of the environment, the 'solution' being selected from the . . . exploratory thought trials according to a criterion which is in itself *sub-*

---

52. *Objective Knowledge*, p. 117.

53. On such potentialities, see also Konrad Lorenz, *Behind the Mirror, op. cit.*, p. 147, where Lorenz contends that exploratory behavior is absolutely objective even with animals: "The raven that investigates an object has no wish to eat it", he writes. "The rat that examines all the nooks and crannies of its territory has no wish to hide; they both want to know whether the object in question *can* be eaten or used as a hiding place. . . . All objects that have been explored and then 'filed away' in this manner have been objectivated in a higher sense, since the knowledge of how to employ them has been both acquired and remembered independently of the pressure of the ever changing motivational situations within the organism as well as of the environmental situations around it." On the role of potentialities in evolutionary theory, see also Michael T. Ghiselin, *The Triumph of the Darwinian Method* (Berkeley: University of California Press, 1969), p. 64. For a general theory of potentiality or "propensity", see the "Metaphysical Epilogue" to Popper's *Quantum Theory and the Schism in Physics*.

stituting for an external state of affairs."[54] In an eco-niche infused with culture – in significant contact with World 3 – one can lead a most abstract existence: 'abstract' with reference to vicariousness and indirectness of one's contact with World 1. One can use World 3 to cut oneself off from World 1, just as one can use World 3 to sharpen one's questions about and one's participation in World 1.

Presentationalists had contended that presentations or sensations are the very stuff of the world rather than being representative of it. Such a view conflicts with two parts of the account just sketched. First, it conflicts with the highly complicated character of human experience itself as revealed by a consideration of cognitive structures. (And only a hint at this complexity has been given in this account.) Second, the layered, hierarchical way in which these structures work together *makes no sense* except by reference to a *common* external world to which they are differentially adjusted in a common task of representation. They are, as it were, independent and complementary witnesses to the reality of this world. Seen from an evolutionary perspective, much sensation has vicarious and indirect *representation* as its main point, teleonomically speaking. The survival-serving function of representation, achieved through the organs, structures, and activities of cognition, is to diminish the need for direct contact with a dangerous environment.

14. The Comparative Study of Cognitive Structures

I now wish to turn to the second step announced above, the comparative examination of cognitive structures in non-human organisms. We must, however, first consider a preliminary point.

As we consider various cognitive structures and their limitations, we notice that *any* cognitive structure or vehicle or carrier of knowledge will have *its own* physical characteristics – that is to say, characteristics peculiar to it *as a vehicle* rather than being characteristics of the object to be represented.[55] Some of these characteristics will aid it in the task of making a representation of something else; others – often the same ones, in other respects – may limit it. And there is always the danger of mistaking the characteristics of the structure or vehicle for the characteristics of the object to be represented. For instance, many cognitive structures use grids. A mosaic is one example. Cross-stitch embroidery is another. Yet another is the ordinary photoprint screen. A photoprint screen cannot produce any points of the object represented finer than those corresponding to the finite elements of the screen. The grain of the photographic negative permits no unlimited enlargement. Only that can be represented which can be "spelled out" on the "keyboard" provided by the grain of the print. Or take the domain resolved with

---

54. Campbell, Chapter III below.
55. For a discussion of vehicular selectors, see Campbell, "Descriptive Epistemology: Psychological, Sociological, and Evolutionary", William James Lectures, 1977, *op. cit.*, mimeograph of October 1978, Chapter 2. See also my application of Campbell's work in Chapter XVIII, below.

the lens of a microscope.[56] The fineness of the smallest structure of the object still visible with the aid of the lens depends upon the relationship between the angle of aperture and focal length. For a structural grating to be seen, the first diffraction spectrum which is thrown by the grating must still fall into the front lens. When this is no longer so, no structure is visible and one sees a smooth brown surface – no matter what is really there.

A presentationalist would hardly deny this; quite the contrary, if he knows his Kant, he understands such matters. *But he wants to make something out of these limitations*, and is preoccupied by the fear that we may mistakenly – and unjustifiably – impute the characteristics of the cognitive structure to the external world that this structure putatively represents. Lest we conclude that an external world is, say, composed of squares from the observation that the grain of the photograph is composed of small squares, we must – so the idealist or presentationalist may suggest – *avoid saying anything at all about an objective world independent of "squareful" representation, and speak only of different manners of arrangement in square.* Substitute "sensations" or "experience" for "squares", and you have a characteristic presentationalist stance.

Now this fastidious prohibition is only plausible (if at all) so long as one ignores the existence of more than one cognitive device. If there were indeed but a single microscope, one might conclude that structures are only "conceivable" up to the fineness resolved by that microscope, and that to speak of finer structures is meaningless. Once one knows of microscopes of different power, one reaches a different conclusion. Suppose, for example, that there is a less strongly resolving lens which registers brown for structures which are still visible as structures by the original instrument. One will hardly be inclined to treat its power of resolution as delimiting reality or our knowledge thereof. Any microscope will be limited in its achievement; even the most powerful lenses have limits as to the fineness of the structure which they resolve. There is, however, no reason to conclude that any *particular* limitation says anything about the character – let alone the conceivability – of the external world.

No particular mode of representation, no particular cognitive structure, is alleged to be perfect or complete. The fact that something is left out of a particular mode of representation gives no license to conclude that it is not there. As Lorenz puts it:

> If one examines methodically what the cross-stitch representation permits to be stated about the form of the thing-in-itself, the conclusion is that the accuracy of the statement is dependent upon the relationship between the size of the picture and the grain of the screen. If one square is out of line with a straight-line contour in the embroidery, one knows that behind it lies an actual projection of the represented thing, but one is not sure whether it exactly fills the whole square of the screen or only the smallest part of it. *This question can be decided only with the help of the next finest screen.*[57]

56. See Konrad Lorenz, "Kant's Doctrine of the A Priori in the Light of Contemporary Biology", *op. cit.*, pp. 112–13.

57. *Ibid.*, p. 30.

15. *About a Frog, Idealistically Disposed*

What is true of *any* cognitive structure, any vehicle or representation or information, is true of the cognitive structures of man and other organisms. And indeed the neural apparatus – with retinas using rods and cones – employed by humans and many animals to organize an image of the world is rather like a photoprint screen, and cannot reproduce any finer points of the external world than are permitted by the net or grid being used. As Lorenz remarks: "Just as the grain of the photographic negative permits no unlimited enlargement, so also there are limitations in the image of the universe traced out by our sense organs and cognitive apparatus."[58] It is trivially true that the validity of no such image, however fine, can be guaranteed: the structure, and with it the possibility of error stemming from that structure, is always there.

Yet by surveying the cognitive structures of animals other than humans – in effect, by consulting *less* fine screens – one undercuts the idea that the limits of the most recent (evolutionarily speaking) human cognitive structures define the limits of the external world. One of the first to distinguish between the subjective visual and tactile spaces of man (and to distinguish both of these from objective space) was the presentationalist philosopher Bishop Berkeley (in *An Essay Towards a New Theory of Vision*). The insight that the subjective spaces of animals may differ from one another and from that of man, and the connection of this to the problem of objective space, came only later. It is now well known, and argued by Simmel, Uexküll, and others, that the phenomenal worlds of animals differ from one another and from man's. Thus color perception is relatively unimportant and undeveloped in the familiar cat, who hunts at night, whereas color constancy is crucial for the honeybee, which searches out particular flower blossoms by means of their color. The boundaries separating what is experienced from what is beyond experience differ for each sort of organism. The frog provides a good example.

The vision of the frog, like radar, ignores many dimensions of the external world that are visually present to humans. An M.I.T. research group devised an experiment in which visual stimulation could be offered to one eye alone of an immobilized frog.[59] The frog was situated so that its eye was at the center of a hemisphere seven inches in radius. On the inner surface of this hemisphere, small objects could be placed – with the use of magnets – in different positions and moved about. Microelectrodes were implanted in the frog's optic nerve to measure electrical impulses sent to the brain by the eye. In the course of presenting various objects, colors, and movement to the frog, the investigators discovered that only

58. *Ibid.*
59. This example is presented in J. Y. Lettvin, H. R. Maturana, W. S. McCulloch, and W. H. Pitts, "What the Frog's Eye Tells the Frog's Brain", *Proceedings of the Institute of Radio Engineers* **47**, 1959, pp. 140–51. Reprinted in Warren S. McCulloch, *Embodiments of Mind* (Cambridge: The M.I.T. Press, 1965), pp. 230–55. See also H. R. Maturana, "Biology of Cognition", Report 9.0, Biological Computer Laboratory, Department of Electrical Engineering, University of Illinois.

four different kinds of messages were sent from the retina to the brain. Regardless of complexity and differences present in the environment, the frog's eye is equipped to transmit only a few different kinds of messages, and filters out – or simply cannot register – any additional information presented.

McCulloch and his associates termed the four different kinds of visual activity registered by the frog: (1) sustained contrast; (2) net convexity; (3) moving edge; (4) net dimming.

The first provides the general outline of the environment. The third enhances response to sudden moving shadows – such as a bird of prey. The fourth responds to a sudden decrease in light, as when a large enemy is attacking. The second responds neither to general changes of light nor to contrast, but only when small dark objects come into the field of vision and move close to the eye.

McCulloch and his group conclude:

> The frog does not seem to see or, at any rate, is not concerned with the detail of stationary parts of the world around him. He will starve to death surrounded by food if it is not moving. His choice of food is determined only by size and movement. He will leap to capture any object the size of an insect or worm providing it moves like one. He can be fooled easily not only by a bit of dangled meat but by any moving small object. . . . His choice of paths in escaping enemies does not seem to be governed by anything more devious than leaping to where it is darker.[60]

Thus the vision of the frog differs from that of men with respect to quantity and quality of information conveyed.[61] The frog does not inhabit a different objective world; he sees fewer details, and these are reproduced through a coarser screen. From the vantage point of our own cognitive achievements we would not take seriously the claim of an idealistically disposed frog that the limits of his experience define the limits of the world, or that it is meaningless to speak of the sorts of things which he cannot perceive.

As the visual world of the frog differs from our own, so does the spatial world of the water shrew. The water shrew masters its living space almost exclusively by path learning acquired through trial and error movement. Whereas a man can master a spatial problem by a simultaneous clear survey, most reptiles, birds, and lower mammals lack this capacity. The water shrew commands its space through kinesthetically ingrained movements known and applied by rote so exactly that hardly any optical or tactile steering or control is needed. The human being can approximately understand how this works, for he is able to behave approximately this way himself – as for example in a strange city for which he has no map. But the water shrew, presumably, would not be able to understand the human's way of mastering space through simultaneous clear survey. As Lorenz puts it: "basi-

60. *Ibid.*, p. 231.
61. A somewhat similar example is that of some sea urchins, which respond only to dimming of light – whether that be from a passing cloud or boat, or from the real danger of an approaching fish. See L. von Bertalanffy, "The Relativity of Categories", *Philosophy of Science*, October 1955, pp. 243–63.

cally, we can comprehend only the lower precursors of our own forms of perception and thought."

The spatial world of an animal may be even stranger than this example would suggest. A primitive animal might have a hunger space that it uses when hungry, a separate thirst space, a separate escape space for escape from each predator, a mate-finding space, and so on for each important activity. *Only with a higher stage of evolution does the hypothesis emerge that these spaces are the same or overlap. This hypothesis amounts to a hypothetical realism or representationalism.*

The white rat, the cat, the dog, the chimpanzee, all have access to this stage, where spatial learning achieved in the service of one activity is at once available for another. Accompanying this there emerges curiosity about all possible spaces, a trait with obvious survival value. "The different *Umwelten* of different animals", Campbell sums up, "do represent in part the different utilities of their specific ecological niches, as well as differential limitations. But each of the separate contours diagnosed in these *Umwelten* are also diagnosable by a complete physics, which in addition provides many differentia unused and unperceived by any organism."[62]

16. A Summary of the Argument

These few examples convey some impression of the kind of argument for representationalism, for realism, that emerges from evolutionary epistemology. They also suggest why anyone informed about biology and evolutionary epistemology finds it incredible that so many philosophers of science should seek to erect on the foundations of human sense experience an entire edifice of justified human knowledge – let alone an entire world.

Briefly to summarize the argument presented: when we consider the indirectness and vicariousness of cognition within any particular animal, and also the differences in cognitive structures from one animal to another, we see that the various vicars and structures make no sense individually or collectively in their mutual integration, hierarchical arrangement, and controls, except by reference to a common external world, in which they function, which they attempt in their various ways *to represent*, and in connection with which they have evolved. Each of the vicars – kinesthetic sense, vision, language, scientific representation, and the various others – has evolved separately and can be explained in terms of survival value *only* by reference to the others and to an external world. The way in which they complement one another, check, and partly compensate for the inadequacies of one another, makes no sense apart from a common reality. From the height of our own cognitive structures we can understand the way in which the spatial and other cognitive equipment of various animals approximate, in however imperfect a way, to devices more elaborately and complexly developed in our-

62. Campbell, Chapter II below, p. 86.

selves; and we can suppose that we and these animals have evolved in our diverse ways while coping with a common environment. We can guess at the features of this external environment as it transcends our evidence by analyzing the onto-logical presuppositions of the various devices, including theories, used by our-selves and animals in cognition. A hypothetical external world plays a crucial role here. If one, however fastidiously and justifiably, omits the external world, one is left with an inexplicable miracle, a piece of "pre-established harmony". It can hardly be said then, as the philosopher Herbert Dingle wrote in defending presen-tationalism in physics: "the external world plays no part at all in the business, and could be left out without the loss of anything. . . . It is thus a useless en-cumbrance . . . a will o' the wisp, leading us astray and finally landing us in a bog of nescience."[63]

It is not only the "less fine structures", the coarser lenses, of animals to which we can appeal here. Modern science, physics, physiology, and psychology give one *finer* structures *from whose standpoint one can even criticize and evaluate one's own cognitive structures*, and identify and correct for distortions and limitations in them. To attain such a standpoint, it is not necessary to make the cognitive structures work differently, or to alter one's actual phenomenal experience. That may indeed be impossible. R. L. Gregory, indeed, has argued, with regard to some optical illusions and paradoxes, that one *cannot* correct one's visual percep-tion of them even when one knows intellectually what is really so and how the illusion is constructed. Yet one *can* still correct conceptually or intellectually. One is by no means trapped by such an illusion, even though one cannot escape its perceptual effects.[64] The supposition that one must be trapped is doubtless con-nected to the presentationalist prejudice that all cognition must be reducible to the perceptual, whereas our minds in fact move in multiple modes and dimen-sions. In this particular example, one in effect corrects one's World 2 by refer-ence to one's World 3. To one who knows about the construction of the illusion, the *experience* of it will then have both perceptual and theoretical or conceptual components – *in conflict*. And we may be able to provide, physiologically, a well tested explanation both of the illusion and of the conflict. Such an illusion arises from the discrepancy between a perceptual and a conceptual hypothesis.

Many philosophers, ignoring the possibility of correcting cognitive structures through theoretical knowledge, have, then, wrongly concluded that we are epistemologically imprisoned in our cognitive structures. (See Part III below.) In fact, as this example shows, we can and do transcend them.

---

63. Herbert Dingle, *The Sources of Eddington's Philosophy* (Cambridge: Cambridge University Press, 1954), p. 25.

64. See Gregory's contributions to *Structure in Science and Art, Third Boehringer Symposium* (Am-sterdam: Excerpta Medica, 1980). See also my remarks there. See also Gregory Bateson, *Mind and Nature* (New York: E. P. Dutton, 1979), p. 37 and chapter 7. See also Gregory, "The Confounded Eye", *op. cit.*, pp. 86 and 49.

17. Why All This Ought Not to be Surprising— And Why It Is

eppur si muove. I feel that I must be flogging dead horses: in the preceding pages I have used a biological theory that is more than a century old to whip a presentationalist philosophy of science that was thoroughly discredited some seventy-five years ago. Surely these facts about evolution, perception, and cognitive structures are well known? In a sense they are: even Mach knew some of these things. So much so, indeed, that one can readily understand F. A. von Hayek's remark: "I suddenly realized how a consistent development of Mach's analysis of perceptual organization made his own concept of sensory elements superfluous and otiose, an idle construction in conflict with most of his acute psychological analysis."[65] Yet Mach, and other presentationalists like him, "know" these things only by fits and starts; they do not put them to the consistent and "systematic development" for which Hayek later calls. Thus, even if the horse is dead, *eppur si muove*.

To understand these matters better, let us stand back from the discussion in which we have engaged. I have used two unfamiliar terms, "presentationalism" and "representationalism", to characterize a debate that would conventionally be posed as being between "idealism" and "realism". These conventional terms are spoilt by years of misuse and inverted usage.[66] I hope that the unfamiliar terms have enabled me to be clear about the issues without being detoured into terminological disputes. I have also written as if presentationalism were characteristic of philosophy of physics, and representationalism characteristic of biology, whereas actual alignments are, of course, more complicated.[67]

The roots of presentationalism go very deep, and affect not only philosophers of physics. Indeed, for such a philosophy to exert the pull that it does, these roots may be not only deep but psychological, and even metaphysical: representationalism, which assigns so much more minor a role to one's subjective experiences, involves a level of acceptance of death that is foreign to presentationalism.

Yet the deep roots I wish to mention again in closing are not psychological but methodological. For it seems to me that philosophers of science do not ordinarily *choose* presentationalism; rather, they are *driven* to it by certain deep structural assumptions that permeate most of western philosophy.

Among these is, first and foremost, *justificationism*. I discussed this in passing earlier (section V) and the second part of this book is devoted to the examina-

65. F. A. von Hayek, *The Sensory Order, op. cit.*, pp. vi and 175–76. See Mach, *The Analysis of Sensations*, p. 126.
66. See Blackmore, "On the Inverted Use . . . ".
67. Indeed, some biologists, such as Maturana, attempt to introduce presentationalism into the heart of science.

tion of it.[68] As I indicate there, most western philosophy is structured *within* this doctrine; indeed it is so much a part of the fabric of western philosophy that many philosophers do not even know that it is there, let alone that it lies at the root of difficulties and might be replaced. Most western philosophies, being structured within justificationism, focus their main attention on subordinate questions that do not even arise unless justificationism is assumed to be correct.

Thus it seems to me that philosophers of physics would never have permitted themselves to be forced into presentationalism had it not been for this deeper assumption. Moreover, the problems which remain with presentationalism, and which dominate most texts in the philosophy of physics, are problems which arise out of the difficulties of justificationism. Thus issues of induction, confirmation, probability theory, and of the "empirical basis" dominate these texts. But what are the problems of induction, confirmation, probability, and empirical basis but problems of justification? When one abandons justification one finds that most of these textbooks in philosophy of physics are not only inapplicable to, irrelevant to, philosophy of biology – to refer again to Mayr's complaint. Nor is it only, as I have argued in this chapter, that they are in conflict with philosophy of biology. Rather the situation is far worse; *these textbooks are utterly useless.* These elaborate, even brilliant, accounts of how to justify in terms of elements are of little interest once one has abandoned justification and elements.

Moreover, once one abandons justificationism one also finds that some other positions commonly associated with, and reinforcing, philosophy of physics, and amounting to an ideology, also diminish in plausibility. These positions include determinism, materialism, monism, reductionism.[69]

Here again, the example of biology is useful. For natural history and the life sciences provide readily comprehensible examples of knowledge processes in which justificationism is not only irrelevant to but flagrantly contradicts Darwinian theory of natural selection. They also provide the material for arguments against determinism and reduction presented elsewhere.[70]

68. See my *The Retreat to Commitment*, and also Popper's discussion of the matter in *Realism and the Aim of Science*. On justification in a biological setting, see Donald T. Campbell, "Unjustified Variation and Selective Retention in Scientific Discovery", cited in footnote 41, above, esp. pp. 139–61. Part I, section 2.

69. There is no conflict, however, with the more restricted sense of reductionism espoused in Campbell, " 'Downward Causation' in Hierarchically Organised Biological Systems", in F. J. Ayala and T. Dobzhansky, eds., *Studies in the Philosophy of Biology, op. cit.*, pp. 179–86.

70. See my "Consciousness and Physics", *op. cit.*, and Chapter XVII below.

Acknowledgements

I am grateful to the following persons for conversation and correspondence which assisted me in the correction and improvement of this essay: Professor John T. Blackmore; Donald T. Campbell; Sir Ernst Gombrich; Richard Gregory; Erwin N. Hiebert; Peter Munz; Sir Karl Popper; Gerard Radnitzky; Walter B. Weimer; and Günter and Dorothy Wächtershäuser. The errors that remain are my own. In preparing this essay I have also made use of material in four earlier papers: "Philosophy of Science" (in Hebrew translation) in Asa Kasher, ed., *New Trends in Philosophy* (Tel-Aviv: Yachdav, 1982); "Philosophy of Science *vs.* Philosophy of Biology", in *Fundamenta Scientiae* 3, 1, 1982, pp. 55–78; "The Philosophy of Karl Popper: Part I: Biology and Evolutionary Epistemology", *Philosophia* 6, 3–4, September-December 1976, pp. 463–494; and "The Challenge of Evolutionary Epistemology", in *Proceedings of the Eleventh International Conference on the Unity of the Sciences* (New York: ICF Press, 1983), pp. 835–880.

Bibliography

F. J. Ayala and T. Dobzhansky: *Studies in the Philosophy of Biology: Reduction and Related Problems* (Berkeley: University of California Press, 1974).

W. W. Bartley, III: "Philosophy of Science", in Asa Kahser and Shalom Lappin, eds.: *New Trends in Philosophy* (Tel Aviv: Yachdav, 1982).

W. W. Bartley, III: "Philosophy of Biology versus Philosophy of Physics", *Fundamenta Scientiae* 3, 1, 1982.

W. W. Bartley, III: "Logical Strength and Demarcation", in Gunnar Andersson, ed.: *Rationality in Science and Politics* (Dordrecht: D. Reidel, 1982).

W. W. Bartley, III: "A Popperian Harvest", in Paul Levinson, ed.: *In Pursuit of Truth* (New York: Humanities Press, 1982).

W. W. Bartley, III: "The Philosophy of Karl Popper: Part I: Biology and Evolutionary Epistemology", *Philosophia*, Israel, 1976, pp. 463–494.

W. W. Bartley, III: "The Philosophy of Karl Popper: Part II: Consciousness and Physics: Quantum Mechanics, Probability, Indeterminism, and the Mind-Body Problem", *Philosophia* 7, 3–4, July 1978, pp. 675–716.

W. W. Bartley, III: "The Philosophy of Karl Popper: Part III: Rationality, Criticism and Logic", *Philosophia* 11, 1–2, February 1982, pp. 121–221.

W. W. Bartley, III: "Ein schwieriger Mensch: Eine Porträtskizze von Sir Karl Popper", in Eckhard Nordhofen, ed.: *Physiognomien: Philosophen des 20. Jahrhunderts in Portraits* (Königstein: Athenäum Verlag, 1980), pp. 43–69.

W. W. Bartley, III: "Remarks", in Peter Medawar & Julian Shelley, eds.: *Structure in Science and Art* (Amsterdam: Excerpta Medica, 1980).

W. W. Bartley, III: "Commentary on Max Jammer's Remarks on the Interaction between Philosophy and Science", in *Proceedings of the Seventh International Conference on the Unity of the Sciences* (New York: International Cultural Foundation, 1979), pp. 929–933.

W. W. Bartley, III: "What Was Wrong with Darwin?", *New York Review of Books*, September 15, 1977.

W. W. Bartley, III: "Theory of Language and Philosophy of Science as Instruments of Educational Reform", in Robert S. Cohen and Marx W. Wartofsky, eds.: *Methodological and Historical Essays in the Natural and Social Sciences* (Boston: Reidel, 1974).

W. W. Bartley, III: "Rationality versus the Theory of Rationality", in M. Bunge, ed.: *The Critical Approach to Science and Philosophy* (Glencoe: The Free Press, 1964), pp. 3-31.

W. W. Bartley, III: *The Retreat to Commitment*, 2nd, enlarged edition (La Salle: Open Court, 1984).

Gregory Bateson: *Steps to an Ecology of Mind* (New York: Ballantine Books, 1975).

Gregory Bateson: *Mind and Nature: A Necessary Unity* (New York: Dutton, 1979).

John T. Blackmore: *Ernst Mach: His Work, Life, and Influence* (Berkeley: University of California Press, 1972).

John T. Blackmore: "On the Inverted Use of the Terms 'Realism' and 'Idealism' Among Scientists and Historians of Science", *British Journal for the Philosophy of Science* **30**, 1979, pp. 125-134.

John T. Blackmore: "A New Conception of Epistemology and Its Relation to the Methodology and Philosophy of Science", *Methodology and Science* **14**, 2, 1981, pp. 95-126.

John T. Blackmore: "Essay Review: Hermann von Helmholtz: *Epistemological Writings*", *Annals of Science* **35**, 1978, pp. 427-431.

John T. Blackmore: "A Reply to Kuhn and Koertge on the Influence of Mach's Positivism", unpublished manuscript.

John T. Blackmore: "Philosophy as Part of Internal History of Science", unpublished manuscript.

John T. Blackmore: "Boltzmann's Concessions to Mach's Philosophy of Science", unpublished manuscript.

Werner Callebaut and Rix Pinxten: *Evolutionary Epistemology: A Multiparadigm Program*, forthcoming.

Donald T. Campbell: "Evolutionary Epistemology", in P. A. Schilpp, ed.: *The Philosophy of Karl Popper* (La Salle: Open Court, 1974), pp. 413-463. [Chapter II below]

Donald T. Campbell: "Descriptive Epistemology: Psychological, Sociological, and Evolutionary", William James Lecture, Harvard University, 1977, Preliminary Draft, October 1978. Mimeographed.

Donald T. Campbell: "Blind Variation and Selective Retention in Creative Thought as in Other Knowledge Processes", *Psychological Review* **67**, 1960, pp. 380-400. [Chapter III below]

Donald T. Campbell: " 'Downward Causation' in Hierarchically Organised Biological Systems", in F. J. Ayala and T. Dobzhansky, as cited.

Donald T. Campbell: "Perception as Substitute Trial and Error", *Psychological Review* **63**, 5, 1956, pp. 330-342.

John C. Eccles: *Facing Reality* (New York: Springer Verlag, 1970).

Richard L. Gregory: *Concepts and Mechanisms of Perception* (London: Duckworth, 1974).

Richard L. Gregory: *Eye and Brain* (New York: World University Library, 1966).

Richard L. Gregory and E. H. Gombrich, eds.: *Illusion in Nature and Art* (London: Duckworth, 1973).

Michael T. Ghiselin: *The Triumph of the Darwinian Method* (Berkeley: University of California Press, 1969).

F. A. von Hayek: *The Sensory Order* (Chicago: University of Chicago Press, 1952).

Erwin N. Hiebert: "The Genesis of Mach's Early Views on Atomism", in Robert S. Cohen and Raymond J. Seeger, eds.: *Ernst Mach: Physicist and Philosopher* (Dordrecht: D. Reidel, 1970).

Erwin N. Hiebert: "The State of Physics at the Turn of the Century", in Mario Bunge and William R. Shea, eds.: *Rutherford and Physics at the Turn of the Century* (New York: Dawson and Science History Publications, 1979).

Erwin N. Hiebert: "Mach", in Charles Coulston Gillispie, ed.: *Dictionary of Scientific Biography* (New York: Charles Scribner's Sons, 1978), Vol. VIII, pp. 595–607.

Erwin N. Hiebert: "Wilhelm Friedrich Ostwald", in Gillispie, ed., work cited, Vol. XV, Supplement 1, pp. 455–469.

Erwin N. Hiebert: "The Energetics Controversy and the New Thermodynamics", in Duane H. D. Roller, ed.: *Perspectives in the History of Science and Technology* (Norman: University of Oklahoma Press, 1971) pp. 67–86.

Erwin N. Hiebert: "Mach's Philosophical Use of the History of Science", in Roger H. Stuewer, ed.: *Historical and Philosophical Perspectives of Science* (Minneapolis: University of Minnesota Press, 1970), pp. 184–203.

Gerard Hinrichs: "The Logical Positivism of Berkeley's *De Motu*", *Review of Metaphysics* 3, 1950, pp. 491–505.

Gerald Holton: "Mach, Einstein and the Search for Reality", in Colin Chant and John Fauvel, eds.: *Darwin to Einstein: Historical Studies on Science and Belief* (London: Longmans, 1980), pp. 235–267.

E. J. Jensen and R. Harre: *The Philosophy of Evolution* (London: Harvester, 1981).

Franz Kreuzer, ed.: *Ich bin—also denke ich* (Vienna: Deuticke, 1981).

Franz Kreuzer, ed.: *Offene Gesellschaft-Offenes Universum: Franz Kreuzer im Gespräch mit Karl R. Popper* (Vienna: Deuticke, 1982).

Konrad Lorenz: *Behind the Mirror* (New York: Harcourt Brace Jovanovich, 1973).

Konrad Lorenz: "Kant's Doctrine of the A Priori in the Light of Contemporary Biology", in L. von Bertalanffy and A. Rapoport, eds.: *General Systems, Yearbook of the Society for General Systems Research*, 1962, pp. 112–14.

Konrad Lorenz: *Evolution and the Modification of Behavior* (Chicago: University of Chicago Press, 1965).

Konrad Lorenz and Franz M. Wuketits, eds.: *Die Evolution des Denkens* (Munich: Piper, 1983).

Konrad Lorenz: *Studies in Animal and Human Behaviour* (Cambridge: Harvard University Press, 1971), two volumes.

Konrad Lorenz: "Gestalt Perception as a Source of Scientific Knowledge", in *Studies in Animal and Human Behaviour*, op. cit., Vol. II, pp. 281–322.

Ernst Mach: "On the Part Played by Accident in Invention and Discovery", *The Monist* 6, January 1896, pp. 161–175.

Ernst Mach: *The Analysis of Sensations and the Relation of the Physical to the Psychical* (New York: Dover, 1959).

Ernst Mach: *The Science of Mechanics: A Critical and Historical Account of Its Development* (La Salle, Ill.: Open Court, 1960).

Ernst Mach: *Knowledge and Error: Sketches on the Psychology of Enquiry* (Boston: D. Reidel, 1976).

Ernst Mayr: "Discussion: Footnotes on the Philosophy of Biology", *Philosophy of Science* **36**, 1969, pp. 197–202.

Ernst Mayr: *Evolution and the Diversity of Life* (Cambridge: Harvard University Press, 1976)

Ernst Mayr: *Populations, Species, and Evolution* (Cambridge: Harvard University Press, 1970).

Jacques Monod: *Chance and Necessity* (New York: Alfred A. Knopf, Inc., 1971).

Karl R. Popper: *Auf der Suche nach einer besseren Welt* (Munich: Piper, 1984).

Karl R. Popper: *Conjectures and Refutations* (London: Routledge & Kegan Paul, 1963).

Karl R. Popper: *The Logic of Scientific Discovery* (London: Hutchinson, 1959).

Karl R. Popper: *Objective Knowledge: An Evolutionary Approach* (London: Oxford University Press, 1972).

Karl R. Popper: *The Self and Its Brain* (with John C. Eccles) (New York: Springer Verlag, 1977).

Karl R. Popper: *Unended Quest* (La Salle: Open Court, 1976).

Karl R. Popper: *Realism and the Aim of Science* (New Jersey: Rowman & Littlefield, 1982), Vol. I of the *Postscript to the Logic of Scientific Discovery*, as edited by W. W. Bartley, III.

Karl R. Popper: *The Open Universe* (New Jersey: Rowman & Littlefield, 1982), Vol. II of the *Postscript to the Logic of Scientific Discovery*, as edited by W. W. Bartley, III.

Karl R. Popper: *Quantum Theory and the Schism in Physics* (New Jersey: Rowman & Littlefield, 1982), Vol. III of the *Postscript to the Logic of Scientific Discovery*, as edited by W. W. Bartley, III.

Karl R. Popper, Konrad Lorenz: *Die Zukunft ist Offen: Das Altenberger Gespräch mit den Texten des Wiener Popper-Symposiums* (Munich: Piper, 1985).

A. Remane: *Die Grundlagen des natürlichen Systems der vergleichenden Anatomie und der Phylogenetik* (Königstein/Taunus: 1971).

Moritz Schlick: *General Theory of Knowledge* (New York: Springer Verlag, 1974).

J. von Uexküll: *Umwelt und Innenwelt der Tiere* (Berlin: Springer, 1920).

J. von Uexküll: *Theoretische Biologie* (Berlin: Springer, 1929).

J. von Uexküll and G. Kriszat: *Streifzüge durch die Umwelten von Tieren und Menschen* (Berlin: Springer, 1934).

Gerhard Vollmer: Review of *The Self and Its Brain*, in *Allgemeine Zeitschrift für Philosophie* 2, 1981, pp. 60ff.

Gerhard Vollmer: Review of Riedl: *Biologie der Erkenntnis*, in *Allgemeine Zeitschrift für Philosophie*, 1982.

Gerhard Vollmer: *Evolutionäre Erkenntnistheorie* (Stuttgart: S. Hirzel Verlag, 1981).

Chapter II

Evolutionary Epistemology

By Donald T. Campbell

An evolutionary epistemology would be at minimum an epistemology taking cognizance of and compatible with man's status as a product of biological and social evolution. In the present essay it is also argued that evolution – even in its biological aspects – is a knowledge process, and that the natural-selection paradigm for such knowledge increments can be generalized to other epistemic activities, such as learning, thought, and science. Such an epistemology has been neglected in the dominant philosophic traditions. It is primarily through the works of Karl Popper that a natural selection epistemology is available today.

Much of what follows may be characterized as "descriptive epistemology", descriptive of man as knower. However, a correct descriptive epistemology must also be analytically consistent. Or, vice versa, of all of the analytically coherent epistemologies possible, we are interested in those (or that one) compatible with the description of man and of the world provided by contemporary science. Modern biology teaches us that man has evolved from some simple unicellular or virus-like ancestor and its still simpler progenitors. In the course of that evolution, there have been tremendous gains in adaptive adequacy, in stored templates modeling the useful stabilities of the environment, in memory and innate wisdom. Still more dramatic have been the great gains in mechanisms for knowing, in visual perception, learning, imitation, language, and science. At no stage has there been any transfusion of knowledge from the outside, nor of mechanisms of knowing, nor of fundamental certainties.

This essay first appeared in Paul A. Schilpp, ed., *The Philosophy of Karl Popper* (LaSalle: Open Court, 1974), pp. 413–463, and is reprinted by permission. The essay was prepared during the author's tenure as a Fellow of the Center for Advanced Study in the Behavioral Sciences, under USPHS Special Fellowship 1-F3-MII-30, 416–01, 1965–66. Revised with the support of N.S.F. Grant GS32073X. The author has had the opportunity to profit from the suggestions of D. M. Armstrong, W. Ross Ashby, H. J. Barr, Gregory Bateson, John Birmingham, Henry W. Brosin, Robert W. Browning, Milič Čapek, Arthur Child, Michael Cullen, Jan Dick, Michael T. Ghiselin, Moltke Gram, R. J. Hirst, Donald D. Jensen, Harry J. Jerison, Gary Koeske, Thomas S. Kuhn, Joseph LaLumia, Arnold Levison, Mark Lipsey, Konrad Lorenz, D. M. MacKay, Wolfe Mays, Earl R. MacCormac, Grover Maxwell, Theodore Mischel, Charles Morris, Thomas Natsoulas, F. S. C. Northrop, Stephen C. Pepper, Burton Perrin, Hugh G. Petrie, John R. Platt, Henryk Skolimowski, Herman Tennessen, William Todd, Stephen E. Toulmin, C. F. Wallraff, Robert I. Watson, Philip P. Wiener, and William C. Wimsatt.

An analytically coherent epistemology could perhaps be based upon a revelation to Adam of true axioms and deductive logic, from which might be derived, perhaps in conjunction with observations, man's true knowledge. Such an epistemology would not be compatible with the evolutionary model. Nor would be a direct realism, an epistemology assuming veridical visual perception, unless that epistemology were also compatible with the evolution of the eye from a series of less adequate prior stages back to a light-sensitive granule of pigment. Also incompatible would be a founding of certainty on the obviously great efficacy of ordinary language. In the evolutionary perspective, this would either commit one to a comparable faith in the evolutionary prestages to modern language, or to a discontinuity and point of special creation. Better to recognize the approximate and only pragmatic character of language at all stages, including the best. An analytic epistemology appropriate to man's evolved status must be appropriate to these evolutionary advances and to these prior stages, as well as to modern man.

We once "saw" as through the fumblings of a blind protozoan, and no revelation has been given to us since. Vision represents an opportunistic exploitation of a coincidence which no deductive operations on a protozoan's knowledge of the world could have anticipated. This is the coincidence of locomotor impenetrability with opaqueness, for a narrow band of electromagnetic waves. For this band, substances like water and air are transparent, in coincidental parallel with their locomotor penetrability. For other wavelengths, the coincidence, and hence the cue value, disappears. The accidental encountering and systematic cumulations around this coincidence have provided in vision a wonderful substitute for blind exploration. In this perspective, clear glass and fog are paradoxical – glass being impenetrable but transparent, fog being the reverse. Glass was certainly lacking in the ecology of evolution. Fog was rare or nonexistent in the aqueous environment of the fish where most of this evolution took place. (Modern man corrects the paradoxical opacity of fog through exploiting another coincidence in the radar wave bands.) The visual system is furthermore far from perfect, with usually overlooked inconsistencies such as double images for nonfixated objects, blind spots, optical illusions, chromatic aberration, astigmatism, venous shadows, etc.

In all of this opportunistic exploitation of coincidence in vision there is no logical necessity, no absolute ground for certainty, but instead a most back-handed indirectness. From this perspective, Hume's achievement in showing that the best of scientific laws have neither analytic truth nor any other kind of absolute truth seems quite reasonable and appropriate. Here description and analysis agree.

1. The Selective Elimination Model

The advances produced in the course of evolution are now seen as due to natural selection, operating upon the pool of self-perpetuating variations which the genetics of the breeding group provide, and from within this pool, differentially propagating some variations at the expense of others. The supply of variations comes both from mutations providing new semistable molecular arrangements of the genetic material and from new combinations of existing genes. Considered as improvements or solutions, none of these variations has any a priori validity. None has the status of revealed truth nor of analytic deduction. Whatever degree of validation emerges comes from the differential surviving of a winnowing, weeding-out, process.

Popper's first contribution to an evolutionary epistemology is to recognize the process of the succession of theories in science as a similar selective elimination process. The theme is expressed clearly, if but in passing, in the 1934 *Logik der Forschung*. Here are two relevant passages:

> According to my proposal, what characterizes the empirical method is its manner of exposing to falsification, in every conceivable way, the system to be tested. Its aim is not to save the lives of untenable systems but, on the contrary, to select the one which is by comparison the fittest, by exposing them all to the fiercest struggle for survival.[1]
>
> . . . How and why do we accept one theory in preference to others?
>
> The preference is certainly not due to anything like an experiential justification of the statements composing the theory; it is not due to a logical reduction of the theory to experience. We choose the theory which best holds its own in competition with other theories; the one which, by natural selection, proves itself the fittest to survive. This will be the one which not only has hitherto stood up to the severest tests, but the one which is also testable in the most rigorous way. A theory is a tool which we test by applying it, and which we judge as to its fitness by the results of its applications.[2]

Fuller expressions of this evolutionary epistemology were contained in his first book (1932) *Die beiden Grundprobleme der Erkenntnistheorie*. In later publications, especially as collected in *Conjectures and Refutations*, the theme is more explicitly presented and elaborated.[3]

These additions add trial-and-error learning by man and animals to the prototypic illustrations of his basic logic of inference (logic of discovery, logic of the expansion of knowledge). They make explicit his willingness to identify the process of knowledge with the whole evolutionary sequence.

> Without waiting, passively, for repetitions to impress or impose regularities upon us, we actively try to impose regularities upon the world. We try to discover similarities in it, and to interpret it in terms of laws invented by us. Without waiting for premises we jump to conclusions. These may have to be discarded later, should observation show that they are wrong.

1. K. R. Popper, *The Logic of Scientific Discovery* (London: Hutchinson; New York: Basic Books, 1959), p. 42. Hereinafter cited as *L.Sc.D.* Reprinted by permission of the author and publishers.

2. *L.Sc.D.*, p. 108.

3. K. R. Popper, *Conjectures and Refutations* (London: Routledge & Kegan Paul; New York: Basic Books, 1963). Hereinafter cited as *C.&R.*; and *Die beiden Grundprobleme der Erkenntnistheorie* (Tübingen: J. C. B. Mohr Verlag, 1979).

This was a theory of trial and error – of *conjectures and refutations*. It made it possible to understand why our attempts to force interpretations upon the world were logically prior to the observation of similarities. Since there were logical reasons behind this procedure, I thought that it would apply in the field of science also; that scientific theories were not the digest of observations, but that they were inventions – conjectures boldly put forward for trial, to be eliminated if they clashed with observations; with observations which were rarely accidental but as a rule undertaken with the definite intention of testing a theory by obtaining, if possible, a decisive refutation.[4]

Hume was right in stressing that our theories cannot be validly inferred from what we can know to be true – neither from observations nor from anything else. He concluded from this that our belief in them was irrational. If 'belief' means here our inability to doubt our natural laws, and the constancy of natural regularities, then Hume is again right; this kind of dogmatic belief has, one might say, a physiological rather than a rational basis. If, however, the term 'belief' is taken to cover our critical acceptance of scientific theories – a *tentative* acceptance combined with an eagerness to revise the theory if we succeed in designing a test which it cannot pass – then Hume was wrong. In such an acceptance of theories there is nothing irrational. There is not even anything irrational in relying for practical purposes upon well-tested theories, for no more rational course of action is open to us.

Assume that we have deliberately made it our task to live in this unknown world of ours; to adjust ourselves to it as well as we can; to take advantage of the opportunities we can find in it; and to explain it, if possible (we need not assume that it is), and as far as possible, with the help of laws and explanatory theories. *If we have made this our task, then there is no more rational procedure than the method of trial and error – of conjecture and refutation:* of boldly proposing theories; of trying our best to show that these are erroneous; and of accepting them tentatively if our critical efforts are unsuccessful.[5]

The method of trial and error is not, of course, simply identical with the scientific or critical approach – with the method of conjecture and refutation. The method of trial and error is applied not only by Einstein but, in a more dogmatic fashion, by the amoeba also. The difference lies not so much in the trials as in a critical and constructive attitude towards errors; errors which the scientist consciously and cautiously tries to uncover in order to refute his theories with searching arguments, including appeals to the most severe experimental tests which his theories and his ingenuity permit him to design.[6]

In the process, Popper has effectively rejected the model of passive induction even for animal learning, and advocated that here too the typical process involves broad generalizations from single specific initial experiences, generalizations which subsequent experiences edit.[7] It is noteworthy that the best of modern mathematical learning theories posit just such a one-trial learning process, as opposed

4. *C.&R.*, p. 46. Reprinted by permission of the author and publishers.
5. *C.&R.*, p. 51.
6. *C.&R.*, p. 52. (See also *C.&R.*, pp. 216, 312–13, 383, and *ad passim*.)
7. For example, *C.&R.*, p. 44.

to older theories which implied inductive accumulation of evidence on all possible stimulus contingencies.[8]

Most noteworthy, Popper is unusual among modern epistemologists in taking Hume's criticism of induction seriously, as more than an embarrassment, tautology, or a definitional technicality. It is the logic of variation and selective elimination which has made him able to accept Hume's contribution to analysis (while rejecting Hume's contribution to the psychology of learning and inference) and to go on to describe that sense in which animal and scientific knowledge is yet possible.

2. Locating the Problem of Knowledge

It is well to be explicit that involved in Popper's achievement is a recentering of the epistemological problem. As with Hume, the status of scientific knowledge remains important. The conscious cognitive contents of an individual thinker also remain relevant. But these no longer set the bounds of the problem. The central requirement becomes an epistemology capable of handling *expansions* of knowledge, *breakouts* from the limits of prior wisdom, *scientific discovery*. While one aspect of this general interest is descriptive, central to Popper's requirement is a logical epistemology which is compatible with such growth.

> The central problem of epistemology has always been and still is the problem of the growth of knowledge. And the growth of knowledge can be studied best by studying the growth of scientific knowledge. . . . A little reflection will show that most problems connected with the growth of our knowledge must necessarily transcend any study which is confined to common-sense knowledge as opposed to scientific knowledge. For the most important way in which common-sense knowledge grows is, precisely, by turning into scientific knowledge. Moreover, it seems clear that the growth of scientific knowledge is the most important and interesting case of the growth of knowledge.
>
> It should be remembered, in this context, that almost all the problems of traditional epistemology are connected with the problem of the growth of knowledge. I am inclined to say even more: from Plato to Descartes, Leibnitz, Kant, Duhem, and Poincaré; and from Bacon, Hobbes, and Locke to Hume, Mill, and Russell, the theory of knowledge was inspired by the hope that it would enable us not only to know more about knowledge, but also to contribute to the advance of knowledge – of scientific knowledge, that is.[9]

I now turn to the last group of epistemologists – those who do not pledge themselves in advance to any philosophical method, and who make use, in epistemology, of the analysis of scientific problems, theories, and procedures, and, most important,

---

8. W. K. Estes, "All-or-None Processes in Learning and Retention", *American Psychologist* **19** (1964), 16–25; F. Restle, "The Selection of Strategies in Cue Learning", *Psychological Review* **69** (1962), 329–43; R. C. Atkinson and E. J. Crothers, "A Comparison of Paired-Associate Learning Models Having Different Acquisition and Retention Axioms", *Journal of Mathematical Psychology* **1** (1964), 285–312.

9. *L.Sc.D.*, pp. 17–19.

of scientific discussions. This group can claim, among its ancestors, almost all the great philosophers of the West. (It can claim even the ancestry of Berkeley despite the fact that he was, in an important sense, an enemy of the very idea of rational scientific knowledge, and that he feared its advance.) Its most important representatives during the last two hundred years were Kant, Whewell, Mill, Peirce, Duhem, Poincaré, Meyerson, Russell, and – at least in some of his phases – Whitehead. Most of those who belong to this group would agree that scientific knowledge is the result of the growth of common-sense knowledge. But all of them discovered that scientific knowledge can be more easily studied than common-sense knowledge. For it is *common-sense knowledge writ large*, as it were. Its very problems are enlargements of the problems of common-sense knowledge. For example, it replaces the Humean problem of "reasonable belief" by the problem of the reasons for accepting or rejecting scientific theories. And since we possess many detailed reports of the discussions pertaining to the problem whether a theory such as Newton's or Maxwell's or Einstein's should be accepted or rejected, we may look at these discussions as if through a microscope that allows us to study in detail, and objectively, some of the more important problems of "reasonable belief".

This approach to the problems of epistemology gets rid . . . of the pseudo-psychological or "subjective" method of the new way of ideas (a method still used by Kant). But it also allows us to analyse scientific problem-situations and scientific discussions. And it can help us to understand the history of scientific thought.[10]

A focus on the growth of knowledge, on acquisition of knowledge, makes it appropriate to include learning as well as perception as a knowledge process. Such an inclusion makes relevant the learning processes of animals. However primitive these may be, they too must conform to an adequate logical epistemology. Animal learning must not be ruled out as impossible by the logic of knowing.[11] Popper notes these broader bounds to the epistemological problem in numerous places in *Conjectures and Refutations*, for example:

Although I shall confine my discussion to the growth of knowledge in science, my remarks are applicable without much change, I believe, to the growth of pre-scientific knowledge also – that is to say, to the general way in which men, and even animals, acquire new factual knowledge about the world. The method of learning by trial and error – of learning from our mistakes – seems to be fundamentally the same whether it is practised by lower or by higher animals, by chimpanzees or by men of science. My interest is not merely in the theory of scientific knowledge, but rather in the theory of knowledge in general. Yet the study of the growth of scientific knowledge is, I believe, the most fruitful way of studying the growth of knowledge in general. For the growth

10. *L.Sc.D.*, p. 22.
11. Russell has made a similar point in identifying himself with an evolutionary epistemology: "There is another thing which it is important to remember whenever mental concepts are being discussed, and that is our evolutionary continuity with the lower animals. Knowledge, in particular, must not be defined in a manner which assumes an impassable gulf between ourselves and our ancestors who had not the advantage of language." Bertrand Russell, *Human Knowledge: Its Scope and Limits* (New York: Simon and Schuster, 1948), p. 421.

of scientific knowledge may be said to be the growth of ordinary human knowledge *writ large.*[12]

Such a location of the epistemological problem differs strikingly from traditional views, even though overlapping them. Given up is the effort to hold all knowledge in abeyance until the possibility of knowledge is first logically established, until indubitable first principles or incorrigible sense data are established upon which to build. Rather, the cumulative achievement of logical analysis is accepted: such grounds are logically unavailable. No nonpresumptive knowledge and no nonpresumptive modes of knowing are·possible to us. The difference between science and fiction, or between truth and error, must lie elsewhere, as in the tests and outcomes of testing of the logical implications of the presumptions. No claims to the refutation of a consistent (and therefore unspoken) solipsism are made. The logical irrefutability of such a possibility is accepted. The problem of knowledge, however, is elsewhere – in truth claims descriptive of a more than non-phenomenal world. This presumptive descriptive character is as inextricable in "direct" observation as in the statement of laws. The interest in the primitive fundamentals of knowledge does not begin or end with the conscious contents or sense data of the philosopher himself.

Another older and also more current statement of the epistemological problem is also eschewed. This is the identification of "knowledge" not as "true belief" but as "true belief" which is also "rationally justified" or "well-grounded." Though widely used in linguistic analysis, this point of view implicitly accepts as valid an inductivist epistemology (giving but superficial lip service to Hume in recognizing such induction as providing only approximate validity). Popper does not limit truth to those statements which have rational support or are well-grounded before they are asserted. Truth rather lies in the outcome of subsequent tests.

> *We do not know: we can only guess.* And our guesses are guided by the unscientific, the metaphysical (though biologically explicable) faith in laws, in regularities which we can uncover – discover. Like Bacon, we might describe our own contemporary science – "the method of reasoning which men now ordinarily apply to nature"– as consisting of "anticipations, rash and premature" and as "prejudices".
>
> But these marvelously imaginative and bold conjectures or "anticipations" of ours are carefully and soberly controlled by systematic tests. Once put forward, none of our "anticipations" are dogmatically upheld. Our method of research is not to defend them, in order to prove how right we were. On the contrary, we try to overthrow them. Using all the weapons of our logical, mathematical, and technical armory we try to prove that our anticipations were false – in order to put forward, in their stead, new unjustified and unjustifiable anticipations, new "rash and premature prejudices".[13]

12. *C.&R.*, p. 216.
13. *L.Sc.D.*, pp. 278-79.

3. A Nested Hierarchy of Selective-Retention Processes

Human knowledge processes, when examined in continuity with the evolutionary sequence, turn out to involve numerous mechanisms at various levels of substitute functioning, hierarchically related, and with some form of selective retention process at each level. While Popper has for most of his career been more interested in the logic of knowing than in a descriptive epistemology, in *Of Clouds and Clocks* he has expanded his evolutionary perspective along these lines. This is a paper which should be read by both epistemologists and those interested in problems of purpose and teleology. A few brief quotations from it will serve to introduce the present section.

> My theory may be described as an attempt to apply to the whole of evolution what we learned when we analysed the evolution from animal language to human language. And it consists of a certain *view of evolution* as a growing hierarchical system of plastic controls, and of a certain *view of organisms* as incorporating – or in the case of man, evolving exosomatically – this growing hierarchical system of plastic controls. The Neo-Darwinist theory of evolution is assumed; but it is restated by pointing out that its "mutations" may be interpreted as more or less accidental trial-and-error gambits, and "natural selection" as one way of controlling them by error-elimination.[14]

He also emphasizes what are called here vicarious selectors:

> Error-elimination may proceed either by the complete elimination of unsuccessful forms (the killing-off of unsuccessful forms by natural selection) or by the (tentative) evolution of controls which modify or suppress unsuccessful organs, or forms of behavior, or hypotheses.[15]
>
> Our schema allows for the development of error-eliminating controls (warning organs like the eye; feed-back mechanisms); that is, controls which can eliminate errors without killing the organism; and it makes it possible, ultimately, for our hypotheses to die in our stead.[16]

Also important is his emphasis on the multiplicity of trials needed at each error-elimination level, the necessity for the profuse generation of "mistakes."

More generally, in *Clouds and Clocks*, Popper has spoken for that emerging position in biology and control theory which sees the natural selection paradigm as the universal nonteleological explanation of teleological achievements, of ends-

---

14. K. R. Popper, *Of Clouds and Clocks: An Approach to the Problem of Rationality and the Freedom of Man* (St. Louis, Missouri: Washington University, 1966), p. 23. This is the Arthur Holly Compton Memorial Lecture, presented at Washington University on April 21, 1965, and printed as a 38-page booklet; reprinted in K. R. Popper, *Objective Knowledge: An Evolutionary Approach* (Oxford: Clarendon Press; New York: Oxford University Press, 1972). This excerpt reprinted by permission of the author and publishers.

15. *OCC*, p. 23.

16. *OCC*, p. 25.

guided processes, of "fit".[17] Thus crystal formation is seen as the result of a chaotic permutation of molecular adjacencies, some of which are much more difficult to dislodge than others. At temperatures warm enough to provide general change, but not so warm as to disrupt the few stable adjacencies, the number of stable adjacencies will steadily grow even if their occurrence is but a random affair. In crystal formation the material forms its own template. In the genetic control of growth, the DNA provides the initial template selectively accumulating chance fitting RNA molecules, which in turn provide the selective template selectively cumulating from among chaotic permutations of proteins. These molecules of course fit multiple selective criteria: of that finite set of semistable combinations of protein material, they are the subset fitting the template. The template guides by selecting from among the mostly unstable, mostly worthless possibilities offered by thermal noise operating on the materials in solution. Turning the model to still lower levels of organization, elements and subatomic particles are seen as but nodes of stability which at certain temperatures transiently select adjacencies among still more elementary stuff.

Turning to higher levels, the model can be applied to such dramatically teleological achievements as embryological growth and wound healing. Within each cell, genetic templates for all types of body proteins are simultaneously available, competing as it were for the raw material present. Which ones propagate most depends upon the surrounds. Transplantation of embryonic material changes the surroundings and hence the selective system. Wounds and amputations produce analogous changes in the "natural selection" of protein possibilities. Spiegelman[18] has specifically noted the Darwinian analogy and its advantages over vitalistic teleological pseudoexplanations which even concepts of force fields and excitatory gradients may partake of.

Regeneration provides an illustration of the nested hierarchical nature of biological selection systems. The salamander's amputated leg regrows to a length optimal for locomotion and survival. The ecological selection system does not operate directly on the leg length however. Instead, the leg length is selected to conform to an internal control built into the developmental system which vicariously represents the ecological selective system. This control was itself selected by the trial and error of whole mutant organisms.[19] If the ecology has recently undergone change, the vicarious selective criterion will correspondingly be in error.

---

17. The most complete recent review of this voluminous literature is William Church Wimsatt, "Modern Science and the New Teleology" (unpublished Ph.D. diss., University of Pittsburgh, 1971); and W. C. Wimsatt, "Teleology and the Logical Structure of Function Statements", *Studies in History and Philosophy of Science* 3, No. 1 (April, 1972). He recognizes the proper understanding of this problem as inextricably involved with an evolutionary epistemology.

18. S. Spiegelman, "Differentiation as the Controlled Production of Unique Enzymatic Patterns", *Symposia of the Society for Experimental Biology, II: Growth in Relation to Differentiation and Morphogenesis* (New York: Academic Press, 1948).

19. H. J. Barr, "Regeneration and Natural Selection", *American Naturalist* 98 (1964), 183–86.

This larger, encompassing selection system is the organism-environment interaction. Nested in a hierarchical way within it is the selective system directly operating on leg length, the "settings" or criteria for which are themselves subject to change by natural selection. What are criteria at one level are but "trials" of the criteria of the next higher, more fundamental, more encompassing, less frequently invoked level.

In other writings[20] the present author has advocated a systematic extrapolation of this nested hierarchy selective retention paradigm to *all* knowledge processes, in a way which, although basically compatible with Popper's orientation, may go farther than he would find reasonable in extremity, dogmatism, and claims for generality. It may on these same grounds alienate the reader. (Disagreement at this point will not rule out accepting later propositions.)

1. A blind-variation-and-selective-retention process is fundamental to all inductive achievements,[21] to all genuine increases in knowledge, to all increases in fit of system to environment.

2. In such a process there are three essentials: (a) Mechanisms for introducing variation; (b) Consistent selection processes; and (c) Mechanisms for preserving and/or propagating the selected variations. Note that in general the preservation and generation mechanisms are inherently at odds, and each must be compromised.

3. The many processes which shortcut a more full blind-variation-and-selective-retention process are in themselves inductive achievements, containing wisdom about the environment achieved originally by blind variation and selective retention.

4. In addition, such shortcut processes contain in their own operation a blind-variation-and-selective-retention process at some level, substituting for overt locomotor exploration or the life-and-death winnowing of organic evolution.

The word "blind" is used rather than the more usual "random" for a variety of reasons. It seems likely that Ashby[22] unnecessarily limited the generality of his mechanism in Homeostat by an effort fully to represent all of the modern connotations of "random". Equiprobability is not needed, and is definitely lacking in the mutations which lay the variation base for organic evolution. Statistical independence between one variation and the next, although frequently desirable, can also be spared: in particular, for the generalizations essayed here, certain processes involving systematic sweep scanning are recognized as blind, insofar as variations are produced without prior knowledge of which ones, if any, will

20. D. T. Campbell, "Methodological Suggestions from a Comparative Psychology of Knowledge Processes", *Inquiry* 2 (1959), 152–82; and D. T. Campbell, "Blind Variation and Selective Retention in Creative Thought as in Other Knowledge Processes", *Psychological Review* 67 (1960), 380–400, and Chapter III of this volume.

21. The use of the phrase "inductive achievements" is for convenience in communicating and does not in the least imply advocacy of the Bacon-Hume-Mill explanation of those achievements nor disagreement with Popper's brilliant criticisms of induction.

22. W. R. Ashby, *Design for a Brain* (New York: John Wiley & Sons, 1952).

furnish a selectworthy encounter. An essential connotation of "blind" is that the variations emitted be independent of the environmental conditions of the occasion of their occurrence. A second important connotation is that the occurrence of trials individually be uncorrelated with the solution, in that specific correct trials are no more likely to occur at any one point in a series of trials than another, nor than specific incorrect trials. A third essential connotation of "blind" is rejection of the notion that a variation subsequent to an incorrect trial is a "correction" of the previous trial or makes use of the direction of error of the previous one. (Insofar as mechanisms do seem to operate in this fashion, there must be operating a substitute process carrying on the blind search at another level, feedback circuits selecting "partially" adequate variations, providing information to the effect that "you're getting warm", etc.)[23]

While most descriptions of discovery and creative processes recognize the need for variation, the present author's dogmatic insistence on the blindness of such variation seems generally unacceptable. As will be seen in what follows, particularly in the discussions of vision and thought, there is no real descriptive disagreement. The present writer agrees that the overt responses of a problem-solving animal in a puzzle box are far from random, and this for several reasons: (1) Already-achieved wisdom of a general sort which limits the range of trials (such wisdom due to inheritance and learning). (2) Maladaptive restriction on the range of trials. (Such biases due to structural limitations and to past habit and instinct inappropriate in a novel environment.) But these first two reasons will characterize the wrong responses as well as the correct ones, and offer no explanation of the correctness of the correct one. (3) Vicarious selection, appropriate to the immediate problem, achieved through vision. (See the subsequent section on this topic.) When, in considering creative thought, Poincaré is followed, allowing for unconscious variation-and-selection processes, opportunity for descriptive disagreement is further reduced. The point is not empirically empty, however, as it sets essential limits and requirements for any problem-solving computer (discussed under "Thought", below). But the point is also analytic. In going beyond what is already known, one cannot but go blindly. If one can go wisely, this indicates already achieved wisdom of some general sort.

Expanding this orientation and applying it to the setting of biological and social evolution, a set of ten more or less discrete levels can be distinguished, and these are elaborated in the following sections.

1. *Non-mnemonic problem solving.* At the level of Jennings's[24] paramecium, stentor, and Ashby's[25] Homeostat, there is a blind variation of locomotor activity until a setting that is nourishing or non-noxious is found. Such problem-solutions are

23. The above five paragraphs have been quoted with some rearrangement and transitional modifications from pp. 380 and 381 of Campbell, "Blind Variation" (note 20).

24. H. S. Jennings, *The Behavior of the Lower Organisms* (New York: Columbia University Press, 1906).

25. *Design for a Brain* (note 22).

then retained as a cessation of locomotion, as a cessation of variation. There is, however, no memory, no using of old solutions over again. Ashby deliberately took Jennings's paramecium as his model, and describes the natural selection analogy at this level as follows:

> The work also in a sense develops a theory of the "natural selection" of behaviour-patterns. Just as in the species the truism that the dead cannot breed implies that there is a fundamental tendency for the successful to replace the unsuccessful, so in the nervous system does the truism that the unstable tends to destroy itself imply that there is a fundamental tendency for the stable to replace the unstable. Just as the gene pattern in its encounters with the environment tends toward ever better adaptation of the inherited form and function, so does a system of step- and part-functions tend toward ever better adaptation of learned behavior.[26]

In a world with only benign or neutral states, an adaptive organism might operate at this level without exteroceptors. Wherever it is, it is trying to ingest the immediate environment. When starvation approaches, blind locomotor activity is initiated, ingestion being attempted at all locations. Even at this level, however, there is needed an interoceptive sense organ which monitors nutritional level, and substitutes for the whole organism's death. In the actual case of Jennings's stentor, chemoreceptors for noxious conditions are present, vicarious representatives of the lethal character of the environment, operating on nonlethal samples or signs of that environment. It is these chemoreceptors and comparable organs which in fact provide the immediate selection of responses. Only indirectly, through selecting the selectors, does life-and-death relevance select the responses.

At this level of knowing, however, the responses may be regarded as direct rather than vicarious. And, as to presuppositions about the nature of the world (the ontology guiding epistemology), perhaps all that is assumed is spatial discontinuity somewhat greater than temporal discontinuity in the distribution of environmental substances: moving around is judged to bring changes more rapidly than staying put. At this level the species has discovered that the environment is discontinuous, consisting of penetrable regions and impenetrable ones, and that impenetrability is to some extent a stable characteristic. The animal has "learned" that there are some solvable problems. Already the machinery of knowing is biasedly focused upon the small segment of the world which is knowable, as natural selection makes inevitable.

2. *Vicarious locomotor devices.* Substituting for spatial exploration by locomotor trial and error are a variety of distance receptors of which a ship's radar is an example. An automated ship could explore the environment of landfalls, harbors, and other ships by a trial and error of full movements and collisions. Instead, it sends out substitute locomotions in the form of a radar beam. These are selectively reflected from nearby objects, the reflective opaqueness to this wave band vicariously representing the locomotor impenetrability of the objects. This vicar-

26. *Ibid.*, p. vi (note 22).

ious representability is a contingent discovery, and is in fact only approximate. The knowledge received is reconfirmed as acted upon by the full ship's locomotion. The process removes the trial-and-error component from the overt locomotion, locating it instead in the blindly emitted radar beam. (The radar beam is not emitted randomly, but it could be so emitted and still work. The radar beam is, however, emitted in a blind exploration, albeit a systematic sweep.) Analogous to radar and to sonar are several echolocation devices in animals. Pumphrey has described the lateral-line organ of fish as a receiver for the reflected pulses of the broadcast pressure waves emitted by the fish's own swimming movements. The all-directional exploring of the wave front is selectively reflected by nearby objects, pressure wave substituting for locomotor exploration. The echolocation devices of porpoises, bats, and cave birds have a similar epistemology.[27]

Assimilating vision to the blind-variation-and-selective-retention model is a more difficult task.[28] It seems important, however, to make vision palpably problematic, in correction of the commonsense realism or the direct realism of many contemporary philosophers which leads them to an uncritical assumption of directness and certainty for the visual process. The vividness and phenomenal directness of vision needs to be corrected in any complete epistemology, which also has to make comprehensible how such an indirect, coincidence-exploiting mechanism could work at all. Were visual percepts as vague and incoherent as the phosphors on a radar screen, many epistemological problems would be avoided. From the point of view of an evolutionary epistemology, vision is just as indirect as radar.

Consider a one-photocell substitute eye such as was once distributed for the use of the blind. To an earphone, the cell transmitted a note of varying pitch depending upon the brightness of the light received. In blind search with this photocell, one could locate some objects and some painted boundaries on flat surfaces, all boundaries being indicated by a shift in tone. One can imagine an extension of this blind search device to a multiple photocell model, each photocell of fixed direction, boundaries being located by a comparison of emitted tones or energies perhaps in some central sweep-scanning of outputs. To be sure, boundaries would be doubly confirmed if the whole set were oscillated slightly, so that a boundary stood out not only as comparison across adjacent receptors at one time, but also as a comparison across times for the same receptors. (The eye has just such a physiological nystagmus, essential to its function.) Similarly, one could build a radar with multiple fixed-directional emitters and receivers. It would search just as blindly, just as open-mindedly, as the single beam and sweep-scanner. In

27. R. J. Pumphrey, "Hearing", in *Symposia of the Society for Experimental Biology, IV: Physiological Mechanism in Animal Behavior* (New York: Academic Press, 1950), pp. 1–18; W. N. Kellogg, "Echo-Ranging in the Porpoise", *Science* **128** (1958), 982–88; and D. R. Griffin, *Listening in the Dark* (New Haven: Yale University Press, 1958).

28. D. T. Campbell, "Perception as Substitute Trial and Error", *Psychological Review* **63** (1956), 331–42.

such multiple receptor devices, the opportunities for excitation are blindly made available and are selectively activated.

Blind locomotor search is the more primary, the more direct exploration. A blind man's cane is a vicarious search process. The less expensive cane movements substitute for blind trials and wasted movements by the whole body, removing costly search from the full locomotor effort, making that seem smooth, purposeful, insightful.[29] The single photocell device seems equally blind, although utilizing a more unlikely substitute, one still cheaper in effort and time. The multiple photocell device, or the eye, uses the multiplicity of cells instead of a multiplicity of focusings of one cell, resulting in a search process equally blind and open-minded, equally dependent upon a selection-from-variety epistemology. The substitutability of cane locomotion for body locomotion, the equivalence of opaque-to-cane and opaque-to-body, is a contingent discovery, although one which seems more nearly "entailed," or to involve a less complex, less presumptive model of the physical world than does the substitutability of light waves or radar waves for body locomotion.

This is, of course, a skeletonized model of vision, emphasizing its kinship to blind fumbling, and its much greater indirectness than blind fumbling, phenomenal directness notwithstanding. Neglected is the presumptive achievement of the visual system in reifying stable discrete objects, stable over a heterogeneity of points of viewing; neglected is the fundamental epistemological achievement of "identifying" new and partially different sets of sense data as the "the same" so that habit or instinct or knowledge can be appropriately applied even though there be no logically entailed identity.[30]

3. *Habit* and 4. *Instinct*. Habit, instinct, and visual diagnosis of objects are so interlocked and interdependent that no simple ordering of the three is possible. Much more detailed work is needed on the evolution of knowledge processes, and such an examination would no doubt describe many more stages than are outlined here. Such a study could also profitably describe the "presumptions" about the nature of the world, or the "knowledge" about the nature of the world, underlying each stage. Certainly the extent of these presumptions is greater at the more advanced levels.

---

29. *Ibid.*, pp. 334–35. Note also the example of left-hand search substituting for right-hand exploration in a blind sorting task.

30. Beginnings on this problem of pattern matching are to be found in Bertrand Russell's discussion of the "structural postulate", pp. 460–72, and 492, of *Human Knowledge: Its Scope and Limits* (New York: Simon & Schuster, 1948); in Konrad Lorenz, "Gestaltwarnehmung als Quelle wissenschaftliche Erkenntnis", *Zeitschrift für experimentelle und angewandte Psychologie* 6 (1959), 118–65, translated as "Gestalt Perception as Fundamental to Scientific Knowledge", *General Systems* 7 (1962), 37–56; and in D. T. Campbell, "Pattern Matching as Essential in Distal Knowing", in *The Psychology of Egon Brunswik*, ed. by K. R. Hammond (New York: Holt, Rinehart & Winston, 1966), pp. 81–106.

31. The formal analogy between natural selection and trial-and-error learning has been noted by many, including James M. Baldwin, *Mental Development in the Child and Race* (New York: Macmillan, 1900); Samuel Jackson Holmes, *Studies in Animal Behavior* (Boston: Gorham Press, 1916); Ashby, *Design for a Brain*; and J. W. S. Pringle, "On the Parallel Between Learning and Evolution", *Behaviour* 3 (1951), 175–215.

The visual diagnosis of reidentifiable objects is basic to most instinctive response patterns in insects and vertebrates, both for instigation of the adaptive pattern and for eliminating the trial-and-error component from the overt response elements. In a crude way, instinct development can be seen as involving a trial and error of whole mutant animals, whereas trial-and-error learning involves the much cheaper wastage of responses within the lifetime of a single animal.[31] The same environment is editing habit and instinct development in most cases, the editing process is analogous, and the epistemological status of the knowledge, innate or learned, no different. Thus the great resistance of the empiricists to innate knowledge is made irrelevant, but in the form of a more encompassing empiricism. It can be noted that all comprehensive learning theories, including those of Gestalt inspiration, contain a trial-and-error component, be it a trial and error of "hypotheses" or "recenterings".[32]

These general conclusions may be acceptable, but the evolutionary discreteness of the two processes is not as clear as implied nor should instinct necessarily be regarded as more primitive than habit. Complex adaptive instincts typically involve multiple movements and must inevitably involve a multiplicity of mutations at least as great in number as the obvious movement segments. Furthermore, it is typical that the fragmentary movement segments, or the effects of single component mutations, would represent no adaptive gain at all apart from the remainder of the total sequence. The joint likelihood of the simultaneous occurrence of the adaptive form of the many mutations involved is so infinitesimal that the blind-mutation-and-selective-retention model seems inadequate. This argument was used effectively by both Lamarckians and those arguing for an intelligently-guided evolution or creation. Baldwin, Morgan, Osborn, and Poulton,[33] believing that natural selection was the adequate and only mechanism, proposed that for such instincts, learned adaptive patterns, recurrently discovered in similar form within a species by trial-and-error learning, preceded the instincts. The adaptive pattern being thus piloted by learning, any mutations that accelerated the learning, made it more certain to occur, or predisposed the animal to certain component responses, would be adaptive and selected no matter which component, or in what order affected. The habit thus provided a selective template around which the instinctive components could be assembled. (Stating it in other terms, learned habits make a new ecological niche available, which niche then selects instinct components.) It is furthermore typical of such instincts that they involve learned components, as of nest and raw material location, etc.

This can be conceived as an evolution of increasingly specific selection-criteria, which at each level select or terminate visual search and trial-and-error learning. In what we call learning, these are very general drive states and reinforcing con-

32. D. T. Campbell, "Adaptive Behavior from Random Response", *Behavioral Science* 1 (1956), 105–10.

33. James M. Baldwin perhaps first proposed the idea. He reprints relevant papers by C. Lloyd Morgan, H. F. Osborn, E. B. Poulton, and himself in *Development and Evolution* (New York: Macmillan, 1902), using the terms "orthoplasy" and "organic selection" to cover the concept.

ditions. In the service of these general reinforcers, specific objects and situations become learned goals and sub-goals, learned selectors of more specific responses. (Even for drives and reinforcers, of course, the environment's selective relevance is represented indirectly, as in the pleasureableness of sweet foods, the vicariousness of which is shown by an animal's willingness to learn for the reward of non-nutritive saccharin.) In the habit-to-instinct evolution, the once-learned goals and sub-goals become innate at a more and more specific response-fragment level. For such an evolutionary development to take place, very stable environments over long evolutionary periods are required.

Popper in his Herbert Spencer Lecture of 1961[33a] makes a creative analysis of the evolution of purposeful behavior which in some ways parallels Baldwin's, but is more explicit on the hierarchical selection of selectors. Using a servomechanism model of an automated aeroplane, he suggests that mutations of "aim-structure" precede and subsequently select mutations in "skill structure".

5. *Visually supported thought.* The dominant form of insightful problem solving in animals, e.g., as described by Köhler,[34] requires the support of a visually present environment. With the environment represented vicariously through visual search, there is a substitute trial and error of potential locomotions in thought. The "successful" locomotions at this substitute level, with its substitute selective criteria, are then put into overt locomotion, where they appear "intelligent", "purposeful", "insightful", even if still subject to further editing in the more direct contact with the environment.

6. *Mnemonically supported thought.* At this level the environment being searched is vicariously represented in memory or by "knowledge", rather than visually, the blindly emitted vicarious thought trials being selected by a vicarious criterion substituting for an external state of affairs. The net result is the "intelligent", "creative", and "foresightful" product of thought, our admiration of which makes us extremely reluctant to subsume it under the blind-variation-and-selective-retention model. Yet it is in the description of this model that the trial-and-error theme, the blind permutation theme, has been most persistently invoked. When Mach in 1895 was called back to Vienna to assume the newly created professorship in "The History and Theory of Inductive Sciences", he chose this topic:

> The disclosure of new provinces of facts before unknown can only be brought about by accidental circumstances . . . [35]
>
> In such [other] cases it is a psychical accident to which the person owes his discovery – a discovery which is here made "deductively" by means of mental copies of the world, instead of experimentally.[36]

33a. In *Objective Knowledge*, pp. 256–80 (note 14).
34. Wolfgang Köhler, *The Mentality of Apes* (New York: Harcourt, Brace, 1925).
35. Ernst Mach, "On the Part Played by Accident in Invention and Discovery", *Monist* 6 (1896), 161–75.
36. *Ibid.*, p. 171.

After the repeated survey of a field has afforded opportunity for the interposition of advantageous accidents, has rendered all the traits that suit with the word or the dominant thought more vivid, and has gradually relegated to the background all things that are inappropriate, making their future appearance impossible; then, from the teeming, swelling host of fancies which a free and high-flown imagination calls forth, suddenly that particular form arises to the light which harmonizes perfectly with the ruling idea, mood, or design. Then it is that that which has resulted slowly as the result of a gradual selection, appears as if it were the outcome of a deliberate act of creation. Thus are to be explained the statements of Newton, Mozart, Richard Wagner, and others, when they say that thoughts, melodies, and harmonies had poured in upon them, and that they had simply retained the right ones.[37]

Poincaré's famous essay on mathematical creativity espouses such a view at length, arguing that it is mathematical beauty which provides the selective criteria for a blind permuting process usually unconscious:

> One evening, contrary to my custom, I drank black coffee and could not sleep. Ideas rose in crowds; I felt them collide until pairs interlocked, so to speak, making a stable combination.[38]
>
> . . . What happens then? Among the great numbers of combinations blindly formed by the subliminal self, almost all are without interest and without utility; but just for that reason they are also without effect upon the esthetic sensibility. Consciousness will never know them; only certain ones are harmonious, and consequently, at once useful and beautiful.[39]
>
> . . . Perhaps we ought to seek the explanation in that preliminary period of conscious work which always precedes all fruitful unconscious labor. Permit me a rough comparison. Figure the future elements of our combinations as something like the hooked atoms of Epicurus. During the complete repose of the mind, these atoms are motionless, they are, so to speak, hooked to the wall; so this complete rest may be indefinitely prolonged without the atoms meeting, and consequently without any combination between them.
>
> On the other hand, during a period of apparent rest and unconscious work, certain of them are detached from the wall and put in motion. They flash in every direction through the space (I was about to say the room) where they are enclosed, as would, for example, a swarm of gnats or, if you prefer a more learned comparison, like the molecules of gas in the kinematic theory of gases. Then their mutual impacts may produce new combinations.[40]
>
> . . . In the subliminal self, on the contrary, reigns what I should call liberty, if we might give this name to the simple absence of discipline and to the disorder born of chance. Only this disorder itself permits unexpected combinations.[41]

37. *Ibid.*, p. 174.
38. Henri Poincaré, "Mathematical Creation", in H. Poincaré, *The Foundations of Science* (New York: Science Press, 1913), p. 387.
39. *Ibid.*, p. 392.
40. *Ibid.*, p. 393.
41. *Ibid.*, p. 394.

Alexander Bain was proposing a trial-and-error model of invention and thought as early as 1855.[42] Jevons in 1874[43] was advocating a similar model in the context of a rejection of Bacon's principle of induction on grounds similar to Popper's.

> I hold that in all cases of inductive inference we must invent hypotheses until we fall upon some hypothesis which yields deductive results in accordance with experience.[44]

> It would be an error to suppose that the great discoverer seizes at once upon the truth or has any unerring method of divining it. In all probability the errors of the great mind exceed in number those of the less vigorous one. Fertility of imagination and abundance of guesses at truth are among the first requisites of discovery; but the erroneous guesses must be many times as numerous as those which prove well founded. The weakest analogies, the most whimsical notions, the most apparently absurd theories, may pass through the teeming brain, and no record remain of more than the hundredth part. There is nothing really absurd except that which proves contrary to logic and experience. The truest theories involve suppositions which are inconceivable, and no limit can really be placed to the freedom of hypothesis.[45]

In his very modern and almost totally neglected *Theory of Invention* of 1881, Souriau effectively criticizes deduction, induction, and *"la méthode"* as models for advances in thought and knowledge. His recurrent theme is *"le principe de l'invention est le hazard"*:

> A problem is posed for which we must invent a solution. We know the conditions to be met by the sought idea; but we do not know what series of ideas will lead us there. In other words, we know how the series of our thoughts must end, but not how it should begin. In this case it is evident that there is no way to begin except at random. Our mind takes up the first path that it finds open before it, perceives that it is a false route, retraces its steps and takes another direction. Perhaps it will arrive immediately at the sought idea, perhaps it will arrive very belatedly: it is entirely impossible to know in advance. In these conditions we are reduced to dependence upon chance.[46]

> By a kind of artificial selection, we can in addition substantially perfect our thought and make it more and more logical. Of all the ideas which present themselves to our mind, we note only those which have some value and can be utilized in reasoning. For every single idea of a judicious and reasonable nature which offers itself to us, what hosts of frivolous, bizarre, and absurd ideas cross our mind. Those persons who, upon considering the marvelous results at which knowledge has arrived, cannot imagine that the human mind could achieve this by a simple fumbling, do not bear in mind the great number of scholars working at the same time on the same problem, and how much time even the smallest discovery costs them. Even genius has need of

42. 1855 is the date of the first edition of Alexander Bain, *The Senses and the Intellect*. The quotations are from the 3d ed. (New York: Appleton, 1874), pp. 593–95.
43. Stanley Jevons, *The Principles of Science* (London: Macmillan, 1892). (1st ed., 1874; 2d ed., 1877; reprinted with corrections, 1892.)
44. *Ibid.*, p. 228.
45. *Ibid.*, p. 577.
46. Paul Souriau, *Theorie de l'Invention* (Paris: Hachette, 1881), p. 17.

patience. It is after hours and years of meditation that the sought-after idea presents itself to the inventor. He does not succeed without going astray many times; and if he thinks himself to have succeeded without effort, it is only because the joy of having succeeded has made him forget all the fatigues, all of the false leads, all of the agonies, with which he has paid for his success.[47]

. . . If his memory is strong enough to retain all of the amassed details, he evokes them in turn with such rapidity that they seem to appear simultaneously; he groups them by chance in all the possible ways; his ideas, thus shaken up and agitated in his mind, form numerous unstable aggregates which destroy themselves, and finish up by stopping on the most simple and solid combination.[48]

Note the similarity of the imagery in the final paragraph with that of Ashby as cited under level 1, above, and that of Poincaré, Mach, and Jevons.

In Souriau's use of the phrase "artificial selection", he seems to refer to the analogy with Darwin's theory of natural selection, but we cannot be certain. Souriau's book is totally devoid of citations or even mentions of the works of any other. William James, however, is completely explicit on the analogy in an article published in 1880.[49] Arguing against Spencer's model of a perfectly passive mind, he says:

And I can easily show that throughout the whole extent of those mental departments which are highest, which are most characteristically human, Spencer's law is violated at every step; and that, as a matter of fact, the new conceptions, emotions, and active tendencies which evolve are originally *produced* in the shape of random images, fancies, accidental outbirths of spontaneous variation in the functional activity of the excessively unstable human brain, which the outer environment simply confirms or refutes, preserves or destroys – selects, in short, just as it selects morphological and social variations due to molecular accidents of an analogous sort.[50]

. . . The conception of the [scientific] law is a spontaneous variation in the strictest sense of the term. It flashes out of one brain, and no other, because the instability of that brain is such as to tip and upset itself in just that particular direction. But the important thing to notice is that the good flashes and the bad flashes, the triumphant hypotheses and the absurd conceits, are on an exact equality in respect of their origin.[51]

James departs from the more complete model presented in Poincaré,[52] Mach,[53] and Campbell[54] by seemingly having the full range of mental variations selected by the external environment rather than recognizing the existence of mental selectors, which vicariously represent the external environment (the selected products,

47. *Ibid.*, p. 43.
48. *Ibid.*, pp. 114–15.
49. William James, "Great Men, Great Thoughts, and the Environment", *The Atlantic Monthly* **46**, No. 276 (October, 1880), 441–59. See also William James, *Principles of Psychology* (New York: Henry Holt, 1890), Vol. II, pp. 617–79.
50. *Ibid.*, p. 456.
51. *Ibid.*, p. 457.
52. "Mathematical Creation" (note 38).
53. "Part Played by Accident" (note 35).
54. "Blind Variation" (note 20).

of course, being subject to further validation in overt locomotion, etc.).

Among the many others who have advocated such a view are Baldwin, Fouillé, Pillsbury, Woodworth, Rignano, Thurstone, Lowes, Tolman, Hull, Muenzinger, Miller and Dollard, Boring, Humphrey, Mowrer, Sluckin, Pólya, and Bonsack.[55] One presentation which has reached the attention of some philosophers is that of Kenneth J. W. Craik, in his fragmentary work of genius, *The Nature of Explanation*,[56] a work which in many other ways also espouses an evolutionary epistemology.

The resultant process of thought is a very effective one, and a main pillar of man's high estate. Yet it must be emphasized again that the vicarious representations involved – both environmental realities and potential locomotions being represented in mind-brain processes – are discovered contingent relationships, achieving no logical entailment, and in fine detail incomplete and imperfect. This same vicarious, contingent, discovered, marginally imperfect representativeness holds for the highly selected formal logics and mathematics which we utilize in the processes of science.

Computer problem solving is a highly relevant topic, and is perhaps best introduced at this point. Like thinking, it requires vicarious explorations of a vicarious representation of the environment, with the exploratory trials being selected by criteria which are vicarious representatives of solution requirements or external realities. The present writer would insist here too, that if discovery or expansions of knowledge are achieved, blind variation is requisite. This being the case, it is only fair to note that Herbert Simon, both a leading computer simulator of thought and an epistemologically sophisticated scholar, rejects this point of view, at least in the extreme form advocated here. For example, he says, "The more difficult and novel the problem, the greater is likely to be the amount of trial and error required to find a solution. At the same time, the trial and error is not completely random or blind; it is, in fact, highly selective."[57] Earlier statements on this have been still more rejective.[58] The present writer has attempted elsewhere to answer in more detail than space here permits,[59] but a brief summary is in order. The "selectivity", insofar as it is appropriate, represents already achieved wisdom of a more general sort, and as such, selectivity does not in any sense explain an innovative solution. Insofar as the selectivity is inappropriate, it limits areas of search in which a solution might be found, and rules out classes of possible solutions. Insofar as the selectivity represents a partial general truth, some unusual solutions are ruled out. Simon's "heuristics" are such partial truths, and a computer which would generate its own heuristics would have to do so by

55. See Bibliography in Callebaut and Pinxten, cited in Bibliography to chap. 1 above.
56. *Ibid.*
57. Herbert A. Simon, *The Sciences of the Artificial* (Cambridge, Mass.: The MIT Press, 1969), p. 95.
58. A. Newell, J. C. Shaw & H. A. Simon, "Elements of a Theory of Human Problem Solving", *Psychological Review* 65 (1958), 151-66.
59. "Blind Variation", pp. 392-95 (note 20).

a blind trial and error of heuristic principles, selection from which would represent achieved general knowledge. The principle of hierarchy in problem solving depends upon such discoveries, and once achieved, can, of course, greatly reduce the total search space, but without at all violating the requirement of blindness as here conceived. For example, one of the heuristics used in Simon's "Logic Theorist" program[60] is that any substitution or transformation which will increase the "similarity" between a proposition and the desired outcome should be retained as a stem on which further variations are to be tried. Any transformation decreasing similarity should be discarded. Similarity is crudely scored by counting the number of identical terms, with more points for similarity of location. This rule enables selection to be introduced at each transformational stage, greatly reducing the total search space. It employs an already achieved partial truth. It produces computer search similar to human problem solving in failing to discover roundabout solutions requiring initial decreases in similarity. Beyond thus applying what is already known, albeit only a partial truth, the new discoveries must be produced by a blind generation of alternatives.

7. *Socially vicarious exploration: observational learning and imitation.* The survival value of the eye is obviously related to an economy of cognition – the economy of eliminating all of the wasted locomotions which would otherwise be needed. An analogous economy of cognition helps account for the great survival advantage of the truly social forms of animal life, which in evolutionary sequences are regularly found subsequent to rather than prior to solitary forms. In this, the trial-and-error exploration of one member of a group substitutes for, renders unnecessary, trial-and-error exploration on the part of other members. The use of trial and error by scouts on the part of migrating social insects and human bands illustrates this general knowledge process. At the simplest level in social animals are procedures whereby one animal can profit from observing the consequences to another of that other's acts, even or especially when these acts are fatal to the model. The aversion which apes show to dismembered ape bodies, and their avoidance of the associated locations, illustrates such a process.[61] In ants and termites the backtracking on the tracks of foragers who have come back heavily laden illustrates such a process for knowledge of attractive goal objects. The presumptions involved in this epistemology include the belief that the model, the vicar, is exploring the same world in which the observer is living and locomoting, as well as those assumptions about the lawfulness of that world which underlie all learning.

Also noted in social animals, perhaps particularly in their young, is a tendency to imitate the actions of models even when the outcomes of those actions cannot be observed. This is a much more presumptive, but still "rational" procedure. It involves the assumptions that the model animal is capable of learning

60. Newell, Shaw & Simon, "Human Problem Solving" (note 58).
61. D. O. Hebb, "On the Nature of Fear", *Psychological Review* 53 (1946), 259–76.

and is living in a learnable world. If this is so, then the model has probably eliminated punished responses and has increased its tendencies to make rewarded
responses, resulting in a net output of predominantly rewarded responses (the
more so the longer the learning period and the stabler the environment).[62]

But even in imitation, there is no "direct" infusion or transference of knowledge or habit, just as there is no "direct" acquisition of knowledge by observation
or induction. As Baldwin[63] analyzes the process, what the child acquires is a
criterion image, which he learns to match by a trial and error of matchings. He
hears a tune, for example, and then learns to make that sound by a trial and error
of vocalizations, which he checks against the memory of the sound pattern. Recent
studies of the learning of bird song confirm and elaborate the same model.[64]

8. *Language.* Overlapping with levels 6 and 7 above is language, in which the
outcome of explorations can be relayed from scout to follower with neither the
illustrative locomotion nor the environment explored being present, not even
visually-vicariously present. From the social-functional point of view, it is quite
appropriate to speak of the "language" of bees, even though the wagging dance
by which the scout bee conveys the direction, distance, and richness of his find
is an innate response tendency automatically elicited without conscious intent to
communicate. This bee language has the social function of economy of cognition
in a way quite analogous to human language. The vicarious representabilities of
geographical direction (relative to the sun and plane of polarization of sunlight),
of distance, and of richness by features of the dance such as direction on a verti-
cal wall, length of to-and-fro movements, rapidity of movements, etc., are all
invented and contingent equivalences, neither entailed nor perfect, but tremen-
dously reductive of flight lengths on the part of the observing or listening worker
bees.[65] The details of von Frisch's analysis are currently being both challenged
and extended. Perhaps the dance language does not communicate as precisely
as he thought. Perhaps sonic, supersonic, and odor-trail means are also involved.

62. Solomon E. Asch in *Social Psychology* (New York: Prentice-Hall, 1952) has argued the
rationality of such imitative or conformant behavior, and the social nature of man's cognition of the
world. See also D. T. Campbell, "Conformity in Psychology's Theories of Acquired Behavioral Dispositions", in *Conformity and Deviation*, ed. by I. A. Berg and B. M. Bass (New York: Harper & Row,
1961), pp. 101–42; D. T. Campbell, "Social Attitudes and Other Acquired Behavioral Dispositions",
in *Psychology: A Study of a Science*, Vol. 6: *Investigations of Man as Socius*, ed. by S. Koch (New York:
McGraw-Hill, 1963), pp. 94–172, and A. Bandura, *Principles of Behavior Modification* (New York: Holt,
Rinehart & Winston, 1969).

63. James M. Baldwin, *Thought and Things, or Genetic Logic* (New York: Macmillan, 1906), Vol.
I, p. 169. Popper has also emphasized this, in his *Postscript to the Logic of Scientific Discovery* (London:
Hutchinson, 1982-3).

64. R. A. Hinde, ed., *Bird Vocalizations* (Cambridge, England and New York: Cambridge University Press, 1969). See especially the chapters by Lorenz and Immelman.

65. Karl von Frisch, *Bees, Their Vision, Chemical Sense, and Language* (Ithaca: Cornell University
Press, 1950); T. A. Sebcok, ed., *Animal Communication: Techniques of Study and Results of Research*
(Bloomington, Ind.: Indiana University Press, 1968); and T. A. Sebcok & A. Ramsay, eds., *Approaches
to Animal Communication* (The Hague, Netherlands: Mouton & Company, 1969). Note especially the
elegant new confirmation of von Frisch by J. L. Gould, M. Henerey, and M. C. MacLeod, "Communication of Direction by the Honey Bee", *Science* **169** (1970), 544–54.

It seems certain, however, that there are effective means of transmitting to other bees the successful outcomes of scout bee explorations in such a manner as to greatly reduce the total wasted exploratory effort over that required of solitary bees.

Given the present controversy over "bee language", it may be well to make the point of a functional-linguistic feature in social insects at a more primitive level. Ants and termites have independently discovered the use of pheromones for this purpose: an explorer who has encountered food exudes a special external hormone on his walk back to the nest. The other workers backtrack on this special scent. If they too are successful, if the food supply remains plentiful, they keep the pheromone track renewed. The "knowledge" of the environment upon which the worker bases his trip is profoundly indirect. This "knowledge" is more directly confirmed if and when the worker finds food (although the also implied information that food is more prevalent in this direction than in most others is not tested at all). But even this confirmation is profoundly indirect at the individual system level, for it involves sense-organ criteria for nourishingness rather than nourishingness itself. These criteria turn out to be approximate within limits set by the prior ecology. Non-nourishing saccharin and ant poison illustrate the indirectness and proneness to illusion in novel ecologies.

For human language too, the representability of things and actions by words is a contingent discovery, a non-entailed relationship, and only approximate. We need a Popperian model of language learning in the child and of language development in the race. Regarding the child, this would emphasize that word meanings cannot be directly transferred to the child. Rather, the child must discover these by a presumptive trial and error of meanings, which the initial instance only limits but does not determine. Rather than logically complete ostensive definitions being possible, there are instead extended, incomplete sets of ostensive instances, each instance of which equivocally leaves possible multiple interpretations, although the whole series edits out many wrong trial meanings. The "logical" nature of children's errors in word usage amply testifies to such a process, and testifies against an inductionist version of a child's passively observing adult usage contingencies. This trial and error of meanings requires more than the communication of mentor and child. It requires a third party of objects referred to. Language cannot be taught by telephone, but requires visually or tactually present ostensive referents stimulating and editing the trial meanings.

Moving to the evolution of human language, a social trial and error of meanings and namings can be envisaged. Trial words designating referents which the other speakers in the community rarely guess "correctly" either fail to become common coinage or are vulgarized toward commonly guessed designations. All words have to go through the teaching sieve, have to be usefully if incompletely communicable by finite sets of ostensive instances. Stable, sharp, striking object-boundaries useful in manipulating the environment have a greater likelihood of utilization in word meanings than do subtler designations, and when used, achieve a greater universality of meaning within the community of speakers. Such natural boundaries for words exist in much greater number than are actually used, and alternate boundaries for highly overlapping concepts abound. Just as certain knowledge is never achieved in science, so certain equivalence of word meanings is never achieved in the iterative trial and error of meanings in language learning. This equivocality and heterogeneity of meanings is more than trivial logical technicality; it is a practical fringe imperfection. And even were meanings uniform, the word-to-object equivalence is a corrigible contingent relationship, a product of a trial and error of metaphors of greater and greater appropriateness, but never complete perfection, never a formal nor entailed isomorphism.[66]

9. *Cultural cumulation.* In sociocultural evolution there are a variety of variation and selective retention processes leading to advances or changes in technology and culture. Most direct, but probably of minor importance, is the selective survival of complete social organizations, differentially as a function of cultural features. More important is selective borrowing, a process which probably leads to increased adaptation as far as easily tested aspects of technology are concerned, but could involve adaptive irrelevance in areas of culture where reality testing is more difficult. Differential imitation of a heterogeneity of models from within the culture is also a selective system that could lead to cultural advance. The learning process, selective repetition from among a set of temporal variations in cultural practice, also produces cultural advance. Selective elevation of different persons to leadership and educational roles is no doubt involved. Such selective criteria are highly vicarious, and could readily become disfunctional in a changing environment.[67]

10. *Science.* With the level of science, which is but an aspect of sociocultural evolution, we return to Popper's home ground. The demarcation of science from other speculations is that the knowledge claims be testable, and that there be available mechanisms for testing or selecting which are more than social. In theology and the humanities there is certainly differential propagation among advocated beliefs, and there result sustained developmental trends, if only at the level of

---

66. The above two paragraphs are condensed from D. T. Campbell, "Ostensive Instances and Entitativity in Language Learning", in *Unity through Diversity*, ed. by N. D. Rizzo (New York: Gordon and Breach, 1973). See also E. R. MacCormac, "Ostensive Instances in Language Learning", *Foundations of Language* 7 (1971), 199–210. Quine has presented a quite similar view, except for his employment of a passive conditioning learning theory in place of a trial and error of meanings, although his trial and error of "slicings" or abstractions is probably equivalent. See W. V. Quine, *Word and Object* (Cambridge, Mass.: MIT Press, 1960), and especially pp. 26–39 of W. V. Quine, *Ontological Relativity* (New York: Columbia University Press, 1969). Austin's faith that distinctions preserved in ordinary language have as referents distinctions in the world referred to, is justified by a similar model of language evolution.

67. For a review of this literature, see Margaret Mead, *Continuities in Cultural Evolution* (New Haven: Yale University Press, 1964); and D. T. Campbell, "Variation and Selective Retention in Sociocultural Evolution", in *Social Change in Developing Areas: A Reinterpretation of Evolutionary Theory*, ed. by H. R. Barringer, G. I. Blanksten, and R. W. Mack (Cambridge, Mass.: Schenkman, 1965), pp. 19–49. Perhaps the first to consider social evolution in explicitly natural selection terms was William James, "Great Men, Great Thoughts" (note 49). Louis Rougier has explicitly posited a competition of and a natural selection from among culturally diverse modes of thought in explaining the development of logical and scientific thinking, in *Traité de la Connaissance* (Paris: Gauthier-Villars, 1955), pp. 426–28.

fads and fashions. What is characteristic of science is that the selective system which weeds out among the variety of conjectures involves deliberate contact with the environment through experiment and quantified prediction, designed so that outcomes quite independent of the preferences of the investigator are possible. It is preeminently this feature that gives science its greater objectivity and its claim to a cumulative increase in the accuracy with which it describes the world.

An emphasis on the trial-and-error nature of science is a recurrent one, perhaps more characteristic of scientists describing scientific method than of philosophers. Agassi attributes such a view to William Whewell as early as 1840: "Whewell's [is] in retrospect a Darwinian view: we must invent many hypotheses because only a few of them survive tests, and these are the ones that matter, the hard core around which research develops."[68] James, Huxley, Boltzmann, Ritchie, Jennings, Cannon, Northrop, Beveridge, Pepper, Auger, Holton, Roller, Gillispie, Caws, Ghiselin, and Monod are also among those espousing such a view,[69] along with Toulmin, Kuhn, and Ackermann, to be discussed in more detail below.

There are a number of aspects of science which point in this direction. The opportunism of science, the rushing in and rapid development following new breakthroughs, are very like the rapid exploitation of a newly entered ecological niche. Science grows rapidly around laboratories, around discoveries which make the testing of hypotheses easier, which provide sharp and consistent selective systems. Thus the barometer, microscope, telescope, galvanometer, cloud chamber, and chromatograph all have stimulated rapid scientific growth. The necessity for the editing action of the experiment explains why a research tradition working with a trivial topic for which predictions can be checked advances more rapidly than research focused upon a more important problem but lacking a machinery for weeding out hypotheses.

A major empirical achievement of the sociology of science is the evidence of the ubiquity of simultaneous invention. If many scientists are trying variations on the same corpus of current scientific knowledge, and if their trials are being edited by the same stable external reality, then the selected variants are apt to be similar, the same discovery encountered independently by numerous workers. This process is no more mysterious than that all of a set of blind rats, each starting with quite different patterns of initial responses, learn the same maze pattern, under the maze's common editorship of the varied response repertoires. Their learning is actually their independent invention or discovery of the same response pattern. In doubly reflexively appropriateness, the theory of natural selection was itself multiply independently invented, not only by Wallace but by many others. Moreover, the ubiquity of independent invention in science has itself been independently discovered.[70]

---

68. Joseph Agassi, "Comment: Theoretical Entities Versus Theories", in *Boston Studies in the Philosophy of Science*, ed. by R. S. Cohen and M. W. Wartofsky (Dordrecht, Holland: D. Reidel, 1969), Vol. V.
69. See Bibliography in Callebaut and Pinxten, *op. cit.*
70. *Ibid.*

Placing science within the selective retention theme only begins the analysis that will eventually be required, for there are within science a variety of trial-and-error processes of varying degrees of vicariousness and interdependence. At one extreme is the blindly exploratory experimentalist who within a given laboratory setting introduces variations on every parameter and combination he can think of, without attention to theory. While such activity does not epitomize science, such research often provides the empirical puzzles that motivate and discipline the efforts of theoreticians. A multiple opportunism of selective systems (or "problems") needs also to be emphasized. Whereas the mass explorations of pharmaceutical houses for new antibiotics may be single-problem oriented, "basic" research is, like biological evolution, opportunistic not only in solutions, but also in problems. The research worker encountering a new phenomenon may change his research problem to one which is thereby solved. Serendipity as described by Cannon and Merton,[71] and the recurrent theme of "chance" discovery, emphasize this double opportunism. Its occurrence implies that the scientist has an available agenda of problems, hypotheses, or expectations much larger than the specific problem on which he works, and that he is in some sense continually scanning or winnowing outcomes, particularly unexpected ones, with this larger set of sieves.

At the opposite extreme from this blind laboratory exploration is Popper's view of the natural selection of scientific theories, a trial and error of mathematical and logical models in competition with each other in the adequacy with which they solve empirical puzzles, that is, in the adequacy with which they fit the totality of scientific data and also meet the separate requirements of being theories or solutions. Popper[72] has, in fact, disparaged the common belief in "chance" discoveries in science as partaking of the inductivist belief in directly learning from experience. Although there is probably no fundamental disagreement, that issue, and the more general problem of spelling out in detail the way in which a natural selection of scientific *theories* is compatible with a dogmatic blind-variation-and-selective-retention epistemology remain high priority tasks for the future.

Intermediate perhaps, is Toulmin's[73] evolutionary model of scientific development, which makes explicit analogue to population genetics and the concept of evolution as a shift in the composition of gene pool shared by a population, rather than specified in an individual. In his analogy, for genes are substituted "competing intellectual variants", concepts, beliefs, interpretations of specific fact, facts

71. W. B. Cannon, *The Way of An Investigator* (New York: W. W. Norton & Co., 1945); R. K. Merton, *Social Theory and Social Structure* (Glencoe: Free Press, 1949).
72. K. R. Popper, *Postscript.*
73. S. E. Toulmin, "The Evolutionary Development of Natural Science", *American Scientist* 55 (1967), 456–71. See also S. E. Toulmin, *Foresight and Understanding: An Inquiry Into the Aims of Science* (Bloomington, Indiana: Indiana University Press, 1961); S. E. Toulmin, "Neuroscience and Human Understanding", in *The Neurosciences*, ed. by Frank Schmitt (New York: Rockefeller University Press, 1968); S. E. Toulmin, *Human Understanding, Vol. I: The Evolution of Collective Understanding* (Princeton, N. J.: Princeton University Press, 1972).

given special importance, etc. The individual scientists are the carriers. Through selective diffusion and selective retention processes some intellectual variants eventually become predominant, some completely eliminated. Some new mutants barely survive until their time is ripe.

The selective systems operating on the variations need also to be specified. As Baldwin and Peirce emphasized, the selective system of science is ultimately socially distributed in a way which any individualistic epistemology fails to describe adequately. Vicarious selectors also must be specified. Whereas the meter readings in experiments may seem to be direct selectors, this is only relatively so, and most of the proximal selection is done on the basis of vicarious criteria, including the background presumptions required to interpret the meter readings, some of which are very general in nature. In keeping with the nested hierarchy evolutionary perspective, a trial and error of such presuppositions would be expected as part of the overall process. Both Toulmin's interpretation of the history of science in terms of shifts in what does not need to be explained and Kuhn's paradigm shifts can be interpreted in this light.[74] This is consistent with Toulmin's own evolutionary orientation. Although Kuhn also uses natural selection analogues, a natural selection of paradigms imputes to surviving paradigms a superiority over their predecessors which he explicitly questions. Ackermann has extended the evolutionary perspectives of Kuhn, Popper, and Toulmin, viewing experimental evidence as providing ecologies or niches to which theories adapt, i.e., which select theories.[75]

4. Historical Perspectives on Evolutionary Epistemology

What we find in Popper, and what has been elaborated so far, is but one type of evolutionary epistemology, perhaps best called a natural selection epistemology. As we have seen, there were both implicit and explicit forerunners of this in the nineteenth century, but they did not provide the dominant theme. Instead, theories of pre-Darwinian type generated the major evolutionary input into epistemology, even though their acceptance was furthered by the authority of Darwin's work. Herbert Spencer was the major spokesman for this school. Although he was an enthusiastic recipient of Darwin's theory of natural selection (and may even have coined the phrase "survival of the fittest"), he was a vigorous evolutionist before he read Darwin, and his thinking remained dominated by two pre-Darwinian inputs. The first was the model of embryological development, and the second was a version of Lamarckian theory in which the animal mind was a passive mirror of environmental realities. Čapek has provided three excellent

74. *Foresight and Understanding* (note 73); T. S. Kuhn, *The Structure of Scientific Revolutions* (Chicago: University of Chicago Press, 1962).

75. Robert Ackermann, *The Philosophy of Science* (New York: Pegasus, 1970).

historical reviews[76] of Spencer's epistemology and its influence. Among his positive contributions was his insistence that knowing had evolved along with the other
aspects of life. Also valuable was his concept of the "range of correspondences",
the range becoming broader at higher evolutionary stages as manifest both in
distance-receptor depth and range of environmental utilization. (His evolutionary
Kantianism will be discussed below.)

What Spencer missed was the profound indirectness of knowing necessitated
by the natural selection paradigm, and the inevitable imperfection and approximate character of both perceptual and scientific knowledge at any stage. Instead,
believing that an infinitely refinable and sensitive human cognitive apparatus had
in the course of evolution adapted perfectly to the external environment, he became a naive realist accepting the givens of the cognitive processes as fundamentally valid. He also viewed human cognition as validly encompassing all reality,
rather than just those aspects behaviorally relevant in the course of human evolution. Čapek sees the major limitations of Mach's and Poincaré's evolutionary
epistemologies as stemming from their residual tendency to follow Spencer in accepting the completeness of cognitive evolution. It was against the Spencerian
version of evolutionarily-produced cognitive perfection and completeness that
Bergson rebelled.[77] The Spencerian evolutionary epistemology had become a quite
dominant view by 1890, a fact difficult to believe so absent has been any evolutionary epistemology in the major philosophical discussions of the last fifty years.
William James, in 1890, speaks of the pervasive "evolutionary empiricists".[78] Georg
Simmel, in 1890, was able to write,

> It has been presumed for some time that human knowing has evolved from the
> practical needs of preserving and providing for life. The common underlying presup-
> position is this: there exists objective truth, the content of which is not influenced
> by the practical needs of the knower. This truth is grasped only because of its utility,

76. Milič Čapek, "The Development of Reichenbach's Epistemology", *Review of Metaphysics* 11
(1957), 42–67; Milič Čapek, "La Théorie Biologique de la Connaissance chez Bergson et sa Signification
Actuelle", *Revue de Metaphysique et de Morale* (April–June, 1959), 194–211; and Milič Čapek,
"Ernst Mach's Biological Theory of Knowledge", *Synthèse* 18 (1968), 171–91, reprinted in *Boston Studies
in the Philosophy of Science*, ed. by R. S. Cohen and M. W. Wartofsky (Dordrecht, Holland: D. Reidel,
1969), Vol. V, pp. 400–21.

77. Bergson also rejected the Darwinian blind mutation and natural selection model of cognitive evolution. However, his emphasis on the utility-perspectival, partial, oversimplified, nature of
human cognition, and its inappropriateness when extended into the subatomic and galactic areas,
is in agreement with the natural selection epistemology advocated here ("La Théorie Biologique").
That Mach and Poincaré were explicitly natural-selectionist rather than Lamarckian both in their
perspective on cognitive evolution and in their treatment of creative thought indicates the need for further analysis. Čapek's attribution to Mach of Spencer's belief in the completeness and perfection
of the evolutionary process is contradicted by this quotation from Mach's contemporary, Boltzmann,
"Mach himself has shown in a most ingenious way that no theory is either absolutely true or absolutely false, and that, moreover, every theory is constantly being improved just as are organisms as
described by Darwin." *Populäre Schriften*, p. 339.

78. *Principles of Psychology*, p. 617 (note 49).

correct conceptions being more useful than wrong ones. This view is common to various schools of epistemology, in realism, where knowing is an inevitable grasping of an absolute reality, in idealism, where knowing is directed by *a priori* forms of thought.[79]

While accepting a natural-selection epistemology, Simmel argues that, for the evolving animal, truth and usefulness are historically one. Anticipating von Uexküll and Bergson, he notes that the phenomenal worlds of animals differ from one to the other, according to the particular aspects of the world they are adapted to and the different sense organs they have.

Pragmatism's relation to natural selection and other evolutionary theories is mixed. In William James's prepragmatism writings, he clearly espoused a natural-selection fallibilism of thought, social evolution, and science, in explicit opposition to Spencer's passive-omniscient Lamarckianism.[80] A vague social-evolutionary orientation appears in his writings on pragmatism, but nowhere as explicit on the issues of importance here. John Dewey's faith in experimentalism was never explicitly related to the variation-and-selective-retention epistemology, and his only reference to natural selection in his book, *The Influence of Darwin on Philosophy*, is in refutation of the argument for God's existence from the wondrous adapted complexity of organisms.[81] In his chapter of that book on the problem of knowledge, no mention of natural selection or trial and error occurs.

Charles Sanders Peirce is profoundly ambivalent in this regard. His concept of truth as "the opinion which is fated to be ultimately agreed to by all who investigate"[82] partakes of the "leftovers" or winnowing model of knowledge which is the particular achievement of the selective-retention perspective. Here is another fragment with this flavor:

> . . . it may be conceived, and often is conceived, that induction lends a probability to its conclusion. Now that is not the way in which induction leads to the truth. It lends no definite probability to its conclusion. It is nonsense to talk of the probability of a law, as if we could pick universes out of a grab-bag and find in what proportion

79. Georg Simmel, "Über eine Beziehung der Selectionslehre zur Erkenntnis-theorie", *Archiv für systematische Philosophie* 1, No. 1 (1895), 34–45. The present writer has had the benefit of access to two unpublished papers, the first is Herman Tennessen, "Brief Summary of Georg Simmel's Evolutionary Epistemology", June, 1968, being an abstract of Herman Tennessen "Georg Simmel's tillemping av selecksjonslaeren pa erkjennelsesteorier", in *Filosofiske Problemer* (Oslo: Norwegian University Press, 1955), pp. 23–30. The second is a preliminary translation of Simmel's paper by Irene L. Jerison. Simmel does not, in fact, cite Spencer, nor any other on this point.

80. *Principles of Psychology* and "Great Men, Great Thoughts" (note 49).

81. John Dewey, *The Influence of Darwin on Philosophy* (New York: Henry Holt & Co., 1910; Bloomington: Indiana University Press, 1965), pp. 11–12.

82. *Collected Papers of Charles Sanders Peirce*, ed. by Charles Hartshorne and Paul Weiss (Cambridge, Mass.: Harvard University Press, 1931–58), 5.407. (All references to Peirce in this paper follow the standard practice of designating volume and paragraph in the *Collected Papers*.) Also quoted in Manley Thompson, *The Pragmatic Philosophy of C. S. Peirce* (Chicago: University of Chicago Press, 1953), p. 83, and in Philip P. Wiener, *Evolution and the Founders of Pragmatism* (Cambridge, Mass.: Harvard University Press, 1949), p. 93.

of them the law held good. Therefore, such an induction is not valid; for it does not do what it professes to do, namely make its conclusion probable. But yet if it had only professed to do what induction does (namely, to commence a proceeding which must in the long run approximate to the truth), which is infinitely more to the purpose than what it professes, it would have been valid.[83]

Another Peirceian imagery that is quite sympathetic is that of a primeval chaos of chance, within which nodes of order emerged, nodes which grew but never exhausted the chaos, a background of chance and indeterminacy remaining. This imagery is preminiscent of that of Ashby.[84] But the mechanism which is used to explain the emergence is not selective retention, but a mentalistic, anthropomorphic, "tendency to habit" on the part of physical matter:

> . . . a Cosmogonic Philosophy. It would suppose that in the beginning -- infinitely remote – there was a chaos of unpersonalized feeling, which being without connection or regularity would properly be without existence. This feeling, sporting here and there in pure arbitrariness, would have started the germ of a generalizing tendency. Its other sportings would be evanescent, but this would have a growing virtue. Thus the tendency to habit would be started; and from this, with the other principles of evolution, all the regularities of the universe would be evolved. At any time, however, an element of pure chance survives and will remain until the world becomes an absolutely perfect, rational, and symmetrical system, in which mind is at last crystallized in the infinitely distant future.[85]

Peirce was thoroughly conversant with the concept of natural selection and recognized it as Darwin's central contribution. Certainly he had in his creative exploration all of the ingredients for a selective retention evolutionary epistemology. Yet, the perspective if ever clearly conceived was also ambivalently rejected, and compatible statements such as those above are few and far between, overshadowed by dissimilar and incompatible elements. Wiener[86] has carefully documented his ambivalence on the issue. In spite of all of his emphasis on evolution, and on the ontological status of chance, Peirce was not a Darwinian evolutionist. Rather he favored the views of both Lamarck and Agassiz, or at least gave them equal status. Wiener is able to quote Peirce as describing Darwin's theory as one which "barely commands scientific respect", and "did not appear at first at all near to being proved, and to a sober mind its case looks less hopeful now [1893] than it did twenty years ago".[87] While later expressing much more Darwinian positions, he hedged by regarding sports (and trial thoughts) as being initiated by lack of environmental fit, and as being formed "not wildly but in ways having some sort of relation to the change needed".[88] Peirce's evolutionism was nostalgic, for if not consistently committed to a God-guided evolution:

83. *Collected Papers*, 2.780.
84. *Design for a Brain* (note 26).
85. *Collected Papers*, 6.33. See also 5.436, 6.200, 6.262, 6.606, 6.611.
86. *Founders of Pragmatism*, Chap. 4, pp. 70–96 (note 82).
87. *Ibid.*, p. 77.
88. *Ibid.*, pp. 87–88.

. . . a genuine evolutionary philosophy, that is one that makes the principle of growth a primordial element of the universe, is so far from being antagonistic to the idea of a personal creator that it is really inseparable from that idea; while a necessitarian religion is in an altogether false position and is destined to become disintegrated. But a pseudo-evolutionism which enthrones mechanical law is at once scientifically unsatisfactory, as giving no possible hint of how the universe has come about, and hostile to all hopes of personal relations to God.[89]

In connection with such a view, however, he had the important insight that natural laws (and perhaps even God Himself) are evolutionary products and are still evolving.[90]

James Mark Baldwin is known to philosophers today only as the editor of the 1901–1905 *Dictionary of Philosophy* for which Peirce wrote a number of entries. Professionally a psychologist, he is perhaps today better remembered by sociologists of the Cooley tradition, or as a contender for the dubious honor of writing the first social psychology text (that by subtitle and preface) in 1897. Always a vigorous evolutionist, Darwinist-Weismannian and anti-Lamarckian, he turned to epistemology in his later years in his several volumes on *Thought and Things or Genetic Logic*.[91] In 1909 he published casually a brief book on *Darwin and the Humanities*[92] which stands in marked contrast with Dewey's contemporaneous *The Influence of Darwin on Philosophy*[93] for its pervasive use of the natural selection and generalized selective retention theme. In this volume Baldwin summarized more concisely points he had made elsewhere, some of which have been cited above:

My favorite doctrines, and those in which my larger books have been in some measure original, seem now, when woven together, to have been consciously inspired by the theory of Natural Selection: I need only mention "Organic Selection", "Functional Selection", "Social Heredity", "Selective Thinking", "Experimental Logic", thoroughgoing "Naturalism of Method", etc. Such views as these all illustrate or extend the principle of selection as Darwin conceived it – that is, the principle of survival from varied cases – as over against any vitalistic or formal principle.[94]
. . . Natural selection is in principle the universal law of genetic organization and progress in nature – human nature no less than physical nature.[95]

89. *Collected Papers*, 6.157, original date 1892.
90. Wiener, *Founders of Pragmatism*, pp. 94–95 (note 82); Peirce, *Collected Papers*, 1.348.
91. James M. Baldwin, *Thought and Things, A Study of the Development and Meaning of Thought, or Genetic Logic*, Volume I: *Functional Logic or Genetic Theory of Knowledge;* Volume II: *Experimental Logic or Genetic Theory of Thought;* Volume III: *Genetic Epistemology* (London: Swan Sonnenschein [in Muirhead's Library of Philosophy]; New York: Macmillan, 1906, 1908, 1911). If these volumes left any impact at all, it was in the French tradition out of which Jean Piaget's recent work on genetic epistemology emerges.
92. James M. Baldwin, *Darwin and the Humanities* (Baltimore: Review Publishing Co., 1909; London: Allen & Unwin, 1910).
93. *Influence of Darwin* (note 81).
94. *Darwin and Humanities*, p. viii (note 92). Reprinted by permission of the American Psychological Association.
95. *Ibid.*, p. ix.

. . . Summing up our conclusions so far with reference to Darwinism in Psychology we may say:

(1) The individual's learning processes are by a method of functional 'trial and error' which illustrates 'natural' in the form of "functional selection".

(2) Such acquisitions, taken jointly with his endowment, give him the chance of survival through "natural", in the form of "organic selection".

(3) By his learning, he brings himself into the traditions of his group, thus coming into possession of his social heritage, which is the means of his individual survival in the processes of "social and group selection".

(4) Thus preserved the individual's endowment or physical heredity is, through variation, directed in intelligent and gregarious lines through "natural" as "organic selection".

(5) Individuals become congenitally either more gregarious or more intelligent for the maintenance of the group life, according as the greater utility attaches to one or the other in the continued operation of these modes of selection.[96]

His distinction between pragmatism and his version of instrumentalism deserves quoting at some length:

The theory of truth becomes either one of extreme "Pragmatism" or one merely of "Instrumentalism".

Instrumentalism holds that all truth is tentatively arrived at and experimentally verified. The method of knowledge is the now familiar Darwinian procedure of "trial and error". The thinker, whether working in the laboratory with things or among the products of his own imaginative thought, *tries out hypotheses*; and only by trying out hypotheses does he establish truth. The knowledge already possessed is used instrumentally in the form of a hypothesis or conjecture, for the discovery of further facts or truths. This reinstates in the sphere of thinking the method of Darwinian selection.

Here Darwinism gives support to the empiricism of Hume and Mill and forwards the sober British philosophical tradition. And no one illustrates better than Darwin, in his own scientific method, the soberness, caution, and soundness of this procedure.

But a more radical point of view is possible. What is now known as Pragmatism proceeds out from this point. It is pertinent to notice it here, for it offers a link of transition to the philosophical views with which we must briefly concern ourselves.

Pragmatism turns instrumentalism into a system of metaphysics. It claims that apart from its tentative instrumental value, its value as guide to life, its value as measured by utility, seen in the consequences of its following out, truth has no further meaning. Not only is all truth selected for its utility, but apart from its utility *it is not truth*. There is no reality then to which truth is still true, whether humanly discovered or not; on the contrary, reality is only the content of the system of beliefs found useful as a guide to life.

I wish to point out that, in such a conclusion, not only is the experimental conception left behind, but the advantages of the Darwinian principle of adjustment to actual situations, physical and social, is lost; and if so interpreted, instrumentalism defeats itself. This clearly appears when we analyze a situation involving trial and error.

96. *Ibid.*, pp. 32–33.

Trial implies a problematical and alternative result: either the success of the assumption put to trial or its failure. When we ask why this is so, we hit upon the presence of some "controlling" condition or circumstance in the situation – some stable physical or social fact – whose character renders the hypothesis or suggested solution either adequate or vain, as the case may be. The instrumental idea or thought, then, has its merit in enabling us to find out or locate facts and conditions which are to be allowed for thereafter. These constitute a *control upon knowledge and action*, a system of "things".[97]

5. Kant's Categories of Perception and Thought as Evolutionary Products

The evolutionary perspective is of course at odds with any view of an *ipso facto* necessarily valid synthetic *a priori*. But it provides a perspective under which Kant's categories of thought and intuition can be seen as a descriptive contribution to psychological epistemology. Though we reject Kant's claims of a necessary *a priori* validity for the categories, we can in evolutionary perspective see the categories as highly edited, much tested presumptions, "validated" only as scientific truth is validated, synthetic *a posteriori* from the point of view of species-history, synthetic and in several ways *a priori* (but not in terms of necessary validity) from the point of view of an individual organism. Popper makes this point in the following quotation:

> The problem "Which comes first, the hypothesis (H) or the observation (O)", is soluble; as in the problem, "Which comes first, the hen (H) or the egg (O)". The reply to the latter is, "An earlier kind of egg", to the former, "An earlier kind of hypothesis". It is quite true that any particular hypothesis we choose will have been preceded by observations – the observations, for example, which it is designed to explain. But these observations, in their turn, presupposed the adoption of a frame of reference: a frame of expectations: a frame of theories. If they were significant, if they created a need for explanation and thus gave rise to the invention of a hypothesis, it was because they could not be explained within the old theoretical framework, the old horizon of expectations. There is no danger here of an infinite regress. Going back to more and more primitive theories and myths we shall in the end find unconscious, *inborn* expectations.
>
> The theory of inborn *ideas* is absurd, I think; but every organism has inborn *reactions* or *responses*; and among them, responses adapted to impending events. These responses we may describe as "expectations" without implying that these 'expectations' are conscious. The newborn baby "expects", in this sense, to be fed (and, one could even argue, to be protected and loved). In view of the close relation between expectation and knowledge we may even speak in quite a reasonable sense of "inborn knowledge". This "knowledge" is not, however, *valid a priori*; an inborn expectation, no matter how strong and specific, may be mistaken. (The newborn child may be abandoned, and starve.)
>
> Thus we are born with expectations, with "knowledge" which, although not *valid*

a priori, is *psychologically or genetically a priori*, i.e. prior to all observational experience. One of the most important of these expectations is the expectation of finding a regularity. It is connected with an inborn propensity to look out for regularities, or with a *need* to *find* regularities, as we may see from the pleasure of the child who satisfies this need.

This "instinctive" expectation of finding regularities, which is psychologically *a priori*, corresponds very closely to the "law of causality" which Kant believed to be part of our mental outfit and to be *a priori* valid. One might thus be inclined to say that Kant failed to distinguish between psychologically *a priori* ways of thinking or responding and *a priori* valid beliefs. But I do not think that his mistake was quite as crude as that. For the expectation of finding regularities is not only psychologically *a priori*, but also logically *a priori*: it is logically prior to all observational experience, for it is prior to any recognition of similarities, as we have seen; and all observation involves the recognition of similarities (or dissimilarities). But in spite of being logically *a priori* in this sense the expectation is not valid *a priori*. For it may fail: we can easily construct an environment (it would be a lethal one) which, compared with our ordinary environment, is so chaotic that we completely fail to find regularities. . . .

Thus Kant's reply to Hume came near to being right; for the distinction between an *a priori* valid expectation and one which is both genetically and logically prior to observation, but not *a priori* valid, is really somewhat subtle. But Kant proved too much. In trying to show how knowledge is possible, he proposed a theory which had the unavoidable consequence that our quest for knowledge must necessarily succeed, which is clearly mistaken. When Kant said, "Our intellect does not draw its laws from nature but imposes its laws upon nature", he was right. But in thinking that these laws are necessarily true, or that we necessarily succeed in imposing them upon nature, he was wrong. Nature very often resists quite successfully, forcing us to discard our laws as refuted; but if we live we may try again.

Kant believed that Newton's dynamics was *a priori* valid. (See his *Metaphysical Foundations of Natural Science*, published between the first and the second editions of the *Critique of Pure Reason*.) But if, as he thought, we can explain the validity of Newton's theory by the fact that our intellect imposes its laws upon nature, it follows, I think, that our intellect *must succeed* in this; which makes it hard to understand why *a priori* knowledge such as Newton's should be so hard to come by.[98]

This insight is the earliest and most frequently noted aspect of an evolutionary epistemology, perhaps because it can be achieved from a Lamarckian point of view, as well as from the natural-selection model which is absolutely essential to the previous points. Herbert Spencer, a Lamarckian for these purposes, achieved this insight, as Höffding conveniently summarizes:

> With regard to the question of the origin of knowledge Spencer makes front on the one hand against Leibniz and Kant, on the other against Locke and Mill. He quarrels with empiricism for two reasons: – firstly, because it does not see that the matter of experience is always taken up and elaborated in a definite manner, which is determined by the original nature of the individual; secondly, because it is lacking in a criterion of truth. We must assume an original organization if we are to understand

98. *C.&R.*, pp. 47–48.

the influence exercised by stimuli on different individuals, and the criterion by means of which alone a proposition can be established is the fact that its opposite would contain a contradiction. In the inborn nature of the individual then, and in the logical principle on which we depend every time we make an inference, we have an *a priori* element; something which cannot be deduced from experience. To this extent Spencer upholds Leibniz and Kant against Locke and Mill; but he does so only as long as he is restricting his considerations to the experience of the individual. *What is a priori for the individual is not so for the race.* For those conditions and forms of knowledge and of feeling which are original in the individual, and hence cannot be derived from his experience, have been transmitted by earlier generations. The forms of thought correspond to the collective and inherited modifications of structure which are latent in every newborn individual, and are gradually developed through his experiences. Their first origin, then, is empirical: the fixed and universal relation of things to one another must, in the course of development, form fixed and universal conjunctions in the organism; by perpetual repetition of absolutely external uniformities there arise in the race necessary forms of knowledge, indissoluble thought associations which express the net results of the experience of perhaps several millions of generations down to the present. The individual cannot sunder a conjunction thus deeply rooted in the organization of the race; hence, he is born into the world with those psychical connections which form the substrata of "necessary truths" (see *Principles of Psychology*, pp. 208, 216; cf. *First Principles*, p. 53. "Absolute uniformities of experience generate absolute uniformities of thought"). Although Spencer is of opinion that the inductive school went too far when they attempted to arrive at everything by way of induction (for, if we adopt this method, induction itself is left hanging in the air), yet, if he had to choose between Locke and Kant, he would avow himself a disciple of the former; for, *in the long run, Spencer too thinks that all knowledge and all forms of thought spring from experience.* His admission that there is something in our mind which is not the product of our own *a posteriori* experience led Max Müller to call him a "thoroughgoing Kantian", to which Spencer replied: "The Evolution-view is completely experiential. It differs from the original view of the experimentalists by containing a great extension of that view. – *But this view of Kant is avowedly and utterly unexperiential.*"[99]

It is of no small interest to notice that John Stuart Mill, who at first demurred at Spencer's evolutionary psychology, afterwards declared himself convinced that mental development takes place not only in the individual but also in the race by means of inherited dispositions. He expressed this modification of his view a year before his death in a letter to Carpenter, the physiologist (quoted in the latter's *Mental Physiology*).[100]

As Wallraff[101] has documented, the demoting of Kant's categories to the level of descriptive rather than prescriptive epistemology began in 1807 with Jacob Fries's effort to interpret the categories as having only a psychological base, as but descriptive of human reason. While such a position was typically accompanied by a thoroughgoing dualism and was purely mentalistic, by 1866 Frederick

99. Harold Höffding, *A History of Modern Philosophy* (London: Macmillan, 1900; New York: Dover, 1955), Vol. II, pp. 475–76.

100. *Ibid.*, pp. 457–58.

101. Charles F. Wallraff, *Philosophical Theory and Psychological Fact* (Tucson: University of Arizona Press, 1961), pp. 10–11.

A. Lange was able to discuss the *a priori* as aspects of a "physicopsychological" organization of the mind,[102] and to posit, with Mill, the possibility of "erroneous *a priori* knowledge". He also wrote:

> Perhaps some day the basis of the idea of cause may be found in the mechanism of reflex action and sympathetic excitation; we should then have translated Kant's pure reason into physiology, and so made it more easily conceivable.[103]

All that was lacking here was an explicit statement of the kind of validation of such physiological biases which a natural-selection evolution provides. Helmholtz's biological interpretation of the Kantian *a priori* categories is similar.[104] Baldwin had the insight in 1902 and earlier:

> As Kant claimed, knowledge is a process of categorizing, and to know a thing is to say that it illustrates or stimulates, or functions as, a category. But a category is a mental habit; that is all a category can be allowed to be – a habit broadly defined as a disposition, whether congenital or acquired, to act upon or to treat, items of any sort in certain general ways. These habits or categories arise either from actual accommodations with "functional" or some other form of utility selection, or by natural endowment secured by selection from variations.[105]

In the tradition of pragmatism, the categories were seen as but pragmatically useful ways of thinking, usually products of culture history rather than biological evolution,[106] although in espousing such a viewpoint, Wright was able to say in passing:

> In a certain sense, therefore, the distinctions involved in some, at least, of the categories, *viz.*, space, time, thing, and person, are present in the sense percepts of animals. . . . It is clear that historically and phylogenetically perceptual elements anticipatory of some of the categories existed prior to the genesis of thought.[107]

Wright's position is extended explicitly by Child[108] who posits both "biotic categories", biological functions shared with animals and of biological survival value, and "sociotic categories" which are cultural products. He says in passing "Since

102. *Ibid.*, p. 11; Frederick Albert Lange, *The History of Materialism* (New York: Humanities Press, 1950), Vol. 2, p. 193. (Reprinting of a translation first published in 1890.)
103. *History of Materialism*, p. 211 (note 102).
104. Čapek, "Mach's Theory of Knowledge" (note 76).
105. The quotation is from James M. Baldwin, *Development and Evolution* (New York: Macmillan, 1902), p. 309. See also his *Mental Development* (Macmillan, 1900), and *Darwin and the Humanities* (note 97).
106. E.g., William James, *Pragmatism* (New York: Longmans-Green, 1907), pp. 170, 182, 193. This is also Rougier's position, *Traité de la Connaissance* (note 67). Marx Wartofsky also emphasizes primarily the social evolution of the Kantian a priori, in "Metaphysics as Heuristic for Science", in *Boston Studies in the Philosophy of Science*, ed. by R. S. Cohen and M. W. Wartofsky (Dordrecht, Holland: D. Reidel, 1968), Vol. III, pp. 164–70.
107. William K. Wright, "The Genesis of the Categories", *The Journal of Philosophy, Psychology and Scientific Methods* **10** (1913), 645–57, esp. 646.
108. Arthur Child, "On the Theory of the Categories", *Philosophy and Phenomenological Research* **7** (1946), 316–35.

Kant, the term 'category' has primarily referred to the presumably pervasive structures of racial mind."[109]

A great many other scholars have considered some kind of an evolutionary interpretation of Kant's categories, usually very briefly and without citing others. In approximately chronological order these include James, Morgan, Mach, Poincaré, Boltzmann, Fouillé, Cassirer, Shelton, Reichenbach, R. W. Sellars, Uexküll, Meyerson, Northrop, Magnus, Lorenz, Piaget, Waddington, Bertalanffy, Whitrow, Platt, Pepper, Merleau-Ponty, Simpson, W. S. Sellars, Hawkins, Barr, Toulmin, Wartofsky, and Watanabe. Quine, Maxwell, Shimony, Yilmaz, and Stemmer have made much the same point without explicit reference to the Kantian categories.[110] Of these, many are essentially biologists generalizing into philosophy. This brief quote from Waddington epitomizes their message:

> The faculties by which we arrive at a world view have been selected so as to be, at least, efficient in dealing with other existents. They may, in Kantian terms, not give us direct contact with the thing-in-itself, but they have been moulded by things-in-themselves so as to be competent in coping with them.[111]

Most of the passages cited are very brief, noting the insight only in passing. In marked contrast is the rich exposition provided by Lorenz.

In his essay, "Kant's Doctrine of the *A Priori* in the Light of Contemporary Biology", Lorenz[112] accepts Kant's insight as to some degree of fit between innate categories of thought and the *Ding an sich*. He accepts Kant's claim that without such prior-fitting categories, no one could achieve in his own lifetime the empirical, experiential, knowledge of the world which he does achieve. He accepts in some sense Kant's skepticism as to the form of knowledge. While to Lorenz more than Kant the *Ding an sich* is knowable, it certainly is only known in the knower's categories, not in those of the *Ding an sich* itself. Thus he accepts Kant as psychologist if not as epistemologist. As with all of those we have cited above, from Spencer on, any validity or appropriateness of the categories to the *Ding an sich* is due to their status as a product of an evolution in which the *Ding an sich* has acted in the editorial role of discarding misleading categories.

Lorenz, like Popper,[113] recognizes that it was to Kant's great disadvantage to believe Newton's physics perfectly true. When Kant then recognized the *a priori* human intuitions of space, time, and causality as fitting Newton's physics (which they do to a lesser degree than Kant thought), he had a greater puzzle on his hands than a modern epistemologist has. From our viewpoint, both Newton's laws of dynamics and the intuitive categories of space perception can be seen as but approximations to a later more complete physics (or to the *Ding an sich*).

109. Child, "Theory of Categories", p. 320.
110. See Bibliography in Callebaut and Pinxten, *op. cit.*
111. "Evolution and Epistemology", *op. cit.*
112. "Kants Lehre vom apriorischen".
113. *C.&R.*, p. 48, quoted above note 98. See also Hans Reichenbach, as reported by Čapek, "Reichenbach's Epistemology" (note 76).

The realization that all laws of "pure reason" are based on highly physical or mechanical structures of the human central nervous system which have developed through many eons like any other organ, on the one hand shakes our confidence in the laws of pure reason and on the other hand substantially raises our confidence in them. Kant's statement that the laws of pure reason have absolute validity, nay that every imaginable rational being, even if it were an angel, must obey the same laws of thought, appears as an anthropocentric presumption. Surely the "keyboard" provided by the forms of intuition and categories – Kant himself calls it that – is something definitely located on the physicostructural side of the psychophysical unity of the human organism. . . . But surely these clumsy categorical boxes into which we have to pack our external world "in order to be able to spell them as experiences" (Kant) can claim no autonomous and absolute validity whatsoever. This is certain for us the moment we conceive them as evolutionary adaptations. . . . At the same time, however, the nature of their adaptation shows that the categorical forms of intuition and categories have proved themselves as working hypotheses in the coping of our species with the absolute reality of the environment (in spite of their validity being only approximate and relative). Thus is clarified the paradoxical fact that the laws of "pure reason" which break down at every step in modern theoretical science, nonetheless have stood (and still stand) the test in the practical biological matters of the struggle for the preservation of the species.

The "dots" produced by the coarse "screens" used in the reproductions of photographs in our daily papers are satisfactory representations when looked at superficially, but cannot stand closer inspection with a magnifying glass. So, too, the reproductions of the world by our forms of intuition and categories break down as soon as they are required to give a somewhat closer representation of their objects, as in the case in wave mechanics and nuclear physics. All the knowledge an individual can wrest from the empirical reality of the "physical world-picture" is essentially only a working hypothesis. And, as far as their species-preserving function goes, all those innate structures of the mind which we call "a priori" are likewise only working hypotheses. Nothing is absolute except that which hides in and behind the phenomena. Nothing that our brain can think has absolute, *a priori* validity in the true sense of the word, not even mathematics with all its laws.[114]

Lorenz portrays for the concepts of space and causality their analogues in water shrew, greylag goose, and man, arguing for each an "objectivity", yet limitedness and imperfection. For a weak microscope, we assume that the homogeneous texture provided at its limit of resolution is a function of those limits, not an attribute of reality. We do this because through more powerful scopes this homogeneity becomes differentiated. By analogy, we extend this assumption even to the most powerful scope. Seeing our human categories of thought and intuition as but the best in such an evolutionary series, even though we might have no better scope to compare it with, generates a parallel skepticism. Actually we do have a better scope, modern physics, which today, at least, if not in Kant's time, provides a much finer-grained view of reality.

114. Lorenz, "Kants Lehre vom apriorischen", pp. 103–4, translation pp. 26–27. Reprinted by permission of the author.

There is a two-sided message in this literature: there is an "objective" reflection of the *Ding an sich* which, however, does not achieve expression in the *Ding an sich's* own terms. Lorenz, and many of the others, have argued that the mind has been shaped by evolution to fit those aspects of the world with which it deals, just as have other body parts:

> This central nervous apparatus does not prescribe the laws of nature any more than the hoof of the horse prescribes the form of the ground. Just as the hoof of the horse, this central nervous apparatus stumbles over unforeseen changes in its task. But just as the hoof of the horse is adapted to the ground of the steppe which it copes with, so our central nervous apparatus for organizing the image of the world is adapted to the real world with which man has to cope. Just like any organ, this apparatus has attained its expedient species-preserving form through this coping of real with the real during a species history many eons long.[115]

The shape of a horse's hoof certainly expresses "knowledge" of the steppe in a very odd and partial language, and in an end product mixed with "knowledge" of other contingencies. Our visual, tactual, and several modes of scientific knowledge of the steppe are each expressed in quite different languages, but are comparably objective. The hydrodynamics of sea water, plus the ecological value of locomotion, have independently shaped fish, whale, and walrus in a quite similar fashion. Their shapes represent independent discoveries of this same "knowledge", expressed in this case in similar "languages". But the jet-propelled squid reflects the same hydrodynamic principles in a quite different, but perhaps equally "accurate" and "objective" shape. The *Ding an sich* is always known indirectly, always in the language of the knower's posits, be these mutations governing bodily form, or visual percepts, or scientific theories. In this sense it is unknowable. But there is an objectivity in the reflection, however indirect, an objectivity in the selection from innumerable less adequate posits.

6. Pragmatism, Utilitarianism, and Objectivity

For both Popper and the present writer the *goal of objectivity* in science is a noble one, and dearly to be cherished. It is in true worship of this goal that we remind ourselves that our current views of reality are partial and imperfect. We recoil at a view of science which recommends we give up the search for ultimate truth and settle for practical computational recipes making no pretense at truly describing a real world. Thus our sentiment is to reject pragmatism, utilitarian nominalism, utilitarian subjectivism, utilitarian conventionalism, or instrumentalism,[116] in favor of a critical hypothetical realism. Yet our evolutionary epistemology, with its basis in natural selection for survival relevance, may seem to

---

115. *Ibid.*, pp. 98–99, translation p. 25.
116. Note that James M. Baldwin as quoted above, *Darwin and the Humanities*, pp. 68–73 (note 97), uses the term instrumentalism in a unique way, in making the very point against pragmatism being made here.

commit us to pragmatism or utilitarianism. Simmel in 1895[117] presents the problem forcibly, as also do Mach and Poincaré.

This profound difference in sentiment deserves much more attention than can be given here, but brief comments from a variety of perspectives may be in order. These are based on the assumption that neither Popper nor the present writer intend to relinquish the goal of objectivity, and must therefore reconcile it with the natural selection epistemology to which that very quest for objective truth has led us.

Where the emphasis on utilitarian selectivity is to counter the epistemic arrogance of a naive or phenomenal realism, we can join it unambivalently. The critical realist has no wish to identify the real with the phenomenally given. Thus the visual and tactual solidity of ordinary objects represents a phenomenal emphasis on the one physical discontinuity most usable by man and his ancestors, to the neglect of other discontinuities identifiable by the probes of modern experimental physics. Perceived solidity is not illusory for its ordinary uses: what it diagnoses is one of the "surfaces" modern physics also describes. But when reified as exclusive, when creating expectations of opaqueness and impermeability to all types of probes, it becomes illusory. The different *Umwelten* of different animals do represent in part the differential utilities of their specific ecological niches, as well as differential limitations. But each of the separate contours diagnosed in these *Umwelten* are also diagnosable by a complete physics, which in addition provides many differentia unused and unperceived by any organism.[118]

Nor do we claim any firmer grounding of the scientific theory and fact of today than do the pragmatists and utilitarians. Indeed, Popper's emphasis on criticism may produce an even greater skepticism as to the realism of present-day science. There is, however, a difference in what it is that is being grounded. Consider a graph of observational points relating the volume of water to its temperature. An extreme punctiform pragmatism or definitional operationism would regard the observations themselves as the scientific truth. A more presumptive pragmatism would fit a least squares curve with minimum parameters to the data, and regard the values of the points on the fitted curve as the scientific facts, thus deviating from some of the original observations. Even at this stage, degrees of pragmatism occur. The departure may be justified purely on the grounds of computational efficiency, or the discrepant observations may be regarded as "errorful", with the anticipation that, were the experiment repeated, the new observations would on the average fall nearer to the "theoretical" values than to the original observations. Most scientific practice is still less pragmatic, more realistic than this: Of all mathematical formulae that fit the data equally well with the same number of parameters, scientists choose that one or those whose parameters can be used in other formulae subsuming other observations. While the search for

117. "Beziehung der Selectionslehre" (note 79).
118. von Bertalanffy, "Relativity of Categories".

such parameters may most often be done as a search for physically interpretable parameters, it can also be justified on purely utilitarian grounds. In extending this series, were Popper's position to be classified as a pragmatism at all it would have to be as pragmatic selection from among formal theories claiming to be universally descriptive of the real world, but not identified as the real world. Even this degree of pragmatism needs to be qualified.

The extremes of pragmatism, definitional operationism, and phenomenalism would equate theory and data in a true epistemological monism. But as elaborated in actual philosophies of science, the dualism of data and theory just described is accepted. Adequately to handle the issues raised in discussions of epistemological monism and dualism[119] we need to expand the framework to an epistemological trinism (trialism, triadism, trimondism) of data, theory, and real world (approximately corresponding to Popper's "second world", "third world", and "first world").[120] The controversial issue is the conceptual inclusion of the real world, defining the problem of knowledge as the fit of data and theory to that real world.

Such a critical realism involves presumptions going beyond the data, needless to say. But since Hume we should have known that non-presumptive knowledge is impossible. As Petrie[121] has pointed out, most modern epistemologies recognize that scientific beliefs are radically underjustified. The question is thus a matter of which presumptions, not whether or not presumptions. Biological theories of evolution, whether Lamarckian or Darwinian, are profoundly committed to an organism-environment dualism, which when extended into the evolution of sense organ, perceptual and learning functions, becomes a dualism of an organism's knowledge of the environment versus the environment itself. An evolutionary epistemologist is at this level doing "epistemology of the other one",[122] studying the relationship of an animal's cognitive capacities and the environment they are designed to cognize, both of which the epistemologist knows only in the hypothetical-contingent manner of science. Thus he may study the relationship between the shape of a rat's running pattern ("cognitive map") and the shape of the maze it runs in. Or he may study the polarization of sunlight (using scientific instruments since his own eyes are insensitive to such nuances) and the bee's sensitivity to plane of polarization. At this level he has no hesitancy to include a "real

119. A. O. Lovejoy, *The Revolt Against Dualism* (La Salle, Ill.: Open Court, 1930); W. Köhler, *The Place of Value in a World of Facts* (New York: Liveright, 1938).

120. K. R. Popper, "Epistemology without a Knowing Subject", in *Logic, Methodology, and Philosophy of Sciences*, ed. by B. van Rootselaar and J. E. Staal (Amsterdam: North-Holland, 1968), Vol. III, pp. 333–73; K. R. Popper, "On the Theory of the Objective Mind", *Akten des XIV internationalen Kongresses für Philosophie* 1 (Vienna, 1968), 25–53. Both are reprinted in *Objective Knowledge* (note 14), pp. 106–52 and 153–90.

121. H. G. Petrie, "The Logical Effects of Theory on Observational Categories and Methodology", duplicated (Northwestern University, June 20, 1969).

122. D. T. Campbell, "Methodological Suggestions from a Comparative Psychology of Knowledge Processes", *Inquiry* 2 (1959), 157; D. T. Campbell, "A Phenomenology of the Other One: Corrigible, Hypothetical, and Critical", in *Human Action*, ed. by T. Mischel (New York: Academic Press, 1969), pp. 41–69.

world" concept, even though he may recognize that his own knowledge of that world even with instrumental augmentation is partial and limited in ways analogous to the limitations of the animal whose epistemology he studies. Having thus made the real-world assumption in this part of his evolutionary epistemology, he is not adding an unneeded assumption when he assumes the same predicament for man and science as knowers.

It is true, of course, that in an epistemology of other animals he has independent data on the "knowledge" and "the world to be known", and thus studying the degree of fit involves no tautology. It is true that in extending this "epistemology of the other one" to knowledge of modern physics, no separate information on the world-to-be-known is available with which to compare current physical theory. But this practical limitation does not necessitate abandoning an ontology one is already employing. (This argument is of course only compelling vis-à-vis those of such as Simmel, Mach, and Poincaré, who base their utilitarian nominalism and conventionalism on an evolutionary perspective.)

We can also examine utilitarian specificity versus realism in the evolution of knowing. Consider the spatial knowledge of some primitive locomotor animal, perhaps Konrad Lorenz's[123] water shrew. It may have a thirst space it uses when thirsty, a separate hunger space, a separate space for escape from each predator, a mate-finding space, etc. In its utilitarianism, there is a separate space for every utility. In a higher stage of evolution, the hypothesis has emerged that all these spaces are the same, or overlap. The realistic hypothesis of an all-purpose space has developed. There is abundant evidence that white rat, cat, dog, and chimpanzee are at or beyond this stage: that spatial learning achieved in the service of one motive is immediately available for other motives. Along with this goes spatial curiosity, the exploring of novel spaces and objects when all utilitarian motives (thirst, food, sex, safety, etc.) are sated and the exploration has no momentary usefulness. Such disinterested curiosity for "objective", all-possible-purpose spatial knowledge-for-its-own-sake has obvious survival value, even though it may transcend the sum of all specific utilities. Scientific curiosity of course goes beyond the specifically utilitarian to a much greater extent. Survival-relevant criteria are rare among the criteria actually used in deciding questions of scientific truth. The science Mach was attempting to epitomize had made most of its crucial selections from among competing theories on the basis of evidence (such as on the phases of the moons of Jupiter) of no contemporary or past utility. And in the history of science, those who took their theories as real, rather than their contemporary conventionalists, have repeatedly emerged in the main stream for future developments.

These several disparate comments scarcely begin the task of relating the critical-realist, natural-selection epistemology to the recurrent issues in the history of the theory of knowledge. Potentially it can provide a dialectic resolution to many old

123. "Kants Lehre vom apriorischen".

controversies. But spelling out the points of articulation with the main body of epistemological concerns remains for the most part yet to be done.

Summary

This essay has identified Popper as the modern founder and leading advocate of a natural-selection epistemology. The characteristic focus is on the growth of knowledge. The problem of knowledge is so defined that the knowing of other animals than man is included. The variation and selective retention process of evolutionary adaptation is generalized to cover a nested hierarchy of vicarious knowledge processes, including vision, thought, imitation, linguistic instruction, and science.

Historical attention is paid not only to those employing the natural-selection paradigm, but also to the Spencerian-Lamarckian school of evolutionary epistemologists, and to the ubiquitous evolutionary interpretation of the Kantian categories. It is argued that, whereas the evolutionary perspective has often led to a pragmatic, utilitarian conventionalism, it is fully compatible with an advocacy of the goals of realism and objectivity in science.

Blind Variation and Selective Retention in Creative Thought as in Other Knowledge Processes[1]

By Donald T. Campbell

1. Introduction

This paper proposes to examine creative thought within the framework of a comparative psychology of knowledge processes, and in particular with regard to one theme recurrent in most knowledge processes. This theme may be expressed as follows:

a. A blind-variation-and-selective-retention process is fundamental to all inductive achievements, to all genuine increases in knowledge, to all increases in fit of system to environment.

b. The many processes which shortcut a more full blind-variation-and-selective-retention process are in themselves inductive achievements, containing wisdom about the environment achieved originally by blind variation and selective retention.

c. In addition, such shortcut processes contain in their own operation a blind-variation-and-selective-retention process at some level, substituting for overt locomotor exploration or the life-and-death winnowing of organic evolution.

Between a modern experimental physicist and some virus-type ancestor there

This essay was first published in *The Psychological Review* **67**, 1960, pp. 380–400, and is reprinted by permission.

1. A partially overlapping version of this paper was presented at the Inter-Disciplinary Conference on Self-Organizing Systems, sponsored by the Office of Naval Research and the Armour Research Foundation of the Illinois Institute of Technology, Chicago, May 5–6, 1959. The author is indebted to Carl P. Duncan for contributing to the development of many of the points involved.

has been a tremendous gain in knowledge[2] about the environment. In bulk, this has represented cumulated inductive achievements, stage-by-stage expansions of knowledge beyond what could have been deductively derived from what had been previously known. It has represented repeated "breakouts" from the limits of available wisdom, for if such expansions had represented only wise anticipations, they would have been exploiting full or partial knowledge already achieved. Instead, real gains must have been the products of explorations going beyond the limits of foresight or prescience, and in this sense blind. In the instances of such real gains, the successful explorations were in origin as blind as those which failed. The difference between the successful and unsuccessful was due to the nature of the environment encountered, representing discovered wisdom about that environment.

The general model for such inductive gains is that underlying both trial-and-error problem solving and natural selection in evolution, the analogy between which has been noted by several persons (e.g., Ashby, 1952; Baldwin, 1900; Pringle, 1951). Three conditions are necessary: a mechanism for introducing variation, a consistent selection process, and a mechanism for preserving and reproducing the selected variations. In what follows we shall look for these three ingredients at a variety of levels. But first a comment on the use of the word "blind" rather than the more usual "random". It seems likely that Ashby (1952) unnecessarily limited the generality of his mechanism in Homeostat by an effort to fully represent all of the modern connotations of random. Equiprobability is not needed, and is definitely lacking in the mutations which lay the variation base for organic evolution. Statistical independence between one variation and the next, while frequently desirable, can also be spared: in particular, for the generalizations essayed here, certain processes involving systematic sweep scanning are recognized as blind, insofar as variations are produced without prior knowledge of which ones, if any, will furnish a selectworthy encounter. An essential connotation of "blind" is that the variations emitted be independent of the environmental conditions of the occa-

---

2. This extended usage of "knowledge" is a part of an effort to put "the problem of knowledge" into a behavioristic framework which takes full cognizance of man's status as a biological product of an evolutionary development from a highly limited background, with no "direct" dispensations of knowledge being added at any point in the family tree. The bibliographical citation of the several sources converging on this approach to the problem of knowledge, and the discussion of its relation to traditional philosophical issues and to the strategy of science are presented elsewhere (Campbell, 1959). Suffice it to say here that the position limits one to "an epistemology of the other one". The "primitives" of knowledge can not be sought in "raw feels" or in "phenomenal givens", or in any "incorrigible" elements. While man's conscious knowledge processes are recognized as more complex and subtle than those of lower organisms, they are not taken as more fundamental or primitive. In this perspective, any process providing a stored program for organismic adaptation in external environments is included as a knowledge process, and any gain in the adequacy of such a program is regarded as a gain in knowledge. If the reader prefers, he can understand the paper adequately regarding the term "knowledge" as metaphorical when applied to the lower levels in the developmental hierarchy. But since the problem of knowledge has resisted any generally accepted solution when defined in terms of the conscious contents of the philosopher himself, little seems lost and possibly something gained by thus extending the range of processes considered.

sion of their occurrence. A second important connotation is that the occurrence of trials individually be uncorrelated with the solution, in that specific correct trials are no more likely to occur at any one point in a series of trials than another, nor than specific incorrect trials. (Insofar as observation shows this not to be so, the system is making use of already achieved knowledge, perhaps of a general sort. The prepotent responses of an animal in a new puzzle box toward the apparent openings may thus represent prior general knowledge, transferred from previous learning or inherited as a product of the mutation and selective survival process.) A third essential connotation of "blind" is rejection of the notion that a variation subsequent to an incorrect trial is a "correction" of the previous trial or makes use of the direction of error of the previous one. (Insofar as mechanisms do seem to operate in this fashion, there must be operating a substitute process carrying on the blind search at another level, feedback circuits selecting "partially" adequate variations, providing information to the effect that "you're getting warm", etc.)

2. *Review of the Theme in Lower Knowledge Processes*

In this perspective, the epistemologically most fundamental knowledge processes are embodied in those several inventions making possible organic evolution. At the already advanced level of cellular life, this is a "learning" on the part of the species by the blind variation and selective survival of mutant individuals. In terms of the three requirements, variation is provided by the mutations, selection by the somewhat consistent or "knowable" vagaries of the environment, and preservation and duplication by the complex and rigid order of chromosome mitosis. Bisexuality, heterozygosity, and meiotic cell division represent a secondary invention increasing the efficiency of the process through increasing the range of variation and the rate of readjustment to novel environments. The selection and preservation processes remain the same. The ubiquity of bisexuality, its several independent inventions, and the multifarious elaboration of the theme, all speak to its tremendous usefulness.

The higher evolutionary developments shift a part of the locus of adaptation away from a trial and error of whole organisms or gene pools, over to processes occurring within the single organism. Such processes are numerous, each being not only a device for obtaining knowledge, but also representing general wisdom about environmental contingencies already achieved through organic evolution, making possible more efficient achievement of detailed local knowledge. One of the most primitive of these is exploratory locomotion, described in the protozoa by Jennings (1906) and accepted as a model for Homeostat by Ashby (1952). Forward locomotion persists until blocked, at which point direction of locomotion is varied blindly until unblocked forward locomotion is again possible. The external physical environment is the selection agency, the preservation of discovery is embodied in the preservation of the unblocked forward movement. At this level, the species has "discovered" that the environment is discontinuous, consisting of penetrable regions and impenetrable ones, and that impenetrability is to some extent a stable characteristic – it has discovered that when blocked it is a better strategy to try to go around than to wait until one can move through.

Insofar as individual organisms without distance receptors (such as paramecia and earthworms) can learn through contiguity, the species has already achieved the more general knowledge that there is some event-contingency stability in the environment. That is, in the degree to which individual learning is useful, there has been the species-level discovery of slower transformation processes on the part of relevant segments of the environment than of the organism. In addition, whereas the ultimate selection is life or death in encounters with the external environment, by the evolutionary stage at which learning is possible, much of this once-external criterion has been internalized. Crude environmental contingencies with low selection ratios are now represented as pleasures or pains, or as reinforcers more generally. The selection becomes much more sharp, but the contact with the environmental realities less direct.

The presence of a fundamental trial-and-error process in individual learning needs no elaboration or defense. Suffice it to say that recognition of such a process is found in all learning theories which make any pretense of completeness, including at least three of Gestalt inspiration (Campbell, 1956a). While higher vertebrate (and higher cephalopod) learning makes far more use of the short circuiting of overt trial and error by vision than is allowed for by the usual learning theory (Campbell, 1956b), for convenience here the multiplication of levels will be avoided by treating trial-and-error learning as a single process level.

The next and most striking class of discoveries are those centering around echo-location and vision. Woodworth (1921) has emphasized the achievement of a percept from the ingredients of sensation through a series of "trial-and-error perceptions". Thurstone (1924) has interpreted perception as a trial and error of potential locomotions placed in a hierarchy of trial-and-error processes including both overt trial and error and ideational trial and error, in a book containing many anticipations of cybernetic concepts. Pumphrey (1950) interprets the primitive sense receptor of the fishes called the "lateral-line organ" as a crude echo-location device, making use of the reflected pulses of the fish's own swimming. Griffin (1958) has documented in detail the use by bats and cave birds of sonic and supersonic vocalizations selectively reflected by obstacles of the environment. Kellogg (1958) has made a similar case for the porpoise. Here is a powerful substitute for blind locomotor exploration. (See Simon, 1957, p. 264, for an estimate of such gains.) In echo location a wave pulse is emitted blindly in all directions. The obstacles of the environment selectively reflect the pulse from certain of these directions, and thus provide a feedback which is substitutable for that which would have been received had the animal locomoted in those directions. Radar guidance systems employ an analogous substitution of a blindly scanning electromagnetic wave pulse, in economical substitution for a blind scanning of the same environment of potential locomotions by full ship or projectile movements.

Visual perception seems interpretable as a substitute search process of similar order (Campbell, 1956b). The full analogy is weakened by the absence of an emitting process on the part of the organism. Instead, advantage is taken of diffuse electromagnetic waves made available from external sources. Consider first a pseudoeye consisting of but a single photoreceptor cell. (Such a device has been distributed for use by the blind in which a photocell output is transformed into a sound of variable pitch.) With such a device, blind scanning as in a radar system is essential. Brightness contours can be located and fixated by continual crossing, as in the "hunting" process in a mechanical servosystem, or as in the vocal pitch control in which a steady note is "held" only by a continuous search oscillation (Deutsch & Clarkson, 1959). To conceive of such an "eye" as a blind searching device substituting for a more costly blind locomotion in the explored directions is not difficult. The eyes of insects and vertebrates and the higher cephalopods differ from such a device by having multiple photocells, making possible selective reflection from objects in multiple directions at once. Each receptor cell can be conceived of as exploring the possibilities of locomotion in a given direction, the retina collectively thus exploring the possibilities of locomotion in a wide segment of potential directions for locomotion. Except as the eye is aimed by other sources of knowledge, these possibilities have been made "blindly" available without prescience or insight. For the "blindness" of an eyeless animal there has been substituted a process so efficient that we use it naively as a model for direct, unmediated knowing. But the process is still one of blind search and selective retention, in the sense employed in this paper.

Vision is a very complex and marvelous mechanism, and the brief presentation here does not do justice even to the random search components involved. Hebb (1949) has well documented the active search of eye movements, correcting the model of the inactive fixed-focus eye which is implicit in both Gestalt psychology and conditioning theory. Riggs (Riggs, Armington, & Ratliff, 1954) and Ditchburn (1955) have documented the essential role of the continuous low amplitude scanning provided by "physiological nystagmus" or "fixation tremor". Platt (1958) has provided a brilliant analysis of the role of a blind "rubbing" process, his "lens-grinding" model, for the achievement of visual acuity and spatial representation in a visual system containing unaddressed elements. These and other considerations convince the present writer that although vision represents the strongest challenge to the generality of a blind-variation-and-selective-retention aspect to all knowledge processes, it is not in fact an exception. These brief comments have not fully justified this conclusion, however.

Taking these echo-location and visual exploratory processes collectively, several general aspects can be noted: all exploit a specific and limited coincidence, i.e., that objects impenetrable by organismic locomotion also are opaque to, or reflect, certain wave forms in the acoustical frequencies and in the bands of electromagnetic waves of the visual and radar spectra. It is this coincidence, unpredictable upon the basis of the prior knowledge available to the more primitive organisms, which makes possible such marvelously efficient shortcuts. Thus while phenomenologically vision is more direct than other knowledge processes, it is seen in this perspective as an indirect, substitute process. As in all substitute knowledge processes, the effectiveness is limited by the accuracy of the coding process, i.e., the translation terms between one level and another. Such coding is never exhaustive (Platt, 1956). It always involves abstraction, and along with this some fringe imperfection and proneness to systematic error. It must finally be checked out and corrected by overt locomotion. Its efficacy is limited by the *relevance* of the coding to the more fundamental level of behavior for which it is a substitute. This relevance was itself initially tested out by a blind-variation-and-selective-retention process at the level of organic evolution or early childhood learning. (Species differ in this regard.) The phenomenal directness of vision tempts us to make vision prototypic for knowing at all levels, and leads to that chronic belief in the potential existence of direct and "insightful" mental processes, a belief which it is one purpose of this paper to deny.

3. Creative Thought

Creative thought provides the next level knowledge process for the present discussion. At this level there is a *substitute* exploration of a *substitute* representation of the environment, the "solution" being selected from the multifarious exploratory thought trials according to a criterion which is in itself *substituting* for an external state of affairs. Insofar as the three substitutions are accurate, the solutions when put into overt locomotion are adaptive, leading to intelligent behavior which lacks overt blind floundering, and is thus a knowledge process. To include this process in the general plan of blind variation and selective retention, it must be emphasized that insofar as thought achieves innovation, the internal emitting of thought trials one by one is blind, lacking prescience or foresight. The process *as a whole* of course provides "foresight" for the overt level of behavior, once the process has blindly stumbled into a thought trial that "fits" the selection criterion, accompanied by the "something clicked", "Eureka", or "Aha-Erlebnis", that usually marks the successful termination of the process.

Today, we find the blind-variation-and-selective-retention model most plausibly applied at the levels of organic evolution and trial-and-error learning of animals, and least palatable as a description of creative thinking. Historically, however, the phrase "trial and error" was first used to describe thinking, by Alexander Bain as early as 1855, two years before Darwin's publication of the doctrine of natural selection. Not only for historical interest, but also to further develop the psychology of creativity, the following quotations from him (Bain, 1874) are provided:

> Possessing thus the material of the construction and a clear sense of the fitness or unfitness of each new tentative, the operator proceeds to ply the third requisite of constructiveness – trial and error – . . . to attain the desired result. . . . The number

of trials necessary to arrive at a new construction is commonly so great that without something of an affection or fascination for the subject one grows weary of the task. This is the *emotional* condition of originality of mind in any department (p. 593).

In the process of Deduction . . . the same constructive process has often to be introduced. The mind being prepared beforehand with the principles most likely for the purpose . . . incubates in patient thought over the problem, trying and rejecting, until at last the proper elements come together in the view, and fall into their places in a fitting combination (p. 594).

With reference to originality in all departments, whether science, practice, or fine art, there is a point of character that deserves notice. . . . I mean an Active turn, or a profuseness of energy, put forth in trials of all kinds on the chance of making lucky hits . . . Nothing less than a fanaticism of experimentation could have given birth to some of our grandest practical combinations. The great discovery of Daguerre, for example, could not have been regularly worked out by any systematic and orderly research; there was no way but to stumble upon it. . . . The discovery is unaccountable, until we learn that the author . . . got deeply involved in trials and operations far removed from the beaten paths of inquiry (p. 595).

In 1881 Paul Souriau presented a still more preponderant emphasis on the factor of chance as the sole source of true innovation. He asserts again and again that "le principe de l'invention est le hasard". In the main, he presents his argument through illustration and through the elimination of rival hypotheses about the inventive process, including deduction, induction, and "la méthode". A positive explanation of the process is hard to find. This sample will illustrate his approach:

A problem is posed for which we must invent a solution. We know the conditions to be met by the sought idea; but we do not know what series of ideas will lead us there. In other words, we know how the series of our thoughts must end, but not how it should begin. In this case it is evident that there is no way to begin except at random. Our mind takes up the first path that it finds open before it, perceives that it is a false route, retraces its steps and takes another direction. Perhaps it will arrive immediately at the sought idea, perhaps it will arrive very belatedly: it is entirely impossible to know in advance. In these conditions we are reduced to dependence upon chance.

In the case just analysed we supposed that we had to solve a problem already stated for us. But how was the problem-statement itself found? It is said that a question well posed is half answered. If so, then true invention consists in the posing of questions. There is something mechanical, so to speak, in the art of finding solutions. The truly original mind is that which discovers problems. But here again, it does no good to speak of method, since method is the application of already existing discoveries. The discovery of a new problem can therefore only be fortuitous. Thus we see the role of logic diminish and that of chance increase as we approach closer to true invention. Chance is the first principle of invention: it is what has produced method, nourished it, and made it fertile. Method can only analyse the ideas which come to it from elsewhere, drawing out their consequences and exhausting their contents. Left to itself method soon becomes sterile. Methodological minds cannot help having a feeling of disdain for adventurous minds which affirm before proving and believe before knowing. But they must recognize that without such audacity, no progress would be possible. The mind is not able to revise itself upon its own foundations. New ideas cannot have prototypes: their appearance can only be attributed to chance (pp. 17–18).

Souriau has not only the notion of chance combinations, but also the concept of their being produced in large numbers which are generally worthless and from which only the rare ones fitting a goal or criterion are selected. These two widely separated quotations illustrate this:

> By a kind of artificial selection, we can in addition substantially perfect our thought and make it more and more logical. Of all of the ideas which present themselves to our mind, we note only those which have some value and can be utilized in reasoning. For every single idea of a judicious and reasonable nature which offers itself to us, what hosts of frivolous, bizarre, and absurd ideas cross our mind. Those persons who, upon considering the marvelous results at which knowledge has arrived, cannot imagine that the human mind could achieve this by a simple fumbling, do not bear in mind the great number of scholars working at the same time on the same problem, and how much time even the smallest discovery costs them. Even genius has need of patience. It is after hours and years of meditation that the sought-after idea presents itself to the inventor. He does not succeed without going astray many times; and if he thinks himself to have succeeded without effort, it is only because the joy of having succeeded has made him forget all the fatigues, all of the false leads, all of the agonies, with which he has paid for his success (p. 43).
>
> . . . If his memory is strong enough to retain all of the amassed details, he evokes them in turn with such rapidity that they seem to appear simultaneously; he groups them by chance in all the possible ways; his ideas, thus shaken up and agitated in his mind, form numerous unstable aggregates which destroy themselves, and finish up by stopping on the most simple and solid combination (pp. 114–115).

The phrase "artificial selection" is reminiscent of Darwin's writings, although Souriau makes no mention of the selective-survival model of evolution (nor does he cite the ideas of any other person whatsoever).[3] Note how similar the final quotation is to Ashby's (1952) phrasing of the inevitable self-elimination of unstable combinations:

> Just as, in the species, the truism that the dead cannot breed implies that there is a fundamental tendency for the successful to replace the unsuccessful, so in the nervous system does the truism that the unstable tends to destroy itself imply that there is a fundamental tendency for the stable to replace the unstable (p. vi).

3. [See previous chapter, p. 65.] Souriau's presentation is in general quite modern in spirit, although associationistic in a way some would find dated, and vigorously deterministic in a way now undermined by subatomic physics, although not necessarily so for the problems of which he treats. He comments wisely on many topics not covered here, including simultaneous independent invention and the Zeitgeist, the social conditions of creativity and invention, the dissonance created by discrepant opinions of others, the congruence of free will and determinism, and both the conflict and interdependency between erudition and innovation. His attacks on both deduction and induction are reminiscent of Peirce's later critiques.

Ernst Mach was another great 19th century thinker about thinking who emphasized this model. We today remember him most as a psychologist-physicist-philosopher who contributed to the present day positivistic recognition of the hypothetic character of our constructions of the world and who first made explicit the empirical presumptions involved in the physicist's assumption of an Euclidian space. But when, at the age of 57 in 1895, he was called back to his alma mater the University of Vienna to assume a newly created position of Professor of the History and Theory of Inductive Science, he chose a quite different theme for his inaugural address, "The part played by accident in invention and discovery".

Poincaré (1908, 1913) in his famous essay on mathematical invention presents a point of view which is also judged to be in agreement. He first gives an example in imagery: "One evening, contrary to my custom, I drank black coffee and could not sleep. Ideas rose in crowds; I felt them collide until pairs interlocked, so to speak, making a stable combination" (Poincaré, 1913, p. 387). Poincaré feels that it is rare for this blind permuting process to rise into conscious awareness, and that as a rule only the successful selected alternatives enter consciousness. Because of the relevance of Poincaré's comments; because Hadamard (1945) has cited him in opposition to the accidentalist position while he is read here as favoring the selective-retention version of it; and because of all of the sources cited he would most generally be respected as truly creative (in the field of mathematics) these longish excerpts (Poincaré, 1913) are read into the record:

> It is certain that the combinations which present themselves to the mind in a sort of sudden illumination, after an unconscious working somewhat prolonged, are generally useful and fertile combinations, which seem the result of a first impression. Does it follow that the subliminal self, having divined by a delicate intuition that these combinations would be useful, has formed only these, or has it rather formed many others which were lacking in interest and have remained unconscious?
>
> In this . . . way of looking at it, all the combinations would be formed in consequence of the automatism of the subliminal self, but only the interesting ones would break into the domain of consciousness. And this is still very mysterious. What is the cause that, among the thousand products of our unconscious activity, some are called to pass the threshold, while others remain below? Is it a simple chance which confers this privilege? – Evidently not; among all the stimuli of our senses, for example, only the most intense fix our attention, unless it has been drawn to them by other causes. More generally the privileged unconscious phenomena, those susceptible of becoming conscious, are those which, directly or indirectly, affect most profoundly our emotional sensibility (p. 391).
>
> . . . we reach the following conclusion: The useful combinations are precisely the most beautiful. I mean those best able to charm this special sensibility that all mathematicians know, but of which the profane are so ignorant as often to be tempted to smile at it.
>
> What happens then? Among the great numbers of combinations blindly formed by the subliminal self, almost all are without interest and without utility; but just for that reason they are also without effect upon the esthetic sensibility. Consciousness will never know them; only certain ones are harmonious, and, consequently, at once

useful and beautiful. They will be capable of touching this special sensibility of the geometer of which I have just spoken, and which, once aroused, will call our attention to them, and thus give them occasion to become conscious.

This is only a hypothesis, and yet here is an observation which may confirm it: when a sudden illumination seizes upon the mind of the mathematician, it usually happens that it does not deceive him, but it also sometimes happens, as I have said, that it does not stand the test of verification; well, we almost always notice that this false idea, had it been true, would have gratified our natural feeling for mathematical elegance.

Thus it is this special esthetic sensibility which plays the role of the delicate sieve of which I spoke, and that sufficiently explains why the one lacking it will never be a real creator.

Yet all the difficulties have not disappeared. The conscious self is narrowly limited, and as for the subliminal self we know not its limitations, and this is why we are not too reluctant in supposing that it has been able in a short time to make more different combinations than the whole life of a conscious being could encompass. Yet these limitations exist. Is it likely that it is able to form all the possible combinations, whose number would frighten the imagination? Nevertheless that would seem necessary, because if it produces only a small part of these combinations, and if it makes them at random, there would be small chance that the *good*, the one we should choose, would be found among them.

Perhaps we ought to seek the explanation in that preliminary period of conscious work which always precedes all fruitful unconscious labor. Permit me a rough comparison. Figure the future elements of our combinations as something like the hooked atoms of Epicurus. During the complete repose of the mind, these atoms are motionless, they are, so to speak, hooked to the wall; so this complete rest may be indefinitely prolonged without the atoms meeting, and consequently without any combination between them.

On the other hand, during a period of apparent rest and unconscious work, certain of them are detached from the wall and put in motion. They flash in every direction through the space (I was about to say the room) where they are enclosed, as would, for example, a swarm of gnats or, if you prefer a more learned comparison, like the molecules of gas in the kinematic theory of gases. Then their mutual impacts may produce new combinations.

What is the role of the preliminary conscious work? It is evidently to mobilize certain of these atoms, to unhook them from the wall and put them in swing. We think we have done no good, because we have moved these elements a thousand different ways in seeking to assemble them, and have found no satisfactory aggregate. But, after this shaking up imposed upon them by our will, these atoms do not return to their primitive rest. They freely continue their dance.

Now, our will did not choose them at random; it pursued a perfectly determined aim. The mobilized atoms are therefore not any atoms whatsoever; they are those from which we might reasonably expect the desired solution. Then the mobilized atoms undergo impacts which make them enter into combinations among themselves or with other atoms at rest which they struck against in their course. Again I beg pardon, my comparison is very rough, but I scarcely know how otherwise to make my thought understood.

However it may be, the only combinations that have a chance of forming are those where at least one of the elements is one of those atoms freely chosen by our will. Now, it is evidently among these that is found what I call the *good combination.* Perhaps this is a way of lessening the paradoxical in the original hypothesis.

Another observation. It never happens that the unconscious work gives us the result of a somewhat long calculation *all made,* where we have only to apply fixed rules. We might think the wholly automatic subliminal self particularly apt for this sort of work, which is in a way exclusively mechanical. It seems that thinking in the evening upon the factors of a multiplication we might hope to find the product ready made upon our awakening, or again that an algebraic calculation, for example a verification, would be made unconsciously. Nothing of the sort, as observation proves. All one may hope from these inspirations, fruits of unconscious work, is a point of departure for such calculations. As for the calculations themselves, they must be made in the second period of conscious work, that which follows the inspiration, that in which one verifies the results of this inspiration and deduces their consequences. The rules of these calculations are strict and complicated. They require discipline, attention, will, and therefore consciousness. In the subliminal self, on the contrary, reigns what I should call liberty, if we might give this name to the simple absence of discipline and to the disorder born of chance. Only, this disorder itself permits unexpected combinations (pp. 392–394).

In addition to these pioneers there of course have been numerous others who in some manner have made a substitute trial and error in a modeled or mnemonic environment an important aspect of their description of thinking. In rough chronology these include Baldwin (1906), Pillsbury (1910), Rignano (1923), Woodworth (1921), Woodworth & Schlosberg (1954), Thurstone (1924), Tolman (1926), Hull (1930), Muenzinger (1938), Miller and Dollard (1941), Craik (1943), Boring (1950), Humphrey (1951), Mowrer (1954), Sluckin (1954), and many others.

4. Objections to the Model

The Gestalt Protest

The trial-and-error theme in learning was of course one part of the syndrome of ideas against which Gestalt psychology eloquently protested. In spite of this, there is judged to be no inherent conflict between the perspectives of this paper and the Gestalt position. To make this interpretation, it is necessary to regard neither traditional associationism nor Gestalt psychology as discrete integrated wholes, but instead to regard each as congeries of which the parts may be separately accepted or rejected.

The Gestaltists are judged to have validly rejected Thorndike's (1898) description of animal problem solving as solely a matter of overt locomotor trial and error. As this writer (Campbell, 1956b) has argued previously, recognizing vision as a substitute trial-and-error process leads to the expectation that some locomotor problems will be solved by this means, obviating overt trial and error. Even more so does the model for thought. To the present writer the Gestaltists were correct descriptively even though epistemologically the trial-and-error process remains fundamental to discovery. In Wertheimer's (1959) specific contrasts between in-sightful problem solving and blind trial and error, it is a trial and error of overt manipulation which is involved. Furthermore, as Humphrey (1951) and Wood-worth and Schlosberg (1954) point out, the Gestalt descriptions of problem solv-ing provide ample evidence of both fortuitous solutions and misleading "insights". The recurrent Gestaltist protest that even the errorful trials are "intelligent" and that the subsequent trials make use of what was learned through the error are taken here as equivalent to the statements that the problem solver had some valid general knowledge to begin with, and that before acting he employed the substi-tute trial and error of thought or vision.

The blind-variation-and-selective-retention model of thought joins the Gestalt-ists in protest against the picture of the learning organisms as a passive induction machine accumulating contingencies. Instead, an active generation and checking of thought-trials, hypotheses, or molar responses is envisaged. The model at the level of thought places essential importance upon internalized selective criteria against which the thought-trials are checked. Poincaré's (1913) esthetic criteria and the Gestalt qualities of wholeness, symmetry, organized structure, and the like can be regarded as built-in selective criteria completely compatible with the model. Pringle (1951) for example, has proposed a selective-retention model of central nervous system action in which systematic temporal patterns provide the selective criteria in a resonance process. Nor does the model here presented specify the nature of the thought-trials employed. There must often be a trial and error among possible general principles, or among rational abstractions, or field reor-ganizations, or recenterings. Both the blind-variation-and-selective-survival model and Gestalt theory emphasize the advantage of breaking out of old ruts, and the disadvantages of set and rote drill (Boring, 1950; Dunker, 1945; Katona, 1940; Luchins, 1942; Wertheimer, 1959). Furthermore, the encountering in thought of an idea which fits can be accompanied at the phenomenal level by a joyful "Aha Erlebnis" or a Gestalt experience of "closure", and at the overt performance level by a sudden and stable improvement signifying "insight". There is no essen-tial disagreement here. Nor is the trial-and-error model without phenomenologi-cal support. Note the highly similar testimony from the disparate historical citations provided above, especially in the imagery of multitudinous, loosened, agitated, teeming, colliding, and interlocking ideas.

This is not to say that a Gestalt psychologist would be happy with the blind-variation-and-selective-retention description of thought processes. Nor are all aspects of the Gestalt syndrome here accepted. While "insight" is accepted as a phenomenal counterpart of the successful completion of a perhaps unconscious blind-variation cycle, its status as an explanatory concept is rejected, especially as it connotes "direct" ways of knowing. Furthermore, when publicized as a part of an ideology of creativity, it can reduce creativity through giving students a feeling that they lack an important gift possessed by some others, a feeling which inhibits creative effort and increases dependence upon authority. Polya (1945, 1954) has described such an inhibiting tradition in the teaching of mathematics.

Individual Differences and Genius

Another prevalent orientation antithetical in spirit to the blind-variation-and-selective-retention model may be called the "mystique of the creative genius and the creative act". This is related to our deeply rooted tendency toward causal perception (e.g., Heider, 1944), a tendency to see marvelous achievements rooted in equally marvelous antecedents. It takes the form of the "fallacy of accident" and of *"post hoc ergo propter hoc"*. Let a dozen equally brilliant men each propose differing guesses about the unknown in an area of total ignorance, and let the guess of one man prove correct. From the blind-variation-and-selective-survival model this matching of guess and environment would provide us with new knowledge about the environment but would tell us nothing about the greater genius of the one man – he just happened to be standing where lightning struck. In such a case, however, we would ordinarily be tempted to look for a subtle and special talent on the part of this lucky man. However, for the genuinely unanticipatable creative act, our "awe" and "wonder" should be directed outward, at the external world thus revealed, rather than directed toward the antecedents of the discovery. Just as we do not impute special "foresight" to a successful mutant allele over an unsuccessful one, so in many cases of discovery, we should *not* expect marvelous consequents to have had equally marvelous antecedents. Similarly, in comparing the problem-solving efforts of any one person; from the selective survival model it will be futile, in the instance of a genuinely innovative achievement, to look for special antecedent conditions not obtaining for blind-alley efforts: just insofar as there has been a genuine gain in knowledge, the difference between a hit and a miss lies in the selective conditions thus newly encountered, not in talent differences in the generation of the trials.

This is not to deny individual differences in creative intellect. Indeed, the blind-variation-and-selective-retention model of creative thought predicts such talent differences along all of the parameters of the process. This is to emphasize, however, that explanations in terms of special antecedents will very often be irrelevant, and that the causal-interpretative biases of our minds make us prone to such over-interpretations, to *post-hoc-ergo-propter-hoc* interpretations, deifying the creative genius to whom we impute a capacity for direct insight instead of mental flounderings and blind-alley entrances of the kind we are aware typify our own thought processes. Ernst Mach (1896) notes our nostalgia for the directly-knowing genius: "To our humiliation we learn that even the greatest men are born more for life than for science in the extent to which even they are indebted to accident" (p. 175).

What are the ways in which thinkers might be expected to differ, according to the trial-and-error model? First, they may differ in the accuracy and detail of their representations of the external world, of possible locomotions in it or manipulations of its elements, and of the selective criteria. Differences in this accuracy of representation correspond to differences in degree of information and intelligence. Second, thinkers can differ in the number and range of variations in thought-trials produced. The more numerous and the more varied such trials, the greater the chance of success. Bain has emphasized the role of fanaticism or extreme dedication in producing large volumes of such explorations. Bain, Souriau, Mach, and Poincaré have all emphasized the role of advance preparation in assembling the elements whose blind permutation and combination make possible a wide range of trials. Many observers have emphasized the role of set and familiarity in reducing the range of variations, and have recommended ways of reducing trial-to-trial stereotypy, as by abandoning the problem for awhile, going on to other things. Devices abound which are designed to increase the likelihood that all permutations be considered and are used by most of us, as in going through the alphabet in finding rhymes or puzzle words. There are no doubt age differences in the rapidity and uninhibited range of thought-trial production. The sociology of knowledge makes an important contribution here: persons who have been uprooted from traditional cultures, or who have been thoroughly exposed to two or more cultures, seem to have the advantage in the range of hypotheses they are apt to consider, and through this means, in the frequency of creative innovation. Thorstein Veblen (1919) has espoused such a theory in his essay on the intellectual preeminence of Jews, as has Robert Park (1928) in writing of the role of "the marginal man" in cultural innovation. (See also Seeman, 1956.) And more generally, it is the principle of variation which leads us to expect among innovators those of personal eccentricity and bizarre behavior. We can also see in this principle the value of those laboratories whose social atmospheres allow wide ranging exploration with great tolerance for blind-alley entrances.

The value of wide ranging variation in thought-trials is of course vitiated if there is not the precise application of a selective criterion which weeds out the overwhelming bulk of inadequate trials. This editing talent undoubtedly differs widely from person to person, as Poincaré (1908, 1913) has emphasized. With regard to selection criteria, one further point should be made. Much of creative thought is opportunistic in the sense of having a wide number of selective criteria available at all times, against which the thought trials are judged. The more creative thinker may be able to keep in mind more such criteria, and therefore increase his likelihood of achieving a serendipitous (Cannon, 1945; Merton, 1949) advance on a problem tangential to his initial main line of endeavor (e.g., Barber & Fox, 1958). Further areas of individual differences lie in the competence of the retention, cumulation, and transmission of the encountered solutions.

It need not be expected that these dimensions of talent all go together. In organic evolution, the variation process of mutation and the preservation of gains through genetic rigidity are at odds, with an increase in either being at the expense of the other, and with some degree of compromise being optimum. Just so we might expect that a very pure measure of innovative range in thought and a very pure measure of rote memory might be even negatively correlated, as Saugstad (1952) seems to have found, and similarly for innovative range and selective precision. Such considerations suggest complementary combinations of talent in creative teams, although the uninhibited idea-man and the compulsive edit-and-record type are notoriously incompatible office mates.

Notice regarding the individual differences thus described that while they do make creative innovation much more likely on the part of some individuals than others, they do not place the joys of creative innovation beyond the reach of the less gifted. Indeed looking at large populations of thinkers, the principles make it likely that many important contributions will come from the relatively untalented, undiligent, and uneducated, even though on an average contribution per capita basis, they will contribute much less, points which Souriau (1881) has noted. The intricacy of the tradition to which innovation is being added of course places limitations in this regard.

The Enormous Domain of Possible Thought-Trials to be Searched

A final type of objection to the blind-variation-and-selective-retention model of thought needs to be considered. This objection is to the effect that the domain of possible thought trials is so large that the solution of a given problem would take an impossibly long time were a search of all possibilities to be involved, either through a systematic scanning of all possibilities where these are enumerable, or through a random sampling of the universe of possibilities. Time and trial estimates thus based can be overwhelming, as Kurt Lasswitz's story "The Universal Library" (1958) dramatically illustrates. Other parodies of our model occur in literature as far back as Swift's portrait of the Academy of Lagado in *Gulliver's Travels* (1941, pp. 166–169). (Ley, 1958, traces such ideas back to Lully, ca. 1200.) Newell, Shaw, and Simon (1958a, 1958b) refer in this vein to what they call the "British Museum Algorithm", i.e., the possibility of a group of trained chimpanzees typing at random producing by chance in the course of a million years all of the books in the British Museum. Such parodies seem effectively to reject the blind-variation-and-selective-retention model through a *reductio ad absurdum*. Needless to say, such a rejection is not accepted in the present paper. As a matter of fact, it is judged to be in the same class as parallel objections to the theory of natural selection in evolution. Similar features in these two instances make the accidentalist interpretation more acceptable.

1. Neither in organic evolution nor in thought are all problems solved, nor all possible excellent solutions achieved. There is no guarantee of omniscience. The knowledge we do encounter is achieved against terrific odds. (Those advocating heuristically-programed problem-solving computers are careful not to guarantee solutions, and this modesty should be extended to all models of creative thought.)

2. The tremendous number of nonproductive thought trials on the part of the total intellectual community must not be underestimated. Think of what a small proportion of thought becomes conscious, and of conscious thought what a small proportion gets uttered, what a still smaller fragment gets published, and what a small proportion of what is published is used by the next intellectual generation. There is a tremendous wastefulness, slowness, and rarity of achievement.

3. In biological evolution and in thought, the number of variations explored is greatly reduced by having *selective criteria imposed at every step.* Thus mutant variations on nonadaptive variations of the previous generation are never tested – even though many wonderful combinations may be missed therefore. Some of the "heuristics" currently employed in logic and chess playing machines (Newell, Shaw, & Simon, 1958a, 1958b) have the similar effect of evaluating all next-possible moves in terms of immediate criteria, and then of exploring further variations upon only those stems passing the screen of each prior stage. It is this strategy of cumulating selected outcomes from a blind variation, and then exploring further blind variations only for this highly select stem, that, as R. A. Fisher has pointed out (e.g., 1954, p. 91), makes the improbable inevitable in organic evolution. This strategy is unavoidable for organic evolution, but can obviously be relaxed in thought processes and in machine problem solving. However, the Pandora's box of permutations opened up by such relaxation can be used to infer that, in general, thought-trials are selected or rejected within one or two removes of the established base from which they start. In constructing our "universal library" we stop work on any volume as soon as it is clear that it is gibberish.

4. When we make estimates of the number of permutations which would have to be culled to obtain a given outcome, we often assume that problem solving was undertaken with that one fixed goal in mind. This overlooks the opportunistic, serendipitous course of organic evolution and of much of creative thinking. The likelihood of a productive thought increases with the wider variety of reasons one has for judging a given outcome "interesting". To neglect this opportunistic multipurposedness gives one a poor base for estimating the probability of encountering the one outcome hit upon and recorded. Thus when Newell, Shaw, and Simon's "Logic Theorist" (1958a, 1958b) sets out to prove the sixty-odd theorems in a given chapter of *Principia Mathematica,* it may face a more formidable task than did Whitehead and Russell in generating them, if, except for the dozen classic theorems reproduced, Whitehead and Russell were otherwise free to record every deduction they encountered which seemed "interesting" or "nontrivial". Wigglesworth (1955) has noted this strategy on the part of "pure" scientists, in commenting on the relationship between pure and applied scientists in wartime:

> In the pure science to which they were accustomed, if they were unable to solve problem A they could turn to problem B, and while studying this with perhaps small prospect of success they might suddenly come across a clue to the solution of problem C (p. 34).

In presenting their case for adding "heuristics" to the program of the "Logic Theorist", Newell, Shaw, and Simon have emphasized the inadequacy of blind trial and error. So has Miller (1959) in advocating the heuristic of searching backward from the goal.[4] There is, however no essential disagreement between their point of view and the one offered here. By adding heuristics mechanical thought processes have indeed been made more like those of human beings, both in adequacy and type of errors. Such innovations have obviated the protests of those such as Wisdom (1952) and Mays (1956) who, while conceding that machines could choose good moves at chess or solve logic problems, have found the machines failing to imitate life just in their orderly inspection of all possibilities. Newell, Shaw, and Simon recognize that a machine which would develop its own heuristics would have to do so by a trial and error of heuristic principles, with no guarantee that any would work. They further recognize that possession of an effective heuristic represents already achieved general knowledge about the domain under search, and that adding to this general knowledge will be a blind search process. (The devices of learning and vision and of coding environmental possibilities for thought-search all represent heuristics in this sense.) They might also agree that most heuristic devices will be limited to the specific domain of their discovery, and can only be extended to other domains on a trial basis. They would probably also agree that no problem solving process will be "direct". The disagreements I have with their excellent paper on the processes of creative thinking (Newell, Shaw, & Simon, 1958b) are thus minor matters of emphasis, but may be worth

---

4. Miller (1959, pp. 244–46) is wrong in implying that the strategy of working backward from the goal eliminates the necessity of symbolic trial and error in creative thinking. His mistake comes from assuming that only one path leads into a goal or subgoal. In the spatial locomotion problems from which his concrete illustrations come, and for the logic problems used by Newell, Shaw, and Simon, the paths into any position are not singular, but are instead typically as numerous as paths leading out. A *pure* strategy of working from the goal back to the start would thus involve exploring just as many permutations as the pure strategy of exploring all paths from the start position. However, there is a useful strategy available to symbolic trial and error and not to overt trial and error, in working concurrently from both ends. This produces a dramatic advantage in the number of permutations generated, and a smaller but still substantial gain in the number of comparisons. In the instance suggested by Miller in which each locus branches into 4 alternatives and in which the start and goal turn out to lie 7 stages apart, either of the pure strategies would generate $4+4^2+4^3+4^4+4^5+4^6+4^7$ or 21,844 permutations (neglecting the probable achievement of success before exhausting the 4^7 generation of alternatives). For the mixed approach, the junction would be encountered at the third stage away from each end, or when $2(4+4^2+4^3)$ or 168 alternatives had been examined. In the pure strategy, there would be 21,845 comparisons involved, that is, the start position and each subsequent alternative would be compared with the goal. In the mixed strategy, many more comparisons per alternative are required. Each permutation must be compared with each of the current and previous permutations on the other stem, which in this instance amounts to 7,225 comparisons. If the comparisons are regarded as equally costly as the generating and storing of alternatives, the savings of the mixed approach over either of the pure approaches would amount to approximately 1 to 6, a very handsome gain for any heuristic. This gain is larger as the number of branches at each stage increases. Advocacy of the heuristic of working backwards in what is essentially this mixed form is present in Polya (1945), Wisdom (1952), and Newell, Shaw, and Simon (1958a, 1958b). In none of these is it claimed that trial and error is eliminated, while all point to the reduction in trials which it can achieve.

stating nonetheless, to further clarify the position here advocated. They say, for example:

> We have given enough estimates of the sizes of the spaces involved . . . to cast suspicion upon a theory of creativity which places its emphasis upon increase in trial and error (p. 63).

The blind-variation-and-selective-retention model unequivocally implies that *ceteris paribus,* the greater the heterogeneity and volume of trials the greater the chance of a productive innovation. Doubling the number of efforts very nearly doubles the chance of a hit, particularly when trials are a small part of the total domain and the repetitiousness among trials is low. But they too recognize unconventionality and no doubt numerosity as a necessary, if not a sufficient condition of creativity (1958b, p. 62). What they would validly stress, is the very frequent tactical advantage of a trial and error of general strategic principles over a trial and error involving no classificatory effort nor attempt to use clues, and, once such general heuristics have been discovered, the advantages of a hierarchized trial-and-error process. The advantage of such a strategy depends upon the ecology, of course, but we are in general justified in expecting solutions to be nonrandomly distributed, and to show significant contingencies with prior clues. Polya (1945, 1954) has, of course, been a major source of inspiration for all efforts to introduce heuristics into problem solving, and for him a trial-and-error approach is a heuristic of fundamental importance.

Another minor point of disagreement may be mentioned. In their efforts to consider how a "logic theorist" might be programmed to learn a general heuristic from hindsight they propose that it keep a record of the outcomes of all past trials, successful and unsuccessful, in order to be able to scan its experience for general principles of strategy (1958b). Implementing this would put a tremendous strain upon memory storage, and would introduce a scanning process as time consuming as the original search process which produced the record. The strategy of organic evolution is to keep a record only of what works, even at the expense of repeating its errors. The general preponderance of wrong tries at every level, plus problems of memory glut and access, suggests a similar strategy for all knowledge processes. Heuristics can probably best be learned through a trial and error of heuristics, tried on new problem sets rather than old.

5. *Status as a Theory*

At the level here developed, one might better speak of an "orientation to", or a "perspective on" creative thought processes, rather than a "theory of". At many points, this perspective merely points to problems, rather than taking that step toward theory of providing guesses at answers: e.g., for the processes here outlined to be possible, theory must not only provide several memory processes, but most importantly, must specify a possible mechanism for the trial-and-error search of these. From such specifications will come the subtlety of prediction characteristic of a developed theory.[5] While the perspective even in its very general state has some unequivocal empirical implications, the major advantage to it may be metaphysical, or at least metatheoretical. Like the theory of natural selection in organic evolution, it provides an understanding of marvelously purposive processes without the introduction of teleological metaphysics or of pseudocausal processes working backward in time.

Note that there are still ambiguities about the status *as theory* of the well established principle of organic evolution through natural selection, even though now buttressed with the detailed genetic model of the variation and retention processes. Scriven (1959) has called it an explanatory rather than a predictive theory. While the present writer feels that Scriven has somewhat undervalued the experimental studies of evolution with viruses, bacteria, and insects, and may have mistaken the past absence of experimental settings appropriate to testing the theory for an inherent attribute of the type of theory per se; he has called attention, nonetheless, to some serious problems. Even Sewall Wright (1960), whose statistical genetic theory of evolution has added subtle details to the overall description of the process, has commented in a similar vein:

> The theory is deterministic only in an exceedingly limited sense. It is essentially a theory of the conditions favorable for an ever continuing process that is essentially unpredictable in its details. There can be no formula for serendipity (p. 148).

The problems which a selective retention theory of creative thinking shares with that of evolution include the following:

1. The basic insight, so useful and so thrilling when first encountered, is close to being an analytic tautology rather than a synthetic description of process: if indeed variations occur which are differentially selected and propagated, then an evolutionary process toward better fit to any set of consistent selective criteria is inevitable.

2. For most applications of the selective retention model, the variation is taken as a descriptive given, as an unexplained part of the explanation. While other predictive theories likewise depend upon unexplained processes at a more molecular level, this instance may seem evasive at a particularly crucial point, and has indeed been taken as a denial of determinism or as a rival metaphysic of "spontaneous change" as presumptive as a teleological one. We are currently getting detailed deterministic explanations of the mutation of genes, but until something comparable is available

5. This paper does not attempt to review theories in this area. Citations to the important contributions of Pringle (1951) and Hebb (1949), do not begin to represent this literature. Note the special problem of a brain analogue to switching. Ashby's (1952) model and most computer memory search involves a spatial displacement of solids impossible in the brain, as in the stepping switch or the rotation of a magnetic memory drum. Computer memory search processes making use of timed pulses require a precision of timing dependent upon a stability of dimension presumably not available in the brain and usually if not always dependent upon a clock within which actual spatial displacement of solids takes place. It is for these reasons that Pringle's (1951) theory seems particularly promising, and one wonders why it has not been more used, or if not usable, more publicly refuted. See Pribram (1959) for a recent contribution to the problem of appropriate brain process models.

to predict the generation of heterogeneous thought trials, this constitutes a weakness of the model.

3. The biological study of the evolution of any species takes the form of a post hoc reconstruction of a unique, "undetermined", historical process. The achievement of any general regularities must be probabilistic in the extreme. Studies starting from specific spectacular achievements in creative thought must be similar in nature.

4. The theory suffers from the multiplicity of possible mediations it posits. Where there are gaps in the historical knowledge, the theory makes available an embarrassing surfeit of possible reconstructions. In this, and in contrast to the successful theories of macrophysics, the theory is less self-disciplining, less specific in its predictions, more evasive of potential disconfirmation. This is perhaps the most important of Scriven's (1959) points, and one equally applicable to the theory of creative thinking.

5. In the usual applications, the environment is not described or describable prior to the organismic achievement of adaptation to that environment. Whereas the theory deals with an iterative process whereby an organism adapts to (achieves knowledge of) an independent environment, the evidences as to the organismic form and environmental parameters are often confounded, in that the same data series is used to infer both. While this is not so for laboratory studies of trial-and-error learning, it is particularly apt to be so for any study of truly great creative thinking in science. (See Campbell, 1959, p. 157 for epistemological citations to this problem.)

There is in addition, a serious problem which the blind-variation-and-selective-retention theory of creative thought faces which is not present in comparable degree in the modern theory of organic evolution. This is the unfavorable ratio of hypothesized unobservable processes to observable input-output variables. Note that even in its sketchy form here given, some six to fourteen or more separately variable parameters are implied. These include: *(a)* A mnemonic representation of environment, varying perhaps in scope, accuracy, and fineness of detail; *(b)* A mnemonic search or thought-trial process, varying in the accuracy with which it represents potential overt exploration; *(c)* A thought trial generating and changing process, varying in rate, heterogeneity, idiosyncrasy, and lack of repetitiousness among successive thought-trials; *(d)* Selective criteria, varying in their number, accuracy of representation of environmental contingencies, and precision, sharpness, or selection ratio; *(e)* A preservation or propagation process, providing a retention for selected thought trials of a quite different order from the memory traces of the nonselected ones, varying perhaps in accuracy and accessibility; *(f)* A reality testing process in which the selected thought trials are checked out by overt locomotion in the external environment, varying perhaps in sensitivity to disconfirming feedback.

This inventory of weaknesses does not, of course, represent argument in favor of rival theories of creative thought, which are judged to be still more amorphous, still less adequate. And as Duncan (1959) makes clear in reviewing the research literature on human problem solving, for all theories there is lacking a disciplined relation both to experimental undertakings and to findings. Even in its present form, however, the theory contains many empirical implications. Manipulation of any one of the 14 variables just listed should increase the number of creative products, providing the other variables can be held constant. Predictions of this order have been specified in the discussion of individual differences. Particularly characteristic are the unequivocal predictions regarding the volume and heterogeneity of thought trials. *Ceteris paribus,* a creative solution is more likely the longer a problem is worked upon, the more variable the thought-trials, the more people working on the problem independently, the more heterogeneous these people, the less the time pressure, etc.

6. Summary

This paper has attempted to make the psychological and epistemological point that all processes leading to expansions of knowledge involve a blind-variation-and-selective-retention process. Processes, such as vision and thought, substituting for an overt trial and error are of course acknowledged. But each of these is interpreted as containing in its very workability wisdom about the environment obtained originally by the blind variation of mutation and natural selection. In addition, each contains a blind-variation-and-selective-retention process at its own level. Supporting the effort to interpret all knowledge processes in this light has been an emphasis upon the tremendous gain in knowledge in the course of evolution and history, a gain which can only be explained by a continual breakout from the bounds of what was already known, a breakout for which blind variation provides the only mechanism available.

The application of this perspective to the process of creative thought antedates its application to trial-and-error learning in animals and to organic evolution, and is illustrated through quotations from Bain, Souriau, Mach, and Poincaré. The model is not in disagreement with the bulk of the Gestalt description of problem solving, nor the work on heuristically-programed problem-solving computers. However, there is an effort to root out a prevailing implicit belief in the possibility of "direct" or "insightful" creative thought processes.

References

Ashby, W. R. *Design for a brain* (New York: Wiley, 1952).

Bain, A. *The senses and the intellect,* 3rd ed. (New York: Appleton, 1874).

Baldwin, J. M. *Mental development in the child and the race* (New York: Macmillan, 1900).

Baldwin, J. M. *Thought and things, or genetic logic,* Vols. I–III (New York: Macmillan, 1906–1911).

Barber, B., & Fox, R. C. "The case of the floppy-eared rabbits: An instance of serendipity gained and serendipity lost", *Amer. J. Social.,* 1958, **64**, 128–36.

Boring, E. G. "Great men and scientific progress", *Proc. Amer. Phil. Soc.*, 1950, **94**, 339–51.
Campbell, D. T. "Adaptive behavior from random response", *Behav. Sci.*, 1956, **1**, 105–10. (a)
Campbell, D. T. "Perception as substitute trial and error", *Psychol. Rev.*, 1956, **63**, 330–42. (b)
Campbell, D. T. "Methodological suggestions from a comparative psychology of knowledge processes", *Inquiry*, 1959, **2**, 152–82.
Cannon, W. B. *The way of an investigator* (New York: Norton, 1945).
Craik, K. J. W. *The nature of explanation* (Cambridge: Cambridge University Press, 1943).
Deutsch, J. A., & Clarkson, J. K. "The nature of the vibrato and the control loop in singing", *Nature*, 1959, **183**, 167–68.
Ditchburn, R. W. "Eye-movement in relation to retinal action", *Optica Acta*, 1955, **1**, 171–76.
Duncan, C. P. "Recent research on human problem solving", *Psychol. Bull.*, 1959, **56**, 397–429.
Dunker, K. "On problem-solving", *Psychol. Monogr.*, 1945, **58**(5, Whole No. 270).
Fisher, R. A. "Retrospect of the criticism of the theory of natural selection", in J. Huxley, A. C. Hardy, & E. B. Ford, eds., *Evolution as a process* (London: Allen & Unwin, 1954).
Griffin, D. R. *Listening in the dark* (New Haven: Yale University Press, 1958).
Hadamard, J. *The psychology of invention in the mathematical field* (Princeton: Princeton University Press, 1945).
Hebb, D. O. *The organization of behavior* (New York: Wiley, 1949).
Heider, F. "Social perception and phenomenal causality", *Psychol. Rev.*, 1944, **51**, 358–74.
Hull, C. L. "Knowledge and purpose as habit mechanisms", *Psychol. Rev.*, 1930, **37**, 511–25.
Humphrey, G. *Thinking* (London: Methuen, 1951).
Jennings, H.S. *The behavior of the lower organisms* (New York: Columbia University Press, 1906).
Katona, G. *Organizing and memorizing* (New York: Columbia University Press, 1940).
Kellogg, W. N. "Echo-ranging in the porpoise", *Science*, 1958. **128**, 982–88.
Lasswitz, K. "The universal library", (first published 1901), in C. Fadiman, ed., *Fantasia mathematica* (New York: Simon & Schuster, 1958).
Ley, W. "Postscript to 'The universal library'", in C. Fadiman, ed., *Fantasia mathematica* (New York: Simon & Schuster, 1958), pp. 244–47.
Luchins, A. "Mechanization in problem solving: The effect of Einstellung", *Psychol. Monogr.*, 1942, **54**(6, Whole No. 248).
Mach, E. "On the part played by accident in invention and discovery", *Monist*, 1896, **6**, 161–75.
Mays, W. "Cybernetic models and thought processes", *Proceedings of the First International Congress on Cybernetics, Namur* (Paris: Gauthier-Villard, 1956).
Merton, R. K. *Social theory and social structure* (Glencoe, Ill.: Free Press, 1949).
Miller, N. E. "Liberalization of basic S-R concepts: Extensions to conflict behavior, motivation, and social learning", in S. Koch, ed., *Psychology: A study of a science.* Vol. 2. *General systematic formulations, learning, and special processes* (New York: McGraw-Hill, 1959).
Miller, N. E., & Dollard, J. *Social learning and imitation* (New Haven: Yale University Press, 1941).
Mowrer, O. H. "Ego psychology, cybernetics, and learning theory", in *Kentucky symposium: Learning theory, personality theory, and clinical research* (New York: Wiley, 1954), pp. 81–90.

Muenzinger, K. F. "Vicarious trial and error at a point of choice: I. A general survey of its relation to learning efficiency", *J. genet. Psychol.*, 1938, **53**, 75–86.

Newell, A., Shaw, J. C., & Simon, H. A. "Elements of a theory of human problem solving", *Psychol. Rev.*, 1958, **65**, 151–66. (a)

Newell, A., Shaw, J. C., & Simon, H. A. *The process of creative thinking*. University of Colorado 1958 symposium on cognition. *Rand Corp. Rep.*, 158, No. P-1320. (b)

Park, R. E. "Human migration and the marginal man", *Amer. J. Sociol.*, 1928, **33**, 881–93.

Pillsbury, W. B. *The psychology of reasoning* (New York: Appleton, 1910).

Platt, J. "Amplification aspects of biological response and mental activity", *Amer. Scient.*, 1956, **44**, 181–97.

Platt, J. "Functional geometry and the determination of pattern in mosaic receptors", in H. P. Yockey, R. L. Platzman, & H. Quastler, eds., *Symposium on information theory in biology* (New York: Pergamon, 1958), pp. 371–98.

Poincaré, H. "L'invention mathematique", *Bull. Inst. Gen. Psychol.*, 1908, **8**, 175–87.

Poincaré, H. "Mathematical creation", in H. Poincaré, *The foundations of science* (New York: Science Press, 1913).

Polya, G. *How to solve it* (Princeton, N. J.: Princeton University Press, 1945).

Polya, G. *Mathematics and plausible reasoning*. Vol. I. *Induction and analogy in mathematics;* Vol. II. *Patterns of plausible inference* (Princeton, N. J.: Princeton University Press, 1954).

Pribram, K. H. "On the neurology of thinking", *Behav. Sci.*, 1959, **4**, 265–87.

Pringle, J. W. S. "On the parallel between learning and evolution", *Behavior*, 1951, **3**, 175–215.

Pumphrey, R. J. Hearing. In *Symposia of the Society for Experimental Biology.* IV. *Physiological mechanisms in animal behavior* (New York: Academic Press, 1950).

Riggs, L. A., Armington, J. C., & Ratliff, F. "Motions of the retinal image during fixation", *J. Opt. Soc. Amer.*, 1954, **44**, 315–21.

Rignano, E. *Psychologie du raisonnement* (Paris: Alcan, 1920); reprinted: *The psychology of reasoning* (New York: Harcourt, Brace, 1923).

Saugstad, P. "Incidental memory and problem-solving", *Psychol. Rev.*, 1952, **59**, 221–26.

Scriven, M. "Explanation and prediction in evolutionary theory", *Science*, 1959, **130**, 477–82.

Seeman, M. "Intellectual perspective and adjustment to minority status", *Soc. Probl.*, 1956, **3**, 142–53.

Simon, H. A. *Models of man* (New York: Wiley, 1957).

Sluckin, W. *Minds and machines* (Harmondsworth: Penguin, 1954).

Souriau, P. *Theorie de l'invention* (Paris: Hachette, 1881).

Swift, J. *Gulliver's travels*, originally published 1726 (Oxford: Blackwell, 1941).

Thorndike, E. L. "Animal intelligence: An experimental study of the associative processes in animals", *Psychol. Rev. Monogr. Suppl.*, 1898, 2(4, Whole No. 8).

Thurstone, L. L. *The nature of intelligence* (New York: Harcourt, Brace, 1924).

Tolman, E. C. "A behavioristic theory of ideas", *Psychol. Rev.*, 1926, **33**, 352–69.

Veblen, T. "The intellectual preeminence of Jews in modern Europe", *Pol. sci. Quart*, 1919, **34**, 33–42.

Wertheimer, M. *Productive thinking* (New York: Harper, 1959).

Wigglesworth, V. B. "The contribution of pure science to applied biology", *Ann. appl. Biol.*, 1955, **42**, 34–44.

Wisdom, J. O. "Symposium: Mentality in machines", in *Proceedings of the Aristotelian Society, Suppl. Vol. 26, Men and machines* (London: Harrison, 1952), pp. 1–26.

Woodworth, R. S. *Psychology* (New York: Holt, 1921).

Woodworth, R. S., & Schlosberg, H. *Experimental psychology,* rev. ed. (New York: Holt, 1954).

Wright, S. "Physiological genetics, ecology of populations, and natural selection", *Perspectives Biol. Med.,* 1959, **3**, 107–51, reprinted: Tax, S., ed. *Evolution after Darwin.* Vol. I. *The evolution of life* (Chicago: University Chicago Press, 1960.)

Chapter *IV*

Campbell on the Evolutionary Theory of Knowledge

By Karl R. Popper

Professor Campbell's remarkable contribution [Chapter II above] shows the greatest agreement with my epistemology, and (what he cannot know) an astonishing anticipation of some things which I had not yet published when he wrote his paper. In addition, it is a treatise of prodigious historical learning: there is scarcely anything in the whole of modern epistemology to compare with it; certainly not in my own work. His historical references are all highly relevant; they are a real treasure house; and they often surprised me greatly.

For me the most striking thing about Campbell's essay is the almost complete agreement, down even to minute details, between Campbell's views and my own. I shall try to develop one or two of these points a little further still, and shall then turn to the very rare and comparatively minor points where there may be some difference of opinion.

I

In my paper "Two Faces of Common Sense",[1] I develop in considerable detail the relationship between my realism and my fallibilistic epistemology. Although I wrote this paper before reading Professor Campbell's contribution, there is the closest similarity (especially with his Summary).

I show in my paper that if we start from a critical commonsense realism (not from a naive realism, and even less from a direct realism which somehow attributes to us the ability to "see" that the world is real) then we shall take man as one of the animals, and human knowledge as essentially almost as fallible as animal knowledge. We shall suppose the animal senses to have evolved from primitive beginnings; and we shall look therefore on our own senses, essentially, as

This chapter was first published in P. A. Schilpp, ed.: *The Philosophy of Karl Popper* (LaSalle: Open Court, 1974), pp. 1059–65. ©Karl R. Popper.
1. Published as Chapter II of *Objective Knowledge* (London: Oxford University Press, 1972).

part of a decoding mechanism – a mechanism which decodes, more or less successfully, the encoded information about the world which manages to reach us by sensual means. There is some reason to think that our senses and our brain operate fairly well together in this business of decoding, but no reason at all to allow them or us any "direct" knowledge of anything immediately "given".

I think this is in complete agreement with Campbell's views; and with the views he attributes to me.

The next step is to look at the function and working structure of our apparatus for gaining knowledge about the physical world ("world 1"). Here we have, like some animals, the senses and the brain, which between them deliver us with knowledge that belongs, if conscious, to "world 2". But the characteristic thing about specifically human knowledge – *science* – is that it is formulated in a descriptive and argumentative language, and that the problems, theories, and errors which are embedded in this language stand in their own peculiar relations, constituting what I call "world 3".

Campbell does not say very much about my theory of world 3, and it is here that I should like to make some remarks in amplification of his.

A point which follows almost directly from this critical realism is what I have described as the *knowledge situation* of animals and men. So far as the knowledge is not, somehow, genetically built into them, animals and men can only gain knowledge if they have a drive or instinct for exploration – for finding out more about their world. Their very existence, to be sure, presupposes a world which is *to some extent* "knowable" or "explorable", but it also presupposes an innate disposition to know and to explore: we are active explorers (explorers by trial and error) rather than passive recipients of information impressed upon us from outside (Lamarckism, inductivism).

But we live in a complicated and partly mysterious world. We seem to know much more about it than the animals do – or anyway much more in a not entirely instrumental or utilitarian sense of "knowledge"; but there is no reason to think that our knowledge is not highly fallible and sketchy. It is only in the last three hundred years that we have begun to know much about the situation of the Earth on which we are living; and it is only one hundred years or a little less since we began to know more about the limitations of our natural senses as detectors, and to build detectors which reveal to us encoded information or messages about the world to which our senses would not be immediately responsive.

Thus it is an almost immediate consequence of critical realism (together with an evolutionary approach) to regard ourselves, and our knowledge, as continuous with the animals and with animal knowledge. This means in my opinion that we must abandon any approach which starts from sense data and the given, and replace it by the assumption that all human knowledge is fallible and conjectural. It is a product of the method of trial and error.

Part of our knowledge consists of innate dispositions and expectations (or of drives or instincts to explore, for example, or to imitate). What is so notable about human knowledge is that it has grown so very far beyond all animal knowledge, and that it is still growing. The main task of the theory of human knowledge is to understand it as continuous with animal knowledge; and to understand also its discontinuity – if any – from animal knowledge.

In all this there is, I believe, complete agreement between Campbell and myself.

II

A point in Campbell's theory seems to me to deserve special mention; it is a point on which I have had to say very little that is useful, if anything, and on which he has to say excellent and enlightening things. I am thinking of what he calls the *"blindness"* of the trials in a trial-and-error method.

I have sometimes compared the human situation in the quest for new knowledge with the proverbial situation of a blind man who searches in a dark room for a black hat which is – perhaps – not there. This is not saying much: but it indicates that the searcher at least acts as if he had a problem. I have often added that the trial movements of the searcher will not be completely random. There are various reasons for this, both positive and negative. The positive ones are in the main that the searcher has a problem to solve, and that this means that he has some knowledge, however fuzzy, previously acquired by essentially the same trial-and-error method; this knowledge serves as a guide, and eliminates complete randomness.[2] A negative argument is that randomness, and the associated idea of (probabilistic) independence in the sequence of trials, are hardly applicable: the tosses with a penny may be random, but only with respect to a definite property – heads or tails. There must be a definite, given *order* if we want to speak of randomness, such as the orderly sequences of tosses with a penny, considered from the point of view of which side comes up: here we have definite "elementary events", which may or may not yield a random sequence.

But although the blind man who searches for a black hat may *bring* some order into his trials, the order is not *given* to him; he may choose or invent one order (method) first, and a different order later; and these choices will be trials too – even though on a higher level. (They may, but need not, be influenced by his earlier experience in somewhat similar or in very different situations.) There is no definite or given order of "elementary events"; we do not even know what is the maximum activity that constitutes *one* trial (event) rather than two.

Nevertheless, the trials are *forays into the unknown*. Campbell, who explains why he does not call them random (see the text between his notes 21 and 24), calls them "blind" (an excellent term) and insists on the fact that, so far as they are trials in a trial-and-error movement – that is, so far as they are forays into the unknown – they are blind; while to the degree that past knowledge enters, their

---

2. David Miller has drawn my attention to the parallelism here with Plato's *Meno* 80 D f. The existence of vague or "fuzzy" knowledge (hardly possible of course for Plato) indicates, I think, how Meno's problem is to be solved.

blindness is only relative: it begins where the past knowledge ends.

I think this is very important. It means that we may at the beginning of an exploration be blinder than we are after even a short time, though after even a short time we may still be blind: we may still not know where the black hat is, but we may know (or think that we know) where it is not.

I regard this idea of the "blindness" of the trials in a trial-and-error movement as an important step beyond the mistaken idea of random trials, which in any case stand under the influence of a (changing) exploratory drive and (likewise changing) problem situation. (See esp. the text to, and following, Campbell's note 57.)

Campbell comes to the conclusion that the trial-and-error method is essentially similar to the attempts of a blind man to feel his way with a stick. It is active. And he shows that our use of our sense organs is essentially of the same nature (see the text following Campbell's note 28): "From the point of view of an evolutionary epistemology, vision is just as indirect as radar."

This shows that nothing is "given" to us by our senses; everything is interpreted, decoded: everything is the result of active experiments, under the control of an exploratory drive.

There is a point here, however, into which Campbell does not go, but which I regard as important. The blind trial stands not only under the influence of the exploratory drive or instinct, but also under the influence of the experience of error – the experience that this is wrong, that this is *not* the solution. This point (which he of course would concede) seems to me so important because it becomes on the human level the basis of our *criticism* of the results of our trials.

III

Campbell's paper also touches on some other points.

There is the question of the decoding (itself yielding an interpretation subject to trial and error) which is partly undertaken by our sense organs and partly by our brain. I conjecture that the deepest basis of this decoding operation is a genetically based, innate drive to find out, to understand, to correlate. This is perhaps the strongest reason why blindness is so different from randomness.

When blind and deaf Helen Keller's teacher "spelt" the word "water" into the hand over which water was running, and Helen Keller "understood"– when she knew that this *meant* water – there must have been at work not only a dispositional ability to learn a language (an "unnatural" language, and one which was hardly "social" at all), but also a deep-seated dispositional *need*, an unconscious *desire* for symbols and for the understanding of symbols.

I conjecture that it is so with all our decoding instincts – for example with vision, including the vision of color. I conjecture that a child who is colorblind (say, red-green blind), but otherwise as healthy and active as Helen Keller, would make use of any help to decode colors and to learn to distinguish red from green. I suggest that if such a child is fitted, for example, with a red lens before the right eye and a green lens before the left eye, he would soon learn not only how to make use of his peculiar experiences in order to distinguish red from green: he would actually learn to *see* red and green; that is, he would, under the influence of his healthy nervous system and its *needs* and *drives,* learn to make use of the distinct experiences available to *decode the encoded messages correctly* ("correctly" according to the guidance of his inborn needs).[3] It is, I think, some support of my hypothesis that a former pupil of mine, the psychoanalyst Dr. Noel Bradley, reports that colorblind children may deeply suffer from their deficiency (which they should not, one would think, experience, unless some instinct is not satisfied), and many even develop a neurosis in connection with it.[4]

IV

I come now to two points where I may possibly slightly deviate from Campbell. The first is connected with his psychological analysis of Kant's *a priori* categories. In this connection, Campbell first quotes at length a passage from me (see the text to his note 98) and then continues: "This insight is the earliest and most frequently noted aspect of an evolutionary epistemology", referring to Herbert Spencer, Harald Høffding, Wallraff, Lange, Baldwin, and Konrad Lorenz.

However, I may perhaps say that in the long passage quoted by Campbell from me there are, I hope, several "insights", and that the insight denoted by Campbell as "this insight" is not the one which I wished to bring out as important.[5]

It is a clear and an almost obvious insight that Kant's idea of *a priori* knowledge can be psychologically interpreted (and has sometimes been so interpreted; sometimes even by Kant himself, and certainly by Fries). That is, our interpretation of events in terms of causality (for example) may be merely psychological, or due to the structure of our brain, without being necessarily *valid* in Kant's sense; valid, that is to say, not only for all possible rational beings, but in the sense that it must be true for the world as we know it. This latter meaning is not psychological but raises a claim to absolute *objectivity;* and the fundamental meaning of Kant's teaching was that his categories (and principles) were *a priori valid* – and *objectively valid* – in this sense, and not merely *a priori* in the sense that

3. There are many variants of this suggested experiment, such as the use of contact lenses, and especially of two contact lenses which are both vertically divided into a red and a green side.

4. This neurosis may, of course, be due to the discovery that they do not see like normal human beings; that is to say, its origin may be a social inferiority rather than a dissatisfied innate drive to decode. I conjecture, however, the latter.

5. In the long passage quoted by Campbell and referred to when he speaks of "this insight", I said, I think, several other things besides this, things which had to my knowledge not been said before by any of the authors whom Campbell quotes. However, I leave it to the interested reader to find out what these other insights are. I may perhaps mention another minor point here: I completely agree with what Campbell has to say about chance discovery. I do not know which unfortunate remark of mine may have created a different impression. (See Campbell, text to note 72.)

they factually preceded our experiences, and were needed for our experiences.

All writers here quoted by Campbell, including myself, have pointed out that we may reinterpret Kant's *a priori* so as not to mean *"objectively valid"* but "prior to sense experience". (I have pointed out too that in some way or other all hypotheses *(H)* are psychologically prior to some observation *(O)*, since observation presupposes an interest, a problem, a conjecture.)[6]

V

I come now to my last comment. It is, I think, an important one, and it is related to the difference between man and animal, and especially between human rationality and human science and animal knowledge.

Campbell speaks very interestingly of the language of the bees (text to his note 65), and he also mentions my stress on criticism; but he nowhere seems to allude to my view that human descriptive language differs from all animal languages in being also argumentative, and that it is human argumentative language which makes criticism possible, and with it science.

There is a world of difference between holding a belief, or expecting something, and using human language to *say* so. The difference is that only if spoken out, and thus objectivized, does a belief become criticizable. Before it is formulated in language, I may be one with my belief: the belief is part of my acting, part of my behavior. If formulated, it may be criticized and found to be erroneous; in which case I may be able to discard it.

The language of the bees may resemble human language in that it can be said (up to a point) to be descriptive. But so far as we know, a bee cannot lie, and another bee cannot deny what the first bee asserted.

I think that the first storyteller may have been the man who contributed to the rise of the ideas of factual *truth* and *falsity,* and that out of this the ideal of truth developed; as did the argumentative use of language. I do not sense any difference in opinion in what Campbell says concerning truth and instrumentalism. But there seems to be a slight difference in emphasis: in my stress on the idea of truth, on the argumentative function of the human language, and on criticism – in brief in my predilection for world 3. But it is very likely that there is no difference here: Campbell's beautiful essay covers a great many things; he may have been reluctant to say more.

6. See the text following Campbell's note 97, and his reference to my *Conjectures and Refutations,* p. 47.

Light and Life: On the Nutritional Origins of Sensory Perception[1]

By Günter Wächtershäuser

Information does not stream into us from the environment. Rather, it is we who explore the environment and suck information from it actively, like food.[2]

Karl Popper

A. Introduction

Popper's philosophy marks a major achievement: the first and only unified theory of knowledge. One single coherent process of knowledge, a problem-solving process, is seen as stretching from the earliest inklings of life to the latest advances of science and technology.[3] We are concerned here with a special aspect of this lifelong process: the evolutionary origins of perception, i.e., the transition from long-term problem solving by biological evolution to short-term problem solving by sensory cognition.

How do we proceed in such an inquiry? Generally speaking, the course of evolution may be unravelled in two directions, forward in time or backward in

This essay is a revised and expanded version of a lecture given May 27, 1984, during the 150th National Meeting of the American Association for the Advancement of Science in a Symposium on "New Directions in Evolutionary Epistemology" arranged by Paul Levinson. Copyright © 1984, 1985, Günter Wächtershäuser.

1. The title alludes to a famous lecture by Niels Bohr, delivered at the opening meeting of the International Congress on Light Therapy, Copenhagen, on August 15, 1932, and printed in *Nature* **131**, 1933, pp. 421–23, 457–59.
   2. Karl R. Popper, in "Evolutionary Epistemology", cited below (footnote 3).
   3. Karl R. Popper, *Objective Knowledge: An Evolutionary Approach* (London, Oxford University Press, 1972); Karl R. Popper, *The Open Universe: An Argument for Indeterminism*, W. W. Bartley III. ed. (London: Hutchinson Ltd., 1982), pp 131–62; Karl R. Popper, John C. Eccles, *The Self and its Brain*, (Berlin: Springer Verlag, 1977); Karl R. Popper, *Unended Quest*, (London: Fontana/Collins, 1976); Karl R. Popper, "Evolutionary Epistemology", in J. W. Pollard ed., *Evolutionary Theory: Paths into the Future*, (Chichester: Wiley & Sons, 1984); see also Chapters IV and VI and for further discussions chapters I and II of this volume.

time. In the first procedure, we follow Popper's method of situational logic.[4] We try to spell out a most plausible initial situation and analyze the problems it poses for some organisms. Next, we try to construct a possible solution to this problem situation guided by considerations of physical, chemical, and ecological plausibility. This will lead to a new problem situation for which we try again to construct a solution. In this fashion, we attempt a theoretical reconstruction of the course of evolution in the form of a speculative concatenation of problems and solutions.[5] In the second procedure, we study the features of modern organisms as they exist today and we try to establish phylogenetic relationships by similarity considerations. The first approach will be taken in section B and the second approach in section C, and we shall see that both approaches lead to compatible results.

Many evolutionary studies focus primarily on the evolution of whole organisms or species. Our study of the origin of perception will focus by contrast on the evolution of features or, more precisely, of biochemical features. The first focus suggests the image of a tree of evolution which grows strictly by a branching process, by bifurcations. It breaks down in cases of symbiosis or endosymbiosis. The focus on biochemical features raises a distinctly different image. It is the image of a flow of evolution where patterns of branching are mixed with patterns of confluence, reaching from the combination of simple chemical compounds to the symbiosis of whole organisms. New features with novel types of functions arise by a combination of previously disconnected features. As an example for such confluence and as a central result of our inquiry, we see the origin of vision as a joint venture of an active locomotion machine with light-receiving pigments derived from the photosynthesis apparatus. Vision began as an active search for nutritive light.

B. The Co-evolution of Photosynthesis and Vision — a Speculative Tale

1. The Origin of Active Locomotion

Once upon a time, some four billion years ago, the earth became inhabited by tiny unicellular organisms, protobacteria. They lived in primeval waters containing, as their only source of food, a large variety of abiotically generated organic substances. Wherever this source of food was available, the organisms thrived and multiplied rapidly, which in turn led to food depletion. To some extent these local food shortage problems were alleviated by passive movement resulting from water currents. But eventually an exploratory food searching behavior by active

---

4. Karl R. Popper, *Objective Knowledge*, pp. 170–90.
5. Excellent examples of this method are found in Hans Kuhn, Jürg Waser, "Selbstorganisation der Materie und Evolution früher Formen des Lebens", in W. Hoppe et al., eds., *Biophysik* (Berlin: Springer Verlag, 1982), pp. 860–907, and in Wolfgang F. Gutman, Klaus Bonik, *Kritische Evolutionstheorie* (Hildesheim: Gerstenberg Verlag, 1981).

locomotion emerged. This must have occurred by a multitude of small steps, which we shall now attempt to reconstruct.

Our speculation begins with the assumption that in primitive organisms the rate of diffusion of nutrients into the cell and waste products out of the cell was a factor limiting the population. Since diffusion velocity increases with relative movement between the cell and the surrounding fluid, a flow of liquid could facilitate nutrient intake. However, in the absence of any flow turbulence (i.e., in laminar flow) diffusion is severely limited by a stagnating surface layer. If this stagnating layer is broken up by turbulence, the diffusion speed greatly increases. Now it is important to realize that tiny fibrous protrusions on the outer surface of the cell wall could induce such turbulence. Therefore, they would have had a strong selective advantage. As a next step, an internally generated *active,* but still uncoordinated movement of these fibrils might have occurred, further promoting turbulence and thus diffusion. Next, by the coordination of movements of many fibrils (i.e., cilia), and with it a further enhancement of diffusion, an active cell locomotion could have emerged. This cell locomotion must at first have been random. But later, in a most decisive moment in evolution, this random and inefficient locomotion may have turned into controlled locomotion by coupling with already existent nutrient receptors in the cell wall (chemoreceptors). The identity between the chemical receptors for nutritives and the signal detectors for locomotion control would ensure that only edible nutrients were searched for. If so, this may have been the earliest inkling of a form of perception (see Section E below). It was fully in service of food acquisition and it arose by a joint venture of active locomotion and detection of nutrients. This active and controlled locomotion was one of the two tributaries in the flow of evolution which led to the formation of visual perception. The other tributary we shall turn to now.

2. *Photosynthesis and Vision under a Friendly Sun*

Eventually, the prebiotic broth, a consommé of sorts, became *globally* depleted. The rate at which it was replenished by the abiotic formation of organic substances became the limiting factor of the sustainable biomass. Life was restricted by the scarcity of food. This global food shortage gave rise to what is one of the most important innovations in the history of life: photosynthesis. It enabled its "inventors" to utilize light for the *internal* biosynthesis of essential organic compounds as a supplement to their ingestion from *external* sources and it eventually led to a global changeover of the fuel base of life. In this early encounter with life, light functioned solely as food.

The photosynthesis apparatus must at first have been rather inefficient compared with modern green plants, wasting most of the received light. Thus, the amount of light was a limiting factor. Moreover, lighting conditions must have always been locally different and temporally changing. For the organisms this posed the problem of finding and staying in a spot of optimum radiation. It was solved by the emergence of light-searching behavior, a light-controlled locomotion (photomovement). This occurred again by a joint venture, a coupling of the already existent active locomotion machine with light reception by the photosynthesis apparatus. It could have come about comparatively easily, since active locomotion needs a fuel and since photosynthesis provides just this fuel. Later the control chain was shortened by the transduction of control signals from the photosynthesis pigments to the locomotion machine.[6] In either case, the primary light-absorbing pigments of bacterial photosynthesis were also used for photomovement. This had an enormous advantage: the type of light searched by photomovement was automatically "edible" light useful for photosynthesis.[7]

Thus, bacterial photomovement, a vision of sorts, is connected with bacterial photosynthesis in a double sense. Biochemically speaking it is a derivative of photosynthesis and functionally speaking it is ancillary to photosynthesis. The search for light began not as a quest for information but as a quest for food.

3. Photosynthesis and Vision under a Hostile Sun

So far, we have only looked at the friendly side of light. But solar radiation also has a hostile, life-destroying aspect due to its ultraviolet components. Let us now unravel that part of the story.

At the beginning of life, our earth was covered by an atmosphere which was utterly different from that of today. It was devoid of any oxygen and as a consequence it did not have a protective ozone layer. Thus, ultraviolet radiation was not absorbed but freely penetrated the atmosphere. Physicists tell us that the sun at that time must have been cooler and hence its radiation less intensive and somewhat shifted away from the ultraviolet range compared to present solar light. But even so, the ultraviolet radiation impinging on the surface of the earth must have been quite intense.

If we now consider that DNA is rapidly destroyed by ultraviolet light, notably near its absorption maximum of 265 nm, we are driven to the question: how could life have ever started under a blazing sun? The answer might be simple: it didn't. According to Hans Kuhn[8] the earliest organisms may have dwelt within tiny pores of submersed sand, which were a substitute for cell walls and which fully sheltered the organisms from light. Later, their quest for food drove some of them to dare the open waters. We know they survived, but why? Water absorbs solar radiation, and it does so particularly in the ultraviolet range. Thus, ultraviolet light decreases with increasing depth of water, until it finally vanishes. Therefore, given sufficient depth, it was possible for our ancestral microbes to dare the open yet shun the light.

By doing so, they made an important discovery. Water absorbs unevenly. It changes not only the intensity of light, but also its spectral distribution. The exact

---

6. Examples may be found in the photokinetic reactions of purple bacteria and cyanobacteria, and in the phototaxic and photophobic reactions of some cyanobacteria. See Manfred Tevini, Donat-Peter Häder, *Allgemeine Photobiologie* (Stuttgart: Georg Thieme Verlag, 1985), pp. 276–78.
7. Jerome A. Schiff, *Biosystems* **14**, 1981, p. 129.
8. Hans Kuhn, *Angewandte Chemi* **84**, 1972, p. 838.

nature of these changes depends on the substances that are dissolved or suspended in natural waters. In the turbid waters of Burly Griffin Lake, Australia, the maximum of light transmission is in the red range near 700 nm, while in the clearest waters of the Sargasso Sea it is in the blue range near 470 nm.[9] Yet, all these waters have one thing in common: as we probe deeper, the toxic ultraviolet radiation decreases faster than nutritive light. For the emergence of photosynthesis, this was decisive. There was always a zone with the necessary protection from ultraviolet rays yet with sufficient exposure to "edible" light. The early photosynthesizers survived in a narrow niche between the devil and the deep blue sea.

Subsequent evolution was marked by a number of important inventions which made bacteria somewhat radiation-resistant and allowed for greater light exposure. The emergence of mechanisms for DNA repair permitted the healing of radiation damage. Protective pigments were incorporated into the cell wall for shielding the sensitive nucleic acids from radiation attacks by converting harmful radiation into harmless heat. It is quite plausible that some simple protective pigments were the precursors of the pigments for photosynthesis and that, to some extent, the evolution of photosynthesis may have been a co-evolution of photoprotective and photoactive pigment functions.

But aside from these somewhat passive strategies, an active protective behavior emerged. We can easily see that a positive photomovement toward ever greater light intensities, while beneficial for photosynthesis, would have been devastating for the organisms. It would have driven an organism to the surface of the water and thus to certain death. Therefore, photomovement came under a dual control enabling not only a search for "nutritive" light but also a flight from "toxic" ultraviolet radiation. With this earliest form of color vision, the quest for light as food became selective.[10]

4. The Advent of Oxygen or the Blue-green Revolution

We will now turn to the formation of the oxygen atmosphere and its significance for the co-evolution of photosynthesis and vision.

Perhaps the most ancient form of photosynthesis is found in purple bacteria, which produce organic compounds by hydrogenating carbon dioxide (CO_2). As hydrogen source they use hydrogen sulfide (H_2S), whereby elementary sulfur (S) is formed as a waste product:

$$2H_2S + CO_2 \overset{h\nu}{\rightarrow} (CH_2O)_x + H_2O + 2S.$$

The requisite life-sustaining hydrogen sulfide, though abundantly contained in the exhalations of the earth, must have been restricted to limited regions, since it was precipitated by metal ions (e.g., Fe^{++}) which acted as H_2S scavengers. Thus, the first photosynthesizers were precariously restricted in a double sense:

---

9. Claus Buschmann, Karl Grumbach, *Physiologie der Photosynthese* (Berlin: Springer Verlag, 1984), p. 184.
10. An example is found in the photomovement of halobacteria (see section C.4 and footnote 21).

not only to light-exposed yet sufficiently deep zones of water, but also to regions rich in H_2S.

The solution to this problem of local restriction came with the emergence of a novel type of photosynthesis of far-reaching consequences: a modification of the bacterial photosynthesis apparatus in blue-green algae (cyanobacteria) which allowed for a change of the hydrogen source: a substitution of water for hydrogen sulfide (H_2S):

$$H_2O + CO_2 \overset{h\nu}{\to} (CH_2O)_x + O_2.$$

Now life was able to colonize the vast expanses of the oceans. For a long time, the waste product of this form of photosynthesis, molecular oxygen, was eliminated by the oxidation of large amounts of reducing metal ions (mainly $Fe^{++} \to Fe^{+++}$). But some 1.7 billion years ago this oxygen sink became exhausted and free molecular oxygen started slowly to accumulate, at first in the waters and later in the atmosphere. A global environmental changeover from a reducing to an oxydizing atmosphere ensued. The consequences were enormous. Most forms of anaerobic organisms became extinct by oxygen-poisoning. They were replaced by a multitude of novel oxygen-tolerating or oxygen-dependent (aerobic) organisms.

More importantly, the atmospheric oxygen gave rise to the formation of a layer of ozone high up in the atmosphere. Ozone absorbs ultraviolet light and its absorption maximum happens to coincide with the absorption maximum of DNA. Thus, it absorbs most strongly those portions of the spectrum which cells cannot tolerate. The ozone layer is an effective filter against the most destructive ultraviolet radiation. Now, by virtue of their light-seeking and ultraviolet-fleeing capabilities, the photosynthesizing organisms could rise higher and higher toward ever greater light intensities and eventually to the surface of the water and even onto land. And so it came to pass that life made the earth globally inhabitable for life.

5. The Parasitic Origin of Animal Vision

The earth was now widely colonized by a microbial ecosystem. The food chains were short: a variety of light-searching photosynthesizers (phototrophs) as primary producers, which in turn served as prey for bacteria-devouring (heterotrophic) organisms (phagocytosis). It is widely believed that in this ecosystem endosymbiosis was a frequent occurrence. A photosynthesizing bacterium, after having been ingested, was not digested but rather maintained as an internal cell organelle, a chloroplast. It was kept in a state of slavery, forced to share its photosynthetic products with its master cell. And we may further speculate that it was also forced to lend its light-searching capability for piloting the endosymbiotic organism into areas of optimum radiation. This endosymbiosis, in conjunction with a number of other poorly understood yet thoroughgoing innovations, gave rise to what may be viewed as the eukaryotic (cells with a nucleus) pro-genitors of all higher multicellular forms of life, plant as well as animal. They may be pictured as freely swimming, vision-guided, partly phototrophic and partly heterotrophic organisms. Some of them gave up their animal-like feeding habits and specialized into full-fledged freely swimming unicellular algae, wholly dependent on photosynthesis and light-searching capabilities. Later, when these algae turned into multicellular rooted plants, such vision-guided locomotion of whole organisms was abandoned. But photosynthesis was maintained and perfected.

Others specialized into algae-hunting protozoa by abandoning photosynthesis but maintaining vision-guided locomotion as a way of tracking down algae. These primitive animals did not hunt by directly detecting their prey, but rather by indirectly searching for well-lit areas, using light as a clue for the occurrence of algae. From this earliest form of animal vision, a most simple capacity for discriminating light intensities, all higher forms of animal eyes may be assumed to have arisen. Animal eyes are the offspring of a contraband, stolen from photosynthesizing bacteria through an act of endosymbiosis.

To make a long story short, over billions of years of microbial evolution, the interaction of life and light was marked by a peculiar coevolution of photosynthesis and vision: the photosynthetic machinery served as the biochemical precursor for the formation of a visual apparatus, which in turn served for finding the light for photosynthesis. Early vision bestowed its beneficial effects on the productivity of the very apparatus whence it arose.

C. Confrontation with Some Facts of Biology and Biochemistry

1. The Photochemical Unity of Animal Vision

So far, we have traced the evolution of photosynthesis and vision by moving forward in time, beginning from a fictitious early starting point and reconstructing a sequence of concatenated problems and solutions. We shall now go backward in time, on the basis of a comparative study of extant organisms. We shall see that both accounts are compatible.

Today, photoreceptor organs are found in most (metazoan) animal groups ranging from the simplest light-sensitive cells of hydrozoa to sophisticated eyes in annelida, arthropoda, mollusca, and vertebrata. Admittedly, there are considerable morphological differences, which led L. von Salvini-Plawen and Ernst Mayr to postulate 40 to 65 independent origins of animal eyes.[11] But these forms of vision seem to be based on one single identical type of visual pigment (rhodopsin): a vitamin A aldehyde (retinal) connected to a membrane protein (opsin). And they

---

11. L. von Salvini-Plawen, Ernst Mayr, "On the evolution of photoreceptors and eyes", in *Evolutionary Biology* **10**, 1977, pp. 206–63.

are all based on the same primary photochemical process: a light-induced cis-trans-isomerization of the chromophore retinal:

$$\xrightarrow{\ h\nu\ }$$

CH=N—Opsin

CH=N—Opsin

George Wald, the Nobel-prizewinning pioneer in visual biochemistry, has attributed this astonishing photochemical unity of vision to an extreme case of an evolutionary convergence of biochemicals:

> Organisms, under the unremitting pressures of natural selection, have no choice but to rediscover again and again . . . the same molecular structure. . . . If one asks how it comes about that certain molluscs, arthropods and vertebrates agree in possessing vitamin A, the answer is not that these animals are related phylogenetically, but that all of them have eyes.[12]

This view seems hardly plausible, and most recently it has been clearly refuted by two independent groups,[13] who found a considerable degree of homology between the genes coding for the visual opsins of *Drosophila melanogaster* and several mammals, i.e., two animal groups which have been separated by over 500 million years of evolution. It may well be expected that throughout the animal kingdom there is also a homology in the enzymes for producing retinal.

It should be mentioned that in two younger branches of the animal tree, retinal derivatives figure in place of retinal. 3,4-Dehydroretinal is used by some fishes and amphibians[14] and another derivative, 3-hydroxyretinal, is used by diptera (e.g., flies) and lepidoptera (e.g., butterflies).[15] Both derivatives emerged as relatively late extensions of the retinal-producing biosynthetic pathway.

Thus, contrary to Wald's opinion, the evolution of the pigments of animal (metazoan) vision appears to be not polyphyletic and convergent, but monophyletic and divergent, with a singular, one-time "invention" of retinal and opsin at its root.

2. The Algal Connection of Animal Vision

Our story suggests the hypothesis that there must be a direct biochemical connection between animal vision and algal photomovement. The first important evidence of this kind has most recently been produced. It appears that retinal, the

12. George Wald, "Phylogeny and Ontogeny at the Molecular Level", in A. I. Oparin, ed., *Evolutionary Biochemistry* (New York: Pergamon Press, 1963), p. 19.
13. Joseph E. O'Tousa, Wolfgang Baehr, Richard L. Martin, Jay Hirsh, William L. Pak and Meredith L. Applebury, *Cell* **40**, 1985, pp. 839–50; Charles S. Zucker, Alan F. Cowman and Gerald M. Rubin, *Cell* **40**, 1985, pp. 851–58.
14. George Wald, *Nature* **139**, 1937, p. 1017.
15. K. Vogt, K. Kirschfeld, *Naturwissenschaften* (1984), pp. 211–13.

universal chromophore of animal vision, is also used as the chromophore of photo-movement by the unicellular green alga *Chlamydomonas reinhardtii*.[16] For even stronger evidence we might predict some sequence homology in the genes of animals and chlamydomonads coding for opsin and for the enzyme of retinal bio-synthesis. With evidence of this kind coming in, our assumption that animal vision and algal photomovement have been inherited from a common ancestral organism would become compelling.

What could this common ancestral organism have been like? In our story, we adopted the view that it was an endosymbiotic organism consisting of a host cell and a photosynthesizing bacterium as endosymbiont, which later turned into the chloroplasts of the green algae such as Chlamydomonas. The recently discovered phototrophic oxygenic Prochlorophyta[17] give considerable support to this view. They have the same photosynthesis pigments as the chloroplasts of green algae and may therefore be considered as closest living relatives of the bacterial endosymbiont.[18] But our account goes beyond this conventional view. It makes the additional claim that the bacterial endosymbiont was also exploited as a pho-todetector for piloting its host organism and that it is the precursor of algal and animal eyes. That is to say a retinal-based photomovement should have existed already on the level of the phototrophic bacteria prior to endosymbiosis. Perhaps the most recently discovered freely swimming Prochlorophyt[19] might prove to show such a photomovement based on retinal as chromophore.[20]

While such direct evidence for the endosymbiotic origin of vision is not yet available, it should be mentioned that a spectacular analogous case has recently been discovered in *Paramecium bursaria*. This is a highly derived protozoon, which feeds on algae. It leaves some of its prey (Chlorella) undigested and forces it to share its photosynthetic products with its host and, more importantly, it has been found that the endosymbiotic Chlorella is also employed as a pilot for the light-seeking movement of its host.[21] Here a tiny plant organism serves literally as the eye of a unicellular protozoon.

Biologists have widely accepted Euglena as the most likely link between unicellular algae and unicellular animals. If this opinion should prove correct, our speculation on the origin of animal vision would be refuted, since the photomovement of Euglena seems not to be based on retinal, but rather on a compound totally unrelated to retinal, a flavine.[22] Happily, most recent findings seem to indicate that the chloroplasts of Euglena have *triple* membranes. This means that they

16. K. W. Foster, J. Saranak, N. Patel, G. Zarilli, M. Okabe, T. Kline and K. Nakanishi, *Nature* **311**, 1984, pp. 756–59.

17. R. A. Lewin, *Nature, 261,* 1976, pp. 697–8.

18. Prochlorophyta contain chlorophyll a and chlorophyll b just like the chloroplasts of green algae.

19. T. Burger-Wiersma, M. Veenhuis, J. J. Korthals, C. C. M. Van de Wiel, L. R. Mur, *Nature,* **320**, 1986, pp. 262–4.

20. Cyanobacteria, which owing to their lack of chlorophyll b are not the likely ancestors of the chloroplasts of green algae, utilize for their photomovement photosynthesis pigments (phycobilins and carotenoids) (see the literature reference in footnote 6).

21. D. Neiss, W. Reisser and W. Wiesser, *Planta* **152**, 1981, pp. 268–71.

22. Häder Tevini, *Allgemeine Photobiologie,* p. 277.

could not have arisen by an early endosymbiosis of a bacterium, which could have only given rise to a *double* membrane. Rather they must have arisen by a more recent endosymbiosis of a eukaryotic alga within a unicellular protozoon.[23] Thus, Euglena can be ruled out as a candidate for the primitive ancestor of animals. It is highly derived rather than primitive, and it must have arisen long after the emergence of unicellular algae and animals.

3. The Biochemical Connection between Pigments of Photosynthesis and Animal Vision

Further, our story suggests a biochemical connection or homology between the pigments of photosynthesis and the pigment of animal vision. However, a quick glance at the formulae of retinal, the chromophore of animal vision, and chlorophyll, the main pigment of photosynthesis, seems to belie any such connection. The structural differences are enormous and the biosynthetic pathways leading to both compounds are unrelated. But chlorophyll is not the only pigment of photosynthesis. Rather, it becomes increasingly evident that β-carotene plays an important role not only as a light-harvesting pigment in the antenna complexes but also as a component of the very reaction center of photosynthesis.[24] Now it is important to note that animals produce their retinal by oxidative cleavage of β-carotene.

But animals cannot synthesize the carotene starting material. Rather, they ingest it with their food. Its ultimate sources are plants and photosynthesizing bacteria, which produce it in a lengthy, multistage biochemical pathway. It appears

23. L. W. Wilcox, G. J. Wedemayer, *Science* 227, 1985, pp. 192–94.
24. R. J. Cogdell and J. Valentine, *Photochemistry and Photobiology*, 38, 1983, pp. 769–72.

plausible that the eukaryotic ancestor of both animals and algae once had the full capacity for the biosynthesis of β-carotene *and* for its conversion to retinal and that in animals, feeding on carotene-rich bacteria or plants, the biosynthesis of carotene became unnecessary and was abandoned.

We can go a little further and look at the conditions for the first emergence of a retinal-based visual system. The multistage biosynthesis of β-carotene constitutes a heavy investment for the cell. Its product, however, pays full dividends due to its important role in photosynthesis. Now, the biosynthesis of retinal as a terminal extension of the carotene pathway *consumes* β-carotene and thus *weakens* the photosynthesis apparatus. Further, it is plausible that in the earliest stages of the emerging retinal biosynthesis, the function of retinal must have been rather inefficient. Therefore, any selective advantage conferred by such inefficient retinal function could be expected as having been small and certainly offset by the selective disadvantage of the loss of precious β-carotene. How then could the evolution of a retinal-based photomovement have ever gained momentum? The answer may perhaps lie in an amplifying feedback effect of sorts.

Retinal, right from its first invention, functioned within an apparatus for seeking light. More light meant more photosynthesis and thus higher returns for the investments into the carotene biosynthesis. Thus, the overall effect even of a poor form of early photomovement on photosynthesis was positive. Early retinal-based photomovement could emerge precisely, because it bestowed its beneficial effects on the productivity of the very photosynthesis apparatus whence it arose.

It might be speculated that this dual connection between algal photosynthesis and photomovement is but an example of a more general principle of innovative evolution. In the field of biochemical evolution, this "principle of dual connectivity" (chemical and functional) may hold whenever a new biochemical with a novel type of function arises as a chemical derivative of a biosynthetic precursor with a different function, and when the precursor is not abundantly available but is rather itself the precious product of a lengthy biosynthetic pathway. Under these conditions, an overall selective advantage exists only if the novel function is ancillary to the function of the precursor.

4. The Generalized Connection between Photosynthesis and Photocontrol Pigments

So far we have looked at the connection between retinal-based vision and photosynthesis. We will now turn to some other forms of photocontrol. As a consequence of the general principle suggested at the end of the preceding section, it might be expected that any kind of photocontrol pigment may be found to be biochemically related to some kind of photosynthesis pigment. What are the facts?

Let us first consider the case of the halobacteria. They exhibit a light-seeking and ultraviolet-fleeing photomovement[25] and also a photosynthesis of sorts (a light-

---

25. L. Spudich and R. A. Bogomolni, *Nature* **312**, 1984, p. 509.

driven proton pump for ATP-synthesis),[26] and *both* are based on pigments consisting of protein-bonded retinal. Thus, the photomovement-photosynthesis-connection is here most evident. The occurrence of *retinal* in the pigments of halobacteria might suggest even a connection with animal vision. It may be speculated that the halobacteria and the original host cell of the eukaryotes derive from one common ancestor, which was the sole one-time "inventor" of retinal. Some simple facts of biochemistry belie such speculation.

There are three kingdoms of life: eukaryotes, eubacteria, and archaebacteria. Halobacteria belong to the kingdom of archaebacteria. Now, the split between the host cell of the eukaryotes and the archaebacteria must have occurred very early in the evolution of life and *certainly long before the change-over to the oxygen atmosphere*. This is clearly evidenced by the fact that the ribosomes and other old and most conservative components of the cell are widely different *between,* yet highly homologous *within* these two kingdoms of organisms.[27] On the other hand, the chemical conversion of β-carotene to retinal requires *free molecular oxygen*.[28] Halobacteria are aerobic and they require an *external* supply of oxygen for producing retinal. Thus, it appears that they could not have acquired a capacity for the biosynthesis of retinal before the advent of an aerobic environment, i.e., before much more than some 1.7 billion years ago. Therefore, retinal appears to have been acquired twice and independently, once within the archaebacterial line of the halobacteria and once within the eubacterial line of the phototrophic bacterial precursors of the chloroplasts of the eukaryotes. The latter could have "invented" retinal before the advent of an aerobic environment since they produce molecular oxygen *internally* by their oxygenic photosynthesis (see Section C.2 on Prochlorophyta). This view on the halobacteria is compatible with the lack of sequence homology between mammal and halobacterial opsins.[29]

Another kind of photomovement is found in *Stentor coeruleus,* a ciliar protozoon. Its pigment is a protein-bonded quinon, stentorin.[30] Recently it was announced by Song that the same organism shows light-driven bursts of ATP formation (a photosynthesis of sorts) which seems to be based on the same or a similar pigment as the photomovement.[31]

As mentioned earlier (section C.2) the photomovement of Euglena[32] and some

26. D. Oesterhelt, W. Stoeckenius, *Proceedings of the National Academy of Science, US* **70,** 1970, pp. 2853–57.

27. C. R. Woese, L. J. Magrum, G. E. Fox, *Journal of Molecular Evolution* **11,** 1978, pp. 245–52.

28. J. A. Olson and O. Hayaistis, *Proceedings of the National Academy of Science US* **54,** 1965, p. 1364; D. S. Goodman, H. S. Huang, M. Kanai and T. Shiratori, *JBC,* **242,** 1967, p. 3543.

29. Yu. A. Ovchinnikov, *FEBS Letters* **148,** 1982, 179–91.

30. P. S. Song, E. B. Walker and M. J. Yoon, in F. Lenci and G. Colombetti, eds., *Photoreception and Sensory Transduction in Aneural Organisms* (New York: Plenum Press, 1980), pp. 241–52.

31. Announced by P. S. Song in the Meeting of the American Society for Photobiology, New Orleans, June 1985, and reported in *The Times-Picayune/The States-Item,* New Orleans, June 27, 1985, p. A-6.

32. G. Colombetti and F. Lenci, eds., *Photoreception and Sensory Transduction in Aneural Organisms* (New York: Plenum Press, 1980), pp. 172–88.

other protists (and also the phototropism of the fungus Phycomyces[33]) seem to be based on a protein-bonded flavine. Here the biochemical connection with photosynthesis is very weak. Flavoproteins occur merely in the electron transport chain of chlorophyll-based photosynthesis. There is no evidence yet for a form of photosynthesis based on a flavine as a light-absorbing pigment.

Let us sum up the situation: in its long encounter with light, life seems to have "discovered" the nutritional value of light on several independent occasions. Photosynthesis is polyphyletic. And the plural types of photosynthesis pigments gave rise in turn to different types of photocontrol or photomovement pigments. Animal vision is situated on just one of these lines of evolution.

D. The Narrow Band of Visible Light—A Test for Explanatory Power

1. The Window of the Atmosphere—a Case of Make-believe Adaptation

We will now show how our account of the origin of vision can explain the visible light range. We will begin with a criticism of the conventional explanation.

All human and animal vision is limited to a tiny band of visible light. Our eyes do not pick up waves above about 700 nm (infrared waves, microwaves, radiowaves) and below 300 to 400 nm (ultraviolet waves, x-rays, γ-rays). As Bartley put it so succinctly: "We live in an electromagnetic sea, as it were, and nonetheless these waves do not register unassisted on our eyes".[34] How can we explain this fact? Let us first consider that the primary reaction of vision must be a photochemical reaction. Photochemistry certainly does not occur throughout the full range of the electromagnetic spectrum, but its range is still as wide as from 100 to 1400 nm.[35] Thus, our problem remains, albeit in a narrower form: why is the range of visible light much smaller than the range of photochemistry?

A widely popularized explanation assumes that the atmosphere has a window of light transmission in the visual range, while it absorbs all the other radiation and that the visual pigments simply adapted to the type of radiation transmitted by this window.[36] However, the proponents of this "window theory" make a cardinal mistake. Instead of adapting the theory of adaptation to the facts, they seem to adapt the curve of light distribution to their theory of adaptation.

Most spectral curves of light drawn in support of the "window theory" show the radiation *energy* plotted against the wavelength, and they exhibit a pronounced

33. M. K. Otter, M. Jayaram, R. M. Hamilton and M. Delbrück, *Proceedings of the National Academy of Science US* **78**, 1981, pp. 266–69.

34. W. W. Bartley, III, Chapter I of this volume.

35. Ultraviolet radiation below 100 nm leads to destructive ionization. Infrared and microwaves above 1400 nm generate merely heat through vibrational and rotational excitations. The range of 100 to 1400 nm is the range of electron excitations, which lead to highly specific chemical reactions. This is the range of photochemistry.

36. G. Vollmer, *Evolutionäre Erkenntnistheorie* (Stuttgart: S. Hirzel, 1981), p. 98; H. von Ditfurth, *Im Anfang war der Wasserstoff* (Hamburg: Hoffman und Campe, 1972), p. 100.

peak in the visible range. Yet eyes are not *light energy meters* but rather *photon counters*.[37] Now, if we convert the published energy distribution curves to photon density curves (the energy of a photon decreases with increasing wavelength by the formula: $e = hc/\lambda$) the radiation peak loses its convincing shape. The infrared range becomes more pronounced, and the radiation maximum is shifted somewhat towards longer wavelengths. In fact, many published curves, when properly converted, show about as many photons in the range of 700 to 1000 nm as in the range of 400 to 700 nm.[38] Thus, the "window theory" is undermined rather than supported by such curves.

But the case of the "window theory" is weaker still. In aqueous habitats, where vision first evolved, the light distribution changes with the type and concentration of impurities and with the depth of water.[39] If we probe deeper and deeper into a body of clear ocean water, the light range becomes increasingly restricted to a narrow band of blue light. Thus, it is admittedly always possible to single out a special depth in a special body of water in order to make the available light range coincide with the visible light range and to claim that animal vision must have started there. But the theory of evolutionary adaptation is a theory for explaining *evolutionary change* by a *change in the environment*. Now animals, by rising to the surface of the water, by crawling onto land and by spreading into a diversity of habitats with demonstrably different ranges of available light (e.g., dense forests vs. open plains; low vs. high altitudes; overcast vs. clear skies; polar vs. equatorial zones) did greatly change their photic environment, but their range of vision hardly changed and there is no convincing correlation between their photic environments and their range of vision. Thus, an adaptation to the available light, while it might have been of benefit, apparently did not occur to any significant extent.[40]

2. The Coincidence between the Bands of Vision and Photosynthesis

We will now show how the range of visible light can be explained by the origin of vision in photosynthesis. We will proceed in two stages. First, we will try to give an explanation of the range of photosynthesis and then we will explain the range of vision with reference to this range of photosynthesis.

Photosynthesis is an energy-consuming chemical reaction. It is driven by the absorption of light energy. Light consists of photons, and the energy of a single

37. Barbara Sakitt, *Journal of Physiology* **223**, 1972, pp. 131–50.
38. H. H. Seliger, Environmental Photobiology, in K. C. Smith, ed., *The Science of Photobiology* (New York: Plenum, 1977), pp. 143–73. U. Kull, *Evolution* (Stuttgart: J. B. Metzlersche Verlagsbuchhandlung, 1977), p. 76, shows a photon density curve with substantially more photons in the range of 700 to 1000 nm than in the range of 400 to 700 nm. Strangely, the same author has adopted the "window theory".
39. See section B.3 and footnote 9.
40. 3-Dehydroretinal (see section C.1 and footnote 14) has an absorption maximum shifted by some 20 nm toward longer wavelengths. But the pattern of its distribution seems to be so erratic that no convincing correlation with the photic environment can be found. (F. Crescitelli, "The vertebrate visual pigments", in H. Gutfreund, ed., *Biochemical Evolution* (Cambridge: Cambridge University Press, 1981), p. 346.)

photon decreases with increasing wavelength. For each elementary photochemical reaction the absorption of a single photon is required.[41] If the energy of a photon is high enough, it will satisfy the energy demand of the elementary photochemical reaction and the reaction will take place. On the other hand, if the energy of a photon is below a certain threshold value, it fails to cause the photochemical reaction.

The oxygen-producing (oxygenic) photosynthesis of bacteria, algae, and plants is based on the abstraction of hydrogen from water. Hence it requires a high amount of energy, and the cutoff point is as low as 700 nm.[42] The anoxygenic photosynthesis of purple bacteria is based on the abstraction of hydrogen from hydrogen sulfide. This requires much less energy. Therefore, some purple bacteria are photosynthetically active with wavelengths up to a threshold value of 1100 nm.[43] Thus, it is possible in principle to explain the cutoff points of the ranges of photosynthesis toward longer wavelengths strictly by reference to considerations of chemical energy demands.[44] There is no need to resort to a process of an adaptation to the photic environment.

The cutoff point of the ranges of photosynthesis toward short wavelengths (350 to 400 nm) is explainable by the toxic effects of the ultraviolet radiation. Thus, photosynthesis is limited to a range of non-toxic and nutritive light. Radiation below this range is poisonous and radiation above this range is not nourishing.

We now turn to the range of vision. There is a peculiar coincidence between the ranges of vision and of oxygenic photosynthesis. Both extend from about 400 to about 700 nm. What does this coincidence mean? According to our story, retinal-based animal vision derived from retinal-based photomovement of algae, which served for finding the light for their (oxygenic) photosynthesis. A photomovement responsive to light above 700 nm or below 400 nm would have been disastrously misleading by maneuvering the organism into non-nourishing or toxic areas. Thus, the restriction of a retinal-based photomovement to the range of 400 to 700 nm had a high selective advantage. Later, when the algal photomovement apparatus was exploited in animal vision for tracking down algae, the responsive range of 400 to 700 nm was still beneficial and simply retained. Thus, the visual range is readily explainable by its historic origin in photosynthesis and no similarly plausible explanation and certainly not an explanation by adaptation to the photic environment seems to be in sight.

Much later, when animals started to use their sense of vision for many purposes other than algae hunting, adherence to the photosynthesis range of 400 to 700 nm was no longer necessary. Thus, the proponents of the "window theory"

41. Albert Einstein, "Über einen die Erzeugung und Verwandlung des Lichts betreffenden heuristischen Gesichtspunkt", *Annalen der Physik* **4**, Folge 17, 1905, pp. 132–48.
42. The energy demand of this reaction is so high that it cannot be met by one photon alone. It requires two photons in a series connection of two elementary photochemical reactions. Anoxygenic photosynthesis requires excitation by only one photon.
43. E.g., *Rhodopseudomonas viridis* (N. Pfennig, *Annual Review of Microbiology* **21**, 1967, p. 285).
44. See also E. Strasburger, *Lehrbuch der Botanik* (Stuttgart: Gustav Fisher Verlag, 1983), p. 250, and J. Schiff, *Biosystems*, p. 141.

should expect an adaptive extension towards the infrared range with its abundance of photons to have taken place. But this did not happen. Instead, in many insects[45] and also in some fishes,[46] the visual range was extended into the low-intensity ultraviolet range and hence in a direction which, in the light of the "window theory", would appear to be counter-adaptive rather than adaptive.

3. The Campbell Coincidence

Donald T. Campbell has discovered a most interesting coincidence: Animal locomotion is blocked by all solid bodies but not by air and water. Similarly the flux of visible light is obstructed by most solid bodies, but again not by air and water. According to Campbell, vision evolved largely by the exploitation of this coincidence as a vicarious (or indirect) substitute for direct exploration by locomotion. In short, vision substitutes for collision.[47]

We shall discuss two aspects of Campbell's coincidence. First, we shall show that it cannot explain the range of visible light. Then, we shall discuss the evolutionary connection with a photosynthesis-derived sense of vision.

Ultraviolet radiation as well as near-infrared radiation are transmitted by air and, to a considerable extent, also by water, while they are obstructed by solid bodies such as stones. Thus, the (in)transparency – (im)penetrability coincidence is not exclusive to the band of visible light. It rather extends far into the ultraviolet and infrared ranges. It follows that the restriction of visible light to the narrow band of 400 to 700 nm cannot be explained as an adaptation to the range of Campbell's coincidence. Further, it should be considered that collision prevention requires some capacity for *contrast* vision, i.e., a higher visual function compared to simple light detection. Thus it is plausible that the range of vision had been established long before eyes for collision prevention emerged.

Our evolutionary story suggests that vision started as a direct process of seeking light for photosynthesis which later turned into an indirect process for the detection of light as a vicarious clue for tracking down algae. How was it possible that, from such simple beginnings, all the sophisticated contrivances of animal eyes could have emerged? Campbell's insight seems to go a long way toward answering this question. The evolution of the higher functions of animal vision might largely be explained as the result of a windfall profit. The range of vision, once established for photosynthesis purposes, happened to fall *within* the range of radiation in which Campbell's (in)transparency – (im)penetrability coincidence exists, and animal eyes could exploit this coincidence in a long evolution of contrast detection. Thus, our speculation on the origin of vision in photosynthesis and Campbell's coincidence are complementary rather than conflicting.

45. See section C.1 and footnote 15.
46. Chr. Neumeyer, "An ultraviolet receptor as a fourth receptor type in Goldfish color vision", *Naturwissenschaften* **72**, 1985, pp. 162–63.
47. See Chapters II and III of this volume.

E. There is More to Vision than Meets the Eye

In the preceding sections, we have inquired into the transition from long-term problem solving by biological evolution to short-term problem solving by sensory cognition. We have located the origin of sensory perception in foraging for food and, more precisely, in a joint venture of a preexisting active locomotion machine with the preexisting receptors for nutritive chemicals or nutritive light. Thus, right from the start, sensory perception is a composite process, arising from two component processes: active locomotion and food absorption. Neither of these two components alone amounts to cognition. But with the conjunction of both comes something radically new: a sensory knowledge acquisition process. In this process, the two contributory components can still be detected, albeit with transformed functions. Active locomotion can now be interpreted as a creative or generative part leading to ever new positional variations, while food reception can be interpreted as a critical or evaluative part for the assessment of each new positional variation. Sensory knowledge acquisition satisfies from the start the Popperian formula[48] of an interplay of creation and criticism.

A model that seems to bear witness to this earliest form of sensory knowledge acquisition is seen in the photomovement of extant purple bacteria.[49] Here, an internally programmed active locomotion leads to ever new and spontaneous changes in position, while light reception serves strictly on the critical or evaluative side by the detection and elimination of bad moves (see also section B.2 and footnote 6). Our story suggests that a continuous, albeit lengthy line of evolution stretches from these lowly beginnings to animal cognition and to man's highest cognitive achievements. By extending Crick's principle of continuity,[50] we may further speculate that, notwithstanding numerous later sophistications, the two basic components of sensory cognition were always maintained: the active and creative component, stretching from the active mind back to active locomotion, and the critical and evaluative sensory component, stretching back to the pigments of photosynthesis and other food receptors. Hence, in principle, the evolution of such a composite cognitive process can be traced back to the confluence of two non-cognitive processes without violating the principle of continuity.

Our evolutionary account agrees nicely with Popper's claim that all processes of short-term problem solving by sensory knowledge acquisition must necessarily be *active* processes and that passive knowledge acquisition does not exist.[51] Indeed, the alternative notion of knowledge acquisition by a *passive* flow of bits of information from the environment through the interface of the outer sensory

---

48. Karl R. Popper, *Die beiden Grundprobleme der Erkenntnistheorie*, (Tübingen: J. C. B. Mohr (Paul Siebeck), 1979), based on manuscripts from 1930 to 1933, see notably pp. 19–32; Karl R. Popper, *Logik der Forschung*, (Vienna: Julius Springer, 1934); Karl R. Popper, *Conjectures and Refutations*, (London: Routledge & Kegan Paul, 1963); see also the references in footnote 3.

49. E. Strasburger, *Lehrbuch der Botanik*, p. 448.

50. F. H. C. Crick, *J. Mol. Biol.*, **38**, 1968, p. 367.

51. See the references in footnote 3.

periphery into the organism would drive us to an absurd position. We can see this if we attempt to trace the notion of a passive sense data flow back through evolution. In this exercise, more and more sophistications will be seen as falling by the wayside, with the alleged flow of sense data becoming ever simpler and shorter until finally all that is left as a most primitive sense datum is the photoexcitation of a photosynthesis pigment molecule. And so it is that the passive theory forces us into the absurd position of interpreting the primary photochemical reaction of photosynthesis as a cognitive process. Thus it appears that the theory of passive knowledge acquisition produces severe difficulties if we try to accommodate it within an evolutionary account. No such difficulties in tracing cognitive processes back to non-cognitive origins arise for the notion of a cognitive process as being *active and composite* from the start.

The cognitive apparatus for performing short-term problem solving through sensory cognition arose by a process of long-term problem solving through biological evolution. Most biologists interpret Darwinian evolution as a process of *passive adaptations* to the environment. However, in Popper's theory of *active Darwinism*, the activity of the organisms is seen as the principal driving force of evolutionary change.[52]

Our account of the nutritional origins of the sensory cognitive apparatus seems to favour Popper's interpretation. In section D, we have seen that one of the main characteristics of visual perception, the restriction of the visible light range, can hardly be understood as a passive adaptation to the environment. It rather seems to be the result of internal biochemical conditions of the organism and its foraging activities within the environment. The situation may be summarized as follows: Perception is not a process of passive acquisition of information from the environment by an apparatus which itself is the result of passive adaptation to this same environment. It is rather a process of active foraging within the environment by means of an apparatus which in its major characteristics is shaped by the organism's own foraging activities. As Popper would have it: organisms by being active seekers are the active makers of their senses.

---

52. Karl R. Popper, *Auf der Suche nach einer besseren Welt*, (Munich: Piper, 1984), pp. 11–40, Karl R. Popper, "The Place of Mind in Nature", in Richard Q. Elvee ed., *Mind in Nature*, (San Francisco: Harper & Row, 1982), pp. 31–59; and *Objective Knowledge*, pp. 256–84.

Chapter VI

Natural Selection and the Emergence of Mind

By Karl R. Popper

It is a great honor to have been invited to give the first Darwin Lecture at Darwin College, in Cambridge, which of all universities is most closely connected with Charles Darwin and the Darwin family.

When I received the invitation, I was worried whether or not I should accept it. I am not a scientist; nor am I a historian. There are Darwin scholars devoted to studying his life and his times; but I have done nothing of the kind. For these reasons, I suppose I ought to have declined the invitation. Yet it was an extremely kind and pressing invitation; and those who invited me were obviously well aware of the fact that I was neither a biologist nor a Darwin scholar, but simply an amateur. In the end I did accept, choosing as my topic a theme which, I believe, is closely linked to two of Darwin's central interests: natural selection; and the evolution of mind.

However, in the first Darwin Lecture a few words should be said about Charles Darwin himself, even by one who has no special qualifications to speak of him. So I may just as well start by saying that Darwin's face and Darwin's name belong to my earliest childhood memories. In my father's study in Vienna there were two striking portraits, the portraits of two old men. They were the portraits of Arthur Schopenhauer and of Charles Darwin. I must have questioned my father about these two men, even before I had learned to read. Schopenhauer's portrait was interesting, though I was not very attracted by it. But Darwin looked most attractive. He had a long white beard, even longer than my father's beard, and he wore a strange dark cloak, a kind of raincoat without sleeves. He looked very friendly and very quiet, but a little sad, and a little lonely. It was the well-known photograph taken in 1881, when he was seventy-two, a year before his death. This is how it is that I have known Darwin's face and name for as long as I can remember. I knew that he was a great Englishman and traveller, and one of the greatest students of animals who ever lived; and I liked him very much.

This is the first Darwin Lecture, delivered at Darwin College, Cambridge, on November 8th, 1977. Copyright © by Karl Popper. The lecture was published in *Dialectica* **22**, 3, 1978, pp. 339–55, and dedicated to the memory of Paul Bernays.

Darwin is not only the greatest of biologists – he has often been compared to Newton – but also a most admirable, venerable, and indeed a most lovable person. I know of few books that can be compared to the five volumes of his letters that were edited by his son Francis, and that contain also his Autobiography. From these books there speaks a human being almost perfect in his simplicity, modesty, and devotion to truth.

The topic of my lecture is "Natural Selection and the Emergence of Mind". Natural selection is, obviously, Darwin's most central theme. But I shall not confine myself to this theme alone. I shall also follow Darwin in his approach to the problem of body and mind, both the mind of man and the animal mind. And I shall try to show that the theory of natural selection supports a doctrine which I also support. I mean the unfashionable doctrine of mutual interaction between mind and brain.

My lecture will be divided into four sections.

In the first section, entitled "Darwin's *Natural Selection* versus Paley's *Natural Theology*", I shall briefly comment upon the Darwinian revolution and on today's counter-revolution against science.

The second section is entitled "Natural Selection and its Scientific Status".

The third section is entitled "Huxley's Problem". It contains the central argument of my lecture, an argument based on natural selection. It is an argument for mutual interaction between mind and brain, and against T. H. Huxley's view that the mind is an epiphenomenon. It is also an argument against the so-called identity theory, the now fashionable theory that mind and brain are identical.

The fourth section, entitled "Remarks on the Emergence of Mind", concludes with a few speculative suggestions on what seems to be the greatest marvel of our universe – the emergence of mind and, more especially, of consciousness.

1. Darwin's *Natural Selection* versus Paley's *Natural Theology*

The first edition of Darwin's *Origin of Species* was published in 1859. In a reply to a letter from John Lubbock, thanking Darwin for an advance copy of his book, Darwin made a remarkable comment about William Paley's book *Natural Theology*, which had been published half a century before. Darwin wrote: "I do not think I hardly ever admired a book more than Paley's 'Natural Theology'. I could almost formerly have said it by heart."[1] Years later in his Autobiography Darwin wrote of Paley that "The careful study of [his] works . . . was the only part of the academical course [in Cambridge] which . . . was of the least use to me in the education of my mind."[2]

1. *The Life and Letters of Charles Darwin*, edited by his son Francis Darwin (London: John Murray, 1887), subsequently cited as *L. L.*, volume II, p. 219. The portrait of Darwin described in the lecture forms the frontispiece to volume III.
2. *L. L.*, volume I, p. 47.

I have started with these quotations because the problem posed by Paley became one of Darwin's most important problems. It was *the problem of design*. The famous *argument from design* for the existence of God was at the center of Paley's theism. If you find a watch, Paley argued, you will hardly doubt that it was designed by a watchmaker. So if you consider a higher organism, with its intricate and purposeful organs such as the eyes, then, Paley argued, you are bound to conclude that it must have been designed by an intelligent Creator. This is Paley's argument from design. Prior to Darwin, the theory of special creation – the theory that each species was designed by the Creator – had been widely accepted, not only in the University of Cambridge, but also elsewhere, by many of the best scientists. There were of course alternative theories in existence, such as Lamarck's; and Hume had earlier attacked, somewhat feebly, the argument from design; but Paley's theory was in those days the one most seriously entertained by serious scientists.

It is almost unbelievable how much the atmosphere changed as a consequence of the publication, in 1859, of the *Origin of Species*. The place of an argument that really had no status whatever in science has been taken by an immense number of the most impressive and well-tested scientific results. Our whole outlook, our picture of the universe, has changed, as never before.

The Darwinian revolution is still proceeding. But now we are also in the midst of a counter-revolution, a strong reaction against science and against rationality. I feel that it is necessary to take sides in this issue, if only briefly; and also, in a Darwin lecture, to indicate where Darwin himself stood.

My position, very briefly, is this. I am on the side of science and of rationality, but I am against those exaggerated claims for science that have sometimes been, rightly, denounced as "scientism". I am on the side of the *search for truth*, and of intellectual daring in the search for truth; but I am against intellectual arrogance, and especially against the misconceived claim that we have the truth in our pockets, or that we can approach certainty.

It is important to realize that science does not make assertions about ultimate questions – about the riddles of existence, or about man's task in this world.

This has often been well understood. But some great scientists, and many lesser ones, have misunderstood the situation. The fact that science cannot make any pronouncement about ethical principles has been misinterpreted as indicating that there are no such principles; while in fact the search for truth presupposes ethics. And the success of Darwinian natural selection in showing that the *purpose or end* which an organ like the eye seems to serve may be only apparent has been misinterpreted as the nihilist doctrine that all purpose is only apparent purpose, and that there cannot be any end or purpose or meaning or task in our life.

Although Darwin destroyed Paley's argument from design by showing that what appeared to Paley as purposeful design could well be explained as the result of chance and of natural selection, Darwin was most modest and undogmatic in his claims. He had a correspondence about divine design with Asa Gray of

Harvard; and Darwin wrote to Gray, one year after the *Origin of Species*: " . . . about Design. I am conscious that I am in an utterly hopeless muddle. I cannot think that the world, as we see it, is the result of chance; and yet I cannot look at each separate thing as the result of Design."[3] And a year later Darwin wrote to Gray: "With respect to Design, I feel more inclined to show a white flag than to fire . . . [a] shot . . . You say that you are in a haze; I am in thick mud; . . . yet I cannot keep out of the question."[4]

To me it seems that the question may not be within the reach of science. And yet I do think that science has taught us a lot about the evolving universe that bears in an interesting way on Paley's and Darwin's problem of creative design.

I think that science suggests to us (tentatively of course) a picture of a universe that is inventive[5] or even creative; of a universe in which *new things* emerge, on *new levels*.

There is, on the first level, the theory of the emergence of heavy atomic nuclei in the centre of big stars, and, on a higher level, the evidence for the emergence somewhere in space of organic molecules.

On the next level, there is the emergence of life. Even if the origin of life should one day become reproducible in the laboratory, life creates something that is utterly new in the universe: the peculiar activity of organisms; especially the often purposeful actions of animals; and animal problem solving. All organisms are constant problem solvers; even though they are not conscious of most of the problems they are trying to solve.

On the next level, the great step is the emergence of conscious states. With the distinction between conscious states and unconscious states, again something utterly new and of the greatest importance enters the universe. It is a new world: the world of conscious experience.

On the next level, this is followed by the emergence of the products of the human mind, such as the works of art; and also the works of science; especially scientific theories.

I think that scientists, however sceptical, are bound to admit that the universe, or nature, or whatever we may call it, is creative. For it has produced creative men: it has produced Shakespeare and Michelangelo and Mozart, and thus indirectly their works. It has produced Darwin, and so created the theory of natural selection. Natural selection has destroyed the proof for the miraculous specific intervention of the Creator. But it has left us with the marvel of the creativeness of the universe, of life, and of the human mind. Although science has nothing to say about a personal Creator, the fact of the emergence of novelty, and of creativity, can hardly be denied. I think that Darwin himself, who could not "keep out of the question", would have agreed that, though natural selection was an idea which opened up a new world for science, it did not remove, from the picture

3. *L. L.*, volume II, p. 353.
4. *L. L.*, volume II, p. 382.
5. Cp. K. G. Denbigh, *The Inventive Universe* (London: Hutchinson, 1975).

of the universe that science paints, the marvel of creativity; nor did it remove the marvel of freedom: the freedom to create; and the freedom of choosing our own ends and our own purposes.

To sum up these brief remarks:

The counter-revolution against science is intellectually unjustifiable; morally it is indefensible. On the other hand, scientists should resist the temptations of scientism. They should always remember, as I think Darwin always did, that science is tentative and fallible. Science does not solve all the riddles of the universe, nor does it promise ever to solve them. Nevertheless it can sometimes throw some unexpected light even on our deepest and probably insoluble riddles.

2. Natural Selection and its Scientific Status

When speaking here of Darwinism, I shall speak always of today's theory — that is Darwin's own theory of natural selection supported by the Mendelian theory of heredity, by the theory of the mutation and recombination of genes in a gene pool, and by the decoded genetic code. This is an immensely impressive and powerful theory. The claim that it completely explains evolution is of course a bold claim, and very far from being established. All scientific theories are conjectures, even those that have successfully passed many severe and varied tests. The Mendelian underpinning of modern Darwinism has been well tested, and so has the theory of evolution which says that all terrestrial life has evolved from a few primitive unicellular organisms, possibly even from one single organism.

However, Darwin's own most important contribution to the theory of evolution, his theory of natural selection, is difficult to test. There are some tests, even some experimental tests; and in some cases, such as the famous phenomenon known as "industrial melanism", we can observe natural selection happening under our very eyes, as it were. Nevertheless, really severe tests of the theory of natural selection are hard to come by, much more so than tests of otherwise comparable theories in physics or chemistry.

The fact that the theory of natural selection is difficult to test has led some people, anti-Darwinists and even some great Darwinists, to claim that it is a tautology. A tautology like "All tables are tables" is not, of course, testable; nor has it any explanatory power. It is therefore most surprising to hear that some of the greatest contemporary Darwinists themselves formulate the theory in such a way that it amounts to the tautology that those organisms that leave most offspring leave most offspring. And C. H. Waddington even says somewhere (and he defends this view in other places) that "Natural selection . . . turns out . . . to be a tautology".[6] However, he attributes at the same place to the theory an "enormous power . . . of explanation". Since the explanatory power of a tautology is obviously zero, something must be wrong here.

6. C. H. Waddington, "Evolutionary Adaptation", in S. Tax, ed., *Evolution After Darwin: volume I – The Evolution of Life* (Chicago: Chicago University Press, 1960) pp. 381–402; see p. 385.

Yet similar passages can be found in the works of such great Darwinists as Ronald Fisher, J. B. S. Haldane, and George Gaylord Simpson; and others.

I mention this problem because I too belong among the culprits. Influenced by what these authorities say, I have in the past described the theory as "almost tautological",[7] and I have tried to explain how the theory of natural selection could be untestable (as is a tautology) and yet of great scientific interest. My solution was that the doctrine of natural selection is a most successful metaphysical research program. It raises detailed problems in many fields, and it tells us what we would expect of an acceptable solution of these problems.

I still believe that natural selection works in this way as a research program. Nevertheless, I have changed my mind about the testability and the logical status of the theory of natural selection; and I am glad to have an opportunity to make a recantation. My recantation may, I hope, contribute a little to the understanding of the status of natural selection.

What is important is to realize the explanatory task of natural selection; and especially to realize *what* can be explained *without* the theory of natural selection.

We may start from the remark that, for sufficiently small and reproductively isolated populations, the Mendelian theory of genes and the theory of mutation and recombination together suffice to predict, *without natural selection*, what has been called "genetic drift". If you isolate a small number of individuals from the main population and prevent them from interbreeding with the main population, then, after a time, the distribution of genes in the gene pool of the new population will differ somewhat from that of the original population. This will happen even if selection pressures are completely absent.

Moritz Wagner, a contemporary of Darwin, and of course a pre-Mendelian, was aware of this situation. He therefore introduced a theory of *evolution by genetic drift*, made possible by reproductive isolation through geographical separation.

In order to understand the task of natural selection, it is good to remember Darwin's reply to Moritz Wagner.[8] Darwin's main reply to Wagner was: if you have no natural selection, you cannot explain the evolution of the apparently designed organs, like the eye. Or in other words, without natural selection, you cannot solve Paley's problem.

In its most daring and sweeping form, the theory of natural selection would assert that *all* organisms, and especially *all* those highly complex organs whose existence might be interpreted as evidence of design and, in addition, *all* forms of animal behavior, have evolved as the result of natural selection; that is, as the result of chance-like inheritable variations, of which the useless ones are weeded out, so that only the useful ones remain. If formulated in this sweeping way, the theory is not only refutable, but actually refuted. For *not all* organs serve a *useful*

7. *Objective Knowledge* (Oxford: Clarendon Press, 1972), p. 241. See also my "Metaphysical Epilogue" to *Quantum Theory and the Schism in Physics*, vol. III of the *Postscript to the Logic of Scientific Discovery*, ed. W. W. Bartley, III (London: Hutchinson, 1982).

8. See *L. L.*, volume III, p. 158f.

purpose; as Darwin himself points out, there are organs like the tail of the peacock, and behavioral programs like the peacock's display of his tail, which cannot be explained by their *utility*, and therefore not by natural selection. Darwin explained them by the preference of the other sex, that is, by sexual selection. Of course one can get round this refutation by some verbal maneuver: one can get round any refutation of any theory. But then one gets near to rendering the theory tautological. It seems far preferable to admit that *not* everything that evolves is *useful*, though it is astonishing how many things are; and that in conjecturing what is the *use* of an organ or a behavioral program, we conjecture a possible explanation by natural selection: of *why* it evolved in the way it has, and perhaps even of *how* it evolved. In other words, it seems to me that like so many theories in biology, evolution by natural selection is not strictly universal, though it seems to hold for a vast number of important cases.

According to Darwin's theory, sufficiently invariant selection pressures may turn the otherwise random genetic drift into a drift that has the appearance of being purposefully directed. In this way, the selection pressures, if there are any, will leave their imprint upon the genetic material. (It may be mentioned, however, that there are selection pressures that can operate successfully over very short periods: one severe epidemic may leave alive only those who are genetically immune.)

I may now briefly sum up what I have said so far about Darwin's theory of natural selection.

The theory of natural selection may be so formulated that it is far from tautological. In this case it is not only testable, but it turns out to be not strictly universally true. There seem to be exceptions, as with so many biological theories; and considering the random character of the variations on which natural selection operates, the occurrence of exceptions is not surprising. Thus not all phenomena of evolution are explained by natural selection alone. Yet in every particular case it is a challenging research program to show how far natural selection can possibly be held responsible for the evolution of a particular organ or behavioral program.

It is of considerable interest that the idea of natural selection can be generalized. In this connection it is helpful to discuss the relation between selection and instruction. While Darwin's theory is selectionist, the theistic theory of Paley is instructionist. It is the Creator who, by His design, molds matter, and instructs it which shape to take. Thus Darwin's selectionist theory can be regarded as a theory that explains by selection something that looks like instruction. Certain invariant features of the environment leave their imprint on the genetic material as if they had molded it; while in fact, they selected it.

Many years ago I visited Bertrand Russell in his rooms at Trinity College and he showed me a manuscript of his in which there was not a single correction for many pages. With the help of his pen, he had instructed the paper. This is very different indeed from what I do. My own manuscripts are full of corrections – so full that it is easy to see that I am working by something like trial and error;

by more or less random fluctuations from which I select what appears to me fitting. We may pose the question whether Russell did not do something similar, though only in his mind, and perhaps not even consciously, and at any rate very rapidly. For indeed, what seems to be instruction is frequently based upon a roundabout mechanism of selection, as illustrated by Darwin's answer to the problem posed by Paley.

I suggest that we might try out the conjecture that something like this happens in many cases. We may indeed conjecture that Bertrand Russell produced almost as many trial formulations as I do, but that his mind worked more quickly than mine in trying them out and rejecting the non-fitting verbal candidates. Einstein somewhere says that he produced and rejected an immense number of hypotheses before hitting on (and first rejecting) the equations of general relativity. Clearly, the method of production and selection is one that operates with negative feedback.

More than forty years ago I proposed the conjecture that this is also the method by which we acquire our knowledge of the external world: we produce conjectures, or hypotheses, try them out, and reject those that do not fit. This is a method of critical selection, if we look at it closely. From a distance, it looks like instruction or, as it is usually called, induction.

What a painter does is often strikingly similar. He puts on his canvas a spot of color and steps back to judge the effect, in order either to accept it, or to reject it and to go over the spot again. It does not matter for my discussion whether he compares the effect with an object painted, or with an inward image, or whether he merely approves or disapproves of the effect. What is important here has been described by Ernst Gombrich by the excellent phrase "making comes before matching".[9] This phrase can be applied with profit to every case of selection, in particular to the method of producing and testing hypotheses, which includes perception, and especially *Gestalt* perception. Of course, the phrase "making comes before matching" can be applied also to Darwinian selection. The making of many new genetic variants precedes their selection by the environment, and thus their matching with the environment. The action of the environment is roundabout because it must be preceded by a partly random process that produces, or makes, the material on which selection, or matching, can operate.

One of the important points about this roundabout method of selection is that it throws light on the problem of downward causation to which Donald Campbell and Roger Sperry have called attention.[10]

9. See under "making comes before matching" in the index of E. Gombrich, *Art and Illusion* (London: Phaidon, 1960 and later editions).
10. See D. T. Campbell, "'Downward Causation' in Hierarchically Organized Biological Systems", in F. J. Ayala and T. Dobzhansky, eds., *Studies in The Philosophy of Biology* (London: Macmillan, 1974), pp. 179–86; R. W. Sperry, "A Modified Concept of Consciousness", *Psychological Review* 76, 1969, 532–36; and "Lateral specialization in the surgically separated hemispheres", in F. O. Schmitt and F. G. Worden, eds., *The Neurosciences: Third Study Programme* (Cambridge, Mass.: M.I.T. Press, 1973), pp. 5–19.

We may speak of downward causation whenever a higher structure operates causally upon its substructure. The difficulty of understanding downward causation is this. We think we can understand how the substructures of a system cooperate to affect the whole system; that is to say, we think that we understand upward causation. But the opposite is very difficult to envisage. For the set of substructures, it seems, interacts causally in any case, and there is no room, no opening, for an action from above to interfere. It is this that leads to the heuristic demand that we explain everything in terms of molecular or other elementary particles (a demand that is sometimes called "reductionism").

I suggest that downward causation can sometimes at least be explained as *selection* operating on the randomly fluctuating elementary particles. The randomness of the movements of the elementary particles – often called "molecular chaos"– provides, as it were, the opening for the higher-level structure to interfere. A random movement is accepted when it fits into the higher level structure; otherwise it is rejected.

I think that these considerations tell us a lot about natural selection. While Darwin still worried that he could not explain variation, and while he felt uneasy about being forced to look at it as chancelike, we can now see that the chancelike character of mutations, which may go back to quantum indeterminacy, explains how the abstract invariances of the environment, the somewhat abstract selection pressures, can, by selection, have a downward effect on the concrete living organism – an effect that may be amplified by a long sequence of generations linked by heredity.

The selection of a kind of behavior out of a randomly offered repertoire may be an act of choice, even an act of free will. I am an indeterminist; and in discussing indeterminism I have often regretfully pointed out that quantum indeterminacy does not seem to help us;[11] for the amplification of something like, say, radioactive disintegration processes would not lead to human action or even animal action, but only to random movements. I have changed my mind on this issue.[12] A choice process may be a selection process, and the *selection* may be *from* some repertoire of random events, *without being random in its turn*. This seems to me to offer a promising solution to one of our most vexing problems, and one by downward causation.

3. Huxley's Problem

The denial of the existence of mind is a view that has become very fashionable in our own time: mind is replaced by what is called "verbal behavior". Darwin lived to see the revival of this view in the nineteenth century. His close friend, Thomas Henry Huxley, proposed the thesis that animals, including men, are automata. Huxley did not deny the existence of conscious or subjective experiences,

11. Cp. my *Objective Knowledge*, chapter 6, pp. 226–29.
12. See also p. 540 of J. C. Eccles and K. R. Popper, *The Self and Its Brain* (Berlin, Heidelberg, London, New York: Springer-Verlag, 1977).

as do now some of his successors; but he denied that they can have any effect whatever on the machinery of the human or animal body, including the brain.

"It may be assumed", Huxley writes,[13] " . . . that molecular changes in the brain are the causes of all the states of consciousness . . . [But is] there any evidence that these states of consciousness may, conversely, cause . . . molecular changes [in the brain] which give rise to muscular motion?" This is Huxley's problem. He answers it as follows: "I see no such evidence . . . [Consciousness appears] to be related to the mechanism of . . . [the] body simply as a collateral product of its working . . . [Consciousness appears] to be . . . completely without any power of modifying [the] working [of the body, just] as the steam-whistle . . . of a locomotive engine is without influence upon its machinery."

Huxley puts his question sharply and clearly. He also answers it sharply and clearly. He says that the action of the body upon the mind is one-sided; there is no mutual interaction. He was a mechanist and a physical determinist; and this position necessitates his answer. The world of physics, of physical mechanisms, is causally closed. Thus a body cannot be influenced by states of consciousness. Animals, including men, must be automata, even if conscious ones.

Darwin's view of the matter was very different. In his book on *The Expression of the Emotions in Man and Animals* he had shown in great detail how the emotions of men and of animals can and do express themselves in muscular movements.

One direct reply of Darwin's to his friend Huxley, whom he greatly admired and loved, is most characteristic. A charming letter to Huxley written three weeks before Darwin's death, closes with a characteristic mixture of tenderness, irony, and wit: " . . . my dear old friend. I wish to God there were more automata in the world like you."[14]

In fact, no Darwinist should accept Huxley's one-sided action of body upon mind as the solution of what is called the mind-body problem. In his *Essay* of 1844, in his *Origin of Species*, and even more so in his much larger manuscript on *Natural Selection*, Darwin discussed the mental powers of animals and men; and he argued that these are a product of natural selection.

Now if that is so, then mental powers must help animals and men in the struggle for life, for physical survival. It follows from this that mental powers must be able to exert in their turn an important influence on the physical actions of animals and men. Animals and men could not, therefore, be automata in Huxley's

---

13. See T. H. Huxley, "On the hypothesis that animals are automata, and its history" (1874), chapter 5 of his *Method and Results* (London: Macmillan, 1893), pp. 239–40. While the passage quoted in the text refers to animals, Huxley follows it up, a few pages later, by saying " . . . to the best of my judgment, the argumentation which applies to brutes holds equally good of men; and, therefore, . . . all states of consciousness in us, as in them, are immediately caused by molecular changes of the brain-substance. It seems to me that in men, as in brutes, there is no proof that any state of consciousness is the cause of change in the motion of the matter of the organism . . . We are conscious automata . . . " (*ibid.*, pp. 243–44). I have discussed these views of Huxley's in my paper "Some Remarks on Panpsychism and Epiphenomenalism", in *Dialectica*, volume 31, Nos 1–2, 1977, pp. 177–86, and in my contribution to *The Self and Its Brain* (see note 12 above).

14. *L. L.,* volume III, p. 358.

sense. If subjective experiences, conscious states, exist – and Huxley admitted their existence – we should, according to Darwinism, look out for their use, for their adaptive function. As they are useful for living, they must have consequences in the physical world.

Thus the theory of natural selection constitutes a strong argument against Huxley's theory of the one-sided action of body on mind and for the mutual interaction of mind and body. Not only does the body act on the mind – for example, in perception, or in sickness – but our thoughts, our expectations, and our feelings may lead to useful actions in the physical world. If Huxley had been right, mind would be useless. But then, it could not have evolved, as it did, by natural selection.

My central thesis here is that the theory of natural selection provides a strong argument for the doctrine of *mutual interaction* between mind and body or, perhaps better, between mental states and physical states.

Of course, I am very much aware of the fact that the doctrine of *mutual interaction* is utterly old-fashioned. Still, I propose to defend interaction, and old-fashioned dualism (except that I reject the existence of so-called "substances"); I even defend *pluralism*, since I hold that there are three (or perhaps more) interacting levels or regions or worlds: the world 1 of *physical* things, or events, or states, or processes, including animal bodies and brains; the world 2 of *mental* states; and the world 3 that consists of the *products of the human mind*, especially of works of art and of scientific theories.

I am afraid that I do not have time to say more about world 3 here. I must confine myself to formulating the conjecture that the world 1 of physical objects, and the world 2 of mental states, interact, and that the world 3 of scientific theories, for example of medical theories, also strongly interacts with the world of physical objects, *via* the psychological world 2.

The present fashion is either to deny that anything like mental experience exists, or to assert that mental experiences are somehow or other *identical* with physical states of the central nervous system.

I do not think the first of these fashions – the suggestion that we don't have experiences – is very interesting. For we have good intersubjective tests of the hypothesis that we do have such experiences. And all that ever seems to have been said against our hypothesis is that the universe would be a simpler place by far if we did not have experiences – or since we do have them, if only we could keep mum about them.

However, there is what seems to be a more serious position than the bare denial of mind. It is the currently most fashionable theory that mental states are in some sense identical with physical states: the so-called identity theory of body and mind.

Against the identity theory I think that I can use the same argument from natural selection that I used against Huxley: the identity theory seems to me to be incompatible with the theory of natural selection. For according to the identity theory, the world of physical objects or states is closed. All causation is physical causation. Thus even the identity theorist who admits consciousness cannot attribute to it any independent causal function in the physical world.[15] It cannot have evolved by natural selection. The situation of the identity theorists is the same as that of T. H. Huxley.

4. Remarks on the Emergence of Mind

I conjecture that life, and later also mind, have evolved or emerged in a universe that was, up to a certain time, lifeless and mindless. Life, or living matter, somehow emerged from nonliving matter; and it does not seem completely impossible that we shall one day know how this happened.

Things look far more difficult with the emergence of mind. While we think we know some of the preconditions of life, and some of the substructures of primitive organisms, we do not have the slightest idea on which evolutionary level mind emerges. H. S. Jennings said in 1906, in his great book on *The Behaviour of the Lower Organisms*, that, in observing the behavior of the amoeba, he could hardly help attributing to it consciousness. On the other hand, some students of biology and some students of human language do not wish to attribute mind or consciousness to any animal except man. And, as I have mentioned before, there are philosophers who deny the existence of mind altogether; who regard talk of mind or of conscious states as sheer babble: as a verbal habit that is bound to disappear, like talk about witches, with the progress of science, especially of brain research.

In contrast to these philosophers, I regard the emergence of mind as a tremendous event in the evolution of life. Mind illuminates the universe; and I regard the work of a great scientist like Darwin as important just because it contributes so much to this illumination. Herbert Feigl reports that Einstein said to him: "But for this internal illumination, the universe would be just a rubbish heap."[16]

As I said earlier, I think we have to admit that the universe is creative, or inventive. At any rate, it is creative in the sense in which great poets, great artists, and great scientists are creative. Once there was no poetry in the universe; once there was no music. But then, later, it was there. Obviously, it would be no sort of explanation to attribute to atoms, or to molecules, or even to the lower animals, the ability to create (or perhaps to proto-create) a forerunner of poetry, called proto-poetry. I think it is no better explanation if we attribute to atoms or molecules a proto-psyche, as do the panpsychists. No, the case of great poetry shows clearly that the universe has the power of creating something new. As Ernst Mayr once said, the emergence of real novelty in the course of evolution should be regarded as a fact.

15. If, as Spinoza says, the order and connection of things is the same as the order and connection of ideas, then the order and connection of ideas is, from an evolutionary or Darwinian point of view, clearly redundant for the identity theorist.

16. See Herbert Feigl, *The 'Mental' and the 'Physical'* (Minneapolis: University of Minnesota Press, 1967), p. 138. I have made a small change to the wording.

In view of the difficulty, if not the impossibility, of testing the conjectural ascription of mental powers to animals, speculation about the origin of mind in animals will probably never grow into a testable scientific theory. Nevertheless, I will briefly offer some speculative conjectures. At any rate, these conjectures are open to criticism, if not to tests.

I will start from the idea, stressed by ethologists such as Thorpe, that the behavior of animals, like that of computers, is programmed; but that unlike computers, animals are *self-programmed*. The fundamental genetic self-program is, we may assume, laid down in the coded DNA tape. There are also acquired programs, programs due to nurture; but what can be acquired and what cannot—the repertoire of possible acquisitions—is itself laid down in the form of the fundamental genetic self-program, which may even determine the probability or propensity of making an acquisition.

We may distinguish two kinds of behavioral programs, *closed behavioral programs* and *open behavioral programs,* as Mayr calls them.[17] A closed behavioral program is one that lays down the behavior of the animal in great detail. An open behavioral program is one that does not prescribe all the steps in the behavior but leaves open certain alternatives, certain choices; even though it may perhaps determine the probability or propensity of choosing one way or another. The open programs evolve, we must assume, by natural selection, due to the selection pressure of complex and irregularly changing environmental situations.

I can now state my conjecture as follows:

Ecological conditions like those that favor the evolution of *open behavioral programs* sometimes also favor the evolution of the beginnings of consciousness, by favoring conscious choices. Or in other words, consciousness originates with the choices that are left open by open behavioral programs.

Let us look at various possible stages in the emergence of consciousness.

As a possible first stage there may evolve something that acts like a centralized warning, that is, like irritation or discomfort or pain, inducing the organism to stop an inadequate movement and to adopt some alternative behavior in its stead before it is too late, before too much damage has been done. The absence of a warning like pain will lead in many cases to destruction. Thus natural selection will favor those individuals that shrink back when they receive a signal indicating an inadequate movement; which means, anticipating the inherent danger of the movement. I suggest that pain may evolve as such a signal; and perhaps also fear.

As a second stage, we may consider that natural selection will favor those organisms that try out, by some method or other, the possible movements that might be adopted *before they are executed*. In this way, *real* trial-and-error behavior may be replaced, or preceded, by *imagined* or vicarious trial-and-error behavior. The

---

17. See Ernst Mayr, *Evolution and the Diversity of Life* (Cambridge, Mass.: The Belknap Press, Harvard University Press, 1976), p. 23.

imagining may perhaps initially consist of incipient efferent nervous signals, serving as a kind of model, or symbolic representation of the actual behavior, and of its possible results.

Richard Dawkins has brilliantly developed some such speculations about the beginnings of mind in considerable detail.[18] The main points about them are two. One is that these beginnings of mind or consciousness should be favored by natural selection, simply because they mean the substitution of imagined or symbolic or vicarious behavior for real trials which, if erroneous, may have fatal consequences. The other is that we can here apply the ideas of *selection* and of *downward causation* to what is clearly a choice situation: the open program allows for possibilities to be played through tentatively – on a screen, as it were – in order that a *selection* can be made from among these possibilities.

As a third stage, we may perhaps consider the evolution of more or less conscious aims, or ends: of purposeful animal actions, such as hunting. Unconscious instinctive action may have been purpose-directed before, but once vicarious or imagined trial-and-error behavior has started, it becomes necessary, in situations of choice, to evaluate the end state of the imagined behavior. This may lead to feelings of avoidance or rejection – to *anticipations* of pain – or to feelings of eager acceptance of the end state; and the latter feelings may come to characterize a consciousness of aim or end or purpose. In connection with open choices, a feeling may evolve of preference for one possibility rather than another; preference for one kind of food, and thus for one kind of ecological niche, rather than another.

The evolution of language and, with it, of the world 3 of the products of the human mind allows a further step: the human step. It allows us to *dissociate ourselves* from our own hypotheses, and to look upon them critically. While an uncritical animal may be eliminated together with its dogmatically held hypotheses, we may *formulate* our hypotheses, and criticize them. Let our conjectures, our theories, die in our stead! We may still learn to kill our theories instead of killing each other. If natural selection has favored the evolution of mind for the reason indicated, then it is perhaps more than a utopian dream that one day may see the victory of the attitude (it is the rational or the scientific attitude) of eliminating our theories, our opinions, by rational criticism, instead of eliminating each other.

My conjecture concerning the origin of mind and the relation of the mind to the body, that is the relation of consciousness to the preceding level of unconscious behavior, is that its usefulness – its survival value – is similar to that of the preceding levels. On every level, making comes before matching; that is, before selecting. The creation of an expectation, of an anticipation, of a perception (which is a hypothesis) *precedes* its being put to the test.

If there is anything in this interpretation, then the process of variation fol-

18. See R. Dawkins, *The Selfish Gene* (Oxford: Oxford University Press, 1976), pp. 62f.

lowed by selection which Darwin discovered does not merely offer an explanation of biological evolution in mechanical terms, or in what has been slightingly and mistakenly described as mechanical terms, but it actually throws light on downward causation; on the creation of works of art and of science; and on the evolution of the freedom to create them. It is thus the entire range of phenomena connected with the evolution of life and of mind, and also of the products of the human mind, that are illuminated by the great and inspiring idea that we owe to Darwin.

Appendix: On Light and Life

(This Appendix is translated, in slightly modified form, from the third section of my paper: "Festvortrag: 40 Jahre Naturwissenschaften", in Otto Molden, ed.: *Der Beitrag Europas: Erbe und Auftrag: Europäisches Forum Alpbach 1984* (Vienna: Österreichisches College, 1985).)

I should like to report here, very briefly, a lecture that was given a few months ago at a meeting of the American Association for the Advancement of Science under the title "Light and Life", a title that is perhaps known to some of you from a lecture by Niels Bohr given in 1932. Comparing these two lectures, I can only say that I greatly prefer the new lecture to Bohr's, even though Bohr's lecture made a great impression on me at that time. The author of this new lecture is Dr. Günter Wächtershäuser.

The content of his lecture is fascinating. In this brief space I cannot do justice to it. Essentially it is a theory of the evolution of vision. The single-celled organisms which made the great chemical discovery that one can use light as nourishment – for nourishment is the taking in of energy – must more or less simultaneously also have discovered phototropism, the active movement towards light, and with it, sensitivity to light. Without that they would have starved. From the light-eating microbes there evolved first the green plants and, later, animals. Animals are descended from the plant-like microbes; but they have forgotten the secret of nourishing themselves from light. Instead, they became profiteers and parasites; for they nourished themselves from the green plants, and hence only indirectly from sunlight. By nourishing themselves on plants, these animals obtain substances that they themselves cannot produce, including what are called vitamins. These substances enable them to be sensitive to light and so they make it possible for them to develop eyes.

One of Wächtershäuser's central hypotheses is this. The search for light begins not as a search for information, but rather as a search for nourishment. That is a quite uncommonly interesting proposition. Through it, a problem of evolutionary epistemology is closely linked with problems of biology and indeed of molecular biology.

Wächtershäuser's hypothesis can be tested, and he himself has found exceedingly interesting data in the biological literature. Perhaps the most sensational is a paramecium, a single-celled creature, that feeds on green algae, that is, on plants. One among these plants – an algae – is called chlorella. This chlorella is not only used as food by the paramecium. Rather, the paramecium uses many individuals of the species chlorella literally as eyes. It sticks the chlorella on itself like a badge and then enters into a symbiotic relationship with this algae – which, however, it later eats. As long as the chlorella serves as an eye, it helps to steer the movement of the whole symbiotic organism, just as a driver steers a car. But it functions simultaneously as a stomach – for it gives back part of its light nourishment to its host. Eventually, however, it is eaten up.

I conclude with the remark that animals, including ourselves, after becoming human, forgot the secret discovery of the plants about how to use light as a source of energy. Our biochemists too, up to now, have not rediscovered the secret – apart from some highly inefficient methods. Its rediscovery is one of our most important scientific problems. Its solution would turn all atomic energy plants into scrap iron.

Emergence, Reduction, and Evolutionary Epistemology: A Commentary

By Rosaria Egidi

An argument implied in the discussions of evolutionary epistemology by Bartley and Vollmer seems to me to deserve special attention: the problem of "emergence" and the cluster of *methodological* issues which connect it with the topic indicated by Popper by the metaphorical expression "third world".[1] I emphasize the word "methodological" because the level of analysis I shall consider does not deal with *ontological* or *substantialistic* emergence, but to the *logical* theses, including that of Popper, about novelties and unpredictable elements of knowledge which have been investigated within the analytical tradition.

Accordingly the problem of methodological emergence and also of the trial-and-error-method, which is the Popperian connotation of emergentism, is radically different from the ontological doctrines which from the beginning of the twentieth century have been called "emergent" or "creative evolution" (C. D. Broad, Samuel Alexander, Lloyd Morgan, W. M. Wheeler, H. Bergson). These doctrines, which have perhaps been too quickly discarded, are connected to the claim to explain the variety, diversity, and novelty of phenomena without recourse to mechanistic, vitalistic, or reductionistic models of explanation. Thus, "emergentism" is a label for all the theories which assert the presence, in the realm of living beings and organic life, of elements which are not continuous with what went before and which are therefore "emergent", or irreducible to the already known elements.

In opposition to Darwinian evolutionism and to the view of a continuity and gradualness of development in structural changes and in the formation of new configurations (gestalts), the first theorists of emergence and of emergent evolution maintained that beings and events which occur for the first time in the universe are discontinuous with beings and events which precede them in space and time. The manifold and different structures which occur in the evolution of the

---

1. Karl R. Popper, *Objective Knowledge: An Evolutionary Approach* (Oxford: Clarendon Press, 1972), pp. 153–90.

organic world as in the whole universe constitute a long chain of "levels" of increasing complexity. They are mutually irreducible and are provided with qualitatively new features, which are unexpected on the basis of those of lower levels. This view has been called "ontological" or "substantialistic" emergence, since the emergence appears as an intrinsic characteristic of new facts and events, which occurs in the evolution of nature and the cosmos not as a mere sum of pre-existing elements but as a unique, unrepeatable fact, which cannot be explained on the basis of already known facts. In this sense Broad and Alexander spoke of emergences such as "human mind" or "deity" within the history of the universe.

The most vigorous criticism of ontological emergence has come from the reductionistic epistemology of logical positivism. A. Pap, C. G. Hempel, G. Bergmann, and E. Nagel insist on eliminating the "misconception that certain phenomena have a mysterious quality of absolute unexplainability".[2] They deny that emergence is a property of objects, states, processes, and entities, and maintain that emergence is instead a property of concepts and laws of science, and depends on the status of theories in scientific language. The meaning of emergence has no objective reference and depends on the explanatory and predictive power of theories in specific fields of a certain science. Thus the concept of emergence does not refer to a property "inherent in some phenomena" but has a methodological function, indicative of the scope of our knowledge.[3] Thus they do not speak of *absolute* emergence as a characteristic of essential elements of a totality but of *relative* emergence in the sense that a certain property which seems emergent in terms of a certain theory may not be emergent with respect to different theoretical contexts. They admit the emergence of laws and theories in the language of science, the presence of new and unpredictable concepts and laws in scientific knowledge, only as long as they are not considered intrinsically new, but are viewed as not reducible to the standard systems of laws and theories. There are of course certain areas of natural and perhaps of human sciences which resist reduction. It is conceivable that chemistry and biology will be completely reduced to physics and physiology (that is, chemical and biological concepts and laws to physical and physiological concepts and laws), if indeed such a reduction has not already taken place. Nevertheless in some cases, as Popper says, we could even produce arguments to show why the first area cannot be reduced to the second one. This is one case in which we may have an example of genuine "methodological emergence".[4]

In the past few decades the reductionistic/methodological theory of emergence has been subjected to several attacks. One of these attacks comes from Popper in his defense of the growth of knowledge as "a progress without reduction". The debate about the dichotomy 'emergence versus reduction' is really only one as-

2. Carl G. Hempel, "The Logic of Explanation", in *Readings in the Philosophy of Science,* ed. H. Feigl and M. Brodbeck (New York: Appleton-Century-Crofts, 1953), p. 335.
3. *Ibid.,* p. 336.
4. Popper, *op. cit.,* p. 295.

pect of the problem of the growth of knowledge, the possibilities and modalities of scientific progress. Needless to say, Popper's conception is in no sense a revival of ontological emergentism, but a critical attempt to offer a rational account of emergent evolution which avoids the evil of reductionism. Since reductionism is for Popper a synonym for inductivism and determinism and, as Bartley points out, for all justification-philosophies, it is easy to understand that the primary concern of the Popperian analysis of the growth of knowledge is to distinguish its own version of emergence from the reductionistic, inductivistic, deterministic connotations of the methodological concept. I agree with Bartley's arguments against justificationism, but it seems to me that some questions remain open. What is the context to which emergence belongs?

Besides the "emergence of entities and processes" suggested by the theorists of emergent evolution and the "emergence of concepts and theories" defended by the logical empiricists, Popper introduces an "emergence of problems, of new problems", which seems to occupy an intermediate position between those two.[5] Because of the analogy he sees between the evolution of organisms and the growth of cognitive processes (i.e., the adoption of a common selective eliminative model), his version of emergence approximates the old doctrines of emergent evolution and implies their creativistic, metaphysical presuppositions. But, because of the role which the question of method plays in the evolutionary processes of knowing, that is, in the trial-and-error method, Popper's concept of emergence is of a methodological or logical nature. In this light emergence seems to belong to the context of justification.

Another and perhaps the most interesting argument concerning the role of emergence in the growth of knowledge is found in the Popperian attempt to prove the *nonempirical* but *logical-rational* character of the emergence concept. The emergence of a new problem is a matter which does not belong to the "second" but to the "third" world. Unfortunately none of the arguments in favor of emergentism are explicitly formulated. Here I shall do no more than indicate some points worthy of examination and development. Analysis of the role played by emergence in the growth of knowledge is necessarily connected with the question of the adequacy of the evolutionary model, with the compatibility of this model with Popper's general epistemology, and with an analysis of his basic epistemological rules and the limits of their applicability.

Popper's rejection of reductionism and determinism in order to make room for emergentism is sketched in *Objective Knowledge* and developed in his later works.[6] It is worth noting that he has never made clear the essential distinction between emergence as a concept of unpredictability and emergence as a doctrine of indeterminism. Many authors have often pointed out that unpredictable ele-

---

5. *Ibid.*, pp. 287–89.
6. Popper, "Scientific Reduction and the Essential Incompleteness of All Science", in his *The Open Universe: An Argument for Indeterminism*, ed. W. W. Bartley, III (Totowa: Rowman & Littlefield, 1982), pp. 131–62.

ments of knowledge, emergent novelties, creative, noncumulative factors determining scientific languages do not necessarily imply a denial of determinism.[7] Accordingly the unpredictability of properties of such organic wholes or complexes as chemical compounds, organisms, and social groups on the basis of the properties of their component parts such as chemical elements, cells, individual persons is a *logical* problem, based on the patterns of the logic of whole/part relations, and on the deductive/nomological model of scientific explanation. Emergence in the sense of unpredictability indicates therefore the impossibility of reducing the parts to the wholes, i.e., of deducing the properties of the parts from the properties of the wholes. But unpredictability and nonderivability are in no sense an argument against determinism, that is, against the possibility of explaining organic wholes by means of deterministic theories. As Feigl contended, "the argument for genuine emergence along with the arguments for (irreducible) holism appear plausible only as long as they are couched in *epistemic* terms. That is to say, if the properties of the parts or components have explored only in 'splendid isolation', there would hardly be any clue as to what sort of wholes (compounds, organisms, etc.) they might form when brought into interaction with each other".[8]

The gist of Popper's attempt to offer a rational account of emergence is that reduction can be accomplished, if and only if the concepts of the theories or laws which are to be reduced are definable in terms of the concepts of the reducing theory or law. But in reply to this argument it might be contended that, since definability is a necessary but not a sufficient condition, emergence in the sense of unpredictability or nonderivability may yet obtain, even if the definability condition is satisfied. The problem of emergence is therefore not a logical question, as Popper insists, but an *empirical* one.

This is not the occasion for discussing what is common to the empiricist and the rationalistic conceptions of emergence. Within an empirically oriented conception, it does seem appropriate, however, to conclude with two critical remarks on the Popperian version of emergentism and its compatibility with an evolutionary account of knowing procedures and with an indeterministic conception of the growth of knowledge. The first remark is related to Vollmer's contribution. I would suggest adding a further argument to his table of circularities which some critics have assigned to evolutionary epistemology. This argument refers to the consistency of Popper's defense of emergentism with his logical and methodological presuppositions. Popper's plea for deductive methods of explanation in natural and in social sciences, his discussion of emergence in the context of "third world" problems, are instances of ineliminable presuppositions, which have their

7. Cf. Gustav Bergmann, *Philosophy of Science* (Madison: University of Wisconsin Press, 1957); Herbert Feigl and Paul E. Meehl, "The Determinism-Freedom and Body-Mind Problems", in *The Philosophy of Karl Popper*, P. A. Schilpp, ed., (La Salle: Open Court, 1974), pp. 520–59; Ernst Nagel, *The Structure of Science* (London: Routledge & Kegan Paul, 1961), pp. 366–80; Kenneth Schaffner, "Antireductionism in Molecular Biology", in *Science* 157, 1967, pp. 644–47.
8. Feigl and Meehl, "The Determinism-Freedom and Body-Mind Problems", *op. cit.*, p. 256.

roots in the logic of fundamental whole/part relations. Thus one could remark that Popper's emergentism does not follow from his conception of the growth of knowledge but from a monistic model of rational explanation.

My second remark refers to teleology, a key notion for a number of recently re-examined epistemological doctrines connected with methodological emergentism. Although Popper stresses that "such nonphysical things as *purposes, deliberations, plans, decisions, theories, intentions, and values* can play a part in bringing about physical changes in the physical world",[9] teleology and related problems do not play any role in his analysis of the growth of knowledge, or in his concept of emergent, new problems in natural and social sciences and in history. The special attention he pays to physical and ethical indeterminism[10] makes it evident that for him teleological problems constitute an essential part of the matrix in which the D-N model of rational explanation has its roots. However, since teleological concepts and explanations do not constitute obscure and metaphysical constructions but an extensive chapter of the logic of decisions and human actions, it seems to me that here again it is imperative to an evolutionary theory of knowing procedures to re-examine methodological emergentism and to refute the objections raised so far to various rationalistic solutions.

9. *Objective Knowledge, op. cit.*, p. 256.
10. *Ibid.*, pp. 226–34; *The Open Universe, op. cit.*, pp. 113–30.

═ Chapter *VIII* ══════════

On Supposed Circularities in an Empirically Oriented Epistemology

By Gerhard Vollmer

Evolutionary epistemology as a theory of knowledge is based on empirical facts.[1] There are several objections against such a way of arguing. Most of them blame evolutionary epistemology for committing a logical fallacy, for proceeding by a *petitio principii*, for begging the question, for assuming as a premise what' is to be proved – in short, for being *circular*. Although the serpent biting its own tail is, since the times of gnosticism, a symbol of philosophy, the charge of being circular is not very flattering. It might, therefore, be worthwhile to examine those attacks. They can be divided in three groups saying either

- that epistemology in general is impossible, or
- that any epistemology which draws on empirical findings must be circular, hence empty or inconsistent, or
- that at least evolutionary epistemology is circular.

All these claims are erroneous. Therefore, this contribution divides into three parts. Part *A* defends epistemology in general, *B* supports epistemologies which are empirically oriented, and *C* advocates evolutionary epistemology in particular.

A. "Epistemology is Impossible."

This claim might sound somewhat surprising, epistemology being such a distinguished philosophical discipline and of such venerable age. It will be of no help, however, to point to the history of philosophy and to enumerate so many epistemological systems. In fact, all of them *might* be fallacious. The very fact that there are so many of them even *contradicting* one another, shows that some of them must be false. Why, then, not all of them?

1. Presentations of evolutionary epistemology are given in Gerhard Vollmer, *Evolutionäre Erkenntnistheorie* (Stuttgart: Hirzel, 1975, 3rd ed. 1981); and in Vollmer, "Mesocosm and Objective Knowledge – On Problems Solved by Evolutionary Epistemology", in Franz M. Wuketits, ed., *Concepts and Approaches in Evolutionary Epistemology* (Dordrecht: D. Reidel, 1984), pp. 69–121.

In fact, there are attacks, superficial or sophisticated, regarding the whole enterprise of epistemology as impossible. Most of them claim to have disclosed a vicious circle which would frustrate all epistemological efforts, past and future. Four of these supposed circles will be discussed – and refuted.

A1. "We lack a criterion of knowledge."

a. The argument reads:

Epistemology is the science which investigates the validity of knowledge. It sees knowledge as fundamentally problematic and in need of justification, of proof, of validation, of foundation, of legitimation. For an investigation of the validity of knowledge we need a *criterion* which shows whether and when knowledge is *valid*, a criterion which tells supposed knowledge from *genuine* knowledge, a criterion which is sufficient to classify knowledge as *true* knowledge.

Such a criterion would be either a piece of knowledge itself, or not. As a piece of knowledge it would itself be problematic, being in need of a criterion of validity. This leads to a circle or to an infinite regress.

Now, if the criterion is not a piece of knowledge, what else could it be? Could it be a *convention*? No, because a convention could never *justify* knowledge; at least, it would be a matter of doubt and in need of yet another criterion or convention whether conventions can legitimate anything at all. This would contradict the declared goal of epistemology to give a final criterion of knowledge. It could be the *accordance* or unanimity of knowing subjects; it could be the degree of *evidence*; it could be the *usefulness* of knowledge. But whatever it might be, it would have to be an *object* of knowledge, even of empirical knowledge. Therefore, in order to *recognize* it as a criterion of objective knowledge, we would be, in turn, in need of a pertinent criterion. This leads to another circle or infinite regress. There is, then, no sufficient criterion of knowledge. Hence epistemology is impossible.

b. This argument was put forward several times.

In criticizing Kant, Schelling already wrote:

> Kant's critique is based on the following idea: Before we might claim to know anything, it is necessary first to examine our cognitive abilities. At first sight, this idea seems to be quite obvious. On closer inspection, however, we find that what is at stake, is our knowledge of knowledge. Therefore, we would need a previous investigation concerning the possibility of such knowledge of knowledge, and in this way we could inquire all the way back to infinity.[2]

A more drastic formulation was given by Hegel:

> The investigation of knowledge cannot proceed except by knowing and that is as absurd as learning to swim without going into the water.[3]

---

2. F. W. Schelling, *Zur Geschichte der neueren Philosophie, Sämtliche Werke*, Band 10, 1861, p. 78.
3. G. W. F. Hegel, *Enzyklopädie der philosophischen Wissenschaften*, 1827, section 10.

The argument was further expounded by Leonard Nelson.[4] Therefore, it is jokingly called "full Nelson" (which is a very effective hold in wrestling).

c. The argument is logically sound,
    i.e., its conclusion follows from its premises. There is no contradiction, no circularity, no infinite regress. It does not say that *knowledge* is impossible – which would contradict itself – but only that a *theory of knowledge* in the above sense is impossible. *If* epistemology is indeed meant to justify knowledge, to produce sufficient criteria of truth, to establish necessary propositions, then it is useless, barren, impossible, stillborn. *If* we set out doubting the validity of every piece of knowledge, no knowledge can be justified. As Russell put it:

> If we adopt the attitude of the complete sceptic, placing ourselves wholly outside all knowledge, and asking, from this outside position, to be compelled to return within the circle of knowledge, we are demanding what is impossible, and our scepticism can never be refuted. For all refutation must begin with some piece of knowledge which the disputants share; from blank doubt, no argument can begin. Hence the criticism of knowledge which philosophy employs must not be of this destructive kind, if any result is to be achieved. Against this absolute scepticism, no logical argument can be advanced.[5]

d. The fact that epistemology cannot meet excessive and self-contradictory requirements does not mean that it is impossible.
    We rather have to correct our conception of epistemology. It is, therefore, the *premise* of the "full Nelson" which is in need of correction. Epistemology does not prove the existence of knowledge; it *presupposes* knowledge. It relies on convictions, intersubjective evidences, successful conjectures, confirmed hypotheses. It is neither infallible nor unfailing and should not claim to be. It works hypothetico-deductively, as any other scientific discipline does.

But in contradistinction to empirical science, it has both descriptive and normative (critical and advisory) elements; it combines matters of fact and matters of obligation, is-problems and ought-problems, explanatory and explicatory tasks. It takes an unbiased *review* of statements which generally pass for knowledge and sets *norms* for a rational and methodologically sound concept of knowledge.

And also in contradistinction to empirical science, the presuppositions of epistemology are themselves open to epistemological investigation. Therefore, the general statements of epistemology must be self-applicable. Now, we learn from logic that self-applicable statements *may* lead to paradoxes. This is a hint to another supposed circularity to which we shall devote the next section.

A2. "Self-reference leads to contradictions."

a. The argument
    Human thinking has come across many paradoxes. Some of them are just surprising phenomena, in conflict with our expectations; others are serious defects,

---

4. Leonard Nelson, *Über das sogenannte Erkenntnisproblem* (Göttingen, 2nd ed., 1930), p. 444f.
5. Bertrand Russell, *The Problems of Philosophy* (London: William & Norgate, 1912), Chapter 14.

contradictions whose conflicting parts seem to be equally reasonable or justified. In what follows, only serious paradoxes (antinomies) are dealt with.

The first paradoxes turned up in antiquity. Well known are Zeno's paradoxes, the liar paradox ("I'm lying now"), the solicitor paradox ("I'll pay you for teaching me after having won my next lawsuit"). Of later origin are the barber paradox ("I'm shaving all men who don't shave themselves") and the paradox of the unexpected execution or examination ("it will take place next week, but you will not know the day in advance"). But whereas for thousands of years such paradoxes were looked upon as rather exotic, funny, more or less sophistical and removable in principle, Russell's paradox ("the set of all sets which do not contain themselves as elements"), disclosed in 1901, initiated a deep crisis in the foundations of logic and mathematics.

It can be seen that all (serious) paradoxes have their origin in *self-reference*, in the fact that a concept or a statement refers to itself, in the attempt to apply it to itself, hence in circularity. And all paradoxes disappear if self-application is prevented.

Now, epistemology is a clear case of self-reference, hence of suicidal circularity. Therefore, epistemology is impossible.

b. *This argument is fallacious.*

It is true that epistemology is self-referring. It sets out to investigate knowledge and to reflect its *own* methods, principles, presuppositions, results. Of course, we could deliberately decide to restrict epistemology to the investigation of *other* disciplines. It would, then, be an ordinary meta-discipline talking brightly about other branches of science, but leaving us in the dark about its own pretensions, premises, strategies, foundations. This could not satisfy us at all. If epistemology claims to yield knowledge about knowledge, it must include itself. Its self-referential character is conceded and unavoidable.

But *not every case of self-reference will lead to a paradox*. There are many self-referential structures (concepts, statements, real systems) which are free of contradiction: "I'm telling the truth" (this statement, if referring to itself, is empty but harmless), "the book which catalogues all catalogues which cite themselves", "the set of all sets which contain themselves as element".

Real-world cases of nondestructive self-reference should also be mentioned, though without pretension to formal rigor.

Why do the teeth not chew themselves? In fact, they do, but all at once, hence with small force per tooth. Thus, they are wearing out only slowly compared to man's lifetime. In herbivorous animals, chewing much more than omnivorous primates, the teeth must constantly be renewed, either by growing permanently (horses) or by being replaced by new ones (six times for elephants).

The stomach secretes hydrocholoric acid that dissolves metals and kills living cells. *Why does the stomach not digest itself?* In fact, it would, but has a protecting barrier of epithelial cells keeping off hydrogen ions and being renewed every three days.

As there are so many cases of harmless self-reference, it would be unreasonable, viz., too radical, to prohibit *all* kinds of self-reference. This would be as stupid as amputating a leg for the sake of an infected toe. Self-reference is, though liable to paradox, indeed indispensable in everyday life, in nature, in language, in science, in philosophy. That a self-referential epistemology is *bound* to lead to contradiction, has not been shown. It is true, there are epistemological statements which contain or lead to inconsistencies, for instance: "There is no (not even hypothetical) knowledge", "No rule without exception", "All universal statements are wrong", "A proposition that is only probable, is probably false". Yet, the fact that these statements are paradoxical just betrays that they are meaningless or false, but not that epistemology is impossible.

What is more, self-reference is not only harmless in many cases; very often it is even fruitful, yielding deep and unexpected results. There are not only vicious circles, but also virtuous circles. They will be dealt with in *B3*.

Typical cases of such virtuous self-reference are Gödel's incompleteness theorems (cf. *B3c*). Paradoxically enough, it is just these theorems which are sometimes used as arguments against epistemology. This subject deserves a separate section.

A3. "But Gödel says . . . "

We are not done yet with problems of self-reference. Whereas the preceding section dealt with supposed *inconsistencies*, paradoxes, contradictions in self-referential systems, we will now be confronted with some supposed *disabilities* of such systems. A most impressive and widely discussed argument of this type refers to meta-mathematical results, notably to Gödel's theorems.

a. The argument

Epistemology is the attempt of a special system, viz., man's cognitive system, to search into itself, to elucidate its structure, to understand its inner workings, to explain its achievements and failures, to find out its own limits. This is a clear case of self-application. But Gödel has shown (it is said) that

- no system can prove all truths about itself,
- no system can know itself,
- no system can explain itself,
- no system can understand itself,
- no system can transcend itself.

Hence, epistemology is impossible.

b. Formal systems

The argument is defective. It is confused and partly false. It is not the premise that is faulty, this time, but first and foremost, the presentation and interpretation of Gödel's results. In order to understand them and to draw epistemological consequences, we will first have to study what Gödel has in fact shown.

Kurt Gödel (1906–1978) was an ingenious logician and mathematician who proved several deep theorems. His completeness theorem of 1930 asserts the completeness of the predicate calculus and has nothing to do with our problem. In 1931, he proved two *incompleteness* theorems. These theorems deal with properties of formal systems. To understand them one must know what a formal system is. Without going into details, let us just give a sober definition and some illustrative examples.

A formal system is a triplet $<L, A, R>$ consisting of

- a formal language L,
- a set A of axioms (formulated in L), and
- a set R of rules of derivation (formation, deduction, possible moves) such that
- there is a least one axiom or one rule (i.e., $A \cup R \neq \emptyset$).

Formal systems are, for example, the calculi of logic, axiomatic systems (e.g., of mathematics), rules of games, algorithmic procedures, generative grammars, computer programs.

c. Gödel's theorems

Gödel's *first incompleteness theorem* reads:
For any formal system S which is

- consistent (i.e., free of contradictions) and
- rich enough to contain number theory,

there are statements which

- can be formulated in S, yet
- cannot be proved (nor refuted) in S, but nevertheless
- are true and
- can be proved to be true by richer means.

The theorem says that any Gödel system (that is, any consistent, formal system containing arithmetic) is *incomplete*, because it contains statements it cannot prove, although they are true. It shows that *truth* and *provability* are not coextensive, do not embrace the same set of statements. The concept of truth is *wider* than the concept of provability: For any Gödel system S there are more true statements than statements provable in S. (A hint at how Gödel reached his results will be given in *B3c*.)

All Gödel sentences (true, but not provable in S) are *self-referring*: They say something about the system S and even about themselves. A typical example is the Gödel sentence G: "This statement G is not provable in S." It is easy to see *from outside* (semantically) that G must be true, for, if it were false, it would be provable in S, hence contradict itself.

Let it be stressed that by no means *all* self-referring sentences in S are unprovable in S. Thus, self-reference is not damned to prevent provability (much less, to be inconsistent, hence destructive, as was pointed out in *A2*). A self-referring statement which *can* be proved in S is: "If S is consistent, then G is true."

Now, *if* the consistency of S were provable in S, then, according to the last theorem, we could prove G in S. But this would contradict our previous result, that G *cannot* be proved in S. That means, that the consistency of S is *not* provable in S. This is Gödel's *second incompleteness theorem*: No Gödel system (consistent formal system containing arithmetic) can prove its own consistency.

How can we apply those results to the human mind?

d. Application to cognitive systems

It is plain that our cognitive system contains *arithmetic*. It is also reasonable to suppose that it is *consistent*, i.e., free of contradictions (because within an inconsistent system one can prove anything, and that does not *seem* to be the case with us). Now, let's assume that our cognitive system may be regarded as a *formal* system (i.e., that it is isomorphic to *some* formal system).

Under those assumptions, our cognitive system can be treated as a Gödel system. Therefore, Gödel's incompleteness theorems apply. What do they say? They say that we cannot *prove* all truths, in particular, that we cannot *prove* that we are consistent. What a pity! But does that mean that epistemology is impossible? Not at all.

α. First of all, although according to Gödel we cannot prove *all* truths, we might be able to prove *most* truths. The truths we are prevented from proving are of a very special kind: They are self-referring.

β. Of course, such self-referring statements are still highly relevant to epistemology. But those which refer to themselves (to their truth, consistency, provability) are not too frequent. Moreover, most of them are either vacuously true ("I'm telling the truth") or meaningless ("I'm lying"). And those which refer to the cognitive system itself, saying something, for instance, about its consistency, are not as restrictive as they seem to be. I cannot prove my consistency, and you cannot prove your consistency; but perhaps I can prove your consistency, or you mine? Although I cannot prove all truths about myself, I might still be able to prove all truths about other, cognitively "lower" systems – computers, animals, children, or myself when I was a child. All this is not excluded by Gödel's results.

γ. In fact, I might "understand" (prove all truths about) *all* other cognitive systems. Or they might understand me. Would that not be an excellent state of affairs? It is not excluded by Gödel's theorems either.

If I can do something you cannot do, am I superior? I can see your face, stand on your shoulders, you can't; am I superior? No, because you, in turn, can do something I cannot do. The situation is perfectly symmetric. It *might* also be symmetric in epistemology.

δ. Even if a cognitive system cannot *prove* all true statements about itself, it might still *find* them, formulate them, discuss them, criticize them, and give intuitive arguments for (or against) them. That is enough for a sound epistemology.

ε. We might also point to the fact that our epistemological research (in a broad sense, including psychology, neurophysiology, etc.) is still far off the limit set by

Gödel's theorems. Although we would not mind having a consistency proof of our thinking, we know too well that, for lack of precision and of scope, we would not have the slightest chance for such a proof, even if Gödel's limitative results were inapplicable or nonexistent. Whether we actually *feel* those limits, is, at any rate, a practical question, not one of principle.

ς. All this is not meant to belittle Gödel's achievements, neither their metamathematical deepness nor their epistemological impact. On the contrary, the incompleteness theorems are of great epistemological relevance. They indicate a fundamental limitation of formal methods. The mind is incapable of formalizing all its mathematical intuitions. If it has succeeded in formalizing some of them, this very fact yields new intuitive knowledge, e.g., about the consistency of this formalism. Gödel himself calls this fact "the incompletability of mathematics". According to Emil Post, this is even a "law of nature concerning the mathematizing power of Homo Sapiens". And Heinrich Scholz sees Gödel's results as "a second *Critique of Pure Reason*". Thus, far from rendering epistemology impossible, Gödel's results are essential *contributions* to epistemology.

η. Cognitive systems might not be formal systems, after all. One might reject our previous assumption for intuitive or for other reasons. Then, one important premise of Gödel's theorems is not satisfied, and we cannot apply them at all. We would have to resort to other arguments. We might think in terms of complexity, claiming that any cognitive system must be more complex than the objects it tries to explain. This argument will be treated in the next section.

A4. "No system can explain itself."

a. The argument from complexity

A favorite argument against the possibility of (parts of) epistemology, especially of self-knowledge, has the following tenor: *Any cognitive system must be more complex than the object it tries to explain.* This argument is intuitively plausible. It does not even seem to need clarification or support by arguments. But is it cogent? We could cast doubt on it by presenting an analogous statement of equal plausibility: *Any system must be more complex than the object it produces.* As everybody knows from school and from daily life, organisms do reproduce themselves, preserving their complexity. And, as will be shown in *C4*, even machines can reproduce themselves. The fact, however, that systems of sufficient complexity can *reproduce* themselves, does not *prove* that they can explain themselves. It should bring home, at least, that the intuitive plausibility of such inability arguments is worth nothing. What we need here are not confessions, but rather precise arguments. Well, what arguments are relevant to the claim that no system can explain itself?

b. Does Gödel help?

Once again, we might be tempted to resort to Gödel's results (cf. *A3c*) or to the undecidability theorems of metalogic. But this will not do. According to Gödel – provided we allow ourselves to be likened to formal systems – we cannot prove our own consistency and some other highly sophisticated self-referring statements. According to other (Church's and Tarski's) theorems, there are more statements we cannot prove or disprove. But does this prevent self-explanation or self-understanding?

To be sure, it would be convenient to have at hand a clear-cut explication of "understanding" and "explanation". But it should be clear that the burden of definition (as well as of proof) lies with the party asserting inabilities.

For centuries, mathematicians had invented and used *algorithms* without having a clear concept of what an algorithm is. As long as any kind of problem seemed to be solvable by some newly invented procedure, there was, in fact, no need to clarify this concept. Yet in our century, the suspicion arose that *some* problems were not amenable to algorithmic solution. Now, in order to show for a certain problem, that it cannot be solved by *any* algorithm, we must know how *all* algorithms work. It became necessary to give a precise definition. This was done by Post, Turing, Church, and others. Only then did it become possible to prove that algorithms are not omnipotent, i.e., to specify problems which cannot be solved algorithmically.

Likewise, the contention that some systems are *not* capable of self-understanding, can be substantiated only by a clear definition of "self-understanding". It should be safe, however, to say that *a proof of self-consistency will not be necessary for self-understanding* (although, of course, consistency is). Moreover, even if we cannot *prove* all true statements, we still might *find* and integrate them in a consistent hypothetico-deductive system.

c. Limits to cognitive systems?

We may even go one step further. *If* we allow ourselves to be regarded as formal systems or, equivalently, as highly complex machines, then we might as well compare ourselves to Turing machines. And here, Turing proved another very important theorem, viz., the existence of a *universal Turing machine*. A universal Turing machine can simulate any other Turing machine. That is, whatever any arbitrary Turing machine can do, whatever problem it can solve, whatever question it can answer, whatever algorithm it realizes – the universal Turing machine can do the same, solve the same problem, answer the same question, realize the same algorithm. That means that all *universal* Turing machines are, in principle, equivalent. Now, if we regard ourselves as formal systems or Turing machines, it will be appropriate to liken us to universal Turing machines. (This might even be too ambitious, as Turing machines may have infinitely many states, whereas we may not. Finite automata are, by the way, much easier to handle and to understand than Turing machines. But we shall disregard that point for now.)

Representing a universal Turing machine, each human cognitive system would be able to achieve everything which *any* universal Turing machine can do. There is, then, no *known* limit to our cognitive capacities for want of complexity, intuition, consciousness, or self-transcendence. Once we *are* universal Turing machines, there is no problem we couldn't solve if any formal system, algorithm, or Turing machine can solve it. *Nor is there any limit to self-understanding of cognitive systems*, which could substantiate the contention in (*a*).

Finally, we might reject the idea of regarding ourselves as (isomorphic to) formal systems. We are not Turing machines, then, the brain is not a biochemical machine, it does not work algorithmically, we cannot apply Gödel's or Turing's or other metamathematical results. What rigorous argument do we have then? For the time being, none. It might well be suspected that there are no rigorous arguments at all. We shall, therefore, feel entitled to take epistemology seriously.

d. *"Objective self-knowledge is impossible."*

This contention is, in a way, inverse to the previous claim (*A4a*), that no system can understand itself. For, it says that it is just the "self" that can know itself. But, although it can know about itself from self-consciousness, it cannot learn about other "selves". Epistemology aims, of course, at intersubjective and, if possible, objective knowledge. But if knowledge of the self, in an *objective* sense, is impossible, then epistemology as an objective science would be impaired. The concept of objective self-knowledge would be self-contradictory, inconsistent, a vicious circle.

This argument was put forth by Kant. He maintained, for instance, that "I cannot obtain the least representation of a thinking being by means of external experience, but solely through self-consciousness."[6] This might have been true in Kant's time. Until recently, knowledge of the self was possible only through introspection. But, in the meantime, we have developed cognitive technologies which free the study of the self from subjectivism.[7] Psychology, neurobiology, artificial intelligence provide insights into the workings of the self. Although this will remain extremely difficult and although we *might* never get the information we want, the study of the self has been objectified.

As an illustration take the localization of the self. For Kant, this question was meaningless.

> For, if I were to visualize the location of my soul, that is, of my absolute self, somewhere in space, then I must perceive myself by just the same sense through which I also perceive the matter surrounding me . . . – Now, the soul can perceive itself only by the inner sense, the body, however, (be it inside or outside) only by outer senses, hence it can, by all means, not determine a place for itself, because in order to do that, it would have to make itself an object of its own outer intuition and to displace itself outside of itself; which is a contradiction. – To ask metaphysics for a solution of the problem concerning the residence of the soul, leads, therefore, to an impossible concept ($\sqrt{-2}$).[8]

Kant's reference to the "impossible" number $\sqrt{-2}$ is quite telling. In his time, "imaginary numbers" still were looked at as meaningless concepts. Of course,

---

6. Immanuel Kant, *Critique of Pure Reason*, 1781, p. A347; see ed. by Norman Kemp Smith (London: Macmillan and Co., Ltd., 1953).

7. This point is quite lucidly made in P. Levinson, "Evolutionary Epistemology Without Limits", in *Knowledge: Creation, Diffusion, Utilization* 3, 1982, pp. 465–502, esp. pp. 487ff.

8. Kant, *Über das Organ der Seele*, p. A86.

there is no real number whose square could be negative. But as was shown by Gauss and others, the concept of "number" may be reasonably extended to include such strange objects. An analogous process had taken place before when, in Plato's time, it was detected that there were quantities (e.g., lengths) which cannot be expressed as *ratios* of integers. That is why they were called "irrational". Later, however, they were quite rationally accepted as "real" numbers. $\sqrt{-2}$ is an impossible concept only under certain preconceptions still held widely in Kant's time, but superseded by wider concepts and new knowledge.

The same is true with the "impossible" concept of a localized soul. We know that the self resides inside the human body. Moreover, we know it to be localized in the brain. There it is restricted to special areas. We have not succeeded in narrowing down this localization further. This might be achieved in a further step. It is also thinkable, however, that consciousness is an integrative phenomenon, covering large areas of the brain, moving back and forth. Be that as it may, the localization of consciousness and self is not a problem that *necessarily* defies all scientific investigation.

e. Conclusion

Epistemology, being metadisciplinary and self-referring, is not an easy task; but it is not impossible either. One serious difficulty is our immense lack of knowledge about ourselves, about our brain, about our mind, about cognition, about knowledge. This problem might be alleviated by future findings of empirical science. But then a new problem arises: How far may epistemology rely on empirical facts? Will an empirically based epistemology not be circular? To this problem we turn next.

B. "Epistemology is Possible, but any Empirically-Oriented Epistemology is Circular."

B1. The argument

Epistemology tries to search both into human knowledge in general and into empirical knowledge in particular and to justify cognitive claims. Now, any justification is as reliable as the premises it uses. If epistemology starts with empirical facts, its outcome has – at best – the reliability of just those empirical findings. Thus, epistemology can justify empirical knowledge just as far as empirical knowledge *is* already justified.

What is worse, empirical knowledge is, in fact, uncertain, hence in *need* of certification. All this implies that an empirically based epistemology cannot do what it sets out to do – it is an impossible enterprise. Trying anyway leads to a vicious circle. It is just that difficulty which shows the fundamental *difference* between empirical science and epistemology proper.

Evolutionary epistemology admittedly is such a discipline. It relies heavily

on empirical facts – on the existence of knowledge, of subjective cognitive structures, of impressions, sensations, perceptions, recollections, thoughts, inferences,
of communication, language, and understanding, on the partial fit between subjective and objective structures, on facts of science in general and of evolution
in particular, on the fact that there are structurally *different* cognitive devices cul-
minating in man's central nervous system.

If the above argument is sound then evolutionary epistemology is a failure,
missing the decisive epistemological point from the very start. It might, at most,
survive as a purely descriptive discipline, as a conglomerate of biological, psychological, and historical fragments, being worth perhaps an entry in the cata-
logue of the sciences, but definitely not ranking as a philosophical discipline. In
a similar vein, other allegedly philosophical but empirically-oriented disciplines,
such as Piaget's genetic epistemology or Chomsky's deep structure grammar, would
be so many phony, just empirical, disciplines, having nothing in common with
epistemology.

The preceding argument is erroneous. This we shall show in three independent steps:

- The premise of the argument as to the goal of epistemology is false. (*B2*)
- The circularity in question is not a *vicious* circle, but rather a virtuous one.
  (*B3*)
- Indeed, it is not a circle at all, but a self-correcting feedback structure. (*B4*)

(The special charge, that evolutionary epistemology, subscribing to hypothetical
realism and asserting a partial congruence between world and knowledge, is circular, will be treated in *C2*.)

B2. The task of epistemology

*a. It is not the goal of epistemology to give absolute justifications for claims to
knowledge or truth.*

This was already made plausible in *A1*. An absolute justification of human
knowledge is *not possible*. Every such attempt to pull ourselves out of the swamp
of uncertainty leads to a threefold impasse, namely

- either in a circle – which is logically faulty,
- or in an infinite regress – which is practically impossible,
- or to an arbitrary suspension of the postulate of justification – which leads
  to dogmatism.

This treble alternative of dead ends was aptly called the "Münchhausen
trilemma" by Hans Albert,[9] after Münchhausen, a (fictive) baron who reported
to have pulled himself out of a swamp by his hair.

---

9. Hans Albert, *Traktat über kritische Vernunft* (Tübingen: J. C. B. Mohr (Paul Siebeck) Verlag,
1968), p. 13; now available in English translation as *Treatise on Critical Reason* (Princeton: Princeton
University Press, 1985).

The trilemma is all-pervasive in justificational contexts. We may spot it in traditional epistemologies (except, of course, skepticism and agnosticism). It obtains for the definition of concepts, for the derivation of statements, for the validation of norms, for the justification of values. Of course, we would not *mind* such an absolute justification of knowledge if it were at hand. But Münchhausen was a notorious liar, and the justification hoped for by traditional epistemology is not possible.

But it is *not necessary* either. What could drive us, anyway, to look for such a justification? It could be, first, our *wish* to have perfect knowledge. But wishes are guaranteed to be fulfilled only in fairytales. So far, no fairy has yielded to our quest for certainty. It could be, second, the pure *existence* of perfect knowledge. If we had such knowledge, true, reliable, universal, objective knowledge, epistemologists might feel the obligation to explain how such is possible. But so far, nobody has exhibited a single piece of perfect knowledge. Thus, there is nothing to explain; the problem simply does not exist.

b. For Kant, the problem did indeed seem to exist.

He had to face a glaring contradiction, which Stegmüller[10] calls "*the paradox of experience*". The following four statements were taken to be true by (pre-critical) Kant:

α. Newton's theory is absolutely true.

This was the unshakable conviction of Kant and most of his contemporaries.

β. A scientific theory is justified as absolutely true if and only if it is either logically derived or empirically verified.

Both rationalists and empiricists had shared this point of view.

γ. Newton's theory cannot be proved by logical means.

That was realized by Kant when he spotted the flaws in Leibniz's and Wolff's rationalistic systems.

δ. Newton's theory cannot be verified empirically.

This Kant had learned from Hume.

These four statements are in mutual contradiction. Kant tried to remove this contradiction by declaring β incomplete: A further chance to justify knowledge should be *synthetic judgments a priori*. They would be true without being analytic or derived from experience. Newton's theory, then, would be true because and as far as it contains synthetic *a priori* principles.

10. W. Stegmüller, "Gedanken über eine mögliche rationale Rekonstruktion von Kants Metaphysik der Erfahrung", Ratio **9**, 1967, pp. 1–30 and **10** (1968), pp. 1–31, esp. p. 22.

Yet the character of those principles is very special. They provide perfect knowledge, but – alas – only of appearances or *phainomena*. What we know through them is just how the world *appears* to us, not how it *is*. But that was our actual concern – knowledge about the real world, knowledge without subjective admixtures, *objective* knowledge. Kant's epistemology gives us absolute knowledge, but knowledge about nothing (real). Must we leave it at that?

There are, of course, deficiencies in Kant's epistemology. We might be tempted to criticize it for different reasons, which will be passed over for now. Defects might be repaired. The decisive point is this: Do we have a better solution? There is no doubt that transcendental philosophy is a possible solution to the paradox of experience. And if statement α is to be kept, i.e., *if* Newton's theory – or, for that matter, any other theory referring to reality – passes for perfect knowledge, Kant's answer *might* even be the only possible one.

But is Newton's theory absolutely true? No! Not only had we to learn that it is fallible, that it *might* be false, we even know that it *is* actually false. It does *not* describe adequately the motion of planets, the expansion of electromagnetic waves, or the running of clocks in gravitational fields, the behavior of collapsed stars, the state and evolution of our universe. Thus, we may as well remove the paradox by skipping statement α or by replacing it with a weaker contention. Then Kant's problem has disappeared; in fact, it didn't exist to start with!

Concerning objectivity, we are much better off, now. Our knowledge – uncertain, imperfect, conjectural, preliminary, fallible as it might be – finally has a *chance*, at least, to be objective, to be true for the real world as it is.

Perfect knowledge about nothing, or imperfect knowledge about the real world – what do we prefer? Of course, there is no choice (Newton's theory *is*, in fact, false); but if there were a choice, would we not choose the second alternative?

c. In short, we must and can do without perfect knowledge.

As was shown in *A1d*, this does not undermine epistemology. Although we cannot get what we might have wanted (perfect knowledge), we are still better off than in the subjectivistic transcendental prison. What, then, is the real task of epistemology? Its task is

- the *explication* of our concepts of knowledge,
- the *analysis* of the presuppositions and consequences of such a commitment,
- the *investigation* of our cognitive abilities,
- the *distinction* of subjective and objective structures, of descriptive and normative concepts, of constitutive and regulative ideas, of factual and conventional elements in knowledge,
- the *elucidation* of the methodological conditions for the rise of knowledge,
- the *specification* of limits to knowledge.

B3. The existence of virtuous circles

Even if the premise of the argument produced in *B1* is false, the conclusion could still be true. And the idea that an empirical orientation makes epistemology circular is, indeed, rather suggestive and very common. (It is also the favorite excuse of traditional philosophers who decline to take evolutionary epistemology seriously.)

But there is no vicious circle here. Having abandoned the idea of perfect knowledge, we no longer mind starting with empirical facts. Even traditional epistemology has to take *some* facts for granted, e.g., the existence of knowledge and the possibility of communicating, of passing on information to other beings. We don't even mind our knowledge being preliminary. On the contrary, epistemologists just *live* on its imperfections.

If there is, indeed, a circle, it is not a vicious circle, not a fatal blind alley, not a sterile trap of self-confirmation. It is rather a *virtuous circle*, a *circulus virtuosus*, a fruitful self-correcting *feedback loop*, a system with *new properties* which none of its parts possessed at the outset, and with effects which neither of its individual elements could have produced. It is worthwhile to study some exemplary cases. (For *a* through *d* some familiarity with formal logic will be helpful.)

a. Recursive definitions:

There are, of course, circular definitions.
Here are some examples:

> A chicken is a chicken. A raven is a bird which is a raven. A boomerang is a tool which, if it is thrown and does not come back, is not a boomerang (von Kutschera). A great truth is a truth, whose opposite is also a great truth (Niels Bohr). Time is what happens if nothing else happens (Feynman).

Such definitions are irreparably defective. But not every definition which at first sight looks circular is really circular. Typical cases are recursive definitions:

> *x* is a *predecessor* of *y* if and only if *x* is a parent of *y* or *x* is a parent of a *predecessor* of *y*.

Similar definitions may be given for "descendant", "successor", "epigone", "copy", "superior", "inferior", "subordinate", "cause", "effect", "smaller", "greater" (for natural numbers). Here, the definiendum occurs in the definiens. This seems to be an exemplary case of a vicious circle. But a recursive definition is sound if in every single case the definiendum can be *eliminated* from the definiens. This is done by tracing back the definitional chain until one hits the basic predicate (parent, child, imitator, immediate cause . . .). For such an eliminative process to be successful, *circles must be excluded* and it must be secured that *an end will be reached* after finitely many steps. These conditions are met in all finite hierarchies (of logic, of genealogy, of competence, etc.). There, recursive definitions are perfectly legitimate.

b. Can we give a definition of "definition"?

Would we not have to know what a definition is *before* we give a definition? Would we not, therefore, need a definition of "definition" before we can give it? *Are we not trapped in a vicious circle?* There is doubtless *some* circularity, but no vicious circle. The definition we are looking for must meet several requirements.

α. It must have the formal properties of a *nominal definition*: It must be a propositional equivalence between definiendum and definiens; the definiendum must be atomic, contain the same variables as the definiens, each of them just once; and it must be new.

β. Moreover, as we already have some idea of what a definition is, our definition must comply with the adequacy conditions of an *explication* (or real definition): It must for instance be precise, neither too narrow nor too wide, fruitful and simple.

γ. Because of its self-reference it must be *consistent*: It must not contradict itself; it must fulfill the requirements it implies; it must have itself the formal properties it imposes on any definition.

A possible solution to this puzzle would be the following definition of "definition": A *definition* is a stipulation (convention) that a certain new symbol has the same meaning as a certain combination of symbols whose meaning is already known. This solution is perfectly self-applicable, but not circular. Definitions and even explications being partly conventional, it is, of course, not the only solution.

Likewise, the following structures are self-referring, but *may* be perfectly consistent:

- a theory which explains the coming into being and development of theories,
- an axiomatized theory of axiomatics,
- an epistemology which includes epistemological theories,
- a methodology which reflects its own methods,
- a historiography which describes its own history,
- a law concerning the acceptance of legal norms,
- "nomic", a game which consists in changing its own rules (cf. *C4d*),
- an advertisement betraying the methods of subliminal advertising,
- a neurophysiologist investigating his own brain.

c. The method Gödel used to prove his incompleteness theorems is an impressive case of useful self-reference.

In dealing with formal systems, we usually distinguish object language from metalanguage. In arithmetic, for instance, to which the following discussion is confined, concepts like "number", "sum", "smaller than", "divides by", "prime number", belong to the object language, whereas "theorem", "derivable", "consistent", "complete", belong to the metalanguage. The distinction is common, clear-cut, and useful. Semantical paradoxes (as "I'm lying") are avoided by such a distinction.

Yet, Gödel invented a method to relate meta-theoretical expressions to numbers, that is, to concepts of the object language. All of a sudden, propositions *on* arithmethic can be translated into propositions on numbers, i.e., into arithmetical statements. This (reversible) translation is called "arithmetization of metamathematics" or "gödelization". It becomes possible for an arithmetical proposition to refer to itself, to "talk" about itself, to assert its own derivability or consistency.

Such a procedure seems to be hopelessly circular. It blurs the clear-cut and intuitively necessary distinction between object and metalanguage. Before Gödel, nobody would have dreamt of such a frivolous construction except in a nightmare.

But Gödel succeeded not only in doing the impossible, but also in preventing inconsistencies and, moreover, in finding and *proving* some of the most important theorems of metamathematics, nay, of human thinking (cf. *A3c*). Gödel's method – instead of being fatal to epistemology – is an outstanding example of a *virtuous circle*.

The same is true of many other important results of metalogic, notably of Church's and Tarski's theorems ("there are no decision procedures for theoremhood or for truth in Gödel systems"). They follow from skillful *self-referential* constructions.

d. It is the idea of critical examination

which had to replace the ideas of cognitive certainty, of perfect knowledge, of absolute foundations. As no logical derivation can be given for our most general principles, theories, norms, etc., we rather have to judge them by their consequences. We cannot prove, but we can invent and check. This method of trial-and-error elimination of bold conjecture and rigorous test, lies also at the heart of critical rationalism[11] (or – more adequately – rational criticism). Of course, we cannot reasonably call in question our premises all at once (cf. *A1c*), but we should be ready to examine *each* of them in due time. In this way, we would be able to criticize them and to replace any of them if necessary. According to critical rationalism, nothing would be exempt from scrutiny and potential rejection, not even the most fundamental principles of logic.

Not even of logic? Well, the intuitionistic discussion about the law of the excluded middle (*tertium non datur*) clearly shows that even parts of logic are open to revision. But the method of trial-and-error elimination *presupposes* itself some modest logical means.[12]

If we stick to the idea of critical examination, then we need the following logical tools:

- We must be able to draw conclusions, to find consequences, to make inferences, to say "if – then", i.e., we need some kind of *implication* or entailment ($\rightarrow$), which is reflexive ($A \rightarrow A$) and transitive (from $A \rightarrow B$ and $B \rightarrow C$ go over to $A \rightarrow C$).
- We further need the traditional *modus* (*ponendo*) *ponens* or *rule of detachment* (from A and $A \rightarrow B$ go over to B).
- We must be able to discuss, to make objections, to say "no", to reject something, i.e., we need some kind of *negation*.
- We need the principle of the *excluded contradiction* (else any proposition would be derivable, which would be irrational).

11. See Gerard Radnitzky, "In Defense of Self-Applicable Critical Rationalism", Chapter 14 of this volume.

12. Hans Lenk, "Philosophische Logikbegründung und rationaler Kritizismus", *Zeitschrift für philosophische Forschung* **24**, 1970, pp. 183–205.

- We need, of course, the traditional *modus (tollendo) tollens* or *rule of contraposition* (from $A \rightarrow B$ and non-B go over to non-A), which allows indirect proofs, reduction to absurdity, rejection of premises on the strength of wrong or unwanted conclusions.

This "logic of consequences with negation" is an *indispensable* part of rational critique. We could not reject it for rational arguments, because *to reject it would mean to apply it*. As tolerance must be intolerant against the enemies of tolerance (if it does not want to tolerate its own extinction), so rational criticism must be dogmatic about the elementary tools of rational critique (lest it should be expelled by dogmatism). That is, if we subscribe to the idea of critical examination, we must also embrace the aforementioned set of logical rules. The idea and the rules of rational critique are constitutively and inseparably coupled to each other. This is a kind of circle, but, as should be clear now, it is a *virtuous circle*, installing rationality and critical examination.

e. How about the "circle of understanding" or "hermeneutic circle"?

Without digging deeper into this problem we may formulate the following alternative: Either there is no *circle* at all, as Stegmüller and even Heidegger have it (then it is quite strange that so many philosophers are so enthusiastic about this nonexisting circle), or there *is* a circle, but we understand each other all the same, and the circle is not a vicious one (as many other thinkers contend).

f. Predictions of voluntary acts

may influence the final choice of the actor. If persons are likely to vote for a candidate who is *expected* to win, we have a "bandwagon" effect (if against, rather an "underdog" effect). If the traffic is predicted to be heavy, people might avoid traveling by car. In all these cases the predictions seem to invalidate themselves. Is it at all possible to make correct predictions if the published prediction changes the outcome? Is this not a vicious circle, a self-refutation by feeding back?

There is, indeed, some kind of circularity involved, but not a vicious circle. If the predictor knows the inclination (probability, propensity) of people to change their mind according to published predictions, he can take that into account.[13]

To be specific, let us suppose that elections are predicted to result in a 70 percent vote for party A and a 30 percent vote for party B. Let the bandwagon-effect be expressed by the percentage equation

$$\text{actual outcome} = 70 + 0.2 \, (\text{predicted outcome} - 50).$$

If the pollster publishes his prediction (70 for A), the actual outcome will be 74, i.e., the prediction will be falsified. If he publishes 74, the actual outcome will be 74.8, etc. Whatever he predicts, he is bound to refute himself. Is he? No, he

---

13. A. I. Goldman, "Actions, Predictions, and Books of Life", *American Philosophical Quarterly* 5, 1968, pp. 135–51, sec. VI.

is not. He need only require that the actual outcome equal the predicted outcome. This additional equation leads to a unique solution:

$$\text{actual outcome} \overset{!}{=} \text{predicted outcome} = 75.$$

Thus, the pollster can predict an outcome of 75 percent for A, knowing that his prediction adds 5 percent to the A-score, and also knowing that (thereby) his prediction will come true.

g. The "bootstrap mechanism"

was introduced into elementary particle physics by the physicist Geoffrey F. Chew.[14] The designation "bootstrap" derives from the expression "to pull oneself up by one's own bootstraps", which means just the same as the Münchhausen trick. In its broadest sense, the bootstrap idea says that nature is as it is because this is the only way for nature to be *consistent* with itself. To describe nature correctly would mean to recognize all its traits as necessary; no arbitrary fundamental constants or laws would be tolerated. Elementary particles would not consist of even smaller particles, but would constitute dynamic structures which owe their *existence* to the same forces by which they *interact* with each other.

A familiar picture, developed by Hideki Yukawa, qualitatively describes a pair of nucleons (protons or neutrons) as being held together by the exchange of mesons. Now, what are mesons? A meson would be, in turn, a bound state of two nucleons, namely just the state it helps to build up. The mass of the meson would then have to be the mass of the two-nucleon system bound by the meson. This chain of inclusions would continue indefinitely: mesons are pairs of nucleons which are pairs of mesons which are pairs of nucleons, etc.

"Particles consist of themselves". If this sounds circular, don't be afraid: It is circular by intention. But, there is no vicious circle involved. Whether nature is indeed "bootstrapped" is not yet clear. In any case, the bootstrap concept is a consistent, sound, and fertile scientific idea.

h. Which was first, hen or egg?

If the hen – from which egg did it crawl? If the egg – by which hen was it laid? This venerable puzzle of evolution or rather of evolutionary theory has been solved only recently. As evolution did not start with birds, it will be legitimate to translate "hen" into "function, represented by proteins", and "egg" into "information, represented by nucleic acids". Which, then, was first, function or information? If function – how was it encoded? If information – how was it decoded and duplicated?

The answer is this. Life started with macromolecules (RNA-molecules) representing, at the same time, *function and information*. Those first self-replicating molecules, which started molecular evolution, were folded chains of nucleotides. Their *information* was the sequence of their elementary building blocks, being

14. G. F. Chew, "'Bootstrap': a Scientific Idea?", *Science* **161**, 1968, pp. 762–65.

duplicated without enzymes, therefore not in need of being decoded. Their *function* was to replicate as fast, as faithfully, and as durably as possible. And because different sequences (i.e., different informations) differ in stability and in replicative speed and precision (i.e., have different functions), those first self-replicative units must have met with different success in multiplication (or with a well-known, though highly misleading, phrase: in the struggle for life). Thus, biological evolution could take off from those first self-replicating systems, leading, in due time and course, to more and more complexity and, finally, to cognitive systems, pondering over this baffling non-vicious circle.

What do we learn from those examples? We learn

- that the world and science are full of circles,
- that not every circle is a vicious circle,
- that, on the contrary, many circles are not only consistent, but also fruitful, productive, constitutive for rational enterprises, in short,
- that *there are virtuous circles*.

The circle supposed to occur in empirically-oriented epistemologies is such a virtuous circle. If there is any circularity at all, it is not a *petitio principii*, because there is no principle to be begged. Evolutionary epistemology is a hypothetico-deductive system which starts from a combination of factual and epistemological premises, trying to draw conclusions, to check them for consistency and for truth, and to correct them if necessary.

It is time by now to look deeper into the structure of this supposed circularity, of this creative feedback loop, of this self-correcting process. On closer inspection, we might find that there is no circle after all. This deserves a new section.

B4. The nature of the supposed circularity

a. The strategy of epistemology

If epistemology is a scientific discipline, it must specify its object, its task, its method. Its object is knowledge; its task is analysis; its method is hypothetico-deductive reasoning. In more detail, epistemology starts with some specific questions, e.g.: What do we know? How do we know? Why do we know? Although these are epistemological problems, we don't need any theory of knowledge to formulate them. This is an important point: We begin right in the midst of everyday situations, usual knowledge, household language, naive questions. To answer our questions, we turn to the object of our investigation, to factual knowledge, be it everyday or scientific. We try to analyze it, to classify, to structure, to systematize, to give definitions, explications, derivations, proofs, to find (at least necessary) criteria of adequacy, of truth, of objectivity, of demarcation, of rationality.

With those epistemological tools – concepts, categories, distinctions, standards, norms – we *turn back* to knowledge, structural, empirical, and epistemological knowledge. Now, we feel qualified to discriminate – naive convictions and proved hypotheses, "hard" facts and "mere" interpretations, descriptions and explanations, observational and theoretical levels, primitive and defined concepts, axioms and theorems, object- and metalanguage, analytic and synthetic statements, extensional and intensional equalities, necessary and sufficient conditions, syntactic, semantic, pragmatic aspects, logical, ontological, epistemological and methodological arguments, heuristic strategies and rational reconstructions, context of discovery and context of justification, intuitive plausibility and logical cogency, prediction and retrodiction, pseudoscience and good science, etc. Thereby we *improve* our knowledge, rendering it more precise, more coherent, more consistent, more systematic, more objective, more reliable.

And with such improved knowledge at our disposal, we *turn back* again to epistemology, reflecting, controlling, criticizing, correcting, sharpening, cleaning, restricting, rejecting. And all that only to *turn back* to perception, experience, science, to all kinds of knowledge including epistemology, testing, modifying, reorganizing . . .

When does this process end? Never. It is a continuous interplay, a perpetual give and take, a never-ending critical co-operation, an endless mutual correction.

This process is not circular. We might rather liken it to a *spiral*. This spiral structure obtains both historically and systematically: New knowledge has necessitated new epistemologies, and new epistemological concepts have helped the advancement and the understanding of scientific theories. Many epistemological systems, meant to be unshakable and final, turned out to mirror the respective knowledge of their times (or, even worse, the nescience of their creators). Cases in question are Francis Bacon, John Locke, René Descartes, David Hume, Immanuel Kant, Hermann von Helmholtz. It would be worthwhile to review the history of science and of philosophy under this *feedback* aspect. We cannot, however, dwell upon this interesting point here.

In order to gain a deeper insight in the spiral structure of many systems *supposed* to be circular, we shall discuss some illustrative examples.

b. Examples

α. How is a hammer made? Usually it is forged with a sledge hammer. And how was the blacksmith's hammer forged? With another hammer! But, then, who made the first hammer? *How can there exist hammers if you need a hammer to hammer a hammer?* Is this a circle? No! Just think of an ever-improving series of hammers, starting with stones (or, for the sake of iron, with cast-iron).

β. How do you make sure that a clock is isochronal, that it specifies equal time-intervals as *equal*? You check with another, preferably better, clock. But who controls the better clock? Who made the best clock, the ultimate isochronometer? A circle? Well, we know that a pendulum swings periodically, isochronously, don't we? How do we know?

The history of science is quite illuminating. The isochrony of any clock depends on some repetitive process – dropping of water, rotation of the earth, swinging of a pendulum. It was Galileo who (in 1581) detected the isochrony of the pendulum. Sitting in the cathedral of Pisa, he observed the lustre hanging from the ceiling and swinging slowly. By comparing with his heartbeat (!), Galileo realized that the period of swinging (of the lustre) was independent of its amplitude. Much later (in 1656) Huygens used this fact to construct reliable clocks, i.e., to keep their pace constant. Still later, clocks were improved by other periodic mechanisms. And today, a doctor uses his watch to measure the pulse of a patient. Use heartbeat to control isochrony, and use isochrony to control heartbeat? A circle?

No, a *sequence of ever-improved chronometers* – heartbeat, pendulum, balance, quartz crystal, molecules, atoms, nuclei . . . And, of course, improved chronometers may be used to detect deficiencies in the supposed isochrony of their predecessors: The heartbeat is known to be irregular, the circular pendulum does *not* swing isochronously (not even Huygens's cycloidal pendulum which does much better), nor do balances or crystals. *Nothing is perfect, but we may improve upon everything.*

γ. *How are temperatures measured?* Usually by the length of a mercury or alcohol column. This works because those substances expand with higher, contract with lower temperatures. The length of the column is measured by comparison with a standard length, represented by a standard object. But how can we have a standard object if objects change their length with temperature? A circle? Yes and no.

Again, we use a procedure of *successive approximations*: Start with marks on a standard stick, use it to produce a scale of temperatures, with its help find a table or function which accounts for the thermal expansion and contraction of your stick, e.g.,

$$L(T) = L(T_0) \cdot [1 + \beta(T - T_0)],$$

by this corrected length scale improve your temperature scale, use the latter to find a better relation between length and temperature, etc. Continue until no significant corrections are left to be made.

The procedure described here is an iterative process of corrections and meta-corrections, a feedback structure which leads (converges) to a point, where length and temperature measurements are consistent with each other. At that stage, which depends on the precision available or required, the procedure stops. Although there is some *apparent* circularity, the actual procedure is, clearly, not circular.

δ. *The "self-consistent field method"* of quantum mechanics, invented by Hartree and Fock in 1930, is a method to find the distribution of electrons in atoms with more than one electron. We start with a special distribution of electrons. This initial estimate is arbitrary (but will be, of course, our best guess). Now, one electron is regarded as moving in the combined field of the atomic nucleus and all *other* electrons, wherefrom its resulting motion (or charge distribution) is computed. This is done for *every* electron. Thus, we get a new (and better) distribution of all electrons. This new information is used again, and for every electron we compute how it would move in the new field, thus getting a new distribution, and so on. This "circular" procedure is repeated until it gives no more correction. The field is then said to be "self-consistent": the electron distribution is such that the field it produces causes precisely this very electronic motion and charge distribution. Although this may sound circular, it is not, of course. It is rather a self-correcting approximative procedure of great value.

ε. Any other iterative process could be called upon. *The approximate procedures of mathematics* are uncountable. Very simple, but still very impressive are the traditional methods to find approximative solutions to equations, notably of higher degree, or – what amounts to the same – zeros of functions. Let us mention "regula falsi" (the rule of the false estimate, used widely in the 16th century) and "Newton's method of approximation", using derivations.

A very useful (viz., elegant) method to compute the square root of a (real) number z to any desired degree of precision, is the iterative ("circular") formula

$$a_{n+1} = \frac{1}{2}\left(a_n + \frac{z}{a_n}\right).$$

We *start* with any positive estimate a_o, compute, in a first step, $a_1 = \frac{1}{2}\left(a_o + \frac{z}{a_o}\right)$, then a_2, a_3, and so on. As an example we produce the successive values of $\sqrt{2}$, starting with $a_o = 1$ as a first guess.

$$a_o = 1$$
$$a_1 = 1.\underline{5}$$
$$a_2 = 1.41\underline{7}$$
$$a_3 = 1.414\underline{22}$$
$$a_4 = 1.414213\underline{5}$$

Here, the last (respectively underlined) digit is not final, but is improved upon by the next step. As can be seen the algorithm yields two more correct decimal places in every step. Thus, it is much faster than the usual "pedestrian" method for the computation of square roots. It is another example of a useful self-correcting feedback structure.

ζ. *The foundations of logic* have intrigued many thinkers since Aristotle. Every attempt to lay down absolute foundations is bound to end up in the Münchhausen trilemma (cf. *B2a*). In the case of logic, the dead end is usually a circle of a very special kind. For, in order to justify rigorously rules of logic, that is, of valid inference, we would have to *derive* them from something else. But any derivation already uses logical rules, hence *presupposes what it is supposed to produce*. This is a *vicious circle*. No absolute justification of logic can exist.

This does not preclude, however, every chance for improvement. It is still possible to search into the structures of logical inference and to lay deeper their *preliminary* foundations. The best illustration for this contention is the history of logic itself.

Since the existence of an argumentative language, people could have verbal disputes on what to do and what to believe. Law-courts served to keep such debates peaceful and orderly. Sophists invented conversational contests, verbal controversies *for their own sake*. (This was a first step to logic.) They liked paradoxes and they might have detected that the validity of arguments may depend both on content and on structure. Aristotle was the first to investigate systematically the structure of *formally* valid inferences (a second step to the foundations). He even devised a logical calculus, a neat *system* of formal inferences, his syllogistics (a third step). During the 19th century, it was detected that Aristotle's analysis of inferential procedures was incomplete. New calculi of logic were devised. Logical inference was *symbolized* (a fourth step). Now, object- and *metalanguage* could be distinguished and questions as to completeness, minimality, consistency, independence, decidability could be asked and answered (a fifth step). In our century, logical inference is mechanized and delegated to *machines* (a sixth step). Alternative inferential systems, even contradicting each other, are formulated, and the question naturally arises which of them is most *adequate*. To answer it, intuition, constructivity, effectiveness, habits of dialogues are invoked (a seventh step).

The history of logic shows that there can be improvement by feedback, even if absolute foundations are impossible. This was seen and stressed already a hundred years ago by the past master of logic, Gottlob Frege:

> It is impossible, they say, to advance science by a *Begriffsschrift* [conceptual symbolism]; for, the invention of the latter already presupposes the perfection of the former. But the same fictitious difficulty arises already in language. The latter is said to have made possible the development of reason; but how could man create language without reason? The appliances of physics serve to investigate the laws of nature; they can be manufactured only by advanced engineering which, in turn, rests on knowledge of the laws of nature. In all cases, the circle is dissolved in the same manner. Progress in physics implies progress in engineering, and the latter helps in building new devices which, in turn, promote physics. The application to our case is evident.[15]

c. Characteristics of a spiral feedback structure

The *common structure* of all these apparent circles should by now be transparent. Actually, it is not a circle but a feedback process. Its development in time might be likened to a spiral. There must be a *starting position* which might be rather arbitrary, just serving as an ignition mechanism and providing the system with a first kick.

Then, there is a *feedback strategy* turning back and back again, an iterative process whose states act back on the system. Whether thereby the system really

---

15. G. Frege, "Über die wissenschaftliche Berechtigung einer Begriffsschrift", *Zeitschrift für Philosophie und philosophische Kritik*, N. F., **81**, 1882, pp. 48–56, esp. p. 55.

changes its state and where it will develop in time, depends on the system itself. In all cases discussed so far the process leads to "improvement"– hammers, time keeping, measurement of length and temperature, electron distributions, solving equations, foundations of logic, development of physics and engineering.

There is, finally, the fact that some systems approach *a final, stable, stationary state*, a fixed point or "point of convergence", where no alteration or improvement is possible any longer. But such a convergence is not an inevitable property of all feedback loops or approximative procedures. The system in question might be unstable, it might explode or collapse, it might waver between different states, it might have several stable states, such that the final state reached depends on the starting point. There might also be evolutionary processes leading to more and more complexity without reaching a final state.

On the other hand, the structure of the system might allow us to *predict* the existence, the multiplicity, the location of such stationary states and the chance to reach them. Because the existence of such states is a *structural* property it is explored by *structural* science, in particular by mathematics. Mathematicians try to specify the conditions of convergence. For such criteria to be applicable to factual science, the systems in question must allow of precise descriptions. Such are, of course, not always at hand. Then, it will be a question of trial and error to check for convergence. And it will be necessary to make such test procedures as *systematic* as possible. One necessary (and *usually* sufficient) criterion of convergence is that subsequent corrections become smaller and smaller.

Whether an iterative process is a convergent one, might be left to subsequent judgment, to trial and error, to success and failure. But to get it started, *initial state and feedback strategy* are indispensable. A good scientist does not keep in mind all minute details, he uses a *strategy* to find them from less specific information. Initial data and search strategy are complementary: If the data are scanty, the strategy must be rich, and vice versa. The extreme cases (only data or only strategy) are viable in principle, but memory- or time-consuming. For efficient problem solving, a combined value ("sum" or "product") of data and strategy has to be minimized. We are touching here on some interesting questions of methodology, which cannot be treated here.

Coming back to epistemology, we see immediately that the interaction between empirical knowledge and theories of knowledge is, so far, not a candidate for a mathematically precise description. We therefore have to rely on trial and error. But even then, it is not a matter of course to compare epistemologies, to specify deviations and to give a quantitative measure thereof.

The idea of convergence is, however, by no means useless. As science seems to converge somehow – claims as to "incompatibility" or "incommensurability" notwithstanding – so the feedback loop between knowledge and theories of knowledge might converge accordingly. The *regulative idea* in this process of epistemological convergence is, of course, *truth*. Although we cannot prove the existence of reality, of objective knowledge, of truth, we still act under the assumption that reality, objective knowledge, and truth exist.

With these assumptions, we are sometimes successful, sometimes not. But why? No subjectivist, no agnosticist, no positivist, no instrumentalist, no conventionalist can *explain* this amazing partial success. The *realist* can: Some theories describe reality, are objective, are true. Therefore, they are successful, others are not. It is this *surplus of explanatory power* which justifies ontological, epistemological, and methodological realism. And if realism is right, then the idea of convergence makes sense in epistemology.

Our knowledge – including our knowledge of knowledge – is supposed to refer to a real world which *includes* knowing subjects. The fact that epistemology is based on (or starts with) empirical knowledge, does not preclude consistency or improvement. We have learned to view this relation as a self-correcting feedback loop which may be hoped to evolve to a stationary state.

But this is also the thesis of evolutionary epistemology. It is, therefore, about time to examine whether this particular theory of knowledge is circular, although – as we have seen – not every epistemology and not even every empirically oriented epistemology is so.

C. "Epistemology Might be Based on Empirical Knowledge, but Evolutionary Epistemology, at Least, is Circular."

C1. "Hypothetical realism is self-refuting."

a. The argument

Evolutionary epistemology is inseparably connected with hypothetical realism. This is a modest form of critical realism.

Its main tenets are: All knowledge is hypothetical, i.e., conjectural, fallible, preliminary. There exists a real world, independent of our consciousness; it is structured, coherent, and quasi-continuous; it is at least partially knowable and explainable by perception, experience, and intersubjective science.

According to this position all knowledge is hypothetical, i.e., uncertain. This claim is itself part of a theory, hence of knowledge. It must, therefore, apply to itself. But this must lead – it is said – to a contradiction. It would be the same kind of inconsistency as in the liar paradox "what I'm saying is false" or as in the phrase "no rule without exceptions". If the latter is a rule – and what else should it be? – it must apply to itself. This means that there must be exceptions to it. There are, then, rules without exceptions. But this evidently contradicts the original contention. It is inconsistent. The same is true for the main tenet of hypothetical realism.

b. This argument is quite common, but nevertheless erroneous.

The phrase "what I'm saying is false" is, of course, *self-contradictory*. For, if it is true, it must be false, *and*, if it is false, this is just what it says, hence it is true. The rule "no rule without exceptions", however, is just *false*. For, if taken to be true, it turns out to be false, whereas from the assumption that it is false, it does *not* follow that it is true. It is therefore simply false. No serious paradox, no antinomy, is involved here.

Now, how about the alleged main thesis of hypothetical realism "all statements are hypothetical" (i.e., either false or, if true, then unprovable)?

This statement is, indeed, false. It is false due to the fact that at least some statements, tautologies in particular, are provable. They are provable if only we accept certain rules of logical inference. And we have shown already that the idea of critical examination is inseparably connected with certain elementary logical rules which we could not give up without abandoning the very idea of rational critique. Thus, our "main thesis" would be false even if we did *not* construct it self-referentially.

Hypothetical realism does not, however, declare *all* statements hypothetical. It rather claims all *synthetic* statements to be hypothetical. This is a *weaker* contention. It doesn't refer to *all*, but rather to all nonanalytic statements, hence to statements which are not just logically true.

Now this statement is itself either analytic or synthetic. If it is analytic, it is not self-applicable because it doesn't say anything about analytic statements. It is, however, not evident whether it is analytic or not. For, not every nonanalytic statement is *necessarily* hypothetical, hence unprovable. Some nonanalytic statements could *possibly* be provable in some way or other, by synthetic a priori principle, for instance, or by induction. Thus, we must consider the possibility that our statement is synthetic.

Let's suppose, then, our statement "all synthetic statements are hypothetical" to be itself synthetic. Then it should be true for itself, hence self-applicable. It then claims to be itself, *qua synthetic*, also hypothetical, that is, false or true-and-unprovable. In particular, it *might* be false: There could exist, as was mentioned above, *provable* synthetic statements. Should they exist, then the main thesis of hypothetical realism would be false. But this does not – despite all self-reference – lead to any contradiction. According to hypothetical realism it is of the very essence of synthetic statements to be possibly false.

Our statement could not be provable, however. For, assuming it to be provable, it would become *false*, hence unprovable again. The assumption that it is *unprovable* does not, on the other hand, lead to a contradiction. For, this is precisely what it asserts for itself.

C2. *"The real world is nothing but the world of our experience."*

a. The argument

Evolutionary epistemology distinguishes between a real world and our knowledge of it, be it innate or acquired, naive or sophisticated. What is more, this knowledge is alleged to be true, to be congruent or correspondent (in part) with the real world. Subjective cognitive structures are claimed to "fit" outside structures, to be "adapted" to them, to "match" with them, to be "isomorphic" to them.

It is said, for instance, that our perceptual apparatus *reconstructs three-dimensional structures* from two-dimensional retinal information (which is true), and then, that outside objects are *really* three-dimensional.

It is said that our cognitive device gives a *causal interpretation* to temporal sequences of events (which is true), and then, that the world is *indeed* causally connected.

It is said that we make intuitively a sharp *distinction between past and future* (which is true), and then, that this distinction is *objective*.

From these (and many other) pretended congruences it is concluded that our cognitive apparatus is quite good in coping with reality (though it might be even better). Finally, these successes (and the failures) of human cognition are *explained* by an adaptive evolutionary process, which in turn is said to have epistemological consequences.

All this – the critical argument continues – is mistaken. How on earth could we know what the world (or nature or reality) is like? This we can never know. What is more, *we cannot even have the slightest idea how the world is in itself*. All we can get to know is how the world *appears* to us, how it *seems* to be, how it *looks* to our cognitive system. The world we see, hear, feel, search into (and destroy), is once and for all determined by the structures of that very cognitive system.

Things are said to be three-dimensional because we construct them that way.

The world is said to be causally connected because we cannot help interpreting sense data causally.

Time is said to be asymmetric because we cannot have any other experience.

Moreover, space and time and causality are structures contributed to knowledge by the cognitive system (or subject). No wonder, then, that we find those congruences between the real world and our knowledge. "The real world" is nothing but our knowledge of it. Thus, it *must* be as we know it; otherwise there is no knowable world at all.

To take the real world and our knowledge of the world apart is misleading. To assert congruences, conformities, isomorphies between world and knowledge is redundant, meaningless, tautological, circular. There is nothing to be explained, neither by evolutionary epistemology nor by any other theory. Thus, the very starting-point of evolutionary epistemology is fallacious, circular, nonexistent.

b. This argument against evolutionary epistemology is erroneous.

It represents, of course, the point of view of transcendental philosophy, of Kant and his followers. In *B2b*, we have shown which problem Kant tried to solve, why he solved it as he did, and why and how we can give a much simpler solution. Of course, much more could be said about the relation of evolutionary epistemology to transcendental philosophy.[16] Here, we shall restrict ourselves to the

16. Vollmer, "Kant and Evolutionary Epistemology", *Proceedings of the 7th International Wittgenstein Symposium*, 1982 (Vienna: Hölder-Pichler-Tempsky Verlag, 1983), pp. 185–97.

supposed circularity concerning the congruence of real world and human knowledge. We shall show that there is no vicious circle, that it makes perfect sense to assert such a congruence, to claim, for instance, physical space to be "really" three-dimensional. How can that be?

Evolutionary epistemology agrees with transcendental philosophy on the existence of *subjective cognitive structures*. They are – as Kant would have it – prior to and constitutive for any individual experience, but they are – contrary to Kant – neither necessary nor universally valid. Moreover, they *apply to perception and everyday experience, but not to theoretical knowledge*. This is a most important point, overlooked by most critics and even adherents of evolutionary epistemology. It will, ultimately, dissolve the ostensible circularity.

This distinction is highly significant. Our forms of intuition and our categories of experience, the qualities of our perceptions, and the basic elements of inference, of classification, of abstraction, are, according to evolutionary epistemology, innate, ontogenetically *a priori* and constitutive for mesocosmic knowledge, but *not for scientific theories*. Perception cannot transcend perception – theoretical knowledge can; everyday knowledge cannot correct everyday knowledge – theoretical knowledge can. In perception and everyday experience, we are bound to and limited by our genetically determined ratiomorphous apparatus – in science, we are (relatively) free.

Kant failed to make this decisive distinction.

> The scope of theoretical knowledge extends no further than the objects of the senses.
>
> – Kant[17]

> Kant wrote his *Critique* in order to establish that the limits of sense experience are the limits of all sound reasoning about the world.
>
> – Popper[18]

His forms of intuition, categories of experience, and general principles of factual knowledge were supposed to apply to everyday experience and also to theoretical knowledge. But, faced with the most successful theories of modern physics, *most of those principles turn out to be false*. For the description of nature we do not use Kant's allegedly "universally and necessarily valid" *a priori* principles. Elementary particles, atoms, molecules, neutron stars, black holes are quite different from all those mesocosmic objects we cope with in perception and everyday knowledge.

However, the theories of modern physics are, of course, *empirical* theories. They refer to the real world, are testable, tested, and confirmed empirically (though not *proved*, as must be stressed again and again). Which shows that we *can* have experiences, observations, measurements, which *contradict* our mesocosmic expectations. Experiences made with household tools (forms of intuition and categories) teach us that microcosm and megacosm teem with structures which contradict those very household tools.

---

17. Kant, *Welches sind die wirklichen Fortschritte, die die Metaphysik seit Leibnitzens und Wolf's Zeiten in Deutschland gemacht hat?* (Königsberg: Goebeels und Unzer, 1804), p. A45.

18. K. R. Popper, *Conjectures and Refutations* (New York: Harper & Row, 1968), pp. 179ff.

c. Take an example, concerning dimensionality.

Let us start with something familiar, the shape of the earth. To anybody (except to astronauts) the earth looks like a flat disk. Thus, for millions of years, it was supposed to be, indeed, a flat disk. But, there are *observations* which suggest that it is actually a sphere: ships sinking below the horizon, the earth's disk-like shadow during moon eclipses, Magellan's tour, etc.

Now, let clever ants inhabit and investigate the surface of the earth. Let them be equipped with a spatial intuition of only two dimensions (which, however, meets all their needs as their world, their mesocosm, is essentially two-dimensional). Naturally, they would think of their world as flat (as even we did). Let some of them develop geometry and survey their habitat with standard sticks and goniometers. They would find the angles of triangles adding up to more than the 180 degrees due in a two-dimensional Euclidean world.

After some time of perplexity and instrument checking, there would come a Copernican mind who would explain these strange results to his fellow-ants by the hypothesis that their world is – contrary to their intuition – three-dimensional, in fact, a sphere. He might even succeed in explaining other strange observations, e.g., an age-old legend, hitherto defamed as a fairy-tale, of a certain *Magellant* who had completely rounded the earth. Although none of these ants could *visualize* a sphere, their scientists could perfectly well cope with its properties, draw testable conclusions, test them, confirm them. Thus, purely two-dimensional observations (measuring of angles, e.g.) would lead to theoretical knowledge which *contradicts* the initial (and final!) intuitions. The situation is seemingly paradoxical, but nevertheless, without contradiction.

It should be clear, then, that *empirical* theories may depart from and even contradict our mesocosmic intuitions, categories, principles. Thus, it makes perfect sense to ask whether the world is as it appears to be on our mesocosmic cognitive level, and to try to find out that empirically. This has been done by scientists for hundreds of years.

d. It is thinkable that our world is actually four-dimensional

(or of even higher dimensionality) and that, mesocosmically, we just get three-dimensional *projections* of four-dimensional objects. It is also thinkable that our mesocosmic experiences could be much better accounted for by the hypothesis of such a four-dimensional world. (Recall the case of the ants!) Many scientists have worked out and tested this hypothesis – it is *wrong*. There is not the slightest hint at a deviant dimensionality, no contradiction in theories presupposing three-dimensional space, no fact which could be explained by four, but not by three dimensions.

It is true, special relativity combines space and time to a space-time continuum of four dimensions. But even there, space remains three-dimensional, time one-dimensional. Space and time are just more narrowly interwoven with each other than classical physics had supposed.

There are even *proofs* that, under very general conditions which are empirically confirmed by nonspatial experiences (e.g., resound-free propagation of waves, closed planetary orbits, possibility of living systems), macroscopic physical space *must* be three-dimensional. Were it not, some things in our world would not be possible or would be quite different from the way they are. Thus, it is perfectly sound to claim dimensional congruence between the structure of the world and its perceptional reconstruction.

It is *thinkable* that our world is *not* causally connected, that only regular temporal successions exist, and that we cannot help giving causal interpretations. Causality, however, is – contrary to Hume and modern empiricism – *more* than regular succession. Whenever we speak reasonably of a causal connection, there is also an energy transfer.[19] No energy transfer – no causality; no cause, no effect. This energy transfer may be *empirically* controlled and confirmed. Thus, whether our intuitive causal interpretation of a specific sequence of events is correct, is a sensible question which can be investigated empirically. And we also know quite well that in some cases our causal perception is erroneous. And still, although we know better rationally, our ratiomorphous apparatus sticks to its wrong causal interpretation. Thus, our causal interpretation of events holds true sometimes, sometimes not. The question, whether it does, is, at any rate, meaningful.

It is *thinkable* that our intuitively safe distinction between past and future has no counterpart in the real world, that it is only our subjective way of experiencing a timeless or time-symmetric world. Still, we could find that out. We are not inevitably committed to time-directed theories. In fact, although all our everyday experiences are impregnated with the arrow of time (few observable processes are reversible, most are dissipative, i.e., entropy-increasing), *all fundamental theories of physics are time-symmetric.* Physics has not found time-asymmetry in the basic regularities of nature, as one would have expected.[20] This surprising and still somewhat mysterious fact shows that, by empirically confirmed theories, we can perfectly well overcome (though not suspend) our intuitive way of seeing the world.

The temporal symmetry of the basic equations of physics does not mean, however, that the world is known to be indeed time-symmetric. It just indicates that the arrow of time might not be due to the laws of nature, but possibly due to the initial conditions of our universe.

Again, it makes perfect sense to claim the distinction between past and future to be objective, i.e., to obtain in the real world, to assert a congruence between subjective cognitive structures and objective structures. This congruence, established by scientific findings, is, by the way, another striking example of a *virtuous circle* (cf.*B3*).

19. Vollmer: "Ein neuer dogmatischer Schlummer? Kausalität trotz Hume und Kant", *Akten des 5. Int. Kant-Kongresses 1981* (Bonn: Grundmann, 1981), pp. 1125–38. See also Chapter 8 of my contribution to the volume edited by Wuketits, cited in note 1.

20. P. C. W. Davies, *Physics of the Time Asymmetry* (Berkeley: University of California Press, 1977).

We start from the observer – a living system – who can make a distinction between future and past, and we end with dissipative structures which contain, as we have seen, a "historical dimension". Therefore we can now recognize ourselves as a kind of evolved form of a dissipative structure and justify in an "objective" way the distinction future-past we had introduced at the start. This circularity implies no vicious circle, as the distinction between future and past, once the concept of dissipative structures is recognized, is much more precise than the initial one which was assumed at the start.[21]

Our last example – the arrow of time, the existence of dissipative structures, the possibility of developmental and evolutionary processes – leads to another building block of evolutionary epistemology, to evolution. Problems of circularity concerning evolution are the subject of the next section.

C3. *"The theory of evolution is circular."*

a. *"The concept of evolution is inconsistent."*

When scientists speak of cosmic, chemical, molecular, biological, cultural evolution, they refer to processes going on in time and ending, as a rule, with systems *other* than they had started with. Thus, the concept of "evolution" is meant to apply to sequences of events where something *new* is coming into being.

Etymologically, however, "to e-volve" means "to roll out, to un-roll, to unwind, to un-fold". But we can unroll only things which are already there. Thus, "evolution" cannot mean what it is intended to mean. Whatever comes up in evolution, must have existed, possibly unseen, somewhere to start with. The same is true of related concepts such as "development" (to de-velop $\underline{\Delta}$ to un-wrap), "emergence" (to e-merge $\underline{\Delta}$ to dip out).

This argument is, of course, a complete failure. The meaning of a concept is given by its definition, by its explication, by its use, by its context, by propositions relating it to other concepts, but never by etymology. The historical origin of a word is interesting in itself and might furnish helpful *heuristic clues* as to its meaning. The appeal, however, to what a word "originally" meant, to "its very essence", or to the "revealing character of language" will never decide on its meaning. There are even words which have changed their meaning to the near opposite.

A very good example of this is found in the word *nice*, which some teachers still tell children really means 'precise' or 'exact' as in *a nice distinction* or *a nice point*. But this, except in these expressions, is what it *used* to mean, not what it means now. The trouble about appealing to older meanings is that there is no obvious time at which we can stop. For if we go back a little further we shall find that *nice* meant 'foolish' or 'simple', not far away in meaning from the Latin *nescius* 'ignorant', from which it is derived. But the Latin word comes from a negative prefix *ne-* and a root which, though it has the meaning 'to know' in Latin, originally meant 'to cut' and is related to *schism* and *shear*. So originally it should

---

21. I. Prigogine, "Time, Irreversibility and Structure", in J. Mehra, ed., *The Physicist's Conception of Nature* (Dordrecht: D. Reidel, 1973), pp. 589f.

have had the meaning 'not cutting' or 'blunt' (almost the opposite of the prescribed meaning of 'precise'). So how far back do we go for an "original" meaning?[22]

Likewise, the word "evolution" means what we make it to mean, and not what Romans might have meant when coining or using it. Nevertheless, we might as well (or even better) designate the rise of new traits, properties, structures, objects, systems, in evolution by *another* word, for instance, by the scholastic term "fulguration", as was proposed by Konrad Lorenz.

Moreover, it is not true that new, "fulgurative" features are impossible. Science deals extensively with such novelties; systems theory tries to understand the specific character of "emergent" properties, and philosophy of science struggles with the related problems of reduction. There are still many intriguing questions to be answered, but none of them roots in the alleged circularity.

b. "Darwinism is tautological."

α. *How far does evolutionary epistemology depend on Darwinism?* There are, of course, many objections to the theory of evolution, notably to Darwin's theory and its modern successors. They will not be treated in this contribution which is restricted to supposed circularities. Be it mentioned, however, that evolutionary epistemology does not depend on every minute *detail* of evolutionary theory. Evolutionary epistemology is, therefore, not refuted if some specific contention of evolutionary theory is falsified. It does depend, however, on some basic evolutionary concepts and principles such as

- the *common origin* of most, if not all, organisms on earth,
- the phylogenetic *relationship of Man* to animal ancestors, especially to primates,
- the (nearly) *invariant reproduction* of organismic systems,
- the *inheritability* of anatomical, physiological, behavioral, and cognitive traits,
- the diversification of organismic types by *mutations,*
- the differential reproduction due to different fitness, called *"natural selection"* (or "survival of the fittest"),
- the ensuing *adaptive* process.

This collection of principles might, indeed, pass for a sketch of Darwinism. Whether there are still other factors ruling evolutionary processes, e.g., gene recombination, fluctuations of population size, annidation, isolation, or what have you, is, though relevant, not decisive for evolutionary epistemology.

Evolutionary epistemology would be at a complete loss, however, if one of the previous characteristics of biological evolution were false. There is, indeed, a serious attack impeaching the concept of Darwinian selection of being *circular.*

β. *The alleged tautology.* According to Darwinism, the reproductive success of a species depends on the *fitness* of its members. In a competitive population

22. F. Palmer, *Grammar* (Penguin, 1971), pp. 23f.

of different individuals, higher fitness entails more food, more space, more partners, more offspring, hence a predominance of the more adapted individual and,
in the long run, an increasing frequency of the respective genotype. This principle of *survival of the fittest* is a cornerstone of evolutionary theory.

Yet, how is fitness defined or tested? How can we measure adaptation? The
only chance is to look for the actual success in reproduction. The individuals or
species with many descendants are the fit ones; others, which did not survive,
must have been unfit. Obviously, the decisive criterion for fitness is survival. The
above principle then only asserts the *survival of the survivor*. The cornerstone of
evolutionary theory degenerates to an empty circularity, to a mere tautology.

γ. *Refutation of the circularity claim.* This attack can be rebutted. It is, in fact,
possible to give a precision definition of "fitness" without resorting to survival
rates. Fitness or degree of adaption or selection value is a specific combination
of three functional parameters:

- *stability* of system,
- *speed* of reproduction (how many descendants in what time?), and
- *quality* (precision, faithfulness, invariance) of reproduction.

How these parameters can be combined to yield a quantitative "value function", was shown by Manfred Eigen in 1971. For self-replicative molecular structures and perhaps for viruses and unicells, this selection value or fitness may even
be measured or theoretically predicted. For higher organisms, such measurements
or predictions will be too difficult for some time to come. However, the decisive
point is not how well fitness can be measured, but whether and how it can be
defined and understood without recourse to the concept of survival. Modern bio-
genetics has finally settled this problem. The supposed circularity or tautology
in the theory of evolution does not exist.

C4. "Evolution cannot lead to more complexity."

a. The argument

Any system must be more complex than the object it produces. If a system
can construct something, it must contain a complete description of the object
to be constructed. It must have, *in addition,* special appliances which interpret
the description and perform the suitable operations. Thus, the producing system
must be more complex than the product. That means that the transition from
producer to product will show some decrease of complexity. Therefore, a
complexity-preserving process of reproduction is not feasible, much less a process showing increasing complexity. A sequence of systems, each of which produces
the next one, must exhibit *continuous degeneration.*

b. The case for reproducing organisms

If there were no organisms (except, of course, some tough philosophers), adherents of circularity would certainly declare self-reproduction impossible. Yet,

there are organisms (and even self-reproducing philosophers). Thus, the question is not whether there can be such systems, but how self-reproduction is possible.

Well, first of all, no organism – and, for that matter, no system at all – *produces* itself. There are only systems which *copy* themselves thereby producing other, though similar or even structurally identical, systems. In "real life", this comes about through an appropriate combination of information and function, the *informational* units coding for the functional ones (DNA for proteins), and the *functional* units managing both the expression and the duplication of the informational units (enzymes "reading" and multiplying DNA-molecules). There is no vicious circle involved. (For the question how this "circular" process might have started, see *B3h.*)

c. The case for reproducing machines

Now, we might try to set aside living systems as being too complex and not understood completely. Maybe we prefer to talk about machines. They are artifacts, and we understand them completely because we design them and construct them. Let machines produce machines which, in turn, produce other machines and so on – will they, at least, follow our conviction that complexity will necessarily decrease? To answer that question, we need a clear concept of what a machine is and what it can do. Such a concept was put at our disposal by Alan Turing. He devised a machine which is simple enough to allow of a rigorous formal description and still complex enough to perform all algorithmic tasks, i.e., to solve all problems which can be solved by *algorithms*. And John von Neumann has shown that such *Turing machines, given a clever program and enough material, can reproduce themselves.* Our conviction as to the impossibility of self-reproducing systems is simply false. As to the problem of complexity, von Neumann comes to a remarkable conclusion:

> "Complication" on its lower levels is probably degenerative, that is, every automaton that can produce other automata will only be able to produce less complicated ones. There is, however, a certain minimum level where this degenerative characteristic ceases to be universal. At this point automata which can reproduce themselves, or even construct higher entities, become possible.[23]

Von Neumann points to the fact that, for reproduction, a certain *minimal complexity* is indispensable. How complex this minimal system must be is not fixed (and not known). It certainly depends on environmental conditions. If they favor reproduction, our system might be relatively simple; if not, it has to rely on its own, must be more autonomous, hence more complex. It is also significant that von Neumann, in giving a formal description of a self-reproducing machine in 1951, distinguishes, for reasons of principle, informational and functional units without knowing, of course, that and how this very bipartition is realized in nature.

23. J. von Neumann, "The General and Logical Theory of Automata", in L. A. Jeffress, ed., *Cerebral Mechanisms in Behavior* (New York: Wiley, 1951). As an introduction, L. S. Penrose, "Self-Reproducing Machines", *Scientific American* **200** (June 1959), pp. 106–14.

The last remark in von Neumann's above quotation hits on the problem of *increasing* complexity. This will be the concern of our last section.

d. The case for increasing complexity

We have seen that complexity may be preserved in reproduction. Our final point will be the question how complexity might even *increase*. This is, of course, the most fascinating aspect of any evolutionary process, be it cosmic, astrophysical, chemical, molecular, biological, cultural, or social.

As for *formal systems*, it might be worthwhile to ponder on a self-developing social game invented recently[24] and called "nomic". The game starts with rules as every game does. But these rules are not fixed once and for all; they may be changed during the game. In fact, *the game consists in alterations of its rules*, in the removal or modification of subsisting rules or the introduction of new ones.

"Nomic" is played clockwise. Every "move" consists in a player's proposal to change the rules. If the proposal is accepted by vote, the player gets "points" on his score. Whoever reaches 100 points first is the winner. The rules have different degrees of mutability. For different changes, different majorities are necessary. But *no rule is completely taboo*. Even the rules and meta-rules mentioned so far might be changed.

"Nomic" is a paradigmatic structure which is able to change or to replace every single trait (i.e., rule) of itself, a perfect example of a self-referring system evolving (possibly) to more and more complexity.

As for *machines*, the problem of a complexity-increasing evolution was also touched on by von Neumann at the end of his aforementioned article. He remarked that arbitrary alterations in the informational unit of his self-reproducing machine could be kept in subsequent generations, being destructive as a rule, but occasionally neutral or even helpful. They would play, then, the role of mutations in the genetic set-up of organisms. Although the fear of super-intelligent machines, envisaged by science fiction authors and by clever journalists, is groundless for centuries to come, there is, *in principle*, no limit to an autonomous evolution of sufficiently complex machines.

As for *organisms*, it is evident from the facts of evolution that an increase of complexity has taken place. The human genome contains about 10 billions of nucleotides, which might be likened to the informational content of a thousand books, about a thousand pages each!

As was mentioned in *b*, the problem for science is not *whether*, but *how* such an increase of information, of order, of complexity, was possible. We are just beginning to understand this process by principles of nonequilibrium thermodynamics. It certainly is not a problem of circularity any longer.

According to a recurrent objection, the second law of thermodynamics, the law of entropy increase, should prevent the rise of structures. This is completely

---

24. See Hofstadter's description of "Nomic" in *Scientific American* **246** (June 1982), pp. 16–25.

mistaken. First, contrary to a popular belief, entropy is not a measure of disorder (such that the inevitable increase of entropy would hinder the rise of order or structure). Second, the law of entropy applies only to *closed* systems, whereas organisms are *open* systems, producing entropy but passing it over to the environment and keeping their own entropy content low. Third, under special conditions (low total energy *and* existence of attractive interactions or confinement by external forces), the increase of entropy in fact *implies an increase of order and structure*. Thus, the law of entropy does not contradict the existence of organisms, but might even help to explain it.

As for *cognitive systems,* there is no reason why – regarding complexity – their case should be different. There are, at present and in history, different cognitive levels, and we might boast a supreme one. Cognitively, we are, indeed, superior to all other systems on earth. Although this is not our merit, but rather a result of evolutionary processes, there is no reason why we should not take advantage of our superiority.

Though superior, our cognitive system is not necessarily final. It arose by evolution and it will evolve further, for better or for worse. It might gain more complexity and power. It is *thinkable* that an improved cognitive system could

- visualize four-dimensional objects (we can't; only three-dimensional projections are amenable to our spatial intuition);
- visualize non-Euclidean structures (we can't; that's why it took an Einstein to devise general relativity);
- visualize the temporal reversal of any process (we can't; just think how difficult it is for us to speak words or sentences backwards or to recognize the retrograde of a melody);
- learn and use fluently all natural languages on Earth (nobody can);
- view arbitrarily (but still finitely) many logical consequences of any statement or set of statements;
- develop an *intuitive* understanding of feedback structures, of cybernetical causality, of exponential growth, of statistical independence.

We could extend this list of fictive improvements at will. But *biological changes are not really relevant*. The pace of evolution is simply too slow to be of actual significance for our present cognitive system. Considerable changes of genetically determined traits take thousands and millions of years. Thus, we should not place our hopes (or fears) on biological evolution. Instead, we should rely on cultural evolution. In fact, it seems that our brains could be used much better. Our brain capacity is wasted, so to speak, most of the time by most people. We can do better. We can use books, computers, artificial memories, rich formal systems, elegant algorithms, strong theories, effective teamwork, etc.

There is *no known limit* to the complexity of the cognitive super-systems we might develop and use in the future. And it is superfluous to point to the fact that we might badly need such powerful cognitive tools.

Conclusion

We set out to investigate alleged circularities in evolutionary epistemology. It turned out that the charges were of a different character. Some of them are directed at evolutionary epistemology itself, others at the use of empirical facts in epistemology, and some even at epistemology in general. All these attacks are unfounded. In most cases, the supposed circular structures proved to be non-vicious, consistent, fertile, self-correcting feedback loops which we termed "virtuous circles".

Problems of circularity were seen and analyzed by philosophers. Many of these problems were declared unsolvable, whereas scientists, motivated by the conviction that nature cannot be circular or self-contradictory, simply solved those problems in a pragmatic way: They developed iterative, recursive, evolutionary procedures. They, in turn, did not realize that they had at hand elegant solutions to some intriguing epistemological puzzles.

This situation might seem curious; but perhaps it is not that strange, after all. The common ground between science and philosophy, their mutual connections and interactions, the flows of information, are still rather scanty. Might this contribution, might the problem of circularity, might evolutionary epistemology help to correct this state of affairs? Science is, after all, philosophy with new means.

Theory of Rationality and Problems of Self Reference

Chapter IX

Theories of Rationality

By W. W. Bartley, III

1. Introduction

The second part of the present volume debates a theory of rationality that I advanced in 1962 in the first edition of *The Retreat to Commitment*, and have developed in numerous publications in subsequent years.[1] My theory attempts to build on, to interpret, to correct, and to generalize Popper's theory of falsifiability. I have at different times named my account "comprehensively critical rationalism" and "pancritical rationalism", and the abbreviations CCR and PCR are also often used in the literature to refer to it.

My account of rationality was developed in order to combat a contention that lies at the heart of all classical dogmatism, fideism, relativism, and scepticism – a claim to the effect that there is an inescapable limit to criticism and thus to rationality, in that argumentation necessarily involves an end-point or presupposition (Wittgenstein called it a "hinge") that must be accepted without evaluation or criticism. I denied the logical necessity of such dogmas; contended that arguments for their inescapability depended on a *fusion* between the idea of justification and the idea of criticism; and introduced the notion of *non*justificational criticism.

One expression that I used to indicate the dispensability of dogma was that everything is open to criticism – including the principle that everything is open to criticism. It is this expression on which the debate presented here is trained.

In a series of three essays, John F. Post argues that my account fails in that my claim that everything is subject to criticism, including this claim itself, leads to semantic paradox – and to uncriticizable statements. Watkins also offers various statements that he alleges to be uncriticizable, although, unlike Post, he does

---

1. *The Retreat to Commitment* (New York: Alfred A. Knopf, Inc., 1962; London: Chatto & Windus, 1964); 2nd ed., revised and enlarged (La Salle and London: Open Court, 1984); "Rationality versus the Theory of Rationality", in Mario Bunge, ed., *The Critical Approach to Science and Philosophy* (New York: The Free Press, 1964); "Theories of Demarcation Between Science and Metaphysics", in I. Lakatos and A. E. Musgrave, eds., *Problems in the Philosophy of Science* (Amsterdam: North-Holland Publishing Company, 1968); "Rationality, Criticism and Logic", *Philosophia* 11, February 1982, pp. 121–221; "Non-Justificationism: Popper *versus* Wittgenstein", in *Epistemology and Philosophy of Science, Proceedings of the 7th International Wittgenstein Symposium* (Vienna: Hölder-Pichler-Tempsky, 1983), pp. 255–61. See also the references and bibliography in the 2nd ed. of *The Retreat to Commitment*, and in Chapter XIII below.

not limit his discussion to semantical paradox. Gerard Radnitzky, on the other hand, defends my account of rationality from the objections of Post and Watkins; and in the final essay, I attempt to rebut Post's and Watkins's arguments.

As indicated in the Introduction to this volume, and as also will be apparent from Gerhard Vollmer's essay, there is a close connection between its first and second parts: Darwinian variation and selection are, as Popper and Campbell have pointed out, *nonjustificational*; and there are parallels, explored in Part I, between evolution – which is a knowledge process – and the growth of human knowledge. In Part II, the question is raised and confronted, whether any nonjustificational theory of criticism and rationality – and thus of the growth of human knowledge – is possible without paradox and contradiction.

In this opening chapter, I attempt to orient the reader to the background of the debate by presenting a very brief statement of my position. For a fuller account, the reader is referred to the greatly enlarged second edition (1984) of *The Retreat to Commitment*.[2]

2. Theories of Rationality: Comprehensive Rationality

Rationality is action and opinion in accordance with reason. What that amounts to is a matter of dispute among rationalists and other philosophers. What I call theory of rationality has grown from this disagreement.

Three such theories can usefully be distinguished. Here I shall call them *comprehensive rationality, limited rationality,* and *pancritical rationality.*

According to the first two of these, rational action and opinion must be justified or given a foundation. From such a perspective, theory of rationality is concerned with how to justify – i.e., verify, confirm, make firmer, strengthen, validate, make certain, show to be certain, make acceptable, probabilify, cause to survive, defend – whatever action or opinion is under consideration.

Comprehensive rationality (or *panrationality*) dominates traditional philosophical approaches, and remains today the most common account of rationality. It is explicitly stated as early as Epictetus (*Discourses*, Chapter 2), and combines two requirements: a rationalist accepts all and only those positions that can be justified by appeal to the rational authority.

But what is the *nature* of this rational authority? Here defenders of comprehensive rationality differ among themselves, their answers falling into two main categories:

1. Intellectualism (or Rationalism), according to which rational authority lies in the Intellect or Reason. A Rationalist justifies his action and opinion by appealing to intellectual intuition or the faculty of reason. This position is associated with the philosophies of Descartes, Spinoza, Leibniz.

2. Empiricism (or Sensationalism), according to which the rational authority

2. *Op. cit.*

lies in sense experience. An empiricist justifies his action and opinion by appealing to sense observation. Associated with this view are the philosophies of Locke, Berkeley, Hume, Mach, Carnap.

All such comprehensive accounts of rationality – or comprehensive justificationism or foundationalism – are widely thought today to have failed. There are a number of reasons for this, of which I shall cite only four:

First, the two main candidate authorities – pure reason and sense observation – are hardly authoritative. Sense observations, for example, are psychologically and physiologically impure, as it were: they are theory-impregnated, subject to error and illusion.

Second, even if such difficulties are overlooked, neither authority is adequate to do what is required. In particular, both are *too narrow and too wide*. Clear and distinct ideas of reason let in too much, are too wide, in the sense that they can justify contradictory conclusions – as Kant showed with his antinomies of pure reason. Sense observation, on the other hand, is logically inadequate to justify scientific laws, causality, memory, and the existence of other people and the external world. In this sense it excludes too much and is too narrow for the purpose in hand.

Third, the two requirements for comprehensive rationality – that *all* and *only* those positions that can be justified by appeal to the rational authority be accepted – are mutually incompatible. Thus if we accept the second we must justify the first. But the first requirement is not justifiable by sense observation, intellectual intuition, or any other rational authority ever proposed. Moreover, any such justification of the practice of accepting the results of argument, even if it could *per impossible* be carried out, would be pointless unless it were already accepted that a justification should be accepted at least here – which may be at issue. So if the first requirement cannot be justified, either theoretically or practically, the second requirement forbids that one hold it. Worse, the second requirement also cannot be justified by appeal to known criteria or authorities. Therefore it appears to assert its own untenability and must, if correct, be rejected.

Fourth, no version of comprehensive rationality can defeat the ancient argument about the limits of rationality that can be traced to Sextus Empiricus and the ancient sceptics, to the effect that there are essential limitations to justification. This argument is a commentary on the fact that any view may be challenged by questions such as "How do you know?", "Give me a reason", or "Prove it!" When such challenges are accepted by citing further reasons that justify those under challenge, these may be questioned in turn. And so on forever. Yet if the burden of justification is perpetually shifted to a higher-order reason or authority, the contention originally questioned is never effectively defended. One may as well never have begun the defense: an infinite regress is created. To justify the original conclusion, one must eventually stop at something not open to question *for which one does not and need not provide justificatory reasons*. Such a thing – e.g., a standard, criterion, authority, basic presupposition, framework, way of life –

would mark the halting point for rational discussion, the limit of rationality.

To sum up these four difficulties in comprehensive rationality: the first two argue that all proposed authorities are, for various reasons, inadequate to their task; the third argues that the position is inconsistent; the fourth, that it demands unlimited justification whereas justification is essentially limited.

3. Limited Rationality

There have been several different sorts of reactions to these difficulties – reactions which can be placed in the category of *limited rationality*. There is little essential difference between these reactions, mainly differences of emphasis.

The first such reaction is frankly irrationalist, or fideist. It joyfully takes any difficulties to mark the breakdown of an over-reaching reason. The fideist makes a claim. I will not call it quite an argument: for the radical fideist is concerned with argument only to the extent that it is an effective weapon against someone, such as a rationalist, who is moved by argument. This claim is simple. Since an eventual halt to rational justification is inevitable and cannot be made with objective and universal reason, it must be made with unreason, subjectively and particularly. Thus the fideist deliberately makes a final, unquestionable subjective commitment to some particular authority or tradition or way of life, or some framework or set of presuppositions. Such a way of life creates and defines itself by reference to the limits of justification accepted within it: by reference to that to which commitment is made or imposed, in regard to which argument is brought to a close.

Although this limit to justification is a limitation to rationality, and although reason is now relativized to it, it remains a *logical* limitation. This point is emphasized, in order to press home the attack on rationalism. For if no one can escape subjective commitment, then no one may be criticized rationally for having made such a commitment, no matter how idiosyncratic. If one *must*, then one *may*: any irrationalist thus has *a rational excuse for subjective irrationalism*. He has a "*tu quoque*" or boomerang argument. To any critic, the irrationalist can reply: "*tu quoque*", reminding him that those whose rationality is similarly limited should not berate others for admitting to the limitation. The limitation is the more telling in being accompanied by the remark that in those things which matter most – one's ultimate standards and principles – reason is incompetent; and that those matters which reason can decide are of comparatively little importance. Kierkegaard, in his *Fear and Trembling*, in his *Johannes Climacus*, or *De Omnibus Dubitandum Est*, is one of many writers who have used such an argument to reach such a conclusion.

The second main sort of reaction to the difficulties of comprehensive rationality does not differ structurally from the one I have just described; and it reaches some of the same conclusions. Yet there is a marked difference of emphasis and mood. It too is often called "fideism", and yet if it is so, it is a fideism "without glee". It is taken up by some, such as Wittgenstein, who, far from having any particular animus against rationality, rather indicate their respect for rational argument by taking the arguments against comprehensive rationality seriously, and by attempting to chart a more adequate, limited – i.e., *non*comprehensive – approach to rationality.

Such a limited view of rationality is common within British philosophy of the analytical sort, and also within American "neo-pragmatism". Taking such a general approach, but differing greatly in their individual emphases and attitudes to rationality, are Sir Alfred Ayer, Robert Nozick, Hilary Putnam, W. V. Quine, Richard Rorty, Morton White, and many others. It is now difficult to find a professional philosopher who does *not* take some such approach, however reluctantly.

Despite differences, virtually all who take this limited approach to rationality nonetheless share at least two assumptions: one about commitment and the limits of justification; the other about description as the only alternative to justification.

First, they accept that grounds or reasons or justifications must be given if something is to be rational, but insist that the standards – criteria, authorities, presuppositions, frameworks, or ways of life – to which appeal is made in such justification cannot and need not be themselves justified, and that a commitment must hence be made to them.

A few examples may be given. In *On Certainty*, Wittgenstein states:

> Must I not begin to trust somewhere? . . . somewhere I must begin with not-doubting; and that is not, so to speak, hasty but excusable: it is part of judging.(150) . . . regarding (something) as absolutely solid is part of our *method* of doubt and enquiry.(151) . . . Doubt itself rests only on what is beyond doubt.(519) . . . The *questions* that we raise and our *doubts* depend on the fact that some propositions are exempt from doubt, are as it were like hinges on which those turn.(341) . . . If I want the door to turn, the hinges must stay put.(343) . . . Whenever we test anything, we are already presupposing something that is not tested.(163) . . . At the foundation of well-founded belief lies belief that is not founded.(253) . . . Giving grounds . . . justifying the evidence, comes to an end; – but the end is not certain propositions' striking us immediately as true, i.e., it is not a kind of *seeing* on our part; it is our acting, which lies at the bottom of the language-game.(204) . . . The language-game is . . . not based on grounds. It is not reasonable (or unreasonable).(559) . . . if the pupil cast doubt on the justification of inductive arguments . . . the teacher would feel that this was only holding them up, that this way the pupil would only get stuck and make no progress. – And he would be right . . . this pupil has not learned to ask questions. He has not learned *the* game that we are trying to teach him.(315)

Wittgenstein's own statements are clear, and to make matters clearer his student Norman Malcolm has explained, in his essay on "The Groundlessness of Belief", that Wittgenstein means that justification occurs *within* a system and that there can be no rational justification of the framework itself. Rather, as Malcolm puts it: "The framework propositions of the system are not put to the test." It is, he maintains, *a conceptual requirement that inquiries stay within boundaries*.[3]

---

3. Norman Malcolm, "The Groundlessness of Belief", in Stuart C. Brown, ed., *Reason and Religion* (Ithaca: Cornell University Press, 1977), pp. 143-57.

Scientific and religious frameworks are said to be on a par here. In line with Wittgenstein's own remarks about the justification of induction, Malcolm states: "the attitude toward induction is belief in the sense of 'religious belief'– that is to say, an acceptance which is not conjecture or surmise and for which there is no reason – it is a groundless acceptance . . . Religion is a form of life . . . Science is another. Neither stands in need of justification, the one no more than the other."

Yet there is a difference between Wittgenstein and the gleeful fideist who glories in the limitations of reason and calls for *deliberate* commitment to the absurdity of one's choice. Malcolm reports that, on the Wittgensteinian view, one does not *decide* to accept framework propositions. Rather, "we are taught, or we absorb, the systems within which we raise doubts . . . We grow into a framework. We don't question it. We accept it trustingly. But this acceptance is not a consequence of reflection." Or as Wittgenstein says: "It is not reasonable (or unreasonable)."

Sir Alfred Ayer takes a similar approach. In *The Problem of Knowledge* (1956), departing from the comprehensive rationality of *Language, Truth and Logic*, he maintains that the standards of rationality enjoy an immunity from any need for justification. It is impossible to judge them to be irrational, he argues, since they set the standards on which any such judgement would have to be based.

There is, however, an obvious objection to what Ayer says. It is true that *if* some particular standards of rationality *are* correct, then there can exist no other correct rational standards which conflict with them. This "if", however, marks a crucial assumption: this is precisely what is at issue. Thus this approach begs the question, is itself a variety of fideism, and hence is no answer to it.

So much for the first assumption made by proponents of "limited rationality". Their second assumption is that the task of the philosopher, once he has seen that any attempt to *justify* standards or frameworks or ways of life must be made in vain, is to *describe* them. That is, the task of the philosopher is the neutral description of all standards and frameworks – a description in terms of which no particular set of standards is given any authority over any other. "Standards", here, taken in the widest sense, include not only the principles of different ideologies, but also those of different academic disciplines, and those of different "ways of life" or "language games".

An obvious difficulty in this approach is that, within it, not only justification is limited: criticism and evaluation are also limited: "the framework propositions are not put to the test"; they are *merely* described.

We have now reviewed in a general way several sorts of comprehensive rationality and several sorts of limited rationality. Most contemporary philosophers assume that there are no other options, and consider none. But in this they err, for there is another option entirely . . .

4. Pancritical Rationality

My own approach differs from the theories of rationality just rehearsed in that it provides a *nonjustificational* account of rationality. In this account, *ratio-*

nality is unlimited with regard to criticism (although there are of course various other limitations to rationality which are not denied[4]).

My approach is based on, interprets, partially corrects, and generalizes Popper's approach. Before stating it briefly, I would like to note briefly the corrections to Popper's position, since otherwise one might become sidetracked in textual exegesis.

In some of Popper's early works, there are occasional passages which might lead one to count him as a limited rationalist, or even as a fideist. These appear in *Die beiden Grundprobleme der Erkenntnistheorie*, in *The Logic of Scientific Discovery*, and also in the first three editions of *The Open Society and Its Enemies*. Thus in *The Open Society* (Chapter 24), Popper urges an "irrational faith in reason" by which we "bind" ourselves to reason. In *The Logic of Scientific Discovery* (Chapter 5), a "decisionism" emerges briefly in his discussion of the acceptance of basic statements; and in *Die beiden Grundprobleme*, a fideism of sorts appears in passing in his remarks about the selection of aims and goals, and in his acceptance of "Kant's idea of the primacy of practical reason".[5]

In my view, these early fideistic remarks are relatively unimportant; they play no really significant role in Popper's early thought and none at all in his later thought, but are superfluous remnants, out of line with the main thrust and intent of his methodology, empty baggage carried over from the dominant tradition. They may be dropped without loss, as Popper himself has done, with considerable improvement in consistency, clarity, and generality in the position as a whole. Thus, in 1960, when I proposed a contrast between justificationist and nonjustificationist theories of criticism as a generalization of his distinction between verification and falsification, he dropped the remaining fideism from his approach, and adopted instead the approach that I am about to describe. Our contrast between justificationist and nonjustificationist accounts was introduced at that time.

The alternative approach, which Popper continues to call "critical rationalism", and which I prefer to call "comprehensively critical" or "pancritical" rationality, is then an attempt to overcome the problem of the limits of rationality by generalizing and correcting Popper's original approach.[6]

Our approach begins by denying both assumptions of limited rationality mentioned above: that is, it denies that justifications must be given for something to be rational; and it does not turn to description when justification proves impossible. Rather, *it abandons all justification whatsoever.* And *it sees criticism, not description, as the alternative to justification.*

While agreeing with proponents of limited rationality that principles and standards of rationality, or frameworks and ways of life, cannot be justified rationally,

---

4. See the Introduction to the 2nd edition of *The Retreat to Commitment* for a statement concerning other limitations on rationality.

5. K. R. Popper, *Die beiden Grundprobleme der Erkenntnistheorie* (Tübingen: J. C. B. Mohr (Paul Siebeck) Verlag, 1979); esp. p. 395; *The Logic of Scientific Discovery* (London: Hutchinson, 1959); *The Open Society and Its Enemies* (London: Routledge & Kegan Paul, Ltd., 1945).

6. See Popper's discussion in *Realism and the Aim of Science* (London: Hutchinson, 1983), Part I, section 2.

we regard this as a triviality rather than as an indication of the limits of rationality. For we contend that nothing at all can be justified rationally. *Not only do we not attempt to justify the standards; we do not attempt to justify anything else in terms of the standards.* We do not think that there is any such thing as "well-founded belief" anywhere in the "system".

Rather, we locate rationality in *criticism*. A rationalist is, for us, one who holds *all* his positions – including standards, goals, decisions, criteria, authorities, and *especially* his own most fundamental framework or way of life – open to criticism. He withholds nothing from examination and review. He does wish, by contrast to Malcolm, to put the framework propositions of the system to the test. We believe that the framework is held rationally to the extent that it is subjected to and survives criticism. Thus we wish to enhance the role of "reflective acceptance" of frameworks, not to deny it. In connection with our examination of frameworks, we have gone so far as to challenge the very existence of inductive reasoning, and obviously neither "believe" in induction nor regard it as immune from criticism. Anyone who will return to reread the final selection from Wittgenstein quoted above will see that we very definitely are, then, from his point of view, "bad pupils".

Some may object to our position that it is simply impossible – not only practically so, as it may well be, but also *logically* impossible. *They will insist that all criticism is in terms of something which must be taken for granted as justified, and which is hence beyond criticism.* They may add that it is a mark of our being bad pupils that we do not understand this.

But we *do* understand it: we understand what the claim means and know that many philosophers make such claims all the time. We also understand something of the historical background of the claim. This claim is itself a "framework" or structural feature. *But we deny it.* We deny that it is correct: we deny that it is logically necessary to trust something – a "hinge" as it were – that is beyond doubt. "Regarding something as absolutely solid" is *not* part of *our* method of doubt and enquiry. Nor do we suppose that something that is not tested must be presupposed whenever a test is made.

For the distinctive character of our position lies in its novel separation of the question of justification from the question of criticism. *Of course* all criticism is "in terms of" something. But this "something" in terms of which the criticizing is done need not be taken for granted as justified or beyond criticism – indeed, it need not be taken for granted at all. One example of such nonjustificational criticism is Popper's account of corroborability. To test a particular theory, one determines what sorts of events would be incompatible with it, and then sets up experimental arrangements to attempt to produce such events. Suppose that the test goes against the theory. What has happened? The theory definitely has been criticized in terms of the test: the theory is now *problematic* in that it is false relative to the test reports; whereas the test reports *may* at the moment be unproblematic. In that case, the theory may be provisionally and conjecturally rejected because it conflicts with something that is unproblematic or less problematic. Does this prove or establish or justify the rejection of the theory?

Not at all. Test reports are hypothetical, criticizable, and revisable – forever – just like everything else. They may *become* problematic: they are themselves open to criticism by the testing of their own consequences.

This *process* of criticism is of course potentially infinite: one can criticize criticisms indefinitely. Rationality is in this sense unlimited. But no infinite *regress* arises since there is no question of proof or justification of anything at all. This approach may produce in one who is unaccustomed to it an uncomfortable feeling of floating, of having no firm foundation. That would be appropriate: for it is floating; it *is* doing without a foundation. But this approach does not produce paradox: nor is floating logically impossible, however difficult it may be in some physical environments. Thus the *tu quoque* argument is defeated: no commitment is necessary; all commitments may be criticized.

In sum, we have separated justification and criticism; whereas in virtually all other philosophical approaches and accounts of rationality, justification and criticism remain fused. The unconscious fusion of justification and criticism that permeates such thought explains why so many philosophers turn, relativistically and sceptically, to *description* of frameworks and standards when justification of them proves impossible. For criticism only appears as an *alternative* to justification after the two notions are separated.

5. The Ecology of Rationality

The new problem of rationality – of criticism and the growth of knowledge – now becomes the problem of the *ecology of rationality*. Instead of positing authorities in terms of which to guarantee and to criticize action and opinion, we aim to construct a philosophical program for fostering creativity and counteracting error. Within such a program, the traditional "How do you know?" question does not legitimately arise. For we do not know. A different question becomes paramount: "How can our lives and institutions be arranged so as to expose our positions, actions, opinions, beliefs, aims, conjectures, decisions, standards, frameworks, ways of life, policies, traditional practices, etc. – whether justifiable or not – to optimum examination, in order to counteract and eliminate as much error as possible?"

Thus a general program is demanded: a program to develop methods and institutions that will contribute to the creation of such an environment. Such methods may be expected to be generally consistent with, but not restricted to or limited to, science.

John Dewey was right to say, in his essay "On the Influence of Darwin on Philosophy", that *The Origin of Species* had introduced a mode of thinking that should transform the logic of knowledge. The basic method of the growth of human knowledge, as suggested in Part I of this volume, is the method of variation and selection found in living organisms: and evolutionary adaptation in organisms is also a knowledge process, a process in which information about the environment is incorporated into the organism. Human knowledge – like other knowledge processes – grows by evolution and adaptation in terms of the method of conjecture (blind unjustified variation) and refutation (selective retention).

Why, it may be asked, have twentieth-century professional philosophers, who have known and often advocated Darwinian theory, not already adopted such an approach? Not for want of trying. The problem is that it is impossible, within a justificationist approach, consistently to work out a truly Darwinian epistemology. There is no counterpart in biology to the "justification" that plays so important a role in Wittgenstein and in almost all other professional philosophical writing. Whereas there is a clear counterpart in biological variation and selection to the nonjustificational criticism just presented. Indeed, the concern for justification is pre-Darwinian and even Lamarckian in character (see Chapter I above).

Thus the question of the justification of action and opinion is as irrelevant as any question about whether a particular mutation is justified (or foresighted, or suitable in advance of natural selection, in the Lamarckian sense). The issue, rather, is of the viability of the mutation – or the proposed action or opinion. The question is resolved through exposing it to the pressures of natural selection – or attempted criticism and refutation. Mere survival in this process does not guarantee the survivor: a species that survives for thousands of years may nonetheless become extinct. Just as a theory that survived for many generations may eventually be refuted – as was Newton's. And a framework for thought – such as the myth of inductive reasoning – may eventually be refuted too.

The Possible Liar

By John F. Post

Consider the sentence P, 'This sentence is possibly false', and assume that P is true or false. The law *ab esse ad posse* yields

(1)   That P is false entails that it is possible that P is false.

Should it be possible that P is false, it would follow that P says what is the case.[1] That a sentence says what is the case entails that it is true. Hence

(2)   That it is possible that P is false entails that P is true.
(3)   That P is true entails that P is not false.
(4)   That P is false entails that P is not false (from 1–3).

If a statement entails its negation, then its negation is necessary. This generalization does not depend on identifying entailment and strict implication (though with its converse it does). In any case it follows from (4) that

(5)   It is necessary that P is not false.
(6)   It is not possible that P is false (from 5).
(7)   P is not false (from 5).
(8)   P is true (from 7: by hypothesis P is true or false).
(9)   It is possible that P is false (from 8 and what P says).

This is the Possible Liar (PL). The contradiction between (6) and (9) represents an antinomy, since the very elementary principles used in the derivation are perfectly sound in contexts which do not involve self-reference.

Modal antinomies of self-reference are not new. The PL is new in combining two things. First, the PL uses a weak modality–merely the *possibility* of falsity. We are not surprised to learn that

(10)   J knows that (10) is false

generates an antinomy, for the modality is strong, being the epistemic analogue

---

This chapter was published in *Nous* **4**, 1970, and is reprinted by permission.

1. A slightly more complex version of the Possible Liar meets an objection some may wish to raise at this point, namely that it is only a contingent fact that P refers to itself, hence only a contingent fact that P says that P is possibly false. The difficulty, should it be taken seriously, would not be substantially reduced merely by replacing 'This sentence' in P with 'P'.

of necessity (given suitable assumptions about how much J knows: cf. Kaplan and Montague [6], especially p. 80 and (1) on p. 87; and Cargile [3]). Similarly we are not surprised to learn that 'This sentence is necessarily false' and 'This sentence is provably false' are antinomous. By comparison the PL comes as a bit of a shock, even at this late date in the history of the antinomies.

Second, the modal term in P behaves as a *connective*, forming sentences by attaching to sentences. The sentence to which 'possibly' (or 'it is possible that . . . ') attaches is

(11)   This sentence is false,

where the subject term of (11) refers to P, *not* to (11). Otherwise attaching 'possibly' to (or inserting it in) (11) in order to form the self-referential P would change the reference of (11)'s subject term. This would impeach the status of 'possibly' in P (and in 1–9) as a standard modal connective, since such connectives do not have this effect on the subject terms of the sentences to which they are attached. P is not about its component sentence (11), but about whatever its component is about, which happens to be P.

In contrast, most of the modal antinomies to be found in the literature involve the modal terms as *predicates*, forming sentences by attaching to sentence *names*. The resulting sentences are about their components, as is

(12)   J knows '(12) is false'.

In addition, the modal predicates are given a syntactical interpretation, usually via provability in some formal system (cf. Montague [8] and Bennett [2]). The modal terms in P and (1)–(9) can be given a semantic interpretation, so that P is fundamentally the same as P°: 'There is a world in which P° is false'.

The literature does contain a sentence in which the modal term seems to behave as a connective and in which the modality is weak, being the epistemic analogue of possibility:

C.   J does not know that C is true.[2]

But it is not clear whether the author of C regards it as antinomous. He remarks only that C 'appears to be true but unknowable by J'. Nevertheless it can be shown that J both knows and does not know that C is true (cf. the Fallible Liar antinomy, below).

The PL is the head of a large family of antinomies, including a Possible Grelling (in which a predicate X is p-heterological iff X is possibly not self-predicable), various Strengthened PL's ('This sentence is possibly either false or neither true nor false', 'This sentence is either possibly false or neither true nor false', etc.), a Possible Russell antinomy (turning on the set of all sets which possibly are not members of themselves), and PL's involving indirect self-reference (though the

2. Cargile, [3]. By substituting the epistemic 'not known by J to be not' for 'possibly' in P one obtains 'This sentence is not known by J to be not false', which is fundamentally the same as C.

absolute notions of possibility and necessity must be systematically replaced by conditional notions).

Non-alethic variants can be obtained by substituting different modalities for 'possibly' in P, provided of course that they obey at least the principles employed in (1)–(9). For example, there is a Temporal Liar ('It is sometimes the case that this sentence is false'), as well as a Fallible Liar ('This sentence is not known by J to be true'; by making some innocuous assumptions about what J does know, it can be shown that he both does and does not know that the sentence is true). In addition, various combinations of the foregoing exist, such as a Strengthened Possible Grelling, a Fallible Grelling, a Strengthened Fallible Grelling (in which X is sf-heterological iff either X is not known to be self-predicable or X is neither truly nor falsely self-predicable), and so on.

Much can be learned from the PL family which cannot be learned from the Classical Liar (CL). Discontent with the language-level approach to the antinomies has stimulated attempts to distinguish proper from improper self-reference in such a way that the antinomies all turn out to involve the latter. Without exception these more discriminating solutions have been designed with the CL in mind, together with its familiar variants (including the Strengthened Liar). It is not at all clear that they can be just as successful in solving every member of the rather large PL family.

Indeed I shall argue elsewhere that however successful they may be in excluding the classical antinomies, the criteria proposed by Robert L. Martin [7] and Fred Sommers [10] for distinguishing between proper and improper self-reference in natural language cannot exclude versions of the PL. Similar difficulties are likely to affect other natural-language solutions. They may also affect certain artificial-language solutions which allow a degree of self-reference, depending on how modal terms are to be added to the language (cf. Fitch [4], especially note 3, and van Fraassen [5]).

Broader philosophical implications of the PL begin to emerge in connection with sentences involving generality of reference, such as

(13) Every sentence which belongs to a certain class C of sentences is possibly false – and (13) is possibly false too. ('Except for sentences outside C, no sentence is necessarily true, not even this one'.)

If C includes '(13) is possibly false', but includes neither 'If (13) is true then (13) is possibly false' nor logicians' hypotheticals like '$\Box A \rightarrow A$', '$\Box A \leftrightarrow -\Diamond -A$' and the Tarski paradigm, then (13) is demonstrably false (this is not to say that (13) is antinomous).

The notion of criticizability can be given an explication which allows an analogous demonstration of the falsity of

(14) Every rational, synthetic sentence is criticizable – and this sentence is criticizable as well.

(14) expresses an important aspect of William Bartley's "Comprehensively Criti-

cal Rationalism" [1], and should be compared with Karl Popper's rationalism: "Nothing is exempt from criticism – not even this principle of the critical method itself" [9]. These and related applications of the Possible Liar will be developed in a subsequent study.

Addendum (1985)

The opening assumption, that P is true or false, later proved dispensable, as seen in my "Presupposition, Bivalence and the Possible Liar", *Philosophia* **8** (1979), pp. 645-50. The implications for van Fraassen's solution were explored in the same paper. The argument about the Martin and Sommers solutions appeared in "Shades of the Liar", *Journal of Philosophical Logic* **2** (1973), pp. 370-86, and in "Shades of Possibility", *Journal of Philosophical Logic* **3** (1974), pp. 155-58. An application to show the shortcomings of solutions along the lines of Ryle and Kneale appeared in "Propositions, Possible Languages and the Liar's Revenge", *British Journal for the Philosophy of Science* **25** (1974), pp. 223-34. The "subsequent study" referred to in the last sentence was "Paradox in Critical Rationalism and Related Theories", *The Philosophical Forum* **3** (1972), pp. 27-61, reprinted here as chapter XI.

References

[1] Bartley, William Warren, III, *The Retreat to Commitment* (New York: Knopf, 1962), especially pp. 141-49 and 169-72.

[2] Bennett, Jonathan, review of papers related to [8], *Journal of Symbolic Logic* **XXX** (1965), pp. 101-102.

[3] Cargile, James, review of [6] and related papers, *Journal of Symbolic Logic* **XXX** (1965), pp. 102-103.

[4] Fitch, Frederick B., "Universal Metalanguages for Philosophy", *Review of Metaphysics* **XVII** (1964), pp. 396-402.

[5] van Fraassen, Bas, "Presupposition, Implication and Self Reference", *Journal of Philosophy* **LXV** (1968), pp. 136-52.

[6] Kaplan, David, and Montague, Richard, "A Paradox Regained", *Notre Dame Journal of Formal Logic* **I** (1960), pp. 79-90.

[7] Martin, Robert L., "Toward a Solution to the Liar Paradox", *Philosophical Review* **LXXVI** (1967), pp. 279-311.

[8] Montague, Richard, "Syntactical Treatments of Modality", *Acta Philosophica Fennica* **XVI** (1963), pp. 153-67.

[9] Popper, Karl, *The Open Society and Its Enemies*, 4th ed., vol. II (New York: Harper Torchbooks, 1962), p. 379.

[10] Sommers, Fred, "On Concepts of Truth in Natural Languages", *Review of Metaphysics* **XXIII** (1969), pp. 259-86.

Paradox in Critical Rationalism and Related Theories[1]

By John F. Post

I. Introduction

"Nothing is exempt from criticism – not even this principle of the critical method itself."[2] Some such principle is implicit in all versions of Critical Rationalism (CR), including those of Sellars, Aune, Popper, Bartley, and many others. The idea is not just that there is nothing we may take on authority, or that there is nothing about which we cannot be mistaken. In addition the rational man should accept nothing which cannot be overthrown by criticism. In some sense all his beliefs must be criticizable in principle.[3]

Criticizability is a weak property, logically speaking – much weaker than falsity, for example. Nevertheless the statement that all rationally acceptable statements are criticizable turns out to be invalid, if it is meant to satisfy its own standard. Since this result seems absurd in light of the standard's logical weakness, but still is provably true, we have what Quine calls a "veridical paradox".[4] While paradoxes of this kind are not antinomies, the present result does owe something to a new antinomy, the Possible Liar ("This very sentence is *possibly* false").[5] But the debt is chiefly a heuristic one.

When confronted with the paradox in CR, some critical rationalists may be tempted to deny that their theory of rationality should literally satisfy its own

This chapter was published in *The Philosophical Forum* 3, 1, 1971, and is reprinted by permission.

1. Supported in part by the National Endowment for the Humanities (Grant H69-I-171), and by the American Council of Learned Societies (GIA-9/69). I am especially indebted to the following for their comments on early drafts: Richard Bernstein, Clement Dore, Carl Hempel, Richard Ketchum, Imre Lakatos, John Pollock, Karl Popper, John Watkins, and David Weissman. Naturally this does not implicate them in the difficulties that remain.
2. Popper (1963), 379. Cf. Popper (1968b), 51, 52, 57, and espec. 122.
3. Cf. Sellars (1963), 106–108, 118, 170; Popper (1968b), 228; and Aune (1967), 124–26.
4. Quine (1966), 5.
5. Presented in Post (1970); cf. espec. 409. Popper (1963), 230, discusses a similar connection between the Classical Liar and *uncritical* rationalism, a theory he rejects.

standard. The antinomies, some may say, show that *no* semantic self-reference should be allowed; and there may be much talk of use-mention, language-levels, and Tarski's theory of truth. Unfortunately, critical rationalists pay an even higher price, in rejecting self-reference for their theories, than do some other philosophers who have made the same move when threatened with self-referential trouble.[6] We shall see in § VIII that this move is *inconsistent* with one of CR's most fundamental principles: the rational man should try to improve on his theories by seeking greater content and criticizability.

Of course there is a widespread feeling that certain philosophical theories about theories should apply to themselves, and that *in spite of the antinomies* it is somehow improper to reject self-reference even if doing so preserves the validity of such a theory. But *no one has ever articulated an adequate rationale for this feeling, or explained exactly why rejecting all self-reference is improper in these circumstances.* In § VIII I attempt to do so. The basis of the approach, ironically, is provided by one of CR's own principles.

The problem of whether one can legitimately construe a philosophical theory self-referentially becomes urgent only when it is clear that the theory *is* in trouble if construed so as to apply to itself. To show that CR is in this kind of trouble, we must first develop a faithful account of CR's principles. I attempt to do so both in § II, which considers, among other things, CR's commitment to analyticity; and in § III, which provides a systematic account of CR's notion of criticizability. So far as I know, *critical rationalists themselves have never attempted such an account of their notion of criticizability* (in contrast to falsifiability, or empirical criticizability, of which it is largely a generalization).

Sections II and III are crucial for assessing the derivation in § IV, where it becomes clear that one of CR's key principles is invalid if it is construed self-referentially, and that another of CR's principles is "self-referentially inconsistent". We shall see in § V that (as CR is currently formulated) the self-referential consistency can be restored only at the expense of the sort of *completeness* rationalists generally expect of their theories. That is, *if the principle is self-referentially consistent, then it is incomplete* (unless we have no good reason to accept it in the first place) – an unexpected analogue of Gödel's famous theorem.

In § VI similar results are seen to affect a number of related theories, such as various forms of pragmatism, certain falsifiability theories of cognitive significance, and indeed a *veri*fiability theory of significance.[7] Each is invalid *even if it happens to satisfy its own standard.* This is a stronger point than that sometimes made in the literature, where it has been argued only that one or another of these theories happens not to satisfy its standard. We shall also find that in spite of themselves, these theories make claims which are synthetic *a priori.*

---

6. Cf. Pap (1949), 341–42; and Richman (1953), who criticizes Pap for making this sort of move.

7. In spite of the important differences between CR and verificationist theories, they have two crucial features in common. Both are committed to analyticity, and both imply principle B, below, or a principle essentially similar to B (cf. § VI).

William Bartley's Comprehensively Critical Rationalism (CCR), which definitely is supposed to satisfy its own standard, is shown in § VII to be invalid. In addition, Bartley's theory, and indeed all current versions of CR, imply *a synthetic statement which can only be justified, never refuted*. Even if these theories were not invalid, the presence of such a claim would come as a shock, in light of their rejection of "justificational" procedures.

Finally, we shall see that *Quine's epistemology survives the sort of self-referential criticism which CR and related theories fail to survive*. His theory survives not because he forswears self-reference, but because he abandons analyticity. This is not to suggest that one should therefore embrace Quine's epistemology. Rejecting analyticity may not be the only way out of the paradox in CR and its relatives. But his theory's survival of at least the present sort of criticism sheds new light on how strategic analyticity is for CR and related theories, even if it happens not to increase the pressure on that already beleaguered notion. More on this in the concluding § IX.

II. Formulating CR

CR is not just a theory about theories. In its typical formulations it is also about attitudes toward theories. To that extent, CR has a psychologistic component. It also has a normative component. For CR would have men behave in certain ways toward their own beliefs and toward those who criticize their beliefs. Neither component is readily accessible to logical treatment of the kind employed in § IV. Nevertheless the psychologistic and normative aspects of CR rest on a claim which can be so treated. Roughly, the claim is that every statement (or system of statements) which represents a theory a rational man is entitled to accept is criticizable and so far has survived criticism.[8]

(i) There is a qualification. Logical truths obviously are rational, yet according to CR, they will not always be criticizable. Various systems and principles of logic may be challenged from time to time, to be sure. But in any context or situation in which some theory Θ is up for revision, certain rules of inference are required in order to draw Θ's implications. Whenever one of the implications is false, Θ is false. This "retransmission of falsity" must be guaranteed to obtain in the context if comparison of Θ's implications with experience is to provide a genuine "test" of Θ. We must suppose that in the context, there is nothing which could count against the rules of inference used to draw Θ's implications.[9] Within

---

8. This expresses a necessary, not a sufficient condition of rational acceptability. Cf. Popper (1968b), 228: "What cannot (at present) in principle be overthrown by criticism is (at present) unworthy of being seriously considered; while what can in principle be overthrown and yet resists all our critical efforts to do so . . . is . . . not unworthy of being seriously considered and perhaps even of being believed – though only tentatively." Cf. Sellars (1963), 170, quoted below; Aune (1967), 126, also quoted below; and Bartley (1962), 146–48: a position may be held rationally *"provided that it can be and is held open to criticism and survives severe testing".* Cf. Agassi, Jarvie, and Settle (1971), 44.

9. Cf. Popper (1968b), 64, 207; Bartley (1962), 169–70; and Bennett (1958), 180–88.

the context they are not criticizable, though in some other context they may themselves come up for revision and be criticizable.

This contextual exemption from criticizability of certain logical truths is an important part of what Sellars means when he says,

> Empirical knowledge, like its sophisticated extension, science, is rational . . . because it is a self-correcting enterprise which can put *any* claim in jeopardy, though not *all* at once.[10]

According to the typical critical rationalist, criticism could not even begin, were certain things not provisionally placed beyond criticizability, including, above all, the rules of inference required in the revisability situation. *CR's notion of what it is to criticize, and therefore its notion of criticizability, both presuppose the analyticity of certain logical principles.*[11]

No doubt other sorts of analytic truths should enjoy this contextual exemption from criticizability. Synonymy relations involving various terms in a theory Θ often are required in order to draw Θ's implications. If these relations could be revised instead of Θ, falsity of Θ's implications would not entail falsity of Θ. In this way a theory could be protected against any refutation, contrary to CR's rejection of content-reducing "conventionalist stratagems".[12]

(ii) Strictly speaking, therefore, the claim on which CR rests is

A. Every rational, non-inferential statement is criticizable and has survived criticism.

X is a *rational* statement iff a rational man is entitled to accept X – iff X is "rationally acceptable" (in context, under suitable interpretation). X is *inferential* in a context K iff X is analytic and X is required in order to draw the implications of a theory Θ which is up for revision in K. Clearly, if X is Θ or some statement equivalent to Θ, then X is automatically non-inferential in K.

CR's principle A entails

B. Every rational, non-inferential statement is criticizable.[13]

B expresses an essential part of what Popper has in mind when he says, elliptically, "Nothing is exempt from criticism". The same is true of Aune, when he says,

> The basic structure of empirical reasoning can be essentially the same *regardless of subject matter.* . . . This mode of reasoning is . . . *maximally critical* because it permits us to challenge any one of our assumptions, though not, of course, *all* of them at any one time.[14]

10. Sellars (1963), 170.
11. This presupposition is perhaps most explicit in Bartley (1962), 166–73; but see his note 8, p. 170.
12. Popper (1968a), 82–84; Popper (1968b), 37; Aune (1967), 52, 62, 125; and Sellars (1963), 317, 319, 329, 331.
13. Cp. the Epimenides Possible Liar: "Every Cretan statement is possibly false," in Post (1970), last two paragraphs.
14. Aune (1967), 126; emphasis added.

In contrast, Quine really means it when he states that *no* statement is immune to revision – not even in those contexts in which the statement is required to draw the implications of a theory which is up for revision.

(iii) Some critical rationalists may wish to construe A and B as exemplifying a kind of analyticity. In doing so they would find themselves in the company of certain logical empiricists who construed their own theory (that all meaningful, synthetic statements are testable) as in some sense analytic.[15] These empiricists did so partly in order to deny that their theory should itself be testable, contrary to their metaphysical and theological opponents, who were quick to argue that it is not.

But even if an empiricist's theory is supposed to be analytic, it still must be rationally assessed. It must be criticizable in terms of its fruitfulness, simplicity, superiority over related theories, compatibility with scientific practice, or whatever. The same is true of the critical rationalist's A and B. If A and B are rational, then they should be criticizable. The only question (which we shall pursue in (v) of § III) is what sort of criticism applies to them if they are analytic. We are *not* assuming that A and B are synthetic when we assume that they should be rational, hence criticizable, according to their own standard.

But we *are* assuming that A and B are non-inferential. Obviously they are. For we are attempting to solve an essential part of the problem of whether A and B should be accepted, given the available evidence, by solving the problem of whether they are theories of rationality which are rational by their own standards. That is, the present context K – the problem-situation of this paper – is one in which A and B are up for revision. Therefore, even if A and B are analytic in some sense – even if, say, they give the term "rational" a necessary part of its meaning – they are non-inferential in the present K.

Synthetic statements, if rational, are criticizable, usually but not always in the sense that we can specify what would make them false (as we shall see). Analytic statements, if rational and non-inferential, are also criticizable – not in the sense that we can specify what would make them false (or not necessarily in that sense), but in the sense that we can specify some way in which they could fail to be fruitful, simple, superior to other theories, or whatever.

Of course analytic statements are not the only ones which are criticizable in the latter sense. Synthetic statements can also be criticized for a failure to be fruitful, simple, or superior, as well as for having a false implication. That is, according to CR, *every rational, non-inferential statement X, whether analytic or synthetic, is criticizable in the broad sense that we can either specify something which would result in X's falsity, or specify some way in which X could fail to be fruitful, simple or whatever.* B expresses this apparently harmless claim.

(iv) Probably A is best regarded as expressing a pair of necessary conditions for rationality. Criticizability and survival of criticism, unless construed *very*

15. Ayer (1959) notes this tendency.

broadly, may not be sufficient. For example, they may fail to capture the idea that the rationality of science consists also in its potential for growth. The preferable theory is the one "which tells us more, which has the greater explanatory and predictive power".[16] In short, some sort of excess criticizability is required. Nevertheless criticizability, without reference to any excess, remains a minimal condition for rationality.[17] This is what B expresses.

It is B which in § IV is proved invalid. Since the proof of B's invalidity nowhere presupposes that B is synthetic, it follows from the proof that B is synthetic after all (or at any rate that it is not analytically true; it might be analytically false, though this seems unlikely). The same is true of A, since it entails B; and in view of B's invalidity, A must also be rejected. That is, A will not have survived the present criticism. A is a self-referential theory which implies that it possesses a certain property – the property of having survived criticism – which A turns out not to possess after all. Such a theory is said to be "self-referentially inconsistent".[18]

If B and therefore A are successfully criticized, then of course they are criticizable. *To that extent* they are rational according to the standard CR presents in B (and in A). To paraphrase Popper, once a theory has been successfully criticized, its rational character is secure and shines without blemish.[19] But having failed to survive the criticism, A and B are not *fully* rational by the standard presented in A. In other words, *A and B are self-referentially consistent with respect to criticizability, whereas A is self-referentially inconsistent with respect to survival of criticism.*

III. Criticizability

Roughly speaking, a statement X is criticizable just in case we can specify what would count against X. More precisely, *X is criticizable just in case X has a potential criticizer.* This section is devoted to explaining what a potential criticizer is.

Even with the explanation, it could happen that the resulting notion of criticizability is not exactly what a given critical rationalist has in mind. But if the notion he does accept is to do the work he expects it to do, then it will fundamentally resemble the one developed here. Since, as we shall see, the proof-techniques of the next section are quite general and flexible, they probably could be adjusted to show that his particular theory (a variation on B) would be invalid if construed

16. Popper (1968b), 217. Cf. Aune (1967), 62: "Any theory that increases the possibility of demonstrating error is far preferable to one that minimizes this possibility."

17. Cf. Lakatos (1968), 377–78. Lakatos's methodology of research programs is not caught in a paradox similar to the one in CR, in view of the irrefutability or uncriticizability of the "core" of a research program (cf. Lakatos (1970), 133). His position represents the improved, self-applicable theory of rationality called for in the last sentence of the present paper, as I hope to argue on another occasion.

18. The term and the concept are from Fitch (1952).

19. Popper (1968b), 240. Cf. Agassi, Jarvie, and Settle (1971), 44–45: "The criticizability of any doctrine is never reinforced better than on the occasion of its refutation."

self-referentially. Hence we may regard the present notion of criticizability, together with the proof it generates, as being applicable to almost any workable variety of CR. That the notion accords with what critical rationalists have typically said about criticizability will become clear as we proceed.

We shall say that a statement S is a *potential criticizer* of X iff (i) we can specify S; (ii) S is open to mutual rational control by critical discussion; (iii) S is consistent; (iv) if X is consistent, X does not imply S, and if X is contingent, X's negation does not imply S; and (v) S implies that X is invalid. In the course of explaining these conditions, we shall also see why each is a necessary component of the notion of criticizability hitherto espoused by CR. The question of whether they are jointly sufficient will be treated below, in (vi) of the present section.

(i) A statement S which (at present) we are unable to specify can (at present) play no role in the rational assessment of X,[20] even if (unbeknownst to us) S satisfies (ii)–(v). Thus suppose someone claims that X is criticizable, on the grounds that there exists a statement which, were we ever to become acquainted with it, would be seen to satisfy (ii)–(v). If no one can say *what* the statement is, then on the available evidence we must conclude that the claim is mistaken – X is (at present) uncriticizable. As Popper says, "criteria of refutation have to be laid down *beforehand*", if a theory is to receive real support from any test or attempted criticism of it.[21]

Therefore if X is to be criticizable, then we must be able to present a syntactically well-formed sentence, together with its semantic interpretation, which expresses a statement satisfying (ii)–(v). Clearly our ability to present such a sentence is a function of our imaginativeness, of our powers of analysis, and of how much scientific and philosophical knowledge or technique we possess. Even in the case of low-level empirical statements, criticizability is a function of the "generally accepted experimental technique of the time". [22] Hence criticizability does not depend solely on the logical form of the theory in question (cf. (iii)–(v)). It depends also on certain material requirements.[23]

20. Cf. Popper (1968b), 228. By the way, the notion of criticizability being developed in this section is a genus of which the three levels of criticizability sketched by Agassi, Jarvie, and Settle (1971) seem to be species.

21. Popper (1968b), 38n; emphasis added. Agassi, Jarvie, and Settle (1971), 46, seem to suggest that a version of CR, namely Bartley's CCR, is such that a counter-statement S need not be specifiable beforehand: "What counts as a criticism and when CCR should be given up cannot be specified in advance. . . . This however does not jeopardize Bartley's argument." If they mean that a *potential* criticizer need not be specified, then their view (or Bartley's, *if* they interpret him correctly here) is very much at odds with the spirit of CR, as Popper's remark indicates (in any case, see the last four sentences of (ii) in § IV, below). But if they mean that having specified a potential criticizer S, we cannot or need not specify circumstances in which we would actually have to accept S, or view it as a *successful* criticism and give up CCR, then what they mean is entirely compatible with the present view of criticizability. Indeed a successful criticism often counts as such *only in retrospect*, in light of a *better* theory (cf. Lakatos (1970), 116–22). This is another reason why the availability of Lakatos's improvement over CR is so strategic (cf. note 17, above).

22. Lakatos (1968), 377–78.

23. Popper (1968a), 102, makes this distinction between formal and material requirements. Cf. Popper (1968b), 242.

(ii) One of the latter seems to be that a potential criticizer must itself be intersubjectively criticizable, in the sense that it is open to "mutual rational control by critical discussion."[24] According to CR, "intersubjective testing is merely a very important aspect of the more general idea of intersubjective criticism".[25] Empirical basic statements which count as potential falsifiers must themselves be "testable, intersubjectively, by 'observation'".[26] Hence it seems reasonable to require that a statement's potential criticizers be intersubjectively criticizable by whatever means are appropriate – by observation if they are empirical, by something else if they are not. Potential criticizers should be rationally controllable by critical means that are a function of the kind of statement they are.

(iii) A statement S is *consistent* iff for no Y does S imply Y & −Y. Obviously a potential criticizer must be consistent. Otherwise *any* contingent statement X would be criticizable, and trivially so (where X is *contingent* iff X is neither inconsistent nor analytic). For we could immediately specify a simple contradiction S* (cf. (i)); and if X is contingent, then neither X nor its negation implies S* (cf. (iv)). Condition (v) would hold because a contradiction implies everything;[27] and (ii) would hold because we could show that S* is contradictory simply by analyzing its logical form. Hence without (iii), S* would be a potential criticizer of X. Of course there are other reasons why (iii) should be required, but this one is as telling as any.

(iv) Suppose that X is *inconsistent*. Then X implies everything. If *no* statement were allowed to imply one of its potential criticizers S, then X would have no potential criticizers – X would be uncriticizable. Since an inconsistent statement ought to be criticizable (even if one chooses not to let it be falsifiable), such a statement is allowed to imply S.

Suppose that X is *consistent* and that X does imply one of its potential criticizers S, contrary to the first clause of condition (iv). Suppose further that we "test" X or attempt to overthrow it by trying to establish S, in the sense of seeking considerations which warrant the provisional acceptance of S. If the outcome of such testing or discussion is a decision to *reject* S, then of course we would have to reject X. But this is the opposite of what we want. For if X's potential criticizer S is rejected, then X has survived the test – to some extent, X has been "corroborated" (at least if the test is severe).[28] *Therefore a consistent X should not be allowed to imply S.*

Suppose that X is contingent and that X's negation implies S, contrary to the second clause of (iv). Suppose also that the outcome of a test is a provisional decision to reject S – that is, to call S invalid. Then we would have to call −X invalid. Most contingent theories X are such that if −X is invalid, then X is true (cf. (v), below). Given such a theory, if we rejected S we would have to call X true. But this means that X's survival of the test *verifies* X. This too is the opposite of what we want.

24. Popper (1968a), 44n*1. Cf. Popper (1963), 226.
25. Popper (1968a), 44n*1. Cf. Popper (1968b), 152, and Popper (1963), 217–18.
26. Popper (1968a), 102.
27. Cf. Popper (1943); and Popper (1968a), 91n*2.
28. Cf. Lakatos (1968), 378–82, espec. 380.

Furthermore, if $-X$ were allowed to imply S, *any* contingent X would be automatically criticizable. For given any such X, we could immediately specify a consistent S which implies X's invalidity and which is not implied by X: simply let S be $-X$ or some statement equivalent to $-X$. Unless condition (ii) is construed *very* narrowly, the resulting S would be rationally controllable by *some* sort of critical discussion. Hence if we were to allow $-X$ to imply S, S would be a potential criticizer of X, and trivially so. *Therefore X's negation should not be allowed to imply S, if X is contingent.* It follows from this and the first clause of (iv) that *if X is contingent, then neither X nor $-X$ implies S.*

The reason why X's negation should be allowed to imply S when X is *analytic* is twofold. First, as seen in § II(iii), we want at least some analytic statements to be criticizable (when they are non-inferential). Hence such statements must have potential criticizers. Second, if X is analytic, then $-X$ is inconsistent and implies any statement whatever. Thus if $-X$ were not allowed to imply S, X could have no potential criticizers, contrary to our intent.

(v) Given two statements X and Y, X *implies* Y iff whenever X is true, Y is true (i.e., Y is true in any circumstance or state of affairs in which X is true).[29] Hence S implies X's invalidity iff whenever S is true X is invalid. *Invalidity, however, does not always amount to falsity, nor validity to truth.* Let us see why.

Successful criticism of a theory X may or may not result in the assignment of falsity to X, even if the assignment is highly tentative. That depends on what kind of theory X is and on what kind of consideration is brought against it. Concerning *philosophical* theories, Popper says,

> If we look upon a theory as a proposed solution to a set of problems, then the theory immediately lends itself to critical discussion. . . . For we can now ask questions such as, Does it solve the problem? Does it solve it better than other theories? Has it perhaps merely shifted the problem? Is the solution simple? Is it fruitful? Does it perhaps contradict other philosophical theories needed for solving other problems?[30]

If a theory X shifts the problem, thus failing to be relevant, it does not follow that X should be assigned falsity. In the context of the problem, the question of whether X is true or false simply does not arise. Indeed the question of whether X is valid or invalid in *any* sense does not arise.

Can we say that *if* X is relevant to some problem we are trying to solve, *then* successful criticism of X should result in assigning falsity to X? Not in general. To be sure, more than relevance is required of a rational theory, if relevance means having the syntactical form and semantical significance of an answer to the question which expresses the problem. For there will always be other theories which, in this sense, are relevant to the problem. If we can specify what would count against such a theory X* but are unable to do so for X, then clearly X* is to be

---

29. That is, X *necessitates* Y in the sense of van Fraassen (1968), 138. As to states of affairs, we assume that if P entails Q and P holds in a state of affairs α, then Q holds in α.

30. Popper (1968b), 199. I have benefitted greatly from discussion with Professor John Watkins both on the issue of whether successful criticism always results in the assignment of falsity, and on other aspects of the paper.

preferred. We would at least know how to go about testing or attempting to overthrow X*. It follows that *if X satisfies the check of relevance, then we must still be able to specify considerations which imply X's invalidity.* But it does not follow that they should imply X's falsity.

For suppose X is a philosophical theory which is to be construed as a methodological rule, or perhaps as a convention, proposal, or recommendation. Such theories are commonly taken to be neither true nor false. Provided X is relevant to some chosen problem, we must be able to specify some way in which X could fail to be fruitful, simple, consistent, consistent with other rules we accept, or whatever. A decided failure of this sort would require us to reject X as being *unsound*, especially if there is a viable alternative to X.

But we would not necessarily assign falsity to X. We might assign falsity to X if we held the view that successful criticism of a rule or proposal converts it into a synthetic theory with a truth value. But suppose we held the view that a rule-like X is just not the *sort* of thing which could *ever* have a truth value. In this case, successful criticism of X could not result even in the tentative assignment of falsity to X. Instead we would simply *cease to be guided* by the rule or convention X represents, calling X unsound.

Similarly, suppose X is a philosophical theory which in some sense is analytic. As seen, logical empiricists have occasionally construed their own theory as exemplifying a kind of analyticity. Granting their own theory's relevance, we still must be able to specify some way in which it could fail to be simple, fruitful, superior to other theories, or compatible with scientific practice. Should the theory fail in some such respect, we would reject it as unsound, especially if an alternative theory existed.

But again we would not necessarily assign falsity to X. We might do so if we held the view that successful criticism of an analytic theory converts it into a synthetic one. But if we held the view that X is analytic in some unconditional sense, then rejection of X would not consist in assigning it falsity even tentatively. Instead we would simply cease to use X to illuminate problems in science, epistemology, or whatever. X would be unsound, but not false.

The critical rationalist presumably wants to apply his notion of criticizability to philosophical theories even if they are construed as methodological rules or as in some sense analytic. Indeed *some critical rationalists may construe CR's key principles A and B as themselves rule-like*[31] *or analytic.* Consequently we shall retain the broader notion of criticizability, whereby successful criticism need not result even in the tentative assignment of falsity.

Instead we shall say that *successful criticism always results in the tentative assignment of invalidity*, where a statement X is *invalid* iff X is neither true nor sound. That is, X is *valid* iff X is true or sound. If X is sound, then it need not be true, since X might be neither true nor false. If X is true, then it need not be sound,

---

31. Popper probably would do so, since he construes the principles of rational method in science as rules, or "proposals for an agreement". Cf. Popper (1968a), 37–38, 53.

since X could be true yet fail to be simple, fruitful, superior to another theory, or whatever. It follows that X could be unsound without being false. If X is false, then it need not be unsound, since X could be false and yet be simple, fruitful, or superior to other available theories. But we shall say that *if X is inconsistent, then it is always unsound, hence always invalid.* If X is sound, then −X is unsound, but the converse does not hold in general. For *both* X and −X might fail to be simple, fruitful, superior to some other theory, or whatever. Similarly, if X is valid, then −X is invalid, but not, in general, conversely.

No matter how invalidity is construed, CR requires a generalized analogue of its principle of the retransmission of falsity. The appropriate generalization is that if X implies Y, and Y is invalid, then X is invalid (provided X and Y are both relevant to the problem we are trying to solve in a given context). Let us call this the principle of the *retransmission of invalidity*.[32] It follows at once that if X implies Y, and S implies that Y is not valid, then S implies that X is not valid (again, provided that X and Y are both relevant in the problem situation).

(vi) In summary, then, provided X is relevant to a given problem, X is criticizable just in case we can specify a rationally controllable, consistent statement S such that neither X nor −X implies S if X is contingent, X does not imply S if X is consistent, and S implies X's invalidity.

While conditions (i)–(v) are *necessary*, they may not be quite *sufficient* for S to count as a potential criticizer of X. For example, let S* be 'P knows that −X', where P is any person, X is any synthetic statement, and the concept of knowledge involved is that of justified true belief.[33] Obviously we would not want S* to count as a potential criticizer of X, yet S* may be one by (i)–(v). Clearly S* is specifiable, consistent (since −X is, because X is synthetic), implied by neither X nor −X, and implies X's invalidity. If in addition S* is rationally controllable, as it seems to be, then automatically *any* synthetic X is criticizable, since for any such X we could specify a corresponding S*.

The critical rationalist could add a clause to (i)–(v), to the effect that a potential criticizer S cannot be "trivially stronger" than X's negation (or trivially imply X's invalidity), or to the effect that S is "better corroborated" in the context than X. Granted a suitable explication of "trivially stronger" or of "better corroborated" (which is to grant a lot), S* and related statements involving strong modalities could be excluded. Some such clause may be needed in any case, to exclude a variety of non-modal examples omitted here.

Whether (i)–(v) are sufficient to exclude S* and other degenerate examples is the *critical rationalist's* problem. For it is *he* who owes us an explication of criticizability (in contrast to falsifiability, explications of which he has presented in the literature). In presenting (i)–(v) I have merely done his work for him, or as much as seems practical, given the circumstances. The problem of the sufficiency of

---

32. In the present paper, since X might be neither true nor false, retransmission of falsity will not always hold. Cf. van Fraassen (1968), 137–38.
33. The example is due to Professor Clement J. Dore.

these conditions becomes *mine* only to the extent that contemplated changes in them might affect the derivation in the next section. There it will be clear that at least the clauses just contemplated for handling degenerate examples have no effect on the derivation.

One test of the adequacy of conditions (i)–(v) is the fact that according to them, every falsifiable theory is criticizable. In the case of such a theory X (which is neither analytic nor truth-valueless), the appropriate counter-statements are simply X's potential falsifiers. These are consistent, specifiable statements not implied by X.[34] They imply X's falsity and are rationally controllable by intersubjective testing based on observation. In addition they are not implied by –X. For they are themselves falsifiable, whereas –X is an unfalsifiable, strictly existential statement, being the negation of one which is strictly universal.[35]

Other species of criticizability can be isolated by imposing other, nonempirical conditions on what is to count as a potential criticizer.[36] Conditions (i)–(v) express what is common to all these kinds of criticizability. The critical rationalist's principles A and B must be criticizable in the sense of (i)–(v), if they are to be rational according to their own standard.

IV. Proof

Let 'PSX' stand for 'S is a potential criticizer of X'. That is, PSX iff S satisfies conditions (i)–(v) of § III (provided X is relevant to some problem we are trying to solve). Thus X is criticizable just in case $(\exists S)PSX$. Let 'RX' stand for 'X is rational and non-inferential in the present problem-context K' (cf. § II(ii)). In this notation, CR's principle B – the statement that every rational, non-inferential statement is criticizable – is the same as

B. $(X)(RX \rightarrow (\exists S)PSX)$,

where the variables range over statements.

As seen in § II, B is supposed to be criticizable itself, whether or not it is analytic. Thus the critical rationalist is claiming

C. $(\exists S)PSB$.

As Popper says, "Everything is open to criticism (from which this principle itself is not exempt)."[37] The parenthetical statement is essentially C (or essentially implies C).

34. Cf. Popper (1968a), 100–101.
35. Cf. Popper (1968a), 68–69, 101–102.
36. Lakatos (1967), 199–202, raises the issue of what sorts of conditions are to be imposed in connection with mathematical criticizability.
37. Popper (1963), 378. In effect Aune (1967), 126, is asserting C when he says that his proposed mode of reasoning is a "rational mode of reasoning because it is . . . maximally critical", since what is proposed is to maximize criticizability.

The proof depends primarily on two premises, which will be established in due course. Provided B and C are consistent,

(1) (S)(PSC→PSB)

(2) (S)(PSB→−PSC)

That is, if B and C are consistent, then (1) every potential criticizer of C is a potential criticizer of B, and (2) no criticizer of B is a criticizer of C. From (1) and (2) we have immediately

(3) −(∃S)PSC,

which is to say that C is not criticizable.

Presumably the critical rationalist wants his statements about his theory of rationality to be rational themselves. Thus we may assume that C is rational. But C is also non-inferential, as we shall see. So C is rational and non-inferential, which is to say that RC. Together with (3) this yields

(4) RC & −(∃S)PSC

(5) (∃X)(RX & −(∃S)PSX)   (from 4)

(6) −(X)(RX→(∃S)(PSX).   (from 5)

Line (6) shows that B's negation is valid. *Therefore B is invalid* – provided that B is consistent and that C is consistent and rational. Clearly these provisos are accepted by CR.

(i) We begin the argument for premise (1) by recalling one of the problems CR and its principle B are meant to solve. This is the problem of finding a theory of rationality which itself is rational. Within this problem-context K, B is supposed to be rational and is up for revision. If X is up for revision in K, then automatically X is non-inferential in K (cf. § II(ii)). Thus given that we are operating within K, we may assume that B is rational and non-inferential – i.e., that RB.

Clearly B does not *entail* C. But given that we are operating within K, or given that RB, B implies C.[38] In other words, given that we are in K, or given that RB, whenever B is true, C is true (cf. § III(v)). It follows that so long as we are operating within K, *C's invalidity implies B's invalidity.*

This is only to be expected. Given that we are trying to find a theory of rationality which itself is rational, failure of such a theory to satisfy its own standard of rationality constitutes a damaging criticism of it. Considerations which count against the claim that the theory satisfies its standard count against the theory. Hence for any statement S, if S implies C's invalidity, then S implies B's invalidity. Retransmission of invalidity from C to B holds in K.

Now suppose that PSC, and that C is consistent. In (iii) below we shall see that C is not analytic. Thus, assuming that C is consistent, C is contingent. By

---

38. Cf. the notion of "conditional necessity" in von Wright (1957), 89–126; and Rescher (1968), 26–28. Thus 'B→C' is necessary given that we are in K, or given that RB.

conditions (i)–(v) of § III, it follows that S is a specifiable, rationally controllable, consistent statement such that neither C nor −C implies S, and S implies C's invalidity. Hence S automatically satisfies conditions (i)–(iii). As seen, any S which implies C's invalidity implies B's invalidity. Therefore S also satisfies condition (v) for B. What about condition (iv)?

Suppose that B is consistent and that B does imply S, contrary to the first clause of (iv). Since by hypothesis S implies C's invalidity, it would follow that B implies C's invalidity. That is, whenever B is true, C is neither true nor sound. But because B implies C (given that we are in K), whenever B is true, C is true. If B is consistent, it could never happen that B is true and C both true and not true. Therefore if B is consistent, then B does *not* imply S (where PSC).

In showing that the second clause of condition (iv) holds for B we must be careful not to presuppose that B is contingent, since some critical rationalists might claim that B exemplifies a kind of analyticity. Instead we must show only that *if* B is contingent, *then* −B does not imply S (where PSC).

Suppose, contrary to the second clause of (iv), that B is contingent and that −B does imply S. Since S implies C's invalidity (because by hypothesis, PSC), it would follow that −B implies C's invalidity. But if X implies Y, then X's validity implies Y's validity: there is no retransmission of invalidity without transmission of validity. Hence the validity of −B would imply the validity of C's invalidity, which is to say that whenever −B is valid, 'C is invalid' is valid.

However, the latter implication does not hold, if B is contingent. In that case, it is logically possible for −B to be valid when 'C is invalid' is invalid. That is, there is a (conceivable) circumstance or state of affairs α in which −B is valid and 'C is invalid' is not. (If B were analytic, −B would be inconsistent, and no such α would exist.) Let α be a state in which −B is valid and in which this has been established in the course of testing or criticizing B. In particular, let α be a state in which −B is valid, and in which we have correctly established that some statement S* is one of B's potential criticizers, where S* implies that −B is valid (hence that B is invalid). Thus in α, −B is valid, PS*B, and S* implies −B.

But 'PS*B' entails '(∃S)PSB', so in α, −B is valid and (∃S)PSB.[39] Since '(∃S)PSB' is C, in α −B is valid and C holds. (If C were inconsistent, no such α would exist.) C entails 'C is true',[40] which entails 'C is valid', which entails ''C is invalid' is not valid'. So in α, −B is valid and 'C is invalid' is not. Therefore *if* B is contingent, then −B does not imply C's invalidity, from which it follows that −B does not imply S (where PSC, and C is consistent).

This completes the argument that if PSC, then (i)–(v) hold for S and B, which is to establish premise (1). Clearly, (1) holds *even if B is analytic and even if B has no truth value.* For in establishing (1) we nowhere assume the contrary.

(ii) The intuitive idea behind premise (2) is this. Suppose a critical rationalist succeeded in specifying a statement S which, if accepted, would count as a

39. Cf. note 29, above.
40. Cf. Sellars (1963), 206; van Fraassen (1966), 494; and van Fraassen (1968), 143–48.

criticism of his theory B. He would immediately point to S in order to convince us that B is criticizable – that B satisfies its own standard – on the ground that S is a potential criticizer of B. But to convince us that B is criticizable is to convince us of the truth of C, for in effect C just says "B is criticizable". Thus it is hard to see how S could simultaneously be a potential criticizer of B and imply C's invalidity. Yet S must imply C's invalidity if S is to be a criticizer of C. So if PSB, then −PSC.

Intuition aside, suppose that C is consistent and that PSB. *If* PSC (contrary to what is to be shown), then S implies C's invalidity. But this implication does not hold, when PSB. To see why, let α be a state of affairs in which S is valid and PSB. Because 'PSB' entails '(∃S)PSB', α must be a state in which S is valid and (∃S)PSB. But '(∃S)PSB' is C, so in α, S is valid and C holds. C entails 'C is true', which entails 'C is valid', which entails ' 'C is invalid' is not valid'. So in α, S is valid and 'C is invalid' is not. Therefore if PSB, then S does not imply C's invalidity, and by condition (v) S is not a potential criticizer of C.

Clearly, (2) holds even if B is analytic or truth-valueless. For we nowhere assume the contrary. Note also that in establishing (1) and (2), we have not had to *specify* a potential criticizer of B or of C, let alone specify circumstances in which we would have to *accept* the criticizer, or view it as a *successful* criticism requiring us actually to give up B and C (cf. note 21, above). In effect (1) and (2) assert only that *if* something S could be specified which would count against C then S would count against B, and *if* something could be specified which would count against B then it would not count against C. Hence the two premises can be established in advance of a specification of when we would actually have to give up CR. So too for what they imply, including '−(∃S)PSC' on line (3).

(iii) The only part of the proof which requires further argument is the first conjunct of line (4), namely the claim that RC. As seen, the critical rationalist presumably would say that C is rationally acceptable. He might call what he says about C a proposal or recommendation, and deny that 'C is rational' has a truth value.[41] But he would want to claim validity for 'C is rational', and this is all that (4) commits us to (so far as 'C is rational' is concerned).

In addition to being rational, C is non-inferential in the present revisability-situation K. Indeed C is not analytic in the first place. For suppose C were analytic. Then C would be necessary, and it would be necessary that there is a statement S which we are able to specify and which satisfies the other conditions (ii)–(v) required of a potential criticizer of B. But whether there is such a statement is a *contingent* matter. As noted in § III(i), given any statement X, whether we are able to specify a statement S satisfying (ii)–(v) for X is partly a function of certain material requirements, and depends on such things as the knowledge and technique available at the time. Hence C is not analytic. Since every inferential statement is analytic, C is non-inferential. Together with the validity of 'C is rational', this gives us the validity of 'RC', and with (3), the validity of (4).

---

41. This possibility was brought to my attention by Professor Richard J. Ketchum.

(iv) The proof of B's invalidity nowhere presupposes that B is synthetic or that B has a truth value. Regardless of whether the critical rationalist construes his principle B as a recommendation, convention, methodological rule, or as somehow analytic, the principle turns out to be invalid. That is, B is neither true nor sound. But then it cannot be analytic after all, since if it were, presumably it would be necessarily true (in some sense), hence true. One must conclude that B is highly contingent. *All this is true of A*, since A entails B. (A, once more, is "Every rational, non-inferential statement is criticizable *and* has survived criticism".)

Even though B is invalid, it *is criticizable*, hence self-referentially consistent (cf. § II (iv)). For *B has a potential criticizer in (4)*. Clearly (4) is specifiable, since we have specified it. It is rationally controllable by critical discussion, since both conjuncts could be called into question by finding a mistake in the foregoing arguments for them. (4) is consistent, since it is valid: by (3) its second conjunct is valid; and its first conjunct is valid, as seen, if the critical rationalist wants what he says about B to be rational. Finally, neither B nor its negation implies (4), and (4) implies B's invalidity—C is a counterexample to B.

In addition, (4) is a potential criticizer of A. For (4) is specifiable, rationally controllable, and consistent; neither A nor its negation implies (4); and since A implies B, and (4) implies B's invalidity, (4) implies A's invalidity. Therefore A is criticizable, and in that respect is self-referentially consistent. *But A is self-referentially inconsistent with respect to survival of criticism.* For we have just seen that A is invalid—it is neither true nor sound.

V. Incompleteness

(i) Let us say that a theory of rationality is *incomplete* just in case there exists a statement which we have good reason to accept but which is not rationally acceptable according to the theory's standards. Historical examples of this sort of incompleteness are plentiful. In effect, CR itself charges some of its competitors with incompleteness, by charging that their standards of rational acceptability fail to apply to statements we have good reason to accept. For instance, CR claims that standards which appeal to induction and verification fail to cover most, or even all scientific theories.

Suppose we have good reason to accept A (say, because we have found that A is criticizable and has survived criticism). Since we know that A entails B, we would thereby have good reason to accept B. But B implies C, given that we are in a problem-context in which B is offered as a theory which is rational by its own standard. Within this context, if we have good reason for B, then we have good reason for C. Hence if we have good reason for A, we have good reason for C.

From (1)–(6) and auxiliary remarks, we know that *if* C is rationally acceptable, then B is invalid and A is self-referentially inconsistent. The reason, basically, is that (4) implies −B; and if C is rational (or if 'C is rational' is valid), then (4) is valid. Consequently *CR could restore B to validity, and A to self-referential consistency, by withdrawing the (implicit) claim that C is rational* (or that 'C is rational' is valid).

It follows that unless we have no good reason to accept A, then *if A is self-referentially consistent, it is incomplete,* with C as an example of a nonrational statement we have good reason to accept. The claim that A is criticizable, namely

D. (∃S)PSA,

would be another example of such a statement. For one can show that D is not criticizable, simply by substituting 'A' for 'B' and 'D' for 'C' in (1)–(3) and the arguments for them in (i) and (ii) of § IV. And since we know that A implies D (in the present context), if we have good reason for A, we have good reason for D.

(ii) The notion of criticizability employed in (1)–(6) may not be exactly what a given critical rationalist has in mind. But it is hard to see how one could develop a notion of criticizability which does the epistemological work critical rationalists expect it to do, and which does not satisfy premises (1) and (2). Given (1) and (2), it follows immediately that C is uncriticizable. But C is crucial for CR's self-referential success, since C merely states that B satisfies its own standard.

Premise (1) could be derived from the plausible general principle that if X implies Y, then a potential criticizer of Y is a potential criticizer of X (provided X and Y are both relevant to some problem we are trying to solve). In the present problem-context K, B implies C, so that every criticizer of C would be a criticizer of B. The general principle seems all the more plausible when one reflects that criticizability is largely a generalization of falsifiability, and that if X implies Y, every potential falsifier of Y is a potential falsifier of X.

With regard to premise (2), it is hard to fault the claim that a potential criticizer of B is not a potential criticizer of C. For suppose the critical rationalist were to succeed in specifying some statement S which would count against B. He would try to persuade us that B is therefore criticizable – i.e., that C is *valid* – on the grounds that S is a potential criticizer of B. But if S *is* a criticizer of B, then S cannot logically imply that C is *invalid,* as seen in (ii) of § IV. And on any plausible notion of criticizability, if S does not logically imply C's invalidity, then S is not a criticizer of C.

Thus we may conclude this section with the following "theorem". Suppose we are presented with a notion of criticizability such that (a) if X implies Y, then a criticizer of Y is a criticizer of X (provided X and Y are both relevant in a given context); (b) S is a criticizer of X only if S is consistent and S implies X's invalidity; and (c) the claim C, that B is criticizable, is non-inferential in the context in which B is up for revision. *On any such notion of criticizability, C is not criticizable, B is invalid if C is rationally acceptable, and unless we have no good reason to accept A, A is self-referentially consistent only if it is incomplete.* It seems likely that any notion of criticizability which does the epistemological work CR expects of it will satisfy (a)–(c). If *every* workable notion of criticizability does satisfy (a)–(c), then we may say that A is *essentially* incomplete. Otherwise it is self-referentially inconsistent, or we have no good reason to accept it in the first place.

VI. Related Theories

(i) Logical difficulties at so fundamental a level are likely to affect a wide variety of theories. Indeed *the present sort of paradox affects theories which are not even versions of CR*. For example, suppose a positivist asserts,

(7) Every cognitively significant, non-inferential statement X is verifiable,

where X is verifiable just in case we can specify a test-statement S^* such that S^* is implied by X in conjunction with a certain auxiliary statement A (or conjunction A of statements), and S^* is not implied by A alone.

If X is verifiable in this sense, then we can specify a consistent statement S which implies X's invalidity, namely A & $-S^*$. The positivist's (7) therefore implies

(8) Every significant, non-inferential statement X is such that there is a specifiable, consistent statement S which implies X's invalidity.

(8) is essentially similar to B. Since (8) is up for revision, like B it is automatically non-inferential in the present situation. An adaptation of (1)–(3) easily shows that

(9) There is a specifiable, consistent S which implies (8)'s invalidity,

which states that (8) satisfies its own standard, itself fails to satisfy that standard. (9) is an analogue of C. Clearly (9) is not analytic, hence non-inferential; for whether or not we are able to specify a consistent S which implies (8)'s invalidity is a contingent matter, being a function of our imaginativeness, powers of analysis, and philosophical technique. Therefore (8) is invalid, as is (7).

Furthermore, (9) is *true*. We can specify a consistent statement which implies the invalidity of (8), namely "(9) is significant, non-inferential, and *not* such that there is a specifiable, consistent S which implies (9)'s invalidity". This is an analogue of (4). Hence (9) is synthetic, demonstrably true, but not such that we can specify a consistent S which implies (9)'s invalidity (because (9) fails to satisfy the standard in (8)). It would appear that in an important sense, (9) is synthetic *a priori*.

The positivist could avoid commitment to this synthetic *a priori* statement, and restore validity to (7), by denying that (9) is cognitively significant. But (9) is essential to the self-referential success of (8), hence of (7); so that if it is significant to say that (7) and (8) satisfy their own standards, then we must admit that (9) is significant. Hence (9) would be an example of a significant statement which is not verifiable. (If (9) were verifiable, then it would satisfy the standard in (8), which it does not, as seen.) The price for restoring validity to (7) is therefore a kind of incompleteness for (7). This is true whether or not (7) is regarded as a truth-valueless proposal or as somehow analytic. For we nowhere assume the contrary.

Suppose that a positivist asserts,

(10) Every significant, *contingent* statement is verifiable.

Then (10) implies

(11) Every significant, contingent statement X is such that we can specify a consistent S which implies X's invalidity.

Only if (11) is contingent (as well as significant) does an application of (1)–(3) show that

(12) We can specify a consistent S which implies (11)'s invalidity

fails to satisfy the standard presented in (11). If (10) and (11) are somehow analytic, then their validity can be preserved. Otherwise they are valid only if they are incomplete (assuming that (12) is significant, as it must be if it is significant to claim that (11) satisfies its own standard).

(ii) Consider a falsifiability theory of significance expressed as follows:

(13) Every cognitively significant, non-inferential statement is falsifiable.

The assertion that (13) is falsifiable is non-inferential and presumably significant. According to (13) this assertion should therefore be falsifiable. An adaptation of (1)–(3) then shows that it is not, hence that (13) is invalid; otherwise it is incomplete. The adaptation consists of restricting the range of the variable 'S' to statements which are intersubjectively testable by observation, so that PSX iff S is a potential falsifier of X.

Embattled metaphysicians and theologians have occasionally argued that theories like (7), (10), and (13) fail to satisfy their own criteria of significance. We have a much stronger result. For we now see that even if (7), (10), and (13) *do* satisfy their own criteria, they are all invalid (unless (10) is analytic). Otherwise they are crucially incomplete. The same is true of

(14) Every significant, non-inferential statement is either verifiable or falsifiable,

since it implies (8). For if X is falsifiable, then X has a potential falsifier S, which (among other things) is a specifiable, consistent statement implying X's invalidity.

(iii) Pragmatism takes numerous forms. The varieties relevant here are those which presuppose analyticity and which claim, in effect, that every acceptable, non-inferential statement either has some (direct) experiential cash-value or is a useful instrument (calculational device, methodological rule, or whatever).

Typically a statement is said to have experiential cash-value just in case it is verifiable or falsifiable. Also, a statement X which behaves as an instrument, though neither true nor false, is to be evaluated in terms of its (indirect) experiential payoff. Either X is useful (fruitful, efficacious) in helping to order our experience and serve our needs, or it is not; and according to the pragmatist, X is criticizable in terms of this utility (or lack of it). Successful criticism of an instrumental X consists in bringing considerations to bear which imply the inutility of X.

Inutility is a special case of the unsoundness discussed in § III(v), and therefore a special case of invalidity. For we said that a theory which (in context, relative to a given aim) fails to be fruitful or simple is unsound. Even if X is an instrument and neither verifiable nor falsifiable, the pragmatist wants X to be criticizable in the sense that he can specify a statement S (or a conjunction S of statements) which implies X's invalidity (where presumably S is consistent). Consequently the pragmatist in effect is claiming

(15)   Every acceptable, non-inferential statement X either is verifiable or falsifiable or (though a truth-valueless instrument) is such that we can specify a consistent S which implies X's invalidity.[42]

Clearly (15) implies (8) (with "acceptable" substituted for "significant"), and inherits all the ills which afflict (8). One wonders just how general these self-referential difficulties will prove to be for pragmatism and empiricism.

VII. CCR

William Bartley has done more than anyone to establish the importance of the problem of whether CR is self-referentially consistent. His own theory, which he calls "comprehensively critical rationalism", or CCR, has a psychologistic and a normative component (cf. § II). Nevertheless both components depend on claims which are expressible by A and B.[43] Bartley argues quite rightly that if these claims are rational by their own standards, then skepticism and fideism are deprived of an ancient argument against rationality. This is the *tu quoque* or boomerang argument, to the effect that even the rationalist cannot be fully rational about his deepest beliefs, because his rationality cannot be rationally held.

Bartley does not regard his theory as analytic,[44] and gives no indication that it behaves as a truth-valueless rule or recommendation. On the contrary, he gives every indication of believing that successful criticism of a theory Θ results in the assignment of falsity to Θ.[45] With regard to CCR, he says,

42. Compare this with a version of the Strengthened Epimenides Possible Liar: "Every Cretan statement is either possibly false or neither true nor false." A Strengthened PL ("This very sentence is either possibly false or neither true nor false") appears in Post (1970).
43. Bartley (1962), 146–48, 167–73; and Bartley (1964), 30. Much the same translation of Bartley's claims is presented by Watkins (1969), 58, and Watkins (1971), 57, line (1). The main advantage of B over Watkins' translation is that B allows us to distinguish inferential from non-inferential analytic statements. There is some evidence that Bartley would insist on such a distinction. Cf. Bartley (1962), 153, 170–71.
44. This seems to be the upshot of Bartley (1962), 153–55.
45. With the exception, perhaps, of the check of relevance. Cf. Bartley (1962), 157–59, and espec. 170: "The idea of critical argument presupposes . . . the idea of the *retransmission of falsity.*"

Someone could devastatingly refute this kind of rationalism if he were to produce an argument showing that at least some of the . . . critical standards necessarily used by a comprehensively critical rationalist were uncriticizable. . . . [46]

The claim C, that B is criticizable, may not be what Bartley would call a "critical standard". But it is a claim "necessarily used" when CCR itself is said to be criticizable. Since at line (3) we discover that C is uncriticizable, it follows that CCR has been "devastatingly refuted" – *tu quoque*.

It also follows that Bartley is dead right when he says,

Without any contradiction or other difficulty the practice of critical argument can be criticized. Just as it is possible for a democracy, during the democratic process of voting, to commit suicide, so a comprehensively critical rationalist, who is not committed to the view that his position is the correct one, could be argued out of rationalism.[47]

What he *cannot* be argued out of is C, the claim that his position B is criticizable. For C is uncriticizable. There simply *is* no specifiable, rationally controllable, consistent statement S such that neither C nor $-C$ implies S (unless C is inconsistent), and S implies C's invalidity. In addition, we have established that C is true: because (4) is a potential criticizer of B, B is criticizable.

Since C is demonstrably true, we see that *at the heart of CCR, and indeed of all CR, is a claim – the claim that CR's key principle B is itself criticizable – which can be justified but never refuted.* CR was designed to exclude the justificational ways of thinking which cause so much trouble for its rival, "Comprehensive Rationalism".[48] It is unsettling to find CR making a claim which can be warranted only by positive or "confirming" reasons. Even if C's uncriticizability did not result in B's invalidity (say, because we resign ourselves to B's incompleteness), the critical rationalist would have some explaining to do.

In a couple of papers on CCR, John Watkins asserts that there is no risk that C will ever be refuted.[49] Line (3) shows why Watkins is right: C is uncriticizable. C is also true, as seen. But it does not follow that C is analytic. For we know from an argument in § IV(iii), that C is not analytic. Indeed any assertion that a theory is criticizable is contingent, since criticizability depends on such things as available knowledge and technique.

Thus any argument to the effect that C is analytic must be mistaken. Watkins

46. Bartley (1962), 149. Cf. Agassi, Jarvie, and Settle (1971), 46: "The criticisability of CCR, but not its consistency, is assured if at least one of its standards be criticisable; its consistency, however, depends on *all* its standards being criticisable."

47. Bartley (1964), 30. Contrast this with Lakatos's remark: "No disaster can ever disprove a non-justificationist theory of rationality" (Lakatos and Musgrave (1970), p. 114). The paradox in CR – namely B's invalidity – shows that Lakatos is wrong on this point (unless he uses "disprove" in too strong a sense), and that Bartley is right. It also casts doubt on Michael Martin (1970), 109: "Bartley has not shown that his own position is subject to criticism."

48. Cf. Bartley (1962), 107–109; Bartley (1964), 11–13, 22–26; and Popper (1963), 229–31.

49. The claim he actually talks about is essentially C. Cf. Watkins (1969), 60; and Watkins (1971), 57, remarks following his number (4). In the draft to which Watkins refers in his footnote 7, I did not argue that the claim in question (his (3), essentially the present C) is analytic, but only that it is true in every world of a special kind. My line (3), in § IV above, is a descendant of the earlier result.

presents such an argument.[50] The mistake occurs in his assumption (A3). As he points out, his (A3) trivially implies

(16) All statements that are not rationally acceptable are criticizable.

But (16) trivially implies "All statements that are uncriticizable are rationally acceptable". No critical rationalist would ever agree to this, since it is precisely the opposite of his principle that no uncriticizable statement is acceptable. The reason why there is no risk that C will be refuted is not that C is analytic, contrary to Watkins' argument, but that C is synthetic and uncriticizable. It seems in some sense to be synthetic *a priori*.

There are other ways in which the present paper illuminates recent disputes about CCR.[51] But if CCR is refuted as emphatically as the foregoing indicates, the disputes will seem academic.[52] In any case, the present approach enjoys a generality not to be found in previous criticisms of CCR. The techniques developed in § IV apply to a variety of theories which are not even versions of CR (cf. § V), as well as to versions of CR in which the key principles A and B are alleged to be truth-valueless rules or somehow analytic. Should Bartley choose to escape by construing CCR as analytic or truth-valueless after all, he would still be in trouble.

At this point the alternative of giving up self-reference may seem very attractive. *Perhaps we should give up trying to characterize a class of statements to which our statement of the characterization is itself supposed to belong.* Unfortunately this way out is also closed to Bartley, and indeed to those critical rationalists who have not been so explicit in construing CR self-referentially. Let us see why.

VIII. Self-Reference

Suppose Θ_1 and Θ_2 are competing philosophical theories about acceptable theories, to which they ascribe some sort of semantic property. Suppose Θ_1 and Θ_2 are of such generality that they would naturally be taken to apply to themselves, were it not for some philosophers' rejection of all semantic self-reference. Suppose further that so far as the evidence at our disposal is concerned, Θ_1 and Θ_2

50. Watkins (1971), 57, remarks preceding number (4). Let me add that these two papers of Watkins have forced me to consider certain points I might otherwise have neglected.

51. For example, the notion of criticizability given in § III seems to be stronger than Watkins' $Crit_0$ but weaker than his $Crit_1$, contrary to his conjecture that there is no such notion. Cf. Watkins (1971), 59, (A4). Also the paradox in CR supports Agassi, Jarvie, and Settle (1971), 49: "CCR is much more vulnerable than Watkins appears to have noticed." And the paradox supports their remark on p. 44: "An admissable proof that CCR was in one particular respect uncriticisable [e.g., C] would be proof that in some other respect CCR was criticisable [e.g., B]." On the other hand, our procedure illustrates all too well the danger stressed by Watkins (1969), 59, that in the course of showing that CCR *is* criticizable, one might find oneself going so far as actually to produce "a thumping good criticism".

52. Cf. the debate on CCR touched off by Watkins (1969), which occurs in Agassi, Jarvie, and Settle (1971), Kekes (1971), Richmond (1971), and Watkins (1971).

account equally well for their subject matter, except that Θ_1 is refuted by an argument in which the semantic predicates in Θ_1 are applicable to Θ_1. That is, Θ_1 either is self-referentially inconsistent, failing to have a property it lays down for all acceptable theories; or if it has the property, Θ_1 turns out to be refuted in some other respect (as does B, which is self-referentially consistent, yet invalid if it is complete). On the other hand, Θ_2 is not refuted, so far as we can tell, and in particular not by any such self-referential argument.

Our natural inclination would be to say that Θ_2 is the better theory, because it accounts for everything Θ_1 accounts for and has survived a test which Θ_1 has not survived. Popper himself rejects a rival theory – justificational or uncritical rationalism – on just these grounds: it fails to have a property it lays down for all acceptable theories, namely being "supported by argument or by experience".[53] From this point of view, a philosopher who avoids the refutation of Θ_1, by saying that no semantic self-reference is to be allowed in the first place, has some explaining to do.[54]

Presumably his explanation would be that this so-called "test" of Θ_1 and Θ_2 is no test at all, since it presupposes that some semantic self-reference is meaningful. He would then explain that the safest way out of the antinomies, if not the only way, is to exclude all sentences which mention themselves, or at any rate all sentences which ascribe a semantic property to themselves – especially if we wish to construct a rigorous definition of truth. The result must be a language, or a hierarchy of languages, in which Θ_1 and Θ_2 would be ill-formed if construed self-referentially, and in which the "argument" which "refutes" Θ_1 would also contain ill-formed expressions.

The explanation's *effect*, if not its motive, is to eliminate what many philosophers regard as a proper way of deciding between competing philosophical theories. For example, if all semantic self-reference were excluded, then Popper's own argument against justificational rationalism would contain ill-formed expressions. For his argument presupposes that it is meaningful to assert that this rival theory "can be supported by argument or by experience".[55]

But even the explanation's motive is suspect. Recently it has become much less plausible to suppose that the only way out of the antinomies, or even the only safe way, is by language-levels. Languages have been constructed which allow a high degree of semantic self-reference, which have rigorous Tarski-like truth

---

53. Popper (1963), 230, where Popper's term "inconsistent" means essentially the same as "self-referentially inconsistent". I am indebted to Sir Karl for his spirited criticism of an early draft. The present section is designed in part as a response.

54. Some positivists have chosen to exclude self-reference in order to evade criticism based on a failure of their theories to satisfy their own standards. Cf. Pap (1949), 41–42; and Richman (1953) for objections. Also, cf. Fitch (1952).

55. Popper (1963), 230, and espec. n.1, which appears on 354.

definitions, and which block derivation of the classical antinomies.[56] At least one such system has been shown to be consistent.[57]

Suppose that Θ_1 and Θ_2 are translated into some such consistent system, that they are well-formed in it even when construed self-referentially, and that the argument which refutes Θ_1 is similarly translatable. Then the would-be defender of Θ_1 must capitulate. At best he could revise his theory so as to make it explicitly applicable only to *other* theories.

His revision would avoid the refutation, but at the expense of decreasing the content of his theory, thus making it less criticizable. For *a theory about all theories including itself obviously has greater content than a theory about all other theories,*[58] *and obviously takes the greater risk of refutation* (provided, of course, both are well-formed). Hence this sort of revision of Θ_1 is inconsistent with the aims of CR.

It is inconsistent with these aims if Θ_1, Θ_2 and the argument which refutes Θ_1 happen not to be translatable into one of the self-referential systems that have so far been developed. For there could well be some *other* system into which Θ_1, Θ_2, and the argument could be translated, which allows the kind of self-reference involved in Θ_1 and Θ_2, blocks derivation of the antinomies, and contains an adequate definition of truth. Such a system would be an instrument by means of which we could conduct a "crucial experiment" to decide between Θ_1 and Θ_2, and its development would increase their criticizability. Rejection of all semantic self-reference, or even of that which is involved in Θ_1, would discourage the search for such an instrument and would frustrate its purpose should it be found, thus reducing criticizability.

These considerations lose little of their force *even if we happen not to be acquainted with an alternative theory* Θ_2. It is true that in this case discovery of self-referential trouble in Θ_1 might not, of itself, lead us to abandon Θ_1. We might reject Θ_1 only when an acceptable alternative is found. Nevertheless, if we maintained that the trouble in Θ_1 has no force because it depends on self-reference, we would not even try to find such an alternative. Contrary to CR, we would not try to improve on Θ_1, nor would we try to find a "safe" language in which a decision between Θ_1 and its potential rivals could be made – a language in which the decision could be made even to the satisfaction of those philosophers who would insist on a solution to the antinomies as a precondition of *any* discussion of self-referential theories. That is, we would not try to increase Θ_1's criticizability.

---

56. Cf. van Fraassen (1968), 146–51; Fitch (1964); and especially the language LΘ * of van Fraassen (1970). It seems likely that these languages also block non-classical antinomies such as the Possible Liar, though this has yet to be investigated.

57. This is the System S in Skyrms (1970). The consistency of S means, of course, that the Possible Liar and its relatives cannot be derived in S. Whether this represents a "solution" to the Possible Liar, in the full sense of the term, is another matter. On what counts as a full solution, cf. Martin (1967), 291–92, and Sommers (1969), 260.

58. I owe this point to one of my undergraduate students, Mr. Joseph Blount.

The critical rationalist, therefore, is not free to object that his principle B really ought not to be construed self-referentially. He is not free to object that B is really an inexplicit, elliptical way of expressing the view, say, that at each language-level n, every rational, non-inferential statement is criticizable$_{n+1}$.[59] For B is a philosophical theory about acceptable theories, to which it ascribes the semantic property of criticizability. Also, B is of such generality that it would naturally be taken to apply to itself, were it not for these general worries about self-reference. And (assuming it is complete) B is refuted, as we have seen, by an argument in which the semantic predicates "rational", "non-inferential" and "criticizable" in B are applicable to B. Thus the proposed revision would reduce criticizability. *Critical Rationalism ought to be a Comprehensively Critical Rationalism, as Bartley realized* (though for a different reason).[60]

Furthermore, there are philosophers who will claim that they *are* acquainted with an alternative to B. This is Quine's statement (let us call it Q) that *no* statement is immune to revision (every statement is revisable), even in those contexts in which it is required to draw the implications of some other statement which is up for revision. Clearly Q is a competing theory about acceptable theories, to which it ascribes a semantic property. Q is of such generality that we would naturally suppose that it should apply to itself. Quine would argue that Q accounts at least as well as B for their common subject matter. In effect, of course, he has already argued this.

Yet Q is *not* refuted by the sort of self-referential argument which refutes B (assuming B is complete). The analogue of C is R: "Q is revisable". Q implies R by universal instantiation (assuming both are statements). According to Quine, a statement X is revisable just in case there are circumstances in which we would be inclined to assign falsity to X. Hence the analogue of premise (1) ("Every criticizer of C is a criticizer of B") would be

(1*) Every circumstance in which we would be inclined to assign falsity to R is a circumstance in which we would be inclined to assign falsity to Q.

In spite of the fact that Q logically implies R, (1*) would not hold for Quine, simply because according to him there could be a circumstance in which we would assign falsity to R but not to Q. In such a circumstance we would have rejected universal instantiation instead of Q; retransmission of falsity is not guaranteed. Since even basic laws of logic are revisable for Quine, he can consistently deny (1*). Defending B against Q by refusing to allow the predicates in B to apply to B would hardly accord with the spirit of CR. In general, for a philosopher to plead exemption from self-referential criticism is rather like upsetting the chessboard when losing.

---

59. On the use of predicate-subscripts, cf. Quine (1966), 10.
60. Bartley (1962), 129–31. Bartley's arguments for comprehensiveness seem to have influenced Popper to regard his own version of CR as self-applicable. Compare Popper's (1963), Ch. 24, and Addendum (espec. p. 369, n. 1), with earlier editions of the same work.

IX. Analyticity

Those who share Quine's doubts about the analytic-synthetic distinction (ASD) will find the lesson of this paper all too obvious: CR had better give up the ASD, even in the moderate form presented in § II(i). That is, CR had better give up the presupposition that in every revisability-situation some statements are analytic in the traditional sense and uncriticizable. But if *this* is the lesson, then the elaborate explanations and arguments of the paper are unnecessary, since, according to Quine and his fellow doubters, we already knew that the ASD is untenable. At most, they might say, the paper merely provides another reason for abandoning the ASD by showing how CR and related theories get into self-referential trouble by clinging to a distinction already suffering from a terminal disease.

(i) However, the paper would not provide a reason for abandoning the ASD, or increase the pressure on it, *unless* giving up the ASD were the *only* way out of the paradox in CR, or the *best* way. But there may well be other ways out, other ways of preserving the validity of A and B.

(a) Perhaps the best escape would be to design a notion of criticizability which does the epistemological work required of it but which does not warrant premises (1) and (2). While I have argued that it would be difficult to design such a notion, I have not argued that it would be impossible. For example, there might be a workable sort of criticizability which, unlike falsifiability, is not always re-transmitted from Y to X when X implies Y. Specifically, there might be a workable sort of criticizability according to which not every criticizer of C is a criticizer of B, so that premise (1) would not hold.

(b) Rather than construe CR as a theory about theories, one might present CR as a principle to which the reasoning employed in this paper is inappropriate. Instead, some sort of *practical* reasoning might be appropriate, perhaps of the form

I intend to practice that which is more conducive to end E than is any other practice.
Practicing CR is more conducive to E than is any other practice. So I shall practice CR.

If a suitable end could be specified, *and if the second premise of this argument could be established* – no easy matter – then CR would be "vindicated", in the sense that the argument would constitute a successful "rational" defense of the decision to practice CR. In that case, it would be inappropriate to demand that CR be rationally acceptable according to its own standard.[61]

(c) The last alternative to rejecting the ASD I shall consider here is for CR to give up its implicit claim to completeness. As we have seen, CR can preserve the validity and self-referential consistency of A and B by denying that C and D need be rational according to the standard presented in B. While this is a high price to pay for self-referential consistency, from CR's point of view it would not

61. Cf. Sellars (1967), 409–11, with respect to moral first principles. There is a hint of this in Popper (1968a), pp. 37–38, but on balance he and other critical rationalists so far have presented CR as a theory about theories.

be so exorbitant as abandoning the ASD. For as we have seen, CR's whole idea of how one criticizes something, hence its notion of criticizability, presupposes the ASD. A position which rejected the ASD would be CR in name only. But a position like A, even if incomplete, would retain CR's characteristic features, and would at least be rational by its own standard.

(ii) Suppose for the sake of argument that incompleteness is regarded as too high a price to pay, *perhaps because incompleteness of a theory of rationality would count as a decisive criticism of it.* Suppose further that neither (a) nor (b) nor anything else turns out to be a feasible alternative to abandoning the ASD. Suppose, in short, that giving up the ASD *is* the best way out of the paradox in CR and related theories.

If we grant all these things, then the paradox in CR and the versions of empiricism and pragmatism considered in § VI *would* provide a reason for rejecting the ASD. But *notice how the reason would differ from Quine's.* His argument against the ASD proceeds on the basis of a general scepticism about a distinction. The roots of that scepticism are largely *external* to the philosophies which presuppose the distinction.

In contrast, *we start by granting the legitimacy of the ASD,* and then, with the help of auxiliary assumptions supplied or implied by CR and related theories, we derive a *contradiction* (cf. § IV: (6) is B's contradictory). *If the only feasible way out of the contradiction is to reject the ASD, then the distinction has been reduced to absurdity.* This means that our reason for rejecting the ASD would be specific and *internal* to the philosophies which presuppose it. The critical rationalist and others might not have been moved to reject analyticity by Quine's general, external scepticism. But in order to preserve the consistency of their position they would have to abandon the ASD after all.

Therefore, even if the lesson of the paper were (merely) that CR and related theories had better reject the ASD, *the proof that they had better do so would be logically and epistemologically of a very different order from Quine's.* For what we would have shown is that *even if Quine's external objections to the ASD fail*, these positions would *still* be forced to abandon the ASD. But in any case, we would not have shown this unless giving up the ASD is the only feasible way out of the paradox in CR and related theories. As I have suggested, there may be another way to escape, which, from their point of view, does not involve so high a price. Thus nothing in the paper should be construed as entailing a retreat to some form of irrationalism. What is entailed is a search for a better theory of rationality – a theory which succeeds wherever CR does, but which enjoys full self-referential success as well.

References

Agassi, J., Jarvie, I., and Settle T. (1971), "The Grounds of Reason." *Philosophy* **46**, pp. 43–50.

Aune, B. (1967), *Knowledge, Mind and Nature* (New York: Random House).

Ayer, A. J. (1959), *Introduction to Logical Positivism*, ed. A. J. Ayer (New York: The Free Press).

Bartley, W. W., III (1962), *The Retreat to Commitment*. (New York: Knopf).

Bartley, W. W., III (1964), "Rationality Versus the Theory of Rationality", *The Critical Approach to Science and Philosophy*, ed. M. Bunge (London: Macmillan).

Bennett, J. (1958), "Analytic-Synthetic", *Proceedings of the Aristotelian Society* **59**, pp. 163–88.

Fitch, F. B. (1952), "Self-Reference in Philosophy", Appendix C of his *Symbolic Logic* (New York: Ronald Press), reprinted in Copi and Gould, *Contemporary Readings in Logical Theory* (New York: Macmillan, 1967), pp. 154–60.

Fitch, F. B. (1964), "Universal Metalanguages for Philosophy", *Review of Metaphysics* **17**, pp. 396–402.

van Fraassen, B. C. (1966), "Singular Terms, Truth-Value Gaps, and Free Logic", *Journal of Philosophy* **63**, pp. 481–95.

van Fraassen, B. C. (1968), "Presupposition, Implication, and Self-Reference", *Journal of Philosophy* **65**, pp. 136–52.

van Fraassen, B. C. (1970), "Inference and Self-Reference", *Synthese* **21**, pp. 425–38.

Kekes, J. (1971), "Watkins on Rationalism", *Philosophy* **46**, pp. 51–53.

Lakatos, I. (1967), "A Renaissance of Empiricism in the Recent Philosophy of Mathematics?", *Problems in the Philosophy of Mathematics*, ed. I. Lakatos. (Amsterdam: North-Holland).

Lakatos, I. (1968), "Changes in the Problem of Inductive Logic", *The Problem of Inductive Logic*, ed. I. Lakatos (Amsterdam: North-Holland).

Lakatos, I., and Musgrave, A. (1970), *Criticism and the Growth of Knowledge* (Cambridge: The University Press).

Martin, Michael (1970), "Religious Commitment and Rational Criticism", *Philosophical Forum* **II**, pp. 107–21.

Martin, R. L. (1967), "Toward a Solution to the Liar Paradox", *Philosophical Review* **76**, pp. 279–311.

Pap, A. (1949), *Elements of Analytic Philosophy* (New York: Macmillan).

Popper, K. R. (1943), "Are Contradictions Embracing?", *Mind* **52**, pp. 47–50.

Popper, K. R. (1963), *The Open Society and its Enemies*, Vol. 2 (New York: Harper and Row).

Popper, K. R. (1968a), *The Logic of Scientific Discovery* (London: Hutchinson).

Popper, K. R. (1968b), *Conjectures and Refutations* (New York: Harper and Row).

Post, J. F. (1970), "The Possible Liar", *Nous* **4**, pp. 405–409.

Quine, W. V. (1966), *Ways of Paradox* (New York: Random House).

Rescher, N. (1968), *Topics in Philosophical Logic* (Dordrecht: Reidel).

Richman, R. J. (1953), "On the Self-Reference of a Meaning-Theory", *Philosophical Studies* **4**, pp. 69–72.

Richmond, S. (1971), "Can a Rationalist be Rational about his Rationalism?", *Philosophy* **46**, pp. 54–55.

Sellars, W. (1963), *Science, Perception and Reality* (London: Routledge & Kegan Paul).

Sellars, W. (1967), *Philosophical Perspectives* (Springfield, Illinois: Charles C. Thomas).

Skyrms, B. (1970), "Return of the Liar: Three-Valued Logic and the Concept of Truth", *American Philosophical Quarterly* 7, pp. 153–61.

Sommers, F. (1969), "On Concepts of Truth in Natural Languages", *Review of Metaphysics*, 23, pp. 259–86.

Watkins, J. W. N. (1969), "Comprehensively Critical Rationalism", *Philosophy* **44**, pp. 57–62.

Watkins, J. W. N. (1971), "CCR: A Refutation", *Philosophy* **46**, pp. 56–61.

von Wright, G. H. (1957), *Logical Studies* (London: Routledge & Kegan Paul, Ltd., 1957).

== *Chapter* **XII** ════════════════════════════

A Gödelian Theorem for Theories of Rationality

By John F. Post

A dozen years ago, in a short section of a long paper on critical rationalism and related theories, I floated a Gödelian theorem to the effect that all rationality theories in a certain general class are either self-referentially inconsistent or inherently incomplete.[1] Comment on the paper (which we may call PCRT for short) has tended to ignore the theorem and its generality, concentrating instead on questions of how to interpret particular critical rationalists.[2] In part certain features of PCRT may themselves have been responsible for this. I want now to give the theorem the emphasis I think it deserves, and to explain how, in light of its generality, questions about proper interpretation of particular positions have so far been beside the point.

In its original formulation, the theorem's immediate implications for some theories not treated in detail may not have been so obvious as I had thought. Here, therefore, after sketching the original and portraying its form in the abstract, let us reformulate the theorem in light of possible objections, in order to spell out the implications.

1. Background

To begin the sketch of the original, suppose someone holds the following statement or principle, which presumably expresses a component of one version of Critical Rationalism (CR):

An earlier draft of this chapter was published in *The Proceedings of the Eleventh International Conference on the Unity of the Sciences* (New York: International Cultural Foundation, 1983).

1. Section I of "Paradox in Critical Rationalism and Related Theories", *Philosophical Forum* 3 (1972), pp. 27–61. See also p. 28 and § VI.

2. See Tom Settle, "Concerning the Rationality of Scepticism", Philosophical Forum 4 (1973), pp. 432–37; A. A. Derksen, "The Failure of Comprehensively Critical Rationalism", *Philosophy of the Social Sciences* 10 (1980), pp. 51–66; Thomas F. Gibbons, *Self-Reference, Paradox and Critical Rationalism*, Ph.D. Dissertation, Vanderbilt University (1979); and W. W. Bartley, III, rough draft of Appendix #4 to the new (1986) German edition and translation of *The Retreat to Commitment*, a copy of which he very kindly has allowed me to study.

A.   Every rational, non-inferential statement is criticizable and so far has survived criticism.

The reason for the qualifier 'non-inferential' is that according to the critical rationalist, criticism could not even begin in a situation or context K, were certain
things not (provisionally) placed beyond criticizability in K, including above all
both certain rules of inference (which are held to be analytic) and anything else
required for drawing the implications of the statement(s) up for possible revision
in K. Thus to say that a statement X is non-inferential in K is to say, roughly,
that X is not presupposed background required for drawing the implications of
some Y which is up for possible revision in K.

Next, notice that principle A logically entails statement

B.   Every rational, non-inferential statement is criticizable.

Further, CR holds (in the sense of conjecturing) that

C.   B itself is criticizable.

Indeed in any context in which B is up for possible revision and is held itself
to be rational, B implies C. (Recall Popper, under Bartley's influence: "Nothing
is exempt from criticism – not even this principle of the critical method itself.")[3]
Now suppose the notion of criticizability in A-C is such that

(α)   If X implies Y, then a criticism of Y is a criticism of X ("retransmission
of criticism");
(β)   S is a criticism of X only if S is consistent and implies X's invalidity; and
(γ)   Conjecture C is non-inferential in the context K in which B is under
criticism, hence is up for possible revision.

Conditions (α) – (γ), which are not meant to be jointly sufficient, may seem
to need little argument, though I gave arguments for them in PCRT. The Gödelian
theorem, finally, was this:

TH1.   For any notion of criticizability which satisfies (α) – (γ), C is not
criticizable, B is invalid if C is rational, and unless we have no good
reason to hold A, A is either self-referentially inconsistent or inherently incomplete.

Good reasons here need be no justificationist or foundationalist affair, but a matter
say of survival of criticism to date. Also, we call a principle or theory of rationality *incomplete* iff there is a statement we have good reason to hold but which it
is not rational to hold according to the theory's standards. We call the theory *inherently* incomplete when there is such a statement not "external" to theory but
implied by the theory itself (as C is implied by A via B). And we call principle

3. *The Open Society and its Enemies*, Vol. 2, 1963 edition, p. 379. On the matter of influence,
see Part III of Bartley's "Critical Study of *The Philosophy of Karl Popper*", in *Philosophia* 11 (1982),
pp. 121–221, esp. pp. 146–48.

A *essentially* incomplete iff *every* workable notion of criticizability does not satisfy (α) – (γ).

Details of the argument for TH1 may be found in §§ IV–V of PCRT. In spirit, however, just as Gödel's argument owes something to the antinomy of the Liar ('What I'm now saying is false'), this one owes something to my antinomy of the Possible Liar ('What I'm now saying is *possibly* false').[4] Likewise the debt is largely heuristic. For the crux is a pair of premises which trivially entail that nothing is a criticism of C, hence that C is not criticizable:

(1) Every criticism of C is a criticism of B.
(2) No criticism of B is a criticism of C.

Premise (1) should come as no surprise. Given that we are trying to find a principle of rationality (B, say) which is rational by its own lights, failure of such a principle to satisfy its own standard of rationality (contrary to C) constitutes a damaging criticism of it. In this context, therefore, considerations which count against the conjecture that the principle satisfies its own standard count against the principle. Hence in this context considerations which count against conjecture C count against principle B, so that a criticism of C is a criticism of B.

This argument for (1), I have been slow to see, does not after all presuppose that B implies C, or even that B implies C in any context in which B is up for possible revision and is held itself to be rational. This means that condition (α) – of the retransmission of criticism through implication – is stronger than necessary for derivation of the theorem, though (α) nevertheless not only is sound but is implicit in all versions of CR, given their emphasis on the retransmission of falsity and related measures from conclusion to premises. And since B does imply C in the context of these debates about the self-applicability of rationality theories, (α) gives us a further argument for premise (1).[5]

As regards premise (2), the intuitive idea is that the existence of a criticism of B would entail that B is criticizable, which is just what C says, so this criticism of B could hardly count as a criticism of C. Intuition aside, suppose S is (or expresses) a criticism of B. By condition (β) above, S therefore is consistent. Hence there is an interpretation (model, state of affairs, possible world) m in which S is true. Further, there is an m' in which S is both true and a criticism of B. If there were no such m', we could infer that S is untrue simply from its being a criticism of B. This would mean that we could know *a priori*, as a matter of mere

<hr/>

4. Derived in my "The Possible Liar", *Nous* 4 (1970), pp. 405–49. I there assumed bivalence, an assumption that later proved superfluous. See my "Presupposition, Bivalence and the Possible Liar", *Philosophia* 8 (1979), pp. 645–59. Further applications and implications of the Possible Liar are pursued in my "Shades of the Liar", *Journal of Philosophical Logic* 2 (1973), pp. 370–86; "Shades of Possibility", *Journal of Philosophical Logic* 3 (1974), pp. 155–58; and "Propositions, Possible Languages and the Liar's Revenge", *British Journal for the Philosophy of Science* 25 (1974), pp. 223–34.

5. Gibbons, *op. cit.*, questions the use of (α) to argue for premise (1), on the grounds that while retransmission of invalidity holds when X implies Y, it does not or need not hold when X only implies Y in context (or under an assumption). Whether he is right we need not inquire, in view of the above independent argument for (1).

logic, that no proposed criticism of B could be true. But this is absurd. Our notion of criticizability is such that

(δ) For any S and X, the mere fact that S is a potential criticism of X does not by itself entail that S is untrue.

I have been slow to notice that assumption (δ), which was implicit in PCRT's analysis of criticizability (cf. §III), should be made explicit and added to (α) – (γ), in order to clarify this step in the argument for premise (2). To complete the argument, note that from the fact that in m' S is both true and a criticism of B, it follows that in m' both S is true and there is a criticism of B. Hence in m' both S is true and B is criticizable, which is what C says, so in m' both S and C are true. But then there is an interpretation in which both are true, so S cannot imply C's invalidity. By (β), therefore, S cannot be a criticism of C. Since by hypothesis S is a criticism of B, this establishes premise (2).

From (1) and (2) it follows immediately that C is not criticizable. Yet C is absolutely essential to, because it just is or expresses, CR's claim or conjecture that CR's crucial principle B itself is criticizable. C is no external, adventitious example of an uncontroversial truth which is alleged to be uncriticizable, and which CR is then challenged to prove is criticizable. C is internal, controversial, and uncriticizable; and the challenge to CR is not to prove the contrary, but either to criticize (successfully) the assumptions and inferences in the argument for C's uncriticizability, or else to explain how the argument, though it applies to B and C, does not apply to some other version of CR properly interpreted. As I remarked at the start, comment has tended to concentrate on this matter of proper interpretation, which will be considered below, after a sketch of how the rest of the Gödelian TH1 follows from the uncriticizability of C.

Clearly, C is not required for drawing the implications of B, in the relevant sense; for C *is* one of those implications, in any context (such as the present one) in which B is up for possible revision and is conjectured to be rational itself. So C is a non-inferential statement here (cf. condition (γ)). Further, the Critical Rationalist claims or conjectures that he can hold C rationally. If he is right, then C is a rational, non-inferential statement, yet one which we have just seen is uncriticizable. Hence C is a strict counter-example to B, and B is invalid, as TH1 asserts. Yet of course B is criticizable, hence self-referentially consistent, because we've just now successfully criticized it.

Next, suppose we have good reason to hold A (say because A is criticizable and so far has survived rigorous criticism). Then we have good reason to hold B, since A entails B, and good reason to hold C, since (in context) B implies C ("good reason" is transmissible, even if criticizability and so on may not be). But C is either rational by A's standards or not. If the former, then B is invalid, as just seen, and A too is invalid, since A entails B (retransmission of invalidity). But if we conclude that A is invalid, then A will not have survived the present criticism, and A will be self-referentially inconsistent as regards survival of criticism (though self-referentially consistent as regards criticizability). On the other hand, if C is not rational by A's standards, then C is an example of a nonrational statement we have good reason to hold if we have good reason to hold A, whence it follows that A is incomplete, and inherently so, since A implies C. So we are forced to conclude that unless we have no good reason to hold A in the first place, A is either self-referentially inconsistent or inherently incomplete (and essentially so, if every workable notion of criticizability satisfies $(\alpha) - (\delta)$).

2. The Form of the Theorem

At its most abstract, and under a certain aspect, the form of the theorem and the argument for it, though not given in PCRT, is as follows. Consider

A'. $(\forall X)((FX \ \& \ GX) \to ((\exists Y)YRX \ \& \ HX))$.
B'. $(\forall X)((FX \ \& \ GX) \to (\exists Y)YRX)$.
C'. $(\exists Y)YRB'$.

Now assume either that $(B' \Rightarrow C')$ and

$(\alpha')\ (X \Rightarrow Z) \to (\forall Y)(YRZ \to YRX)$,

or else that if YR ($\ulcorner B'$ satisfies its own consequent$\urcorner$), then YRB'. Either assumption yields

$(1')\ (\forall Y)(YRC' \to YRB')$.

Assume further that

$(\beta')\ YRX \to ((Y \vDash \overline{X}) \ \& \ Y$ is consistent), and
$(\delta')\ YRX \to (\ulcorner YRX \urcorner \nvDash \overline{Y})$.

Then *mutatis mutandis* the argument above for (2) yields

$(2')\ (\forall Y)(YRB' \to \overline{YRC'})$.

Assume finally that

$(\gamma')\ GC'$.

It follows that for any R and G which satisfy $(\alpha') - (\delta')$,

TH2. C' is not R-able (i.e., $(\forall Y)\overline{YRC'}$, from $(1')$ and $(2')$); B' is invalid if FC'; and if $(B' \Rightarrow C')$ and $(\overline{B}' \to \overline{HA'})$, then unless there is no good reason for A', either A' is self-referentially inconsistent as regards H, or else A' is inherently incomplete.

The Gödelian theorem, as formulated in TH2, applies to the class of theories of form A' whose concepts R and G satisfy either $(\alpha') - (\delta')$, or else $(\beta') - (\delta')$ plus the assumption that if YR ($\ulcorner B'$ satisfies its own consequent$\urcorner$), then YRB'.

How general is this class? Very general, evidently, since it includes, as explained in §VI of PCRT, theories that are not even versions of CR, such as positivism, verificationism, instrumentalism, and some forms of pragmatism, even when such theories occur as theories not of rationality but of knowledge, of justification, of meaning, or of truth. Yet the Gödelian theorem has another dimension of generality, beyond its applicability to certain theories of form A'. For the theorem has further formulations, in which it applies to theories not strictly of form A' (or of form A). One such formulation emerges in connection with A1-C1 below, and illustrates the theorem's generality along this other dimension.

3. Possible Objections

With one exception, no criticisms of the argument for the Gödelian TH1 that I am aware of have probed either its assumptions or its inferences.[6] Instead the misgivings have been about my interpretation of CR in A-C, and occasionally about my motives. As regards the latter, it was not and is not my aim to "show that irrational commitment is necessary".[7] Nor was it or is it my aim to find a "rational excuse for irrationalism."[8] As I said at the end of PCRT, "nothing in it should be construed as entailing a retreat to some form of irrationalism" (p. 249). And I explicitly suggested that Quine's theory of rationality, and Lakatos', represent theories which, unlike CR, are not afflicted by these particular self-referential troubles (pp. 247–248, 228 n.17), whatever their other merits.

My motives, when I began the research that led to PCRT, were to answer every extant criticism of Bartley's CCR, convinced as I was of CCR's soundness. I thought that answering the criticisms would be mainly a matter of applying, as no one had yet done, some of the formal techniques of contemporary logic. In the course of trying to represent the debate in formal terms, I began wondering how one might symbolize sentences like 'This very sentence is criticizable' and then, because they were modally simpler, sentences like 'This very sentence is possibly false'. I was shocked when in my notes on the latter I began to find what amounted to steps in the derivation of an antinomy; for I had supposed such sentences would be consistent, indeed provably so (within an appropriate formal system). Worse, it dawned on me that just as the Classical Liar has an Epimenides version ('All Cretans are liars'), so does the Possible Liar. Thus sentences like 'Every sentence in a certain class to which this very one belongs is possibly false' proved paradoxical.[9] But of course they resemble CCR's characteristic principle that every-

6. The exception is Gibbons; see note 5, above. Derksen, *op. cit.*, is actually arguing about how to formulate CCR properly, by means of subscripts on 'criticizable'. But his proposal overlooks the argument in § VIII of PCRT against such subscripting, which would reduce the degree of criticizability of CCR.

7. Bartley, Appendix, *op. cit.*, p. 15.
8. Settle, *op. cit.*, p. 433.
9. See "The Possible Liar", *op. cit.*, p. 408.

thing, including this principle itself, is criticizable. Such reflections were what first shook my confidence in CCR, and I began to reflect on related theories, and on Gödel.

I remain a convinced anti-justificationist, or what comes to the same, an anti-foundationalist. And I am convinced that even C, above, is *revisable in some sense* (Quine's, perhaps), even though C is uncriticizable (in CR's sense, which satisfies $(\alpha) - (\delta)$). The Gödelian theorem, though it clearly applies to a very broad class of theories, does not represent an inherent limit on rationality no matter how rationality is construed. The challenge to us all is to construe rationality by means of an adequate theory which, among other things, is not prey to Gödelian or other limitative theorems. Or as I put it at the end of PCRT, "What is entailed is a search for a better theory of rationality—a theory which succeeds wherever CR does, but which enjoys full self-referential success as well" (p. 249).

As regards proper interpretation of CR, there is first of all the charge that I think proponents of CR must *justify* CR by demonstrating that it satisfies its own standards.[10] To think they must do so would of course be to miss the point of the distinction between justification and survival of criticism, plus the distinction between justificational and non-justificational criticism. But whatever in PCRT—if anything—may have been responsible for the impression that I think the onus is on CR to justify itself, it should be clear from the above sketch that nothing in the argument for TH1 implies any such thing.

For example, the claim C, that B satisfies its own standard, is expressly allowed to be a conjecture. And the world 'claim' itself expressly need not mean "claim as justified", or as true, or probable. Instead it means "claim fallibly, as criticizable and as having so far survived criticism". So too for the words 'hold' and 'good reason'. True, in PCRT I used the word 'accept'. This is a buzz-word for CR, and I knew it at the time; justificationist philosophers use it always to mean "accept as justified", or as proved, or probable, or whatever. But it can also mean "accept fallibly, as criticizable and as having so far survived". This is the way it is used in PCRT.[11] I thought at the time, and still think, that the context made clear this was its use. So too for my use of 'entitled to accept' to mean "fallibly entitled to hold as criticizable and as having so far survived".

As for 'onus' or 'burden of proof', the phrase nowhere occurred, nor did the idea. In any case, I was and am profoundly suspicious of burden-of-proof arguments in philosophy, not only because the intended idea of proof is so often foundationalist, and the standards for who has the burden so amorphous, but because shifting the burden to an opponent is so often question-begging—just as the question is begged against CR if we demand it justify itself. So I deny that CR has any burden of proof. But I affirm that CR has the burden of finding some way out of the Gödelian theorem, if there is one for CR.

10. See Settle, *op. cit.,* pp. 434–35; and Bartley, Appendix, *op. cit.,* p. 8.
11. Contrary to Settle, *op. cit.,* p. 434.

The way out is not to object to some necessary condition for criticizability I proposed in addition to $(\alpha) - (\delta)$. Even when the objection succeeds, it leaves $(\alpha) - (\delta)$ untouched, and $(\alpha) - (\delta)$ suffice to yield premises (1) and (2), hence the theorem. For example, I proposed that if S is to be a criticism of X (or less elliptically, to be a "potential criticizer" of X), then S must be specifiable. That is, we must be able to present a syntactically well formed sentence, together with its semantic interpretation, which expresses a statement that satisfies the other necessary conditions for its being a criticism of X. In part I was encouraged to propose this as a necessary condition of criticizability by Popper's remark that "criteria of refutation have to be laid down beforehand", if a theory is to receive real support from any test or attempted criticism of it.[12]

My interpretation of that remark may have been wrong; and in any case, I have now been persuaded (by Bartley) that specifiability is too strong a necessary condition for something to be a (potential) criticism.[13] But the whole question of specifiability is beside the point, as is the question of whether requiring specifiability would be justificationist in effect.[14] Nothing in $(\alpha) - (\delta)$ or in the rest of the argument for TH1 presupposes specifiability. Indeed I spent a paragraph in PCRT (p. 237) pointing out that the argument for premises (1) and (2) does not require specifiability of a potential criticizer of B or of C (or, by implication, of anything else).

Nor does the way out of the Gödelian theorem consist in arguing that the conditions I proposed for criticizability are not jointly sufficient (even though they were not meant to be). Add as many conditions as you like to $(\alpha) - (\delta)$, the theorem still follows. Only if (but not if) an added condition has the effect of cancelling one of $(\alpha) - (\delta)$ is the theorem thwarted.

A far more promising line, therefore, is cheerfully to admit that TH1 and TH2 apply to A, and thus to anyone so misguided as to express his (version of) CR via A. But CR need not be so expressed, and perhaps should not be. For example, A and B (plus much of the argument for TH1) seem to make rationality an intrinsic property of statements, "whereas rationality is . . . a matter of the way in which a statement is held."[15] It is a matter of a person's attitude or behavior toward the statement and his critics, at a time and over time, in a certain place and historical context.

Likewise A − C seem to make criticizability a property which a statement intrinsically has or not, rather like truth, whereas (as Bartley puts it) "to hold a statement open to criticism is to make the hypothesis, the guess, that the statement may be wrong, and that *some day* some effective criticism, the nature of which we cannot even imagine today, may be produced against it."[16] What would

---

12. *Conjectures and Refutations* (New York: Harper and Row, 1968), p. 38n.
13. Bartley, Appendix, *op. cit.*, pp. 7–10. Perhaps I ought also to have been persuaded by Settle, *op. cit.*, p. 434.
14. As both Bartley and Settle argue.
15. Bartley, Appendix, *op. cit.*, p. 5.
16. Bartley, Appendix, *op. cit.*, p. 8.

even count as a criticism of a statement or theory – whether or not the criticism would be successful – depends on the theory's informative content; and our ability to spell out even a fraction of that content depends heavily on our present background knowledge, and on our present powers of logic and imagination.

Further, CR is primarily a theory not about statements in the first place, but about persons, and about how a rational or critical person might behave. It is a theory about the rationalist identity of persons, not of statements, and about such persons' attitudes and/or positions, whether or not the attitudes or positions are expressible in statements. Again A seems to offend.

Finally, A does offend in the following regard.[17] Even though A requires only the "non-inferential" statements to have survived criticism if they are to be held rationally, still A is too strong. The reason is that much if not all of one's unexamined, unproblematic, provisional background knowledge is presumably not held irrationally, yet not all that much is required for drawing the implications of the statements up for possible revision in the context relative to which this background is unproblematic. Hence, contrary to A, much of this background is not non-inferential and not irrationally held, and yet has not survived criticism precisely because it has not been examined.

My notion of "non-inferential" was meant to cover this, but I now see that strictly it does not. Probably I became preoccupied with the contrast between CR, which presupposes analyticity, and Quine, who does not, and who therefore has a way out of the Gödelian theorem. My preoccupation may have led me to over-emphasize the analytic parts of the provisionally unproblematic background. In any event, I should have spoken not of the "inferential" statements but of the provisionally unproblematic statements, which include the former. Then A would have read, "Every problematic statement (or every statement up for possible revision), if it is to be held rationally, must be criticizable and so far have survived criticism."

Even so, those other objections to A as an expression of CR would remain – the objections that A makes rationality and criticizability intrinsic properties of statements, that A thus ignores matters of personal and historical context, and that CR is not really a theory about statements in the first place, but about one's attitudes and/or positions even when the latter are not expressible in statements.

There were remarks in PCRT which were meant to anticipate such objections. For example, I wrote, "In its typical formulations [CR] is also about attitudes towards theories" (p. 225). "CR would have men behave in certain ways toward their own beliefs and toward those who criticize their beliefs" (p. 225). "X is a *rational* statement iff a rational man is entitled to accept X . . . (in context, under suitable interpretation)" (p. 226). "Criticizability does not depend solely on the logical form of the theory . . . [but] also on certain material requirements" (p. 229). True, I later called criticizability a "semantic property" (p. 247). But in context this clearly was elliptical for "partly semantic" (cf. §§ III and VIII). For I

---

17. As Bartley has pointed out in correspondence.

had explicitly said that criticizability "depends on such things as the knowledge and technique available at the time" (p. 229) which are not purely semantic matters but pragmatic-temporal, or material.

Unfortunately I also wrote, in effect, that these personal, contextual, and normative aspects of CR were not "readily accessible to logical treatment of the kind employed" in the argument for the Gödelian theorem (p. 225). I did not mean that they could not be so treated, only that the treatment would be less simple (as we see below). Also I thought it would be clear how the basic strategy behind the theorem is so flexible as to be applicable even to versions of CR which, unlike A, are explicitly about persons, their occasionally inexpressible attitudes, and so on.

Obviously, none of this was as clear as I thought. Even so, those who objected to A in the above ways needed to do more than conclude merely that they had been misinterpreted. *They needed also to see whether their position, properly formulated, nevertheless is vulnerable to the basic strategy behind the Gödelian theorem.* None, so far as I know, took this necessary further step. Let us now do so.

4. An Application to the Rationality of People

What might a properly formulated version of CR look like? When we take account of all the foregoing objections to A, we arrive at something like the following as (one component of) the version of CR at issue:

> A1.   Consider a person P, a context K, a time *t*, and an attitude, belief, or position X (expressible or not) which is problematic (or up for possible revision) for P in K at *t*. Then P holds X rationally in K at *t* only if: P holds X open to criticism at *t*, and (so far as P can then tell or guess) X has at *t* so far survived criticism.

The heart of A1 is its second sentence. The first merely indicates the range of the implicit universal quantifiers in the second over P, X, *t*, and K. Since A1 is not of the form A', TH2 does not apply. But just as A' entails B', A1 entails

> B1.   P holds X rationally at *t* only if P holds X open to criticism at *t*,

where to say that P holds X open to criticism at *t* is to say (following Bartley) that at *t*, P conjectures, hypothesizes, or guesses both that X may be wrong, and that there is some (potential) criticism of X, the nature of which we may not even be able to imagine at *t*, and which might someday be produced and be seen to be a successful (or effective) criticism of X.[18]

18. See the quote above to which note 16 is attached. The argument-strategy behind the Gödelian theorem can be applied even if P is supposed to conjecture not that there *is* some criticism of X, imaginable or not, which might someday be produced and be seen to be successful, but that *possibly* there is. Merely insert 'necessarily' after 'For P*' in (1*) and (2*), below, in the appropriate sense of 'necessarily', and adjust the rest of the argument accordingly.

Now suppose that P* is the Critical Rationalist himself, who holds A1 and therefore B1, and who understands that A1 and B1 are indeed problematic in the present context K at the present time t. The question thus arises as to whether P* can hold B1 rationally at t, and therefore as to whether P* can hold B1 open to criticism at t. But to say that P* holds B1 open to criticism at t is to say that he conjectures at t both that B1 may be wrong and that

C1.   There is a (potential) criticism of B1, which might someday be produced and be seen to be successful.

Clearly C1 also is problematic in the present context (cf. (γ)), so that if C1 is to be held rationally by P*, then by B1 P* must hold C1 open to criticism, and thereby conjecture that there is a (potential) criticism of C1, the nature of which we need not be able to imagine, but which might someday be seen to count successfully against C1. And P* can genuinely conjecture this about C1 only if he is not compelled by argument from the rest of what he conjectures at t to hold that there is no such (potential) criticism of C1 after all.

The basic argument-strategy behind the Gödelian theorem now applies to A1 – C1 as follows. First,

(1*).   For P* every criticism of C1 is a criticism of B1, whether or not the criticism might someday be produced and be seen to be successful.

The argument for premise (1*) begins by noting that in the present K and t, the Critical Rationalist P* is offering B1 as a principle that is rational by its own standard, hence as a principle about which P* himself makes the conjecture, expressed in C1, that there is some possibly successful criticism of it. But if criticism were to persuade P* that C1 fails – that there is no (potential) criticism of B1 – then he could not genuinely hold B1 open to criticism, which is what C1 says. Hence in the present K, for P* a failure of C1 to be correct would mean that B1 fails to satisfy its own standard (of being genuinely held open to criticism by P*). Thus in K, for P* every consideration which counts against C1 would count against B1, so that for P* every criticism of C1 is a criticism of B1. If in addition P* holds condition (α) above (of the retransmission of criticism), and if P* agrees that B1 implies C1, or at least that B1 implies C1 in the present K, then we have a further argument for (1*) (assuming P* agrees the retransmission holds not only for implication, but for implication-in-a-context).

There is likewise an analogue of premise (2). Again whether or not the criticism might someday be produced and be seen to be successful,

(2*).   For P* no criticism of B1 is a criticism of C1.

The intuitive idea here is much as before: P* would recognize that the existence of a (possibly successful) criticism of B1 would entail C1 (since that is what C1 says), so for P* this criticism of B1 could hardly count also as a criticism of C1. Intuition aside, virtually the same argument works here as worked above for (2):

merely substitute 'B1' for 'B' and 'C1' for 'C' throughout; prefix every operative clause in the argument by 'for P*'; and assume that P* agrees to conditions (β) and (δ). Since by hypothesis P* is a Critical Rationalist, it is hard to see how he could disagree with any of (α) — (δ).

From (1*) and (2*) it follows at once that for the Critical Rationalist P*, there is no (potential) criticism of C1 after all, whether or not such criticism could ever be produced and be seen to be successful. But then P* cannot genuinely conjecture that there is some such criticism of C1, which he must be able to do if he is to hold C1 open to criticism in the relevant sense (which was explained, à la Bartley, in the lines just below B1). And because for P* C1 is problematic in the present context K, it follows that if P* holds C1 rationally in K, then for P* C1 is a strict counterexample to B1, which therefore is false (or invalid) even for P*, though of course B1 is criticizable in view of this very argument for its invalidity.

Next, suppose P* has good reason to hold A1 in K (say because P* rightly holds that A1 has so far survived criticism). Then P* has good reason to hold B1 and C1, assuming he knows that A1 entails B1 and agrees that in K, B1 implies C1. But C2 is either rational for P* by A1's standards or not. If it is, then B1 is invalid for P*, as just seen, as is A1, and P* must conclude that A1 does not survive the present criticism; hence A1 would be self-referentially inconsistent as regards survival. If C1 is not rational for P* by A1's standards, then C1 is an example of something which P* has good reason to hold if he has good reason to hold A1, but which P* does not rationally hold by A1's standards; hence A1 would be incomplete, and inherently so (since A1 implies C1). Thus we are forced to conclude that unless the Critical Rationalist P* has no good reason to hold A1 in the first place, A1 is either self-referentially inconsistent or inherently incomplete (indeed essentially so, if every workable notion of being held open to criticism satisfies (α) — (δ)).

In essence this is just the Gödelian theorem all over again, restated in terms of A1 – C1 instead of A – C. Hence all the above objections to A as an interpretation of CR in general or CCR in particular are beside the point. Such objections fail to address the basic strategy, which is quite flexible and general, and applies even to versions of CR which, like A1, are explicitly about persons, their occasionally inexpressible attitudes, their historical contexts, and so on. It even applies, as noted in connection with TH2 above, to theories that are not versions of CR, such as positivism, verificationism, instrumentalism, and some forms of pragmatism. Hence the strategy also has this other sort of generality, along a dimension we need not now explore, but which stands as a further warning against assuming that the difficulties posed by the Gödelian theorem do not occur at any very fundamental level.

Addendum (1985)

The way out of the Gödelian theorem is not to claim, as Bartley now does, that such a result really comes as no surprise, in view of Tarski's having shown that "any natural language containing semantic terms and the possibility of self-reference may be expected to be inconsistent, and to produce just such paradoxes."[1] For Tarski showed no such thing, whatever he may have thought. He did show that a language which both contains the means of semantic self-reference and satisfies certain further conditions must be inconsistent. But whether natural languages satisfy those further conditions is another matter; most analysts conclude that they do not, and I agree.

Part of Bartley's argument that paradoxes are inevitable is a short derivation of an objection to his own view—a derivation he says is inspired by mine, but simpler.[2] Unfortunately his derivation is unsound. It relies at one point on the unstated assumption that *if a position is false, then there is an argument showing it to be false.* This principle is required if we are to grant Bartley's inference from (i) "if (B) is false, then (A) is false" and (ii) "an argument showing (A) to be false (and thus criticizing it) shows (B) to be true" to (iii) "if (B) is false, then (B) is true".[3] For the inference assumes that if (A) is false, then there is an argument showing (A) to be false. Otherwise the consequent of (i) and what in effect is the antecedent of (ii) will not be connected, as they must be for the inference to (iii) (presumably hypothetical syllogism) to succeed. Yet the assumed principle should be rejected, and not only according to critical rationalists. For it is logically equivalent (by contraposition) to 'If there is no argument showing a position to be false, then it is true'. This principle is what underlies the fallacy of arguing from ignorance, and in any case is inconsistent with a realist conception of truth.

Suppose nevertheless that the critical rationalist uses this sort of "paradoxes-are-inevitable" defense. Then his opponent the justificationist is entitled to use it too. Thus in response to Bartley's argument (or the *tu quoque*) that justificationism is not itself justified, and therefore is self-referentially inconsistent, the justificationist may reply that such a result really comes as no surprise, in view of the inevitable inconsistency of natural language, within which such a theory as his must be expressed. He may go further, as now Bartley apparently does, and adopt a language-level solution to the paradoxes, according to which he should not be interpreted as holding a literally self-applicable position in the first place, so that it is unfair to demand a justification for justificationism itself.

1. W. W. Bartley, III, "The Alleged Refutation of Pancritical Rationalism", Appendix 4 of *The Retreat to Commitment*, 2d ed., revised and enlarged (La Salle: Open Court, 1984), p. 219.

2. *Ibid.*, p. 224.

3. *Ibid.*

Clearly, this is to upset the chessboard when losing, as I argued in detail in § VIII of PCRT; Bartley's portrayal of my argument (outlined in the next paragraph but one) misconstrues it completely. And anyway, if the chessboard were not upset, the justificationist could rightly reject the whole of Bartley's self-referential argument against justificationism, so that much of *The Retreat to Commitment* would make no sense. Because I think it makes excellent sense, some other way out of the Gödelian theorem must be found if there is one.

Popper too adopted a language-level solution to the paradoxes: "semantical antinomies can best be avoided by assuming a hierarchy of (semantical) metalanguages."[4] And despite having written that "Nothing is exempt from criticism – not even this principle of the critical method itself", he subsequently wrote that he should not after all be interpreted as holding a literally self-applicable position: all incautious phrases such as "'[the] principle that everything is open to criticism (from which this principle itself is not exempt)' . . . should read: 'The metalinguistic principle that everything is open to criticism (a principle which, we can say in a metalanguage of higher order, should in its turn be open to criticism).'"[5] This was in response to a draft of PCRT sent Popper in 1969, and it occurs in a footnote that suggests I merely drew his attention to the need to abjure semantic self-reference and rewrite the offending passages in line with a language-level approach.

But of course much more was afoot in PCRT, and to my knowledge Popper never responded to the arguments of §VIII (and elsewhere) that there is substantial independent reason to believe the paradoxes are *not* best solved by a language-level approach, that there are powerful solutions which allow very extensive semantic self-reference (enough certainly to express the self-referential principles of the relevant theories of rationality), and that therefore the effect if not the intent of revising one's (erstwhile) self-referential principles in line with the language-level approach is to make them less criticizable (since a theory about all theories including itself has greater content than one only about all theories at a lower level, and thus takes a greater risk of refutation).

Furthermore, contrary to Bartley, the justificational and nonjustificational approaches are not symmetrical, despite their both being self-referential and expressed in natural language.[6] For it is not the case that "semantical paradoxes could be reproduced as easily in justificational approaches as . . . in nonjustificational."[7] Even though the Gödelian theorem applies to a number of justificational approaches (positivism, verificationism, some forms of pragmatism – see PCRT), clearly it does not apply to them all. And as argued in PCRT, there are nonjustificational approaches (such as Quine's) to which the theorem does not apply. The

4. Karl R. Popper, "Replies to My Critics," in P. A. Schilpp, ed., *The Philosophy of Karl Popper* (La Salle: Open Court, 1974), pp. 1098–99.
5. *Ibid.*, p. 1196 n213.
6. Bartley, *op. cit.*, p. 230.
7. *Ibid.*, p. 230.

result therefore is discriminating enough for us to draw some solid conclusions from it about certain theories of rationality. This is not a night in which all cows are black.

Finally, suppose criticizability and survival of criticism were not necessary but only sufficient for rationality.[8] Then indeed it would still be possible to be a rationalist.[9] In fact it would be all too easy to be one. For then arbitrary dogma, shielded from every criticism, could not be condemned as irrational on the ground that it is uncriticizable; dogmatists and fideists could legitimately claim to be rationalists. This absurd outcome can be avoided only if one's theory of rationality states some necessary condition that arbitrary dogmas and leaps of faith will not satisfy. The justificationist's proposed necessary condition is rejected by the critical rationalist, and rightly. But what necessary condition does the critical rationalist put in its place, if not criticizability and survival of criticism?

For these and other reasons I still believe that the challenge to us all is to construe rationality by means of an adequate theory which succeeds everywhere critical rationalism does, but which is not prey to Gödelian or other limitative theorems.

8. *Ibid.*, p. 238.
9. *Ibid.*

══ *Chapter* **XIII** ══════════════════

Comprehensively Critical Rationalism: A Retrospect

By John Watkins

During the twenty years since its birth my attitude to Comprehensively Critical Rationalism has changed considerably. In this paper I will try to explain why.

1. Bartley's Original Problem

If a philosophical work should be judged more by the problems it poses than by the solutions it offers, then W. W. Bartley's *The Retreat to Commitment* was, and still is, an important book. I found it exciting when I first read it and when I re-read it the other day I was again impressed by its combination of readability and structured argument. Where other philosophical books around that time contain a figure called "the sceptic", Bartley has a figure called "the irrationalist"; but whereas the "sceptic" is a wan, even ghostly, figure who is regularly chided and derided for his absurd obsession with logical rigor, and the question is how best to shrug him off, Bartley's "irrationalist" is a robust fellow, the representative of a sizeable number of real people, mostly Protestant theologians, who glory in discomfitting priggish rationalists and shallow liberals. Far from being shrugged off he is *confronted* head-on. True, he makes only one good point, but he makes it forcibly and effectively and it poses the book's fundamental problem. His point is epitomized by his famous retort to the would-be rationalist: *tu quoque!* A would-be rationalist may pretend to have arrived at his position in a rational way, but if so he deceives himself: he has to make an *irrational commitment* to rationalism. The difference is that the irrationalist makes his irrational commitment openly and honestly. As Bartley put it:

> More extreme irrationalists have gone so far as to suggest that almost *any* deliberate commitment is better than a liberalism which is, they say, typically unaware of its commitments. The soul-impoverished rationalist or liberal, not realizing that he cannot avoid making an irrational commitment, makes one blindly without knowing what he is doing (p. 94).

An earlier draft of this essay was published in *The Proceedings of the Eleventh International Conference on the Unity of the Sciences* (New York: International Cultural Foundation, 1983).

So the problem is posed: is there a viable conception of rationalism such that a rationalist who adopts it is no longer exposed to a *tu quoque*, a conception that would deprive the irrationalist of his sole, yet highly dangerous and effective, argument? As we all know, Bartley answered that there is and that he called it Comprehensively Critical Rationalism.

2. Bartley's Original Solution

I begin with a minor criticism of Bartley's presentation. Someone once observed that Popperians are like Hegelians in one respect: they are very prone to present a triad of views, with the third view coming out on top. Bartley presented three views concerning human rationality. Yet it is clear that the two main antitheses with which he was working yield not three but four positions. One antithesis is between a rationalism that is comprehensive and one that is limited, for instance because it excepts itself from its own requirements. The other is between a rationalism that is justificatory and one that is non-justificatory and critical. We thus have these possibilities:

(1) comprehensively justificatory rationalism
(2) justificatory rationalism
(3) critical rationalism
(4) comprehensively critical rationalism

Bartley's term 'critical rationalism' covers both (2) and (3). This does not matter too much, but it has the awkward consequence that one contemporary philosopher whom Bartley discussed at some length, namely Ayer, gets placed in the same category as Popper. But they surely ought to be put in separate categories, namely (2) and (3) respectively, despite their both having held, in different ways, that rationality is limited. Thus Ayer insisted that there can be no justification (other than self-justification) for the ultimate standards by which rationally accepted statements are justified.[1] And Popper had insisted that his kind of rationalism cannot, for logical reasons, be comprehensive:

> But this means that whoever adopts the rationalist attitude does so because he has adopted, consciously or unconsciously, some proposal . . . ; an adoption which may be called 'irrational'. Whether this adoption is tentative or leads to a settled habit, we may describe it as an irrational *faith in reason*. So rationalism is necessarily far from comprehensive or self-contained. This has frequently been overlooked by rationalists who thus exposed themselves to a beating in their own field and by their own favourite weapon whenever an irrationalist took the trouble to turn it against them.

He added,

1. A. J. Ayer, *The Problem of Knowledge* (London: Penguin, 1956), p. 75.

Accordingly, our choice is open. We may choose some form of irrationalism . . . But we are also free to choose a critical form of rationalism, one which frankly admits its origin in an irrational decision . . . [2]

This choice, he said, is a moral one.

I do not know whether any fideist, Christian or otherwise, has exploited this passage, but Bartley would presumably have said that it plays into the irrationalist's hands. His own view was that the element of fideism (the allegedly irrational faith in reason) could be eliminated from critical rationalism by a rather simple and natural generalization of Popper's critical rationalism. Concerning scientific theories the latter says that it may be rational to adopt one, provisionally, *not* because it is in some sense positively justified (for instance, rendered probably true) by evidence, which it is not, but rather because, although highly testable and although severely tested, it has survived tests. Bartley proposed to generalize this by replacing 'testable' and 'test' by 'criticizable' and 'criticism'. We could then say that a critical rationalist may provisionally adopt a moral, metaphysical, or philosophical position, provided it is highly criticizable, has been subjected to severe critical scrutiny, and has survived criticism; and we can further say that one philosophical position in particular that he may rationally adopt in this way is *critical rationalism*. If that is so, there is an important *structural* difference, and not just a difference in content, between justificatory and critical rationalism: the former cannot, while the latter can, be made *comprehensive* and applied to itself without inconsistency.

When I first learnt of comprehensively critical rationalism from Bartley I regarded it as an important advance: the critical rationalist can be rational about his rationalism. Bravo!

3. The Tricky Question of Uncriticizability

But after a time I became uneasy about this generalization of Popper's idea of rational acceptance within a scientific context to much wider contexts, and the generalization of the idea of empirical testability into that of criticizability. We are sometimes in a position to say unequivocally of two propositions that one is, and the other is not, testable. But can we ever say of two theories that one is, and the other is not, criticizable? Bartley once proposed that the important demarcation is not between falsifiable and unfalsifiable but between criticizable and uncriticizable theories.[3] But would such a demarcation effect a cut? How could the uncriticizability of a theory be established?

2. K. R. Popper, *The Open Society and its Enemies* (London: Routledge & Kegan Paul, Ltd., 4th ed., 1962), Vol. II, p. 231.

3. W. W. Bartley, III, "Theories of Demarcation Between Science and Metaphysics", in I. Lakatos and A. E. Musgrave, eds., *Problems in the Philosophy of Science* (Amsterdam: North-Holland Publishing Co., 1968), p. 49.

This last question will serve to introduce the first criticism of CCR that I published. Bartley held that an unjustifiable position may be held rationally *provided that it can be held open to criticism and survives severe criticism.*[4] So for CCR to be capable of being held rationally it should be capable of surviving severe criticism. But how might one set about trying to criticize it? This question had been raised by Bartley. After describing a possible line of criticism he remarked:

> Although I doubt it, such an argument may be possible. But the onus is on the irrationalist to produce it. I have, in the meantime, done what I can . . . I have just now gone so far as to specify what sort of argument I would accept as a refutation of my position. (p. 149)

The sort of argument that he would accept was this:

> For example, someone could devastatingly refute this kind of rationalism if he were to produce an argument showing that at least some of the unjustified and unjustifiable critical standards necessarily used by a comprehensively critical rationalist were uncriticizable . . .

So the one line of criticism of CCR envisaged by its author was that some essential component of it might be shown to be uncriticizable. But it occurred to me that this line of criticism is *not* available to a would-be critic of CCR. For to show that a philosophical position, or an essential component thereof, has an undesirable property is undoubtedly to *criticize* it. And in view of what CCR says, uncriticizability is an undesirable property. For it says that a rationalist "holds *all* his beliefs . . . open to criticism".[5] Thus if one could show that an essential component of CCR is uncriticizable one would show that it has an undesirable property, which would amount to a strong *criticism* of it, so strong, indeed, that it would "devastatingly refute" CCR. So it is *impossible* to show that either CCR itself or any essential component of it is uncriticizable. The one line of potential criticism of CCR indicated by Bartley never could be actualized. I presented this negative result in 1969.[6]

In a reply to me Agassi, Jarvie, and Settle wrote:

> Watkins is quite correct to claim that the criticizability of CCR is reinforced by every attempt to refute it – this should not be surprising since the criticizability of any doctrine is never reinforced better than on the occasion of its refutation. It does not follow that CCR is thereby rendered immune from defeat.[7]

And Kekes made a similar point: "It is true that no criticism will show the uncriticizability of CCR"; however "nothing [Watkins] says excludes the possibility

---

4. Bartley, *The Retreat to Commitment* (New York: Alfred A. Knopf, Inc., 1st ed., 1962), pp. 147–48. Bartley actually wrote *"survives severe testing"*, but the word 'testing' does not seem right here.

5. Bartley, "Rationality versus the Theory of Rationality", in Mario Bunge, ed., *The Critical Approach to Science and Philosophy* (New York: Free Press, 1964), p. 30.

6. John Watkins, "Comprehensively Critical Rationalism", *Philosophy* **44**, January 1969, pp. 45–51.

7. J. Agassi, I. Jarvie, and T. Settle, "The Grounds of Reason", *Philosophy* **46**, January 1971, pp. 44–45.

of showing the *falsity* of CCR."[8] This is true: there may be other lines of criticism than the one indicated by Bartley in his book, and perhaps one of these will lead to a refutation. Indeed, by the time I received the papers of Agassi *et al.* and of Kekes, I believed that I had hit upon a refutation; and I fear that I rather offended them because in my reply, instead of answering their criticism of my earlier paper, I presented this refutation, in 1971.[9] Perhaps I may now belatedly mention one point of Agassi *et al.* which puzzled me. They wrote:

> . . . it is noteworthy that whereas Watkins amply documents most of the views he ascribes to Bartley, he gives no reference in Bartley's writings for the view that the position that a rationalist can and should hold all his positions open to criticism is a position a rationalist *should hold*. And we can find none.[10]

But surely this did not need *documenting*. The whole thrust of Bartley's argument was that while comprehensive rationalism is a position that a rationalist cannot hold, since it is self-destructive, and critical rationalism is a position that he should not hold, since it exposes him to a *tu quoque*, comprehensively critical rationalism is *the* position that he can and should hold. In Bartleyan language, this is the one rationalist identity that permits rationalist integrity.

4. My 1971 Refutation Updated

My argument was based on two explicitly made assumptions concerning a reasonable interpretation of Bartley's characterization of a rationalist "as one who holds *all* his beliefs . . . open to criticism". The first was that, just as a scientist cannot genuinely hold open to falsification a proposition that is in fact unfalsifiable, so a rationalist cannot genuinely hold open to criticism a proposition that is in fact uncriticizable (we will reconsider this assumption later). The second was that analytic truths, such as '$0 \neq 1$' are, typically though not invariably, uncriticizable (though it may be a criticism of an allegedly substantive thesis to reveal that it has, after all, a merely tautological character). Given those assumptions I took the following proposition A to express what I called the nonpsychologistic core of CCR:

A: All nonanalytic and rationally acceptable statements are criticizable.

Now the distinctive thing about *comprehensively* critical rationalism is that it, unlike critical rationalism, applies to itself. So from A we may proceed to

B: A is a nonanalytic and rationally acceptable statement.

And from A and B we can derive

C: A is a criticizable statement.

8. J. Kekes, "Watkins on Rationalism", *Philosophy* **46**, January 1971, p. 51.
9. Watkins, "CCR: A Refutation", *Philosophy* **46**, January 1971, pp. 56–61.
10. *Ibid.*, p. 46.

Concerning these three propositions I showed that: C is analytic; B is false; and A is either analytic or false.

That C is analytic follows from the fact that if *per impossibile* one could show that C is false, that would constitute a major *criticism* of A, thereby establishing that C is true (the central point of my 1969 note).

As to A: without defining 'criticizable' I did say that it is, surely, an absolutely minimum condition for a proposition p to be criticizable that there exists at least one statement (it need not have been formulated) that bears adversely on p and which is *not self-contradictory*; and I suggested that the next, slightly stronger, condition would require such an adverse statement (what Post calls a "potential criticizer" of p) to be neither self-contradictory nor *certainly false*. I then argued that A would become *analytic* if one adopted the absolutely minimum condition as sufficient for criticizability; for to every nonanalytic statement there corresponds a statement which is not self-contradictory and which bears very adversely on it, namely its negation. If however one adopts the next, slightly stronger, condition as either sufficient, or at least necessary, for criticizability, then A becomes *falsified*. For there are statements (e.g., "There exists at least one sentence written in English prior to the year two thousand that consists of precisely twenty-two words") that are nonanalytic and which we rationally accept just because we find them to be certainly true, and hence uncriticizable in this second, slightly stronger sense.

Now if A is either analytic, as it becomes on the minimum condition for criticizability, or else falsified, as it becomes on the slightly stronger condition, then B must be false. For B says of A, first that it is nonanalytic, and second that it is rationally acceptable; but we have found that if A is nonanalytic, then it cannot be rationally acceptable, because it is falsified by truisms like the above.

I have not been alone in my criticism of CCR. In 1970 John Post proved[11] that the sentence

This very sentence *may be* false

is paradoxical in rather the same way as is

This very sentence *is* false.

And since CCR seems to imply that CCR may be false, he went on to investigate whether CCR is not paradoxical. He concluded that it is.[12] Post, and also Derksen, have cited against CCR nonanalytic truisms like the above. To someone who objects that these are boring and banal, I would reply that an intrinsically boring statement may nevertheless be philosophically interesting. If G. E. Moore had been in the habit of assuring people that he had two hands, or if Descartes had been in the habit of assuring people that he existed, they would have been thought

11. John Post, "The Possible Liar", *Nous* 4, 1970, and Chapter X of this volume.
12. Post, "Paradox in Critical Rationalism and Related Theories", *Philosophical Forum* 3, 1972, and Chapter XI of this volume.

peculiar. I like to think that the above sentence of twenty-two words is not the most interesting one I have ever penned. But it should have a certain interest for someone who has described comprehensively critical rationalism as the position "which holds *everything* [my italics], justifiable or not, open to criticism".[13]

How does Bartley respond to our truistic counterexamples? In a reply to Derksen he wrote: "All I need . . . is to claim that it is *logically possible* [my italics] (without leading to infinite regress, vicious circle, or other logical difficulty) to hold such statements open to criticism."[14] He has also said that critics who concentrate upon the criticizability or otherwise of statements are missing the point, because CCR is a theory about people, and the attitude they should adopt if they seek to be rational, not about statements.[15]

I am entirely sympathetic to the idea that what makes someone a critical rationalist is his attitude to criticisms of his views, rather than the statements he propounds. There are people (I call them "Critical Rationalists" to differentiate them from practicing critical rationalists) whose practice diverges astonishingly from what they preach. Yet I wonder whether CCR was really a theory about *people*. Bartley had said that he was concerned, not with "the practical limitations of rationality such as those explored by Freud – due to human weakness, physical frailty, humanity, but with a so-called *logical* limitation of rationality".[16] That does not sound to me like a theory about people. But let it pass. This emphasis on people directs attention away from the criticizability or otherwise of the statements they accept to the critical or otherwise attitude that they adopt towards them. Their *attitude* might be severely critical, even though some of the statements in question were uncriticizable. Now I admit that I went too far in 1971 when I assumed that "a critically-minded rationalist cannot, presumably, genuinely hold a position open to criticism unless it is actually criticizable in some objective sense" (p. 56); for such a person, not realizing that a certain statement is not actually criticizable in some objective sense, might be very ready to attend to criticisms of it. However, my 1971 refutation still goes through if we withdraw that assumption. We may reformulate CCR, as a doctrine about people and their attitudes, as follows:

> A': A comprehensively critical rationalist can hold open to criticism all the nonanalytic statements that he rationally accepts;
>
> B': A' is one of the nonanalytic statements that a comprehensively critical rationalist rationally accepts;
>
> C': A' is a statement that a comprehensively critical rationalist can hold open to criticism.

13. Bartley, *The Retreat to Commitment, op. cit.*, p. 150.

14. Bartley, "On the Criticizability of Logic – A Reply to A. A. Derksen", *Philosophy of the Social Sciences* **10**, March 1980, p. 77.

15. Bartley, "The Alleged Refutation of Pancritical Rationalism", *Proceedings of the Eleventh International Conference on the Unity of the Sciences*, 1983, Vol. II, p. 1158.

16. Bartley, "Rationality versus the Theory of Rationality", *op. cit.*, p. 5.

As before, we confront A' with our twenty-two word sentence, or something similarly ungainsayable. What would it mean to say that I *can* hold this open to criticism? If it meant that it is psychologically possible for me to do so, it would be false. Having carefully counted the number of words in that sentence several times, I am, as a matter of psychological fact, entirely assured of its truth, and would be unable to take seriously any attempted criticism of it. However, as we have seen, Bartley has taken 'I can hold p open to criticism' to mean only that it is *logically possible* for me to hold p open to criticism. Now it is of course logically possible for me to do anything that is not logically impossible. In *that* sense of 'can', I 'can' swim the Atlantic, doubt that I am over twenty-one – you name it. In that sense of 'can', the sentence 'I can hold open to criticism all the nonanalytic statements that I rationally accept' expresses a logical truth. A statement of that form, understood in that way, would cease to be true only if what is governed by 'can' were logically impossible; in which case, the statement would be a logical falsehood, as is 'I can resist irresistible forces'.

So the present A', like the previous A, is either analytic, as it becomes when 'can' denotes logical possibility, or else falsified, as it becomes when 'can' denotes psychological possibility; which means that the present B', like the previous B, must be false. For B' says of A', first that it is nonanalytic, and second that it is rationally acceptable; but *if* A' is nonanalytic, then it cannot be rationally acceptable, because it is falsified by the existence, for every one of us, of trivial but nonanalytic truths (I have two hands, am over twenty-one, etc.) that we rationally accept just because we are assured of their truth, and are psychologically incapable of holding open to criticism. (If someone approached me with what he claimed to be a cogent criticism of my belief that I am over twenty-one, I would send him packing.) Bartley, in the paper where he said that he needed to claim only that it is logically possible to hold such statements open to criticism, had previously conceded that he "may in fact hold some such views as beyond criticism".

Moreover, in C' above we have a statement that a critical rationalist, who gives the matter thought, knows that he *cannot* hold open to criticism; for he knows in advance that if, *per impossibile*, a good criticism of C' were forthcoming, then that, by *modus tollens*, would be a good criticism of A'; but if it were a good criticism of A', then it would *verify* C'. This is a case where Bartley's retreat from the psychological to the merely logical possibility of holding a statement open to criticism is of no avail. Anyone who understands its simple logic knows that he can no more hold C' open to criticism than he can resist an irresistible force. This is essentially my 1969 point again: integral to CCR is a component that is in principle uncriticizable and hence alien to CCR. So far as I know, this point has never been met.

5. Conclusion

As I said, a serious and interesting problem was posed, and posed in a new way, in *The Retreat to Commitment*. And the solution that Bartley proposed at first seemed, to me at least, simple and elegant. But a seemingly simple and elegant philosophical solution has a troublesome tendency to turn out to involve all sorts of unsuspected difficulties; it may even run into refutations. When that happens, its author may strive to defend and preserve it at all cost; in which case we get what Imre Lakatos used to call a degenerating problem-shift; or he may, as a good practicing critical rationalist, seek a different and better solution.

══ Chapter *XIV* ══════════════

In Defense of Self-Applicable Critical Rationalism*

By Gerard Radnitzky

"It is criticism that, recognizing no position as final, and refusing to bind itself by the shallow shibboleths of any sect or school, creates that serene philosophic temper which loves truth for its own sake, and loves it not less because it is unattainable".†

0. The Problem: Explication of the Concept of Rationality, and of Rationality in Inquiry in Particular

0.1. The Explicandum

Philosophical theories of rationality hinge upon the explication of the concept of rationality. Attempts to explicate a concept make sense only if there is an explicandum, if the intuitive concept – which, according to our proposal, should be replaced in certain contexts by the clarified and improved concept, the explicatum – has a sufficiently stable semantic spectrum. Traditionally a distinction is made between *rationality of means* and *rationality of ends or reasonableness*. In some contexts this distinction is indispensable. However, in both cases rational

---

Earlier versions of this Chapter were published in *The Proceedings of the Eleventh International Conference on the Unity of the Sciences* (New York: International Cultural Foundation, 1983), and, as "Are Comprehensive theories of rationality self-referentially inconsistent?" in *Epistemology and Philosophy of Science. Proceedings of the 7th International Wittgenstein Symposium* (Vienna: Hölder-Pichler-Tempsky, 1983).

* I wish to thank Dr. Gunnar Andersson for many valuable discussions and suggestions and Professors W. W. Bartley, III, and Antony Flew for critical comments on an earlier draft of this paper.
† This quotation – whose concluding passages could be taken from Lessing – is neither from Popper nor from Bartley, but from Oscar Wilde.

discussion and deliberation are possible and necessary.[1] This holds even for so-called "existential decisions" or "ultimate decisions".[2] However, when in every-day speech we talk about rationality *tout court*, we usually mean rationality of means. This concept quite unmistakably refers to the effective and efficient use of means to realize given ends. The use of the concept of efficiency in turn en-tails that cost-benefit analysis will be relevant. In these analyses the appraisal of means is intertwined with an evaluation and critique of ends. Thus the "economic approach" will be relevant throughout because the situation in which the ques-tion of the rational use of means arises will be characterized by scarcity of means and competing ends. However, with respect to inquiry, to cognition, the problem of ends may safely be bracketed because in inquiry, be it everyday inquiry or scien-tific research, the *global* aim, cognitive progress, is already given. This aim can-not be made problematical *within* scientific research because it is constitutive of the very meaning of research.

0.2. The Explicatum

By delimiting our problem to inquiry we have implicitly specified what sort of entities the explicatum is to be predicated of. Primarily it is to be predicated of *actions*, of particular actions, sorts of actions, and of *ways of acting*. Hence, if such a philosophical theory of rationality were to be elaborated, the concepts of intentionality and of success would have to be clarified. In problem-solving activity the sort of action that is of particular interest is adopting a position (the-ory, viewpoint, etc.), rejecting a position, preferring a position over its rivals, and so forth. Following W. W. Bartley, III, I shall here use "position" as an umbrella term for statements, theories, viewpoints, criteria, etc., and sometimes use "con-text" for a way of behaving towards positions or of dealing with positions. Acting

---

1. The criticism of *ends* will in the first place involve the following: (1) Checking whether or not the set of aims or values, the subjective preference structure, is free from *inconsistency*, whether or not it involves empirical impossibility and so forth; (2) drawing attention to *consequences* insofar as these are foreseeable – there will also always be unintended and unwanted consequences – in order to find out whether the "costs" of the means required for realizing the aim are acceptable to the agent.

2. "In order to be able to choose ends and standards in a responsible way critical examination is necessary. Thus such choices do not have to be some kind of blind existential leap into the dark-ness" (Andersson 1984a, p. 10). Walter Kaufmann aptly criticized the moral irrationalist who more or less explicitly holds that reason is irrelevant to ultimate commitments. He writes: "This is a way of saying that while it may be reasonable to keep your eyes open when making relatively petty deci-sions, it makes no sense to keep them open . . . when a choice is likely to mold your future. In other words, be careful when you drive slowly, but when you go over fifty miles per hour shut your eyes!" (Kaufmann, 1973, p. 23). Perhaps most of the so-called "ultimate decisions" ("ultimate" in the sense of being final is probably a rare case – suicide, for instance, or the decision of the kamikaze pilot) can be reconstructed as expressing preferences for future preferences. The typical case would be that of Odysseus and the Sirens or the decision to become a monk. However, when the Kierkegaardian "existential solipsist" holds that for the individual confronted with the question of his personal salva-tion, e.g., when facing death, every scientific or rational argument loses its interest, I wonder whether we have something to oppose him with (Radnitzky, 1968/73, 1973 ed., p. 375). If so, this would limit the impact of the above mentioned quotations from Andersson and Kaufmann.

rationally in the selection of positions (adoption of beliefs, etc.) is in turn a presupposition for success in practical action. In sum, "rationality" (means-rationality) will be predicated primarily of intentional acts (problem-solving activity) and ways of behaving. Only in a derived sense will it be predicated of persons. Rationality in the psychological sense is not a homogeneous personality trait. A person may be rational – most of the time – in one sort of situation while not behaving rationally in others, and moreover this personality trait may lack reliability. (Owing to such considerations, I am departing from Bartley who wishes to predicate 'rationality' primarily of persons.)

This essay will concentrate on the question of the rationality of *ways of dealing with positions* (theories, viewpoints, etc.). In particular it will contrast two such global ways applied in epistemology: the justificationist or foundationalist approach and the non-justificationist or criticist approach. The label "justificationist" indicates that, under the influence of a certain ideal of knowledge, it is presumed that human efforts to know are a quest for certainty or justification.

1. Performance on the Object Level of the Two Global Approaches, the Justificationist and the Non-Justificationist Approaches

1.0. Four Types of Approaches

This distinction appears to be the most important distinction in epistemology. I propose first to outline each of these approaches or contexts as they operate on the object level, and then address myself to the question of the self-applicability of the principle that characterizes each of them. The label *'meta level'* will be used for the level at which the question of self-applicability is dealt with. Thus we will be confronted with *four types: justificationism as not self-applicable and as self-applicable, non-justificatory approach or critical rationalism as not self-applicable and as self-applicable.*

Preview. Justification philosophy *(Begründungsphilosophie)*, a style of thinking based upon the search for epistemic "authorities", has been the dominant style of western philosophy. Karl Popper's approach to knowledge is nonauthoritarian, non-justificationist. Instead of attempting to verify or to probabilify a theory (positivism) or to show at least that it is inductively supported by evidence in the sense of so-called "soft inductivism" (such as, e.g., that advocated by L. J. Cohen), Popper proposes as a methodological maxim that theories be criticized by determining what would count against them, and then subjecting them to severe empirical testing. This removed the trilemma that justification philosophy meets, *viz.*, the trilemma of infinite regress or vicious circle or dogmatic stopping of the justification process. It removed the trilemma on the object level. Bartley attended to the question of the self-applicability of the criticist approach, to the problem on the meta level. He generalized one of the key maxims of critical rationalism, the prohibition against immunizing positions from criticism. He proposed that a way of dealing with positions is rational insofar as it follows the maxim: do not, in principle, dogmatize anything, i.e., keep all positions open to criticism – including this maxim. This explicatum offers a way out of the trilemma of justification philosophy. Underlying it is the insight that we *logically* need not – in order to avoid infinite regress – dogmatize anything, that the alleged dilemma of justification philosophy: "either infinite regress (or circle) or else ultimate commitment" is spurious. What is the import of Bartley's extension of critical rationalism's principle to the meta level? (1) He separated the notions of justification and criticism, so that by adopting the maxim "Hold all positions open to criticism", the trilemma can be avoided. (2) By making this principle self-applicable, he avoids the reappearance of the trilemma on the meta level.

1.1 Justification Philosophy on the Object Level

1.1.0. Aspirations and eventual failure of justificationist philosophy
1.1.0.1. Program and attraction of justification philosophy. Within the context of justification philosophy the main problem of epistemology (or, more accurately, what in this context is perceived as the central problem of epistemology) may be formulated: "When is it rational or, so to speak consistent with one's intellectual integrity, to *accept* a particular position"? The formulation suggests the direction in which the answer is to be sought: "When concerned with a statement, a theory, etc., accept those and only those statements, theories, etc., which not only are true but whose truth has been established." W. W. Bartley summarizes the main type of justificationism (which he calls 'comprehensive rationalism') by two principles: "(1) A rationalist accepts any position that can be justified by appeal to the rational authority; (2) a rationalist accepts *only* those positions that can be justified in this way."[3] This means that it is rational to accept all and only those positions that have been justified by appeal to the "rational authority". This, of course, presupposes that there exists such a rational authority or infallible source of knowledge, and that this source is accessible to human beings. Already at this juncture it becomes clear that the controversy will have to center on the claims of the various contestants to possess this authority.

Justificationism has been and still is dominant among philosophical theories of rationality. *Prima facie* it appears attractive. Since it implicitly acknowledges that not all positions are equally good or bad, it avoids relativism; and it recognizes that something more than and something different from blind belief must be demanded. Yet, in the context of epistemology, "to justify" means more than giving some reason for holding a particular belief. What are to be justified are truth claims. If the distinction between descriptive and (non-instrumentally) evaluative expressions is acknowledged, what is to be justified are primarily *truth claims* with respect to descriptive statements and, analogously, *validity claims* with respect to value judgments. In the context of justification philosophy *(Begründungs-*

---

3. Bartley, 1982, p. 138.

philosophie) the concept of justification is modelled upon the concept of mathematical proof: deduction from premisses. In the undiluted or pure version of justificationism it is claimed that the premisses are true and that their truth has been established (that they are also "known to be true"). This version may be labelled "foundationalism" because it explicitly claims that it is possible conclusively to make good truth claims and hence implies that there is a secure basis upon which to "found" particular statements. In sum, characteristic of the justificationist style in philosophy is that authorities are specified in terms of which to guarantee positions, and that, therefore, criticism is conceived as being in the service of justification. Of course criticism is always *intended* to serve error elimination, but in the justificationist context this immediate aim of criticism is subordinate to the overall aim of justifying in terms of authorities ("Cartesian criticism" so to speak). These remarks refer to the role of criticism on the object level. On the meta level the question arises whether or not it is possible to justify the authorities. Thus it turns out that a coherent account of criticism cannot be made within the context of justificationism (cf. sect. 2.1).

A partial explanation of the popularity of justification philosophy is the widespread tendency to mistake conviction for the guarantee of truth. It is indeed psychologically impossible to doubt certain statements; for instance, Wittgenstein's "ordinary certainties" such as 'Cats do not grow on trees', 'I am more than three months old', and so forth. We have no reasons to doubt them and good reasons not to do so. Yet, a conviction not only does not provide a truth guarantee but is epistemologically irrelevant. That it is psychologically impossible for us to doubt that *p* does not rule out the possibility that we all might be mistaken. The very formulation of the main problem of traditional epistemology: "How do we know?" prejudges the issue because it implies that we *do* know – know in the sense in which "to know" is used in everyday speech. According to this use "to know that *p*" entails that *p;* it entails that if I know *p* then I cannot be wrong with respect to *p,* because if I found out that *p* is false, I would *eo ipso* have to withdraw my knowledge claim.[4] In the history of epistemology the excessive demands and hopes of justification philosophy have led to a peculiar development: a tacking between justificationism and skepticism. Both are inspired by the same ideal of knowledge, an ideal according to which genuine knowledge is secure knowledge (statements with truth-guarantee). They differ in their estimate of man's capacity to know: justificationism overestimates while skepticism underestimates this capacity.

How pervasive the influence of justification philosophy has been can best be seen by looking at areas outside philosophy. For instance, a glance at the history of the disciplines which offer elaborate theories of rationality, economics, and methodology, can illustrate this. In economics there are many examples of "Platonism of models" *(Modellplatonismus).* Neoclassical theories attempt to stylize economic problems as if calculable risk or even certainty, full information, and adequate

---

4. If we use "know" in the sense of Popper's objective knowledge, then the situation is different: "If I know (in the objective sense) I *may* be wrong." Cf., e.g., Radnitzky, 1982d, p. 113.

foresight could be assumed. The manner in which such assumptions are handled shows how much theory formation in economics is influenced by the classical model of rationality offered by justification philosophy. In the methodology of scientific research the very idea of a confirmation theory is governed by the justificationist style of philosophizing. That absolute verificationism has been replaced by probabilistic verificationism or "soft inductivism" does not change the basic orientation.

1.1.0.2. Why is the program of justification philosophy not realizable? That the failure of justificationism is immanent in its program can best be seen by examining its pure version, foundationalism. According to foundationalism it is rational to accept all and only those statements whose truth has been established by deducing them from secure premises. This principle implies a disjunction of exactly three propositions. (i) In order to establish B_0 one deduces it from B_1, in order to establish B_1 one deduces it from B_{1+1}, and so forth; in short, an *infinite regress*. But in this way one cannot establish the sentence which was to be established. Hence the first disjunct is contrary to the principle: when the principle is applied to any arbitrary sentence, it turns out to be logically impossible to satisfy the principle for that sentence. (ii) During the course of justification one uses as a premiss a proposition previously introduced as being in need of justification: a *logical circle*. The second disjunct is also contrary to the principle. Hence these two consequences are ruled out for logical reasons. There remains a third possibility. (iii) The process of justification is broken off at a certain point because one considers oneself to have reached an ultimate stopping point that is epistemologically unproblematic, an Archimedian point as it were. This third disjunct is also contrary to the principle, even more patently so than the first two. From the fact that each of the disjuncts in the statement implied by the principle is inconsistent with the principle itself, it follows that the principle is inconsistent. Therefore it is useless as a regulative principle. The trilemma[5] represents an antinomy not unsimilar to that of The Liar for, if one accepts the demand for deductive justification, it becomes logically impossible to satisfy this demand. The class of nonanalytic statements justifiable in this sense is empty. *This trilemma is inescapable not only in connection with deductive justification—which is but the clearest case—but with all sorts of justification, inductive justification, etc.* Hume's refutation of induction is but a special case of the justificationist trilemma. It is logically impossible to demonstrate the truth or the logical probability of an unrestricted universal conclusion on the basis of premises consisting of a finite and consistent set of singular statements—logically impossible to demonstrate that any X (past, pres-

5. Hans Albert (in Albert, 1968) has given the trilemma an apt label: "The Münchhausen Trilemma": the attempt at absolute establishment of truth is like the attempt of the famous baron in the Münchhausen tales to pull himself out of the swamp by his own hair. In the literature it is mostly referred to as Fries's Trilemma (presented by J. F. Fries in 1828–31). This trilemma is a special case of the general trilemma: as ultimate stopping point (supposed to be nondogmatic) Fries proposes "immediate" experience—a position known under the label of psychologism. Cf. Bartley, 1982, pp. 165 f.

ent, or future) is or must be phi from premisses stating only that so far all observed X's have been phi (even if we assume these "observation sentences" to be true).

Bartley[6] prefers not to speak of a trilemma but to conceive the situation as a dilemma-engendering dilemma. This has the advantage of a longitudinal over a cross-sectional presentation. If you are proving one proposition by another, either you *go on forever or you stop*. Since infinite regress and logical circle (which may be iterated *ad infinitum*) are excluded for logical reasons, one has to stop somewhere. Therefore justificationism is always relative to some ultimate stopping point. *With respect to the stopping point* there are again *two possibilities*. Either you are openly dogmatic and declare that this is your ultimate commitment[7] (a position which, since you consider it beyond criticism, you are not willing to discuss rationally as to its worth) or you attempt to justify it. If you attempt to justify it, you will again be confronted with the dilemma of logically impossible moves or ultimate commitment.

Therefore the key problem of justificationist epistemology is *to show that stopping at the particular ultimate stopping point of your choice is not dogmatic.* (This, again, will involve meta-level considerations.) In the history of epistemology the number of candidates for such an ultimate stopping point is indefinite. The most prominent examples are empiricism and intellectualism. Classical empiricism proposed sense perception (and induction) which proved too narrow. Classical intellectualism proposed intellectual intuition (and deduction), which proved too wide. Kant attempted a synthesis of the two. But the costs of this synthesis were too high: it forced Kant to abandon realism.[8] There have also been attempts to justify the propositions presenting the ultimate stopping point non-propositionally, for instance, by appeal to "immediate" experience (psychologism), or to phenomenological intuition of essences, or to action.[9] It is interesting to note the similarity between the position of Karl Barth, the leading 20th-century exponent of Calvinist "neo-orthodoxy", and Sir Alfred Ayer, a leading figure in analytic philosophy. Barth justifies a particular position by showing that it can be deduced from the "Word of God". For Ayer the rational justification of a particular general statement about the world means that that statement conforms to the rules of inductive reasoning. Both claim to have found an "Archimedian point".[10]

1.1.1. Reactions to the failure of the justificationist context

1.1.1.0. A glance at the recent history of the philosophy of science shows how far-reaching are the consequences of justificationism and, in particular, of its failure. Much philosophy of science is still conducted within the justificationist context. For instance, many methodologists and logicians refuse to acknowledge that

6. Bartley, 1982, pp. 165 f.
7. Such a declaration appears to be already on the meta level, a topic to be dealt with in sect. 2.0.
8. Cf., e.g., Albert, 1982, p. 28.
9. Some of these attempts will be discussed in sect. 2.1.1.3.
10. See Bartley's illuminating discussion of the similarities in Bartley, 1982, esp. p. 135. In sect. 2.1.1.1 and 2.1.1.2 the similarities between Barth's and Ayer's approach will be discussed. It may be interesting to note that K.-O. Apel generalizes Ayer's approach (cf. sect. 2.2.1).

the problem of induction is insoluble in the justificationist context and continue to work on the theory of confirmation.[11] (Sometimes it is asserted that the difficulties confronting Popper's theory of corroboration are no less or even greater than those of the theory of confirmation [e.g., Adolf Grünbaum].) However, what interests us here is the reaction of those who came to the conclusion that the justificationist approach has failed in the sense that its program had turned out not to be realizable. One who recognizes this but nonetheless retains the justificationist ideal of knowledge will become a sceptic.[12] Of the many varieties of scepticism, two play a prominent role in contemporary methodology: relativism and instrumentalism.

1.1.1.1. Relativism. The development of the analytic tradition in the philosophy of science exemplifies the transition from the justificationist-positivist style to the relativistic style. The problem of justifying the ultimate stopping point is eventually regarded as insoluble. There is no way of arbitrating among competing ultimate stopping points. Thus the various intellectual traditions and the "paradigm" underlying them become incommensurable. In this way the domain of justification procedures is limited to the object level and on the object level confined to the particular tradition that happens to be under consideration. Following the later philosophy of Wittgenstein, the framework considerations of the various traditions or "forms of life" are considered to be beyond criticism (criticism in the service of justification). Thus relativists have not just lost, but have abandoned, the problem of rational theory preference. What according to them remains to be done is merely to describe developments – the historist maxim of the methodology of historiography applied to the philosophy of science.[13]

1.1.1.2. Instrumentalism. It is possible to limit the domain of applicability of instrumentalism (as it is possible to limit critical rationalism) to theories. This is often done. The instrumentalist view of scientific theories may be consistently combined with the view that singular statements – "basic statements" – may be categorically and finally known, in some cases at least. It is possible consistently to reject justificationism with respect to theories while retaining it with respect to (some) singular statements. Why should theory instrumentalism be attractive? It offers a quick solution to something which many – wrongly – believe to be a dilemma. If one believes that science aims at true theories and has made some progress in meeting this aim and, like Thomas Kuhn, also believes that scientific theories have all been falsified, then a simple and radical way to resolve the apparent conflict between these three statements is "theory instrumentalism". It abandons all three in one sweep. It does so either by declaring that the question whether a scientific theory has a descriptive function is unanswerable, or by asserting that

---

11. Cf. sect. 1.1.0.2. This has been known since Hume, a point forcibly made by Popper since 1934. For a brief overview see, e.g., Radnitzky, 1982c, sect. 3.
12. See, e.g., Radnitzky, 1980, pp. 194–201 and Radnitzky, 1982c, sect. 7.
13. A brief criticism of Kuhn's position is found, e.g., in Radnitzky, 1982c, sect. 4 and 5.

a theory does not describe, is but a fiction, a black box, that functions as nothing but an instrument for deducing testable consequences. The roots of the instrumentalist view of theories go back at least as far as the two-language approach of logical empiricism. Logical empiricism has totalized the distinction between observation statements and theoretical statements. One recent version of it conceives of a theory as a system of theoretical statements that, so to speak, hovers like a balloon above the ground-level of observation statements (which possess "empirical significance") and is tied down at a few spots by so-called "bridge principles" (as C. G. Hempel has labelled them). These sentences provide an "empirical interpretation" for some of the theoretical terms or some of the theoretical statements. One prefers to ignore that the issues to be faced are *problems of testing* and not *problems of meaning,* and one confounds the concept of truth with methods of ascertaining the truth-value of a particular statement. Instrumentalism has gained an enormous popularity even outside the philosophy of quantum theory. Such a view – as, for example, Wolfgang Stegmüller's "non-statement view of theories" – is but a modern version of instrumentalism interwoven with Kuhn's views in formalistic dress.[14] To summarize: theory instrumentalism appears to be motivated by the insight that a scientific theory cannot be justified. It then concludes that, if justification cannot be had, it is best to dispense with the descriptive function of theories altogether. In this case the failure of justification philosophy led first to efforts to take *just* the theoretical stuffing out of theories and eventually to taking *all* stuffing out of them, reducing them to black boxes.

1.2. The Non-Justificationist or Critical Context on the Object Level

1.2.0. General characteristics

As mentioned, it is possible consistently to limit the critical approach to the object level, e.g., to limit it to theories. Popper's critical rationalism is, however, not restricted in application to the object level. I will sketch some basic features of this approach which bear on the problem of rationality.

(a) The concepts of *concept* and *method* are clearly distinguished. This distinction, applied to the concept of truth, enables us to separate clearly the *concept of truth* and *methods of ascertaining the truth-value of particular statements.* (b) Critical rationalism emphasizes that it is logically impossible (because of the justificationist trilemma) to devise an infallible method of ascertainment that would provide certainty. This is the thesis of *fallibilism.* (c) Thus the concepts of *truth* and *certainty* are clearly separated. As a consequence, the quest for truth can be retained while abandoning the quest for certainty or justification. While fallibilism concerns method, it is simultaneously a global hypothesis about man's capacity to know. And, it is itself fallible. Fallibilism is not only compatible with the concept of (absolute) truth but presupposes it: by stressing the idea of error, it presupposes the concept of falsity and hence that of truth. Moreover, without the concept

---

14. See Andersson, 1979, esp. pp. 8 and 9, or e.g., Radnitzky, 1979, pp. 67 ff.; Radnitzky, 1980, pp. 196–201.

of truth the idea of empirical testing would become meaningless.[15] If the quest for certainty or justification is abandoned, the trilemma on which justificationism foundered does not arise. Since there is no longer a search for an ultimate stopping point that would provide an epistemological "basis" there is no risk of infinite regress. No final state is sought: inquiry and criticism are *open-ended* processes. Methodological criticism of justification philosophy led to the insight that the ideal of knowledge underlying it is utopian and hence incapable of inspiring a regulative principle; and it also led to a revision of our estimation of man's capacity to know. (d) Another consequence of fallibilism is the separation of the concepts of criticism and justification, wherein the sole function of criticism is error elimination. Bartley appears to have been the first explicitly to recognize and emphasize this separation. (e) Pervasive fallibilism does not hinder *cognitive progress.* Science is an *evolutionary phenomenon* in a sense in which art, literature, institutions, etc., are not. Since basic science has the overriding aim of continually improving our understanding of nature, a contribution that achieves more in this respect supersedes those that have achieved less. Thus Einstein supersedes Newton while, e.g., Shakespeare does not supersede Euripides. Methodology has to explicate the concept of cognitive progress (and part of the clarification consists in providing examples of such progress); to indicate methods of ascertaining whether a particular development in the history of science constitutes progress in the sense explicated; and also to spell out methodological rules – broad rules relative to the problem situation – which explicate the concept of rational action in inquiry. Since the function of criticism is error elimination, cognitive progress cannot be achieved with its help alone, but requires the continuous interplay of creativity and criticism.[16] On the human level, deliberate selection – rational choice – has complemented and overtaken natural selection.

By abandoning the justificationist context and, in particular, by separating criticism and justification, *the problem situation has been restructured.* Questions of acceptance are replaced by questions of preference. The justificationist asks: When is it rational to accept a particular theory?, and he suggests an answer on the lines: When it has been verified or probabilified to a sufficient degree. In the critical context the key question is: When is it *rational* (fallibly) to prefer a particular position (statement, view, standard, etc.) over its rival(s)? The answer suggested is along the lines: "It is *rational* (fallibly) to prefer a position over its rivals if and only if it has so far withstood criticism – the criticism relevant for the sort of position at stake – better than did its rivals." Obviously this presupposes – since the process of criticism, like inquiry itself, is open-ended – that all positions (here we are concerned with all positions on the object level) are open to criticism.

---

15. Because the testable consequences deduced with the help of the theory have to be tested; and because even the instrumentalist has to find out whether or not they are correct (true), he too cannot avoid applying the concept of truth at least to "basic" statements. Cf., e.g., Radnitzky, 1982c, sect. 7 and Radnitzky, 1980, pp. 202 ff.

16. The concept of evolution plays an important role in critical rationalism. Creativity and criticism, on the human level, have an analogue on the biological level in the model of "blind variation and retentive selection". See also fn. 26 and sect. *Concluding remarks.*

1.2.1 Which kind of criticism is relevant in a particular case depends upon what sort of position (statement, view, standard, etc.) is under consideration; and the ranking of the various dimensions of criticism will vary with the problem situation.

To elaborate this thesis a taxonomy or typology of sorts of statements and of research situations would be required. Then the question of which sort of criticism is relevant in each type case could be attacked. It is obvious that the criticism relevant for an empirical hypothesis is different from that for a definition, and that each is again different from that relevant for a value judgment, a logical system, etc.[17] Here I will use as an illustration only the situation in which a choice has to be made between competing empirical hypotheses or theories.

1.2.2. Rational action in the situation of theory choice in basic science.

Bartley distinguishes four kinds of non-justificational criticism of theories: check of experience, check of theory, check of a problem, and the check of logic as an organon of criticism.[18] I will present a similar account but change the order and emphasis somewhat.[19] (1) In criticizing a theory the first question to ask is whether it is *relevant for the problem at hand.* Does it potentially offer a solution to it? If it fails to do so yet appears interesting in its own right, the question of problem preference arises, i.e., a problem in internal science policy, which in turn leads to the methodological question of explicating objectively the comparative concept of "the scientific interest" of problems.[20] (2) Criticism that takes place prior to testing consists, besides the routine check of internal consistency, in ascertaining the degree to which the new hypothesis is empirically criticizable. This leads to *comparing the amount of empirical information* carried by the rival hypotheses. Being more empirically criticizable, more falsifiable than its competitors, means being – in principle – more corroborable than they are. Risks have to be matched by chances of unusual profits. Analogously, only a bold theory, a theory with high empirical content, has, in principle, a chance of rendering big returns in terms of new knowledge. (3) Criticism also occurs *after* testing.[21] In selecting theories in basic science it is rational (fallibly) to prefer that theory which we conjecture to be a more accurate description of the relevant aspects of reality than its rivals. If a theory has so far withstood empirical criticism – severe testing –

17. The question which criticism is relevant for a tautology will lead to the argument for a minimal logic as a presupposition of all criticism, since criticism involves the notion of deducibility. A good reason for adopting a particular analytic statement is that certain semantic rules have been accepted: it is true *ex definitione.* A definition in isolation is nothing but a stipulation and hence only a pragmatic criticism is possible. If a definition occurs in a certain context, e.g., in the context of an explication, to criticize it means to criticize the explicatum, which among other things means to ask whether and, if so, in what respect, the explicatum is a better intellectual instrument than the explicandum, i.e., in those contexts for which it is intended (cf. sect. 2.3.4).

18. Bartley, 1982, pp. 161–77.

19. The problem of the adequacy criteria of a theory or the dimensions of criticism relevant for an empirical hypothesis is dealt with, e.g., in Radnitzky, 1972, esp. pp. 219 ff.; Radnitzky, 1974, esp. fig. 4 on p. 90.

20. This is attempted in, e.g., Radnitzky, 1980, sect. 3.5, pp. 211–17.

21. Bartley, 1982, p. 162.

better than its rivals, we have good reasons for *conjecturing* it to be closer to the truth than they are. A statement about *comparative degree of corroboration* is but a rough summary report on the performance in severe testing of two or more competing theories. Although it states what we consider to be our "good reasons", it cannot, of course, provide any guarantee of future success – nor is it intended to do so. For in the non-justificatory context no attempt is made to demonstrate that a particular theory is, say, more probabilified than its competitors. Other dimensions of criticism that are relevant to rational theory preference cannot be discussed here for reasons of space.[22]

In many research situations a *compromise* will have to be made between different desiderata for theories, such as empirical content (as comparative degree of generality and degree of precision), "depth" (which leads to the problem of problem preference),[23] and so on. What *order of preference of the various dimensions of relevant criticism* it is *rational* to adopt will have to be decided from case to case. Nonetheless, some general guidelines can be derived from an analysis of the problem situation. For instance, if we have to choose between two theories both of which are afflicted with "anomalies", the rational global course of action will depend upon the problem situation. In basic research it will sometimes be impossible rationally to prefer one theory over another, and in such cases the only rational thing to do is to suspend judgment and rest content with a detailed description of the problem situation. However, in basic research such an "anomaly" automatically confronts the researcher with a host of new problems – one of the unintended consequences of dealing with that particular theory. Is there a domain where the theory still holds good?; and, if so, why does it hold good only there? What theory might be more promising for that realm where the "old" theory failed?, and so forth. In technological applications, however, the situation is completely different. The decisive question is whether or not the "anomalies" concern the phenomena one has to deal with, i.e., whether or not prognoses made with the help of the theory suffice for the practical purpose at hand. To navigate through a dangerous passage one does not need to know where all the underwater rocks are, but merely where no rocks are. How much accuracy it is rational to request of predictions derived with the help of a theory will depend upon the result of a cost-benefit analysis that focuses on a subjective evaluation of the disutility of failure of the practical action under consideration.

22. For instance, checking whether a new theory is coherent with background knowledge or veteran theories in the discipline. However, the requirement of such a coherence will have to be *suspended* in a situation where the new theory may lead to a shift in perspective, e.g., in connection with so-called "scientific revolutions". Thus, *coherence* appears to be but a *heuristic* principle, which may be suspended, although suspended *pro tempore* only. For, if it were always suspended, periods of so-called "normal science" would become impossible. For each type of criteria, for every dimension of criticism, there exists some type of research situation in which it has to be played down or waived. If any of the adequacy requirements, desiderata, or criteria were universalized, it would not only hamper progress but eventually stop it. This point has been very forcibly made by Paul Feyerabend.

23. See fn. 20.

1.2.3. Non-Inductivist interpretation of our reliance on scientific theories

It is often objected against Popper's methodology that in dealing with practical problems we all proceed like inductivists, that we are convinced of the truth of certain theories and behave accordingly. These objections allude to what Popper refers to as "Hume's psychological problem of induction". A theory of rational action also has to provide a solution to this problem. It often is perfectly rational to be convinced that a particular theory is true and to rely on it in *technological application*. This is so whenever we have reason to believe that the theory is sufficiently well-tested for the purpose at hand. (It need not be the best corroborated theory. Thus in space flight the "old" theory is used, and a cost-benefit analysis will show that this is the rational thing to do.) But the concept of being well-tested, of having so far withstood severe testing, is quite different from the concept of inductive support. One has looked for possible *negative* cases and not for positive cases (as the inductivist would). Thus, to be convinced that a particular theory is true and to rely upon that theory in technological applications may be the rational thing to do and is perfectly compatible with fallibilism. Yet it must be kept in mind that the conviction (a mental entity) and the reliance in practice (an action) are irrelevant to the epistemological issues.

1.2.4. When is it rational to adopt (fallibly) a "basic statement"?

What has been said about theories applies not only to universal statements but also to so-called "basic statements" or "observation reports". A basic statement is a statement of singular form which describes an individuated event (e.g., "At location k there is . . . "). Basic statements are, like theories, fallible and hence cannot provide a secure basis, although they are easier to test than theories. They function as test statements (and also to formulate explananda). Perceptual experience may be the cause of a conviction that a particular basic statement is true and also part of the reasons for the methodological decision to process a particular basic statement from a statement which functions as a (logically) potential falsifier into a falsifying hypothesis, i.e., into a statement which describes a reproducible effect and is hence intersubjectively testable. A basic statement can — notwithstanding our conviction that it is true — be called into question any time. If we wish, we can always derive from it further basic statements which function as test statements *for it*. However, it would be most irrational to problematize a basic statement which we up to now believed to be true unless we had concrete reasons for doing so. The question *when it is rational to problematize a basic statement and when to stop re-checking it depends on a cost-benefit analysis* in which we estimate the marginal utility of additional re-checking (perhaps also with a view to refining it) versus the opportunity costs in terms of time, energy, etc. That is, it is a question of the rational investment of scarce resources.

Relativists such as Thomas Kuhn (Kuhn 1970) often claim that if there are no secure basic statements, then the idea of falsification makes no sense. However, the expression "having been falsified" is elliptical for a logical relation: if the falsifying hypothesis and the auxiliary premisses are true then the theory to be tested is false. Since it is impossible conclusively to establish the truth of the former – there being no infallible method of ascertaining their truth-values – falsification itself remains fallible, in principle falsifiable (falsifiability being a logical relation). Even those who recognize that the *justificationist interpretation* of basic statements as *secure* is untenable, have been unable to free themselves from the justificationist ideal of knowledge; and they thus arrive at the opposite conclusion and interpret basic statements as *conventional*. Critical rationalism has shown that the alleged dilemma: "Either basic statements are secure, in the sense that their truth can be established conclusively, or they are accepted by arbitrary decision or by convention", is spurious.[24] This dilemma is but a special case of the general justificationist dilemma: "Either justification philosophy is viable or scepticism is necessary" (section 1.1.1.0.). Fallibilism entails the perennial willingness to re-examine any position (statement, view, etc.) whenever, and if (but *only if*) there are good reasons for problematizing it. Statements such as Wittgenstein's "ordinary certainties" (e.g., "Cats do not grow on trees", "I am more than three months old", or "The world existed before I was born", and so forth) are no exception. It is rational to believe them because they follow from certain theories (besides, of course, presupposing certain accepted linguistic conventions). But there is *no need to dogmatize them*, neither logically nor otherwise. So far as methodology is concerned they are uninteresting. Problematizing them would not only be a waste of scarce resources of time and energy, but pointless.

1.2.5. Concluding remarks

The trilemma on which foundationalism foundered does not arise in the critical context. The logical problem of induction has been solved or, rather dissolved, there being no induction.[25] (Also the psychological "inductive theory of learning" appears to have been superseded by expectancy theories and other learning theories.) Popper has also solved "Hume's psychological problem of induction". The rationality of relying, in technological applications, upon scientific theories is compatible with fallibilism and anti-inductivism. The systems-theoretical model of the development of knowledge – creativity and criticism – has been shown to be applicable in many fields.[26] In sum, on the object level, Popper's critical rationalism indeed constitutes a Copernican turn.

24. Andersson, 1983b, – to my knowledge, the best account of the problem of "basic statements" so far available.
25. This has been demonstrated, following Hume, by Popper, 1934. For an overview see, e.g., Radnitzky, 1979, esp. p. 222.
26. The comparative study of cognitive apparatuses, the new discipline that is called 'evolutionary epistemology', is but an extension of Popper's methodology to phenomena outside the human sphere. For instance, the interplay of creativity and criticism in research finds an analogue in biology in mutations and natural selection, retentive selection with duplication. Thus this methodology has also proved to have heuristic value outside the study of the human domain.

2. The Meta Level: The Level on which the Question of the Self-Applicability of the Justificationist and of the Criticist Context is Raised

2.0. Comment on the Present use of 'Object Level' and 'Meta Level'

If a linguistic expression, a sentence p, is not used but mentioned then the sentence mentioning it, by using its name ('p'), is on the meta level in relation to the level of p. Hence, strictly speaking, whenever truth claims are made explicit ('p' is true in L), whenever one asserts that the truth of a statement ' . . . ' has been established and that, therefore, this statement is not open to criticism, one has made a statement that stands in a meta-relation to the statement commented upon. What matters here however is not so much the formal distinction between object and meta language; what matters is to distinguish clearly between the level on which the justificationist or the non-justificationist approach is applied to statements that do not talk about the respective approach (the 'object level') and *the level on which the question is dealt with, whether or not a particular approach is self-applicable* (the 'meta level').

2.1. The Question of the Self-Applicability of the Justificationist Context

2.1.0. The three options open to the justificationist

Bartley characterizes the context he calls "panrationalism" (comprehensive rationalism) by two principles: to accept all those positions that can be justified by appeal to rational authority, and to accept only those statements that can be so justified.[27] He then points out that they cannot be held simultaneously: "if the first requirement cannot be justified . . . the second requirement forbids that one hold it . . . [and since the second requirement] too cannot itself be justified by appeal to rational criteria or authorities . . . it must, if correct, be rejected. . . . So a panrationalist not only does not happen to exist, but is logically impossible".[28] This is correct if "panrationalism" refers to the justificationist context regarded as self-applicable. For a philosopher with a justificationist turn of mind the natural thing to do is to be justificationist also on the meta level, and there too to answer the question of the self-applicability of the justificationist context in the affirmative. However, there appear to be at least *three logical possibilities*. Firstly, the justificationist may hold the justificationist context to be *self-applicable*. If he does, he is bound to be confronted with the trilemma of infinite regress, circle or dogmatic stopping – this time on the meta level. Secondly, he may hold the question of the self-applicability of the justificationist context *open*. This is possible without contradiction. Thirdly, he may opt for the justificationist context on the object level and answer the question of the self-applicability

27. Bartley, 1982, pp. 141 f.
28. Bartley, 1982, p. 142.

in the negative, i.e., choose a *dogmatic* stopping at the meta level. This too appears logically possible.

2.1.1. In order to be able to retain justificationism on the object level one is willing to pay a price: dogmatism on the meta level.

2.1.1.0. I propose to look more closely at two options that are exemplified in the literature. (A) *To adopt dogmatism on the meta level—as a minimal concession to the sceptic's arguments—in order to retain justificationism on the object level.* Of course, one will then attempt to argue that this sort of dogmatic breaking off of the justification process is not objectionably dogmatic. (There are also cases where a peculiar sort of relativism on the object level is combined with dogmatism on the meta level.) Such attempts to show that a particular ultimate stopping point is not dogmatic in an objectionable sense mostly argue that there is no other possibility: it has to be done, and hence cannot be objectionable. (B) One attempts *to show that—on the meta level—the justificationist trilemma can be avoided.* Both approaches are indebted to the later philosophy of Wittgenstein.

Let us examine a few cases of prominent philosophers who adopt justificationism on the object level or combine justificationism with fallibilism on the object level, but who limit fallibilism to the statements of science, and who have explicitly addressed the question whether the justificationist approach is self-applicable.

2.1.1.1. A paradigmatic example from theology: the position of Karl Barth.[29] A clear, if only implicit, distinction between object and meta level is made. On the object level the justificationist context is upheld while on the meta level an ultimate stopping point is dogmatized. On the object level the methods for ascertaining the truth-value of a particular theological statement consist in checking whether or not it conforms to the "Word of God". The "Word of God" constitutes the authority and appeal to it is necessary: justification is not only possible, but required. On the meta level that text is dogmatically declared to be *the* source of relevant knowledge—*open fideism.* The Word of God itself is held to be not open to criticism. Indeed as the economist Frank Knight once wrote: "The meaning of religious belief seems to be that it is *sinful to question* it."[30] But a rationale is given for the dogmatizing. It is argued that, to be able to carry on an activity of a certain sort—in this case theology (so to speak, the "form of life" or "language game" of theology)—one must dogmatically accept the authority that governs and defines it. Sometimes (but not in Barth) attempts which are patently circular are made to camouflage the open fideism. Roughly thus: what the authority teaches is the revealed word. How do you know? Because the authority says so. How do you know that it tells the truth? Because it is the very source of truth.[31] In sum,

29. Bartley, 1982, p. 145.
30. Knight, 1947, p. 345.
31. The circle is illustrated in the old Jewish joke about two Chassidim disputing the excellence of their respective tsadiks. " 'Every Friday night', one of them says, 'God converses with our tsadik'; 'How do you know that?', the other asks; 'The tsadik himself told us so'; 'Maybe he lied?', 'How dare you accuse of lying a man with whom God converses every Friday!' " Kolakowski, 1982, p. 218.

in the case of theologians like Karl Barth the source of knowledge is openly dog-matized at the meta level by making the option for it a *nonrational* act. If you wish to engage in theology or in theology of the right sort, then you have to un-conditionally accept certain authorities; but the choice or act involved in wishing to engage in theology or not is neither rational nor irrational. (Popper took a similar stance towards the critical approach.)

It might appear that the Marxist-Leninists operate with a similar circular ar-gument. However, there is a big difference. By contrast to the theologians the Marxist-Leninists are *naive* justificationists. In so far as they insist on the unity of theory and practice, they are committed to saying that everyone who has an adequate understanding of their faith must be in good standing with the (true) party. But they insist that the option for what they claim to be an infallible source, dialectical materialism (with the party holding a monopoly of interpretation and the power to decide what at the moment is to count as heresy), is itself justified because it conforms to the "Iron Law of History". They are naive in their justifica-tionism because they do not raise the question of self-applicability and appar-ently do not even notice the distinction between object and meta level questions. There is, moreover, a further important difference between the worldly, atheis-tic, Marxist doctrine of salvation and the doctrines of most transcendental religions. In the language of religion, "to have found truth" does not mean simply that one has learned certain theological statements but that one has entered onto the path that leads to ultimate deliverance. No philosophy can perform this task.

2.1.1.2. An analogous example comes from the philosophical tradition that is inspired by the later philosophy of Wittgenstein. Bartley can point to striking parallels be-tween Barth's argumentation and that of Sir Alfred Ayer (and of Hilary Putnam).[32] Ayer's way of argumentation can be summarized thus: "In order to be able to carry on with the 'language game' of science we must adopt the so-called 'princi-ple of induction'. For this and certain other principles are presupposed in that sort of activity." On the object level a certain relativism may be conceded, per-haps even the Wittgensteinian idea of incommensurable "forms of life" which can-not stand in judgment on one another.[33] On the meta level they are dogmatized, declared to not be open to criticism. (Likewise Wittgenstein was not willing to subject either the framework propositions of the language game or the "ordinary certainties" to criticism.) The dogmatism is camouflaged by the following type of argument: A particular "form of life", e.g., science or the language game of "our" everyday form of life, has demonstrated its viability and worth by function-ing well in practice. But it cannot function unless certain basic standards, the framework propositions of that form of life, are accepted. Hence, the basic stan-dards of "rationality" for that particular realm cannot be criticized and therefore – criticism being assumed to be in the service of justification – cannot be justified. Why? Because they define what "rationality" means in that particular language

32. Bartley, 1982, pp. 143–46.
33. Bartley, 1973; Radnitzky, 1982a, and 1982b.

game or realm of activity. Therefore, they not only cannot be justified, they *need* not be justified. It would be irrational to request a justification that in principle cannot be had. Therefore, on the meta level – which is the philosopher's domain – nothing more can be done than describing and elucidating, describing for instance the standards that govern "our" form of life, or that particular form of life called "science", and so forth. Philosophy can only describe.[34]

This line of thought has been very influential, and also provides the guiding ideas of Thomas Kuhn's relativism. One consequence that Wittgenstein's later philosophy has within the philosophy of science is that the problem of theory appraisal, the problem of rational theory preference, and the problem of rational problem preference are either lost, as in Kuhn, or deliberately abandoned, as in Paul Feyerabend.[35]

2.1.1.3. Recent attempts to defend a particular stopping point on the meta level by arguing that stopping there is not a dogmatic breaking off of justification, but can be rationally justified. The homeland of the justificationist philosophy is the West; but this kind of move is particularly popular in contemporary German philosophy. At least three prominent philosophers have developed "non-propositional" ways of justifying propositions: K.-O. Apel with his "transcendental pragmatics of language", J. Habermas as a proponent of the so-called "Frankfurt School" or "critical theory" (whose approach is very close to that of Apel), and P. Lorenzen, head of the so-called "Erlangen School". Apel's approach is the most refined and interesting of these.[36] (For empirical science Apel accepts the fallibilist context of the object level, but on the meta level he would not concede that the statement "all knowledge about the empirical world is in principle fallible" is itself fallible.) Since his philosophy is increasingly attracting attention in the English speaking world too, it may be worthwhile to examine briefly how he proposes to circumvent the reproach of dogmatism for the ultimate stopping point of his choice.

Apel is primarily concerned with ethics, not with epistemology. And in ethics he is a justification philosopher, whereas for science he accepts fallibilism. The principle of rationality implicit in his philosophy might be epitomized as follows: A rationalist accepts and follows all those rules that constitute the framework presuppositions of "symmetric" discourse, i.e., a discourse situation in which each partner gets a hearing and each argument is considered on its merits without regard to where it comes from, etc. (Popperians would prefer to speak of the formal requirement for rational discussion and would add that a genuine discussion is the quest for the solution to some problem.) A moral person follows or at least respects the maxims that can be justified by an appeal to these rules. Thus, Apel's principle says much the same as Popper's critical approach. But in Apel it is justified by appealing to an *ultimate stopping point that is claimed to be self-justifying.*

34. Bartley, 1973; Radnitzky, 1982b.
35. E.g., Radnitzky, 1980, p. 197.
36. Apel, 1973.

He finds it in those presuppositions which are constitutive of the meaning of "being-able-to-speak-with-each-other", i.e., in those framework presuppositions in a dialogue which cannot be denied without committing, at least implicitly, a self-contradiction. The central framework presupposition is the existence of language, of a speech community in the sense that linguistic conventions are functioning in a group at least to the extent that they make co-understanding possible. In facts such as, e.g., that we cannot without contradicting ourselves argue that we do not follow any linguistic rules, Apel claims to have found a stopping point for breaking off justification that does not incur the reproach of dogmatism. Rather, it provides the possibility of "ultimate justification" (*Letztbegründung*). In short, he claims to have found a way to justify propositions without being confronted with the trilemma of infinite regress, logical circle, or dogmatic stopping. This way of argumentation is again inspired by the later philosophy of Wittgenstein. The regress undertaken in order to found a statement is terminated not by a vicious circle but by a sort of "hermeneutic circle" which results in an understanding similar to that gained by a child when it gradually becomes a member of a communication community by learning the language – the "form of life". As in Wittgenstein, justification is abandoned only with respect to the framework.

Apel himself has not raised the question whether his principle is self-applicable, but an answer is implicit in his writings. The "option" of accepting the rules that are presuppositions for speaking-with-each-other and, hence, for being-able-to–speak-with-each-other, is no real choice. For as soon as we speak *about* it – attempt to criticize it or to justify it on the meta level – or even to formulate it, we are already using language, engaging in discourse. Apel argues that "opting" for the critical approach, the framework conditions of being-able-to-speak-with-each-other, is "justified" – in the peculiar sense in which he construes 'justifying' (see below)– because it is not criticizable. It is not criticizable because 'criticizing' means using arguments; and using arguments presupposes operating within the critical frame, and hence having "opted" for it – as if this were a real choice situation. This is correct and it constitutes an insight. *If* one wishes to discuss, then one has to use arguments, i.e., one must adopt the "criticist frame". But, from this statement it does not follow that anyone wishes or must wish to discuss; other moves appear possible, e.g., fighting or withdrawing. It is decisive, however, that the assertion that we, when speaking with one another, operate within certain framework presuppositions which cannot be denied without contradiction, is a *synthetic* statement. Hence the methods for ascertaining its truth-value are as *fallible* as they would be for any other synthetic statement. Moreover, even if it is assumed to be true, attempting to deduce a (non-instrumental) norm from it would exemplify the "naturalistic fallacy". On the other hand, if the statement were analytic, no synthetic statement could be deduced from it. Hence in neither case is it possible to justify, to "found", any synthetic statement, let alone a substantive ethics, by appealing to this principle. No guarantee of truth is provided by appealing to this statement or to the insight it formulates.

To the above argument Apel will retort that he has shown, with the help of the "transcendental-reflexive method of ultimate justification" (*"der transzendental-reflexiven Methode der Letztbegründung"*) that there are synthetic truths *a priori* ('SAP' for short). He claims to have found examples of such SAP precisely in the statements that describe those presuppositions of argumentation that cannot be denied without "performative self-contradiction" (*ohne performativen Selbstwiderspruch nicht bestreitbarer Präsuppositionen*). He accuses me of dogmatically assuming that there are no SAPs. To answer Apel's objection, first the concept of SAP has to be clarified. With respect to the distinction synthetic/analytic (in particular language) considerable progress has been made since the time of Kant, thanks to formal semantics. For our present purpose, it is sufficient to say that a synthetic statement has a certain logical relation to facts or possible facts; it says something about the world and not only about the "logical form of the world", as the metaphor goes. With respect to the distinction *a posteriori/a priori* the situation is less satisfactory. First, one must distinguish between genetically *a priori* and *a priori* valid. Evolutionary epistemology has helped us to recognize that there are synthetic truths that are *a priori* (genetically *a priori*) for the individual, but genetically *a posteriori* for the species. But the concept that is relevant for Apel's argument is "validity *a priori*". That a statement is *a priori* valid means that it is true, and its truth-value is independent of empirical facts and, hence, independent of empirical testing. If one takes "valid *a posteriori*" as the primary concept, a critical rationalist would offer the following rough definition: A statement is valid *a posteriori* means that it has been corroborated so far, or better corroborated than its competitors, and that, hence, we conjecture that it is more truthlike than its competitors. Thus, a critical or pancritical rationalist, indeed, denies that there are SAPs in the sense of *a priori* validity. However, this denial is by no means dogmatic. It is supported by the wealth of arguments that W. W. Bartley, III, has offered against the claim that there are ultimate justifiers. Moreover, if a philosopher claims that certain statements exemplify SAP in the sense of *a priori* validity, then he has the *onus probandi*.

It becomes clear that Apel construes 'justifying' and 'founding' (*begründen*) in a peculiar sense: If it has been shown that *x* is a presupposition for activity *y*, then it has been shown that, if you wish to engage in *y*, you have to accept *x*. Apel claims, however, that by showing that *x* is a presupposition (belongs to the "conditions for the possibility") of dialogue he, thereby, has "justified" *x*. But this concept is *different* from the idea of justification in the sense of making good truth claims, of establishing truth or, in general, validity. It appears that the proper functioning of rules of languages, of conventions, has been confounded with the making good of *truth claims*, or, in ethics, where the issue may not be of truth but of right or wrong, of *validity claims*. Problems of justification arise only in connection with truth claims or validity claims. The issue then is whether or not a particular statement can be justified, whether the truth claims or the validity claims made with respect to it can be made good. It is not a matter of linguistic conventions being followed or of the presuppositions of dialogue. In sum, Apel's "transcendental pragmatics of language" turns out to hinge upon a *dogmatic breaking off of the justification procedure on the meta level.*

The so-called "Erlangen School" attempts to justify validity claims or truth claims "non-propositionally" in the following way. It proposes *actions* as the ultimate stopping point. A simple example may illustrate the flavor of its reasoning. Assume that *A* claims that he can stand on his head and then performs this feat. In this event, it is said, *A* has justified the truth claim that he implicitly made by uttering the statement. Thus what is claimed is that *A* has – by his action – proved the truth of his assertion. (If he asserted that he is unable to *X,* it would be claimed that his act of performing *X* falsifies his assertion.) Such an attempt to justify an ultimate stopping point is, however, epistemologically naive. That we, having witnessed the performance, are *convinced* is irrelevant to the epistemological issue. Our perceptual experience of *A* making the utterance and then performing the act mentioned in the utterance constitutes both a motive and a good reason for our asserting that *A* has made a true statement. (This assertion is open to intersubjective criticism, e.g., by other onlookers who may contest it.) But our experience does not provide any infallible method for ascertaining the truth-value of this particular statement, or any truth guarantee. The "Erlangen School" operates consistently with a consensus theory of truth. It offers a "definition" of "truth" which runs as follows: A statement is true if and only if it is such that in an ideal discourse situation ("symmetrical", with all partners having good intentions and being well-informed) all *would in the long run* assent to it. But, this does not provide a definition of the concept of truth; it merely indicates a particular method for ascertaining truth-value – incidentally, a method which cannot be used in any concrete case. Moreover, it would not matter in this counter-factual "method" for the predication of 'truth' whether or not the statement under consideration is true or not.

The guiding ideas underlying this modern version of justification philosophy appear to come from the intuitionist, constructivist philosophy of mathematics, which, particularly by way of Brouwer's philosophy, also inspired the later philosophy of Wittgenstein. Its aspirations and spirit place this school of the philosophy of mathematics squarely within the justificationist camp.

2.2. Non-Self-Applicable Critical Rationalism

2.2.0. The three options open to the critical rationalist

The philosopher who adopts critical rationalism on the object level again has three options. He may adopt critical rationalism on the object level and leave the question of its self-applicability open. Thus he may in his work on methodological problems adopt the critical context, but keep meta questions open. Another possibility is adopting critical rationalism on the object level and attempting to justify it on the meta level. This option is explicitly excluded by Popper. I think it is the only option that he has ruled out. Bartley is the first to have explicitly advocated answering the question of the self-applicability of critical rationalism in the affirmative. I shall first discuss examples of the two first-mentioned options and then turn to Bartley's proposal.

2.2.1. Attempts to justify or dogmatize the criticist context on the meta level

One possible position is: "Hold all your positions open to criticism – *except* this maxim!" To the question: "Why this exception?" either one declares that this stopping point is introduced dogmatically or one attempts to justify it. To my knowledge the most sophisticated attempt to carry out the latter program is that of K.-O. Apel. In section 2.1.1.3 his approach was outlined. Here I will examine his attempt to show that the Criticist Frame [37] not only is not self-applicable but can be *justified on the meta level* – that it not only can be, but must be exempt from criticism since any attempt to criticize it would lead to inconsistency. According to Apel, denying the self-applicability of the critical frame, exempting it from criticism, is not a dogmatic move because it would not be possible to formulate arguments against it – this would be like arguing against argument. Of course, attempting to justify the critical frame on the meta level does not imply also adopting the methodology of critical rationalism on the object level. Likewise, it is logically possible to combine the critical context on the object level with justificationism on the meta level.

Apel's insight that the critical frame, because inseparable from the argumentative function of language, has a very special place in human life appears valuable.[38] In fact, *Apel has generalized Ayer's and Putnam's argumentation*. Ayer and Putnam attempt dogmatically to canonize inductive reasoning on the meta level. Apel replaces the inductivism of Ayer, Putnam, L. J. Cohen, etc., by the critical frame and produces a very tempting argument in favor of the view that this stopping point is not dogmatic since it is self-justifying in the sense that it is logically impossible to argue against it without getting involved in self-contradiction.

Yet, as I have argued above (section 2.1.1.3), Apel's assertion – that we operate within the Criticist Frame whenever we formulate arguments, and (if thinking is regarded as an inner argumentative dialogue) even whenever we think or reason, so that we implicitly continue to endorse it so long as we continue the dialogue – is *synthetic* and hence *fallible*. Any attempt to guarantee its truth will relentlessly lead to the trilemma of infinite regress or circle or dogmatism. To make this clearer let me *reconstruct Apel's argument:* (i) If you wish to conduct an argumentative dialogue, to talk seriously, then you have to accept the Criticist Frame. This is a synthetic statement unless it is conventionalized by defining 'dialogue' with the help of the Criticist Frame. But from an analytic statement only analytic statements could follow. (ii) You have entered a dialogue, you are discussing. This too is a synthetic statement. (iii) Conclusion: you have implicitly adopted, accepted, and endorsed the Criticist Frame.

---

37. The label "criticist frame" (which I proposed in Radnitzky, 1968/73; 1973 p. 366) still appears to me to be suitable.

38. I thought so in 1968 and still regard Apel's argument as important. Radnitzky, 1968/73, pp. 366–77, "The status of the criticist frame and the possibility of its legitimization".

However, neither truth claims with respect to a descriptive statement nor validity claims with respect to a norm can be justified by *action*. Even if everybody were engaged in argumentative dialogue all the time, the Criticist Frame would still not be justified by this fact. Apel's attempt to justify the Criticist Frame on the meta level, although most impressive, is bound to fail in the end. Nonetheless, his insight into the special position of critical rationalism is valuable and his way of attempting to justify it is far more convincing and less dogmatic than those of Ayer, Putnam, and others who have made such attempts.

2.2.2. Popper on the question of the self-applicability of the criticist frame

Popper would reject any attempt to justify the Criticist Frame on the meta level, as contrary to the spirit and flavor of his philosophy. However, he would be in perfect agreement with Apel about its very special position in human life.[39] Popper recognizes, as does Apel, the human freedom to reject reason and argument. The individual has the essential freedom to abandon all speech communities, e.g., by "metaphysical suicide" (from Kierkegaard to Camus), or in psychosis or pseudo-psychosis (as Pirandello's Enrico IV), and perhaps he can stop the inner dialogue (as it is attempted in some yoga exercises).[40] What is logically impossible is to formulate arguments against it and still be consistent. Although it is an inconsistent position if verbalized by arguments, it is psychologically possible to revolt against the Criticist Frame, to reject it. When talking, when making use of the argumentative function of language, I am already within the criticist context – this is the point forcibly made by Apel. But my remaining within it, my adopting it for the future (my preference for certain future preferences) contains a *non*rational element in the sense that it is always possible for me to reject it all: reason, language, and life itself. This much has to be conceded to the existential solipsist or sceptic. In sum, there is an uneliminable element of choice or decision in the adoption of the Criticist Frame – even if it may concern a nonrepetitive, exceptional, ultimate choice – ultimate in the sense that it cannot be reversed, as, for instance, in a successful suicide.

The *locus classicus* for Popper's position on this question is Chapter 24 of *The Open Society and its Enemies*.[41] He asserts that the adoption of the Criticist Frame is based on "an irrational *faith in reason*".[42] He states on the same page: "But we are also free to choose a critical form of rationalism, one which frankly admits its origin in an irrational decision (and which, to that extent, admits a certain priority of irrationalism)." Bartley points out that Popper in response to discussions with him in 1960 "altered the terminology of Chapter 24 of *The Open Society* (fourth and subsequent editions) to mute its fideism . . . he introduced my [Bartley's] distinction between justification and criticism . . . ".[43] In the fourth and

---

39. This can be clearly seen from his discussion of the consequences of the option for or against the criticist frame. Popper, *Open Society*, Chapter 24, p. 233.
40. Radnitzky, 1968/73, p. 375.
41. Popper, *op. cit.*
42. *Op. cit.*, p. 231.
43. Bartley, 1982, pp. 147 f.

subsequent editions Popper formulates his position thus: "The choice before us is not simply an intellectual affair, or a matter of taste. It is a moral decision . . . ."[44] From the pages following the passage quoted it becomes quite clear that he holds the rational discussion of moral decisions to be not only possible, but required and indeed indispensible if one wants to behave morally.

If one holds that for an irrational decision rational discussion is irrelevant, then to declare the option for the Criticist Frame to be "an irrational decision" (*OS* p. 231) appears to be incompatible with declaring it "a moral decision" (*OS* p. 232). However, from the context it is clear that "irrational decision" was merely an unhappy and misleading formulation. For if someone speaks of "an irrational decision", this makes sense only if it is assumed that the kind of decision could also have been rational; since only what can be rational can properly be said to be irrational. What Popper should have said about his position, before his discussion with Bartley around 1960, is that the decision in question was "a *non*rational decision". In the section on Karl Barth (2.1.1.1) I claimed that the decision to engage in science or in theology, etc., at least if taken in isolation, is nonrational. A person must not *eo ipso* be accused of having acted irrationally if he claims that he engages in a certain activity simply because he wants to do it, because he feels that he must do it – provided, of course, that he is also prepared to bear the consequences. As Antony Flew points out[45] when Hume so dashingly proclaimed that reason is and ought only to be the slave of the passions he was certainly not advocating irrationalism. What he was saying was that desires as such are neither rational nor irrational, although it may be very irrational indeed to try to satisfy some desire in a way which is guaranteed in fact to frustrate that desire. Since "rational", in the sense in which the word is used in this essay, is predicated only of actions and ways of behaving, "rational" and "irrational" could *eo ipso* not be predicated of desires, wants, and such like.

In a footnote to the *addendum* of the fourth and subsequent editions of *The Open Society*, Popper explicitly acknowledges that Bartley's criticism has induced him to make important changes in chapter 24 and in the *addendum*. In fact, on p. 379 he writes of "the importance of our principle that nothing is exempt from criticism, or should be held to be exempt from criticism – not even this principle of the critical method itself." From then on, he considered the Criticist Frame to be self-applicable, and he has endorsed Bartley's proposal, although he has not followed up this issue in any detail (except in *Realism and the Aim of Science*, Part I, section 2).

2.3. Self-Applicable Critical Rationalism

2.3.0. Bartley recognized the fundamental weakness in critical rationalism discussed in the preceding section; and he eliminated it by answering the meta-level question of the self-applicability of the critical context in the affirmative. He

44. Popper, *op. cit.*, p. 232.
45. Antony Flew in a personal communication.

declared the philosophical maxim advising that all positions (statements, viewpoints, criteria, etc.) be held open to criticism to be *self-applicable*. Since he had separated the concepts of criticism and justification so that criticism functions only to eliminate errors and thus becomes an open-ended process, and since no attempt is made to find an ultimate stopping point and to declare certain positions justified, regress can never deteriorate into *infinite* regress. There are no exceptions. To concede an ultimate commitment to reason would itself amount to a dogmatization, and would hence be incompatible with pancritical rationalism.

The central regulative principle of critical rationalism is the principle prohibiting the immunization of scientific theories against falsification – be it on the object level through criticism-deflecting devices built into a theory, or by means of *ad hoc* hypotheses, or, on the meta level, through immunizing strategies. Bartley *generalized* the methodological principle prohibiting immunization to empirical theories *into the principle of pancritical rationalism: the principle prohibiting dogmatization of any position.* We logically need not – in order to avoid infinite regress – dogmatize anything, *not even this regulative principle.* To my knowledge Bartley is the first to have separated the concepts of criticism and justification and to have declared the Criticist Frame to be self-applicable. All others have avoided self-applicability probably because they fear that self-reference will engender semantic paradoxes.[46] However, Tarski showed that such paradoxes *can* be avoided.

What I want to make plausible in this essay is above all the following. Firstly, to argue that, by distinguishing the concepts of "criticizable in a language *L*" and "criticizable in a language that stands in metarelation to *L*", semantical paradoxes can easily be avoided. Secondly, to emphasize that the sort of criticism that is relevant in any particular case depends upon the kind of position under consideration.

2.3.1. The concept of potential criticizer

The most prominent critics of Bartley's solution, John F. Post and John W. N. Watkins, have attacked pancritical rationalism with the help of the concept of *"potential criticizer"*. This concept is supposed to be a generalization of Popper's concept of *potential falsifier*. Let us pause first to examine this key concept. The function of Popper's concept of potential falsifier is to prevent immunization: that is to ensure that a theory claiming to be about the empirical world is empirically criticizable and that it will not be immunized against falsification through the addition of *ad hoc* hypotheses. "Potential falsifier" is more than a logical relation, it is a methodological concept. An empirical theory is dealt with *rationally* only if it is accompanied by a declaration stating which experimental results or results of thought experiments would, if true, be regarded as falsifying the theory. The concept of potential falsifier is sufficiently precise and is indispensible in methodology (on the object level).

---

46. Perhaps such considerations prompted Popper not to propose self-application (at least not prior to the *addendum* of the fourth revised edition of *The Open Society*). For a brief discussion of this possibility see, e.g., Radnitzky, 1968/73, pp. 376 and 370.

How does the concept of *potential criticizer* fare? y is a potential criticizer of x if and only if y is well-formed in L (the language in which x is formulated) and y "bears adversely on" x. By this definition Popper's concept of potential falsifier has been generalized in three respects. (i) A potential falsifier has to be a singular statement. This requirement is waived; general statements also qualify as potential criticizers. (ii) A potential falsifier describes an observable event. This requirement too is waived; theories also qualify. (iii) A potential falsifier contradicts the theory of which it is a potential falsifier. This logical relational concept has been generalized into the relational character "x bears adversely on y". This concept is, however, itself left unspecified and hence is so vague as to be practically useless. Moreover, since all sorts of theories are in principle capable of functioning as potential criticizers (provided merely they "bear adversely" on the position under consideration) and since we cannot know in advance what theories we may get, the concept of potential criticizer is not only vague but also appears to be empty. I conclude that the attempt to generalize Popper's methodological concept of potential falsifier into the concept of potential criticizer is a *cul-de-sac*. It does not help us to present Bartley's position more clearly: that the rational way of dealing with any position is to hold it open to criticism – including this principle itself.

2.3.2. *Criticizability* tout court *versus sensible objections*

It is advisable to distinguish between two relational characters which a position (statement, viewpoint, etc.) may exemplify: between "being held open to criticism" or, more accurately, "being criticizable in principle" (*logical* possibility) and "being such that *sensible objections to it are feasible*". According to pancritical rationalism all positions are open to criticism. However, in most problem situations the interesting issue will be whether or not sensible objections to the position under consideration are feasible. The answer to this question will depend not only on the position in question, as John Watkins's use of his examples appears to suggest (a twenty-two word sentence asserting that there is a sentence with exactly twenty-two words and Wittgenstein's "ordinary certainties"). It depends also on the problem situation and the background knowledge. Take, for instance, the statement "$2 + 2 = 4$". In the context of a calculus with mathematical interpretation no sensible objections to it are feasible. In the context of the application of arithmetic the question can be decided only if we have information about the domain. For example, if the plus-sign is interpreted as the operation of physically putting together, the statement is false if it is made to refer to a population of mercury drops. Therefore, whether the decision to problematize a particular statement in a particular problem situation is *rational* will depend not upon its criticizability *tout court* – this is a property shared by every position (at least from the viewpoint of pancritical rationalism) – but it will depend upon whether sensible objections to it are feasible at the moment. If there are, the question will be whether or not it is rational to re-examine the statement under consideration. This question will have to be answered by reference to the results of a cost-benefit analysis (cf. section 1.2.4).

In addition, it is imperative to distinguish the concepts of "criticizable" (logical possibility) and "being such that sensible objections to it are feasible" from the concept of "being such that it is *psychologically impossible to doubt it*" (e.g., Wittgenstein's "ordinary certainties" like 'I am more than three months old'). The fact that it is psychologically impossible to doubt these is irrelevant for their epistemological appraisal.

2.3.3. On the criticizability of logic.

Criticism essentially involves deducing consequences from the position to be examined. Hence the concept of *deducibility*, the relational predicate of the metalanguage: "x is deducible in the language L from y", is indispensible. The idea of deducibility includes the requirement that transformation rules are *truth preserving*.

Bartley declares that logic too is open to criticism and he is even willing to hold the law of excluded middle open to criticism.[47] Bartley writes that the intuitionist approach "maximizes criticism". Yet – I would like to add – it does so in the context of the quest for secure foundations, which it hopes to find in what has been "constructed". (Moreover, the adoption of the justificationist spirit in this field would lead to a mutilation of mathematics.)

Logic is, in principle, criticizable. But, of course, not all logic could be criticized at the same time. Rather, certain logical systems or parts of such systems may be criticized, but only with the help of some other parts of logic. Possibly some parts of logic, e.g., the sentential calculus, are logically true and, in this sense, trivial. Moreover, certain features appear indispensable. For instance, one needs a kind of negation or functional equivalent to it in any functioning logical system.

What sort of criticism is relevant for logical systems? The only function of a logical system is to codify truth-preserving moves. Hence, the decisive criticism is either: (i) that the system is "too strong": that it can be shown that it is possible to deduce from true premises a false conclusion; or (ii) that it is "too weak": some deductions which we have good reasons to regard as valid according to our "intuitive logic" (take, e.g., that from 'p & q' is deducible 'p'), cannot be stylized by it. If neither of these two sorts of criticism applies, there remains criticism on pragmatical grounds: simplicity, ease of handling, "elegance", etc. Popper has attempted to argue that a logical system should be constructed by starting from the concept of deducibility. This surely appears the most natural way to proceed even if it so far has not got the support of many logicians. But what is important

---

47. Bartley, 1982, p. 182. Intuitionists do not criticize the use of the law of the excluded middle in ordinary logic. What the intuitionist philosophy of mathematics doubts is that this "law" applies to *infinite* sets. This has to do with the *concept of infinity* used in this school of the philosophy of mathematics, and it leads to highly technical problems. Incidentally, to associate here to three- or many-valued logics would be misleading. Such attempts have nothing to do with the intuitionist philosophy of mathematics. In my opinion, the idea of a three-valued logic is based upon confounding logical with epistemological problems; roughly: p is true or p is false – or the truth-value of p is unknown. It is impossible for a three-valued logic to provide a proper interpretation, because on some meta level one will have to use a natural language, and natural language is two-valued.

here is that pancritical rationalism does not and does not need to dogmatize any logical system.

2.3.4. *What sort of criticism is relevant for a tautology?*

In case of an uninterpreted formula we could not speak of truth-value but only of some sort of validity specified for the system. This validity is guaranteed by the form of the type expression (literally by its shape). Hence, it cannot be criticized within the system. This does not preclude the possibility of criticizing it with the help of a metalanguage. What sort of criticism is relevant for an *analytic* statement? An analytic sentence of the language L is true in L in force of certain definitions available in L. The statement cannot be criticized within the system, but only with the help of a metalanguage. A *definition* – as a conventional abbreviation – cannot in isolation be criticized. It can be criticized if it is placed in the context of some problem situation, e.g., as a means of introducing the term which has been chosen to designate the explicatum. To answer the question what sort of criticism is relevant for an *empirical hypothesis* we would refer to Popper's methodology. In sum, the interesting problem is what good reasons can be given for the assertion that for a particular position a certain kind of criticism is relevant, and also to show how a position which is not criticizable on the object level can be criticized with the help of a language which stands in meta relation to the language of the object level.

If somebody declared that he can produce a serious criticism against, say, *modus ponens* as a transformation rule of the sentential calculus or against, say, deducing 'p' from 'p and q', is the pancritical rationalist morally obliged – by his basic principle – to listen to him? I would answer that he is not obliged to listen to every critic, and that in any concrete case whether or not it is *rational* to embark on a discussion will depend on a cost-benefit analysis involving a risky estimate of the returns in terms of cognitive progress to be gained from a discussion with this particular dialogue partner on this particular problem, as well as a risky estimate of the opportunity costs in terms of time, etc. This is surely not a theoretical but a practical problem.

3. On the Alleged Semantical Paradoxes of Self-Applicable Critical Rationalism

3.0. *Natural language with its contextualist semantics usually has no problem with semantical paradoxes.*

Since a natural language contains its meta levels, there may arise semantical paradoxes. Since antiquity it has been known that certain statements about truth such as "This statement is not true" (S) lead to the so-called Liar Paradox: If S is true, then it is false, and vice versa. Philosophers have used this to criticize the concept of truth. However, such paradoxes are easily "inactivated" by context and background knowledge, i.e., the costs of "inactivating" them are negligible compared with the utility of *the convenience of being able to express different meta levels with the same symbolism.* Incidentally, even the famous Liar Paradox is innocuous. For, if a Cretan asserts that all Cretans always lie, then the puzzle would dissolve by reference to background knowledge. If the Cretans form a functioning speech community then it cannot be the case that they are always lying. If they did, the communication would have broken down long since. We know that this is not so. Hence, the assertion that all Cretans always lie must simply be false.

One of the advantages of formalized or partially formalized language systems is that the truth-value and even the meaning of an expression is independent of context. Therefore, some device has to be introduced to avoid semantical paradoxes. There are many such devices. (Ernst Zermelo, Bertrand Russell, Paul Bernays and others proposed such devices.) The most efficient device is that introduced by Alfred Tarski. Philosophers have used the semantical paradoxes to criticize the concept of truth. Tarski's so-called semantic definition of truth – by means of which the predicate expression ' . . . is true in the object language L' is introduced into the metalanguage – showed that the Liar Paradox does not arise if object language and metalanguage are distinguished.

3.1. Dissolving Semantical Paradoxes

Several philosophers have attacked the idea of self-applicable critical rationalism on the ground that self-applicability would necessarily involve semantical paradoxes. Above all, Post and Watkins (since 1969) have brought forward such objections.[48] I shall briefly examine the structure of some of their critical arguments.

Bartley's critics appear to suppose that something analogous to the Liar Paradox ("This sentence is not true") would arise with sentences of the form "This statement is not *criticizable*". Assume that it is claimed that all components of x are held open to criticism and that "holding open to criticism" entails "being criticizable". Then, if a component of x can be shown to be uncriticizable, x has thereby been criticized. Thus *prima facie* the situation appears to be that by showing y to be uncriticizable, y has been criticized. That means that by showing y to be uncriticizable, it has been shown to be criticizable. Hence, pancritical rationalism must be self-referentially inconsistent (Watkins). Post in 1972 proposed a Gödelian theorem to the effect that all rationality theories in a certain general class are either self-referentially inconsistent or inherently incomplete.

Watkins's alleged paradox dissolves when object level and meta level are distinguished. By showing that it is logically impossible to criticize y in the object language L, i.e., by showing that y is logically true in L, one has made a comment about y in the metalanguage. This comment constitutes a successful criticism of x (of which y is a component) only if it has been claimed that no component

---

48. I am uncertain about the chronology: who first produced this particular criticism against pancritical rationalism? An extensive bibliography is provided in W. W. Bartley's "Reply" (Chapter XV, this volume).

of x is logically true in L. However, self-applicable critical rationalism does not need to make this claim. Moreover, if some of its components have been shown to be logically true in the object language, this component has by no means been *eo ipso* shown to be trivial. After all mathematics and logic too are logically true in this sense and are by no means trivial. Hence, Bartley's retort[49] that "criticizable" in this context means the *logical* possibility of holding such statements open to criticism (without leading to infinite regress, vicious circle, or other logical difficulty) appears to me to be basically correct.[50]

Watkins then constructs a dilemma. He claims to have shown that the statement A (supposedly expressing the nonpsychologistic core of comprehensive critical rationalism), viz., "All nonanalytic and rationally acceptable statements are criticizable", is either analytic or false.[51] This dilemma is spurious. If "-able" in "criticizable" is construed as a psychological possibility, then A is false. It is indeed psychologically impossible to doubt such statements as, e.g., Wittgenstein's "ordinary certainties" ('I am more than three months old', etc.) and hence criticism of them would be Pickwickian. But this fact is irrelevant for the epistemological issue. To deny this would be a case of psychologism – a special case of ultimate stopping point in the above mentioned trilemma. If "-able" is construed as a logical possibility, then A is analytic in L. A statement p is rationally acceptable (as Watkins uses the phrase) only if p has withstood criticism. If it has, then it has been criticized; hence, it has been shown to be criticizable. Hence, A boils down to "All statements that have been criticized are criticizable". Hence A is analytic in L. But, as just mentioned with respect to the alleged paradox, this need not be a default of pancritical rationalism. Concerning the reproach of triviality, I would point out that an analytic truth need not be trivial, nor need the act of proving a statement to be analytic be trivial. When a hitherto unknown theorem in a system is deduced, its novelty is, strictly speaking, merely psychological because the information provided by the theorem is contained in the postulates. Hence, before the theorem was derived the information existed in the sense in which certain entities of Popper's World-3 exist, e.g., problems not yet discovered – discoverable problems. Having derived the theorem may, nonetheless, be a great intellectual achievement.

Watkins appears to be of the opinion that Bartley's extension of Popper's position is merely designed to provide, or merely capable of providing, arguments against certain theologians.[52] However, Karl Barth functions in Bartley's great essay of 1962 merely as an example of the dogmatic breaking off of the justification procedure at the meta level while retaining justificationism on the object level (in much the same way as, e.g., in Ayer and Putnam).

Post argues that the costs of language stratification à la Tarski are a reduction

49. Bartley, 1986, MS p. 12.
50. Bartley, 1980, p. 77.
51. Watkins, 1983, MS p. 10, an earlier version of chapter 13 of *this volume*.
52. Watkins, 1983, *op. cit.*, pp. 1 f.

of the information content of the statement "x is criticizable" (since "x is criticizable in L" has a lower information content than the first-mentioned statement does). These costs are said to be unbearably high for a pancritical rationalist who should wish to maximize criticism. This argument is not convincing. Firstly, it is not possible to paraphrase the basic principle of pancritical rationalism with the help of the concepts of criticizability and potential criticizer (cf. section 2.3.1); and secondly, the argument contains a false premise. It imputes to the pancritical rationalist (or, for that matter, to the critical-rationalist methodologist) that in each and every problem situation he has to give high content top priority. However, to do so would be irrational since there are problem situations in which other desiderata supersede content. (To take Bartley's example: 'The planets move in circles' has higher empirical content than 'The planets move in elliptical orbits'. Nonetheless it is rational to prefer the hypothesis with the lower content of empirical information.)

Concluding Remarks

Bartley generalized the central principle of Popper's methodology, the prohibition against immunization, and answered the question of the self-applicability of critical rationalism in the affirmative. Thereby he removed one of the most important, perhaps *the* most important difficulty, of critical rationalism. The critical rationalist's account of rationality happens to be parallel to the neo-Darwinian account of *evolution*. The question whether or not a particular mutation is justified is meaningless. The issue is, as Bartley rightly emphasizes, whether or not it is *viable*, and this issue is resolved by exposing it to the pressure of natural selection. Similarly, the question whether or not a position (statement, viewpoint, standard, etc.) can be justified is misleading. The issue is whether it can *survive* when exposed to systematic criticism. We know, in the sense of our objective but conjectural knowledge, that, in spite of so-called "living fossils", each species has but a limited life span.[53] Analogously, the fact that a theory has so far survived severe criticism is no guarantee of its future success. Yet we also know that in spite of the pervasive human fallibility there has been and still is cognitive progress. Adoption of the critical frame – which, as pancritical rationalism, has recognized that we logically need not dogmatize anything – will be an indispensable presupposition for the rational use of the powers that scientific progress and its consequences have bestowed upon man; for a rational economic policy; and for the maintenance and the improvement of the Open Society.

---

53. This theme is dealt with, e.g., in Radnitzky, 1983a, 1983b, where references to the literature are also given.

References

Agassi, J., and Cohen, R. S., eds. *Scientific Philosophy Today*, Boston Studies in the Philosophy of Science, vol. 67 (Dordrecht: Reidel, 1982).

Agassi, J., Jarvie, I., and Settle, T. "The Grounds of Reason", *Philosophy* **66**, (1971) pp. 43–53.

Albert, H. *Traktat über kritische Vernunft* (Tübingen: J. C. B. Mohr, 1968); English translation (Princeton: Princeton University Press, 1985).

Albert, H. *Traktat über rationale Praxis* (Tübingen: J. C. B. Mohr, 1978).

Albert, H. *Die Wissenschaft und die Fehlbarkeit der Vernunft* (Tübingen: J. C. B. Mohr, 1982).

Andersson, G. "Presuppositions, problems, progress", Introduction to Radnitzky and Andersson, 1979, pp. 3–18.

Andersson, G. "Naive and critical falsificationism", in Levinson, 1982, pp. 50–63.

Andersson, G. "Creativity and criticism in science and politics", in Andersson, 1984, pp. 1–14. (1984a)

Andersson, G. "How to accept fallible test statements? Popper's criticist solution", in Andersson, 1984c, pp. 47–68. (1984b)

Andersson, G., ed. *Rationality in Science and in Politics,* Boston Studies in the Philosophy of Science, vol. 79 (Dordrecht: Reidel, 1984). (1984c)

Apel, K.-O. *Transformation der Philosophie.* 2 vols. (Frankfurt: Suhrkamp, 1973); abridged English translation, *Towards a Transformation of Philosophy* (London: Routledge and Kegan Paul, 1980).

Ayer, A. *The Problem of Knowledge* (London: Penguin Books, 1956).

Bartley, W. W., III. *The Retreat to Commitment* (New York: Alfred A. Knopf, Inc., 1962 and London: Chatto & Windus Ltd., 1964); 2nd edition, revised and enlarged (La Salle: Open Court, 1984).

Bartley, W. W., III. *Wittgenstein* (Philadelphia and New York: Lippincott, 1973); 2nd edition, revised and enlarged (La Salle: Open Court, 1985).

Bartley, W. W., III. "On the Criticizability of Logic", *Philosophy of the Social Sciences* **10**, (1980) pp. 67–77.

Bartley, W. W., III. "A Popperian harvest", in Levinson, 1982, pp. 249–90. (1982a)

Bartley, W. W., III. "The philosophy of Karl Popper: Part III: Rationality, criticism, and logic", *Philosophia*, Israel **11**, (1982) pp. 121–221. (1982b)

Bartley, W. W., III. "Rationality", in Radnitzky and Seiffert, 1986, *forthcoming.*

Bunge, M., ed. *The Critical Approach to Science and Philosophy* (Glencoe: The Free Press, 1964).

Cappelletti, V., Luiselli, B., Radnitzky, G. and Urbani, E., eds. *Saggi di storia del pensiero scientifico dedicati a Valerio Tonini* (Roma: Società Editoriale Jouvence, 1983).

Derksen, A. "The Failure of Comprehensively Critical Rationalism", *Philosophy of the Social Sciences* **10**, (1980) pp. 51–66.

Feyerabend, P. *Against Method: Outline of an Anarchistic Theory of Knowledge* (London: New Left Books, 1975).

Feyerabend, P. *Probleme des Empirismus. Ausgewählte Schriften,* Bd. 2 (Braunschweig/Wiesbaden: Vieweg, 1981).

Grmek, J., Cohen, R., and Cimino, G., eds. *On Scientific Discovery: The Erice Lectures 1977,* Boston Studies in the Philosophy of Science, vol. 34 (Dordrecht: Reidel, 1981).

International Cultural Foundation. *The Search for Absolute Values and the Creation of the New World,* Proceedings of the Tenth International Conference on the Unity of the Sciences, Seoul, Nov. 1981 (New York: International Cultural Foundation Press, 1982).

International Cultural Foundation. *The Search for Absolute Values and the Creation of the New World,* Proceedings of the Eleventh International Conference on the Unity of the Sciences, Philadelphia, Nov. 1982 (New York: International Cultural Foundation Press, 1983).

Kaufmann, W. *Without Guilt and Justice: From Decidophobia to Autonomy* (New York: Wyden, 1973).

Kekes, J. "Watkins on rationalism", *Philosophy* 46, (1971), pp. 51–53.

Knight, F. *Freedom and Reform: Essays in Economics and Social Philosophy* (New York and London: Harper & Bros., 1947).

Kolakowski, L. *Religion* (London: Oxford University Press, 1982).

Kreuzer, F., and Riedl, R., eds. *Evolution und Menschenbild* (Hamburg: Hoffmann und Campe, 1983).

Kuhn, T. S. *The Structure of Scientific Revolutions* (Chicago: Chicago University Press, 1962, 2nd enl. ed. 1970).

Kuhn, T. S. *The Essential Tension: Selected Studies in the Scientific Tradition and Change* (Chicago: University of Chicago Press, 1977).

Levinson, P., ed. *In Pursuit of Truth: Essays on the Philosophy of Karl Popper on the Occasion of his 80th Birthday* (New York: Humanities Press, 1982).

Popper, K. *Logik der Forschung* (Wien: Springer, 1934, 6. verb. Aufl., Tübingen: J. C. B. Mohr (Paul Siebeck), 1976).

Popper, K. *The Open Society and Its Enemies.* 2 vols. (London: Routledge and Kegan Paul, 1945, 11th ed. 1977).

Popper, K. *Conjectures and Refutations* (London: Routledge and Kegan Paul, 1963, 7th rev. ed. 1978).

Popper, K. *The Logic of Scientific Discovery* (London: Hutchinson, 1959, 9th rev. ed. 1977 (transl. of Popper, 1934)).

Popper, K. *Objective Knowledge* (Oxford: The Clarendon Press, 1972, 5th rev. ed. 1979).

Popper, K. *Quantum Theory and the Schism in Physics. From the Postscript to the Logic of Scientific Discovery,* ed. W. W. Bartley, III (London: Hutchinson, 1982).

Popper, K. *The Open Universe: An Argument for Indeterminism. From the Postscript to the Logic of Scientific Discovery,* ed. W. W. Bartley, III (London: Hutchinson, 1982).

Post, J. "The Possible Liar", *Nous* 4, (1970) pp. 405–69.

Post, J. "Paradox in Critical Rationalism and Related Theories", *Philosophical Forum* 3, (1972) pp. 27–61.

Post, J. "Shades of the Liar", *Journal of Philosophical Logic* 2, (1973) pp. 370–86.

Post, J. "Presupposition, Bivalence, and the Possible Liar", *Philosophia* 8, (1979) pp. 645–49.

Post, J. "A Gödelian Theorem for Theories of Rationality", *Chapter XII of this volume.*

Radnitzky, G. *Contemporary Schools of Metascience.* (Göteborg: Akademiförlaget, 1968; 2nd rev. ed., New York: Humanities Press, 1970; 3rd rev. enl. pa. ed., Chicago: Regnery, 1973; Chicago: Gateway Editions, 1977).

Radnitzky, G. "Towards a Theory of Research Which is Neither Logical Reconstruction nor Psychology or Sociology of Science", *Quality and Quantity* 4, (1972) pp. 193–238.

Radnitzky, G. "From Logic of Science to Theory of Research", *Communication and Cognition* 7, (1974) pp. 61–124.

Radnitzky, G. "Justifying a Theory vs. Giving Good Reasons for Preferring a Theory. On the Big Divide in the Philosophy of Science", in Radnitzky and Andersson, 1979, pp. 213–56.

Radnitzky, G. "From Justifying a Theory to Comparing Theories and Selecting Questions", *Revue Internationale de Philosophie* 34, (1980) pp. 179–228.

Radnitzky, G. "Progress and Rationality in Research", in Grmek *et al.*, 1981, pp. 43–102.

Radnitzky, G. "Analytic Philosophy as the Confrontation between Wittgensteinians and Popper", in Agassi and Cohen, 1982, pp. 239–86. (1982a)

Radnitzky, G. "Entre Wittgenstein et Popper. Philosophie analytique et théorie de la science", *Archives de Philosophie* (Paris) 45, (1982) pp. 3–62. (1982b)

Radnitzky, G. "Popper as a Turning Point in the Philosophy of Science", in Levinson, 1982, pp. 64–82. (1982c)

Radnitzky, G. "Knowing and Guessing. If All Knowledge is Conjectural, Can We Then Speak of Cognitive Progress?", *Zeitschrift für Allgemeine Wissenschaftstheorie* 13, (1982) pp. 110–21. (1982d)

Radnitzky, G. "Disappointment and Changes in the Conception of Rationality: Wittgenstein and Popper", in International Cultural Foundation, 1982, pp. 1193–1233. (1982e)

Radnitzky, G. "Die Evolution der Erkenntnisfähigkeit des Wissens und der Institutionen", in Kreuzer and Riedl, 1983, pp. 82–120. (1983a)

Radnitzky, G. "The Science of Man: Biological, Mental, and Cultural Evolution", in Cappelletti *et al.*, 1983, pp. 369–401. (1983b)

Radnitzky, G. "Réflexions sur Popper", *Archives de Philosophie* 48, (1985) pp. 79–108.

Radnitzky, G. "Cost-Benefit Thinking Applied to the Methodology of Research", in Radnitzky and Bernholz, 1986.

Radnitzky, G., and Andersson, G., eds. *Progress and Rationality in Science*, Boston Studies in the Philosophy of Science, vol. 58 (Dordrecht: Reidel, 1978).

Radnitzky, G., and Andersson, G., eds. *The Structure and Development of Science*, Boston Studies in the Philosophy of Science, vol. 59 (Dordrecht: Reidel, 1979).

Radnitzky, G., and Andersson, G., eds. *Voraussetzungen und Grenzen der Wissenschaft* (Tübingen: J. C. B. Mohr, 1981. Rev. and enl. German version of Radnitzky and Andersson, 1979).

Radnitzky, G., and Bernholz, P., eds. *Economic Imperialism. The Economic Approach Applied Outside the Traditional Areas of Economics* (New York, NY: Paragon House Publishers, 1986).

Seiffert, H., and Radnitzky, G., eds. *Handlexikon zur Wissenschaftstheorie* (München: Ehrenwirt Verlag, 1986), *forthcoming*.

Settle, T. "Concerning the Rationality of Scepticism", *Philosophical Forum* 4, (1973) pp. 432–37.

Watkins, J. "Comprehensive Critical Rationalism", *Philosophy* 44, (1969) pp. 45–51.

Watkins, J. "Comprehensive Critical Rationalism: A Refutation", *Philosophy* 46, (1971) pp. 56–61.

Watkins, J. "Comprehensively Critical Rationalism: A Retrospect", *Chapter XIII of this volume*.

== *Chapter* **XV** ==================================

A Refutation of the Alleged Refutation of Comprehensively Critical Rationalism

By W. W. Bartley, III

PART I

In a number of essays[1], four of which are included in this volume, John F. Post and J. W. N. Watkins have, separately, argued that comprehensively critical rationalism (or, as I now prefer to call it, pancritical rationalism) leads to semantical paradox and other difficulties and is hence refuted.[2] I reply to them in the following.

1. J. W. N. Watkins, "Comprehensively Critical Rationalism", *Philosophy*, vol. 44, no. 167 (January 1969), pp. 57–62; "CCR: A Refutation", *Philosophy*, vol. 46, no. 175 (January 1971), pp. 56–61; and "What Has Become of Comprehensively Critical Rationalism?", *Proceedings of the 11th International Conference on the Unity of the Sciences*, 1983, pp. 1087–1100 and Chapter XII of this volume; John F. Post, "Paradox in Critical Rationalism and Related Theories", *Philosophical Forum*, vol. 3, no. 1 (1972), pp. 27–61; and "A Gödelian Theorem for Theories of Rationality", *Proceedings of the 11th International Conference on the Unity of the Sciences*, 1983, pp. 1071–86 and Chapter XII of this volume. Related papers by Post include: "The Possible Liar", *Nous*, vol. 4 (1970), pp. 405–409 and Chapter X of this volume; "Shades of the Liar", *Journal of Philosophical Logic*, vol. 2 (1973), pp. 370–86; "Propositions, Possible Languages and the Liar's Revenge", *British Journal for the Philosophy of Science*, vol. 25 (1974), pp. 223–34; "Shades of Possibility", *Journal of Philosophical Logic*, vol. 3 (1974), pp. 155–58; and "Presupposition, Bivalence, and the Possible Liar", in *Philosophia*, vol. 8 (1979), pp. 645–49. Post has also permitted me to read his manuscript, "The Modal Liar: Paradox in Self-Referential Falsifiability".

2. The term "comprehensively critical rationalism" was my original term, introduced in the original American edition of *The Retreat to Commitment* (1962). I now prefer the term "pancritical rationalism" introduced in the first German translation (*pankritische Rationalismus*) in 1964, and also now used in the revised and enlarged edition (1984) of *The Retreat to Commitment*. My reply to Post and Watkins first appears in "The Alleged Refutation of Pancritical Rationalism", *Proceedings of the 11th International Conference on the Unity of the Sciences*, pp. 1139–79, and is incorporated, as Appendix 4, in the second edition of *The Retreat to Commitment*. See also my "Rationalität", in G. Radnitzky and Helmut Seiffert, eds., *Handlexikon zur Wissenschaftstheorie* (Munich: Ehrenwirth Verlag, 1986); my "Non-Justificationism: Popper *versus* Wittgenstein", *Akten des 7. Internationalen Wittgenstein Symposiums*, pp. 255–61; my "A Popperian Harvest", in Paul Levinson, ed., *In Pursuit of Truth*. See also Popper's discussion in *Realism and the Aim of Science*, ed. W. W. Bartley, III, vol. 1 of the *Postscript to the Logic of Scientific Discovery*, part 1, sec. 2. See also my "Transformation of Philosophical Thought: Recent Contributions", and my "On the Differences between Popperian and Wittgensteinian Approaches", both in the *Proceedings of the 10th International Conference on the Unity of the Sciences* (New York: ICF Press, 1982), pp. 1169–71 and 1289–1304.

1. Prospectus.

I shall summarize my approach briefly in sixteen points which will then be developed in the remainder of this chapter.

1. There is a serious distortion running throughout this discussion, the major issue of which is the statement that all statements are open to criticism. In *The Retreat to Commitment* this statement was given a concrete context in which the notion of "criticism" had a distinctive sense. In the discussion, this context has been ripped away, with the consequence that my original statement is deprived of its original meaning, and is having other meanings imposed upon it. I discuss this matter in parts II and V of this chapter.

2. Watkins's arguments distort my position, and are invalid. Moreover, they have been replied to by other writers on several occasions.[3] I shall indicate some additional objections of my own in part V below, and shall also refer to Watkins's argument occasionally elsewhere in this chapter.

3. The bulk of my attention will, however, be on Post's view, which has received less attention.[4]

4. Post contends that my position – that all positions, including my own, are open to criticism – produces semantical paradox,[5] and generates an *uncriticizable* statement. The argument in which he initially couched this claim relied heavily on assumptions that are both false and foreign to my approach; so that my first reaction was simply to point out the error of these assumptions.[6]

5. Post has responded by accepting my objections, and then recasting his paradox without those assumptions to which I had objected.

3. Critical reviews of Watkins's work on pancritical rationalism include: Joseph Agassi, I. C. Jarvie, and Tom Settle, "The Grounds of Reason", *Philosophy*, vol. 46, no. 175 (January 1971), pp. 43–49; John Kekes, "Watkins on Rationalism", *Philosophy*, vol. 46, no. 175 (January 1971), pp. 51–53; Sheldon Richmond, "Can a Rationalist Be Rational about His Rationalism?", *Philosophy*, vol. 46, no. 175 (January 1971), pp. 54–55; Tom Settle, I. C. Jarvie, and Joseph Agassi, "Towards a Theory of Openness to Criticism", *Philosophy of the Social Sciences*, vol. 4 (1974), pp. 83–90; Noretta Koertge, "Bartley's Theory of Rationality", *Philosophy of the Social Sciences*, vol. 4 (1974), pp. 75–81; Gerard Radnitzky, "In Defense of Self-Applicable Critical Rationalism", *Proceedings of the 11th International Conference on the Unity of the Sciences*, 1983; W. D. Hudson, "Professor Bartley's Theory of Rationality and Religious Belief", *Religious Studies*, vol. 9 (September 1973), pp. 339–50; N. H. G. Robinson, "The Rationalist and His Critics", *Religious Studies*, vol. 11 (1975), pp. 345–48. See also Michael Martin, "Religious Commitment and Rational Criticism", *Philosophical Forum*, vol. 2 (Fall 1970), pp. 107–21. See also Jagdish Hattiangadi, "Bartley's Defense of Reason", pp. 1119–23; and Angelo M. Petroni, "What Has Become of Watkins' and Post's Criticism of Self-Applicable Critical Rationalism?", pp. 1125–38, and Walter B. Weimer, "CCR is not Completely Confused Rhetoric", pp. 1101–18, in *Proceedings of the 11th International Conference on the Unity of the Sciences*.

4. The only published notices of Post's work of which I know are: Tom Settle, "Concerning the Rationality of Scepticism", *Philosophical Forum*, vol. 4, no. 3 (Spring 1973), pp. 432–37; and A. A. Derksen, "The Failure of Comprehensively Critical Rationalism", *Philosophy of the Social Sciences*, vol. 10 (1980), pp. 51–66.

5. What is involved is not an antinomy but what Post, following Quine, calls a "veridical paradox". See Post, "Paradox in Critical Rationalism", p. 27; and W. V. Quine, *The Ways of Paradox* (New York: Random House, 1966), pp. 5f, 14, 18.

6. I did this in a draft manuscript, circulated among the parties to the dispute: "On Alleged Paradoxes in Pancritical Rationalism", sometimes referred to as "Appendix" in the pertinent literature, since it was a draft for an appendix to the second edition of *The Retreat to Commitment*.

6. I have reservations about his revised argument, and about some of his remaining underlying assumptions. But this is irrelevant, since I have myself been able to produce a quite similar paradox (inspired by Post's work), using no assumptions that are not acceptable to me. (But see point 12 below.)

7. I am, however, neither surprised nor disturbed to find that a *semantical* paradox of this sort can be produced from my statement of pancritical rationalism. On the contrary, I discussed this possibility at length with Popper in 1961 when I was writing the manuscript of the first edition of *The Retreat to Commitment*.

8. The situation is rather simple. My position refers to itself as criticizable: i.e., it is "self-referential". Moreover, my position employs, although not exclusively, an interpretation of criticizability in terms of possible falsity – and thus involves the semantical concepts of truth and falsity. Finally, my position has always been expressed in natural language: i.e., it has not been formalized.

Since, as Tarski has shown,[7] any natural language containing semantic terms and the possibility of self-reference may be expected to be inconsistent, and to produce just such paradoxes, such results could, of course, be expected from the expression of pancritical rationalism.

When I was writing this book, I believed – as I continue to believe – that such paradoxes can be dealt with as they arise, through means similar to those that Tarski himself had suggested, through distinctions of levels of language, through the use of the notion of object and metalanguages. Gerard Radnitzky, in his discussion of the controversy among Post, Watkins, and myself, makes a similar suggestion.[8]

9. Thus, despite appearances, the real issue between Post and me is not the production of a semantical paradox. Rather, the real issue is that (a) Post does not, in general, appear to favor Tarski-type resolutions of semantical paradoxes[9];

---

7. See Alfred Tarski, "The Semantic Conception of Truth and the Foundations of Semantics", in Herbert Feigl and Wilfrid Sellars, eds., *Readings in Philosophical Analysis* (New York: Appleton-Century-Crofts, 1949), pp. 52–84, esp. pp. 56–60; and Alfred Tarski, *Logic, Semantics, Metamathematics* (Oxford: Clarendon Press, 1956), chap. 8 *(Added 1985). In his "Addendum 1985" to "A Gödelian Theorem", Post suggests that "most analysts conclude" that Tarski *showed* no such thing, but only *thought* that he had done so. Post gives no evidence to support this claim.

8. Gerard Radnitzky, "Are Comprehensive Theories of Rationality Self-Referentially Inconsistent?", *Proceedings of the 7th International Wittgenstein Symposium* (Vienna: Hölder-Pichler-Tempsky, 1983); and "In Defense of Self-Applicable Critical Rationalism", in *Proceedings of the 11th International Conference on the Unity of the Sciences*, pp. 1025–69. See Chapter XIII of this volume.

9. For Post's views on these matters, see the essays cited in footnote 1 above, esp. "Propositions, Possible Languages and the Liar's Revenge", "Presupposition, Bivalence, and the Possible Liar", "Shades of the Liar", "The Possible Liar", and "Relative Truth and Semantic Categories". See also Y. Bar-Hillel, "Do Natural Languages Contain Paradoxes?", *Studium Generale*, vol. 19 (1966), pp. 391–97; R. L. Goodstein, "On the Formalization of Indirect Discourse", *Journal of Symbolic Logic*, vol. 23 (1958), pp. 417–19; R. L. Martin: "Toward a Solution of the Liar Paradox", *Philosophical Review*, vol. 76 (1967), pp. 279–311; F. Sommers, "On Concepts of Truth in Natural Languages", *Review of Metaphysics*, vol. 23 (1969), pp. 259–86; Avrum Stroll, "Is Everyday Language Inconsistent?", *Mind*, vol. 63 (1954), pp. 219–25; B. C. van Fraassen, "Presupposition, Implication and Self-Reference", *Journal of Philosophy*, vol. 65 (1968), pp. 136–52; and Tyler Burge, "Semantic Paradox", *Journal of Philosophy*, vol. 76 (1979), pp. 169–98.

and (b) Post believes that such a course – even if it were possible generally – is closed to me by certain other presuppositions of pancritical rationalism.[10]

10. This is not the place to argue the first point: many ways have been developed for dealing with semantical paradoxes; and I agree with the majority of logicians who believe that there is some acceptable way of dealing with them – whether by type and language-level solutions, Zermelo-type solutions, category solutions, radical exclusion of all self-reference, or various other solutions.[11]

11. I shall, however, show that the presuppositions of pancritical rationalism in no way hinder me – contrary to Post's contentions – from adopting some such escape from these paradoxes.

12. *This means that Post's "uncriticizable" statement is, after all, criticizable. Accordingly, Post's argument collapses.*

13. I then argue that Post's own alternative proposals – having to do with what he wrongly supposes to be the approaches of Quine and Lakatos – are unacceptable.

14. I then contend that even if Post were right – if I had no escape either from the semantical paradoxes generally or from the particular "uncriticizable statement" that he produces – such a result would have no impact on the heart of the position presented in *The Retreat to Commitment.*

15. Having replied to Post, I then return to some details of Post's presentation; for a discussion of our differences of assumption – although not needed for the final argument – is of methodological interest, and may also help prevent further misunderstanding. This detailed review of Post's assumptions forms part IV of this chapter; the reply to the Postian argument itself forms part III.

16. Finally, I discuss briefly my differences with Watkins, concentrating on some points which have not been covered by previous writers. This is done in part 5.

PART II

2. The Background of the Debate.

Some of my differences with Post rest on misinterpretations of my position; some rest on disagreements of substance between us; and some rest on my own

10. Post, "Paradox in Critical Rationalism", sec. 8.

11. See K. R. Popper, "Self-Reference and Meaning in Ordinary Language", *Conjectures and Refutations* (London: Routledge & Kegan Paul, 1963), chap. 14; Ernst Zermelo, "Untersuchungen über die Grundlagen der Mengenlehre", *Mathematische Annalen*, vol. 65 (1908), pp. 261–81; Adolf Fraenkel, *Einleitung in die Mengenlehre* (Berlin, 1919); Bertrand Russell, "Mathematical Logic as Based on the Theory of Types", *American Journal of Mathematics*, vol. 30 (1908), pp. 222–62; J. von Neumann, "Eine Axiomatisierung der Mengenlehre", *Journal für reine und angewandte Mathematik*, vol. 154 (1925), pp. 219–40; Paul Bernays, *Axiomatic Set Theory*, with a historical introduction by Abraham A. Fraenkel (Amsterdam: North-Holland Publishing Company, 1958); William and Martha Kneale, *The Development of Logic* (Oxford: Clarendon Press, 1962), esp. chap. 11; Alfred Tarski, *Logic, Semantics, Metamathematics* (Oxford: Clarendon Press, 1956), esp. pp. 152–278; Robert L. Martin, ed., *The Paradox of the Liar* (New Haven: Yale University Press, 1970); Alan Ross Anderson, "St. Paul's Epistle to Titus", in Robert L. Martin, ed., *The Paradox of the Liar.*

failure to state my position sufficiently clearly and adequately in the first place. Before turning to my reply, I would like to recall the background context of our debate.

My original treatment of these matters was, among other things, an examination of the main rationalist traditions of the West, in the course of which I uncovered and identified certain unconscious and mistaken assumptions about rational argumentation which – so long as they were retained – systematically undermined rationalist goals. I advocated removal of these assumptions for the sake of reconstructing and strengthening the rationalist tradition.

In particular, I was confronting the contention – as ancient as Sextus Empiricus and the Greek sceptics,[12] as contemporary as Wittgenstein, Ayer, Rorty, Karl Barth[13] – that there is an essential logical limitation to rationality: that rational defense and examination of ideas *must*, for *logical* reasons, be terminated by an arbitrary and irrational appeal to what may be called *dogmas* or *absolute presuppositions*. These dogmas or presuppositions earned their names from their characteristics, which included the following: (1) such dogmas and presuppositions, chosen arbitrarily and irrationally, or forced on one by the circumstances of fate or history, marked the limits of rationality; (2) they were not subject to review or criticism; (3) they were incapable of justification; (4) all of one's positions that were rational were justified or defended in terms of these presuppositions or dogmas: that is, any rationality in one's life was rationality *relative to* irrational bases. All of one's rational positions could be derived or induced from, or were somehow warranted by, such dogmas and presuppositions.

To rebut this cluster of contentions, I argued: (1) that *nothing* of any interest can be justified in the way required: the demand for justification is a red herring which has nothing whatever to do with the demands of logic or science, but is rather a piece of ancient methodology carried forward uncritically into modern discussion; (2) criticism is nonetheless possible provided one first *unfuses* justification and criticism (all traditional and most modern accounts of criticism are justificationist); (3) there are no limits to rationality in the sense that one *must* postulate dogmas or presuppositions that must be held exempt from review in order to conduct an argument at all; (4) it is false that those of one's positions that are held rationally are those that are deduced, induced, warranted, or otherwise defended in terms of dogmatically held presuppositions.

Post concentrates on one particular element of my discussion to which I myself happened to give some importance – namely, the claim that "Everything is open to criticism". The remainder of my argument, and the problems I was confronting, are not discussed, and are barely alluded to. Now, even if Post were right about the single conclusion that he does discuss (and he is *not* right even

---

12. Sextus Empiricus, *Works,* Harvard-Loeb Library edition.
13. Wittgenstein, *On Certainty* (Oxford: Blackwell, 1969); A. J. Ayer, *The Problem of Knowledge* (New York: Penguin Books, 1956); Richard Rorty, *Philosophy and the Mirror of Nature* (Princeton: Princeton University Press, 1979); Karl Barth, *Church Dogmatics.* See my "Non-Justificationism: Popper versus Wittgenstein", *Proceedings of the 7th International Wittgenstein Symposium.*

here), this would leave the remainder of my argument, and my solutions, conclusions, and suggestions (including all those just rehearsed) completely unaffected. I shall return to this point in section 7 below; but it should be borne in mind throughout.

3. What Did I Mean in Declaring That Everything Is Open to Criticism?

Just as the background just reviewed has been ignored in most of the discussion, neither has anyone paused to consider carefully what I meant when I declared that everything was open to criticism. What did I have in mind?

The classic account of criticism, which pervades almost all philosophical literature, from the Greeks to the present day, is a *justificationist theory of criticism*. According to this account, the way to examine and criticize an idea is to see whether and how it may be justified. And to justify an idea is to derive it from an authority in terms of which such evaluation and criticism is to be made. In short, such justification combines the following two requirements:

> (1) an authority (or authorities), or authoritatively good trait, in terms of which evaluation (i.e., demarcation of the good from the bad ideas) is ultimately to be made;
> (2) the idea that the goodness or badness of any idea is to be determined by reducing it to (i.e., deriving it from or combining it out of) the authority (or authorities), or to statements possessing the authoritatively good trait.[14]
> That which can so be reduced is justified; that which cannot is to be rejected.[15]

To cite one familiar example of how this works, take the case of Hume. Hume wished to use sense observation as his authority in criticizing and evaluating the controversial issues of his day. Being a freethinker, he was able to show, in short order, that the ideas of God, freedom, and immortality, and of the human soul, could not be reduced to sense observation; and hence he rejected them. But to his surprise and dismay, he also found that scientific laws, the idea of causality, the idea of other minds and an external world, and the statements of history could also not be reduced to sense observation, and hence – by *his* authority and on *his* analysis – should also be rejected.

There are many many difficulties in these justificationist theories of criticism. One problem is the problem of logical strength; the conclusions that their advocates want to draw are almost invariably logically stronger than any available

---

14. See my "Logical Strength and Demarcation", in Gunnar Andersson, ed., *Rationality in Science and Politics* (Boston: D. Reidel, 1984), and appendix 2 of *The Retreat to Commitment*, 2nd edition.
15. This is what I call a "justificational strategy of criticism".

authority;[16] another difficulty – and the one that concerns us here – is that the authorities themselves are, of course, not justified. It is even inappropriate to ask for justification of them, for that would simply engender an infinite regress. If one could continue to ask: "How do you know?", that line of questioning would never end: it would engender an infinite regress. Thus it is supposed that one must stop with an authority – or dogma, or presupposition – *which acts as justifier.* Since this justifier cannot itself be justified, and since the only way to criticize something is to attempt to justify it, these justifiers cannot be criticized. Dogmas, it is concluded, are *necessary.* The logical structure of argumentation itself appeared to vouch for, even to require, dogmatism.

What I did in *The Retreat to Commitment* was to show that *no authorities or justifiers in this sense were needed in criticism.* I separated the notions of justification and criticism (for the first time explicitly) and showed that criticism can be carried out successfully and satisfactorily without engendering any infinite regress, and hence without requiring any resort to justification whatever: without any resort to dogmas or authorities. That is, when I declare that all statements are criticizable, I mean that it is not necessary, in criticism, in order to avoid infinite regress, to declare a dogma that cannot be criticized (since it is unjustifiable); I mean that it is not necessary to mark off a special class of statements, the justifiers, which *do* the justifying and criticizing but are not open to criticism; I mean that there is not some point in every argument which is exempted from criticism; I mean that the criticizers – the statements in terms of which criticism is conducted – are themselves open to review.

I doubt that either Watkins or Post would want to contest what I have just written. Hence, had they kept the statement that all statements are open to criticism in its original context, I do not think that they would have raised or would have wanted to raise their objections. *But they have dropped this context. They take "criticism" outside this context and use it in a very wide, uncontrolled sense; and they have thus pursued a discussion which, however interesting in its own terms, is irrelevant to the problems that I have been facing in my work on rationality.* Neither Post nor Watkins has ever even tried to show that the process of argumentation itself requires that I reserve some core of doctrine from risk; that I must either accept this core dogmatically or else accept infinite regress, circularity, or some other logical difficulty. But they would need to do just this to refute my argument.

Having made this statement about the background of my argument, and thereby protested against the procedure adopted by Post and Watkins, I shall drop this point, and attempt to answer their arguments *on their own terms.* For they are wrong on *their* terms too.

---

16. See my "Logical Strength and Demarcation".

PART III

4. A Postian Paradox.

In part 4 below, I give a detailed review of Post's original and revised statements of his paradox in critical rationalism. As I indicate there, I disagree with many of the particulars, and with many of the presuppositions, of his discussion.

In this part, I present a modified argument of my own devising, which involves no appeal to presuppositions which I reject, in order to create the same kind of objection to my own position that Post himself is aiming for. My own argument is thoroughly inspired by Post's, but perhaps simpler.

The argument revolves around my contention that all positions are open to criticism – including the position that all positions are open to criticism. (We may neglect here the question of whether it is a necessary or sufficient condition for being a rationalist that one so hold all one's positions. This question is discussed in section 13 below, but is not needed for the argument.)

Take the following two claims:

(A) All positions are open to criticism.

(B) A is open to criticism.

Since (B) is implied by (A), any criticism of (B) will constitute a criticism of (A), and thus show that (A) is open to criticism. Assuming that a criticism of (B) argues that (B) is false, we may argue: if (B) is false, then (A) is false; but an argument showing (A) to be false (and thus criticizing it) shows (B) to be true. Thus, if (B) is false, then (B) is true. Any attempt to criticize (B) demonstrates (B); thus (B) is uncriticizable, and (A) is false. And hence, so Post would contend, my position is refuted.[16A]

5. An Argument against Post.

Post says he was surprised by such a result; and he is evidently disturbed by it. I am neither surprised nor disturbed, for I have assumed since 1961 that some such result would turn up. No doubt other such examples could also be constructed.

Such a result was virtually inevitable. My statement of pancritical rationalism, in claiming that all positions are criticizable, including this very claim, is obviously self-referential. And although my understanding of criticism and criticizability is not restricted to interpreting them in terms of possible falsity, such possible falsity is assumed in a large part of my discussion – and thus the semantical concepts of truth and falsity are drawn in. Finally, I have never tried to formalize

---

16A. *(Added 1985.) In his "Addendum 1985" to "A Gödelian Theorem", Post states that my argument here rests on the unstated assumption that if a position is false, then there is an argument showing it to be false. I make no such assumption here or elsewhere; this is *his* assumption, akin to his assumption about the specifiability of potential criticisms (for which see part 4 below).

my position, but have always expressed it in natural language. Yet Tarski has shown that any natural language that contains semantic terms and thus the possibility of generating self-reference may be expected to be inconsistent and will produce just such paradoxes. Thus I, a pancritical or comprehensively critical rationalist, almost *predictably* have on my hands something like the result that the statement that my position is open to criticism is uncriticizable; and that the statement that all positions are criticizable is false.

But what is really the impact of this apparently damaging result? Am I, for instance, now *committed* to this uncriticizable statement? *Hardly.* I would give it up in an instant. I don't *like* it at all; I don't *believe in* it; I don't take it as a *presupposition or dogma;* I have no *faith* in it.

Now is my *lack of faith* blind? Is my complacency foolish? Or do I have some reason to suppose that there may be some way of avoiding such conclusions? In fact, there is plenty of reason for supposing that this problem in self-reference – along with most of the other self-referential paradoxes – may be avoided.

Remember: our statement (B) is uncriticizable only in terms of the (Postian) argument in which it was cast. That argument, however, is certainly criticizable; and there is good reason to suppose that the whole line of argumentation may be avoidable, and with it, these paradoxical conclusions.

I believe that such paradoxes can be dealt with, as they arise, through means similar to those that Tarski himself suggested, through the use of the notion of object- and metalanguages and distinctions of levels of language. But one is not limited to Tarski's approach. There is a rich literature, reaching from Russell's discovery of the paradoxes in Frege's work, through Russell's theory of types, through Tarski's distinction between object and metalanguage, to the present day. This literature suggests various ways for avoiding semantical paradoxes: type and language-level solutions, Zermelo-type solutions, category solutions, radical solutions that exclude all self-reference, and others.[17]

In fact, if we assume that some such means might be devised to avoid Post-type arguments, then the criticizability of (B) can be restored. *The mere possibility of such a solution to the semantical paradoxes makes (B) criticizable after all: it suggests a potential means for invalidating the argument that produces the conclusion that (B) is uncriticizable.* And thus *Post* is refuted!

Post anticipated that I might reply in this way, for he constructs an argument to show that I *ought not* to make any such attempt since it would go contrary to the other goals of pancritical rationalism. And here, I believe, we reach the heart of the true substantive difference between us. (The production of the semantical paradox is not the real issue.)

Post argues that if I were to take such an approach, I

would avoid the refutation, but at the expense of decreasing the content of the theory, thus making it less criticizable. For *a theory about all theories including itself obviously*

17. See footnotes 7 and 11 above.

322   *Theory of Rationality*

has greater content than a theory about all other theories, and obviously takes the greater risk of refutation . . . this sort of revision . . . is inconsistent with the aims of CR . . . The critical rationalist, therefore, is not free to object that his principle *A* really ought not to be construed self-referentially. He is not free to object that *A* is really an inexplicit, elliptical way of expressing the view, say, that at each language-level *n*, every rational, non-inferential statement is criticizable$_{n + 1}$.[18]

But this argument is unacceptable. An argument about content cannot be used to eliminate in advance any language-level route out of the paradoxes. High content (used here by Post in Popper's sense) is indeed an important desideratum in any theory, but obviously does not possess overriding force. To take an example, the hypothesis that all orbits of heavenly bodies are circles has greater content than Kepler's hypothesis that all orbits of heavenly bodies are ellipses. Yet in view of the refutation of the circular hypothesis, it would be absurd to demand that any hypothesis that resorts to ellipses be rejected *a priori* on the grounds that it has less content than the circular hypothesis!

Similarly, if Tarski is right in maintaining that *no* consistent language can possibly contain, within itself, the means for speaking about the meaning or the truth of its own expressions, it is absurd to demand unlimited self-reference in natural language (and to foist this demand on the pancritical rationalist) simply on the grounds that such a theory would have greater content. An inconsistent statement does indeed have "great content", being incompatible with everything!

Thus I assumed from the outset – critically, on the basis of the information available – that any statement of pancritical rationalism in natural language may produce semantical paradoxes – at least to the extent to which criticizability is interpreted in terms of possible truth. And I also took for granted that some formal metalinguistic or other tampering would be necessary whenever such semantical paradoxes appeared.[19]

I am aware, from his other publications, that Post not only objects to my taking this route, but also in general opposes language-level and category solutions to the paradoxes, and particularly to those paradoxes that are related to the possible-liar paradoxes.[20] Yet, notwithstanding his arguments, I do not believe that Post would contend that he has *shown* that none of the language-level or other more traditional approaches to semantical paradoxes can possibly work; in which case the work of the majority of contemporary logicians, who believe that such an approach to such paradoxes generally can be successful, stands in criticism of the *line of argument* that produced the Post-like paradoxes in the first place. *And this renders (B) criticizable after all. And thus Post's argument collapses.*

18. Post, "Paradox in Critical Rationalism", pp. 52–53.
19. See Quine, *Ways of Paradox;* Popper, "Self-Reference and Meaning in Ordinary Language"; and the other works cited in footnotes 7 and 11.
20. See the works by Post cited in notes 1 and 9 above.

6. Post's Own Alternative.

Lurking behind my disagreement with Post about how to approach the paradoxes, there is a more serious disagreement. I shall refer to it only briefly; for Post's own statements about it have been troublingly programmatic, and he would need to spell out his ideas before one could properly respond.

I am referring to his suggestion that the way to escape semantical paradoxes in critical rationalism is to adopt the philosophy either of W. V. Quine or of Imre Lakatos.

First, as to Quine: Post reports that Quine rejects the "analytic-synthetic distinction" and thus is able to abandon the rules of logic – including the law of the retransmission of falsity.[21] But this would enable him, so Post alleges, to deny that any criticism of (B) is a criticism of (A), and thus avoid the Post-type semantical paradox. Hence Post appears to suggest that the "lesson" of his paper may be that pancritical rationalism (and related theories) had better abandon the analytic-synthetic distinction, and do so *just* to avoid semantical paradoxes.[22]

This line of argumentation is thoroughly untenable.

The confusion begins with two errors of reporting. Post misrepresents Quine's own position with regard to the paradoxes. For in his own extensive treatments of the semantical and other paradoxes, Quine has not suggested that they should be avoided by giving up the fundamental principles of logic. Rather, he has suggested the same sorts of repair measures that I listed above: Zermelo's method, the method of subscripts, and others.[23] By such procedures, Quine maintains, such paradoxes may be "inactivated". Post also misreports my own position. I do not, contrary to what he says, hold to the analytic-synthetic distinction.[24] I have explicitly repudiated it (and I shall return to this point later, when I discuss Watkins's criticisms).[25] I have also argued that *all* positions – including what are often called "analytic truths" as well as the fundamental laws of logic – are criticizable. Thus the escape route that Post suggests – if it were such a route – would be as open to me as it might be to Quine.

(What Post is referring to in supposing that Quine and I are in disagreement here is my distinction between *criticism* and what I call *revision* within the Quinean argument situation.[26] I suggest that certain limits are imposed on Quine, willy-nilly, by his own characterization of an argument situation; and I argue that such

21. Post, "Paradox in Critical Rationalism", pp. 53–56.

22. *Ibid.*, pp. 54, 56.

23. See notes 7 and 11 above.

24. See my "Limits of Rationality: A Critical Study of Some Logical Problems of Contemporary Pragmatism and Related Movements", Ph.D. dissertation, University of London, 1962; my "Rationality, Criticism, and Logic", esp. pp. 174–86; my "On the Criticizability of Logic"; and appendix 5 of *The Retreat to Commitment*, 2nd edition.

25. See my "Limits of Rationality"; my "On the Criticizability of Logic"; and *The Retreat to Commitment*, 2nd. edition, chap. 5, sec. 4, and appendix 5.

26. See appendix 5 of *The Retreat to Commitment*, 2nd edition. This appendix also sketches some points on which I disagree with Gerhard Vollmer's discussion, in section B3 of his contribution to this volume, concerning the logical presuppositions of argument.

an argument situation presupposes deducibility and retransmission of falsity, which hence cannot be revised within that situation, and can be given up only by stepping outside that situation. (I have also indicated several circumstances in which one might, indeed, be led to step outside that situation.) This in turn led me to suggest a "revisability criterion" which can provide a clear demarcation in an area where Quine said no clear demarcation was possible. All this is discussed in appendix 5, as well as, very briefly, in chapter 5 of *The Retreat to Commitment*, 2nd. edition.)

Whatever the real positions taken by Quine and myself on these matters may be, it is Post's argument which is at stake here. His argument seems to me: (1) if we abandon logic, then the paradoxes do not arise; (2) hence we should abandon logic in order to avoid the paradoxes.

But such a proposal is quite odd. The whole interest of the paradoxes is that they are reached in the course of *rigorously logical argument.* Therein lies their importance, their telling power, and their threatening character: using logic, and presupposing logic, one reaches illogic. The whole point of the mathematical investigation of paradoxes conducted so vigorously during the past eighty years or so has been to avoid the paradoxes *without endangering logical argument.* If the paradoxes could not be avoided, then one might be led deeply to mistrust logic and rational argumentation. Indeed, one might well be led to abandon logical argumentation altogether.

What can Post even mean to suggest in claiming that we might *"consistently* deny the retransmission of falsity", or that we could or should abandon logic *in order to* avoid the paradoxes? True, we would not have any such paradoxes after such moves. But we also would no longer have rational argumentation either.

No one previously, to my knowledge, has advocated such a means for resolving the paradoxes – *and certainly not Quine.* It will not do simply to appeal to Quine as if Quine had provided an example of what Post may have in mind. If Post really wants to advocate such a course as part of a superior "theory of rationality", he must spell out its character in detail, stating what sort of "rationality" would be left.

This brings me to Post's brief declaration of faith in Imre Lakatos's highly schematic theory of research programs.[27] Post reports that "in view of the irrefutability or uncriticizability of the 'core' of a research program", Lakatos's position presents an "improved, self-applicable theory of rationality" which succeeds whenever pancritical rationalism does, but which enjoys full self-referential success as well. This suggestion is also odd. For there is no intrinsic connection between self-reference and uncriticizability. One could not escape semantical paradox by making the "core" of one's research program irrefutable and uncriticizable *unless,* say, the core of one's research program *happened* to be an uncriticizable statement produced by a semantical paradox (as Post wrongly alleges is so of the core of my own view). And that alone would not provide an *improved* theory of rational-

27. Post, "Paradox in Critical Rationalism", p. 57, n. 17.

ity, or indeed a theory of *rationality* at all. For every dogmatist irrationalist makes his position uncriticizable and irrefutable.

In sum, Post appears to believe that – instead of "inactivating" the semantical paradoxes in one of the more usual ways advocated by the majority of contemporary logicians (ways which, however clumsy and unnatural, do render them harmless) – it would be preferable, part of a "better theory of rationality", to give up logic (retransmission of falsity) and deliberately to render the "core" of one's "research program" irrefutable and uncriticizable. Neither Quine, who was my teacher, nor Lakatos, who was my colleague and for many years my friend,[28] would be well-disposed to such an approach.[28A]

Such an approach is the harder to comprehend in that Post declares that he is *not* an irrationalist, and that it is *not* his aim to show that irrational commitment is necessary or to find a rational excuse for irrationalism, and that nothing in his paper should be construed as entailing a retreat to some form of irrationalism.

7. What if Post Were Right about the Paradoxes?

It should be clear that, and why, I reject Post's argument. But what if Post were right? What if it were indeed *impossible* to avoid semantical paradoxes in the statement of pancritical rationalism? How would that affect the argument of *The Retreat to Commitment?* Although the question is worth asking, it should be emphasized that this section is entirely hypothetical, since I do believe that the semantical paradoxes can be inactivated.

(1) I would not have to abandon the claim that all positions are criticizable, but would have to stress more emphatically than I did originally the way in which this claim is meant (see section 3 above), i.e., to deny the logical necessity for a dogma. I should also note, again for clarity, that some statements that are produced by semantical paradox – e.g., (B) – are, in a very different and very attenuated sense, not criticizable.

(2) My characterization of the rationalist would remain essentially intact. He would remain one who holds all his positions, including his most fundamental standards and his basic philosophical position itself, open to criticism in the

28. See my "On Imre Lakatos", in Paul K. Feyerabend and Marx Wartofsky, eds., *Essays in Memory of Imre Lakatos* (Dordrecht: Reidel, 1976), pp. 37–38.

28A. *(Added 1985.) In his "Addendum 1985" to "A Gödelian Theorem", Post repeats his claim that Quine is a non-justificationist. This is a construction of Quine after the fact; for when Quine was writing "Two Dogmas of Empiricism" the distinction between justificational and non-justificational approaches was unknown. Moreover, it is a misconstruction. As I remark in *The Retreat to Commitment* (2nd edition, Appendix 5, p. 257 & n), Jonathan Bennett published in the late 'fifties and early 'sixties explicitly justificationist expositions of Quine's position – expositions which Quine, in *Word and Object* (Cambridge: Wiley, 1960), pp. 67–68n, did not object to. See Jonathan Bennett, "Analytic-Synthetic", *Proceedings of the Aristotelian Society*, 1958–59, and "On Being Forced to a Conclusion", *Aristotelian Society Supplementary Volume 35*, 1961. Another follower of Quine, Morton White, takes an explicitly justificationist approach, writing for instance in *Toward Reunion in Philosophy* (Cambridge: Harvard University Press, 1956), p. 288, that an *a priori* statement is one that we believe quite firmly and therefore "make immune" to overthrow.

intended sense that he does not, and logically need not, declare a dogma. The only "uncriticizable" statements he would harbor would be "uncriticizable" in a different sense: those forced on him by semantical paradox in the course of *rational* argument using natural language; and he would neither be committed to these nor have been led to them by faith. Nor would they have been forced on him by the need to stem an infinite regress. (It would also continue to be possible for the pancritical rationalist to argue himself out of his position in the other ways that I have described.)[29]

(3) All my other claims, my analysis of the problem-situation, and my solution to the problems of fideism and scepticism, would remain intact. In particular:

(4) My crucial distinction between justificational and critical argument would remain intact.

(5) It would remain impossible, within a justificational or authoritarian theory of knowledge, to resolve the dilemma of ultimate commitment. My critique of justificational argumentation would remain intact.

(6) Thus our historical observations about the Western justificationist tradition would be unaffected (e.g., it would remain authoritarian in structure; within it, justification and criticism would remain fused; within it, the assumption that tokens of intellectual legitimacy are logically transmitted would be retained).[30]

(7) An alternative, non-justificational, nonauthoritarian approach to philosophy, using non-justificational criticism, would remain open.

(8) Within such a non-justificational approach, it would still be possible to resolve the dilemma of ultimate commitment. For the case for arbitrary commitment rested on the claim that rationality was so limited logically that such commitment was inescapable. But *nothing in the semantical paradoxes invokes limits to rationality or requires ultimate commitment—not even to the statement (B) that is "uncriticizable".*

(9) Thus my refutation of the *tu quoque* argument would also remain intact. The uncriticizability of (B) would in no way show that the rationalist must be committed to it, or that he must make a dogma out of it, or that he could use it to cut off argument about some contested position.

For with regard to the semantical paradoxes, the justificationist and non-justificationist approaches—*both* being self-referential, *both* being expressed in natural language—appear to be symmetrical. Semantical paradoxes could be produced as easily in justificational approaches as they can evidently be produced in non-justificational critical approaches. The problems in earlier theories of rationality had nothing to do with possible semantical paradox but arose from much more serious logical difficulties. The justificationist program, for instance, led to the unwelcome choice between infinite regress and dogmatism. *Its difficulties arose not from inconsistencies that appear in, and are intrinsic to, all natural languages in*

29. See appendix 5 to *The Retreat to Commitment*, 2nd edition.
30. See my "Rationality, Criticism, and Logic", sec. 10; my "Rationality versus the Theory of Rationality", pp. 24–29; and appendix 6 to *The Retreat to Commitment*, 2nd edition.

which there is self-reference, but from particular philosophical and methodological errors and assumptions of the justificationist tradition.

The two approaches are, however, crucially *asymmetrical* in that one (justificationism) forces this choice between infinite regress and dogmatism, whereas for the other (non-justificationism), such a choice does not arise. Within a non-justificational approach, there is no occasion or need to stem infinite regress or circular argument; and thus the twin difficulties on which justificational approaches foundered do not arise.

It is this crucial difference, this asymmetry, that permits a solution to the problem, and an escape from the *tu quoque.* Previously, the question was whether something had to be accepted as uncriticizable *in order to* stem infinite regress and avoid circular argument. Whereas the kind of uncriticizable statement that is forced on one by the semantical paradoxes is of no use in stemming infinite regress and circular argument.[30A]

(10) Even if someone did make an article of faith or dogma out of (B), there is virtually nothing he could do with it. (B) has insufficient content to be used to justify other claims. Similarly, those semantical paradoxes that arose within the justificationist approach have never been turned into dogmas: they are useless for that purpose.

PART IV

8. A Review of Post's Earlier Formulations.

The previous seven sections of this chapter contain a full answer to Post, and most of what is needed to answer Watkins as well. In this section, I review some of the details of Post's arguments. Although this review is not necessary for the argument, some of the points that arise are intrinsically interesting. And by reviewing these matters I may also help to prevent further misunderstanding of my positions.

30A. *(Added 1985.) In his "Addendum 1985" to "A Gödelian Theorem", Post states that the "justificational and non-justificational approaches, contrary to Bartley, are not symmetrical". But this is not my argument. I argued, as any reader of the preceding four paragraphs can see, that the two approaches are symmetrical in some respects and asymmetrical in others.

Moreover, the *tu quoque* argument, which is presented in detail in *The Retreat to Commitment,* is not, contrary to Post, a semantical argument about the self-referential inconsistency of justificationism. The difficulties of justificationism arise independently of the issues of semantical paradox; and semantical paradoxes are usually not even referred to in this connection in the classical justificationist and sceptical literature, from Epictetus and Sextus Empiricus to Kierkegaard to the present. To be sure, the justificationist could (however unfaithfully to the historical record) attempt to reconstruct or construe some of his difficulties semantically, and accordingly might try a metalinguistic resolution of them. *But as long as he retained his justificationism this would not work: he would simply generate an infinite regression of metalanguages.* It is only in the absence of justificationism that an effective metalinguistic approach is available to me.

While Post's first reference to my work appeared earlier,[31] his first detailed discussion of it was his "Paradox in Critical Rationalism and Related Theories".[32]

There he claims that pancritical rationalism rests on this principle:

A.   *Every rational, non-inferential statement is criticizable and has survived criticism.*[33]

From *A*, there immediately follows, as Post argues:

B.   *Every rational non-inferential statement is criticizable.*

All this can readily be formalized. Post suggests that '*PSX*' stand for '*S* is a potential criticizer of *X*'. Thus *X* will be criticizable just in case $(\exists S)PSX$. '*RX*' stands for '*X* is rational and non-inferential in the present problem-context *K*'. Thus *B* becomes:

B. $(X)\ (RX \rightarrow (\exists S)PSX)$.

Since *B* itself is supposed to be criticizable, there follows:

C. $(\exists S)PSB$.

To elicit a paradox from these, Post needs two additional premises:

(1) $(S)\ (PSC \rightarrow PSB)$
(2) $(S)\ (PSB \rightarrow -PSC)$.

(Post introduces these two premises as if they were just two additional premises, and neglects to mention the quite extraordinary role they play. For these premises, taken together, prove that $PSC \rightarrow -PSC$; or $-C \rightarrow C$. And thus *C* is always proved, no matter what *A*, *B*, and *C* may happen to be. Thus the two premises are themselves a *recipe* for paradox. Presumably Post intended to say that these two premises are forced on me by my position.)

Premise (1) means that every potential criticizer of *C* is a potential criticizer of *B*. (2), on the other hand, means that no potential criticizer of *B* is a potential criticizer of *C*. If a statement *S* were specified which, if accepted, would count as a criticism of *B*, then that would also show the truth of *C*, and thus could not count against *C*. That is, any criticism of the statement that *B* is criticizable would be a criticism of *B;* and any criticism of *B* would provide an example of, and hence confirm, the criticizability of *B* – i.e., *C*, the statement that *B* is criticizable.

31. See Post, "The Possible Liar", Chapter IX above.
32. *Op. cit.*
33. Post adds that any given statement *X* is a rational statement if and only if a rational man is entitled to accept it – that is, if and only if *X* is "rationally acceptable". Hence *A* could presumably be rewritten:
A_1.   *Every noninferential statement that a rational man is entitled to accept is criticizable and has survived criticism.*
Presumably *A* could also be rewritten, as Post interprets it, as follows:
A_2.   *Every rationally acceptable non-inferential statement is criticizable and has survived criticism.*

But from premises (1) and (2) together, there follows:

(3) $-(\exists S)PSC.$

That is, C is not criticizable.

If we assume that C is rational and non-inferential, however, it follows that B is false. And thus – so Post argues – pancritical rationalism is refuted. The claim that all rational statements can be criticized is incorrect, for the claim that this claim can be criticized itself cannot be criticized.

Post goes on to argue that C, although uncriticizable, is demonstrably true; that B, which is criticizable, is self-referentially consistent but invalid; and that A, which is also criticizable, is invalid and self-referentially inconsistent. B could be restored to validity, and A to self-referential consistency, only by withdrawing the claim that C is rational. But in that case A would be incomplete, contrary to the comprehensive aims and claims of pancritical rationalism. This leads Post to his "Gödelian theorem" that all rationality theories in a certain class that includes my own (and also Popper's)[34] are either self-referentially inconsistent or inherently incomplete.

9. The Rationality of Statements *versus* the Rationality of People.

Post's argument, which is directly derived from his work on possible-liar paradoxes, does not accurately interpret the core of my own position; and thus my own position is not subject to or refuted by his arguments and is not encompassed by his theorem.

Post's argument is, in its original form, a discussion of what makes a *statement* rational; and what makes a statement rational, on his account, is an alleged *semantic* (or partly semantic) *property* of statements called *criticizability*. It is, however, one of the merits of pancritical rationalism, and of *The Retreat to Commitment,* that it presents a theory about people, not statements. It is, quite explicitly (pp. 35, 76, 84–85, and especially p. 86), an account of the *essence of being a rationalist.* It is an account of how a rationalist or critical person might behave. It is not an account – although it may have some relevance to an account – of rational statements or of rational belief. As I wrote (p. 86): "emphasis on the criteria for rational *belief* is suitable only for the history of panrationalism and critical rationalism. The important structural shift to pancritical rationalism involves a change of emphasis to the problem of how to tell a genuine from a non-genuine rationalist." One certainly does not tell a rationalist from an irrationalist simply by looking at the beliefs or the statements which he holds.[35]

---

34. See Post, Chapters X, p. 220, and XI, p. 223. Post also demands that any criticizable statement must meet certain other requirements. These additional requirements do not concern me here. In correspondence, Post has told me that he now wishes to construe criticizability not as semantic but only as "partly semantic". See Chapter XI.

35. On whether a belief can be rational, see Joseph Agassi and I. C. Jarvie, "Magic and Rationality Again", *British Journal of Sociology,* vol. 24 (June 1973), esp. p. 236.

I doubt the merit of discussing the problem of rationality in terms of the rationality of statements ("rationality" being taken as a semantic or "partly semantic" predicate). For statements are intrinsically neither rational nor irrational. The *rationality* of a claim, as expressed by a statement, is much more dependent on time and place and historical context than is the *truth* of a statement. The claim that the earth is flat would not, in most of Europe, in the twelfth century, have been irrational for most people. The rationality of a statement has more to do with the way that it is *held* than it does with its content. Thus, while I happen to believe that the Christian God does not exist, I tend to be embarrassed when I meet the "village atheist", one who makes this claim dogmatically – and irrationally. One could, of course, say that he holds a rational claim irrationally. But why not speak more clearly and say that he holds an accurate statement in an irrational or rigid way?

As this last remark indicates, *rationality is really very different from truth.* The truth of a statement does depend importantly on the statement: it depends on whether it corresponds with the facts; whereas rationality is not a property of statements but is a matter of the way in which a statement is held, and also of the *history* of that statement, of the way in which the statement has been examined.[36]

10. The Problem of the Specification of Criticism.

Thus pancritical rationalism does not involve, and I have never developed, a theory of rationality as a property of statements.

Yet if I were to develop such a theory, it would differ from Post's. For essential to Post's discussion, as he has pointed out, is his claim that criticizability is a semantic property of statements in the sense that for a statement to be criticizable we must be able to *specify* its "potential criticizer".[37] For any statement to be criticizable, Post requires that we be able to *present* a syntactically well-formed sentence, together with its semantic interpretation, which expresses a statement that, if correct, would render the statement under examination false, or unsatisfactory in some other way (e.g., unfruitful, inappropriate, irrelevant, etc.).

What Post means by "specification" and "presentation" is unclear, – as is the way in which the criticizable statements would be demarcated from the uncriticizable statements in terms of this requirement. In so far as I understand this requirement, it seems to me to be unreasonable. It is no part of pancritical rationalism to insist that one must be holding a statement irrationally and uncritically unless one can immediately produce a statement which would, if accepted, constitute a rebuttal.[38] Momentary inability to specify a potential criticism may

36. See my "Rationality, Criticism, and Logic", secs. 4, 20.
37. Post, Chapter XI, esp. sec. 3.
38. For a review of the issue of specifiability and rationality, see Walter B. Weimer, "For and Against Method", *Pre/Text*, vol. 1, nos. 1–2 (Spring–Fall 1980), pp. 161–203, esp. p. 185.

mark a failure of imagination, or may simply indicate that one has not yet sufficiently investigated the theory in question in its relation to its problem situation and to other theories. *Lack of interest* in potential criticism, or *hostility* to potential criticism, would be quite another thing: that would indeed probably mark a dogmatic or at least uncurious attitude. What I had in mind when writing of a pancritical rationalist was one who holds his claims open to review even when – and particularly when – he is unable to imagine, let alone specify, what would count against them.

Post's demand acquires what plausibility it may have from his insistence that to deny it would be to go against the spirit of Popper's philosophy; thus he quotes Popper's remark that "criteria of refutation have to be laid down beforehand". But Post misconstrues Popper. First, this remark has to do with science, not with criticism in general; second, the remark comes from a *footnote* explaining under what circumstances an observation counts in support of a theory, not from an account of what Popper means by "criticizability". (Popper gives no such account.) Again, Popper speaks here of specifying *criteria* of refutation in advance, *not* of specifying a refuting statement or counterexample. Thus one might say that if a theory were found to be inconsistent, that would suffice for its rejection; or that if it were found to be contradicted by empirical observation, that would suffice for its rejection. But one would not be able to specify specific inconsistencies or contrary evidence in advance!

It is, of course, valuable and important, *whenever possible,* to specify in advance what sorts of things would count against a theory. It is also characteristic of the evaluation of scientific theories that one can quite often make such specifications in advance – and that one can indeed not only specify the *sorts* of things that would countermand a theory but can also sometimes point to specific counterexamples. Popper himself notes how Einstein was able to specify in advance what would count against relativity theory, whereas Freudians and Marxists (despite their claims to scientific status for their theories) are unable (and perhaps also unwilling) to specify what would count against their views.

But I was in no way restricting myself to science when I wrote of criticizability: I was concerned with a broad range of ideas, with religion, ethics, theory of value, and metaphysics, as well as with science. In this broader domain there is not the slightest reasonable hope of always being able to specify potential criticisms in advance, although one may try even here to specify the *sorts* of things that would be critically effective.[39] Yet there is all the more reason, in such circumstances, to continue to hold such theories as open to criticism.

Moreover, Post's account seems to involve justificationism at this point (elsewhere he declares himself a non-justificationist). To demand for every putatively criticizable statement a specification or presentation of a potential criticizer is in

---

39. I make an attempt to specify some of the sorts of things that count as criticism in chap. 5, sec. 4, of *The Retreat to Commitment.* See also "Rationality, Criticism, and Logic", secs. 13–19.

effect *to demand a justification of the claim that that statement is criticizable and to refuse to hold that claim hypothetically* (which is to say, critically).

Post had intended his demand to be in the spirit of Popper's critical philosophy. In fact, it runs against that spirit. I am thinking, in particular, of Popper's strong reminder that *we never know what we are talking about.*[40] Thus, there is an infinity of unforeseeable and nontrivial statements belonging to the informative content of any theory – as well as an exactly corresponding infinity of statements belonging to its logical content. Hence it is impossible to know the full implications or significance of any theory. It is thus impossible to know what will refute it. We cannot specify (or predict) today what we shall know only tomorrow.[41]

The way in which one criticizes a theory will depend on how one understands it. One gets to understand a theory through working on it: through criticizing it. An important part of this process is to discover its logical relations to the existing network of theories, problems, and evidence in the relevant field: that is, its relation to what Popper calls the objective "problem situation". But there is no way to know or specify in advance how this process will go, or what sorts of potential objections to the theory under investigation will emerge during the course of this enterprise. Thus on Popper's account the understanding of a theory – and hence its criticism – is a never-ending task, although, in the course of time, the theory may come to be understood better and better.

The informative content of a theory includes any theory incompatible with it – and thus any future theory that may supersede it. So the informative content of Newton's theory – and thus its potential criticizers – includes Einstein's theory. But Einstein's theory could not possibly have been predicted when Newton's theory was put forward. Nor, lacking Einstein's theory, could the relevant sorts of empirical falsifiers have been specified: i.e., those basic statements which clash with Newtonian theory but which could not possibly even have been stated prior to the creation of Einstein's theory. Nor could the statements that could be relevant to a crucial experiment between Newton's and Einstein's theories be specified. And thus the sorts of potential criticizers of Newton's theory that eventually became important historically were unspecifiable during the first several hundred years of life of Newton's theory.

---

40. Popper, *Unended Quest* (La Salle and London: Open Court, 1982), sec. 7. See my discussions in my "Wittgenstein and Homosexuality", in Robert Boyers and George Steiner, eds., *Salmagundi*, Fall 1982–Winter 1983, pp. 166–96; and in my "Ein schwieriger Mensch: Eine Porträtskizze von Sir Karl Popper", in Eckhard Nordhofen, ed., *Physiognomien: Philosophen des 20. Jahrhunderts in Portraits* (Königstein: Athenäum Verlag, 1980), pp. 43–69. See also the discussion by Renée Bouveresse in *Karl Popper* (Paris: J. Vrin, 1981), pp. 59–63. (See also my "Alienation Alienated", this volume, Chapter XVIII.)

41. See Popper's discussion in *The Open Universe: An Argument for Indeterminism*, vol. 2 of the *Postscript to the Logic of Scientific Discovery*, esp. chapters 2 and 3.

11. The Paradox Reconsidered.

Having mentioned these differences between Post's account and my own – concerning certain assumptions in which his argument is couched, but which I reject – I now wish to turn to his argument itself.

Post's argument purports to make use of the "core statement" of pancritical rationalism. In fact, it makes use of something rather different. Take his statement *A*:

A.   *Every rational, non-inferential statement is criticizable and has survived criticism.*

Post means this as a report of my remark (*Retreat*, 2nd. ed., p. 119) that a "position may be held rationally without needing justification – *provided that it can be and is held open to criticism and survives severe examination*". That is,

A'.   *Every position which is held open to criticism and survives severe examination may be held rationally.* (And there is no need to go into the question of its justification.)

A and *A'* are, however, very different. Even if we allow my "position" to be interpreted by his "statement", Post's *A* reverses and crucially alters *A'*. Post's *B* does not follow from my *A'*. Nor does a reversed version of *B* follow from *A'*.[42] Thus someone who holds *A'* need not hold *B'*:

B'.   *Every criticizable statement is rational and non-inferential.*

Nor does Post's *C* follow from my *A'*. Thus his paradox, *as originally constructed*, does not capture pancritical rationalism.

12. The Paradox Reformulated.

In "A Gödelian Theorem for Theories of Rationality", Post takes account of some of the objections that I have just stated.[43] He insists that he does not demand justification of pancritical rationalism; he abandons his requirement of specifiability as a necessary condition for a potential criticism; and he is willing to drop the suggestion that criticizability is an intrinsic or semantic property of statements, and instead to try to formulate the matter in terms of the ways in which people hold statements.

---

42. The first critic to misrepresent pancritical rationalism in this way, and who may be responsible for Post's error, is J. W. N. Watkins, in his "CCR: A Refutation" (see note 1 above and the discussion below), p. 57. See Watkins's statement (1).

43. Printed as Chapter XII of the present volume. My objections to his earlier work were communicated privately, especially in the unpublished draft manuscript: "On Alleged Paradoxes in Pancritical Rationalism".

Having conceded the correctness of most of my objections to his views, Post then immediately produces a new formulation of his argument which, he believes, overcomes my objections.

His reformulated first premise, *A1*, now reads as follows:

> *A1.* Consider a person *P*, a context *K*, a time *t*, and an attitude, belief, or position *X* (expressible or not) which is problematic (or up for possible revision) for *P* in *K* at *t*. Then *P* holds *X* rationally in *K* at *t* only if: *P* holds *X* open to criticism at *t*, and (so far as *P* can then tell or guess) *X* has at *t* so far survived criticism.

From *A1* there follows *B1*:

> *B1.* *P* holds *X* rationally at *t* only if *P* holds *X* open to criticism at *t*.

We also obtain *C1*:

> *C1.* There is a (potential) criticism of *B1*, which might someday be produced and be seen to be successful.

Go through a similar line of argument as before – stated in full in Post's paper – and his alleged refutation of my claim is restored.

13. Necessary or Sufficient?

While attempting to take *most* of my objections into account, Post ignores the objections in section 11 above. And thus his paradox, as reformulated, also does not capture the core of my position.

Our difference here concerns the question whether criticizability and survival of criticism are necessary or sufficient conditions of rationality. I intended them as sufficient conditions and usually expressed them as such in *The Retreat to Commitment*. But I was careless in my expression, and occasionally I stated them as if they were necessary conditions or requirements. Thus it is fair for Post to read them in this way.

But how *should* it be? Am I correct to construe them as sufficient conditions? Or is Post correct not only that I sometimes expressed them as necessary conditions, but also that they *should*, from my point of view, be so construed?

The answer to this question emerges directly from the argument of *The Retreat to Commitment* itself. My characterization of pancritical rationalism stemmed from a critical examination of the panrationalist (or comprehensive rationalist) account, according to which *comprehensive* justification was a *necessary* condition of rationality. (The traditional account was indeed put as a necessary condition.) Since such justification was impossible, it followed that a rationalist was impossible, and thus the question with which I began my book: "Is it possible to remain a rationalist?" (p. xxvi, pp. 83 ff., and passim).

My answer – after discovering the existence of non-justificational criticism – was that the sort of justification that had traditionally been required is not only impossible but also quite unnecessary. Rather, non-justificational criticizability was a *sufficient* condition for rationality. Since this can readily be obtained, it is possible to be a rationalist.

The question whether these criteria are necessary or sufficient could be argued at length. I do not propose to do so here. For, as I have shown in section 4 above, a similar paradox can be generated without reference to this question.

14. Criticizability Is Not Captured by Possible Falsity Alone.

As indicated above, the chief claim Post attributes to me – that every rational, non-inferential statement is criticizable and has survived criticism – is weaker than the one I really hold. My view is that *all* statements are criticizable – not just the rational and non-inferential ones, whatever they may be.[44]

With this claim alone, as I have shown, a similar paradox can be created, and the question of necessary versus sufficient conditions for rationality, as discussed in the last section, loses most of its importance in the present context.

Post's line of argumentation, however, seems to rest on (or at any rate to stem from) the assumption (so far unexamined) that *for a statement to be criticizable is for it to be possibly false.* If I were to accept this assumption, I would be forced to maintain that all positions are possibly false.

But this position – that all positions are possibly false – is, so it seems to me, obviously false. And it is so quite apart from Post's paradoxes. For if all statements are possibly false, then there are no necessary truths (*and* is it a necessary truth, then, that there are no necessary truths?).

I believe not only that not all positions are possibly false, but also that there are indeed necessary truths.[45] And since I also have been maintaining that all positions (including necessary truths) are criticizable, I hardly suppose that criticizability and possible falsity are so closely linked as Post has assumed throughout his discussion – including, especially, his early articles on the paradoxes of the possible liar.

To indicate what I have in mind here, it may be helpful to say something about the background in which *The Retreat to Commitment* was conceived. I had begun to work on the problems underlying it in 1956, when I was at Harvard, being thoroughly indoctrinated at that time by my teachers W. V. Quine and Morton White in the inadequacies of the distinction between analytic and synthetic statements. Although it was only after beginning to study with Popper in London that I found a way to solve my problems, I never abandoned the approach taken by Quine and White on this matter (although I later – see section 6 above and

44. See my "On the Criticizability of Logic", pp. 67–77; and footnote 2; and appendix 5 of *The Retreat to Commitment,* 2nd edition.

45. See Popper's discussion of natural necessity in *The Logic of Scientific Discovery* (London: Hutchinson, 10th impression, 1980), Appendix *x, "Universals, Dispositions, and Natural or Physical Necessity", pp. 420–41, including the new Addendum to p. 441.

appendix 5 to *The Retreat to Commitment,* 2nd edition – set a limit on the applicability of Quine's argument). My doctoral dissertation (1962), which incorporated part of *The Retreat to Commitment,* was entitled: "Limits of Rationality: A Critical Study of Some Logical Problems of Contemporary Pragmatism and Related Movements", referring to the pragmatist connections of Quine and White. The thesis was concerned chiefly with the controversy over the analytic-synthetic distinction. My view that the analytic-synthetic distinction is not viable was very much confirmed and enriched by my seven-year association with Imre Lakatos. I watched closely as *Proofs and Refutations,* his brilliant essay on the logic of mathematical discovery, was conceived and written. Lakatos emphatically rejected what he called "the logicist demarcation between science and mathematics".[46] One way to describe his book would be as a rich historical study of the ways in which demonstrable and necessary truths which could not possibly be false are in fact revised and rejected in the course of mathematical discovery, *in the course of being examined and criticized.*

In view of this, it is surprising that Post would state that my position "presupposes analyticity", or that Watkins (to whom we shall turn in part V) takes the analytic-synthetic distinction for granted throughout his discussion and in his very formulation of what he supposes to be my position.[47]

I do, of course, agree that for a large range of statements one main thing that one does in criticism is indeed to attempt to show falsity, and that one therein usually does assume possible falsity. That is, for a large class of statements, to hold a statement open to criticism is to conjecture or guess that the statement may be wrong and that some day some effective criticism, the nature of which we cannot even imagine today, may be produced against it. But that is not all there is to criticism.

This is not the place to rehearse the elaborate arguments of Quine and White, or the historical examples of Lakatos, to show how necessary truths, statements that cannot possibly be false, may be criticized, revised, rejected in the course of argument.[48] Although I disagree with Lakatos about many matters, I agree completely with his statement: "But whatever the solution may be, the naïve school concepts of static rationality like *apriori-aposteriori, analytic-synthetic* will only hinder its emergence."[49] This corrigibility of "necessary" truths is sometimes also a matter

46. Imre Lakatos, *Mathematics, Science and Epistemology, Philosophical Papers* (London: Cambridge University Press, 1978), vol. 2, p. 91.

47. Another critic of my position, A. A. Derksen, realizes that I do not hold to the analytic-synthetic distinction. See his "The Failure of Comprehensively Critical Rationalism", pp. 51–66, esp. note 1.

48. See Imre Lakatos, *Proofs and Refutations: The Logic of Mathematical Discovery* (London: Cambridge University Press, 1976); and *Mathematics, Science and Epistemology,* esp. chaps. 1, 2, 4, 5, 7. See also W. V. Quine, *From a Logical Point of View,* esp. chaps. 2 and 3; *Word and Paradox* (New York: John Wiley & Sons, 1960); *The Ways of Paradox and Other Essays* (New York: Random House, 1966); and W. V. Quine and J. S. Ullian, *The Web of Belief* (New York: Random House, 1978). See also Morton White, *Toward Reunion in Philosophy;* and *Religion, Politics and the Higher Learning* (Cambridge, Mass.: Harvard University Press, 1959).

49. Lakatos, *Mathematics, Science and Epistemology,* pp. 40–41.

of possible falsity. Often, however, it may be a matter of the revision, the narrowing or stretching and adjustment of concepts. In this process, one may come to revise those conditions which serve to render a certain statement impossible to be false. It is not so much a question of truth and possible falsity as a question of context and of how to arrange and order. Or it may be argued that someone did not prove what he set out to prove – not that what was proved was false or possibly false. Or that the statement of an argument or proposition is inelegant or uneconomical. And so on. The idea that "necessary" truths cannot be revised is probably due to a failure of imagination and a lack of knowledge of the history of mathematics and of science. For our intellectual history contains many examples of ardently and most sincerely believed claims that have been declared to be demonstrable, or necessary truths, synthetic *a priori* true, self-evident, and such like. In Kant's philosophy, for instance, Newtonian physics, Euclidean geometry, and Aristotelian logic were given such a privileged position. But all three have since been displaced – by Einsteinian physics, by non-Euclidean geometries, and by modern logic.

In attempting to hold such "necessary" truths open to revision, the issue is really not one of sincerity, but one of intellectual policy when one is considering the scope of criticism, and when one has the maximization of criticism as one of one's aims.

PART V

15. On Watkins

> For any proposition there is always some sufficiently narrow interpretation of its terms, such that it turns out true, and some sufficiently wide interpretation such that it turns out false . . . concept-stretching will refute *any* statement, and will leave no true statement whatsoever.
>
> *Imre Lakatos*[50]

Watkins's papers have been replied to by a number of writers,[51] but he has ignored most of these criticisms. I shall not rehearse the objections of other writers here, although I think that most of them are sound, but will add only a few points that others have not mentioned.

Watkins's first argument against pancritical rationalism was similar to Post's; but instead of developing it in terms of serious (if irrelevant) problems of semantical paradox, he chose to use it as obvious evidence that I

---

50. Lakatos, *Proofs and Refutations*, p. 99.
51. For replies to Watkins, see references in footnote 3, above. For a reply to Derksen, see my "On the Criticizability of Logic", pp. 67–77.

had developed a "dictatorial strategy". That is, Watkins claims that pancritical rationalism was a perfect example of a dictatorial strategy in the sense that it permits me to win however the argument may go: a defender of pancritical rationalism, he contends, is *assured* victory over his critics however good their criticisms, for his position is never at risk.

Watkins's argument went like this: suppose a critic of pancritical rationalism produces a cogent argument showing that pancritical rationalism is *not* open to genuine criticism. This would *be* a damaging criticism; hence it would be impossible for a critic ever to show that pancritical rationalism is uncriticizable. To show that pancritical rationalism is *un*criticizable is to criticize it, and hence to prove that it is criticizable after all.

Outside the context of semantical paradox – and there is no such context in Watkins's work – this is a deplorable argument. If someone were to come forward with a cogent argument against pancritical rationalism, and if I were then to reply: "Oh, you see, *that just goes to show* that I was right in saying that my position is open to criticism", I would be laughed at. And we all know from Charlie Chaplin that one thing that dictators cannot stand is to be laughed at.

Popper teaches that we should take systems of thought as a whole and appraise them (metalinguistically, of course) as connoisseurs, as it were, searching to identify components within them that could possibly be used to deflect criticism or to immunize those systems in any way against criticism and thereby to turn them into what he calls "reinforced dogmas". Popper's own favorite examples included Freudian and Marxist theory, and also, to a lesser extent, positivism and the Copenhagen interpretation of quantum mechanics. Ernest Gellner did the same sort of thing with Wittgensteinian and Oxford philosophy.[52] In *The Retreat to Commitment,* and also in *Morality and Religion,* I tried to do this sort of thing with various contemporary theological systems. The "game" here was to identify criticism-deflecting strategies (such as the theory of resistances in Freudian theory), *ad hoc* changes in definitions of key terms, *ad hoc* adoption of auxiliary hypotheses (e.g., epicycles), and such like. Another whole context that served to immunize almost all systems from criticism was, I argued, justificationism as such: justificationism explicitly called for uncriticizable dogmas which were off-limits from the outset, and which also *rendered* off-limits anything that could be derived from them.

Let us suppose that some critic of pancritical rationalism, in the course of an appraisal of the position as a whole, finds it guilty of all the devices and ploys I have just mentioned, and also gives concrete examples of how these work in the actual practice of the position. Now, if the proponent of such a system – our hypothetical pancritical rationalist – is indeed, working within his system, already entangled in, ensnared in, such devices, then maybe he *would* interpret the outsider's criticism as confirmation of his own (evidently dogmatic) contention that

52. Ernest Gellner, *Words and Things.*

his position is open to criticism. As Popper has argued, anyone who is ensnared by such criticism-reducing strategems *will* tend to interpret all his or her experience as being confirmatory of, rather than threatening to, his or her position: everything will verify it; nothing will falsify it.

Someone *could*, in the name of pancritical rationalism, behave in such a way: he could declare as his fundamental position that everything he held was criticizable; and then, whenever he was criticized, he could take that as evidence of the truth of his statement.

Anything may be misused. Only by putting an argument in its context can one gauge whether it is being used in a critical or uncritical way. Let us take a look again at the appropriate context for our own discussion. A number of things need to be noticed.

First, such behavior on the part of this hypothetical individual who has declared himself a pancritical rationalist *will in no way invalidate the critic's contentions.* Watkins misses the fact that there is no such thing as "uncriticizability" in general, or uncriticizability in a vacuum, as it were. A system that is uncriticizable is uncriticizable in some *particular, specific,* respects. That is, it must use a *particular* criticism-deflecting strategem; it must use a *particular ad hoc* device; and so on. And the critic will, of course, identify these. Although the fact of this particular criticism will show that the system is in *some* respect criticizable, it won't make those of its features which diminish its criticizability, or which even render it virtually uncriticizable in particular circumstances, disappear.

Second, any such behavior on the part of Watkins's hypothetical pancritical rationalist would in fact be self-defeating. For it would strengthen the hand of the critic, who could now add to his previous indictment. The critic would now say that, in addition to having all those criticism-reducing strategems *at his disposal,* the pancritical rationalist was also putting them *into practice* to the extent of using any criticism of his position as evidence of the correctness of his position. Worse, the poor man was even ignoring all the laughter.

Moreover, the whole situation becomes more complicated when we take account of the different possible points of view in this hypothetical situation, and look at the whole situation more realistically than Watkins's one-dimensional approach allows.

The fact that a system of thought has been criticized *by an outsider* in one particular respect does not make of it a system that is held *by its proponents* in a way that exposes it to criticism generally. This only shows that it is able to be criticized by an outsider; it does not show that it functions in such a way as to permit an insider to be affected by that very criticism. The fact that a criticism has been raised and noted (by outsider or insider) does not make that point of view criticizable in the sense of making criticisms *effective* against the holder of such a viewpoint.

The issue is not whether there are criticisms available: the issue is whether these criticisms can be and are used in such a way as to be effective in regenerating the system and transforming those who hold it. Any system that encouraged the kind of behavior that Watkins suggested – i.e., using criticism as evidence of criticizability at the expense of not taking criticism seriously – would be grossly defective with regard to the very possibility of regeneration.

But there is no evidence that pancritical rationalism ever has been or very effectively could be held in such a way. Pancritical rationalism *explicitly* aims to create a way of life that would be exposed to *optimum* effective criticism with optimum effect on those who hold it; and it undertakes this aim in the spirit of Popper's statement that we must decide that "if our system is threatened we will never save it by any kind of . . . *stratagem*".[53]

Watkins fails to take this into account. He juggles with the words "criticizable" and "rational" and ignores a systems and contextual approach. Above all, he ignores the context in which the theory was put forward.

This brings me to Watkins's second line of criticism, which is to produce trivial examples of true statements that are "obviously" uncriticizable. This is a commonsense "know-nothing" approach, reminiscent of Johnson's "refutation" of Berkeley.

To show its irrelevance, I want to state again the two contexts in which I claimed that all positions are criticizable.

The *first*, which I reviewed in section 3 above, is that all positions are criticizable in the sense that: (1) it is not necessary, in criticism, in order to avoid infinite regress, to declare a dogma that could not be criticized (since it was unjustifiable); (2) it is not necessary to mark off a special class of statements, the justifiers, which *did* the justifying and criticizing but was not open to criticism; (3) there is not a point in all argument, the *terms*, which is exempted from criticism; (4) the criticizers – the statements in terms of which criticism is conducted – are themselves open to review.

In this first sense, all Watkins's examples are irrelevant: his examples could hardly serve as examples of dogmas or terms of argument or justifiers; they will hardly interest the commitment merchant; they lend no credence to the supposition that such dogmas or justifiers are ever necessary; they are in no way parallel to the "unjustifiable" positions of earlier theories of rationality. Such examples of "uncriticizable" statements are not, for instance, needed *in order to criticize;* whereas, in justificationist philosophies, unjustifiable statements are needed in order to justify. These examples do not unravel the crucial distinction between justification and criticism; they do not affect the rebuttal of the *tu quoque;* they are truly irrelevant to the problem of irrationality. In such a discussion, the problem of rationality is forgotten. The problem has shifted – and degenerated.

But I also had a *second* sense of "criticizability" in mind, a sense which is largely independent of the first. I have already alluded to this sense in section 6, and written of it in section 14. This second sense in which I advocated that all positions are criticizable was in no way intended to be an original claim on my part

53. *The Logic of Scientific Discovery*, p. 82.

and also is not really needed to refute the sceptical and fideistic positions against which I have been contending. In this sense, when I said that all positions are open to criticism I meant that statement in the sense in which Quine (and White, Lakatos, and others) had argued against the analytic-synthetic distinction, claiming the revisability of all statements (including "analytic statements" and "necessary truths"), and also in the sense in which Popper had insisted on the theory-impregnation (and hence revisability) of even the most obvious observation statements.[54]

Thus, in bringing forth his examples of an incontestably true nineteen (or twenty-two)- word sentence, and other examples, such as: "I am more than three years old", and "During 1969 Mr. Nixon was President of the U.S.A.", Watkins is not just taking me on, but is combatting a well-developed position in contemporary philosophy to which I happen to adhere. But even if Watkins should be right in rejecting this position (if he does reject it), that would not affect my argument. I like this position, and find it congenial to the pancritical rationalist's goal of maximizing criticism. But my refutation of scepticism and fideism, and of justificationism, and my treatment of the limits of rationality, do not depend on this second sense of "criticizability".

This is hardly the place to review the controversy over the analytic-synthetic distinction or the issue of the revisability of observation statements. I would, however, like to conclude with a brief remark on Watkins's "obviously true" twenty-two-word sentence

(S)   There exists at least one sentence written in English prior to the year two thousand that consists of precisely twenty-two words.

Watkins says that this is "*certainly true* and hence uncriticizable".

But this statement *is* criticizable or revisable in my sense – and in the senses of Quine, White, and Lakatos that I had in mind. Nor is it even farfetched to suppose how it might be revised: although I have recently heard that it is no longer possible to send an inland telegram in Britain, Watkins could find that, in many countries, for the purpose of costing telegrams by the "word", certain sorts of words are grouped together in ways that differ from the *principles of counting* on which the truth of his statement depends: many would, for instance, take "twenty-two" to be one word, not two.[55]

---

54. *Ibid.*, chap. 5.

55. See Lakatos, *Mathematics, Science and Epistemology*, p. 14, where he writes: " '*Class*' and '*membership-relation*' turned out to be obscure, ambiguous, anything but 'perfectly well known'. There even emerged the completely un-Euclidean need for a consistency proof to ensure that the 'trivially true axioms' should not contradict one another. All this and what followed must strike any student of the seventeenth century as *déjà vu*: proof had to give way to explanation, perfectly well known concepts to theoretical concepts, triviality to sophistication, infallibility to fallibility."

Part III

Rationality and the Sociology of Knowledge

Chapter XVI

Philosophy and the Mirror of Rorty

By Peter Munz

> "*Rorty, Rorty on the wall,*
> *Who is the fairest of us all?*"

1. Rorty, champion of Oakeshott and Foucault, becomes a knight errant in quest of culture. Culture as relativism, historicism, conversations, and parlor-games.

Apart from Michael Oakeshott's own writings, Richard Rorty's *Philosophy and the Mirror of Nature*[1] is the most Oakeshottian book I have ever come across. Comfortably protected by the nebulous charm of Cambridge's Common Rooms, Michael Oakeshott produced, soon after the end of the Second World War, a number of papers in which he attacked ideologues both in philosophy and in politics. Oakeshott argued that wherever there are civilized men, there is culture; and culture enshrines ways of traditional behavior which one learns, be one a politician or a philosopher, by cohabiting with other politicians and other philosophers — slowly and thoughtfully imitating their ways, conversing in their idiom, and doing what past experience has taught politicians and philosophers to do, whatever that might be. Fundamental questions and elemental thoughts ought never to be permitted to cross the threshold of the circle, for the existence of the circle was its own automatic legitimization. Prejudice, he echoed Burke, is a state of mind based on experience. Into this cultured environment, Oakeshott argued, there had come a number of ideologues who pretended to know what was good for mankind, if they were politicians; and who pretended to know something special about knowledge, if they were philosophers. Possessed of this special knowledge, Oakeshott continued, these ideologues first claimed that they could teach others what was

---

This chapter was published in *Philosophy of the Social Sciences*, June 1984, and is reprinted by permission.

1. Richard Rorty, *Philosophy and the Mirror of Nature* (Princeton: Princeton University Press, 1979).

good for mankind and how people know, and then proceeded to issue invitations to the rest of mankind to follow their advice and change traditional forms of behavior. At that time there existed in England a very go-ahead educational enterprise run by or named after a Mr. Pelman. This enterprise offered to teach anybody anything in order to help people go places and make money. Oakeshott, in countless witty asides, likened the political and philosophical ideologues to Pelman's school and hinted that these ideologues were motivated, as Mr. Pelman was, by the desire to make money by teaching people to improve the lot of mankind or to improve the reliability of knowledge. Stretching comfortably back in one of Cambridge's innumerable armchairs, Oakeshott always ended by reminding his listeners of the futility of Pelmanism. In an established culture, he smilingly demonstrated by stretching himself even more comfortably and clasping one hand within the elegant fingers of the other, people do what comes naturally and just as politicians have no recipe for improving society, so philosophers have no recipe for knowledge. They are just politicians and philosophers as other people are bakers and bankers, good or bad at their job, as the case may be.

In his *Philosophy and the Mirror of Nature*, Rorty has now provided us with a widely sweeping repetition of this argument. The thirty years which have elapsed between Oakeshott and Rorty seem to have made no difference except that where Oakeshott had relied on the simple good sense of his argument, Rorty, less confident in that simple good sense, takes nearly 400 pages to come to Oakeshott's conclusion by way of careful and well argued analysis of the history of philosophy both ancient and modern. This difference between Oakeshott and Rorty is, however, crucial. One could accept Oakeshott's reasoning or reject it. It was very much a matter of taste and of the degree of comfort one experienced in the position which society had deigned to ascribe to one. Not so with Rorty. Since Rorty chooses to reach his Oakeshottian conclusion by lengthy analysis, we are in a position where we can analyze this analysis and criticize it. With Rorty, Oakeshott's position ceases to be a question of taste and becomes a matter for rational reflection.

To the detriment of Rorty I have to mention that there is, however, just one little matter of style after all, which is not open to rational criticism. Following Oakeshott, Rorty stresses that there is no such thing as 'philosophical method' which might enable professional philosophers, *ex officio*, to have 'interesting views about, say, the respectability of psychoanalysis, the legitimacy of certain dubious laws, the resolution of moral dilemmas', and so forth. He described their activity as 'useful kibitzing' (p. 393). Gilbert Ryle used to illustrate his ruminations with examples from cricket; J. H. Hexter, from baseball. Oakeshott preferred racehorses. They all agree that philosophers are simply people who are unusually smart and need to know nothing in particular. Oakeshott, however, when writing, defined the philosopher as the only man who can afford to have read nothing at all (Introduction to his edition of Hobbes' *Leviathan*, Oxford 1957, p. xiii). Put in this inimitable way, the statement sounds almost convincing. Oakeshott would never have described philosophizing as "kibitzing" even if that was what he meant.

This is, ultimately, I admit, a question of style. There is a world of difference between saying "Philosophy springs from a certain bent of mind" (Oakeshott, loc. cit.) and describing it as kibitzing, even if one does mean the same thing!

If Oakeshott is Rorty's avowed mentor, one must also be impressed by the fact that Rorty's book is the first major book written in English which shows the marked influence of Michel Foucault. There is no denying Foucault's learning, his wit, and his *esprit*. But when all is said and done Foucault is old wine in old bottles – the most old-fashioned of all old-fashioned historists. Like Greek and Hebrew and medieval Christian myth-makers, like Auguste Comte and Sir James Frazer and Oswald Spengler, Foucault believes that as time passes, mankind comes to be subject to changes in taste, knowledge, and practical habits in regard to insanity, sex, and morals.

The thinkers who believed that the changes are random are called historists; and those who believe that the changes are determined by a developmental law are called historicists. Unlike Comte and Frazer and the Biblical myth-makers who were all historicists, Foucault is a simple historist, for he cannot say why the changes occur and does not even think that the question is worth asking. Spengler is betwixt and between historism and historicism. He is a plain historist in that he says that civilizations succeed one another in a random fashion; and a genuine historicist in that he says that a civilization once there grows and decays according to a 'biological' law of growth.

The verve with which this strange anti-scientific belief has been propounded for millennia to be revived so fashionably by Michel Foucault in the middle of the twentieth century is only matched by the utterly incomprehensible lack of interest shown by all historists in why these changes should have taken place in the order in which they undoubtedly did take place. One would have thought that the question whether and why the relationship between the passage of time and the coming of changes was not random would have occupied the minds of these observers more than any other question. Being, to a man, absorbed in the changes, they have not only shown no interest in the question, but also gloried in the view that one need not show any interest because with every change there dawns a new epoch the contents, habits, practices, and views of which are incommensurable with those of the preceding and those of the succeeding epochs. We have here not only a lack of interest – which might be forgiveable enough. After all, why should every man be interested in everything? We have something much worse, something which is not forgivable. We find that the lack of interest is elevated to the rank of a scientific dogma. It appears as the view that whatever happens in any one epoch cannot be related to what happens in other epochs because it is incommensurable with anything outside its own epoch. Here we find that what might at best be described as a lack of interest is turned into a scientific theory. Or is it that the scientific theory is the cause of the lack of interest? Whichever way one takes it, the frame of mind which sustains the two views is utterly absurd. If all avenues for discovering the nature of the relationship between change and the passage of time had been explored (though how could one ever claim that *all* had been explored?) one might eventually settle for the view that the relations *are* random and that every epoch is incommensurable with every other epoch. But since there is no sign that these old-fashioned historists have explored any avenue, let alone several, there can be no reason why we should have to settle for such a conclusion.

Historicists account for the changes by reliance on a developmental law. Historists do not account for the changes and justify their refusal to account by an arch-historist argument. The wish and the ability to account stems from a historical outlook. Historical outlooks, the argument continues, are proper to and comprehensible in, say, the civilization of the nineteenth century, dominated as it was by historical outlook. Once that century is over, "historical outlook" ceases to be relevant or comprehensible and therefore an attempt to account for changes as they succeed one another in time is not only outmoded in the present century, but irrelevant and incomprehensible. Historicists at least think that their historical outlook transcends the limitations and the incommensurability of their own epoch. Historists like Rorty and Foucault do not.

To guard against confusion, I would argue that thinkers like Marx, Hegel, and Toynbee, who are conventionally considered to have cast their thoughts in the same historicist mold, should be exempt from these strictures. There is not even a superficial likeness. One may disagree with their theories, but Marx, Hegel, and Toynbee are definitely non-historicist because they have subjected the question as to why the relation between the passage of time and the advent of changes is not random to the most searching analysis. They have all come up with the findings that in every epoch there are instabilities and a lack of homeostasis so that the passing of time can be intelligibly related to the coming of changes. As a consequence, in the theories of Hegel, Marx, and Toynbee there is no talk of incommensurability. Stoicism and the unhappy consciousness, feudalism and capitalism, can be measured against one another.

Michel Foucault, however, whom Rorty twice invokes with approval, is an old-fashioned, unsophisticated historist. On p. 322 Rorty invokes Foucault's theory of incommensurability and Foucault's radical relativism in support of his contention that whatever people believe and practice in any one circle is valid inside that circle and cannot be measured by the standards of another circle. On p. 391, note 29, Rorty actually quotes p. 231 of Foucault's *Archeology of Knowledge*[2] in support of his own effort to relativize all knowledge and comments: "If we could only see the desire for a permanent, neutral, ahistorical, commensurating vocabulary as itself a historical phenomenon, then perhaps we could see the history of philosophy less dialectically and less sentimentally than has been possible hitherto." I will return to the results of Rorty's efforts to re-write the history of philosophy "less sentimentally" in the last section of this paper. At this point I merely wish

2. (London: Tavistock Publications, 1972).

to draw attention to the degree to which Rorty is indebted to Foucault's old-fashioned historism and relativism.

How are we to evaluate the relative strengths of the influence of Oakeshott and Foucault on Rorty? I have a certain nostalgic sympathy with Oakeshott and take little exception to him because he discoursed and wrote very little in defense of his manner of discoursing. I have no sympathy at all with Foucault, because Foucault uses his *ésprit* to lull people into uncritical acceptance of the plainly stated theories of old-fashioned historism. If it were not for the incessant talk about sex and insanity – both very modish subjects – one might just as well read the Old Testament or Hesiod as Foucault in order to get the idea that epochs succeed epochs and that the whole succession of epochs is just one of the many damned mysteries. But when it comes to the necessity for evaluating the influences of Oakeshott and Foucault on Rorty, the question is quite tricky. As I shall demonstrate, Rorty, thanks to Oakeshott, starts with a presupposition which also turns out to be his conclusion. This procedure is dubious, to say the least, and must weaken the soundness of Rorty's conclusion. But one might forgive the Oakeshottian presupposition that philosophy is something that is done in certain cultures and that philosophers ought not to set themselves up as ideologues. Not so with Foucault. Foucault's radical relativism is used in order to justify Wittgenstein's language-games and Kuhn's paradigms. In Rorty's philosophical universe there are a large number of circles inside which philosophers sit together and meet to play language-games. It is here that Rorty uses Foucault to great advantage. Like Foucault's *epistemes*, each circle is a sort of poker-school where a game is going on, where philosophers meet to smoke and chat and do the occasional bit of philosophizing. Each game is incommensurable with the other games; behavior is relative to the rules inside each circle; there is no accounting for the absence or presence of certain circles in certain areas and all circles remain laws unto themselves, sublimely and serenely untroubled by critical overseers or ideologues trying to compare the rules and standards of one game with those of another to assess them according to external criteria. One learns by being part of the school, and only somebody as vulgar as Mr. Pelman would set himself up to teach anybody at all to play in a school as if he were a *real* member. Rorty uses Foucault's highly questionable view of history not only to justify his own unquestioning and uncritical acceptance of Wittgenstein and Kuhn and the whole theory that truth is whatever satisfies the rules obtaining in a given speech-community but also in order to license himself to re-write and re-interpret the history of philosophy in an unscrupulous manner so that he can come up with the conclusion that certain philosophers like Descartes and Kant were ideologues in Oakeshott's sense and that Wittgenstein, Heidegger, and Dewey were nice philosophical blokes who spent their lives playing nice language-games inside their own circles but are nevertheless quite useful because they provide useful kibitzing – whatever that might mean. There is, of course, something very civilized about Oakeshott. Had Rorty confined himself to Oakeshott, he could have cashed in on the esteem commanded by Oakeshott's civilized realization that all human beings are fallible, that there is no absolute truth in politics and in science, that dogmatism is wrong and that we must be both cautious and gentle at all times and that tolerance and scepticism ought to be infinite. I would gladly have extended my liking for Oakeshott to Rorty were it not for the fact that Rorty has tried to smuggle in under Oakeshott's umbrella (carried by Foucault) Wittgenstein and Heidegger. I would have thought that at least an invitation to imitate Oakeshott would obviate the need for a recourse to these two dour, unironical, and humorless Teutons. As to Rorty's third person in his Holy Trinity, Dewey, I have no great objection. I quite like him and would not have thought that it might require a book of 400 pages and an umbrella to commend him.

Before launching into a critical analysis of Rorty's analysis, I would like to admit one point. It strikes me as inherently plausible to analyze a culture as a going concern and as a closed system so that the question as to whether it is good or bad, efficient or inefficient, does not arise. One cannot only look at a society's culture in this way as a functionally integrated whole; but also at various subsystems of any culture. A hospital, for example, can be viewed as a system in which some people are in beds and other people wear white coats. One can describe their interaction and the manner in which they depend on one another without asking whether the system serves any purpose or whether the quality of the behavior of the people in white coats serves the purpose of getting the people who are in beds out of those beds and whether the behavior of the people in white coats is good enough to achieve that purpose. In short, all systems can be viewed as systems before one starts asking whether they serve a purpose and whether failure to achieve that purpose is reason for changing the system. Given this admission, there is a *prima facie* case in favor of Oakeshott and against Pelman, even though this case is only a partial case.

2. Our hero's astonishing craftsmanship and some trivial fallacies.

As far as I am concerned, Rorty's book has passed the acid test of any serious book. I read it from cover to cover in the cramped space of economy class on a long flight from New Zealand to New York and back. Any book which can pass such a test over a distance of 18,000 miles (equal to a journey three-quarters around the world!) deserves to be taken seriously. It is written with vigor and elegance and bears the hallmark of a genuine literary work: one can detect the master's style by the unfailing identity with which he dots his 'i's' or paints fingernails, nostrils, or ear lobes. That, at any rate, was the standard of genuinely personal style defined by Morelli when he looked at an old painting. Equally, one can detect a piece by Bach or by Mozart by the occurrence of vignettes which are specific to Bach and Mozart. Rorty's 400 pages are not hack work, no matter how professional. They stand as a piece of literature by the repetitiveness of certain arguments and the insistent consistency of observations which crop up at least once in every chapter, thus allowing the reader to identify the craftsmanship of the author and enabling him to identify each section of the work as part of a whole.

Such is the literary momentum of Rorty's craftsmanship that, like a true artist, he does not notice frequent pieces of shoddy reasoning which any moderately intelligent schoolchild could have picked out. On p. 372, for example, there is a *petitio principii*. Rorty says that "we have to see the term 'corresponds to how things are' as an automatic compliment paid to successful normal discourse rather than as a relation to be studied and aspired to throughout the rest of the discourse". This statement only makes sense if one grants his prior argument that all discourse is a language-game in Wittgenstein's sense. If one grants this then "correspondence" can indeed only mean "fits into a language-game". On any other assumption the statement is nonsensical. To all non-Wittgensteinians "correspondence" means something quite different.

On p. 37 he maintains that the "problem of personhood is not a 'problem' but a description of the human condition". I have never heard anybody say that personhood is a "problem". The reason why we think it a "problem" is that there are many different descriptions of personhood. The problem is caused by the fact that many of these seemingly plausible descriptions are incompatible with one another, not by the fact of personhood itself.

On p. 341 he maintains that since a certain historical problem has admitted of several different answers nobody knows "what might count as a good answer". Rorty writes that, since there has been a variety of answers, it must be obvious that there can be *no* answer.

On p. 354 he argues that "torturers and brainwashers are, in any case, already in as good a position to interfere with human freedom as they could wish; further scientific progress cannot improve their position". This argument is plainly wrong on two counts. There have been people who have defied excesses of torture and brainwashing and we have every reason to believe that one could brainwash more effectively if we "knew" more about the brain. I cite these odd examples not so much in criticism of Rorty as to indicate the powerful momentum of the book as a whole which permits the author to carry himself, if not the reader, over hurdles of this kind without flinching.

On p. 32 Rorty places the convention that the Constitution is what the Supreme Court thinks it is on the same level as the view that a man has the pain he says he is feeling. Such remarks may be vintage Wittgenstein but can hardly be taken as final reasoned propositions.

On p. 33, in comparing philosophizing to psychiatry he states that the patient does not need to be told that he made a mistake when he thought that his mother wanted to castrate him and that he was identical with his father. What the patient needs, Rorty says, is to be made to understand how he came to make such mistakes. I cannot vouch for philosophers. But I do know that psychiatrists consider the making of such mistakes and the reasons for making them all of a piece[3].

On p. 29 he wonders why people keep thinking that *epistemic* distinctions reflect *ontological* distinctions. He gives as an example "feelings". "Feelings just *are* appearances. Their reality is exhausted in how they seem. They are pure seemings". I happen to agree with this view and could not have put it better myself. But I would have thought that the fact that feelings are pure seemings and that therefore statements about them are incorrigible makes them something very special so that, by this very fact, they *are* ontologically distinct and belong to a different realm of being. Contrary to Rorty, I would maintain that his own example is final proof that at least in this case the epistemic distinction reflects an ontological distinction.

On pp. 81–83 Rorty seeks to solve the question of the Identity Theory about mind-body by envisaging Antipodeans who have developed well-nigh perfect knowledge of neurons. Why, they may ask, can we not see that talk of mental states was merely a "place holder" for talk of neurons? (p. 81). If there is no way in which we can communicate to the Antipodeans our worries about the relationship between minds and bodies, "ought we not to face up to the possibility that the 'materialist' Antipodeans . . . are right?" (p. 83). I would have thought that our inability to so much as make the Antipodeans understand our worries proves precisely the opposite, i.e., that neurological knowledge is the result of linking neurons to other material or physical events; and mental knowledge or awareness, the result of linking mental states to other mental states: *omne cogitans ex cogitato.* Rorty may well be right about mental states. But the argument he is using proves the opposite of what he thinks it does.

On p. 340 he quotes Kuhn with great approval: "If science did progress by virtue of some shared and binding algorithm of choice, I would be equally at a loss to explain its success"[4]. One cannot hold Rorty responsible for Kuhn's fallacies; but one is entitled to expect that Rorty, in quoting this remark, should point out that the expression "at a loss" is meaningless. If science did proceed by such an algorithm, its success *would* be explained.

All this without even mentioning that on p. 343 Rorty confuses Kant's noumenal world with Kant's phenomenal world, ascribing the transcendent self to the latter!

I suppose Rorty would say with Marshal MacLuhan that the trouble with me is that I think that his fallacies are all wrong. But in addition to these fallacies, there is a fundamental flaw in the main line of the book's argument. On p. 356

3. Citing random references, see E. Jones, *Sigmund Freud*, London 1958, Vol. II, p. 320; Hanna Segal, "Notes on Symbol Formation", *International Journal of Psychoanalysis* **38**, 1957, pp. 391–92; Ch. Rycroft, "Symbolism and Its Relationship to the Primary and Secondary Processes", ibid. **37**, 1956; D. Beres, "Symbol and Object", *Bulletin of the Menninger Clinic* **29**, 1965, p. 3 ff.
4. *Essential Tension* (Chicago: University of Chicago Press, 1977), pp. 332–35.

Rorty insists that there is something basically wrong with the mirror model of knowledge. Knowledge, whatever it is, is not a reflection in a mirror, and those philosophers who have made themselves the keepers of the mind's mirror are self-styled keepers of something that does not even exist. On p. 370, however, when Rorty is elaborating on his distinction between systematic and edifying philosophers, he makes an impassioned plea for the edifying philosophers because they "want to keep space open for the sense of wonder which poets can some-times cause – wonder that there is something new under the sun, something which is *not* an accurate representation of what was already there . . . ". Here Rorty is quite happily accepting that such knowledge as we do have – and even he would admit that such as it is, there is quite a lot of it – is a reflection in a mirror. Having spent 350 pages odd to tell us that the mind is not a mirror he now turns round and tells us that it is and that that mirror never produces anything new but merely produces a "duplicate" so to speak of "what was already there". So now there is nothing wrong with the mirrors. The only thing that is wrong is that they are so boring! Surely, if Rorty had followed his own lead he would by p. 370 have come up with the idea that if the mind is not a mirror, then knowledge cannot be a reflection of reality in a mirror and therefore, *not* being a duplicate, is not boring but something 'new'.

3. The mirror philosophers and their failings: a good diagnosis of a timely demise. Much ado about nothing.

Having paid a handsome compliment to Rorty's artistic integrity and to the momentum of his rhetoric, we must now come to the heart of the matter.

The heart of the matter is, Rorty maintains, that since Descartes, philosophers have believed that they are ideologues who know something special about knowledge. The special information which they believe they have about knowledge is that the mind is a mirror or possesses a mirror and that the mind's eye looks into that mirror to gain knowledge. The world is believed to be reflected in that mirror. Rorty attacks philosophers who from Descartes onwards have claimed that they have such special information and that they know something about knowledge which other people do not know. Having such knowledge, they have vied with one another in making suggestions as to how that mirror could best be polished to provide the most accurate reflection so that the mind's eye could see most clearly what the world is like.

One must take this contention piece by piece. First, there is the animus against philosophers who claim to know something special about knowledge. They are, though Rorty does not spell this out, like Oakeshott's politicians who claim that they know something special about social justice and equality or economic wealth and prosperity which other people do not know.

The sentence that the philosopher is a man who is believed to know some-thing special about knowledge which other people do not know only occurs on

p. 392. But Rorty's intention is made plain in the Introduction, pp. 3–13. The *real* philosopher, Rorty says, is a member of a culture, not an ideologue. Rorty is only interested in "philosophers", that is, in people who are institutionally or conventionally called "philosophers". He is not interested in philosophy or in those tasks and problems in which some philosophers happen to be specialists. Rorty wants to make sure that philosophers should not usurp the role of the magus or necromancer. They should not claim to know something special about knowledge. Such a claim would be typical of the ideologue's presumption which consists in not playing a traditional part in a traditional culture but in arrogating to himself the right to lay down guidelines for the reform of culture. Rorty does not actually use the term "ideologue". He calls the philosophers who claim to know something about knowledge and who are therefore critical of those cultures in which knowledge is mishandled or perverted "cultural overseers" (p. 317). The question whether under certain circumstances some cultures need reform is never asked by Rorty. He takes it for granted that none of them ever do.

As it stands, this attack is quite unwarranted. There is indeed something to be known about knowledge, just as there is something to be known about equality and wealth. There are many different opinions held by different people and all people interested in knowledge or in politics must pay attention to these opinions and weigh them and evaluate them. Then there are some people who do not engage much in politics or in science themselves but who prefer to specialize in the question as to what we can know or how we can promote or, for that matter, prevent, social justice. Whether we call these specialists philosophers and politicians or not does not really matter. The only thing that matters is the acceptance of the fact that there is something to be known about all these things; that it is better to know something about them than not to know anything about them; and, finally, that practicing scientists as well as ordinary citizens must sooner or later face up to the question as to what is known about knowledge or about strategies for promoting equality. Rorty, against all this, maintains that there is nothing special to be known because he presupposes, good disciple of Oakeshott that he is, that in any culture people carry out a traditional function: some are philosophers, some are politicians, some are bakers, and some are soldiers. If they continue their traditional callings and do not pretend any special expertise in any of the fields they are professing, there will be no problems and all will be well in the world.

Second, we must take a closer look at Rorty's general characterization of what it is philosophers claim to know about knowledge. He sums up their claim by telling us they all believe that inside the mind there is a mirror, that it must be polished, and that the mind has an eye so that it can look at the mirror. Granted all the metaphors, the claim is not as absurd or contrary as Rorty makes out. Every statement about reality must be a statement about a relation between a knower and a known. It may well be too simplistic a metaphor to liken this relation to the relation which obtains between a mirror and the objects mirrored.

If Rorty had confined himself to criticizing this particular metaphor one would accept his criticism, but the whole book would have lost its punch. Rorty does not confine himself to this criticism. He goes on to lampoon the notion that the mind has an eye with which it inspects the mirror. He calls this view the "ocular metaphor". That metaphor is not as silly as Rorty thinks. Of all the human senses, the sense of vision has a very special significance. Unlike other animals, we depend more on vision than on smell, feel, or touch or hearing. There are well known neurological reasons for this and it has something to do with our bipedal, upright posture. Hence also our common speech habits. When we want to say that we understand we say "I see!" but not "I hear" or "I smell". For that matter, Jews and Muslims shrink from making God visible; but have no compunction in claiming to have "heard" Him. Whether these speech habits are fully justified or not is hard to say; but the fact that they are widespread and deeply ingrained points to the very special position occupied by the human eye. All this is much more subtly intimated by the title of Douglas R. Hofstadter's latest book *The Mind's I* (though not so much by the content) than by Rorty's labored attempts to demonstrate that the ocular metaphor is misplaced. As Hofstadter's pun suggests, it is less misplaced than Rorty imagines!

If metaphor and Hofstadter's pun on the metaphor are not arguments, some reflection on modern theories of vision will show how wrong Rorty's objection to the ocular metaphor is. Rorty thinks that the ocular metaphor has been ingrained and maintained itself because philosophers imagine that knowledge must be knowledge of something immutable and that knowledge is contemplation. Now the activity of the eye is more like contemplation than any other activity, or so it might have seemed to the Greeks and possibly even to C. D. Broad whose 1923 book on *Scientific Thought* Rorty quotes on p. 39, note 6, in support of his contention that philosophers get their belief in the mind's eye from their conviction that the eye's steady gaze can be fixed on something immutable.[5] More recent literature would have been more helpful[6]. Rorty might also have looked at Holst's "Active Function of Human Visual Perception" to learn that to "gaze" is to take in movement and change.[7] In so far as Rorty's objection to the ocular metaphor is based on the idea that it is linked to the eyes' "steady gaze" on immutability and that once we give up the notion that knowledge is perception of immutability, the ocular metaphor ceases to be justified, Rorty is quite simply wrong. The ocular metaphor may have had its origins among the Greeks who did not know much about optics and neurology. But if it is to be abandoned, there must be better reasons than a reference to Greek ignorance and to an example used by Broad in 1923.

5. C. D. Broad, *Scientific Thought*, 1923, p. 39.
6. C. F. von Weizsäcker, *Der Garten des Menschlichen* (Munich, 1978), has an enlightening chapter, pp. 209 ff., on the unity of movement and visual perception, and the whole of chapter 7 of Richard Gregory's *Eye and Brain* (London, 1966) is a very detailed explanation of the subtle complexity which makes the eye more than any other organ capable of taking in movement.
7. E. V. Holst, *The Behavioural Physiology of Animals and Man* (Eng. trans., London, 1973), Vol. 1, ch. 7.

Third, there are the historical doubts. Rorty's effort to make out that from Descartes onwards all philosophers before Wittgenstein subscribed to the mirror metaphor is, to say the least, highly original. Less kindly, we might argue that it is idiosyncratic. Descartes certainly thought he had discovered something special about knowledge. But it was not that knowledge consists in the mirror image. His discovery was that all thought can only come from thought and that, since knowledge is, in a way, a thought, it must be based on a prior thought: *omne cogitatum ex cogitato*. Had he put it this way, I would have felt happy to be a Cartesian. However this may be, Descartes can only by a stretch of the utmost historical imagination be credited with the view that knowledge is a mirror image of nature.

In so far as Descartes speaks of knowledge in general terms, one might, stretching one's imagination, think that he thinks of "having knowledge" as "looking into a mirror". But when one examines what he has actually written, one realizes that no amount of stretched imagination will help to reach this conclusion about Descartes. Re-reading the *Fourth Meditation* one sees clearly that Descartes wanted to find out what knowledge was left over when all knowledge which is in the least bit doubtful has been removed. Descartes was not interested in knowledge as such; but in certainty. Descartes' certainty did not depend on the degree of accuracy with which the mind mirrored nature, but on the deducibility of knowledge from a premise which was not open to doubt. For Descartes the central issue was not mirroring but deduction.

One must have even greater misgivings about Rorty's portrait of Kant. Unlike Descartes, Kant did perhaps think of the mind as a sort of mirror. But he did not think that we ought to polish that mirror (p. 12). He believed that that mirror had a certain shape or quality and that whatever we saw as being mirrored would be structured by that shape or those qualities. As he put it, the argument was a little fantastic. Why should the mirror have a certain shape? Kant never addressed himself to that question. Today, with the help of evolutionary biology we can think of a perfectly good answer. The mirror, if it indeed is a mirror, has a certain shape because it was formed, like the rest of the human nervous system, by natural selection. Of all possible shapes, *some* shapes survived in the struggle for survival because they produced a more fitting mirror image than other shapes. They may still be a little wrong and produce a distorted image. But given the biological success of the human race as against all other animals (except, perhaps the insects) the knowledge mirrored by the human mind cannot possibly be totally misleading. Hence the very reasonable assumption that the polishing of the mirror was not done by philosophers, as Rorty alleges Kant suggested; but by nature, i.e., the environment, itself.

There is a peculiar irony in Rorty's treatment of Kant. In Rorty's view, Kant believed that one had to keep on polishing the mirror to make sure it would reflect accurately. In 1973 Konrad Lorenz published a book entitled *Behind the Mirror*[8].

8. English translation (New York: Harcourt Brace Jovanovich, 1977).

The book was a "search for a natural history of human knowledge" and began with a criticism of Kant. But Lorenz's criticism of Kant was very different from Rorty's. Lorenz argued that Kant had failed to realize that the mirror is the product of evolutionary adaptations. The mirror, in Lorenz's view, reflects accurately enough, though not with complete accuracy. It does so because it has evolved and would not have evolved had it made too many mistakes. Lorenz holds that Kant was too modest about the mirror. Kant thought that the mirror could never mirror the world as it really is. Lorenz explained that in some respects the mirror *must* be mirroring the world as it really is, for if it did not, it could not have been the product of progressive selections by the environment, i.e., by the world as it really is. It is inconceivable, as Lorenz states, that the world as it really is would have fashioned by chance mutations and selective retention an instrument of cognition which would grossly and consistently mislead us about that world. In order to find out how this has come about and why the mirror is broadly reliable, Lorenz suggests we take a closer look *behind* the mirror. Lorenz shares Rorty's misgivings about the mirror; but suggests that these misgivings can be dispelled if we look at the obverse of the mirror. That obverse has evolved and is in the same category of objects as the objects the mirror reflects. Thus Lorenz proceeds from Kant's transcendental idealism to a hypothetical realism. This means that he recognizes that the appearances in the mirror, which Kant took to be the ultimate beyond which we cannot conceive or perceive, result from a kind of interaction between the things-in-themselves and ourselves. (The last part of the last sentence is a direct quotation from Karl Popper, *The Logic of Scientific Discovery.*) In his heart of hearts, Lorenz says, Kant himself, less logical but far wiser than all Kantians, was not so completely convinced that what appeared in the mirror and the real world in itself were completely unconnected. If the heavens which aroused such sense of wonder in Kant, had been a mere appearance and not the *real* heavens, they would most probably not have aroused in him a sense of wonder comparable to the sense of wonder aroused in him by the moral law. One must appreciate the difficulties Rorty has with mirrors. If, however, he had read Lorenz on mirrors, most of these difficulties would have been removed. Rorty keeps saying that philosophers want to polish the mirror to make sure it reflects more than imaginings and appearances. Lorenz tells us that if one needs an assurance that the mirror reflects more than appearances and imaginings, one only needs to look behind it and grasp that the obverse of the mirror is an adaptive response to the world as it really is.

Leaving evolutionary epistemology's reinterpretation of Kant aside, we can still see Rorty's gross misrepresentation of Kant. Kant, if he did think of a mirror, realized that no amount of polishing it would make it into a more precise instrument for representing nature. On the contrary, Kant realized that the mirror has a distorting shape of its own and therefore sought to demonstrate that whatever we see in that mirror is not nature or the thing-in-itself; but the world of appearances, the phenomena, i.e., reflections in the mirror of our mind. His famous demonstrations that the picture we see in the mirror *must* differ from what is out there in the world proves that Rorty's idea of Kant is quite wrong. Whatever can be said against the mirror metaphor does not apply to Kant.

For the time being, let us give Rorty the benefit of doubt and even credit for his original version of what Descartes and Kant said. What they really said and why they said what they did is a problem of historical knowledge and not even in history can one attain certainty. Rorty's attempt to rewrite the history of philosophy requires only special scrutiny when he uses his vision of the history of philosophy to buttress his conclusions. Of this more later.

Having established that from Descartes onwards philosophers claimed to be ideologues who knew something special about knowledge and having established that the special claim consisted in maintaining that we have knowledge when the mind's eye inspects the mind's mirror to see what nature is mirrored in it, Rorty then proceeds to show that there is no way in which this account of knowledge can be justified. From whatever angle he looks at it – and his examination is thorough and varied – he always can show that this account of knowledge is false. There is no eye, there is no mirror, and there is nothing which is mirrored to be inspected by an eye. He shows that there is something wrong with the view that knowledge is true because it is mirrored. This argument, in one form or another, occurs no less than thirteen times, i.e., on pp. 8, 10, 35, 41, 43, 157, 178, 209, 269, 299, 320, 368, 389, 392. On every one of those pages and in every one of its thirteen forms, I find this argument completely convincing. Rorty, and this is the heart of the matter, shows that whatever knowledge we have cannot be *justified* by the mirror metaphor.

Rorty has many variations on this theme. On p. 3 he says that the mirror metaphor commits us to thinking that to know is to represent accurately what is outside the mind. On p. 368 he points out that the mirror metaphor must be wrong because the words we use to describe what we see in the mirror are "not transparent to the real". On p. 389 he says that knowing is not an "essence" to be described by scientists or philosophers. The most convincing and telling consideration against the mirror is Rorty's contention that the mirror philosophers are committed "to the construction of a permanent, neutral framework for inquiry" (p. 8). All this is quite unexceptionable.

When one comes to examine the details of Rorty's strategy for destroying the notion that the mind mirrors nature and that such mirroring constitutes knowledge, I feel less happy. Since the expression "mirror" occurs neither in Descartes nor in Kant, it is obviously a metaphor invented by Rorty or somebody else to sum up a certain conception of knowledge as representation, true if it is "caused" in a certain way rather than because one can advance certain reasons for it. I will let that go because it is indeed an acceptable metaphor and a convenient summary of certain kinds of epistemology, even though I would argue that it sums up most conveniently an epistemology which is quite non-Cartesian and non-Kantian – that is, the epistemology enshrined in the adage *nihil est in intellectu quod non prius fuerit in sensu.* But for argument's sake I will not insist on such fine distinctions and go along with Rorty's metaphor.

The disturbing feature of Rorty's strategy for attacking the view enshrined in the metaphor is that he proceeds from p. 17 onwards as if the metaphor were a literal truth. The whole of Part I and Part II of his book, i.e., pp. 17–312, are devoted to a very detailed discussion of the implications of the view that the mind is a mirror and that that mirror is inspected by the eye of the mind! Since there cannot be a glass mirror inside our head, talk of a mirror must refer to something "mental". And so he goes off to discuss the mind-body problem, the notion that our knowledge of universals is "mental", the implications of calling something "mental", the incorrigibility of so-called "mental" states, and so forth. Some of his views I find acceptable; others I don't. All of them sound plausible enough. But with a little ingenuity one could easily persuade oneself in every case that the opposite is true or at least equally plausible. For this reason I find the bulk of the book, strange as it may sound, the least interesting part. But this is not the point. The point – a very disturbing point – is that he starts by using a convenient metaphor and then proceeds to destroy its credibility by assuming that it is not a metaphor and that it embodies or commits its users to a certain view about the relationship of mind to body and of the mental to the neural; and that the metaphor must be dropped if one can show that the mentalistic views which would follow if the metaphor were not a metaphor are false. This is disturbing enough; but, perhaps, only redundant. For the foundational and representational epistemology contained in the mirror metaphor can be disposed of much more readily and quickly by the simple consideration advanced (*pace* Rorty) by both Descartes and Kant: in all knowledge the sensory input is smaller than the "epistemic" output; or, as Popper is wont to say: the mind is not a bucket. Once one grasps that, there is no need for treating the mirror metaphor as a literal statement and for attacking the mentalistic consequences which would follow if it were literally true that the mind is a mirror of nature and that we look at that mirror with the eye of the mind.

The ultimate reason why knowledge cannot represent and why it cannot be like a mirror, a map, or a portrait is that knowledge is mainly and mostly knowledge of hypothetical regularities and has therefore to be couched in terms of universals, be they words or concepts. Moreover, for knowledge to be communicable – and it has to be if it is to be discussed and criticized – it has to be expressed in words and sentences. Since the number of words and the permissible forms of arrangements of words in sentences must be limited and since the contents to be communicated must be unlimited (i.e., we use a finite number of media to carry infinite numbers of messages) the words and sentence forms must have "universal" features. Universals, however, cannot be perceived as such and therefore cannot be represented mirror-fashion. This consideration, simply and conclusively, puts paid to all representational or foundational epistemologies. This simple consideration obviates the need for Rorty's lengthy excursions through mentalism.

The value and the merits of Rorty's superfluous strategy are further diminished by the fact that he introduces his presuppositions into his discussions of the mind-body problem. Having set out to make the world safe for the practice of what he calls "philosophy", that is, for the formation of speech communities and language-game circles, he is always predisposed to adopt a Wittgensteinian and Sellarsian stance towards all conceivable arguments that there are mental events, and time and again comes up with the contention that the truth about mental events is what the speech conventions obtaining in any one circle dictate. He even argues, more Wittgensteinian than Wittgenstein himself, that the only (sic!) reason why we think that statements about pain are incorrigible and uncriticizable is that the language-game we are playing says so (p. 32). If I recall Wittgenstein correctly, Wittgenstein used the fact that statements about our pains are incorrigible to prove that we are always engaged in language-games. Wittgenstein considered the incorrigibility of pain-statements to be a statement about the nature of pain. Rorty appears to take it the other way round. He presupposes that we are playing language-games and infers from this presupposition that statements about our pains are incorrigible because if they were open to criticism we would not be playing a language-game.

My disagreement with Rorty starts when he adds on every occasion that knowledge, if it is to count as true knowledge, ought to be justified. Since it cannot be justified by the mirror metaphor, it ought to be justified in a different way. I grant that there must be an alternative. My own alternative is that of Karl Popper: knowledge need not be justified and we can take it as true or as provisionally true, as long as it is not falsified. Rorty, on the other hand, is firmly wedded to the view that knowledge, to be true, must be justified knowledge. He cannot and does not envisage the possibility that it can be hypothetical. Since he can show that it cannot be justified by the mirror metaphor, he seeks an alternative justification.

My real quarrel with Rorty is that he confronts us only with two alternatives. He thinks all knowledge is only worthy of that name if it can be "justified". He has shown over and over again that it cannot be justified as representational. But since it has to be justified, Rorty sees only one alternative. If knowing does not have an essence (p. 389) then we have the "right to believe" what "current standards" recommend. If words are not transparent to the real (p. 368) then we must "deconstruct" them and accept that they acquire their privileges from the men who use them. In short, Rorty gives us a choice between justificationism and relativism which latter amounts to holding that proposition to be justified which has the consensus of a given community. So the real choice, according to Rorty, is between straight justificationism and relative justificationism. Rorty never considers the possibility that there is a genuine third possibility – the possibility that we consider as knowledge a proposition which is *not* justified, neither by the fact that it "represents" nor by the fact that it has found the acclaim of a speech community.

4. Heroic alternatives: language-games, speech communities, and epistemic authority. Who is in, who is out, and who does the deciding? Is kibitzing valuable?

Rorty's alternative justification of knowledge consists in the consensus of specified people or in the authority of an epistemic community. This amounts to saying that we can justify knowledge by showing that it is something agreed to in a circle of people. This alternative argument which Rorty believes to be the correct argument occurs thirteen times, i.e., on pp. 175, 186, 187, 210, 226, 319, 320, 333, 357, 358, 361, 368, 372. In stating and repeating this alternative justification of knowledge, Rorty shows a wide variety of strategies. Now he presents it in its Wittgenstein form as a recourse to language-game; now in its Sellars or Quine or Kuhn shape. The Wittgenstein form is indeed the most common version. We have no justified knowledge, Wittgenstein used to say, but we *do* play language-games, and any proposition has to be judged not by its truth about an external world but whether it is intelligible according to the rules of a specified language-game. But on pp. 175 and 187 it is presented in the form invented by Quine and by Sellars; on pp. 320 and 333 it appears in the shape of a Kuhnian paradigm. Whichever way we look at it, it comes to the same thing. People form speech communities and the rules obtaining in each community have a sort of epistemic authority. If a proposition is approved by that authority, it is justified knowledge; if not, it is not. Finally, to give the thrust of the reasoning real dramatic effect, Rorty invokes Gadamer. Here the epistemic authority of the speech community appears with a genuine crescendo. All we must do, Gadamer is made to say, is to sit down and converse. We must use hermeneutics to find out what it is we are saying. When a speech is examined hermeneutically and approved of, it is justified knowledge; and if not knowledge, it is still a good speech.

Although there is a sense of real intellectual excitement in this progression from Wittgenstein to Gadamer via Quine, Sellars, and Kuhn, we ought to take a closer look at these people and see what it really is they all have in common so that they can be used in this fashion, as an alternative to the mirror philosophers, by Rorty.

With the exception of Gadamer they all have indeed very much in common. They all share the conviction that knowledge must be justified but that there can be no real representational justification of knowledge. We therefore have to accept that all we can get is the consensus of a given community of people in conversation with each other. Each such community represents a closed system as it were, and one cannot really measure what is being approved of in one closed system by the standards of another closed system. I find such a view completely stultifying and uninteresting, though not wholly wrong. Obviously, one can explain a hospital or prison or Parliament as a closed system and if one does, it would seem indeed a trifle churlish to criticize a hospital because it is not run like or does not function as a Parliament. At the same time, and this is where the stultification comes in, a hospital exists obviously for making sick people feel better; and Parliament exists for conducting political debates and for reaching peaceful decisions. While one cannot compare the running of a hospital with the running of Parliament, one can definitely judge the running of each system by testing whether it fulfills a purpose or to what extent it fulfills that purpose. This has to be done by reference to outside events and cannot be done simply by watching the rules of each system as if they had no reference to outside events. All the same, we owe thanks to Rorty for highlighting the fact that the closed systems philosophy is something common to Wittgenstein and Sellars and, at times, to Quine and always to Kuhn.

We are indebted to Rorty for showing us so vividly what these philosophers have in common and for showing us that they all have recourse to the speech community as an epistemic authority because they all believe that knowledge, to be genuine knowledge, has to be *justified* and that, since it cannot be justified by the fact that it "represents" it must be *justified* by the fact that it has the consensus of a given community. We are less grateful to Rorty for his failure to adopt a critical stance to this recourse. Since that recourse is more or less implicit in his Oakeshottian presupposition, he feels honorably exempt from examining its wisdom.

We also owe him a debt because, unbeknown to him, he has pinpointed where the great divide in philosophical thought lies. It does not lie, as he overtly argues, between the upholders of foundational epistemology and the participants in speech communities or language-games – for those upholders and those participants are all justificationists. It lies, as we can learn by reading between Rorty's lines, between the justificationists of all persuasions and Popperian falsificationists.

First of all, the obvious relativism inherent in the recourse to paradigms, language-games, speech communities, or whatever, is reminiscent of Linnaeus' effort to do biology by classifying all known species and by considering them to be immutable. Rorty, in other words, is seeking to put the philosophical clock back to pre-Darwinian days and to commend to us a philosophical Linnaeanism. Linnaeus somehow thought that all species are equidistant from God. The less said about their evolution and the more said about their incommensurability (allowing, of course, for genus and families) the better. Rorty follows suit.

Let us have a closer look at how Rorty defines these communities which have epistemic authority. On p. 187 he says that we are under rules when we enter the community where the game governed by these rules is played. If we do not enter, we are not bound by any of these rules. On p. 188 the emphasis is shifted a little. There he says that philosophy (meaning, I suppose, rational criticism) cannot reinforce or diminish the confidence in our assertions which the approval of our peers gives us. We could not wish for a better description of closed circles, of utter relativism, and of total incommensurability. And all this because Rorty imagines that all knowledge has to be justified and, since it cannot be justified as a representation, it must be justified as having the approval of a community. In passing, though this is a minor consideration, I doubt whether the expression "epistemic authority" of such a community is not an attempt to confuse the issue. One can see that community approval could in some weird way be said to "justify" any piece of knowledge. But one can hardly maintain that it is "epistemically" justified. It is justified by consensus, by obedience to the rules of a language-game, by peer approval, and so forth. But none of these senses of justification qualify for the adjective "epistemic". These communities may have sociological or psychological authority. But how can they have "epistemic" authority, since the approval of peers, supposing that they could be liars or lunatics, could never really validate a piece of knowledge as "epistemologically grounded"? However, this may be a semantic question and we will let it pass and continue with the substance of the argument.

Once the mirror metaphor is disposed of and once one is not prepared to look "behind the mirror" or seek an alternative epistemology, one is left in fact with a sort of argument which is based on a very real psychological experience and which creates – as everybody who has had that experience knows – a sort of epistemological euphoria. With the mirror metaphor out of the way, knowledge ceases to be a relation between knower and known (whatever they might be) and becomes, instead, something like a state of mind. One knows what one knows. One moves in a circle of friends who are more or less of like mind. There is no real risk of contradiction, and therefore no need to legitimize what one knows, for agreement is more or less universal in that circle. Provided one keeps to this circle, there is little chance of contradiction, and knowledge can be identified as the residual state of mind after the things which can be opposed by friends of like mind have been opposed. Eventually one turns round and proclaims the epistemic authority of that circle of friends and, finally, of any circle. Outsiders are not encountered, because most of us do indeed move *in* a circle of like-minded friends. If they are encountered, their objections are dismissed because they stem from the outside. "If you do not share my framework", the argument then runs, "you cannot be expected to agree and your very objection is indeed a confirmation of my knowledge". Thus one gets a euphoria of consensus and from that euphoria there is only a small step to the philosophical argument that the consensus of one's friends has epistemic authority.

Wittgenstein's non-relational view of knowledge and his assertion that knowledge is what one knows when one obeys the rules of the language-game one happens to be playing is well brought out by Bertrand Russell. "I told him", Bertrand Russell said, "he ought not simply to *state* what he thinks true, but to give arguments for it, but he said arguments would spoil its beauty, and that he would feel as if he was dirtying a flower with muddy hands . . . "[9].

9. Quoted by K. Blackwell in I. Bocke, ed., *Perspectives on the Philosophy of Wittgenstein* (Oxford: Blackwell, 1982).

The establishment and consolidation of such philosophical conviviality is taken by Rorty to be an adequate and appropriate substitute for the human condition in which knowledge is a relationship between a knower and a known. There is something reminiscent of G. E. Moore here. Moore used to make short shrift of all arguments about the nature of "the good". He showed time and again that attempts to define the good as what is useful or what is to be recommended universally or what is pleasurable to oneself or what is pleasing to others are logical fallacies which proceed by arbitrarily defining A as B or as C. He concluded therefore that all such attempts ought to be abandoned and that the good was simply the good. This conclusion was impeccable but neither helpful nor enlightening. Rorty's substitution of philosophical conviviality for relational knowledge is less impeccable, no more enlightening, and really quite unnecessary. One will grant that knowledge as a relation between the "inner" and "outer", where "inner" is mind and "outer", matter, or between mental and material events (as it was envisaged by the mirror philosophers) is a chimera. But it does not follow that knowledge is a state of mind to be confirmed and supported in a non-relational way by the consensus of one's friends or one's peers. It merely follows that whatever knowledge is a relation of, it is not a relation between mental and material events. Instead we say that when we know, we mean that the system controlled by or under the hegemony of any one set of DNA stands in a certain relation to all systems not controlled by that specific bit of DNA. With this view we avoid the theory that there is a ghost in the machine – for there is nothing "mental" about DNA and we avoid the view that knowledge is a relation between something mental and the rest of the world. But our relational view of knowledge reconfirms the distinction between "inner" and "outer". Rorty thinks that the disappearance of the mind-matter distinction involves the disappearance of the inner-outer distinction and makes knowledge, therefore, a non-relational state of "mind". This is not so. The inner-outer terminology is merely shorthand for describing the relation involved in knowledge. The shift brought about in our modern knowledge is not a shift away from knowledge as a relation; but a shift away from the view that the relation involved in knowledge is a relation between a knowing mind and the rest of the world. The correct and acceptable shift is towards the view that when there is knowledge, there is a relationship between a system under the hegemony of a specific DNA and systems not under the hegemony of that specific DNA. Rorty, it would seem, has thrown out the baby with the bath water.

If knowledge is to be regarded as the prevailing state of mind in a convivial community, as Rorty has it, the real crux of the matter then is the question as to who is included and who is excluded in these communities. Does everybody have access? Is membership by nomination or by inheritance? As far back as 1919 Irving Babbitt in a then rightly celebrated and now largely forgotten book *Rousseau and Romanticism*, argued that the question of inclusion in such communities is ultimately a matter of ethics. He was discussing the basis for aesthetic judgements. Having found that aesthetic judgements are purely subjective, he argued in favor of giving them an objective basis by linking them to the consensus of certain communities or institutions, the membership of which was to be controlled by the "ethical" consideration that people of low birth and vulgar behavior ought to be excluded from them. In this way he hoped to arrive at an "ethically" grounded objective set of aesthetic judgements. There is no mention of Babbitt in Rorty's book, and I suspect that Rorty not only does not know of Babbitt, who taught at Harvard long before Rorty was born, but also that Rorty would probably like to be thought to belong to a different end of the political spectrum. All the same, the appeal to the importance of moral consideration in the formulation of inclusion and exclusion rules occurs in Rorty on p. 191. Rorty there says that this appeal to morals follows from Sellars. Perhaps Sellars's attention was drawn to it by Babbitt.

Babbitt and his right-wing politics apart, the question is crucial. Apart from the isolated remark on p. 191, Rorty never really fronts up to it, unless one considers his discussion as to whether pigs rather than koalas should be admitted a discussion of this question (p. 190). I cannot get myself to find the discussion of the relative merits of pigs and koalas conclusive. And even if one does, what about the Hitler clones supposedly being bred in Brazil? When they are grown up, should they be allowed in? Or being clones, might they be allowed in before they are grown up? The possibility of clones, whether they are *Boys from Brazil* or not, is very relevant to the question of the authority of these language-games or speech communities. Suppose that there is a majority of clones in any one of these circles. Clones would never criticize one another and could easily out-vote or swamp – whichever method obtains – the rest even though one million clones only represent one voice! People who take Quine and Wittgenstein seriously, as Rorty does, ought to give this matter some serious thought! If we are to accept Rorty's advice that *"conversation* (is) . . . the ultimate context within which knowledge is to be understood" (p. 389), we are entitled to the utmost care in the choice of our partners in conversation. Oakeshott has been able to bypass this important question because he had argued from the safe position of the charmed Cambridge Colleges whose composition at that time was still controlled by a mixture of snobbery and a sort of ethnic-cum-class structure even though the presence in Cambridge in 1946 of British ex-servicemen under rehabilitation and of American veterans under the GI Bill of Rights ought to have made him a little wary about the traditional stability of his conversational circles. Any one of them might have refused to be "acculturated" (cp. p. 265) and their very presence bore witness to the important role played by those naughty ideologues and Rorty's despised "overseers" (p. 317) of culture, who had dared to be critical of the possibility that men who had sacrificed years of their lives should be left to fend for themselves. Wittgenstein was completely careless of this question and often confessed to total relativism, except that he would not admit "tourists" and other casual visitors to his language-games styled "seminars". A language-game is a language-game is a language-game, he might have paraphrased Gertrude Stein. But then he was never one for appealing to authority. Kuhn, of course, is more serious and demands membership of a recognized scientific laboratory as a criterion of qualification. But unlike all these others, Rorty is not so honorably exempt from the need to face this problem, for he sets out, avowedly, in the Introduction to determine the rightful place of philosophers in culture and claims in the last section to have solved the problem. For one who cannot claim exemption from considering the question he has remarkably little to say on the subject. It is granted that these communities have to consist of philosophers and that those philosophers who are ideologues because they claim to know something special about knowledge which other people do not know, are to be excluded – who then are these "philosophers"? Are they the people who earn their living by teaching philosophy? Surely not; for they would then come under the strictures placed by Plato on the Sophists. Or are they people who have passed certain specified examinations? Or are they people who have the correct Platonic "metal" in their souls? I doubt whether Rorty would be happy with the Platonic solution. Would he go back to Irving Babbitt's moral standards? If Babbitt's proposal is to be accepted then the question of Heidegger's Nazism and of Wittgenstein's homosexuality would become supremely relevant. And yet, Heidegger and Wittgenstein are two of the three heroes whose example Rorty invites us to follow.[10]

On p. 38 Rorty states that the question of inclusion or exclusion is not a question of knowledge but a matter of decision. We simply have to "decide" whom we accept into fellowship. This may all be very well and not differ from all sorts of situations in which we have to make decisions not based on knowledge. But the delicate precariousness of the whole question and the fine balance between knowledge and decisions is clearly brought out when Rorty, p. 226, quotes Quine on the subject. Quine makes very concrete proposals as to who is to be accepted into the fellowship. "An observation sentence", Quine is quoted (*Ontological Relativity*, pp. 86–87), "is one that is not sensitive to differences in past experience within the speech community". Rorty adds that Quine thinks that the blind, the insane, and a few more occasional deviants ought to be excluded from that speech community. I suppose one must be grateful for small mercies because one shudders to think what would happen if only those observation sentences could be called true which had the consent not only of *l'homme moyen sensuel* but also of the blind, the insane, and other occasional deviants! Seriously speaking, however, Quine's list of exclusions highlights the dubiousness of the whole idea that there is epistemic authority in a conventionally defined group. Why should the blind be excluded if the deaf are allowed in? Who exactly are "occasional deviants"? Homosexuals like Wittgenstein or Nazis like Heidegger? Or simply the

10. The circumstances of Heidegger's Nazism are discussed in Walter Kaufmann, *Discovering the Mind* (New York: McGraw-Hill, 1980), Vol. II, p. 235; those of Wittgenstein's homosexuality in W. W. Bartley, III, "Wittgenstein and Homosexuality", in R. Boyers and George Steiner, eds., *Homosexuality: Sacrilege, Vision, Politics*, in *Salmagundi*, Fall 1982-Winter 1983, pp. 166–96; and in the "Afterword 1985" to Bartley's *Wittgenstein* (La Salle and London: Open Court, 1985).

flower children of California or convicted criminals or all people referred to in *The West Side Story?* If such questions are difficult to decide, the third category, the category of the insane, is even more elusive. In the very early part of this century, the Swiss psychiatrist Kraepelin had no difficulty in deciding who was insane. But since then the boundaries of sanity have become very frayed.

The question of the exclusion of the insane is specially interesting in view of Laing's almost Quinean contention that since there is no independent way of determining a person's insanity, "insanity" is nothing but a label given to some people by the "epistemic authority" of those people who are institutionally defined as "psychiatrists". A better Quinean than Quine, Laing would certainly challenge Quine's categorical exclusion of the insane. Has Quine ever read Thomas S. Szasz (*The Myth of Mental Illness*, 1962) or R. D. Laing (*The Divided Self,* 1960) on the subject? If not, why not? His essays collected under the title *Ontological Relativity* from which the above quotation is taken appeared in New York in 1969. There is no excuse for not having taken Szasz and Laing into consideration before re-printing this passage. And if Quine is ignorant, what is Rorty's excuse?

5. The case of Hans-Georg Gadamer.

There remains the finale about Gadamer with its crescendo. Here the invocation of Gadamer becomes not only weak but basically futile. Gadamer's famous book is difficult to read in German. The English translation which appeared in 1975 as a "Continuum Book" published by The Seabury Press in New York, is one of those pieces of translation which is only comprehensible to people who are familiar with the original language in which it was written and, for this reason, is not helpful to people who have no German. Rorty therefore had recourse (p. 358, n. 1) to Alasdair MacIntyre's article on Gadamer's book which appeared in 1976 in the *Boston University Journal* under the title "Contexts of Interpretation". But Rorty was not well served by his guru. MacIntyre is no reliable Virgil to Rorty's Dante. MacIntyre assimilates Gadamer to Feyerabend and makes Gadamer look like a Teutonic sort of Oakeshott who is alleged to have recommended that philosophers abandon the search for truth and merely sit around in circles and carry on civilized conversations.

MacIntyre may not be the original culprit in this saga of Gadamer misinterpretation. MacIntyre himself quotes a long paper by Charles Taylor published in *The Review of Metaphysics* in 1977 (Vol. XXV, pp. 1 ff.). In this paper, Taylor misses the nature of the problem posed by Gadamer and thus laid the foundations for MacIntyre and, eventually, for Rorty. Taylor misses the problem in saying that hermeneutics are needed when we have a text which is confused, incomplete, cloudy, and seemingly contradictory. He does *not* add that we must always presume (though there are exceptions) that it was *not* so to the author of the text. The author understood what it meant; or, at least, thought that he understood what he meant. The reader of the text, as distinct from the author, needs hermeneutics not to make the cloudy clear; but to understand what an author of a text which appears cloudy to the reader, meant. The task of hermeneutics is the recovery of the meaning intended by the author and the recovery of any meanings not intended by the author. Hence the standard of hermeneutic achievement is, first: have we got the author right; and, second: are there non-cloudy meanings beyond the ones intended by the author?

Taylor writes as if hermeneutics were simply a search for meaning or an explication of something that is lacking in clarity so that the success of the enterprise can never be assessed in terms of true or false. The truth of the matter is that hermeneutics, even Gadamer's hermeneutics, is a search for knowledge – first for knowledge of what the author had in mind; and then for knowledge of all the things the author might have meant without actually having had them in his mind. Taylor's misrepresentation of hermeneutics set the stage for MacIntyre's and Rorty's belief that hermeneutics is explication of meanings and not a search for knowledge.

MacIntyre's Gadamer may well belong with Wittgenstein and Kuhn; but the real Gadamer does not. The real Gadamer stood firmly in the tradition of German philologically oriented hermeneutics. The purpose of such hermeneutics was not to seek and interpret the rules prevailing in any one closed circle of conversationalists but to seek the meaning of any proposition by seeking to understand what its author had intended to mean. Gadamer's important contribution to this German tradition was his insistence that any proposition can have meanings beyond the meanings intended by its author and that, therefore, hermeneutics is not just the science of finding out what the author of a statement meant but also and especially of finding out the unintended meanings and the implied meanings as well as the archetypal meanings. Gadamer has met with much opposition from the hermeneutical purists led in Italy by Emilio Betti and in America by E. D. Hirsch. Whichever side one is on, there seems no obvious link between Gadamer and Kuhn and between German hermeneutics and the closed language system philosophy propagated by Wittgenstein. Rorty's misrepresentation of Gadamer and his inclusion of Gadamer in the circle of closed circle philosophers may be tolerated as a sort of Wagnerian finale to a very readable book but cannot be accepted as additional proof that the closed system philosophy is viable or interesting.

The question of the correct interpretation of Gadamer is crucial to Rorty's whole book. As an appeal to authority it is not important, for in the English-speaking world Gadamer does not enjoy the authority of Sellars and Kuhn, let alone of Wittgenstein; nor is his name surrounded by the aura which surrounds the name of Heidegger. The recourse to Gadamer is therefore a question of substance and has to be treated as such. For Rorty the alternative to the philosophy of mirrors' permanent neutral framework and to foundational epistemology (p. 315) is Gadamer's hermeneutics which in turn is to be considered to cap the language-game philosophies we have encountered in earlier chapters. Epistemology, Rorty states, assumes that all statements are commensurable. Hermeneutics, Rorty believes, is a struggle against this assertion (p. 316).

One can do no better to show how wrong Rorty is than by going back to the grand source of modern hermeneutics, to Dilthey. Dilthey had a very clear grasp of what is involved if one wants to understand people who do not speak the same language and who belong to a different culture. He developed hermeneutics to deal with this problem. At the heart of his hermeneutics stands the realization that we can only understand other people if, in a deeper sense, we have understood them already. This contention is circular and is commonly known as the methodological circle of hermeneutics. If there is no common ground at all, Dilthey said, there can be no understanding and no amount of hermeneutics can help. Had Dilthey lived after instead of before Chomsky he would probably have said that when one wishes to do hermeneutics to understand people one must share their "deep structure". This hermeneutic project assumes that all statements are commensurable. It admits that their "surface structures" may not be but proposes that one can overcome the incommensurability of the surface structures by delving into the deep structure. Rorty is plainly excluded from even trying this project because he holds that basically the statements allowed in one language-game are incommensurable with those allowed in another language-game. There is no, he repeatedly has assured us, deep structure behind the several and separate epistemic authorities to which we have to defer if we want our knowledge to be justified. To suggest, as Rorty does, that hermeneutics is a struggle against the assumption that all contributions to a given discourse are commensurable (p. 315) is the very opposite of the truth. Hermeneutics is the attempt to lay bare the commensurabilities wherever they are not immediately apparent; not to deny commensurability. Hermeneutics was invented by Dilthey and developed by Gadamer to praise commensurability, not to bury it!

Rorty's whole description of Gadamer is a scandalous caricature. Rorty asserts on p. 359 that Gadamer is not interested in "what is out there" but in "what we can get out of nature and history". It is perfectly true that Gadamer is not a natural scientist but a humanist or, in the jargon of his own German tradition, a philologist not primarily interested in the truth of what is out there but in the truth of our knowledge of what we have thought about what is out there. His interest is a sort of secondary science. He is not concerned with whether Galilei or Aristotle were right; but in whether our knowledge of Galilei and Aristotle is right. Then he went on to explain – and this is his special contribution to the subject – that these men have often thought things the meaning of which far transcended their own intentions. As an example one might choose Darwin. Darwin was ignorant of genetics and of the correct age of the earth. The traditional hermeneuticist would seek to explain what Darwin consciously meant and then, I suppose, write him off; because given this intentional meaning, he must have been wrong about evolution. It could not have happened by natural selection if the earth was as young as he thought and unless genetics plays a crucial part in it. Here then comes Gadamer's improved hermeneutics. Gadamer would add that Darwin's personal and conscious intention is only half of the truth about Darwin. Now that we know the correct age of the earth and understand genetics, we can have a much clearer understanding than Darwin himself could have had of himself. It is almost a commonplace and perfectly true that people have meanings which transcend their own conscious intentions, and for that matter a conclusion shared by Karl Popper who has next to nothing in common with Gadamer. For Popper says in the last but one paragraph of his *Unended Quest:* "As with our children, so with our theories, and ultimately with all the work we do: our products become largely independent of their makers. We may gain more knowledge from our children or from our theories than we ever imparted to them". Gadamer himself would never refer to Popper or use Darwin as an example. His upbringing and his humanist orientation would make him always choose historians and humanists and poets and writers as examples. But for Rorty to pretend that Gadamer is a relativist in his (Rorty's) sense and a sort of latter day Deweyan pragmatist who believes that to be true is that which is useful for the time being, is absurd.

Rorty really carries this scandal to extreme lengths. On p. 364 he makes his Gadamer try to get rid of the classic picture of man as essentially a knower and to replace it by the picture of man as an edifying Oakeshott. Nothing can be farther from the truth. Gadamer is more subtle and more complex. Gadamer explained that man is not just a knower of facts (as the positivists had had it) but also a knower of knowers whose meanings often transcend their intentions. Thus Gadamer, far from reducing science to hermeneutics, showed that one must add hermeneutics to science in order to make science truly scientific. This is a Gadamer very different from an Oakeshottian conversationalist!

This point is not labored. Since Rorty uses Gadamer to crown his whole argument, it is important to understand how wrong Rorty is in using Gadamer. According to Rorty and Oakeshott science is *reduced* to *Bildung* and culture. It is just one of the pursuits of mankind in some cultures and there are other cultures which get on perfectly well without the scientific ingredient. Gadamer's allegedly anti-scientific hermeneutics are supposed to prove that science is simply part of *Bildung* and that there can be *Bildung* without science. In this view science is considered as just one more of the many parts of the conversation of idle humanists (p. 361). Nobody would mind if science were used for *Bildung*, i.e., to enhance the quality of culture. But to argue as Rorty does that science is just one of many optional *Bildungen* is wrong. And if it is not wrong, it is wrong to impute this view to Gadamer.

6. *Adhering to justificationism through thick and thin, our hero has to flee from the dread reflection he sees in his mirror and hides behind the epistemic authorities. Karl Popper's pleas for nonauthoritarian hypothetical realism are cruelly ignored.*

The really puzzling aspect of Rorty's strategy is his sets of alternatives. Knowledge, he assumes, cannot be knowledge unless it is justified. Since the mirror metaphor does not justify it, it can only be justified by recourse to the authority of a language community. If men of good sense and good will, who are in intelligible linguistic communication with each other, agree that something is so, then it is so. Although such a conclusion strikes me as basically absurd, this is what Rorty asserts. He asserts it not in passing, but on no less than thirteen separate occasions! All the same, Rorty is obviously in good company here, even if we definitely have to discount his appeal to Gadamer. Wittgenstein and Sellars and Kuhn are no mean supporters and I would not really dare to challenge the united voice of such men if it were not for the fact that Rorty's recourse to these men is not really necessary.

On every one of the thirteen occasions I accept his rejection of the mirror as a justification of knowledge. But I cannot see for the life of me that Rorty is left with only one alternative. There is a second alternative which he never so much as mentions.

The second alternative was first proposed by Karl Popper nearly half a century ago. Popper argued that though knowledge cannot be *justified* – not by induction and not by a bucket theory of the mind and not by a mirror metaphor – we nevertheless have knowledge. Since we obviously *do* have some knowledge and since it cannot be justified, Popper showed that the truth of knowledge does not depend on our ability to justify it. He showed that every piece of knowledge is a proposal or a hypothesis which could, in principle, be falsified and that as long as it is not actually falsified, we are entitled to regard it as provisionally true. More than Popper himself suspected or could have known in the thirties when he first proposed this view of knowledge, this theory of knowledge has proved amazingly fertile. It has since turned out that it applies not only to the history of modern science but that it obtains right through the whole realm of biological evolution which, like the hypotheses of scientists, proceeds by random mutations and selective retention of those mutations which fit the environment, that is, which are not falsified by the environment. It is totally incomprehensible how Rorty could have written in the seventies of this century and succeeded in completely ignoring this Popperian alternative to the justification of knowledge by the mirror metaphor. There is a sizable literature on the subject by Konrad Lorenz and D. T. Campbell as well as by Rupert Riedl and Gerhard Vollmer – to mention only the most obvious examples. This alternative to foundational epistemology obviates the recourse to the idea that a language community in Wittgenstein's sense is an epistemic authority. By showing that we can have knowledge without "foundation" or induction or mirror images, Popper has filled the vacuum left by the demise of foundational epistemology. In the words of Gerhard Vollmer, we have a perfectly viable alternative to foundational epistemology without seeking a way out by an appeal to the epistemic authorities of language-games or the consensus of other arbitrarily established communities whose verdict is relative to that particular game and incommensurable with the verdict of all other games. Like Rorty himself, Vollmer rejects the traditional attempts to account for knowledge by an inward turned reflection upon our "mind". We cannot succeed in finding out about knowing, he writes in the third paragraph of his review of Riedl's *Biology of Knowledge (Allgemeine Zeitschrift für Philosophie,* 1981), by introducing a mirror into the alleged mirror of our mind. Rorty himself could not have put it better! But unlike Rorty, Vollmer does not seek refuge in the arms of the epistemic authority of a speech community or the *consensus omnium.*

"Our cognitive apparatus", Vollmer writes instead in another place, "is the result of evolution. Our subjective cognitive structures fit the world because they have been formed in the course of evolution by adaptation to the real world. They correspond (in parts) with the real structures because only such correspondence made survival possible".[11]

Rorty's refusal to entertain evolutionary epistemology as an alternative to the epistemic authority of language-games and speech communities and paradigms is quite tantalizing because in many places his own formulations of the shortcomings of foundational epistemology cry out for the alternative offered by evolutionary epistemology. On p. 3 he says that "to know is to represent accurately what is outside the mind". He finds no difficulty in showing that this claim for knowledge is a chimera. But he does not consider that evolutionary epistemology provides a very plausible answer as to how we know and why we know what is outside. Evolutionary epistemology, however, places a very important stricture on this answer. It limits the degree of accuracy. Rorty proceeds throughout on the assumption that knowledge is not knowledge unless it is completely accurate. Evolutionary epistemology admits that the cognitive apparatus which has evolved by natural selection and without which we would not be sitting here to discuss it, does not yield complete accuracy – only enough accuracy to assure survival relative to competing species. If Rorty could only disabuse his mind from the notion of complete accuracy, he could very well entertain evolutionary epistemology as an alternative before seeking solace in the arms of his epistemic authorities. Or again, on p. 157, he says that to know is to have truths which are certain because they have "special" causes. He has no difficulty in disposing of the idea that there are "special" causes and one must agree with him. Then he rushes again to his epistemic authorities. He would have done better to scrutinize the notion of "certainty". Evolutionary epistemology shows that the reason why we cannot be "certain" is because the cognitive apparatus which has evolved by natural selection has evolved and is surviving only provisionally. This is the real reason why in any piece of knowledge we have, we can be confident that, provided it has survived selection, it is hypothetically true, but not "certainly" so. On p. 197 Rorty again makes exaggerated claims for mirror realism. The part of his argument which is wrong is the exaggerated claims. He sets his sights too high; indeed, unnecessarily high. Mirrors are supposed to represent complete reality. They cannot do so and Rorty is right in dismissing them. But evolutionary epistemology does not

11. My translation from Vollmer's *Evolutionäre Erkenntnistheorie,* 3rd edition (Stuttgart: S. Hirzel Verlag, 1981), p. 102.

claim to have justified knowledge of complete reality. It supports nothing more than hypothetical realism, to use Donald Campbell's term. There is no need to give up realism altogether simply because what we know of reality is neither completely accurate, nor certain nor complete. Or take the notion of objectivity. Rorty thinks that only those pieces of knowledge which are completely, accurately, and certainly justified are known objectively. It is much more realistic to expect less, to realize that the cognitive apparatus which has evolved by natural selection yields less and that therefore "justification" is not a necessary condition of objectivity. If the exaggerated and unnecessary demands of completeness, accuracy, and certainty are given up, one can consider evolutionary epistemology as an alternative to language-games and epistemic authorities. Such a consideration is all the more commendable because language-games and epistemic authorities do not really inspire much confidence in knowledge about the outside world. True, inside each game and as a subject of any one epistemic authority one has certainty, accuracy, and completeness; but it is the certainty, accuracy, and completeness of playing a game and belonging to a peer-group – not the certainty and accuracy and completeness which were the will-o'-the-wisps of the representational and foundational epistemology of the mirror metaphor. So when all is said and done, Rorty does not even gain anything. But perhaps he is not out to!

Rorty's ignorance and neglect of Popper is a very striking feature of his strategy. On p. 315 he states that the vacuum left by the demise of foundational epistemology had to be filled. By the time he spells this out, he has already indicated five times that it is to be filled by recourse to the language-game (pp. 175, 186, 187, 210, and 226). From p. 315 onwards he therefore feels relieved of the obligation to consider the Popperian alternative and goes on to show how one can do philosophy by occupying one's time with "discourse" – i.e., by Oakeshottian conversation.

The only explanation which comes to mind for this flagrant neglect is Rorty's dogmatically held belief that knowledge is not knowledge if it is not justified. If the mirror image fails, Rorty concludes, knowledge can only be justified by the consensus of the participants in a language-game. The real explanation for Rorty's insouciant neglect of Popper's alternative has therefore to be sought in his belief that knowledge is not worthy of the name if it cannot be *justified*. This belief blinds him to the much more attractive Popperian alternative that we can have knowledge provided it can be falsified in principle and that there is no need for basing it upon or founding it on inductively gathered experience. He could not consider this alternative because he could not get himself to entertain the possibility that we can have knowledge which is not inductively justified. Had he considered it, he would have seen that the road from the demise of the mirror metaphor does not lead to Wittgenstein and Kuhn and Alasdair MacIntyre's Gadamer, at least not necessarily so.

One might object at this point that Rorty is under no obligation to consider that Popperian alternative. If he sincerely believes as so many pre-Wittgenstein and pre-Kuhn philosophers have done that all knowledge must be justified and founded upon inductively gathered experience, he can well afford to bypass Popper.

7. Since the conclusions are identical with the presuppositions, there is no room for maneuver and our hero is forced into a studied neglect of evolutionary epistemology.

There are two recurring facets in Rorty's book which seem to invalidate such an objection to my criticism. First of all there is a colossal *petitio principii* in the manner the book is built up; and second, Rorty goes out of his way to make it impossible for himself to consider the Popperian alternative and its consequence, an evolutionary epistemology, in place of a foundational epistemology.

Let us take these two points one by one. First, the *petitio principii*. The book ends with the conclusion that in every culture there are philosophers just as there are politicians, bakers, scientists, etc. Rorty recommends that everybody keep his place and pursue his job with competence and honesty so that the sum total can be the "conversation of mankind" in Oakeshott's sense. This conclusion is skillfully foisted upon the reader as the result of the language-games people must play because language-games are the only sensible alternative to the mirror metaphor. Since the mirror metaphor is wrong as an account of how we have knowledge, we can only consider as knowledge the sort of propositions which occur in the conversation of people who participate in a language-game. If this conclusion is not inevitable for people who are acquainted with the Popperian alternative to the language-game, one must grant that it looks inevitable to readers who, like Rorty, are convinced that knowledge must always be justified and that if it cannot be justified by induction or mirrors then it must be considered justified if it obtains the consensus of the participants of a language-game. Those readers, however, who recall the Introduction (pp. 3-13) will hardly be surprised by the conclusion, for the conclusion is precisely stated in the Introduction as a presupposition. The presupposition says in Oakeshottian terms that it is wrong to imagine that philosophers know something special about knowledge which other people do not know. One can hear Oakeshott speaking: it is wrong to think that politicians are people who know something about equality or happiness which other people do not know. Starting with the presupposition that philosophers are simply part of culture and that we do wrong in attributing to philosophers special knowledge about knowledge, Rorty is right from the start in a homemade straightjacket. He *must* be looking for a foundation of knowledge in a language community so that his conclusion that there ought to be language communities is nothing but an explication of his presupposition. The whole of his conclusion is contained in the sentence which occurs in the middle of p. 9: "If we have a Deweyan conception of knowledge *as what we are justified in believing*, then we will not imagine that there are enduring constraints on what can count as knowledge, since we will see 'justification' as a *social* phenomenon rather than as a transaction between the 'knowing subject' and 'reality'" (my italics). The recommendation that philosophers are people who carry on conversation rather than people who know something special about knowledge is not the result of his analysis of the mirror image at all; but it is implied by the presupposition that knowledge is a social phenomenon and that philosophers like bakers and bankers, like soldiers and politicians, simply occupy a given place in a culture and should pursue their calling of carrying on conversation. The *petitio principii* apart, one must really be at a loss as to what it is philosophers of this ilk ought to be doing. One can easily imagine what a baker and a soldier and a banker ought to be doing. But what is it that a philosopher ought to discourse about if it is not the conditions and nature of knowledge? Rorty's attempt to give philosophers a new self-image is not only the result of a vicious circle but is essentially hollow.

Next we come to Rorty's studied effort to make it impossible for himself to consider the Popperian alternative. Although it was not part of Popper's original proposal in *The Logic of Scientific Discovery* of 1934 to develop a theory of knowledge which would link scientific progress with biological evolution, it has been shown that the most fruitful success of Popper's proposal was the insight that problem solving by the invention of falsifiable hypotheses is common to Darwinian evolution and to the progress of science. There is a continuity from the amoeba to Einstein, as Popper himself remarked in his *Objective Knowledge* of 1972. This continuity depends on the fact that the amoeba is 'ratiomorphous' to use Egon Brunswik's term and that Einstein is "rational"– both have expectations of regularities in the environment. The amoeba and all other protozoic organisms are adaptations to these regularities while Einstein can consciously formulate linguistic summaries of such regularities so that we can say that his scientific consciousness is "adapted" to them. If one focuses on such expectation of regularities, one can see that all organisms embody knowledge, albeit at different levels of unconsciousness and consciousness. An organism is an embodied theory about the environment; and an unfalsified but falsifiable theory is a disembodied organism adapted to the environment. Neither is "justified" by the environment; but both are hypothetically true. This is not the place to discuss the many problems surrounding this view of the growth of knowledge by evolution – by mutation or invention and by selective retention. But this is the place for saying that Rorty is making a studied effort to avoid the necessity for considering and weighing this view.

In no less than ten places, widely dispersed throughout the book, Rorty takes pains to claim that human beings are completely unique and totally different from animals and all other organisms. In a sense this is patently true. But when one is considering knowledge, one cannot write as if we were living before Darwin and as if Karl Popper, Egon Brunswik, and D. T. Campbell and Konrad Lorenz and Rupert Riedl had never written. Nor can one pretend that our whole knowledge of biology does not show us that there are very striking and remarkable continuities between human beings and pre-hominid animals and other organisms. And yet, the argument that human beings are totally separate and unique occurs in Rorty's book on pp. 35, 38, 43, 44, 183, 184, 186, 189, 190–91, and 232. Why does Rorty protest so much? Not only does he protest too much in ten places; but on pp. 188–91 he seeks to buttress his protests by a singularly wrong-headed argument. He says that in reverting to community as a source of epistemic authority, we ought to take into account the possibility of including in such communities beings who have non-conceptual knowledge and that we ought to consider for potential membership in this community babies and the "more attractive sorts of animals" whom we can credit with "having feelings". If one is seeking criteria for establishing such communities for "epistemic authority", I think this ploy is worthwhile. If applied consistently, it might even draw the reader's attention to the continuum of organic evolution. But two pages later Rorty argues that we are reasonably quite "irrational" in extending this courtesy to koala bears but not to pigs. Since koalas are cute and pigs are not, we form societies for the protection of koalas but send pigs to the slaughterhouse. This argument not only reveals the utter frivolity of Rorty's reasoning and his inability to understand evolution and the growth of knowledge in evolution; but reveals that his studied effort to avoid the whole question of evolution in regard to knowledge leads him to genuine confusion. We protect koalas because they are an endangered species. We also protect seals, or try to; even though they are less "cute" than koalas. We breed pigs so we can eat them because, unlike koalas, they are very meaty. And at any rate, as any visitor to some remote parts of New Guinea would have told Rorty, the exclusion of pigs from this epistemic authority community is by no means universal. In those parts of New Guinea pigs are suckled by women like babies![12] Rorty is not interested in such information about human and animal behavior as we have to hand. He is merely interested in inventing habits to show that the playing of language-games is a more or less arbitrary custom and that we are quite absurdly though justifiably irrational in deciding who is to be allowed into the game and who is to be excluded. The least he might have said is that epistemic authority founding communities are *not* chosen arbitrarily; but, if one *has* to formulate the matter in terms of communities which constitute an "authority" for knowledge, then one could at least think of species and of human "pseudo-species"– culturally circumscribed societies, to use a term invented by Erikson and since adopted by Sennett. One would then see that there is nothing arbitrary in the decision as to who is in and who is out; but that inclusion is a matter of selective retention of the constitution of the gene-pool (for species) and of the constitution of collective knowledge (for human societies or pseudo-species).

If the argument about koala bears and pigs is merely wrong-headed, there are other arguments to establish the uniqueness of man which are not just wrong-

---

12. Cp. e.g., A. Dupeyrat, *Mitsinari, Twenty-One Years Among the Papuans* (London: Staples Press, 1954), Chapter XXXV and the photograph facing p. 145; B. Dean and V. Carell, *Softly, Wild Drums* (Sydney: U. Smith, 1958), p. 153 and the photograph facing p. 136; Anne Chowning, "Pigs, Dogs and Children in a Melanesian Economy", paper given at a Symposium on Domestic Animals, AAAS, Denver, Colorado, December 1961.

headed but downright false. On pp. 183–84 Rorty claims that the difference between a child and a photoelectric cell's sensitivity to pain is absolute. This is incorrect. The cell has a discriminative response to pain. The child, in learning a language, starts slowly from a discriminative response and advances to a descriptive response. Organisms with a descriptive as well as a discriminative response are better adapted than organisms with nothing but a discriminative response. There is no reason for thinking that there is an absolute discontinuity between discriminative and descriptive response. A perusal of Chapter 1, "Life as a Process of Learning" of Konrad Lorenz's *Behind the Mirror* would have made this amply clear.

Rorty is nothing if not persistent. On p. 43 he comes up with a different reason for believing that man is unique. With the koala bears he was wrong-headed; with the photoelectric cells, he was wrong. With the argument from universals he is perverse. He says on p. 43 that philosophers are reluctant to abandon the idea that human beings have knowledge of universals because they believe that the knowledge of universals is proof of man's uniqueness. "To suggest there are no universals", Rorty writes, "is to endanger uniqueness". I would describe this false argument as perverse because the truth is exactly the other way around. If man had no knowledge of universals, as Rorty thinks, he would be totally unique in the whole realm of living organisms. All organisms, even the simple paramecium (cp. Konrad Lorenz, op. cit., p. 54) is ratiomorphous in that it survives because of its "knowledge" of a dependable relationship between carbon dioxide and the bacteria on which the paramecium feeds. It is not equipped to detect bacteria; but it can respond to the presence of carbon dioxide. It can grasp only one single piece of information. But since it expects this information to be information about a regularity in nature, it survives. In a dim way the paramecium has "knowledge" of a universal. Now it may well be true as Rorty believes that human beings have no knowledge of universals. If Rorty is right, then human beings would be truly unique. However this may be, Rorty must be wrong in thinking that philosophers have resisted giving up the idea that we have knowledge of universals lest such lack of knowledge would make us like animals and put an end to our uniqueness.

It is very natural for people to make mistakes. We are all fallible and nobody would hold it against Rorty that he makes mistakes. But there are mistakes and mistakes. The mistake about knowledge of universals being the criterion of the uniqueness of man is a very special kind of mistake. Its falsity hits the nail so precisely on the head that one is forced to conclude that it was not based on ignorance or carelessness but on uncanny insight. It reminds me of a lecture on French worker-priests which I attended many years ago. The lecture was given by a Catholic priest who defended the papal ban against worker-priests by the argument that it is wrong for a priest who is supposed to be a sort of Jesus figure, to look like a common carpenter. Had the lecturer said plumber or welder the audience might have been impressed. But the choice of "carpenter", of all trades, was too much for them. Like the priest, Rorty, in his heart of hearts, knows that he is wrong.

If one views the growth of knowledge as an evolutionary process in which knowledge grows, either in the shape of organisms or in the shape of theories, by random mutation and selective retention, one must pay special attention to the selected retention in all organisms of the ability to expect regularities in their environments. If one assumes that there are no regularities one is compelled to drop the idea of evolution altogether or replace its mechanism by something other than random mutation and selective retention. With an uncanny and almost unconscious sense of direction Rorty makes sure on p. 38 that the question of regularities and of the knowledge of universals to which they might give rise, does not come up or, at least, does not have to be faced as one of the crucial questions in philosophy. He says there that "there would not have been thought to be a problem about the nature of reason had our race confined itself to pointing out particular states of affairs – warning of cliffs and rain, celebrating individual births and deaths". But, alas! Rorty continues, poetry speaks of man, birth, and death as such. He seems to consider this to have been the philosophical Fall from grace; the ultimate, philosophically original sin. Once people thought of universals, the road was open for Plato's misconstruction of their nature and for the notion that universals are entities to be contemplated with the eye of the mind – and hence the unfortunate ocular metaphor which is so deeply ingrained in the notion that the mind mirrors nature.

Many readers will readily agree that Plato's and Aristotle's treatment of these universals was not above reproach. Especially the attribution of spirituality to universals seems questionable; for such attribution clearly derives from the fact that as such they are not to be seen by the eye but only by the "eye of the mind" – or should we take up Douglas Hofstadter's appropriate pun and say that they are to be seen only by the mind's I, thus drawing attention to the close connection between personhood and awareness of universals. I doubt very much whether the ubiquity of the ocular metaphor and our habit for treating "I understand" and "I see" as synonymous really stems exclusively from Plato's recognition that universals play some role in our knowledge. However this may be, it is significant that Rorty thinks the world would have been a better place if universals had never been heard of. He, for his part, obviously seems to find no great difficulty in orienting himself in his environment without abstract universals or general concepts. One must wonder how he could have managed to master the English language sufficiently to write a four hundred page book and the mind boggles when it tries to fathom what Rorty's private environment might look like or be like if he thinks he could find his way from A to B without the help of abstract universals. The real point is that Rorty is here putting up an old nominalist argument and thus unwittingly barricades any road which might lead to thoughts of evolution.

8. The proof of this pudding is not in the eating but, supposedly, in the history of philosophy. In the excitement generated by the effort to conceal his vicious circle, it has escaped our hero that in eschewing knowledge as the philosopher's domain, he has deprived himself of the right to appeal to historical knowledge.

The study of history has always been held to lead to special insights and recommendations about the present and the future. I do not mean that odd people have often thought that they might learn odd lessons from odd historical examples. We all learn from our mistakes and sometimes even from other people's mistakes. But Rorty like many other people before him, is studying the history of philosophy ("taking stock" of it, as he calls it on p. 38) in order to determine the role of the philosopher in culture. In conclusion I would point out that there are two major objections to such a project.

First of all, intelligent men do not really care about philosophers or what they should be doing. We all search for knowledge. I find philosophers interesting if they have something special to say about the search for knowledge. For that matter, if a scientist or a politician has something interesting to say about that question, I regard him with the same interest as I regard a philosopher. But Rorty assumes that being a philosopher is a sort of intrinsically virtuous occupation which ought to be justified and defended. He takes great care to ensure that philosophers should not become ideologues or overseers and claim to know something which other people do not know. To me all this seems a pseudo-question. Einstein was a scientist; but I regard his so-called philosophical pronouncements and reflections with infinitely greater interest and respect than I regard the ruminations of Wittgenstein, even though Wittgenstein was alleged to have been a "philosopher". Unlike Rorty, I have never believed, to start with, that philosophers are people who know something special about knowledge *ex officio*. On the contrary. I consider those people who specialize in what we all have to know about knowledge as philosophers. Einstein knew a lot about knowledge, but happened not to specialize in that knowledge. In short, the whole question of what officially-designated "philosophers" are doing or not doing is of no interest at all and Rorty's attempt to map out their position in culture is the most boring attempt I have ever come across. One has to have a pretty weird notion of "culture" before one can contentedly sit back and designate some people as "philosophers", and then give those philosophers who claim to be just discoursing intelligently ("kibitzing", p. 393) to pass the time, good marks. If philosophers have nothing much to do, I should be quite happy for them to disappear or, at least, lose their jobs. Rorty's obsessional interest in "philosophers" rather than in questions of knowledge and questions of morals is a very unpromising sign. If he were interested in the roles of farmers or peasants, teachers or scientists, I would listen. But an interest in philosophers as such seems hardly warranted.

Above all, Rorty appears to forget that one cannot take stock of history before history is written. History, even the history of philosophy, is not something which we can all *see* and inspect (another ocular metaphor!) and then derive conclusions about. History and the history of philosophy has first to be written. Then we can look at what has been written and see what we can make of it. (I feel I must apologize for these dreadful ocular metaphors necessitated by English usage.) Such inspection, however, will not be very helpful for there are many ways of writing the history of philosophy and in inspecting so many histories, one cannot claim privileged status for any one and draw conclusions from the history to which one has chosen to accord privileged status. Our knowledge of history depends on an epistemology; and as I have tried to show in my *The Shapes of Time*[13], time, even the time of philosophy, can have many shapes. For some reason which I as a professional historian find very hard to understand, there are always scientists and philosophers, not to mention other people, who think that History is simply a Given, a *datum*, and that one can observe it and reach conclusions about it. They are perfectly aware that neither Nature nor Mind is that kind of a *datum*; but History is widely believed to be an exception. Two decades ago we were treated by Kuhn to a history of science which was supposed to prove that changes in science are due to paradigm shifts. Kuhn's own history of science certainly bore out this contention; except that Kuhn completely forgot that he had, in the first instance, composed his history of science in order to bear out this particular contention. Whatever the merits of this contention, it cannot be proved by looking at the so-called objective history of science. And now Rorty has done something even worse.

Kuhn is a scientist who used historical knowledge to prove that all knowledge is dependent on more or less arbitrarily established paradigms, thus assuming for his proof that historical knowledge, unlike scientific knowledge, is not dependent on paradigms. Rorty goes one better. He is a philosopher who claims to know nothing about knowledge but uses *historical* knowledge to make good the claim that those philosophers who thought they knew something about knowledge were wrong, thus assuming for his proof that historical knowledge, unlike all other knowledge, can be had for the asking. How, one must ask, can one use knowledge to prove that one knows nothing about knowledge?

On p. 356 he sums up his argument by saying that it would make for philosophical clarity if we just *gave* the notion of "cognition" to science. As this is a purely semantic question, I have no objection. I am interested in cognition and it is a matter of total indifference to me whether it is dealt with by scientists or by philosophers. However, our knowledge of history is very much a matter of cognition. The mind-boggling proposal, made by Rorty, is that we should prove

---

13. (Middletown: Wesleyan University Press, 1977.)

something from an appeal to historical *knowledge* and that what we should prove is precisely that philosophers ought not to busy themselves with knowledge. Since this is a philosophical argument to end the philosophical arguments about cognition, how does Rorty imagine that we can prove from cognition of history that the argument is correct?

Rorty invites us to believe that his historical inspection of philosophy has shown that "epistemology-centered philosophy (is) . . . an episode in the history of European culture" (p. 390). The new episode, so his reading of the history of philosophy tells him, is an episode in which philosophers "just say something – they participate in a conversation" rather than contribute to an inquiry (p. 371). Thus Rorty "takes stock" of the history of philosophy – as if it were an object like a table or the contents of a warehouse so that one can take stock of it – and tells us that having taken stock, it is clear that philosophers are people inside most cultures who sit back in armchairs and carry on elegant discourse, a sort of conversation of mankind; but have been wrong in thinking of themselves from Descartes to Bertrand Russell or thereabouts, as ideologues who knew something special (which other people do not know) which could be used to improve culture. Whether Rorty is right or wrong in this claim, it cannot be established by an inspection of the history of philosophy.

Rorty glosses over the fact that "history" is not given and cannot be looked at or inspected by using the odd expression "taking stock" of history. This is a very vague notion. What Rorty really means by using this metaphor from stockbrokers and accountants is: let us look at what is *given* in history to see what choices are offered to us. His mentor Oakeshott also believes that one can simply "abate the mystery" of how and why things are the way they are if one feels one's way from one particular event to the next as each event succeeds another in time (*On Human Conduct*, Oxford, 1979, p. 106). On p. 33 Rorty recommends that "philosophy needs to relive its past in order to answer its questions", again suggesting, this time with the help of a phrase from Collingwood ("relive"; Collingwood actually called it "re-enact"), that there is no doubt as to what happened. If the phrase is Collingwoodian, the meaning is lamentably un-Collingwoodian. For Collingwood realized that in order to "relive" one has to use thoughts – either the thoughts which were used by the subject whose experiences one wants to relive or re-enact, or the thoughts which are available to us. Thoughts are required to link particular events. Such employment of thoughts for the reliving of what happened in the past is a very delicate procedure and never leads to certain knowledge as to what happened. And certainly never to knowledge certain enough to derive arguments from or base arguments on. Rorty seems to be quite unaware of this problem. History and sociology, he seems to think on p. 226, unlike the world outside our minds (i.e., the reality of nature) are *data* and are known with such simple clarity that we can base our evaluation of philosophy and epistemology on them. How does he imagine one can get knowledge of sociology and history without epistemology? Is what happened in history not as much an "object of knowledge" as what happened in nature? If there is no mirror of nature, why can there be a mirror of history?

In his heart of hearts he seems to have known this all along; for he had to proceed first to write his own curious history of philosophy, complete with an original interpretation of Descartes, with the proposition that Plato never thought in terms of mirroring the world and that Heidegger, Wittgenstein, and Dewey between them showed that philosophical ideology is misplaced and obnoxious. The claim about Descartes is intriguing, but probably wrong. Kant is misrepresented and Plato misunderstood. The idea that the mind mirrors nature (or is a bucket, as Popper is wont to say) really belongs with Locke and Hume whose role is far too unspectacular to be given much attention by Rorty. And any history of philosophy which can link Heidegger and Wittgenstein as bedfellows has to be seen (sorry! for "seen" read "read" even though the avoidance of the ocular metaphor makes nonsense of the English idiom) to be believed. Karl Popper is not even mentioned though one would have thought that the pioneer of non-inductive, nonrepresentational, and non-foundational epistemology would merit at least an honorable mention in a book dedicated to the destruction of representational and foundational epistemology. Equally surprising is the omission of Wittgenstein's own pilgrim's progress from the *Tractatus* to the *Philosophical Investigations*; or from Wittgenstein I to Wittgenstein II. If Popper has led the attack on foundational epistemology, Wittgenstein I, the early Wittgenstein of *Tractatus* fame, had championed it in its purest form. By any reckoning, the *Tractatus* had been the classical exposition of foundational and representational epistemology couched in linguistic terms so that, by comparison, mere mirror philosophers like Descartes and Kant are non-starters. Propositions picture the world, Wittgenstein I had said, by representing the structure of facts. Thus the *Tractatus* is the archest of all arch-mirror philosophies, exhibiting all its weaknesses and none of its strengths.

When writing the *Tractatus* Wittgenstein certainly thought that he knew something about knowledge. After the *Tractatus*, Wittgenstein discovered all the countless arguments against mirrors and pictures, and being unable to answer them, dropped the mirror and advanced to language-games. There is no better and more telling illustration of the demise of representational epistemology and the consequent recourse to the alternative of language-games than Wittgenstein's biography – a much more convincing and more amply documented story than the rise of Descartes and Kant, their decline, and the emergence of language-games, all as if the *Tractatus* had never existed and Wittgenstein II had been born fully grown, like Venus herself, from the ocean's foam in which the mirrors had foundered. The least Rorty could have done was to hold up Wittgenstein's progress as a shining example of his own history of philosophy: from mirrors to games. It is as if Wittgenstein had lived up to Haeckel's biogenetic law. His ontogenesis was a perfect recapitulation of the phylogenesis and Rorty's history is Wittgenstein's progress writ large.

I do not know why Rorty chose to delete Popper from his stocktaking. But I think I can offer an explanation of the deletion of Wittgenstein's progress. Rorty claims that in taking stock of the history of philosophy, he has found the demise of the mirror philosophers and the emergence of language-games and epistemic authorities. A "neutral" study of history, whatever that might mean, would have revealed no such thing and would in fact not have revealed much at all. But if one comes to the history of philosophy with a ready-made idea of what one hopes to find, the past, if properly ransacked, will yield some evidence to support all but the most absurd ideas. Its infinite store of facts, each of which is made more infinite by the fact that it is, in turn, infinitely sub-divisible, will respond to almost any probing. "Search me", the past beckons, "and you shall find!" Rorty came to history's infinite bounty with the ready belief that Wittgenstein's progress was the progress of all progresses and that its sum was the ascent from the *Tractatus* to the *Investigations*, from mirrors to games. He searched and found that the history of philosophy is indeed a movement from mirrors to games and that the biogenetic law held good even in philosophy and that Wittgenstein had recapitulated the longer process in his own lifetime. But had he mentioned all this, he could not have called this search for the historical validation of his preconceived idea a "stocktaking". Had he admitted that there was a preconceived idea in the shape of Wittgenstein's progress and that he had held fast to this idea because he loved Wittgenstein and considered his progress the paradigm of philosophical virtue, he would have let the cat out of the bag. The whole exercise would then have appeared not like stocktaking of the powerful verdict of history, but merely as a project of Wittgenstein's errant from A to B, from one form of justificationism to another. To make it look like the verdict of history, Wittgenstein's own progress, which furnishes the initial idea, had to be left out. Therefore Rorty was unable to point out that if his phylogenetic story was true, Wittgenstein had recapitulated it ontogenetically. For the truth of the matter is that it only *looks* as if Wittgenstein had recapitulated. In reality Rorty has fabricated the phylogenetic story by using Wittgenstein's ontogenesis. Rorty has used Wittgenstein's biography and transformed it into *the* history of philosophy.

Rorty writes as if Wittgenstein had invented language-games; or, rather, as if Wittgenstein had thought up the idea that meaning equals use and that when we are asserting something, its meaning does not depend on what it means but on whether we are saying it according to the rules of any particular language-game. Nothing could be further from the truth. Though Rorty obviously thinks that Wittgenstein was God's gift to the world in its hour of need, the truth is that Wittgenstein simply fell back, when he found himself in difficulties largely created by his own *Tractatus*, on a very understandable though hardly forgivable device: one of the oldest, though not *the* oldest, professions in the world. When outside references prove troublesome to account for, Wittgenstein, as so many people had done before him, proclaimed: *extra ecclesiam nulla salus!* (There is no salvation outside the church!)

It is notoriously difficult to account for the fact or explain the reasons for the allegation that linguistic expressions refer to something other than other linguistic expressions. They seem to and are purported to. Their grammar, their syntax, and all vocabularies create the expectation that they do. But nobody has ever quite managed to say how it is done. From time to time Rorty's philosophical overseers have come along and offered rule-of-thumb explanations. At the beginning of this century it was fashionable to say with the positivists that there are events like protocol-statements or experiences like sense-data which form a sort of bridge between what we say and what there is. These bridges are very tenuous and it is a rather unsatisfying experience to cross any of them. Although the problem is very old, and although nobody really enjoyed walking on any of these bridges, positivists never entertained the thought that it might be sagacious to dispense with them.

There is an analogous problem when one is looking at human societies. At any one moment in time all human societies seem to be working. Some better than others. One can see how they work by being inside; but one can also see how they work by watching them. One knows, however, that none of these societies is static and one knows that every one of them has developed out of another. But how can one explain this development and account for the fact that the present working is causally dependent on and partially determined by past workings? How, in short, does any society at any one moment refer to its past? The problem is parallel to the other problem as to how any set of linguistic statements can refer to something outside the set. This problem was, for example, thought to have been solved by the positivists and their bridges. The problem of how societies refer to their past was, for example, solved by historicists who claimed that societies refer to their past because the past, by a developmental law, causes the past to turn into the present and then causes the present to turn into the future, and so forth. Positivists and historicists are great bridge builders and believe that their bridges explain how and why systems refer to something outside themselves. Both explained all meanings understood by people inside a system *via* events that are outside the system. Positivists went *via* nature which they said was mediated by sense-data or protocol statements. Historicists went *via* the past, which determined the present state of the system by the operation of a developmental law.

If it was no pleasure to walk on the bridges built by positivists, it was a downright nausea-making experience to cross from the present into the past or back on any one of the suspension bridges built by historicists. Positivism and historicism, of course, are only two of many methods to show how systems relate to something outside themselves. No matter which method was tried, it has always proved hazardous. For this reason almost every experiment in devising a method has led to a full retreat. If the bridges are unsatisfactory—well then! let us stay inside the system. After all when we are speaking, be it about pains in our hearts or about galaxies or about sub-atomic particles, we usually understand each other and that is really all that matters. And when we are living in a society, we usually know more or less what we are supposed to do and what is expected of us. Since there is little doubt in these regions, why worry about what is going on in the outside world and why worry about the past even if it *does* stand in some weird causal relation to the present? This strategy of retreat is so obvious, so satisfying, and so homely that it always recommends itself with irresistible persuasiveness. We could call it a sort of philosopher's Oedipal Project. Why marry out and face all the toils and troubles which alliances, especially nuptial ones, with strangers always bring about when we have a perfectly good mother in the house? Oedipus, Schmoedipus . . . who cares as long as the boy loves his mother! In all societies known to anthropologists such retreat or such determination to stay at home is considered extremely polluting. But philosophers are more liberal and less guilt-ridden. They recommend it freely, at least as an intellectual exercise. They are so free in their recommendation because it is satisfying and viable, instead of explaining meaning *via* the world, to explain meaning by the manner people listen to each other and to philosophers, and react to each other as well as to philosophers.

In the present century the first such recommendation was actually made by an anthropologist who ought to have known professionally about incest and exogamy. I have always found this very surprising. But we will let this pass. When Malinowski considered the frailty of Tylor's and Morgan's and Frazer's historicism, he suggested not unreasonably that one can understand all societies perfectly well as functioning systems. One can understand so much about them that there is really no need to inquire how much more one can understand if one investigated their past and their origins. A full glass is a full glass and it makes no sense to say that a larger glass would be "fuller". By this argument Bronislaw Malinowski obviated the need for historicism and, indeed, for all other historical thinking and suggested that every society is a closed system which can be described fully without reference to its past.

Wittgenstein's originality did not consist in his invention of this kind of Oedipal Project. If an award for originality has to be made, it should surely go to Sophocles or perhaps even to the historical Oedipus of Thebes. In any case, in the present century this kind of philosophical Oedipal Project was first launched by Malinowski. Wittgenstein's originality consists in the fact that he transferred the Project from the study of societies in general, to our understanding of speech behavior in particular. As with societies, so with sentences. There is no reference to the outside world intended and all resemblances to the outside world are purely coincidental. When we speak, we are performing according to the rules of a language-game and the old question *how*, in spite of the fact that we are performing according to rules, the products of these rules, our sentences, can refer to something other than the game itself, simply ought not to be asked. The reason: they are not intended to refer to something outside. If outside references are not intended, the pontifical bridge-building by positivists is superfluous. Similarly with Malinowski. If there are no fossils in any society and if any society is a functioning system as it stands at any one moment, the pontifications of historicists are redundant. Full marks to Wittgenstein for transferring the Project from societies to language; but no marks for anything else. The profession of the Project is very old indeed.

Nobody disputes that it is extraordinarily difficult to explain or account for outside reference, be it in societies (to their past) or in linguistic expressions to a world of real events. Nobody would dispute, furthermore, that the bridges envisaged by both historicism (to the past of societies) and by positivism to the outside world are extremely shaky. But one ought to dispute that the recommendation that therefore one ought to stay at home and regard language use as a language-game governed entirely by its own rules, is a viable alternative. At least one ought not to resign oneself to this alternative before one has weighed the suggestion that we can think of the relationship in question as a relationship of pattern matching. Linguistic expressions, one could argue, "make" an image. This image or the propositions describing it – it is difficult at the moment to be very precise – can then be "matched" against the outside world and adjusted to make a better "fit". This process could be thought of as a selection of the best "fits" and would therefore require the making of a very large number of proposals, so that there is something to be selected from. Even if one is not prepared to entertain possibilities other than those offered by Positivism or by other mirror philosophies, there still remains the fact that the Malinowski-Wittgenstein strategy of withdrawal to the inside is an old strategy and that if one is taking stock of the history of philosophy one ought to see it as such and not credit Wittgenstein with the invention of the withdrawal stratagem. That stratagem has been proposed whenever there has been unease about relationships. It was practiced by Spengler before Malinowski and by Herder and Voltaire before Spengler. This is the line of succession where Wittgenstein belongs. The ideas of the later Wittgenstein who was running away from the shaky bridges necessitated by his *Tractatus* and its picture sentences, belong with Voltaire, Herder, Spengler, Malinowski, and Ruth Benedict. Rorty does not think so. He considers Wittgenstein's stratagem to have been original and he puts Wittgenstein together with Kierkegaard, Goethe, Santayana, and William James on the periphery of philosophy (p. 367) – where the philosophers who, in Rorty's words, "distrusted the notion that man's essence is to be a knower of essences" are. This is not a bad description of these philosophers, though I would include Kant in this group and exclude Wittgenstein. Kant's apotheosis of the noumenal self and his distinction of the noumenal self from the phenomenal self surely qualifies for inclusion in this distinguished group. But if Rorty had included Kant, he would have weakened his claim that all these splendid fellows are on the periphery. As I observed before, Wittgenstein only qualified, if at all, for inclusion in this group by transferring the Malinowski stratagem from sociology to linguistics. With the inclusion of Kant, the distrust of the notion that man's essence is exhausted by the ability to "know" ceases to be peripheral.

The glaring idiosyncracies of Rorty's history of philosophy amply show that he is not just taking stock of the history of philosophy. He is writing his own special version of it in order to prove that Oakeshott was right. There are many people who have suspected this all along. For them, Rorty's effort to prove it by an appeal to homemade – or ought we say to Rorty-made history? – is redundant. There are many other people who have never believed it. They are quite unlikely to be won over by Rorty's historical method.

Nevertheless, Rorty's book has merit and it was not for nothing that I devoured it with unflagging attention in the most uncomfortable circumstances conceivable. I have ever since my student days in Cambridge been very fond of Oakeshott. I have always found Heidegger particularly repulsive and Wittgenstein totally uninteresting. Rorty now has demonstrated that if one flirts with Oakeshott one will end up in the arms of Heidegger and Wittgenstein, a fate worse than death. This realization, if nothing else, will wean me permanently from Oakeshott.

9. *The Conversation of Mankind. A tragi-comedy entitled* Kibitzing *in one act. The resemblance between the opinions expressed by the characters and some real opinions is not accidental.*

Rorty is curiously silent about the sort of talk that would be going on in these charmed circles where edification rather than knowledge holds sway. It is all very well to determine the philosophers' place in culture and define what they may and what they may not do in that place. But readers are entitled to be told what the conversation of mankind actually consists of. This is not just a question of idle curiosity but of real importance. On p. 370, Rorty is very uncomplimentary about the search for knowledge and dismisses it as a very boring search for duplicates of what we already have out there – duplicates in the mind, I suppose, of what is already out there, outside the mind. Having first dismissed the mirror metaphor as inadequate he now accepts it and says that knowledge is just reflections in the mirror and therefore very boring. I would have thought that with all that criticism of mirrors on the preceding 369 pages, he would feel it encumbent either to say nothing about knowledge or to provide an alternative description. But to dismiss it now as just "boring" because it is nothing but a double of what is out there sounds as if he accepted the mirror philosophies after all but was merely bored by the kind of knowledge mirrors provide. I think that if Rorty really found out what happens when we have knowledge, he would not be bored at all. His trouble is that he first paints a caricature of knowledge as reflections in a mirror and then says that the knowledge which consists of such reflections is boring and that he, for one, prefers the open spaces where new things happen to the world of mirror images. But, I suppose, Rorty is no worse than any of us.

Once we have made up our minds that we do not like something, in this case knowledge, we make a caricature of it so that we can pretend we have good reason for not liking it. We have examined the inadequacies and failings of Rorty's caricature at some length. But we are now entitled to know what the alternative which Rorty likes so much, really is. It is fortunate that, in the absence of any clear information from Rorty, I am able to make good this omission and flesh out Rorty's fantasies by drawing on my own memory of a recent conversation of mankind which was indeed memorable and which I had the good fortune to attend.

I had arrived a day early in town and had a free evening. I stayed at the Hotel de la Gare which was all I expected – cheap, old-fashioned, solidly comfortable. I dined in the restaurant and ate one of my favorite meals – two *oeufs cocotte à la crème*, a large *sole meunière* (The place was close enough to the sea. The fish of the local river are inclined to be muddy), and an adequate Camembert. I drank a well-iced pint of Rosé d'Anjou and had a Hennessy Three Star with my coffee. After dinner I looked in the local gazette for announcements of entertainments and to find out what the bears in the backroom were doing that night. As it happened there was a tremendous choice that evening. Somebody was lecturing on the bronze statues by Phidias which had been recovered from the Mediterranean off the coast of Calabria. There was a seminar about somatic responses and adaptive evolution in which a young Canadian biochemist promised to communicate startling discoveries about immune responses of the body which might support some form of Lamarckism after all. In another place there was a discussion about time-warps and black holes; and, in another, somebody was lecturing on newly discovered skulls and the earliest hominids. Being naturally of a curious bent of mind, my mouth was beginning to water when my eyes fell on an advertisement of a symposium on witchcraft. Mary Douglas was to introduce the Senior Witch from Boro-Boro-Land who would outline witch responses to certain forms of stomach cramps. I knew perfectly well that witchcraft was not very fashionable at the moment and well aware that its temporary demise had nothing to do with the dawn of rational enlightenment. On the contrary, it had lost much ground since we have had strong central government which has enabled us to look upon ambitious upstarts as noxious perverts. Being on the side of centralized orthodoxy, we do not need to take witches seriously. But then, who knows, what with punks and trade unions and inflation, central government may soon be weak again. Then the idea that there are witches will be manipulated by the border against abuses of power at the center and our so-called rational enlightenment will make way for witchcraft just as, a few centuries ago, witchcraft had given way to science – not because it was a dark shadow put to flight by the dawn of reason but because the social border had become weak and power at the center had grown strong. Shifts in power manipulation, however, are always temporary and in ten years from now some knowledge of witchcraft may again command a great deal of respect. Anyway, knowledge is knowledge and there is very little to choose between one form and another. It was also very hard to choose among all the other offerings.

After all, black holes is all very well and so is biochemistry. But who is to say whether such knowledge is worthwhile or more worthwhile than a lecture on phlogiston or on Newtonian mechanics? I was at a loss to decide.

As the time passed and I was still undecided I became a little drowsy with the wine I had drunk and the glass of Cointreau with which I had washed down the Port I had had after dinner did not exactly help. At the moment just when I was staring disconsolately into the middle distance with my glassy eyes, the bartender recognized me for the famous cardsharp that I was and lent across the table: "If I may say so, Sir", he whispered, "the high rollers are in town tonight; it's aces high and deuces wild in there tonight. Real classy culture, Sir"; and then, leaning even further towards me, with a furtive glance around the room lest anybody was listening: "Real high stakes, them is", he said, "at No. 1 Oakeshott Lane, in the cellar. But mind the cultural overseers. Them have been very active these days, them have! They are now in uniform and trained by Mr. Pelman. Real nasty them is these days". He was gone before I could express an interest in the information. But I recalled that I had heard earlier that some of the finest minds of America had flown in to take part in a game and that the waiter who had held back patiently as I was scouring the wine list, had whispered discreetly: "If I may say so, Sir, Quine and Davidson and Kripke are in town". My mind was made up in a jiffy. This game was for me. "To hell with knowledge", I said to myself. Has not my great teacher Rorty taught me that this century's superstition is nothing but last century's triumph of reason and that the latest vocabulary borrowed from the latest scientific achievement does not say anything about truth and reality; but that it is just another of the potential infinity of vocabularies in which the world can be described? (p. 367). Fortified by such advice and confronted by all these tedious and arbitrary alternatives, not even instruction in a fine skill like witchcraft seemed very attractive. If today's superstition is yesterday's reason, tomorrow's reason is likely to be the superstition of the day after tomorrow. In any case, having just spent six weeks skiing in Colorado, my need for culture was greater than my desire for knowledge, so-called. I decided, at the drop of a hat, to seek admission to the conversation of mankind promised for this evening. The very thought of some real culture in place of all that doubtful knowledge made my mouth water. I suddenly realized how delighted I would be if I could hear Kenneth Minogue say: "If it is true that today we are all Marxists, we still have a choice between Karl and Groucho". And if not Minogue, I might catch some such snippet from Stuart Hampshire as "Ordovico or Viricordo, teems of times and happy returns" even if it was only a quotation from Joyce. Or perhaps I would be privileged to hear Urmson and Hampshire argue about Austin. Hampshire thought that Austin thought that language is perfect and that its distinctions and nuances reflect *real* necessity. Urmson has maintained that Austin never thought that common speech is adequate but had merely wanted to show how one can do certain things with certain words. I once heard Lévi-Strauss say that contrary to Austin one can do words with things and ever since I have wanted to get this matter settled. I was not optimistic, though. Lévi-Strauss was, after all, an outsider and I hardly expected him to be able to take an intelligent interest in this great question. But Hampshire and Urmson had both known Austin personally and their fundamental disagreement as to what it was he had said was truly astonishing and proof of the profundity of all disagreements. These and similar expectations made my mind reel with wonder. I became really excited at the thought of so much edification. All that knowledge about black holes and hominids, witchcraft and biochemistry that was being bandied about is, at best, merely an accurate representation, a sort of double, of what is already there. I was dying, I mused, to hear edifying philosophers keep space open for the sense of wonder which poets can sometimes evoke – wonder that there is something new under the sun, something which is not just a duplicate of what is already there (p. 370).

The way to the *Conversazione* led me along large avenues with beautiful vistas, past well-lit windows and open halls. There were crowds of people everywhere, merry and noisy. I thought of all those duplicates of what was already there which were being dished out in those open halls, behind those lit-up windows and did not envy the throng waiting patiently at the open gate to the hall where the lecture on time-warps was to take place. "I wonder how they will accurately represent time-warps", I said to myself. "They are out there, beyond the moon", I mused. "Who cares to have a duplicate in the hall?" I certainly did not envy all those people who were queuing to see nothing more exciting than a duplicate of a time-warp. I wondered, as I quickened my step, why so many people are so keen to have duplicates of what is there. It must be some kind of greed, I supposed. Like preferring two cans of beer to one. "Funny peculiar! that human greed which stops people being really cultured!" I said to myself. "Well, it is not for nothing that greed is a deadly sin. It's nothing much to do with morals, sin has. It is sinful to be greedy because it keeps you away from culture. Just look at all these greedy people, shoving and pushing one another to get duplicates – just plain greed. Why can't they be satisfied with the one time-warp that they already have out there? Why do they need two? And when they have two, I bet they will want a third!" I was beginning to feel really pure now, as I firmly directed my steps away from knowledge, towards the pursuit of culture. Not those dens of vice for *me*! I was longing for the open spaces of real culture, where greed was despised and distrusted and new things would be happening all the time. "What's new, though?", I started to wonder. "Knowledge could be new; but distrust just by itself is really old hat". However, I quickly dismissed such doubts from my mind. The thought of those open spaces lured me on and put all doubts to rest.

As I was hastening along, I could not help having more doubts. They just kept lingering. "I wonder how they will actually make a double of a time-warp", I said to myself. "After all, it is not visible and will not show up in a mirror, not even in the mirror of the mind. So what would a 'double' look like? And when they come to the Quantum Mechanics of it, and when they are trying to make a double of the path of a photon, will that double look like a corpuscle or like a ray? And how does one make 'doubles' of things which are either in a certain place or take a certain time but never both at once? They must be real wizards", I told myself and shook my head. I became so intrigued by this conundrum about duplicates that I had a good mind to turn back to find out. I even pursued the thought about duplicates. "When I identify something as a table, that identified image is not just a duplicate, surely! In identifying an object as a table, I must be abstracting, I must be spotting regularities. But regularities can never be duplicates of anything because the mere idea that there are regularities goes beyond anything I can see or watch and therefore is much more than can show up in a mere mirror". I was on the point of turning back when I suddenly pulled myself together. "Naughty, naughty? Stop being so greedy and don't try to rationalize your greed by saying that you are curious. You are just greedy, for Rorty has told you that knowledge is just a duplication of what is there and now you want to go back to that lecture on time-warps to get another time-warp dished up, as if the one that was out there wasn't enough for you. You are only making it worse by saying to yourself that time-warps cannot be duplicated and that if somebody is talking knowledgeably about them, he is not duplicating them. More like a double-talk, he, he, he . . . " I chuckled. "And don't come back with that old story, even though it is one of Rorty's own stories, which says that knowledge is not what is being mirrored for minds aren't mirrors. True, Rorty once said so; but he knows it is nonsense all the same and that to know is nothing more than having a double". I comforted myself with my photographic memory and saw p. 370 clearly black on white in front of my eyes. I hastened down the road and took a right turn.

My way led me away from the madding crowd into dark alleys, and eventually into a cul-de-sac. The windows of the houses became smaller and darker and I noticed as I was approaching my destination that the street lights had gone out. There was hardly a soul to be seen in this part of town. My heart began to beat faster when I was suddenly and rudely stopped by a posse of uniformed men. They were the cultural overseers, dressed neatly in their uniforms. These guards, mockingly referred to by some of my frivolous friends as philosopher kings, had always been in mufti until, quite recently, they had been allowed to wear uniform. For while for centuries recruitment had been fairly lax, there now was a new rule which stipulated that only graduates from Mr. Pelman's Correspondence School in Rationalism were to be admitted to be cultural overseers. These new people showed all the arrogance of their predecessors but displayed a new nastiness. For as graduates of Mr. Pelman's Correspondence Courses, they had not really become steeped in many of those charming old doctrines about knowledge. They had instead been taught how to behave *as if* they knew all about knowledge. They had been taught to sport the outward appearance, rather than the deeper know-how which, at any rate, comes only from class and tradition and cannot be taught. And now I was being questioned as to my business by these ruffians.

"What do you hope to find down here?", they demanded to know. "Have you passed the right examinations?" And "How do you know that the men taking part in the *Conversazione* conform to the requirements for culture? Or are you just guessing?" To be sure, none of these fellows knew the answer either. But the graduates of Mr. Pelman had learnt to behave as if they did. And since I did not know the answers, I was really in a spot, for I knew that these cultural overseers could easily prevent me from joining the conversation of mankind if I failed to pass their tests. Their standards were very rigid – as rigid and brittle as only mirrors can be. There was no arguing with them, for they *knew*, or so they said. I quickened my step and just as their leader grabbed me by my lapels, I gained the steps leading into the dark cellar where the *Conversazione* was about to begin. "What cheek", I said to myself. "Here are these half-educated louts who call themselves cultural overseers just because they have some special knowledge about knowledge. I bet they would like to stop me listening to the conversation of mankind and make me attend one of those dreary lectures on biochemistry instead". I wondered whether they would have been more approving of me had I been on my way to the Seminar on witchcraft. I doubted it. Their rigid standards would have made them frown on all but the most fashionable cognitive pursuits.

As I was wending my way down the spiral stairway into that dark cellar which was to be illuminated by *real* culture, I was very nearly disappointed; only, this time by a legitimate impediment. I discovered what I ought to have expected: I had some real difficulty in gaining admission. Naturally, as some kind of game was to be played and as the rules were to be binding on all members and since no prior rules were available, they had to be very careful as to who would be allowed in. For once inside, I would be part of the rule constituting group and naturally, they scrutinized me carefully at the door. There seemed to be general agreement that the blind, the insane, and other obvious deviants would not be allowed in. Now I am not blind, but I am deaf in one ear and I do confess to some rather kinky sexual tastes. But then deafness was no bar, though blindness was. And whatever I am, I am not insane and my kinky tastes are not obvious to the naked eye even though they might have been to some naked bodies. I was lucky then that a certain sense of decorum prevailed at the door and that, for scrutiny, they used the eye even though ocular metaphors were, as a whole, frowned upon. All the same, there was some quarreling at the door. There were some who insisted that the scrutinizing guardians at the door were no better than the cultural overseers and that training or absence of training by Pelman was irrelevant and might constitute only a difference in degree. Rorty seemed a bit floored by this argument but Oakeshott came to his rescue. The overseers, he said, exercised their tyranny on the basis of knowledge and existed to ostracize people who had wrong knowledge. But the guardians of the *Conversazione* performed their duty purely on moral and political grounds. They would never deny access to fools, only to people guilty of improper or dubious conduct.

Once inside I was immediately enveloped in a warm air of conviviality. Outside there had been a ferocious storm with hail and sleet. But inside, the windows were covered by heavy curtains. The light was dim and there was the welcoming crackle of an open fire. Everybody was seated in comfortable armchairs and for all we knew, the heavy curtains separated us from the thundering inclemency of the equinoxial gales. Inside, we were sheltered and able to forget the driving rain through which we had fought our way to reach this sheltered enclosure.

As I was nestling back in my chair, I realized that in a sort of mild way, the culture had already started. There had indeed been some kind of an argument as to what sort of game was to be played. Dummett wanted us to play Tarot and had brought with him his heavy tome on that delightful game. But Rorty had insisted that Tarot was not sufficiently cultural and that we should play kibitzing instead. Nobody knew the rules; but since we were all neither blind nor obvious deviants and none of us insane, this was finally deemed to be sufficient guarantee that the rules would be understood and observed by all. And so, just as I was stretching my legs comfortably, the conversation of mankind began. We were all confident that knowing the rules of kibitzing none of us would make a blunder. That much we all remembered from our Wittgenstein.

I will now report the conversation of mankind as faithfully as I can remember. I have to speak, of course, from memory, as it is one of the rules of the game of kibitzing that no notes are to be kept lest there might be argument afterwards, about the good sense of what the participants had said and lest they be committed to what they had said in the game of kibitzing when they were playing other games. This rule really followed from the idea that a blunder is only a blunder in a particular game. Thus there would be no point in taking notes and then keeping people when they were playing a different game, say Tarot, to the views they had expressed when playing kibitzing. Anyway, subsequent arguments would not have been very edifying, and edification, it was agreed, was the sole purpose of the whole exercise. Arguments are never edifying. "Is it not lucky", Alice said, "that I do not like arguments. For if I did, I would have to pursue them and I would not like that at all!"

QUINE: One can't distinguish between matters of fact and of definition. When a native agrees that bachelors aren't married, we can never know whether they are forced to say so by their own language or simply because they have never experienced anything to the contrary.

KRIPKE: How do you know?

RORTY: He does not have to *know*. Knowledge is boring and vulgar and smacks of the disagreeable arrogance of the overseers who waylaid most of us. In here we are all gentlemen and are playing a game. Quine says what he says because the rules of our game permit him to say it. Knowledge would just be a duplication of what there is. One thing out there is quite enough. Who wants a replica in his mind? Quine is kibitzing, not pretending to know something. He is doing it so well that he has just scored a full house. I declare him to be the kibitz of the night!

(Applause)

QUINE: Well, yes, thank you very much. Now let me see. After all, bachelors might be 'gavagais' if we heard a native say 'gavagai' when he sees a bachelor. But how do I know when I listen to the native that he is interested, when he says 'gavagai', in medium-sized enduring physical objects. He might mean space-time objects whose sexual goals are non-bonded and indeterminate, sex-parts, so to speak, rather than one sex-role.

GOODMAN: I must say, I like that. I have always insisted that all bachelors are unmarried. But those bachelors who were unmarried before last Christmas are bleen bachelors. Don't you agree? To a native, they would be bleen gavagais. I certainly could get myself to talk about bleen gavagais. But I would find it very hard to get myself to say that any gavagai is grue. Only emeralds tested for color before last Christmas are grue. Gavagais never! Grue gavagais, indeed! Grue gavagais would be a pain.

SELLARS: I wonder! When I say I am in pain, I do not give an accurate description of my experience. So why should a gavagai not be grue? If I tried to describe experience I would be prey to the myth of the given. The real question is whether we can doubt that a gavagai is grue. I doubt it. All I can say, I repeat, is that I accept my own report about my pain because I cannot see how I could doubt it. Somewhat negative, you might say. Thank God, I am not in real pain.

DAVIDSON: Negative or not—people *are* neurological systems and our understanding of these systems cannot be displaced by people as passive instances of historical patterns. In this matter, I am a truly methodological humanist.

MALCOLM: I do not like this at all. It seems to me that you are questioning the framework propositions of the system, whether neurological or not. The framework propositions, however, are not to be put to the test.

DAVIDSON: No, I cannot agree. The truth conditions have to be found. To find them, we must adopt a principle. We must correlate sentences of the language under study with those of one's own language in such a way as to make speakers of the language under study emerge as saying what one takes to be true.

QUINE: This really sounds amazing to me. Gavagai is not a rabbit? How can you know that it is?

KRIPKE: I know that it is because meaning does not determine reference. We name things by baptizing them. We do not create them out of a list of qualities. Names are rigid designators.

RORTY: Well now, you really *are* exploding a bit of a bomb.

DUMMETT: I'll say! It is the other way around. Meaning determines reference. Names are shorthand for the list of qualities we have decided to use to identify occasions on which we shall use a name.

KRIPKE: I am not given to hiding behind authorities but I would like to know whether you have ever heard that Heidegger said that language is the home of being. He meant that things are born together with their names.

RORTY: Jolly good! I like the way you drag Heidegger in. I do not think you should say "I like to know" because that sounds as if you were a foundational epistemologist and knew what the universally valid framework of knowing is. But I do like the way you bring in Heidegger. I really like that. I know that if he were alive, he couldn't come into this game, not now that we know of his moral turpitude with Hannah Arendt. We do have standards of admission. But I do like to think that if he had not had an affair with Hannah Arendt he could have come in.

GEACH: I agree. Actually, I think that Heidegger could have come in anyway. After all if we can have the Dalai Lama, we can have Heidegger. And I do know that at any time the Dalai Lama *is* some man.

QUINE: I can't accept this. Any temporal stage of the Dalai Lama is a *stage* of some man. This division over time does not go deep.

GEACH: Oh, yes, it does! If you do not recognize such alternatives *in rebus* you make hay of law and morals.

QUINE: You are a good one to talk of morals when you are willing to let Heidegger in. After all, I used to know Hannah Arendt. But I will let you use the Dalai Lama. Nevertheless, temporal stages of objects are objects. At least I regard them as objects.

GEACH: These objects are mere dreams of our language.

MALCOLM: Dreams *are* language.

STRAWSON: I think the trouble with Quine is that he supposes that the real vehicles of reference are bare logical variables shorn clean of descriptive content.

FODOR: Excellent. I call this the language of thought.

DAVIDSON: I'm not so sure. Language, action, and belief are to be approached as a whole. Our interpretation of another person's speech is a theory about one unified thing. After all, language, action, and belief are a unity.

GEACH: No, I maintain that mental utterances are an interior language. When we judge, the mind exercises concepts. The content of a judgement comprises a complex of ideas which represent things. I would suggest that these ideas be identified with words. To judge that the sky is blue is to say in one's heart "the sky is blue".

FODOR: No, not at all. The representational theory of mind is a substantive thesis *and* an empirical thesis and its success is not as a meta-language but depends on whether it serves the theoretical needs of psychologists.

DAVIDSON: I have a grand idea: The core of a theory of language is a specification of its truth conditions!

DUMMETT: What do you mean by that?

DAVIDSON: I mean – to specify the conditions under which sentences are true.

DUMMETT: You are going too fast. Help! Help?

AYER (who had been hiding under a chair, suddenly appears as a *Deus ex cathedra*, disguised as Tom Stoppard): I think that if Dummett is shouting for help we ought to rescue him. After all, he *is* the most distinguished philosopher writing at present in the English language. It is rather worrying that he should be shouting for help.

DUMMETT: We confer meaning on our words one by one. I atomize Davidson.

QUINE: How can so many of these atoms claim to be Davidson?

GEACH: I have solved the problem why different crowds of atoms claim to be Davidson.

STRAWSON: Linguistic notions of reference and predication belong to the metaphysical categories of particular and general.

GEACH: I do not agree and I protest. It is wrong to account for grammatical asymmetry between referring terms and predicates by means of metaphysical distinctions between spatio-temporal particulars and general concepts.

STRAWSON: No, it is not!

GEACH: Oh yes, it is! Even the attempt to do so is a mistake.

STRAWSON: Why do you not accept that the referential function of proper names is entirely indexical?

GEACH: Because not all concepts individuate objects. But there are various legitimate diachronic identifications of physical objects.

QUINE: I find that very gratifying, but it does seem strange to me that I seem to be agreeing with Geach.

GEACH (after a short pause): I have solved the problem why different crowds of atoms compete for the claim to be Davidson or the table. Being the same *A* is equivalent to being many different *B*'s. After all, in an extensional system with single predicates we can stipulate what happens to a fixed vocabulary. I stipulate that these atoms be Davidson.

QUINE: I wonder whether this can be true. After all Davidson thinks and stones do not. Yet Geach's stipulation could also be made of stones. Stones never think, as it happens. Probably an accident; but nevertheless, they do not think.

RORTY: I wonder. On this difficult question we will have to consult the epistemic authority of the meeting.

KRIPKE: I do not think that will be necessary. I maintain, though I have no epistemic authority, that we baptize things which do not think "stones". "Stone" is simply the designator of stones. Simple!

DUMMETT: Not at all simple. "Stone" is but the shorthand of a list of qualities which, when we detect them, entitle us to call a thing a stone.

GEACH: Dummett's trouble is that he wants to know what thoughts *are*. Who cares what we think of stones?

DUMMETT: I do not care, but I do want to push the question further back. What is the list of qualities which entitle us to use the shorthand "thoughts"?

KRIPKE: "Thoughts", "stones", "unicorns"– it all comes to the same. We cannot even say under what circumstances there would have been unicorns.

QUINE: Now I really must protest. Of course we can say under what circumstances there would have been unicorns. We know perfectly well why horned animals have two horns. If the evolutionary pressures would have been different, we might have had animals with one horn. It is really a question of biological knowledge.

RORTY: Now you are bringing in knowledge again. This is against the rules. Knowledge is science and science is ruled out because it is just a duplication of what there is.

GEACH: The trouble with "science" is that it lets in the fishy enterprises of psychology and evolution; but excludes history. The trouble with Quine is that he loves science.

QUINE: Well, I do feel a bit guilty for loving science. But let me assure you – and I am very keen on getting this straight lest you expel me from the conversation of mankind and make me join those uncouth cultural overseers who are roaming the streets of our clean little town – that it is really only an accident that I believe in physical objects and not in Homer's gods. In point of epistemological footing the objects and the gods differ only in degree, not in kind. Those physical objects of science (even if I do love them) are conceptually imported into the situation as convenient intermediaries, not by definition in terms of experience, but simply as irreducible posits comparable epistemologically to the gods of Homer. Now, can I stay? Does this make me qualify for the conversation of mankind?

There was a round of applause. Quine had played the game, even though he loved science. He would not be expelled. But as he was talking, my mind had begun to wander a little. When Geach had said: "The trouble with Quine is that he loves science" I was reminded of another famous conversation of mankind I had once seen in a movie. The film was called *La Grande Bouffe* and showed a charmed circle of four famous film stars closeted for a weekend in a country house where they were doing nothing but cooking and overeating. On Saturday evening Marcello Mastroianni had become a little bored and proposed that he go out and find a couple of girls to help with the entertainment. The others were against the idea because the girls and sex would distract them from eating. But one of them said: "Let him go. The trouble with Marcello is that he loves life. He is a coward. He is afraid to die!" Well, fortunately for Quine, he did love science; but not too much. His confession of faith in culture was accepted and unlike Marcello Mastroianni, he did not really pursue his apostasy – at least not far enough to be expelled. My mind was boggling at this display of edifying culture. Boy, oh boy! Was I edified! When Quine had confessed to a love of science and then retracted and when Geach had attacked evolution, my mind began to over-boggle. These were indeed not just mind-boggling but truly mind-blowing displays of culture. What wit! What repartee! My memory begins to fail me. All I can remember, after these last words, is that the evening passed like a flash of lightning. One good kibitz chased another and there was no end, mind everlasting. Oh for the joys of real culture! by comparison with which the idle thrills of curiosity gratified in the pursuits of science and knowledge, are dwarfed and obliterated. Here, where kibitz is as kibitz does, was the real conversation of mankind, compared to which all other human activities are but vanity, the vanity of vanities.

Enough said. With this kind of conversation in full swing, philosophers would always be assured of a place in culture. Provided they could, like Quine, keep a check on their love of science and control their curiosity, philosophers, if nobody else, would be certain of a bright future. At one stage the proposal to make Quine the kibitz of the evening was repeated and greeted with a round of thunderous applause and repeated shouts of "bravo!" For the rest of the evening, the conversation of mankind seemed drowned by joviality, conviviality, and fraternization. From time to time I thought I detected even cries of "bis!" so that I thought myself, for a moment, in the Teatro della Scala itself, than which there could be nothing *more* cultural. I realized then that there would always be job opportunities for philosophers and that with such cultured demands for more, philosophers for one would never be out of jobs – no matter what the current rate of unemployment might be.

Chapter XVII

Must Naturalism Discredit Naturalism?

By Antony Flew

> *When we hear of some new attempt to explain reasoning or language or choice naturalistically, we ought to react as if we were told someone had squared the circle or proved $\sqrt{2}$ to be rational: only the mildest curiosity is in order—how well has the fallacy been concealed?*
>
> Peter Geach, *The Virtues**

I. Preface

This paper is a sermon preached on the above text. Part I distinguishes evidencing from motivating reasons for believing, arguing that the presence of the latter does not foreclose on the possibility of someone having and knowing that they have the former also: the psychologizing and sociologizing of believers is, therefore, no substitute for the rational examination of beliefs. Part II ridicules and refutes certain reckless and arrogant claims, made on behalf of both psychoanalysis and the sociology of belief, claims which imply that there is no such thing as knowledge properly so called. Part III contends that it must be similarly suicidal to pretend to have discovered that we humans are all subject to a total necessitation, and incapable of choice: the crux is that knowing presupposes a capacity, in the light of criticism, either to maintain or to abandon beliefs; and this is a matter of choosing. Part IV shows that science does not have to be committed to the intellectual suicide of denying to man the peculiarities and potentialities which alone make knowledge possible: the key suggestion here is that only agents – creatures able both to do and to do other than they do do – could even understand the concepts either of choice or of natural necessitation and the contrary-to-fact. Finally it is noted that the protagonist of a naturalistic worldoutlook does not have to become committed to any self-discrediting claims about

---

An earlier version of this chapter has been published in the *Proceedings of the 11th International Conference on the Unity of the Sciences* (New York: ICF Press, 1983).

* Peter Geach, *The Virtues* (Cambridge: Cambridge University Press, 1977), p. 52.

the impossibility of objective knowledge or the unreality of choice; it is just that too many do!

Properly understood, the motto of the present paper expresses a maxim as sound as it is fundamental. The logical geography is, however, quite complicated. So there is a lot to be done if we are to come to appreciate both the implications and the limitations of this motto, as well as the reasons for insisting that we must make it ours. Whereas most of the other contributions to the present volume are concerned with the nature of scientific rationality, and hence with its promotion, mine tries to ward off subversive intellectual threats to the entire enterprise. Choice and language come in only and precisely in as much as, and in so far as, the capability of both is a presupposition of rationality; and, of course, of irrationality also.

II. Explanation as the Answer to Questions

1. In explaining and justifying our chosen motto the first points to seize are: that every explanation is an answer to a question; and hence that, whenever more than one question can be asked, there must be room for more than one answering explanation. Such alternative explanations, therefore, will not necessarily be rivals for the same logical space.

(a) The primary contention that explanations are answers to questions can be somewhat frivolously enforced, yet enforced none the less effectively, by reference to a recent Andy Capp comic strip. The tried and suffering Flo is shown protesting: "There was twelve light ales in the pantry this mornin'– now there's only ONE! 'ow d'yer explain THAT?" To which her incorrigible husband responds, with deadly predictability: "It was that dark in there, I didn't see it." The cartoonist Smythe felt no call to spell out the ways in which the intended question – about the eleven – differed from the question answered – about the one. Any such superfluous and heavy-footed spelling out should have taken notice also of the fractionally less obvious truth that the original challenge was, as so often, rather to justify the questionable than to explain the perplexing.

(b) The corollary of this primary contention – which is that explanations or, for that matter, justifications directed at different questions do not of necessity have to be competitors – had better be illustrated in a less light-hearted and more abstract way.

So consider next the speech act of asserting the familiar, colorless proposition p. There are certainly two, and indeed more than two, categorically different questions which can be asked about this pedestrian performance. One, in requesting an explanation why the performer believes that p, asks for a statement of that performer's warrant for so believing. It asks, that is to say, for his or her evidencing reasons for harboring the belief that p; for his or her evidencing justification for so doing.

The other, in requesting an explanation why the same person chose this particular occasion to express the belief that *p,* asks what was the point and purpose of this particular speech act. It asks, that is to say, for his or her motivating reasons for so acting. The answer given is always in the first instance an explanation, though sometimes it may also constitute an attempt at justification.

2. The crucial distinction between these two kinds of reason – the two senses, that is, both of the word 'reason' and of several associated terms and expressions – can be fixed firmly in mind by reflecting on Pascal's Wager.

(a) In presenting that argument Pascal begins by assuming that we have no sufficient evidencing reasons for holding that the propositions of the Roman Catholic religion are true. He then offers motivating reasons why we should nevertheless labor to become persuaded of their truth.[1] Once the key distinction has been mastered we are well on the way to losing all temptation to assume that evidencing reasons exclude motivating ones, or the other way about. It becomes easy to recognize that one and the same person can at one and the same time have both the strongest of motivating reasons for wanting to believe that *p,* and completely sufficient evidencing reasons to justify their in fact holding that boring old belief that *p.*

(b) A further source of temptation lies in the fact that most people make inquiries or press charges about possible motivating reasons for believing or not believing only when they feel entitled to assume that the available evidencing reasons provide insufficient warrant. They are thus inclined to construe all suggested motivating reasons as shoddy and shiftless substitutes for what is assumed to be lacking – what may even have been shown to be lacking; namely, adequate evidencing reasons. They and others then proceed to mistake it to be, in order to discredit any disfavored belief, both necessary and sufficient simply to provide motivating reasons why their opponents might want to harbor and express that belief. (By preference, of course, these suggested motivating reasons will be thoroughly sordid and self-interested.)

3. The psychologizing and sociologizing of believers thus replaces the rational examination of beliefs. It is a development which cannot but be attractive to those who have contrived, notwithstanding their own inadequacies, to grasp the critical initiative. It is the more attractive when these people are both aware of and even embarrassed by their manifest inability to meet their opponents in fair and

1. See, for instance, "Is Pascal's Wager the Only Safe Bet?" in my *God, Freedom and Immortality* (Buffalo: Prometheus, 1984); or Chapter VI Section 7 in *An Introduction to Western Philosophy* (Indianapolis and London: Bobbs Merrill, and Thames and Hudson, 1971).

open intellectual combat; and in such combat straightforwardly to refute what the more formidable of those opponents does actually maintain.[2]

Attempts by the means described in the previous paragraph to discredit are certainly not the prerogative of any particular place, or period, or party. But it is, I think, fair to say that in Britain during the last fifteen or so years the most persistent offenders have been on the left; and especially among the radical ultras. And what they have been most inclined to try to blow away with barrages of sociological and psychological speculation have been precisely those works seen as constituting very inconvenient, because scarcely answerable, intellectual and moral challenges.

Perhaps the most impressively scandalous examples of such still favorite controversial tactics were produced in treating – or, strictly, in avoiding treating – both the successive *Black Papers* and the so-called Gould Report.[3] However, for present purposes unfortunately, most of these performances appeared either in somewhat ephemeral publications or through the electronic media. So I now instead draw two complementary illustrations from one recent specimen of a sort of which has for many years been pouring from many of the most prestigious presses, and into the libraries and the reading lists of our departments of education.

(a)   Maidan Sarup promises "A Marxist Perspective" in *Education, State and Crisis*.[4] Reviewing what he in fact gives us we have to sympathize with that mellower Marx who is said to have sighed: "Thank God I am not a Marxist." For, when Sarup wants us to dismiss, say, "The attack on progressivism from the Right" (p. 6), it never enters his head actually to quote any of these dexterous attackers. Nor does he even attempt by reason to show either that their assertions are false, or that their arguments are invalid. Perhaps with the sheepishly uncritical students whom he and his sympathetic colleagues have, one presumes, gathered around their feet at Goldsmiths' College, it is indeed for their own indoctrinative purposes enough simply to have described the thoughts to be rejected as 'right-wing'? Certainly for Sarup himself it is both necessary and sufficient to sketch a speculative sociology of such alleged enemies of the workers' class. For instance: "What is important about Bennett's

2. In indicating these attractions I do, of course, come near to employing what I have myself found to be the only halfway effective countertactic: this consists in first developing some plausible yet aggressively unflattering account of the motivation of the original offenders; and then urging a general ban on all such weapons of intellectual mass destruction, in order to clear the way for face to face discussion of whatever substantive and first order issues may be in dispute.

3. C. B. Cox and A. E. Dyson, eds., *Fight for Education: A Black Paper* (London: Critical Quarterly, 1968); C. B. Cox and A. E. Dyson, eds., *Black Paper Two* (London: Critical Quarterly, 1969); C. B. Cox and A. E. Dyson, eds., *Black Paper Three* (London: Critical Quarterly, 1970); C. B. Cox and Rhodes Boyson, eds., *Black Paper 1975* (London: J. M. Dent, 1975); C. B. Cox and Rhodes Boyson, eds., *Black Paper 1977* (London: Temple Smith, 1977); and Julius Gould and others, *The Attack on Higher Education: Marxist and Radical Penetration* (London: Institute for the Study of Conflict, 1977).

4. London: Routledge and Kegan Paul, 1982.

book[5] is not what is contained within it, but how it came to be *used* in the ideological struggle" (p. 7; italics original).

(b)   More remarkably, this sort of largely *a priori* psychologizing and so-ciologizing serves Sarup as an ever-ready, thought-saving, dual-purpose substitute: not only for the labor of trying to refute what he instructs us to reject, but also for the toils of collecting and deploying some evidencing reasons for believing what he requires us to accept. "A Marxist Perspective" just is the one appropriate to, if not perhaps at present al-ways in fact cherished by, the approved social groups; and that putative sociological or psychological fact is itself all the warrant which that per-spective needs. Elements of Sarup's magisterium are thus presented as the *credenda* of an irreligious revelation. (No doubt, under the "repres-sive regime" established in the red base at Goldsmiths' College, students are directed, on pain of ploughing, to note down and on occasion to re-produce whatever agitprop the authoritarian indoctrinators see fit to propagate?)

For instance, Sarup offers a short and entirely abstract summary of the main contentions of Lenin's pamphlet *Imperialism, the Highest Stage of Capitalism*. This summary is offered as if it were by itself fully suffi-cient to show "how capitalism has grown into a world system of colonial oppression, and how in its economic essence imperialism *is* monopoly capitalism" (p. 94; italics original). Nowhere from beginning to end is there one single naming reference either to any actual colony—whether oppressed or otherwise—or to any particular private firm, whether in truth, or only alleged to be, enjoying and exploiting a monopoly position.

By the way: *aficionados* of the Popperian controversy between methodological holism and methodological individualism might put Sarup to a good use as their paradigm case of the former.[6] For Sarup is forever dogmatizing about the scurvy doings of such hypostatized ab-stractions as imperialism, racism, and capitalism. To him, it seems these are the real and ultimate historical agents, with mere flesh and blood human beings their almost never mentioned creatures. He is even pre-pared outright to denounce the "assumption that the individual is more important than the group or class . . . " (p. 9).

5. Neville Bennett, *Teaching Styles and Pupil Progress* (London: Open Books, 1976).
6. The best epitome I know of what this was or is about has been given in a private letter from J. W. N. Watkins, quoted in John O'Neill, ed., *Modes of Individualism and Collectivism* (London: Heinemann, 1973): "the real issue is something like this: social scientists can be roughly and crudely divided into two main groups: those who regard social processes as proceeding, so to speak, under their own steam, according to their own nature and laws, and dragging the people involved along with them; and those who regard social processes as the complicated outcome of the behaviour of human beings" (pp. 335–36n).

III. There is no Knowledge; They Know?

The first point made to elucidate and to defend the motto from Geach was that every explanation is an answer to a question; and hence that, wherever more than one question can be asked, there must be room for more than one answering explanation. In Part I the concentration was upon cases in which a particular explanation in terms of motivating reasons is mistaken either to preclude or to be an adequate substitute for an explanation or justification in terms of evidencing reasons. Consider now the far more devastating cases in which it is either asserted or assumed that the same holds absolutely and in general.

1. Take, as a terse and suitably textbook example, the reckless claim made by one who was in his day our leading British Freudian psychoanalyst:

> The analyst must above all be an analyst. That is to say he must know positively that all human emotional reactions, all human judgements, and even reason itself, are but the tools of the unconscious; and that such seemingly acute convictions which an intelligent person like this possesses are but the inevitable effect of causes which lie buried in the unconscious levels of his psyche.[7]

If this is truly knowledge, then what is here said to be known must be – for a start – true. Yet, if every time that anyone asserts anything their speech acts are nothing "but the inevitable effect of causes which lie buried in the unconscious", then, surely, the implication is that there cannot be – or at any rate that we cannot have and realize that we do have – good evidencing reasons for believing any of these assertions. But, if this goes for everyone, then it must have gone for the whole Fellowship of the Ring; not excluding even Dr. Freud himself.

In that case no one at all – not even the Founding Father – has ever known what we have just now been assured that at least every single working analyst must "know positively". The immediate consequence of Berg's Bombshell is thus simply that no one at all knows either *it*, or indeed anything else whatever. (How fortunate that all the rest of us can know as false what the psychoanalytic in-group are supposed to "know positively" as true, to say nothing of our knowing a good deal more besides!)

The psychoanalysts have got themselves into this preposterous predicament by the deft execution of a familiar yet misguided maneuver. It is a maneuver which has in the past been executed, and will in the future be executed again, both by recognized internal leaders of, and by self-appointed ideological commissars for, many other disciplines. Its nerve consists in turning a modest confession of professional limitation into a piece of aggressively deflationary metaphysics. What the spokesperson for psychoanalysis is perhaps both entitled and required to say, is that analysts must, *in their analytic hours,* limit their inquiries to the conscious and especially to the unconscious motives, purposes, intentions, and so forth of all the speech acts and other – as the behaviorists would say – behaviors of their patients. What such spokespersons are so often and so strongly tempted to do,

---

7. Charles Berg, *Deep Analysis* (London: George Allen and Unwin, 1946), p. 190.

is to insist that their own professional kind of questions is the only kind which can ever legitimately be asked and answered by anyone. The claim then is that their own prized and precious discipline has discovered that reality has, and can have, no aspects other than those with which it is itself exclusively concerned.

Other more or less significant tokens of the same type of maneuver are the claims, more or less seriously made: that nutritional studies have shown that foods consist in nothing else but so much protein, so much carbohydrate, and so much what-have-you, and that any gustatory characteristics which we might uninstructedly attribute are only "in the mind"; that an Aldiss Lamp being intelligently and competently employed can be fully described and fully understood without reference to the semantics of that signaling use; and that physics has revealed that things and happenings in the universe around us possess in reality only those primary qualities which physicists have found it possible to measure, and profitable to incorporate into their most fundamental theories.

2. Turning next to what is still stubbornly miscalled the sociology of knowledge, I confess my failure to lay hold on any parallel claim quite so forthright or quite so reckless as Berg's Bombshell. Yet it would, I fear, be much too flattering to suggest that all or even many of the currently most prominent practitioners are anxiously aware of the intolerable paradox implicit in such pronouncements, much less that they have acquired and learnt to handle the several critical concepts and categorical distinctions needed in order to avert such catastrophic explosions of self-discredit.

David Bloor, for instance, in attending to mathematical beliefs, suggests that his sociologist's conception of knowledge might replace that of the sociological layperson or of the philosopher; and hence that an account of the evidencing reasons for believing that *p* must be a rival to a sociologist's or an historian's explanation of why some group or some individual does or did in fact believe that *p*. First, "the sociology of knowledge might well have pressed more strongly in the area currently occupied by philosophers, who have been allowed to take on themselves the task of defining the nature of knowledge." Second, "when men behave rationally or logically it is tempting to say that their actions are governed by the requirements of reasonableness or logic . . . . If this is so it is not the sociologist or the psychologist who will provide the most important part of the explanation of belief." And, third, "the sociologist is concerned with knowledge, including scientific knowledge, purely as a natural phenomenon. His definition . . . will therefore be rather different from that of either the layman or the philosopher. Instead of defining it as true belief [not *justified* true belief?], knowledge for the sociologist is whatever men take to be knowledge."[8]

---

8. David Bloor, *Knowledge and Social Imagery* (London: Routledge and Kegan Paul, 1976), pp. 1, 2, and 5. My extensive Critical Notice of this book, under the title "A Strong Programme for the Sociology of Belief" appeared in *Inquiry* 21 (Oslo, 1983), pp. 365–78. This incorporates some material from "Is Scientific Enterprise Self Refuting?", in *Proceedings of the VIIIth International Conference on the Unity of the Sciences: Los Angeles 1979* (New York: International Cultural Foundation, 1980), Vol. I.

Two years earlier, in *Science Studies* for 1974 and under the strange, obnoxious title "Popper's Mystification of Objective Knowledge", Bloor had written:

> To appraise an argument for validity is to apply the standards of a social group. It cannot be other, or more, than this because we have no access to other standards . . . the objectivity of knowledge resides in its being the set of beliefs of a social group. This is why and how it transcends the individual and constrains him . . . The authority of truth is the authority of society. (pp. 75–76)

This phrase must, surely, have precisely the same ruinous force as the "merely" and the "nothing but" of our psychoanalyst. If so, then "objective knowledge" can be defined only as the approved beliefs of some approved social group.

Such a definition forbids us to assert, or even to assume, that there actually is what is ordinarily meant by "knowledge", as opposed to "whatever men take to be knowledge". Nor, this move having been allowed, may we maintain, even on non-sociological occasions, that any proposition is old-time true. What and all we may say is that some proposition is what some social group has – no doubt after negotiation – agreed to endorse as being what they take to be the truth.

How then are these groups supposed themselves to interpret their own claims? And what remains as the rational basis of anyone else's or even of their own pretensions to epistemological authority? Despite – indeed because of – the great offense which this pressing always and most significantly causes, we must never fail to press the question of the cognitive status of the professional productions of these same sociologists of belief themselves; and of those of all similar militants of an intellectual revolution of destruction!

It seems too that we have here in this proposed sociological redefinition of "knowledge" one more problem from the ancient stable of Plato's *Euthyphro:* "Is it good because the gods command it, or do the gods command it because it is good?"[9] Are known truths nothing but whatever beliefs some or any in-group endorses, or are they endorsed only because – hopefully – they embrace known truths?

3. The first of two more manifestly absurd examples of the same stubborn refusal to admit any genuine knowledge, as opposed to "whatever men take to be knowledge", is provided by Bloor's Edinburgh colleague Barry Barnes. In what was in effect a companion volume on *Scientific Knowledge and Sociological Theory*[10] Barnes opens the chapter entitled "The sociologist and the concept of rationality" by asserting:

9. In strict accuracy the *Euthyphro* (9C ff) discusses holiness rather than goodness: compare, for related passages in such other classical sources as Hobbes and Leibniz, the *Introduction* mentioned in note 1, above. Here and elsewhere Bloor and his like lay themselves wide open to Paul Feyerabend's objection to Kuhn: "He has failed to discuss the *aim* of science." See I. Lakatos and A. Musgrave, eds., *Criticism and the Growth of Knowledge* (Cambridge: Cambridge University Press, 1970), p. 201. This objection remains both fundamental and sound despite the deplored fact that its maker appears now himself to have abandoned that aim in favor of a frivolous and irresponsible Maoism. See his *Against Method* (London: New Left Books, 1975).

10. London: Routledge and Kegan Paul, 1974.

If due weight is given to the preceding arguments, no particular set of natural beliefs can be identified as reasonable, or as uniquely "the truth". . . . What is implied is . . . that the sociologist cannot single out beliefs for special consideration because they are *the* truth. (p. 22; italics original)

Had this passage stood alone it should perhaps have been construed in some alternative, more charitable way. But before the chapter ends Barnes is going to go on to make both himself and his aspiring discipline ridiculous by repudiating a rival sociologist's claim to know even what in my young day our elders used to pick out as "the facts of life". Poor Steven Lukes, who might as a Radical activist have hoped for rather more sympathetic treatment, is put down first for his "rampant inductivism". Worse still: "Lukes refers to the ignorance of physiological paternity among some people and their 'magical' notions of conception; he regards these notions as in violation of objective rationality criteria without making any attempt to show why" (p. 36). May we for our part not make so bold as to conjecture that Lukes, like most if not quite all contemporary adults, knows – repeat, *knows* – that those ignorant or magical beliefs are not merely thought to be, but nothing more nor less than are, false? For Lukes himself does not appear to be inhibited by any philosophical muddles or misconceptions requiring him to pretend to a heroically total nescience.

4. The second of our more manifestly absurd sociological examples is drawn from a book setting "New Directions for the Sociology of Education".[11] To appreciate the importance of this book you need to know that for ten or more years its profoundly obscurantist and educationally subversive doctrines have been preached as revealed truth both from the electronic pulpits of the Open University and in the more conventional lecture halls of the University of London Institute of Education. A substantial proportion of all Britain's potential or present state school teachers, therefore, either have been or are being exposed to this stuff.

The key contention, the misguiding thread, is never formulated in a properly terse, explicit, or completely categorical form. It is, nevertheless, perfectly clear what it is: the mere possibility of developing some sociological account of the desires and interests supporting the making of some kind of discrimination constitutes a sufficient demonstration that there is no objective basis for anything of the sort; that there are, that is to say, no corresponding differences "without the mind". The reason for describing this doctrine as educationally subversive is, therefore, quite simply, that it is. It forecloses on the possibility that any distinctions made by examiners may correspond to actual differences in the quality

11. M. F. D. Young, ed., *Knowledge and Control* (London: Collier-Macmillan, 1971). Compare both my "Metaphysical Idealism and the Sociology of Knowledge", in *Sociology, Equality and Education* (London, and New York: Macmillan, and Barnes and Noble, 1976), and Graham Dawson's "Unfitting Teachers to Teach: Sociology in the Training of Teachers", in A. Flew and others, *The Pied Pipers of Education* (London: Social Affairs Unit, 1981). The first is a systematic critique, the second argues for a substantial saving of counterproductive public expenditure by excising this cancer from the curriculum.

of the work and of the candidates examined. So what, please, are teachers supposed to be doing if it is not helping to bring out real improvements in the capacities and performances of their pupils?

The editor of this dreadful book, in a note to his own contribution, faults the authors of "an otherwise excellent paper" for "drawing a *metaphysical* 'out there' in terms of which, they claim, we must check our theories . . . " (p. 43n; italics original).[12] Again, Nell Keddie, one of his favorite contributors, after noting that "teachers differentiate . . . between pupils perceived as of high and low ability", forthwith dismisses the very idea that such perceived differences might actually subsist between those teachers' pupils: "The origins of these categories are likely to lie outside the school and within the structure of the society itself in its wider distribution of power" (p. 156).[13]

You may think this bad enough. Nevertheless, compared with Alan Blum, Nell Keddie could almost pass as an alert and unprejudiced research worker. Blum's bizarre essay is written from New York University. I will not resist quoting its climactic claim to a collective divinity of sociologists: "it is not," he says, "an objectively discernible, purely existing external world which accounts for sociology, it is the methods and procedures of sociology which create and sustain that world . . . sociologists have managed to negotiate a set of practices for creating and acting upon external worlds" (p. 131).

The Blessed and Undivided Trinity, therefore, has now to yield place to the American Sociological Association! Our immediate concern here, however, is with Blum's less megalomaniac yet equally wrong-headed denial of any genuine knowledge:

> Scholars who have traditionally sought to discover "objective" knowledge have had to contend with the fact that the search for and discovery of such knowledge is socially organized. . . . The implication is this: if objective knowledge is taken to mean knowledge of a reality independent of language, or presuppositionless knowledge, or knowledge of the world which is independent of the observer's procedures for finding and producing the knowledge, then there is no such thing as objective knowledge. (p. 128)

---

12. A contribution which contains, by the way, a commendation of "countries like North Korea" (p. 40) as opposed to "capitalist societies" (p. 28). Remarkably, the former are praised for what in the latter is abused – the providing of education relevant to future employment: one more example, it would appear, of radical bad faith.

13. From a great wealth of similar material in widely sold recent books I select an editorial pronouncement by R. Blackburn, ed., *Ideology in Social Science* (London: Collins Fontana, 1972): "the assumption that there exists a realm of facts independent of theories which establish their meaning is fundamentally unscientific" (p. 10). The apparent implication that no theory can be, by its failure to fit the theory-independent facts, shown to be false is, of course, most congenial to all those, like Blackburn himself, committed to the propagation of the most famous of all falsified sociological theories. For evidence that Marx himself already recognized essential elements of his system to be false see, for instance, Leopold Schwartzschild, *The Red Prussian* (London: Hamilton, 1948); and, for the continuing indifference to all falsification in our own Marxist contemporaries, compare R. G. Wesson, *Why Marxism?: The Continuing Success of a Failed Theory* (New York and London: Basic, and Temple Smith, 1976).

It is thus clear that Blum too believes that the sociology of belief reveals the impossibility of knowledge. Indeed one of the two sentences omitted from the passage quoted indicates that he has in his own fashion recognized this as a slightly awkward consequence of his position, although not as one for him to worry about: "Philosophically, this has often constituted a dilemma."

About Blum's too modestly minimized "dilemma" there is nothing more for us to say now. But even at this stage it is worth insisting that if he is not being merely slovenly in his word ordering, and if he does really mean to deny "knowledge of a reality independent of language", then his denial is grotesque. For it is indeed just plumb grotesque to maintain that – say – the stars in their courses are in any way dependent on what we say or do not say; and it is not for any sociologist to deny the claims of the natural scientists to know that this earth existed long before it bore any language-using creatures. If, on the other hand, Blum really intends to deny only propositional knowledge independent of language, then this is unexceptionable. Or, rather, it is unexceptionable so long as it is not mistaken to imply that the truths which we have to express in a particular form of words would not be true at all until and unless someone had formulated those truths in these or equivalent words. The crucial distinctions are: first, between knowing, and the truths which are known; and, second, between knowledge of a reality which is independent of language, and knowledge which is itself independent of language.

It is one thing, and scarcely disputatious or exciting, to say that the extent of our knowledge must be limited by, among other things, the quality and the quantity of the conceptual equipment which happens to be available to us. It is quite another, and as we have been reminding ourselves, utterly paradoxical and preposterous to hold that every reality of which we can have knowledge must be dependent upon our presence, and our activities, and our "observer's procedures", and our having the concepts required to possess and to express that knowledge. Embarrassing though the observation is, it does appear to be true that the shamefully simple confusions removed in this and the previous paragraph have been and remain perennial chief sources of the demoralizing dogma that any knowledge which we do possess must be, in some depreciatory and emasculating sense, essentially and only relative and subjective; the dogma – to put it in a brief, brutal and straightforward way – that there really neither is nor can be any such thing as, without prefix or suffix, knowledge.

IV. Knowing Presupposes Choosing

We began from a warning against every "new attempt to explain reasoning or language or choice naturalistically". So far we have concentrated on reasoning, and we have not truly tried to make explicit what Geach has in mind when he speaks of naturalistic explanation. The assumption has been that, at any rate when applied to "reasoning or language or choice", such an offering does not so much pretend to explain as to explain away. It is either mad or mistaken to imply a total rejection of the meaningfulness of any language, of the actuality of human choice, and of the realized possibility of having and giving good reasons. Since the first and last of these rejections must make an incoherent nonsense of the whole project of rational inquiry – the very project of which they are offered as a fruit – it is indeed right for us in those cases at least "to react as if we were told someone had squared the circle or proved $\sqrt{2}$ to be rational".

Yet nothing said in either Part I or Part II even begins to establish either that the same applies to all attempts to show that there is no such thing as choice, and how choice is as much a presupposition of rationality as is language; or that there can be no question of discovering causally sufficient psychological conditions of all the speech acts and other ongoings which are in fact involved when someone is truly said to have come to recognize the excellent evidencing reasons for believing – and hence perhaps to know – this or that.

1. Consider now one throwaway statement from a generally excellent book described by *Fortune* magazine as "A powerful indictment of the American criminal justice system".[14] This statement runs:

> Stated another way, if causal theories explain why a criminal acts as he does, they also explain why he *must* act as he does, and therefore they make any reliance on deterrence seem futile or irrelevant. (p. 58; italics original)

This, in what is here the appropriate sense of "cause", is false. It is as essential as it is uncommon to distinguish two fundamentally different senses of the word "cause". In one of these – the sense in which we speak both of the causes of astronomical phenomena and of ourselves as agents causing movements of inanimate objects – causes truly do, *pace* Hume and the whole Humean tradition, (not compel but) necessitate their effects.[15] Given the total cause, then nothing except a miraculous exercise of Supernatural power can prevent the occurrence of whatever is in fact the due effect. In this first, physical or necessitating interpretation, complete causal theories do indeed explain why what does happen *must* happen.

Yet it is only in a second, quite different, personal or inclining sense that we can talk of the causes of human action; whether criminal or otherwise. If I give you good cause to celebrate – perhaps by sympathetically informing you of some massive misfortune afflicting your most detested enemy – then I provide you with a possible motivating reason for celebration. But I do not thereby necessitate the

14. James Q. Wilson, *Thinking about Crime* (New York: Random House Vintage Books, 1977).

15. I first began to dispute with "the good David" on these issues in Hume's *Philosophy of Belief* (London, and New York: Routledge and Kegan Paul, and Humanities Press, 1961), Chapters VI–VIII. But it is only much more recently that I have begun to feel confident that I do at last know my way around. Therefore see, rather: *A Rational Animal* (Oxford: Oxford University Press, 1978), Chapter III and passim; "Inconsistency within 'a reconciling project' ", in *Hume Studies* 4 (1978); "Of the (Other) Idea of Necessary Connection", in *Philosophy*, 1982; and a Commentary on *Hume and the Problem of Causation*, in *Philosophical Books*, 1982, pp. 135–39.

occurrence of appropriate celebrations. You yourself remain not merely an agent but, as far as this goes, an altogether free agent.

Certain criminologists, seeking the supposed concealed causes of crime, once asked a convicted multiple bankrobber: "Why did you rob banks?" He replied, with the shattering directness of an Andy Capp: "Because that was where the money was." Not yet corrupted by any supposedly rehabilitatory Open University courses in sociology, he did not pretend that his criminal actions had been anything but actions. As an agent he was not, and could not have been, inexorably necessitated. This has to be true since, from the mere fact that someone was in some respect an agent, it follows necessarily that they were in that respect able to do other than they did.

Once this basic distinction between the two causes is mastered it becomes obvious that we need a parallel distinction between two determinisms. Certainly, to say that some outcome is fully determined by physical causes does carry rigorous necessitarian implications. But, equally certainly, to say that someone's actions are completely determined by causes of the other sort—earlier called motivating reasons—is, if anything, to presuppose the contrary. The "psychic determinism" to which Freud appealed in the psychological area is thus not the local application of a universal determinism of the first, necessitating sort. Instead the two appear to be flatly incompatible.[16] It is, therefore, diametrically wrong to try to conscript what historians and other social scientists offer as explanations of human actions *qua* actions to serve as support for a necessitarian determinism. On the other hand, if a naturalistic explanation is to be construed as one which provides a complete account in terms of necessitating physical causes, then Geach must be dead right to dismiss the possibility of any such explanation for the phenomena of choice.

2. The conclusions of the previous section 1 still leave room for both a question and an objection. The question is what is the link between choice, in this libertarian understanding, and rationality? The objection is that, if this is what choice implies, then there neither is nor could be any such thing. A suggestion in answer to the former comes from the second volume of the *Postscript* to Sir Karl Popper's *The Logic of Scientific Discovery*. But in order to overcome the latter I shall in my final Part IV have, without much apology, to defy his warnings against plunging "into the morass of language philosophy".[17]

---

16. The situation is complicated by the rarely noticed fact that the development of the notions of unconscious motivation involved not one but two conceptual innovations: it is not only a matter of attributing motivations to persons who are themselves unaware that they are being so moved; but also of construing as expressions of such unconscious desires, purposes, and what have you behaviors which are not actions, and hence not under the conscious volitional control of the patient—compulsive symptomatic tics and psychogenic paralyses, for instance. See, again, *A Rational Animal*, Chapters 8-9.

17. K. R. Popper, *The Open Universe: An Argument for Indeterminism* (London, and Totowa, N. J.: Hutchinson, and Rowman and Littlefield, 1982), p. xxi.

Popper quotes an argument deployed in *The Inequality of Man* by J. B. S. Haldane:

> I am not myself a materialist because if materialism is true, it seems to me that we cannot know that it is true. If my opinions are the result of the chemical processes going on in my brain, they are determined by the laws of chemistry, not those of logic.[18]

As it stands this argument is vitiated by a false antithesis. Suppose we elaborate and refine upon the illustration offered and the distinctions made in section 1 of Part I, above. Then we can now distinguish a third kind of question to be raised about all the ongoings involved in what would normally be described as the speech act of asserting the proposition *p*. This kind of question asks about the physical necessitating causes of some or all these events. If we discount for the moment the necessitarian implications of such physical causation, then there would seem to be no inconsistency in asking at one and the same time both for the evidencing reasons which the person had for believing *p*, and for the causes of all the various events which occurred in the course of that person's expressing the belief that *p*. On that first, temporary, discounting assumption no incompatibility subsists between – as Haldane at that stage put it – determination by the laws of chemistry and determination by the laws of logic.

But, after noticing that Haldane himself later repudiated both this argument and the conclusion which it was offered to support, Popper nevertheless urges that what Haldane really meant was something else:

> This is precisely Haldane's point. It is the assertion that, if "scientific" determinism is true, we cannot, in a rational manner, know that it is true; we believe it, or disbelieve it, but not because we freely judge the *arguments or reasons* in its favour to be sound, but because we happen to be so determined (so brainwashed) as to believe it, or even to believe that we judge it, and accept it, rationally.[19]

Now the heart of the matter becomes not whether our beliefs were caused by evidencing reasons, rather than by chemical processes in our brains, but whether we could by any means have believed other than we did. Unless we could we cannot take credit for having, as rational beings, judged that these beliefs are true. Popper proceeds to add an important, correct comment:

> This somewhat strange argument does not, of course, refute the doctrine of "scientific" determinism. Even if it is accepted as valid, the world may still be as described by "scientific" determinism. But by pointing out that, if "scientific" determinism is

18. *Ibid.*, p. 89.
19. *Ibid.*, pp. 92–93; italics original. I treated various versions of the argument which Haldane did actually use in an article "A Rational Animal", for J. R. Smythies, ed., *Brain and Mind* (London, and New York: Routledge and Kegan Paul, and Humanities Press, 1965). But I did not either at that time or for several years later appreciate the full force of the different argument which Popper too generously attributes to Haldane.

true, we cannot know it or rationally discuss it, Haldane has given a refutation of the idea from which "scientific" determinism springs.[20]

This seminal idea is, we must assume, part of what Geach would call naturalism; and naturalism is in this way refuted in as much as such a naturalist can be taken, as surely he must be, to be claiming nothing more nor less than to know that his scientifically grounded naturalism is nothing more nor less than true. If, however, this argument is to go through it has to be allowed that no computer or other device the ongoings in which are completely determined by necessitating causes can correctly be said to know that any of its operations are valid or that any of its output is true. I myself gladly accept and affirm this essential limitation upon the potentiality of all such artefacts. Yet to Popper it might seem uncomfortably like a finding of the despised "language philosophy".

3. Before plunging headlong into that forbidden morass we must in passing notice, both that much if not all belief is immediately necessitated, and that this fact can be used to bring out one particular corollary of the previous contention. This is a corollary which cannot but be agreeable to anyone who has ever been to school with Popper.

That at least some beliefs are immediately inescapable is best seen by recalling Hume's doctrine of what Kemp Smith christened "natural beliefs"– the belief, for instance, that in perception we are directly aware of some mind-independent reality.[21] The congenial corollary is that, the more beliefs we find which are in certain circumstances immediately inescapable, the more vital it becomes to try to withdraw from such possibly deceiving situations; and, in a cool hour and a quiet place, to expose ourselves and both these and other beliefs to the full force of all rational objections – that is, to criticism. (Away therefore from the backgammon and the socializing, Mr. Hume; and back to the study, or the stove!)

Such constant willingness to expose ourselves to serious criticism is, beyond doubt, always, if not always quite immediately, within our power. It is also, as

---

20. Entirely by the way: Popper is, surely, again both too charitable and mistaken in his assertion in the same book that "since St. Augustine, at least, Christian theology has for the most part taught the doctrine of indeterminism; the great exceptions are Luther and Calvin" (p. 5). Certainly the *De Libero Arbitrio* of St. Augustine is in its title diametrically opposed to the *de Servo Arbitrio* of Luther. Nevertheless I believe that careful examination reveals that their authors here differ in emphasis and in tone of voice rather than in substance. See my *God: A Critical Inquiry* (La Salle, Illinois: Open Court, 1986), §§2. 34–36, and also my *God, Freedom and Immortality* (Buffalo, N.Y.: Prometheus, 1984), p. 9.

21. See N. Kemp Smith, *The Philosophy of David Hume* (London: Macmillan, 1949), pp. 116 ff. and passim; and note that the name phrase chosen by Kemp Smith is not one of the several employed by Hume. On belief generally see H. H. Price, *Belief* (London, and New York: Allen and Unwin, and Humanities Press, 1969).

I have argued elsewhere,[22] the one sure criterion of the sincerity of our personal commitment to the theoretical search for truth, as well as being, as I also argued there, the telling touchstone of the genuineness of our professed dedication to the stated objectives of whatever practical policies we may choose to favor.

V. Only Choosers Know Either Choice or Necessity

At the beginning of *The Open Universe* Popper announces his intention to present "my reasons for being an indeterminist". At once he adds: "I shall not include among these reasons the intuitive idea of free will: as a rational argument in favour of indeterminism it is useless" (p. 1). His warrant for saying that any such direct appeal to experience is useless, a reason which he formulates in a fashion too misleading to quote here, is that he may be mistaken even about the nature of what the Behaviorist would call one of his own behaviors. In so far as this is a token of a Cartesian kind of argument – one contending that, in any area where we may conceivably be mistaken, we can never truly know – its validity, if it were valid, would have to be recognized as putting an insuperable obstacle in the way of the achieving by any fallible being of any knowledge whatsoever.[23]

Even Popper's original disclaimer, referring as it does to "the intuitive idea of free will", is importantly misleading. For the crucial question is not whether we ever act of our own free will, but whether we ever act at all. When we say of someone that they acted not of their own free will but under compulsion, still they did act. The case of the businessman, who received from the Godfather "an offer which he could not refuse", is thus vitally different from that of the errant mafioso, who was without warning gunned down from behind.

We may both truly and colloquially say of the former, offered the urgent choice of having either his signature or his brains on a document within thirty seconds, that he had no choice, and hence that he could not have done other than he did. (He signed away the whole family business to – if that is the correct phrase – The Organization.) But of course these everyday idioms must not be misconstrued, as so often they are, at the foot of the letter. For in more fundamental senses the businessman who acted under compulsion did have a choice, and could have acted other than he did, however understandably intolerable the only alternative remaining open to him. In these same more fundamental senses, to have a choice, to be able to do otherwise, is essential to what it is to be an agent. In these same

22. "Sincerity, Rationality and Criticism", in *Proceedings of the IXth International Conference on the Unity of the Sciences: Miami 1980* (New York: International Cultural Foundation, 1981), pp. 161–67.

23. Contemplate the devastation wrought by firing off both barrels in the first paragraph of Part IV of the *Discourse on the Method:* "on the grounds that our senses sometimes deceive us, I wanted to suppose that there was not anything corresponding to what they make us imagine. And because some men make mistakes in reasoning . . . and fall into fallacies . . . I rejected as unsound all the reasonings which I had hiterto taken for demonstrations." I give my own reasons for rejecting this argument type in Chapter IX of the *Introduction* mentioned in note 1 above.

more fundamental senses, again, the errant mafioso actually did have no choice; and, because he did not do anything, he could not have done otherwise. For, in that moment of unexpected and sudden death, he ceased both to do and to be.[24]

What this final Part IV is going to sketch is an argument for saying that the two mutually exclusive notions of physical necessity and of being able to do otherwise only are understood, and only can be, by people who have had, and who throughout their lives continue to enjoy, experience of both realities. They – which is to say we – have enjoyed and are continuing to enjoy experience both of unalterable necessity and of effective agency. It is, therefore, just not correct to maintain that the entire Universe is subject at every point to ineluctable necessity. Were this claim true we should not be able even to understand it.

1. By far the best place from which to start to establish our last contention is the splendid chapter "Of Power" in John Locke's *Essay concerning Human Understanding*. This is a chapter the message of which was missed by Hume – "one of the very greatest philosophers of all time".[25] He missed it, as Kant also later did, because he could not entertain any idea of necessity other than the logical, and because he had to defend his insight that causal propositions could not compass any necessity of that logical kind. Locke starts with a statement of what he proposes to prove:

> Every one, I think, finds in himself a power to begin or forbear, continue or put an end to several actions in himself. From the consideration of the extent of this power of the mind over the actions of the man, which every one finds in himself, arise the ideas of liberty and necessity. (II (xxi) 8: here, and in later quotations, seventeenth century typographical exuberance has been tamed down to contemporary dull convention.)

Locke's technique for enforcing this point about our familiarity with our agent powers – our experience of them – is to contrast what we do know or may know about what we cannot do. Unfortunately, Locke, like Popper, wrongly assumes that the sixty-four-thousand dollar question is: not whether we are, and can know that we are, agents choosing this alternative when we could have chosen that; but whether we are, and can know that we are, free agents choosing between alternatives at least one of which we find passing tolerable. This fault we have simply to discount, making the necessary mental transposition as we go along:

> We have instances enough, and often more than enough, in our own bodies. A man's heart beats, and the blood circulates, which 'tis not in his power by any thought or volition to stop; and therefore in respect of these motions, where rest depends not on his choice, nor would follow the determination of his mind, if it should prefer it, he is not a free agent. Convulsive motions agitate his legs, so that he wills it never

24. For a fuller development of these points, see *A Rational Animal*, Chapters III (2.3), IV (2), and IX.
25. *The Open Universe*, p. xix.

so much, he cannot by any power of his mind stop their motion (as in that odd disease called *Chorea Sancti Viti*), but he is perpetually dancing. He is not at liberty in this action but under as much necessity of moving, as a stone that falls, or a tennis ball struck with a racket. On the other side, a palsy or the stocks hinder his legs from obeying the determination of his mind, if it would thereby transfer his body to another place. In all these there is want of freedom . . . . (II (xxi) 11)

What truly there is want of, we must repeat, is not *freedom* but *agency;* not the lack of any tolerable and uncoerced alternatives, but the lack of any alternatives at all. Against this straightforward appeal to experience Popper would argue that it is always conceivable that we are mistaken about what is or is not in fact subject to our wills: that some of us in the past have been afflicted by sudden paralyses; or that we any of us may now have suddenly acquired powers of psychokinesis. Certainly this is conceivable: we are none of us either infallible or all-knowing. But the great mistake is to assume that knowledge presupposes infallibility; that, where we may conceivably be mistaken, there it is impossible for us ever to know. The truth is that we need only to be in a position to know, and to be claiming to know something which is in fact true.

Locke goes on to suggest, albeit in a less satisfactory terminology, that where action is not, there necessity reigns; that the human behaviors which are not actions must be necessary. Thus he writes: "Wherever thought is wholly wanting, or the power to act or forbear according to the direction of thought, there necessity takes place" (II (xxi) 13). And, a page or two earlier, we read:

A tennis ball, whether in motion by a stroke of a racket, or lying still at rest, is not by anyone taken to be a free agent . . . because we conceive not a tennis ball to think, and consequently not to have any volition, or preference of motion to rest, or *vice versa;* and therefore . . . is not a free agent; but all its both motion and rest come under our idea of necessary, and are so call'd. . . . So a man striking himself, or his friend, by a convulsive motion of his arm, which it is not in his power . . . to stop, or forbear; . . . every one pities him as acting by necessity and constraint. (II (xxi) 9)

Once again, of course, the reason why we should pity such persons is not that they would be acting under constraint, but that their behaviors would be completely necessitated, and therefore not actions at all. Especially to those familiar with Hume's criticisms of this chapter, in his discussions both "Of Liberty and Necessity" and "Of the Idea of Necessary Connection", what is most curious is Locke's actual failure to go on to emphasize that, notwithstanding that those behaviors which are actions cannot have been necessitated, since the agents must as such have been able to do other than they did, still the behaviors aforesaid may themselves necessitate. For actions may bring about effects, making one alternative contingently necessary and another contingently impossible.[26]

26. See, for a filling of this gap, Max Black, "Making Something Happen", in S. Hook, ed., *Determinism and Freedom* (New York: New York University Press, 1958); reprinted as Chapter VIII of Black's *Models and Metaphors* (Ithaca, N.Y.: Cornell University Press, 1962).

We know how Hume would have tried to dispose of this contention, had Locke developed it. We know because, though Locke did not, Hume did. Hume, like Popper, insisted upon the perennial conceivability of alternatives: it must always be conceivable that what does usually happen one day will not. And, again like Popper, Hume draws an invalid inference, although not the same invalid inference, from this true premise. Hume's inference is that, since there cannot be logical necessities linking those events or sorts of events which happen to be causes with those events or sorts of events which happen to be their effects, therefore there cannot be and are no objective necessities and no objective impossibilities in the nonlinguistic world. But this is false, and our consideration of choice has shown how we can know it to be false. It is precisely and only from our altogether familiar experiences as agents making things happen, yet agents always limited in the scope of their agency, that we can and must derive two – if you like – metaphysical basics. For this is the source both of our ideas of agency and of this kind of necessity, and of our knowledge that the universe provides abundant application for both these ideas.

2. Section 1 of the present Part IV has, surely, done a good deal to warrant the second and more easily supportable of these two claims. To back the first the best which can be done here and now is indicate that and why Hume and his followers have so totally failed to come to terms with the notions of contingent (as opposed to logical) necessity and of contingent (as opposed to logical) impossibility. Attempting an empiricist philosophy as a contribution to a systematically naturalistic world-outlook, they have wanted to promulgate their universal reign of necessitating causality without being able to excogitate any halfway plausible and consistent account of the nature of such necessity.[27] Hume himself, for example, opens Part I of Section VIII of his first *Inquiry* with a manifesto of necessitarian determinism. This he follows with a review of his official account of necessity as involving – as "a philosophical relation"– nothing but regular succession, with laws of nature reduced to mere material implications; an account which makes universal "necessitation" entirely compatible with the reality of choice. But then in Part II, discussing the agency of God, Hume is happy to reintroduce the vulgar notions of genuine necessitation and of genuine bringing about.[28]

We have suggested already, in the previous section, that Hume was distracted by his overriding concern to expound and defend a great negative insight: "If we reason *a priori*, anything may appear able to produce anything" (IHU XII (iii)). He was also, and even more seriously, crippled by commitment to a narrow, exclusively private, artificial, Cartesian conception of experience. Berkeley had opened the *Principles* by claiming that "the objects of human knowledge" are always and only ideas. This unbelievably pessimistic assertion is in substance repeated

27. For a development of this critique of Hume's account of causation, see the references given in note 15 above.
28. See especially the second of the pieces recommended in the previous footnote.

in the first sentence of the *Treatise,* albeit with the addition of a new distinction of Berkeley's ideas into two kinds: "All the perceptions of the human mind resolve themselves into two kinds, which I shall call *impressions* and *ideas.*"

We have here to remind ourselves that, whereas the plain person confines his talk of perceptions to cases in which some creature of flesh and blood is immediately aware of a mind-independent reality, Hume's "perceptions of the mind" carry no such external implications; while their subjects seem usually to be thought to be – just as in Descartes and in Berkeley – incorporeal. His empiricism is thus one which construes experience as consisting in the passive reception of impressions – a sort of gormless gawping at, and inert acceptance of, what an earlier philosophical generation used to call "the given". This is holus bolus different from the down to earth, active empiricism which has so strong an appeal to realistic common sense.[29] For that everyday, out-of-the-study empiricism sensibly insists that, for instance, anyone claiming to have had experience of cows is claiming to have perceived and in one way or another manipulated a fair number of real flesh and blood cows. Their claim is to have herded and milked, felt and smelt, Gertrude and Mary and Elsie and Jemima and a whole lot of others. There would, and rightly, be short shrift down on the farm for job applicants admitting only to their past enjoyment of cowish sense-data, while daring to deny the very possibility of actual knowledge of either real flesh and blood cows or any other three-dimensional denizens of the External World!

Hume, however, was committed to the contention that the philosophically initiated cannot but embrace such a narrow, artificial, exotic, Veil of Appearance, conception of experience.[30] He thus presents what many years ago I dubbed "a paralytic's eye view" of causation.[31] All that such an inert and passive observer can discern in "the given" is indeed the constant conjunction and regular succession of (sorts of) ideas and (sorts of) impressions. In mere observation he most certainly cannot become aware of contingent necessity, of bringing about, and of causal connection – the connection that is, which warrants, and is perhaps itself constituted by the truth of, contrary-to-fact conditionals.

Like much else in Hume this bold attempt – made "by one of the very greatest philosophers of all time" – has its highest value as an unintended demonstration of what surely cannot be done. However could any pure observer, the incorporeal

29. It is all too easy today to find philosophers, especially radical philosophers, who announce the demise of empiricism without ever making the absolutely crucial distinction developed in the text. The radicals at least cherish theories which they must know to have been struck down by the Supreme Court of Experience; and they may, therefore, be suspected of hoping through such confusion about the extension of the word "experience" to discredit that properly decisive judgement.

30. See, for instance, IHU XII (i) where Hume tells us that "the slightest philosophy" dictates that "the existence which we consider, when we say *this house* or *that tree,* are nothing but perceptions in the mind. . . ."

31. "Can an Effect precede its Cause?", in *Proceedings of the Aristotelian Society, Supplementary* Vol. XXVIII (1954): pp. 49–50.

subject of essentially private experience, acquire these three most elementary notions? However could they be acquired, if not as they surely are in fact acquired, in and through our everyday experience as agents; experience, that is, as corporeal things causing effects upon other corporeal things; experience too as agents who, in their understanding of the possibility of doing otherwise, grasp the crucial concept of the contrary-to-fact? If someone believes that it either is or could be done in some alternative way, then we will have to respond, with the archetypically incredulous man from Missouri: "Show me!"

VI. Epilogue

This whole paper has tried to explain and defend the Geach motto from which we began. We must not stop without reiterating that it has at best provided a refutation only of those imprudently aggressive forms of naturalism which promise to banish "reasoning or language or choice". But such claims in truth are not, though they are often believed to be, essential to naturalism. Consider, for instance, the consistently Aristotelian naturalism of Strato of Lampsacus, who was next but one to The Philosopher himself as Director of the Lyceum. Neither he nor his followers seem to have suggested anything of the sort: they had – poor things – never heard of the sociology of belief; nor did they feel bound to labor to explain human action in the same necessitarian terms as were found convenient in astronomy or meteorology.[32] If we are to accept Geach's motto, then we must interpret the words "explain . . . naturalistically" as entailing discredit, denial, and explaining away. In that understanding, but in that understanding alone,

> When we hear of some new attempt to explain reasoning or language or choice naturalistically, we ought to react as if we were told someone had squared the circle or proved $\sqrt{2}$ to be rational: only the mildest curiosity is in order – how well has the fallacy been concealed?

32. Why, by the way, are some of our own contemporaries so keen to insist that the most complicated creatures known are subject to a total necessitation, while equally eager to maintain that the simplest particles discovered by microphysics are exempt from the rule of necessitating causality? Surely, if there is any indeterminism in the universe, this is more likely to be found among the most complex rather than the least?

Chapter XVIII

Alienation Alienated: The Economics of Knowledge versus the Psychology and Sociology of Knowledge

By W. W. Bartley, III

1. A Problem Shift in the Discussion of Marxism

In early 1946, Rudolf Carnap wrote to Popper to congratulate him on the publication of *The Open Society and Its Enemies*. Carnap was impressed by it, but, as the ensuing correspondence revealed, he was also puzzled. He was puzzled by two things especially: why had Popper given a profuse acknowledgement to F. A. von Hayek, whom Carnap had met at the University of Chicago, whose *The Road to Serfdom* Carnap had heard a lot about but not read, and who had the reputation of being a reactionary? And could it possibly be that Popper himself was not a socialist?

In his response, Popper strongly defended his friend and intellectual comrade Hayek, and also mentioned casually that he was having difficulties in placing *The Open Society* with an American publisher.[1] Carnap replied sympathetically and indignantly, commenting that *that just went to show that scientific publishing should not be in private hands.*

An earlier version of this chapter has been published in Kurt Leube and Albert Zlabinger, eds., *The Political Economy of Freedom* (Munich: Philosophia Verlag, 1985). © 1985 W. W. Bartley, III.

1. *The Open Society and Its Enemies* was of course soon accepted by Princeton University Press, and has been in print, in America as well as in Britain, ever since. Carnap seems to have assumed that it was commercial interest that deterred publishers – twenty of them – from accepting Popper's two-volume work. But it was not at all that: it was the reactions of academic readers to his stinging critique of Plato and Hegel. Hayek had a comparable experience with *The Road to Serfdom*. As he reports in his new Foreword to the book (pp. iv–v), politically prejudiced readers went so far as to declare his book "unfit for publication by a reputable house". It hardly seems likely that a government bureaucracy would have acted any differently. The difference is that, had the matter been under the central control of the government, the books would perhaps never have been published at all. There is an oblique reference to this anecdote in Hayek's "Preface 1976" to *The Road to Serfdom*.

The incident is revealing. Carnap was no Marxist, and he did his best to examine analytically the issues that confronted him. Some of his work was intended to combat what he conceived of as superstition, and one of his most famous essays had been entitled: "The Elimination of Metaphysics through Logical Analysis of Language".[2] But he was, to the core, what Hayek would later call a "constructivist rationalist" and what Popper called an "uncritical" or "comprehensive" rationalist; his personal philosophy and the sensibility in which it was couched contained many of the "superstitions", as Hayek calls them,[3] of twentieth-century thought. An eminent logician, Carnap nonetheless believed, contrary to logic,[4] that every statement could be given a rational justification; a great probability theoretician, he nonetheless believed, contrary to the fundamental rules of the probability calculus, that evidence could probabilistically warrant universal scientific hypotheses.[5] A social thinker of more modest dimensions, he declared – contrary to Hayek's later work on complex and spontaneous orders, and contrary to what is known independently from evolutionary theory and anthropology – that morality is no more than the expression of individual wishes.[6] And he believed – even immediately after reading, and liking, *The Open Society* – that scientific publication should not be left in private hands, but should be put under government control. No doubt this would be a benevolent, rationally planning government, one whose bureaucrats would be so wise as to give rational justifications, or at least probabilistic warrants, to all their statements.

I have told this story not to criticize Carnap, who was in many ways a sympathetic individual, but to conjure up again the intellectual climate of casual socialism and uncritical rationalism in which *The Road to Serfdom* and *The Open Society* were first published.

The intellectual climate has changed since then. The work of Popper, Hayek, and some others has altered the character of the debate: a "problem-shift" has occurred. Hayek and Popper themselves are rarely mentioned except polemically by writers of the left; but many such writings still circle round their unmentionable presence. Claims relating to planning and control, and to historical

2. Rudolf Carnap, "Die Überwindung der Metaphysik durch logische Analyse der Sprache", *Erkenntnis* **2**, 1932, reprinted in A. J. Ayer, ed., *Logical Positivism* (Glencoe: The Free Press, 1959), pp. 60–81.

3. *Law, Legislation, and Liberty*, Vol. III (Chicago: University of Chicago Press, 1979), p. 176.

4. The problem is that such attempts at comprehensive justification lead to an unacceptable dilemma: either infinite regress or irrational dogmatism. See the treatment of the problem in my *The Retreat to Commitment*, and Part II of the present volume. See Carnap's *The Logical Structure of the World* (Berkeley and Los Angeles: University of California Press, 1967), Preface to the First Edition, p. xvii.

5. See Carnap's *Logical Foundations of Probability*, and the discussion of Carnap's work on probability by K. R. Popper, *Conjectures and Refutations* (New York: Basic Books, 1963), Chapter 11.

6. See Carnap's *Logische Syntax der Sprache*. On positivism and values, see also Victor Kraft, *Der Wiener Kreis* (New York: Springer Verlag, 1968), esp. Section B.III.4; and A. J. Ayer, *Language, Truth and Logic* (New York: Dover, 1952).

determinism – once in the forefront of discussion – have been relegated more to the background. Hayek himself suggests that the "hot socialism" against which *The Road to Serfdom* was directed – the "organized movement toward a deliberate organization of economic life by the state as the chief owner of the means of production"– may have died in the West in the late 'forties.[7] But new claims have been thrust forward to replace the old ones; and while more modest, less doctrinaire, and altogether cooler, these new themes continue to shore up a way of thinking which, in its aggregate effect, endangers liberty.

For this chapter I have selected two such current themes. I shall discuss them critically to give a sample, an illustration, of the quality and tendency of contemporary social thought. They illustrate that – despite the change in our intellectual climate during the past forty years – the full implications of Popper's and Hayek's thought have not yet even begun to be assimilated.

My first theme has to do with Marx's "Paris Manuscripts" and problems of "alienation"; the second, with the sociology of knowledge. Neither has the same social and political importance as older claims about state planning and control, and historical laws. But they both are popular; and they are closely related to those older claims.

Threaded through my treatment of both themes are certain important epistemological motifs. These epistemological ideas, which undermine Marx's ideas of alienation as well as the sociology of knowledge, will become apparent very quickly; but a brief clue can be given right away that will help to identify them.

The clue, which can be used as a sort of koan to attain epistemological enlightenment, is this: when people ask me what I have learnt from Popper and Hayek I frequently reply by saying that *I learnt from Popper that we never know what we are talking about,* and *I learnt from Hayek that we never know what we are doing.*

A koan is not much good unless one is endarkened and wants to be enlightened. And similarly, I suppose, a clue in the abstract, even when it is an abstract clue, is not much use unless one has a particular mystery to use it on. So here is the mystery: what does not knowing what we are talking about and not knowing what we are doing have to do with alienation and the sociology of knowledge?

But first to the Paris manuscripts themselves, and a report on "Marxist scholarship".

---

7. Hayek's remarks about "hot socialism" appear in *The Road to Serfdom,* Foreword, pp. vii–viii. Readers interested in exploring the differences between Popper and Hayek are directed, initially, to two places. Popper and Hayek differ, clearly, with regard to the possible and desirable extent of government intervention, and Popper is more of an interventionist. See for example *The Open Society and Its Enemies,* Vol. II, pp. 125–27, where Popper argues for political intervention to an extent that Hayek would not countenance or even believe possible. Popper and Hayek also differ about the use of evolutionary arguments to support tradition. Compare, for example, Hayek's "Epilogue" to *Law, Legislation and Liberty,* Vol. III, with Popper's remarks in F. J. Ayala and Theodosius Dobzhansky, eds.: *Studies in the Philosophy of Biology* (Berkeley: University of California Press, 1974), p. 375.

2. Marx's Paris Manuscripts

Western literature on Marx is vast, and there is little point in generalizing about it. Yet it seems that many leading western Marxists – such as those influenced by such thinkers as Ernst Bloch, Walter Benjamin, Erich Fromm, Karl Korsch, and Herbert Marcuse – now tend to accept an interpretation of Marx that is wholly hostage to Marx's "Paris manuscripts", his early philosophical and economic writings of 1844.

Marx, it is claimed, was in fact not an "historicist", not a believer in historical laws; and his work is thus undamaged by criticisms such as those of Popper. Of course the myth that Marx was an historicist was, it is conceded, not Popper's fault. Rather, "what everyone knows about Marx is very largely a construct of the elderly Engels"[8] – a construct begun in Marx's own lifetime and thrust into prominence on his death, when, in his speech at Marx's graveside in Highgate Cemetery, Engels stated: "Just as Darwin discovered the law of development of organic nature, so Marx discovered the law of development of human history. . . . Marx also discovered the special law of motion governing the present-day capitalist mode of production and the bourgeois society that this mode of production has created. . . . Such was the man of science."[9] This account of Engels was taken over by and strongly promoted in the second and third Communist Internationals, and became a widely accepted popular understanding of Marx.

This account is supported in several ways. Textual and comparative studies suggest that differences of doctrine and emphasis occur throughout the works of Engels and Marx; and qualifying phrases are highlighted – phrases in which both writers warned their readers against "Hegelian-style construction". But the chief support comes from the Paris Manuscripts themselves, which were published only in 1932, documents which, until the 'fifties, were difficult to obtain and had received little scholarly attention. As Herbert Marcuse put it in 1932: "The publication of the economic and philosophical manuscripts . . . must become a crucial event in the history of Marxist studies. These manuscripts could put the discussion about the origins and original meaning of historical materialism, and the entire theory of scientific socialism, on a new footing."[10]

8. See Terrell Carver, "The Marx-Engels Intellectual Relationship", in *The Times Higher Education Supplement,* March 11, 1983, p. 16. See also John Gray, "The System of Ruins", *Times Literary Supplement,* December 30, 1983, and Gérard Bekerman, *Marx and Engels: A Conceptual Concordance,* trans. Terrell Carver (Oxford: Blackwell, 1983). Naomi Moldofsky points out that there is evidence that some central themes of Marxist political economy are already to be found in essays written by the young Engels – for example, in his essay "Outlines of a Critique of Political Economy" (1844). (See W. O. Henderson, ed., *Engels: Selected Writings,* 1967.)

9. Quoted by Tom Bottomore, "The Legacy of Marxism", in *The Times Higher Education Supplement,* March 11, 1983, p. 14.

10. Herbert Marcuse, *Studies in Critical Philosophy* (Boston: Beacon Press, 1972), p. 3. For Marx's early writings, see Karl Marx, *Early Writings,* translated and edited by T. B. Bottomore, with a fore-

Just such a "new footing" has been attempted. These manuscripts are supposed to show that the core of Marx's thought, best illustrated by his doctrine of alienation, is "humanistic", indeed resonates to contemporary existentialism and psychoanalysis, and has little if anything to do with historicism and determinism – and thus is unaffected by arguments concerning historical determinism and planning, which are rejected as dated and irrelevant, as not applying to Marx himself at all, and applying to Marxism only as it happened to be presented at some particular times and places. Such a new footing is recommended not only by western writers such as those already mentioned; similar interpretations of true Marxism are also sometimes advocated in Czechoslovakia, Poland, and Yugoslavia to combat official – "vulgar Marxist" – Communist theory. (The idea of alienation itself, of course, arises already in Hegel, in his attack on the supposed objectivity of the world of nature, in the contention that everything is a facet of human self-consciousness. Here the connection to what was later to be called the sociology of knowledge is obvious. But it is with Marx, rather than Hegel, that we are concerned in the Paris manuscripts.)

What is to be said in response to these radical reinterpretations of Marx?

We may pass quickly over some obvious points. For instance, it almost goes without saying that the argument works both ways: if these critics are correct about Marx himself, what they say is also largely irrelevant to what Hayek and Popper were chiefly trying to do – namely, to deal with the chief doctrines of Marxism and socialism as they have been presented and advocated during the past hundred years. Any such defense of Marx thus protects him from criticism at the cost of considerably diminishing the historical importance of his thought. These critics themselves implicitly concede as much, insofar as they differentiate their own true Marxism from the "vulgar" Marxism of the Soviet Union and some other countries of the eastern bloc: in other words, from those whose view of Marxism, vulgar or not, is the one held – at least officially – by most Marxists the world over.

Yet these critics are not right about Marx, and what they say about him has now been shown to be false. The contention that the theme of alienation lay at the heart of Marx's thought has always been dubious. For Marx never published the Paris manuscripts, and in his later *published* work – in *The Communist Mani-*

---

word by Erich Fromm (New York: McGraw-Hill, 1964); Karl Marx, *Early Texts,* translated and edited by David McLellan (Oxford: Basil Blackwell, 1971); Karl Marx, *Early Writings* (New York: Vintage Books, 1975); Karl Marx, *Economic and Philosophic Manuscripts of 1844,* edited by Dirk J. Struik (New York: International Publishers, 1964); Robert Payne, *The Unknown Karl Marx,* ed. Robert Payne (New York: New York University Press, 1971). There have from the start been many different interpretations of Marx: there always have been warring schools, such as those of the "revisionists", Leninists, Trotskyists, Stalinists, Maoists, structuralists, situationists, and Eurocommunists; such schools began to proliferate in the 1890's. On alienation, see Richard Schacht, *Alienation,* with an introductory essay by Walter Kaufmann (New York: Doubleday, 1970), and Walter Kaufmann, *Without Guilt and Justice* (New York: Wyden, 1973). See also Lewis S. Feuer, "Marx and Engels as Sociobiologists", *Survey* **23,** 4 (Autumn 1977-78), pp. 109-36, esp. pp. 109-10.

festo (1848) for example – he refers to talk of alienation as "philosophical nonsense", and expressly condemns those who use the term (section III.1.c). Already in 1846, in *The German Ideology,* Marx's only explicit references to alienation are derisive. Long-standing suspicions about the status of these manuscripts now seem to be confirmed by the work of a Dutch researcher, Jürgen Rojahn, who, in December 1982, in Linz, at an international conference of labor historians, reported on nearly a decade of work on the Paris manuscripts. These manuscripts, preserved in Amsterdam, are, he argues, no more than a collection of rough ideas and working notes, chiefly concerning the young student Karl Marx's reading of Hegel, Adam Smith, and others. Noting that the manuscripts were often loose and in random order, Rojahn scrutinized page size, page numbers, Marx's own writing, number of columns used, and such like, and concluded that these manuscripts were clearly never *intended* for publication, and probably should have no formal status at all.

These conclusions, although hardly a surprise, were immediately taken as a serious blow to the work of the so-called humanistic Marxists, such as Marcuse, and Fromm, and as welcome news for Soviet Marxists and Leninists who have long opposed such approaches. Eric Hobsbawm, economist and social historian at the University of London, evaluated Rojahn's findings, if correct, as "nothing short of a depth charge in the world of Marxist scholarship."[11]

These findings suggest that Hayek's and Popper's original approaches were appropriate after all. Their critiques – which aim to show that Marxism and socialism are both incorrect and also (contrary to Engels's judgement about Marx "the man of science") *unscientific* – attempt to confront the real economic and political doctrines of the past hundred years, Communist ideology, historicism, determinism, and socialist doctrines of planning. And they are directed not only to western Marxists, socialists, and political thinkers, but also at regimes of the eastern bloc that continue to justify their policies by reference to Marx's "scientific" achievements.

But even if the older Marx had not abandoned the idea of alienation, there would still be every reason to reject it. What did he say about alienation?

3. Marx on Alienation

Whatever difficulties may arise in interpreting Marx's early manuscripts, it seems clear that he was indeed concerned with the alienation of man, and with what he saw as the devaluation and perversion of life. Marx was truly a sort of humanist, and his humanism permeates his later work as well as his early student notes.

---

11. Paul Flather, in *Times Higher Education Supplement,* January 14, 1983, pp. 1 and 28. See my remarks in "Die offene Gesellschaft", in Franz Kreutzer, ed., *Karl R. Popper/Konrad Lorenz: Die Zukunft ist offen* (Munich: Piper Verlag, 1984).

Marx's remarks on alienation provide an account of the relationship between economic conditions and states of mind. These ideas are introduced in the Paris manuscripts, and are indeed more or less restricted to the early work. But echoes of these themes – in different form, and in very different language – sound occasionally also later. Thus in *Capital*, while developing the labor theory of value, Marx writes: "The character of independence and estrangement which the capitalist modes of production as a whole give to the instruments of labor and the product, as against the workman, is developed by means of machinery into a thorough antagonism" (Vol. I, 432).

But it is with the early notes that we are concerned here, and there Marx contends that an individual's products are all-important to his very humanity in the sense that they are externalized expressions and reproductions of his most essential being, through which he actualizes what would otherwise be only implicit. He is the subject, the initiator, of the process, who, ideally, creates his own world. In his labor the individual develops his physical and spiritual energies, and can fulfill himself. Since his work stems from his most intimate self, it is – so it is inferred – his very own, part of his identity.

Marx sees a threat to this self-actualizing, self-fulfilling process – one that, in his view, arises especially in capitalist society. Namely, the fruits of the worker's labor – the very expressions of his being – are wrested away from, alienated from, made strange or foreign to him. They can be surrendered or given away or over to the control of another; they can be taken away by individuals or by impersonal historical, social, or natural forces. When this happens, his product *ceases to be within his own control* and *"stands opposed to him as an autonomous power . . . which he no longer experiences as his own"*. In *The German Ideology*, Marx bemoans the *"consolidation of our own product into an objective power over us that outgrows our control, crosses our expectations, and nullifies our calculations"*.

Behind Marx's argument is the assumption that man does not, yet ought to, control his fate; that man ought not to be dependent on, or under the control of gods, of other men, of the market process; that in liberating oneself from such control lies the path to freedom. To the extent that men turn over their destiny to other beings or to processes beyond their control, they surrender what is proper to them, what is their own, and thus lose themselves. The theme of control that emerges here is central to all socialist thought. As one writer on Marx has put it, his "central point is that man has lost control of his own evolution".[12] "Things are in the saddle and ride mankind." Socialism aims to put man back in the saddle, to have man, by use of his reason, regain control of his fate. This theme is perhaps its most attractive feature but also its fatal flaw. It is attractive because man

12. See the discussion by David McLellan, "Alienation in Hegel and Marx", *Dictionary of the History of Ideas* (New York: Charles Scribner's Sons, 1973), Vol. I, p. 39a.

is indeed so creative, and is by no means entirely the victim of, entirely controlled by, the circumstances of his existence, but can, and often does, overcome them. As Popper writes:

> Climbing high mountains, climbing Everest for example, always seemed to me a striking refutation of the physicalist view of man. To overcome difficulties just for the sake of doing so; to face grave dangers, just for the sake of doing so; to go on at the point of utter exhaustion: how can these ways of fighting all our natural inclinations be explained by physicalism or behaviourism? Perhaps, in a few cases, by the ambition of achieving great distinction: some mountaineers have become famous. But there were, and there are, many mountaineers that scorn notoriety and fame: they love mountains, and they love the overcoming of difficulties for their own sake . . . (*The Self and Its Brain,* p. 146)

But that one can occasionally, even often, heroically triumph over circumstances does not mean that one can be in full control. That man is not controlled by gods does not mean that man himself is godlike. When one abandons the idea of the gods, one must shed as well the idea of godlike control. One is not all-powerful or all-controlling, by reason or will or otherwise. Especially, one cannot expect never to have his expectations crossed, or his calculations nullified. Here, as we shall see in the following sections, is the root of Marx's error. And these reflections about the limitations of reason are themselves, as we shall see below, the results of reasoned reflection.

4. A Moment with Freud

If the issues that we are discussing were not so serious, we could pause here to have some fun with Freud. For the Paris manuscripts are favorites not only of sociologists and philosophers but also of psychologists – and even psychoanalysts – of knowledge. (And as we shall see below, sociology and psychology of knowledge are often closely bound together.) Thus Herbert Marcuse, Karen Horney, Erich Fromm, and other writers have used these manuscripts to link Marx's ideas to those of Freudian psychology and existentialism.

Sophisticated in psychology as these writers are, they have nonetheless failed to train their analytical skills on Marx himself, and thus have failed to notice the apparent underlying psychopathology of Marx's discussion – or the conflict between Freudian and Marxist ideas here.

For if one is committed to the psychology of knowledge, one should not fail to notice that, from that point of view, the early Marx has a very odd attitude to human products: *we must not let them go.* We must not relinquish control of them to anyone else, and, if we do so, *we lose ourselves.* But this – at least in Freudian theory – involves an absurd, unhealthy, and even pathological *identification* with one's products.

I am not myself an admirer of psychoanalysis, and later in this chapter I criticize and reject the very basis on which some writers have attempted to reduce a thinker's ideas to psychopathology; but I could understand why a Freudian might, *from his or her own point of view,* be forced to suspect Marx of something like "anal retentiveness" to a pathological degree.[13] And it is indeed often said that Marx suffered from hemorrhoids. Marx himself, in his discussion of alienation, takes what a Freudian would almost have to interpret as a "fetishistic" attitude to human products. But Marcuse, Horney, and Fromm never notice – or at least do not mention – anything of the sort. Were they too bourgeois to make such a connection? Have such features in Marx become *unmentionable?*

I hope that my readers will appreciate what I am doing here. I am not myself suggesting that there is any connection between Marx's alleged hemorrhoids and his views on alienation; and later in this chapter I argue against the whole program of trying to make such connections. Rather, what I want to know is why the Freudian-Marxists, such as Marcuse and Fromm, for whom such connections *are* all-important, never noticed them *in this particular case* – that is, in the case of Marx.

(When I asked this question at a recent conference in Madrid, a well-known American Marxist protested in strong terms, objecting that Marx's ideas should not be discussed "in terms of urine and spit". I could not agree more; but hemorrhoids have nothing to do with urine and spit; and my point about western bourgeois Marxist-Freudian intellectuals is thus reinforced: they become incapable of thinking simultaneously about feces and Marx. Such connections are for them not only unmentionable but also unthinkable. "Cognitive dissonance" and intellectual compartmentalization, which are already aroused when such people attempt to think at once in scientific and in Marxist-Freudian terms, prevent them from critically training Marxism and Freudianism on one another. The result is that most unedifying spectacle: a practical stupidity woven into and undermining some exceptionally brilliant minds – a practical stupidity in which, in effect, two and two no longer reach four. (See Milton Rokeach: *The Open and Closed Mind* (New York: Basic Books, 1960)).)

In matters such as these, Hegel, from whom Marx had borrowed the idea of alienation, was evidently healthier. For Hegel, the act of turning something over to another, and thus "alienating" it from himself, may be *simply giving it up.* For Hegel, nothing essential is lost; whereas for Marx, one *surrenders* one's product, and in so doing one gives up an essential part of one's being. Marx also differs

---

13. See Sigmund Freud, "Character and Anal Erotism", in *Collected Papers,* Vol. 2 (New York: Basic Books, 1959), pp. 45–50, esp. pp. 47–48 and the footnote on those pages, where Freud reports his patient's discussion of how the "shameful substance which has to be concealed turns into a secret which enriches the world . . . the world was trying to get this valuable secret from me, but . . . I carefully kept it to myself ". Or on the apparent difference between the attitudes of Marx and Hegel here, see Freud, "On the Transformation of Instincts with Special Reference to Anal Erotism", in *Collected Papers,* Vol. 2, pp. 164–71, esp. p. 168, where Freud writes: "The process of defaecation affords the first occasion on which the child must decide between narcissistic and an object-loving attitude. He either parts obediently with his faeces, 'offers them up' to his love, or else retains them for purposes of auto-erotic gratification and later as a means of asserting his own will."

from Hegel in supposing that surrendering one's product to another implies denying one's own interests and submitting to those of the other, thus allowing one's
own product to contribute to one's own oppression.[14]

But the problem is not simply one of psychopathology. It is more serious:
Marx's account of alienation demands something that is both logically and physically impossible. For the key to his own argument is his opposition to permitting
our products to become autonomous powers that will *"outgrow our control, cross
our expectations, and nullify our calculations"*. Yet there is simply no alternative.

5. Why We Never Know What We Are Talking About or What We Are Doing

The passages from Marx that I have just italicized are important. They conjure up images of a process both violent and unjust, in which the strong tears
away from the weak what is dearest to him, and then uses what he has stolen
to torment his victim. Our hearts go out to the victim; our minds cry out for
reform.

Yet any such reform cannot be along the lines that Marx himself suggests.
For he is demanding something that is both logically and physically impossible.

To explain why Marx's demand is impossible, I need first to talk briefly about
knowledge, to call on the notion of *objective knowledge;* and also to illustrate why,

---

14. Marx's approach here, quite apart from any question of psychopathology, is also socially primi-
tive – another matter that tends to go unnoticed. On such matters, consult the rich material Helmut
Schoeck has assembled in his *Envy: A Theory of Social Behaviour* (London: Secker & Warbug, 1969).
Schoeck, Gerardo, and Alicia Reichel-Dolmatoff, and others have, for instance, reported the patterns
of existence and interrelationship in primitive societies such as the Aritama of North Colombia. (See
G. and A. Reichel-Dolmatoff, *The People of Aritama. The Cultural Personality of a Colombian Mestizo
Village* (Chicago, 1961).) To give only one example, Aritama society is frozen by envy: literally *frozen,*
for it is dominated and controlled by certain assumptions that prevent modern economic and cultural
institutions from developing. For example, there is the assumption that there is only one explanation
for any misfortune: the envious black magic of another villager. And to be sure, the individual practice of just such black magic, intended to harm others, is widespread.

How does this relate to our discussion? In many ways, particularly through the act of exchange
as discussed by Marx: thus someone who buys a piece of property in Aritama must assume that the
seller will hate him, *and will pursue him vindictively for the remainder of his life.* The seller here also
"cannot let go". His claim to his property persists; he envies the buyer's superiority in being able
to pay, and feels that he has been cheated of something substantial in return for something as evanes-
cent and transitory as money (Schoeck, pp. 52–53).

In modern exchange societies, it is harder for primitive emotions to arise in such settings: the
institutions foster a more benign attitude. For anonymous mass production of goods enables one to
purchase practically anything at least without having to reckon with the envy of the producer. Such
an anonymous exchange economy has, at least in this respect, a civilizing effect. Yet it is still common
among social romantics (as Marx shows himself occasionally to be) to glorify primitive society, as
when they deplore the impersonality of modern relationships, and plead for a return to the days when
one had a personal relationship in economic transactions, when nearly every article had to be pur-
chased from some known individual. As Schoeck puts it, in such a setting, "the romantically inclined . . . have no idea how subtly the relationships between producer and customer strangled the
circulation of goods."

because of the objective character of knowledge, we never know what we are talking about.

The dominant western approach to knowledge has been subjective: it has come to explain knowledge as a *relationship* – that of generation, or acquisition, mastery, ownership, control, belief – between a subjective mind and a known object. Thus it takes knowledge as something generated or acquired, mastered, owned or possessed, controlled or believed, by a knowing subject. And it often treats the judgements or beliefs supposed to constitute this relationship as the due *expressions* of the mental states of the subjective mind.

Of course, the generation of knowledge does indeed involve such "knowing subjects" – and the expression, acquisition, control, believing, and possession that they may engage in. The question is whether our epistemologies may not have overestimated the importance of this knowing subject. In fact, the main questions of knowledge can, and ought to be, treated quite independently of a knowing subject.

Usually, however, such questions and possibilities are not considered. In the expressionist theory of art, for instance, an individual's work – not only his artistic products, but his ideas, and the things that he makes and does with them – is viewed as an expression of his inner state,[15] as something that he has caused and for which he is responsible, and whose worth or quality depend on the health and other qualities of his mental state.

It is not only in epistemology and in art that one finds such expressionism. The same line of assumptions – and a similar subjective and possessive expressionism – underlie Marx's approach to alienation. His early manuscripts are written in this tradition, as even his terminology shows: for him, one's work, one's products, are externalized expressions and reproductions of one's self, through which the individual actualizes himself. Since they stem from one's most intimate self, it is even plausible to identify with them, as indeed belonging to the self. Of course Marx does not restrict his own discussion to knowledge-products; but most human products are in a sense knowledge-products; and most of what applies to the discussion of knowledge-products applies to other human products, and to action, as well.

This subjective and expressionistic approach, although still widespread, is innocent of any understanding of biology or evolutionary theory; it is *pre-evolutionary*. As we saw in Part I of this volume, Popper, Hayek, D. T. Campbell, Konrad Lorenz, and others, who are pioneering an "evolutionary epistemology", are attempting to chart a different, objective approach to knowledge that will be informed by and compatible with evolutionary theory.[16]

15. See K. R. Popper, *Objective Knowledge* (Oxford: Oxford University Press, 1972); my "Ein schwieriger Mensch: Eine Portraitskizze von Sir Karl Popper", in Eckhard Nordhofen, ed., *Physiognomien: Philosophen des 20. Jahrhunderts in Portraits* (Königstein/Ts: Athenäum, 1980), pp. 43–69; and my "Wittgenstein and Homosexuality", in *Homosexuality: Sacrilege, Vision, Politics, Salmagundi* **58–59**, Fall 1982–Winter 1983, pp. 166–96.

16. See my account in Chapter I of this volume where a bibliography is given.

Such an approach treats human knowledge as an exosomatic product, independent of its installation in any particular human mind, that is comparable in some ways to the exosomatic products of various animals – such as the spider's web, the beaver's dam, the path worn in the forest by the deer, the bird's nest. Objective knowledge consists of such things as linguistically formulated expectations, or theoretical systems. These objects, stored more importantly in books, articles, or programs than in minds, can be studied, investigated, or examined critically, independently of any question about who if anyone believes them or originated them. To large parts of our objective knowledge – the table of logarithms is a trivial example – any question of belief is irrelevant. And as Hayek has pointed out, important parts of our objective knowledge – such as traditions, morality, the law, language, and institutions such as the market, in all of which an immense amount of knowledge has been tacitly stored in the process of their evolution – are manifestations of "spontaneous orders" which were never originated or designed by anyone. The market, for instance, is not a product of human design, and those guided by it usually do not know why they are made to do what they do. Literally, "they do not know what they are doing".[17]

To be concerned with objective knowledge then is to be concerned less with the original production of ideas, and more with their function and objective content, and with such matters as problems and problem situations, with the current state of a discussion or of a critical argument. It is to be concerned with the content, structure, function, growth, use, and development of the product known as knowledge. One can study the structure and function of knowledge objectively just as one can investigate the products of various animals. A biologist may become interested in the nonliving structures that animals produce – such as webs, dams, and nests; and the epistemologist may become interested in the nonliving structures, thought-structures, created by men. One can try to understand the chemical composition, the physical characteristics, the geometrical properties, the engineering soundness of a dam or a nest; and also the biological function of these structures in serving the survival of the species in question. Similarly, one can investigate the structure and function of a theory, its integration with other theories, whether and how it stands in relations of incompatibility with them, whether it solves a problem that has been posed in current discussion, its compatibility with observation, what its function may be in case it is retained in a situation where it no longer solves its original problem or is in conflict with the facts, and so on.

---

17. See Hayek, *Law, Legislation, and Liberty*, Vol. I (Chicago: Chicago University Press, 1973), esp. Chapter 2. It is not of course suggested that those engaged in the market have no information at all or that their behaviour is unintelligent. Quite the contrary, to be guided by and act intelligently on market prices they must be alert to changes in prices, and must have certain specific goals, such as attainment of profit and avoidance of loss. But they do not and often cannot know why and how prices are changing, and also cannot know the unintended consequences of the actions of themselves and others.

The nature of this latter sort of knowledge – an understanding of which demands a kind of connoisseurship of intellectual structures independent of any belief in them – is virtually unexplored in traditional epistemology, although contemporary evolutionary epistemologists are trying to remedy this. It can be shown, although I shall not do this here, that such objective knowledge is more basic and important than subjective knowledge, in the sense that problems of the subjective production of ideas can be understood only *after* acquiring a sound understanding of the nature of the structures or products themselves.[18]

One important characteristic of objective knowledge is that, once created, it takes on a life of its own and exists independently of or autonomously of any knowing subject. The larger part of objective knowledge arises as an unintended by-product of the production of other items (such as books, essays, and other cultural products). Like the path of the deer, these unintended by-products came into existence without being planned, and, once existing, may be put to uses different from any that would previously have been envisioned. What is crucial about an item of objective knowledge – a book, for instance – is its *potential* for being understood, or being utilized (whether by an entrepreneur in the market or an abstract thinker in the "marketplace of ideas") in some way that has not yet been imagined, a potential that may exist without ever being realized. Objective knowledge forms a major component of our ecological niche – which, itself, may be considered as a "field" of potentialities; it acts on it, interacts with the individuals living in that niche, and thus may transform the niche itself. And it develops in a way that is analogous to, although not identical with, the way in which biological growth, the evolution of plants and animals, occurs. The market order again is an example: it is an objective product which is not fully understood, a method on which mankind stumbled as a way of using individual knowledge to deal with the lack of total or comprehensive knowledge.

We are now in a position to return to Marx and the subject of alienation.

6. *Marx, Alienation, Autonomy, and Knowing What We Are Talking About*

Objective knowledge is autonomous in just the sense that Marx had in mind: it outgrows our control, crosses our expectations, and nullifies our calculations. Knowledge is a product not fully known to its producers.

As one simple example, one might mention how mathematics, once created, generates problems that are wholly independent of the intentions of its creators. The distinction between odd and even numbers, and such questions as whether there exists a highest prime number, are unintended consequences of the creation of the sequence of natural numbers. The history of mathematics is full of wonderful surprises and crossed expectations – as illustrated by the extraordinary

18. See Popper, *Objective Knowledge*, op. cit., p. 114.

discoveries of Gödel and Church relating to incompleteness and undecidability. Again, the question whether certain theories are incompatible is a matter of logic, independent of the question whether anyone has noticed any incompatibility or desires the theories to be one way or the other.

While all this is a bit abstract, it can be understood by noticing that it implies that *we never know what we are talking about.*

To put it differently, our knowledge is, at any given time, *unfathomed.* It is the unfathomed, and unfathomable, character of knowledge – more than anything else – that makes it impossible to meet Marx's demands.

When we produce and affirm a theory, we also propose its logical implications. (Otherwise we should not have to retract it when these come to grief.) That is, we affirm all those statements that follow from it – as well as further implications that result from combining this theory with other theories that we also propose or assume. But this means that the informative content of any idea includes an *infinity* of *unforeseeable* nontrivial statements. Thus the content of an idea is far from identical with some particular person's thoughts about it. For there are infinitely many situations, themselves infinitely varied, to which the theory may be applicable. Yet many of these situations have not only not even been imagined at the time the theory is proposed; they are also, literally, *unimaginable* then, in terms of the information then available.

For example, part of the informative content of Newton's theory is that Einstein's theory is incompatible with it; yet this could not possibly have been imagined at the time Newton proposed his theory; nor could the test situations or applications that eventually decided against Newton's theory have been imagined then – since such possibilities of observation and testing of *Newton's* theory became *conceivable* only after the invention of *Einstein's* theory. Einstein's theory postulated *new situations and possibilities* not previously imaginable. It in effect instructed physicists that there were certain places that they might look, places which they could, lacking Einstein's theory, not even have imagined, which would, when investigated, give results in conflict with Newtonian theory.

This means that even the inventor of a theory – Newton in this example – cannot possibly fully have understood it. Many historical examples attest the correctness of this observation. Thus Erwin Schrödinger did not fully understand the "Schrödinger equations" before Born gave his interpretation of them (and then he expressed dislike for them); and the content and application of these equations are indeed still a matter of controversy.

Since it is logically impossible, consciously or unconsciously, to anticipate such matters on the basis of what we know about the inventor or discoverer of a theory, it is absurd to think of knowledge-products in terms of "self-expression". The consequences of an idea may not only be unforeseen but also unwelcome to, *contrary* to, the uneducated self-expression of the inventor. The unexpected ramifications of one's own ideas about the world, about society, about the individual, about one's own aims and preferences, may – as one pursues them, as one works with them, as one adopts them as problems – have a radical impact on one's self-conception, and also on one's instinctive life.[19] Far from expressing one's old self and self-conceptions, they may be radically at odds with them. They may work *against* one's self-expression. (This is true even, or especially, of Marx himself: a writer uses his notes and diaries, his musings, just to transcend them and himself. It was after he had put down and worked through his early jottings and notes that Marx became ready in part to transcend his German Hegelianism, and to begin to publish in a very different vein. As the years went by, he dropped more and more of the Hegelian background. For example, after his encounter with Darwin's work in 1859 and 1860, he began to interpret dialectic not in Hegelian but in Darwinian evolutionary terms.)

Developing this result, we can say that expressionist accounts of knowledge production must fail in three fundamental ways. *First,* they suppose that there is a determinate core to the individual, of which his work and thought are an expression. *Second,* they neglect the objectively unfathomable depths of the product. And third, as a consequence, they are unable to capture the nature of the relationship between a man and his work. In sum, subjective, expressionistic approaches to knowledge misunderstand the nature of the individual self; the nature of intellectual work and creativity; and the nature of the relationship between the two. The result is altogether too passive and one-directional.[20]

We have just discussed the second point – the objectively unfathomable content of intellectual products or ideas – on which the entire argument hangs. To take the first and third points briefly in turn: the human self, while no doubt partly resulting from inborn dispositions, is also at least in part held together by theories: these help to provide its unity, its individuality, and its continuity; and it is rich, unfathomable, and growing to the extent to which these theories enjoy these characteristics.[21] Once one has acquired descriptive language, one becomes not only a subject but also an object for oneself: an object about which one can reflect, which one may criticize and change. Self-transcendence is a familiar and all-important characteristic of human life, and is attained in large part through the reflective criticism and examination of the theories that hold the self together; the destruction of some of those theories; and the creation of new theories in their place. Hence, for the reasons already mentioned, we can never fully know ourselves any more than we can know what we are talking about in other areas. For both poles are anchored in descriptive, theoretical, and hence unfathomable language.

19. For a good example, see J. D. Unwin's amusing introduction to his *Sex and Culture* (London: Oxford University Press, 1934). See also my "Ein schwieriger Mensch", op. cit., esp. p. 59.

20. See my "Wittgenstein and Homosexuality", op. cit., and the new Appendix to the German 2nd edition of my *Wittgenstein* (LaSalle: Open Court, 1985). See also the German translation (München: Matthes & Seitz, 1983).

21. See Sir Karl Popper and Sir John Eccles, *The Self and Its Brain* (New York: Springer Verlag, 1977).

The relationship between the unfathomable self and the unfathomable theories which it has somehow produced can then hardly be one of expression of the one by the other. Such an account fails to take account either of the nature of theory, or of the constantly changing flamelike quality of the individual, as expressed in his active cybernetic relationship with his cultural world, including his own cultural products, and the creative, unpredictable character that is intrinsic to that relationship. This relationship is one of give and take between the individual and the work; it depends upon "feedback" amplified by self-criticism. Such feedback is, as is evident from evolutionary theory, part of any growth process; so it is hardly surprising to find it here.

7. Why Our Products Must Escape Our Control

In other words, our autonomous products escape our control whether we like it or not. This is inevitable: and it would happen whether we "surrender" our products to another human being or try to keep them to ourselves. Because of their autonomy, our most important products are also potentially in conflict with our preferences, expectations, and calculations. Our knowledge is unfathomed.

The implications are profound and manifold. But for our purposes – with regard to the ideas of the early Marx – they mean this: *just as we never know what we are talking about, similarly we also never know what we are doing.* (Indeed, it is artificial to separate these two notions: talking, conceptualizing, estimating a situation, acting – these are intimately interwoven.) We cannot predict the consequences of many actions that we take, *including turning over our products to other persons.* It may well happen, as Marx supposed, that these products will be used by another *against* us. But they may also be used *for* us. Another individual – an entrepreneur, say – may take an idea or tool that we have made, discover in it something that we had not noticed, and develop it in a way that aids us. This benefit to us may also occur contrary to the intentions of the person who obtained it from us. No naive benevolence need be assumed. *For the recipient of our products cannot control them either.* These products continue to be autonomous: no matter who owns or "controls" them, they continue to "outgrow our control, cross our expectations, and nullify our calculations".

Hence it is absurd to characterize the process of exchange as Marx does. For we need one another to help objectify and probe our ideas and other products – and thereby to discover the potentialities of what we produce. Especially, we need to be able both to give and receive criticism and correction – not in order to dominate or humiliate one another, but to learn better what we have already produced. In science, and in intellectual life generally, this is supposed to happen through what is often called "the marketplace of ideas".

There is a profound difference here between Popper and Hayek on one hand, and Marx on the other. For the former, theoretical language provides man with an *opportunity* that permits him to dissociate from, to detach from, *to objectify and to alienate himself from* his own subjective states: to make them into *objects,* not subjective states, not identified with himself, which may then be examined. This process of examining such objects is precisely one of *rendering them strange,* and of passing beyond a merely subjective relationship with them. This approach allows us sometimes to "have done with" our subjective states, to pass beyond them, to become free of them, to transcend them. Whereas, for Marx, "objectification" is, as he says, "the practice of alienation" (p. 39); whereas "communism is the positive abolition . . . of human self-alienation" (p. 155).

The line of reasoning developed in this essay may well have been deeply unwelcome to Marx for yet other reasons having nothing more to do with logic than with sphincter control. Marx's concern with "losing control" of his products no doubt relates to what Hayek would call his naive or "constructivist" rationalism,[22] to the attempt to keep everything, and particularly economic events, under central control, whether individual or collective. Marx has to assume that the original producer understands his product best, indeed that it is perfectly well known to him, and that he can best plan for it, make the necessary decisions for it, control its destiny. For Hayek, of course, the object is not and could not be perfectly well known to its producer any more than some central planning board could enjoy total information and control; and there are mechanisms quite different from conscious control in terms of which the effective acquisition and economical use of such knowledge takes place (perhaps the least studied is the example of the market order in society). Even Kolakowski misses this point in his study of Marxism when he writes: "Exploitation consists in the fact that society has no control over the use of the surplus product, and that its distribution is in the hands of those who have an exclusive power of decision as to the use of the means of production." Yet these decision makers do not – and cannot – control the product either.

In his classic essays "The Use of Knowledge in Society" and "Economics and Knowledge",[23] Hayek shows how the market acts as a discovery process. There he identified, as one of the main problems of economic theory, the problem of how to secure the best use of dispersed resources, such as uncommon knowledge, such as information concerning temporary unique opportunities, known to some particular members of society but not available in its totality, even in principle, to any individual or any central board; and he argued that market competition makes fuller use of such existing knowledge than any other method, such as planning.

22. See Hayek, *The Counter-Revolution of Science* (Glencoe: The Free Press, 1955); *Studies in Philosophy, Politics and Economics* (Chicago: Chicago University Press, 1967), esp. Chapter 5; *New Studies in Philosophy, Politics, Economics and the History of Ideas* (Chicago: University of Chicago Press, 1978), esp. Chapter 1.
23. "The Use of Knowledge in Society", *The American Economic Review 35,* **4,** September 1945, reprinted as a pamphlet by the Institute for Humane Studies, Menlo Park, California, 1977; "Economics and Knowledge", *Economica,* N.S. **4,** 1937, both reprinted in *Individualism and Economic Order* (London: Routledge and Kegan Paul, 1949).

One can generalize Hayek's approach in full harmony with his intentions: the problem is not only how to utilize uncommon *existing* dispersed knowledge, but also how to elicit implicit and not yet fathomed knowledge – whether common or uncommon – in the product itself. Competition not only makes the best use of *existing* dispersed knowledge, but also generates new knowledge which *none* of the participants in the process yet possesses. In their interaction, the various participants can bring to bear their dispersed, specialized, individual, and different knowledge on the unknown and unfathomable object-product, and in this process they may discover more of its potentialities and utilize it accordingly. Better understanding of existing objective knowledge results from this competitive interaction, which is itself a knowledge production process. That is, the market process elicits or creates not-yet-existing knowledge about the already existing product, as well as creating new products. If there were a central planning board charged with the responsibility for maximally fathoming the unfathomable depths of existing objective knowledge, that planning board could hardly do better than to delegate the task to something like a market process, a process that could not only tap "uncommon knowledge" not available to any central board, but also use that uncommon knowledge in prospecting for new knowledge not yet available to anyone at all.

8. Acknowledgement and Alienation

Lest what I have just said be misunderstood, I should like to append briefly and incompletely a few remarks concerning the experience that Marx calls alienation.

I happen to believe that it is important to acknowledge what individual people do: their contribution to the processes and activities in which they engage. It is important to remember that, as Hayek points out, every individual does possess unique information and enjoys an advantage in that this information can hardly be used beneficially without his or her co-operation. People are made dreadfully unhappy – indeed, plunged into a sort of insanity – when their work is not acknowledged: when it or their co-operation is taken for granted. They also may become distraught when they are not acknowledged as individuals – when who they are, their humanity, is not acknowledged, as for example when their time is casually stolen by bureaucrats or their work is stolen by thieves or bosses or colleagues.

Appropriate acknowledgement will differ depending on the circumstances: sometimes payment of some sort is in order and also suffices; sometimes no payment, no matter how great, is enough; frequently a 'thank you' or credit of some sort, combined with common courtesy, suffices; sometimes the only fit acknowledgement may be loud and sustained applause. There are of course occasions when *no* acknowledgement could possibly *suffice* to pay tribute to a magnificent action or piece of work; but even then *some* acknowledgement, however inadequate and halting, is due, if only as a gesture in the direction of the impossible. In this context it is worth stressing that the contribution that ordinary working people make to our society often does go unacknowledged; such people are often taken for granted and also made to feel that they are taken for granted. And of course they are often exploited in other ways as well.

Those who do feel acknowledged and appreciated will often willingly and indeed with enthusiasm *give* their products away – provided that they suppose that by doing so they can make a contribution to the community in which they are living. It is often difficult to find a way in which to make a contribution, and thereby in part to overcome the sense that one's life *makes no difference.*

Although those who are *not* acknowledged in these various ways – or who do indeed feel that their lives make no difference – will often have the sort of experience that Marx refers to as "alienation", I have preferred, in stating my own simple, and perhaps simpleminded, views, to avoid his term as much as possible since there is so much mystification and partisanship connected with it.

What I have just written hardly exhausts the subject of alienation. I would like to add one final word about it, to emphasize that, although it may bring some pain, it is not entirely a bad thing. Quite the contrary.

Alienation – distance, separation – is produced in that social process of passing from the closed to the open or abstract society, a path that involves increasingly "abstract or depersonalized" relationships with our fellows.[24] This path involves great strain; and there is much to suggest that Marx himself suffered from it, and craved personal contact – as may be seen in the way he differs from Hegel in insisting that social institutions never suffice to mediate man's social essence, but that one must (again, to overcome alienation) have direct bonds of fellowship with individual fellow workers.

Yet, strain or not, such alienation or estrangement from nature, society, one's fellow men, *and oneself* is an essential part of growing up. We must detach from the womb – from the assumptions of our environment and our communities – in order to become independent persons, individuals. In this process we may come to look upon ourselves, others, and the world about us as strange and perplexing – as alien indeed. Marx, as a great humanist, wanted man to transcend himself, his past, his origins. Yet he did not comprehend that it is only through something like alienation that we can do any such thing: only through alienation is transcendence possible. And it is the objectivity and autonomy of our product that enable mankind to alienate him or herself from it, and thus to attain such transcendence.

9. The Sociology of Knowledge

The sociology of knowledge, our second theme, is closer to the line of thought that we have been pursuing than may be apparent.

---

24. See Popper, *The Open Society and Its Enemies,* op. cit., Chapter 10; and Hayek, *Law, Legislation and Liberty,* Vol. III, "Postscript". See also note 14 above.

Sociology of knowledge is quite diverse, but its practitioners typically are concerned to chart causal relationships between social interests and knowledge, to demonstrate that all knowledge is the expression of and determined by special interests, and is in the last analysis conventional. Marx himself, whose historical determinism cast ideology as a function of material conditions, is clearly the intellectual ancestor of a subject whose other chief figures include writers like Lukacs, Karl Mannheim, and Lucien Goldmann. But any strict dependence on Marx and Marxism is denied by sociologists of knowledge, and the basic ideas of the subject can no doubt be pursued outside the specific context of Marxism.[25]

Some of its early practitioners, such as Mannheim, had exempted some forms of knowledge, and in particular mathematics and the natural sciences, from their strictures, as able to be evaluated in terms of correspondence with reality independently of social context. But many current sociologists of knowledge are more consistent and often go further, putting all knowledge on an equal, socially contaminated, footing.

There is no doubt that social interests and interest groups, including academic professions, in various ways do affect and distort science, just as they affect other areas of ideology. Sociology of knowledge corrects naive popular conceptions of science that present the individual scientist as a "man in a white coat", as a wholly objective and passive observer of reality who is somehow immune to the sway of social and other influences.

Yet sociology of knowledge is badly defective; and it is equally naive in other respects. Most of it, despite its materialistic pretensions, is in the subjective tradition discussed earlier, and concentrates its attention on the production of knowledge while neglecting the nature, content, function, and structure of the knowledge product. Bringing to bear obsolete subjectivist methodology, and uneducated about crucial features of the product, it provides putative causal accounts of the genesis of products that not only fail to take account of but are incompatible with the nature of the products themselves. It could be decisively refuted, straightaway, by applying the arguments already developed above: ideas cannot simply be the expression of a social community any more than they can be so of an individual,

---

25. There is a vast literature on the sociology of knowledge. To start see Karl Mannheim, *Ideology and Utopia* (London: Routledge and Kegan Paul, 1936); Barry Barnes, *Interests and the Growth of Knowledge* (London: Routledge Direct Editions, 1977); David Bloor, *Knowledge and Social Imagery* (London: Routledge Direct Editions, 1976); Barry Barnes and Steven Shapin, eds., *Natural Order: Historical Studies of Scientific Culture* (London: Sage Publications, 1979); Martin Hollis and Steven Lukes, *Rationality and Relativism* (Cambridge: The MIT Press, 1982). See Popper's critique of Mannheim and the sociology of knowledge in *The Open Society*, op. cit., Chapter 23, and in *The Poverty of Historicism* (London: Routledge & Kegan Paul, 1957), esp. sections 21 and 23. See Hayek's critique of Mannheim in *The Road to Serfdom*, pp. 21, 68, and 158. The philosophers Jürgen Habermas, Michel Foucault, Richard Rorty, and Thomas Kuhn are also sometimes considered to be sociologists of knowledge. See Barry Barnes, *T. S. Kuhn and Social Science* (London: Macmillan, 1982); and Ernest Gellner, "The Paradox in Paradigms", *Times Literary Supplement*, April 23, 1982, pp. 451–52. For an account of bias in professional philosophical groups, see my "A Popperian Harvest", in Paul Levinson, ed., *In Pursuit of Truth* (New York: Humanities Press, 1982), pp. 249–89.

and for all the same reasons. Ideas are not fully known to their inventors or to the communities that originally sponsor them; they are autonomous and thus may turn out to have implications and unintended consequences contrary to the interests of their inventors or sponsoring communities. Ideas not only express the interests of communities; they often contradict and sometimes transform the interests of the communities in which they originate. Indeed, from a biological and evolutionary perspective, this is the distinctive function of ideas: we serve our survival by allowing ideas to perish in our stead, and thus we transcend our earlier selves, of which these ideas very possibly were indeed in some sense an expression.[26]

The reader will, however, easily be able to repeat and reapply *this* argument, in these only slightly different circumstances, for himself. I should now like to introduce a different kind of argument – an argument which, like those given above, concentrates on objective knowledge, but which, rather than considering again the unfathomable content of ideas to attain its objective, instead concentrates on what Donald T. Campbell calls the *structural* and *vehicular* characteristics of ideas. My discussion of the sociology of knowledge in this essay can deal with it only in broad outline, and will not treat individual practitioners.

10. Sociology of Knowledge Does Not Go Far Enough

Although it can indeed be shown that knowledge is, in some respects, deeply affected by social interests, sociologists of knowledge seriously overinterpret their results by studying social distortion of knowledge out of context, and failing to see that it is part of a broader problem.

Consider the nature of objective embodied knowledge. Earlier, we discussed the unfathomable content and consequent autonomy of knowledge products. Now we need to turn to something that has not yet been considered: namely, *the nature of the vechicles in which this objectively unfathomable knowledge is embodied.*

In order to make a statement about the world (or about anything else) one needs a vehicle or carrier for the message. For example, vehicles that are used to represent reality include paintings and various other art forms; and they include spoken and written language. Such vehicles cannot be avoided; and any such vehicle can distort the resulting representation or message. For vehicles all possess their own peculiar physical and structural characteristics – vehicular characteristics – that have nothing to do with their intended referent and may indeed even be alien to it; and these characteristics may intrude to distort the accuracy of the message.

---

26. See Popper, "The Death of Theories and of Ideologies", in *La réflexion sur la mort*, 2e symposium international de philosophie, Ecole libre de philosophie "Plethon" (Athens: 1977), pp. 296–329; and "The Rationality of Scientific Revolutions", in Rom Harré, ed., *Problems of Scientific Revolution. Progress and Obstacles to Progress in the Sciences* (Oxford: Oxford University Press, 1975), pp. 72–101. See also my discussion in the "Introduction 1984" to my *The Retreat to Commitment*.

A few simple examples can be given. The first comes from Donald Campbell's William James Lectures. Imagine a mosaic representation of a simple country scene: a meadow, say, with cows and trees and grass, and perhaps a frolicking lad and lass. This mosaic mural will be done in stone fragments which will, in one way and another, limit and distort the accuracy of the portrayal. The size of the stones, their smoothness and "shininess", the color and thickness of the cement used, the range of colors available, restriction to a two-dimensional surface, the requisite rigidity in the total structure, all may contribute to reduce the accuracy of the portrayal. This is obvious when color is considered: and both color and the illusion of three-dimensionality may be further distorted by the circumstances under which the mural is displayed: lighting, surface reflection, and angle of viewing will obviously affect both. The problem will be increased by the very size of the basic components, i.e., the stone fragments, themselves: it will be impossible to represent elements of the scene to be portrayed that are smaller than the smallest stone elements. The problem of rigidity is also particularly important: the vehicle cannot be unlimitedly flexible, but must be kept sufficiently inflexible to hold itself intact, even if this involves distortion of the representation.[27] At least this will be true if we agree that any representation, any map, even distorted, is better than none at all.

All this forms part of a general problem arising in all representation and familiar in common forms of representation even if not recognized as such. The phenomenon is perhaps best known as it appears in the small dots used in ordinary illustrations and newspaper photographs that are rendered with a photoprint screen. People who are unaware of the processes involved may not know that these dots are there; but they can quickly learn of their presence by taking an ordinary magnifying glass to any newspaper photograph. The photograph, like the mosaic, will not be able to reproduce any finer points of the object represented than are permitted by the net or screen being used. No matter how much the photograph of a politician is enlarged, the threads of his jacket will not become visible. Our neural apparatus, our retinal rods and cones, resembles a photoprint screen in some respects, and is similarly limited. As Konrad Lorenz, whom I cited in Chapter I, put the matter: "If one examines methodically what the cross-stitch representation permits to be stated about the form of the thing-in-itself, the conclusion is that the accuracy of the statement is dependent upon the relationship between the size of the picture and the grain of the screen. If one square is out of line with a straight-line contour in the embroidery, one knows that behind it lies an actual projection of the represented thing, but one is not sure whether

---

27. For an account of these structural and vehicular requirements, see Donald T. Campbell's manuscript "Descriptive Epistemology", William James Lectures, cited in Chapter I above. See also his "A Tribal Model of the Social System Vehicle Carrying Scientific Knowledge", in *Knowledge, Creation, Diffusion, Utilization*, Vol. I, No. 2, December 1979, pp. 181–201, and his "Varieties of Neurological Embodiments", in A. Shimony, D. Nails, and R. S. Cohen, eds., *Naturalistic Epistemology: A Symposium of Two Decades*, forthcoming.

it exactly fills the whole square of the screen or only the smallest part of it. *This question can be decided only with the help of the next finest screen."* [28]

One could give many interesting and diverse examples of the phenomenon – using language both spoken and written, mathematical notation, molding clay, magnetic tapes, photosensitive chemicals, plaster-of-paris casts, fixing processes in photography, the choice of woods and stone for sculpture, and so on – but the point has been made. As Campbell sums up: "The end product, knowledge, at its realized best, is some compromise of vehicular characteristics and of referent attributes." [29]

The next point is crucial: in order to correct such vehicular distortion, to re-move "noise" and static, and to increase the accuracy of representations using such vehicles, certain steps may be taken, and have been taken both in natural history and in the history of representation and engineering. In particular, what are called "monitor-and-modulate circuits" may be introduced. These "improve our picture of reality not by being new detectors of aspects of reality, but rather by trans-forming the otherwise detected reality on the basis of assumptions about the na-ture of the world built in in the course of biological evolution". [30] For example, when wave forms are being transmitted (as for example in radio), resonances of the transmitter substance typically get added to the message; and this may be corrected by filtering out specific vehicle harmonics. Of course in those cases where such harmonics were also part of the original message, the result may involve fur-ther distortions: for it was presumed in the correction that such harmonics are not part of the original message but were peculiar to the vehicle. Another exam-ple is the well-known Gestalt brightness and constancy mechanisms. [31] In our vis-ual system, an inhibition takes place of downstream optic nerve rates of firing in response to high levels of firing monitored upstream nearer the eye. Together with adjustment of the iris and other mechanisms, this effects a systematic im-provement of brightness and color constancy in the perception of objects by reduc-ing the distracting effects of changes in level of illumination. These constancy mechanisms are of inestimable value, and yet create distortions of their own, in-troducing a variety of contrast and optical illusions which simpler systems would not show. Cameras provide straightforward examples of how this can work. Ob-viously a sophisticated camera with a photocell light sensor that continually read-justs its aperture will generally take superior photographs; yet circumstances can be imagined and constructed wherein an old box camera with a fixed aperture would do a better job. Thus a photocell will interpret lightness and brightness

28. Konrad Lorenz, "Kants Lehre vom Apriorischen im Lichte gegenwärtiger Biologie", *Blätter für Deutsche Philosophie*, 1941, pp. 94–125; reprinted as "Kant's Doctrine of the A Priori in the Light of Contemporary Biology", *Blätter für Deutsche Philosophie*, 1941, pp. 94–125. See also the other refer-ences to Lorenz in Chapter IV above.

29. Donald T. Campbell, William James Lectures.

30. Ibid., p. 42.

31. See Lorenz's discussion in "Gestalt perception as a source of scientific knowledge", in *Studies in Animal and Human Behaviour*, 2 vols (Cambridge: Harvard University Press, 1971).

of the overall visual field in terms of presumed background illumination; but the photocell will fail in unusual situations as, for example, when contrast in brightness stems from the objects in question rather than from the background illumination.

In sum, as shown in the examples given above, steps taken to correct the vehicle's limitations and render its representation more accurate may have unintended, and distorting, effects of their own in certain circumstances. Yet, nonetheless, on the whole, however imperfectly and incompletely, these means of representing and carrying knowledge can be improved.

How does this relate to the sociology of knowledge?

The scientific community itself is obviously in some sense a vehicle or carrier of scientific knowledge, and is thus subject to the conditions just discussed – conditions that apply to all such carriers. That is, certain characteristics of the community, its structure and organization, may distort its product; and various correctives to that distortion may, in some circumstances, introduce further unintended distortions.

Some simple examples can be given. In order to further the conduct of science, a certain cohesiveness as well as proper acknowledgment is important. And recognition, awards, and incentives of various kinds are introduced to further this. This holds the community together – it serves the stability requirement that must be satisfied in knowledge vehicles – and contributes to its ability to function; but it also, by encouraging not only trust but also other ordinary human emotions such as ambition, may restrain criticism in some circumstances; it may further group loyalty, partisanship, and even dogmatism in others; and in some circumstances the result may come to resemble, even to be, a kind of tribalism. That is, particular vehicular characteristics, the sorts of things that are essential to hold any human community together, may result in distortions of knowledge, may work against its advancement.

Now if the problem that attracts sociologists of knowledge is distortion, then sociologists of knowledge need to take account of all kinds of distorting influences, those that attend all knowledge vehicles, and not only distortions of a social character. *Moreover they need to show why social distortion cannot be corrected, modulated, compensated for (however imperfectly), in the same kinds of ways that are possible in all other vehicles for knowledge and for human action.* Sociology of knowledge has not seriously attempted either of these essential tasks. To the extent that it neglects these tasks it is just sociology and ideology, not science. In restricting its attention to social distorters, the sociology of knowledge does not go far enough, and itself provides a distorted picture of the problem (should I say for its own social interest?).

To the extent that it is legitimate, the sociology of knowledge needs to be made a sub-branch of a more basic subject that might be called the theory of knowledge vehicles or – again – the theory of objective knowledge. This theory should include an account of what Campbell calls "optimal vehicles", an account developed on both physical and social levels, which could include, as an important part, a new social account of knowledge: an account dealing with the question of how to optimize the rules and practices of the community so as to diminish distortion; and which would also investigate the unintended distorting consequences of those very rules that are intended to diminish distortion. Elsewhere I have called this "the ecology of knowledge".[32]

Is there any reason to suppose that it would be impossible to do this even on the social level? I do not think so; on the contrary, there is every reason to suppose that academic and intellectual communities are at least as susceptible to correction of distortion as are other communities. I believe that all this relativism, conventionalism, cynicism, and hand-wringing about academic institutions governed and warped by special interests – and the resulting hopelessness about objective standards and truth – stems mainly from the archaic methodological and philosophical assumptions embedded in professional sociology; and that such conclusions would never have been reached had the investigation of academic institutions been initiated by economists rather than by sociologists.

To defend this claim would require a long essay, and I can indicate what I have in mind only with a few examples. As we have seen, vehicular and institutional problems of distortion, and the correction of distortion, are general, and are in no way confined to vested interests at work in the "knowledge community" and its particular vehicles. They arise, for instance, in politics, when political institutions are found to have departed radically from their original aims; or, on a more particular level, when policies are found to have produced results directly contrary to those intended. Hayek clearly indicated the kind of problem involved in the opening paragraphs of *Law, Legislation and Liberty:*

> When Mostesquieu and the framers of the American Constitution articulated the conception of a limiting constitution that had grown up in England, they set a pattern which liberal constitutionalism has followed ever since. Their chief aim was to provide institutional safeguards of individual freedom; and the device in which they placed their faith was the separation of powers. In the form in which we know this division of power between the legislature, the judiciary, and the administration, it has not achieved what it was meant to achieve. Governments everywhere have obtained by constitutional means powers which those men had meant to deny them. The first attempt to secure individual liberty by constitutions has evidently failed. . . . To me their aims seem to be as valid as ever. But as their means have proved inadequate, new institutional invention is needed.

The problems and program that Hayek indicates here have been pursued not only in his own work, but in the economic theory of institutions and by the "public choice theorists", such as James M. Buchanan, Gordon Tullock, William A. Niskanen, Jr., and Thomas E. Borcherding – thinkers concerned with such questions as why the state grows while increasingly failing to serve the interests for which

32. See my "Rationality, Criticism and Logic", Philosophia **11**, 1–2, February 1982, pp. 121–221, esp. sections III, IV, and XX; my *The Retreat to Commitment,* 2nd edition, esp. Appendices I and II; and Part II of the present volume.

it was created; or why, in terms of cost-benefit analysis, a society equips itself with one system of collective choice rather than another.[33] Public choice thinkers are attempting to develop a theory of collective choice, a *general* theory of the type that has already long existed for microeconomics. They frankly acknowledge, from the outset, the presence of special interests, and the tendency of individuals to advance their own goals. They reject the naive assumption, common in older political theory and some economics, that private individuals and enterprises are governed by avarice, whereas public institutions are run by high-minded idealists and upright civil "servants". If they were to turn their attention from government to the public and semi-public institutions of academic and intellectual life, they would at once insist that members of these institutions also tend to pursue their own self-interests, and are no more likely to be high-minded, objective, selfless searchers for – or "servants of"– the truth than are individuals in other professions or endeavours. So far, there is some agreement with the contentions of the sociologists of knowledge. There is another point of agreement: just as in discussions of classical economics the state tends to be absent, similarly in some pre-Kuhnian philosophy of science, educational institutions are hardly discussed. This is not so for Popper, who had attacked "Robinson Crusoe" individualistic approaches to scientific and social questions; but Kuhn does deserve credit for making methodologists more widely aware of the role of interested institutions and of the intellectual community in science, in the selection for advancement of one theory rather than its rival.

These points of agreement are interesting and encouraging. Yet there is utter disagreement between the sociologists of knowledge and the economic theorists of institutions – not only in basic philosophical and methodological assumptions (the public choice theorists tend to be deeply influenced by Popper and Hayek), but also about what can be done, about the possibility of correction and reform. Public choice theorists are reformers. While they conclude that western democracies are, at present, imprisoned in outmoded political technologies whose framework forces the state to expand while benefitting privileged classes of bureaucrats, they also contend that these same institutions can be reformed so as to come to channel individual self-interest, within an appropriate system of rewards and punishments, to produce what benefits the public at large, rather than to conflict

---

33. See James M. Buchanan, *Freedom in Constitutional Contract, Perspectives of a Political Economist* (College Station and London: Texas A & M University Press, 1977); *Cost and Choice: An Inquiry in Economic Theory* (Chicago: Markham, 1969); *The Limits of Liberty: Between Anarchy and Leviathan* (Chicago: University of Chicago Press, 1975); *The Calculus of Consent* (Ann Arbor: University of Michigan Press, 1962); Thomas E. Borcherding, ed., *Budgets and Bureaucrats: The Sources of Government Growth* (Durham: Duke University Press, 1977); William A. Niskanan, Jr., *Bureaucracy: Servant or Master? Lessons from America* (London: Institute of Economic Affairs, 1973); Gordon Tullock, *The Politics of Bureaucracy* (Washington: Public Affairs Press, 1965). For excellent popular accounts of this work, see Henri Lepage, *Tomorrow, Capitalism: The Economics of Economic Freedom* (La Salle, Ill.: Open Court, 1982), and *Demain le libéralisme* (Paris: Librairie Générale Française, 1980).

with it – and at no extra cost. In short, they believe that institutions can be evaluated in terms of their success or failure in guiding individual intentions to align with general interests. And they believe in the possibility of institutional, vehicular correction of interest-generated distortion.

Such questions of reform, when applied particularly to the intellectual community, demand answers to questions such as the following – answers which, taken together, would provide what I call "the ecology of knowledge". These questions are: How can our intellectual life and institutions, our traditions, and even our etiquette, sensibility, manners and customs, and behavior patterns, be arranged so as to expose our beliefs, conjectures, ideologies, policies, positions, programs, sources of ideas, traditions, and the like, to optimum criticism, so as at once to counteract and eliminate as much intellectual error as possible, and also so as to contribute to and insure the fertility of the intellectual eco-niche: to create an environment in which not only negative criticism but also the positive creation of ideas are truly inspired?

It is not easy to answer such questions, for existing scientific and educational traditions and even most institutions have evolved gradually; they are "complex phenomena": they enjoy a "spontaneously ordered" character and a usefulness that transcend anything that could have been produced by deliberate invention: they are the product of human action but not of human design.[34] Such spontaneous orders may also be fragile and difficult to maintain. Tampering with them is hence fraught with the danger of unintended consequences, with the danger of making things worse rather than better.

11. Marked Knowledge, Defective Knowledge

A first step in approaching such questions is to notice, to begin to identify, what existing traditions and institutions already contribute to goals of eliminating error and distortion and enhancing the advance of knowledge, and which ones work against those same goals. Some apparently trivial existing institutions – some linguistic institutions, for instance – which of course were never developed for such purposes, in fact serve them rather subtly, economically, and effectively. There is, for instance, what I call *"marked knowledge"*, which is a kind of evolutionary precursor to falsified knowledge. We often use standard qualifiers, such as the phrase "so-called", to *mark* concepts or theories or practices about which there is already some doubt or question, which are not yet examined properly, or which are for the moment out of fashion. There are many such markers: others are the use of the phrase "First Draft" to mark a manuscript that is being circulated for critical comments, or the phrase "trial balloon", which one may use self-deprecatingly to offer a fresh but as yet unexamined idea. This sort of device should

---

34. See Hayek, *Law, Legislation and Liberty,* op. cit.

probably be used much more often: it could only do good if every published manuscript were prominently marked "Damaged Goods". Or perhaps promoters of
ideas could, in their own self-interest, stamp them: "We are not sure that it is
in our interest to market these ideas or in your interest to accept them. *Caveat
emptor.*" The use of such markers in the marketplace of ideas proclaims to others
that we are savvy, critical, and aware of, or anticipate, such defects – or are at
least aware that there is some question about such ideas. We use such devices
to get optimum use out of such ideas: for our purpose is not to delete them too
fast, not to eliminate what might be called *defective knowledge* before we have got
as much as we can from it, but *just to mark it as defective.* Such knowledge can
be transmitted *so marked;* whereas in natural selection in nature, there is only deletion (extinction).

To begin to become aware of, and to face, such ecological questions is to begin
artificially to construct and to probe possible social environments for the advancement of science and learning, to imagine a constitution not only for liberty but
for learning. Paramount in such construction will be the ecological question of
balance – for evolution puts its three steps or rhythms (variation, retention, selective elimination) permanently at odds with one another in a matrix of essential
tensions.

In using the language of evolutionary theory to confront and treat problems
relating to the advancement of knowledge, one should not forget that the mechanisms of organic evolution and those of cultural and intellectual evolution are not
identical, despite their close parallels. We have already mentioned that marked
knowledge has no real organic counterpart. There is also no meta-aim governing
the evolutionary development of organisms in accordance with which variation
or lethal elimination needs artificially to be encouraged. The evolutionary development of ideas, however, may be governed by just such a meta-aim, a culturally
instituted "plastic control", namely: the deliberate production of variation and
the deliberate elimination of falsity and poor fit.

Such questions as these force the epistemologist out of the ivory tower, and
make of him a psychologist, an investigator of objective knowledge and its vehicles, a political theorist, a social reformer – even a sociologist of sorts. Since the
advancement of science and learning is not the only desirable goal of social life,
the epistemologist, like all social reformers, will meet with opposition and conflict, as well as with opportunities.

If the sociology of knowledge, as it exists at present, does not go far enough,
it also goes far too far. Its proponents frequently begin from the assumption that
knowledge can be *reduced* to social interest, and that objectivity and validity, progress in knowledge, critical rationality, and the quest for truth itself are illusory.
As the philosopher and sociologist of knowledge Thomas S. Kuhn puts it: "It
is precisely the abandonment of critical discourse that marks the transition to

science". The difficulties in this line of argument have often been discussed, and I have not repeated them here.[35] Rather, I have drawn attention to other strong arguments that are rarely noticed.

12. Concluding Remarks

In conclusion: what we think we know, the knowledge that we have, is unlikely to be right; even if it is right, it is autonomous, independent from us, and imperfectly known to us. *It is unfathomed knowledge.* And whether right or wrong, perfectly or imperfectly known, it is subject to distortion arising even from the very form in which it presents itself. Rather than being a cause for despair, these circumstances make sense of, give point to, rational investigation, the search for truth, and, especially, education. For the fundamental task of education is *unlearning:* making ourselves, and the ideas in which we conceive and create ourselves, strange, alien, to ourselves, and thus transcending our old selves.

Hence it is worth recalling that theories of education today often wrongly yet in accordance with the sociology of knowledge characterize the educational process as no more than a good opportunity, provided by the state, for teacher and student to express themselves. No doubt part of the intention is thereby to reduce alienation. But education, because of the nature of objective knowledge, is far more than organized mutual self-expression. It is at once the enactment, the reconstruction, and the creation of culture. The teacher must present a structure of knowledge that he does not fully understand to a student who also cannot hope fully to understand it. This is perhaps the smallest social unit in the "marketplace of ideas", but it illustrates, once again, how – despite all distortions – such a market acts as a discovery process. This is part of "The Use of Knowledge in Society". And it illustrates, again, that "we never know what we are doing".

35. See Kuhn's *The Essential Tension* (Chicago: University of Chicago Press, 1977). Many additional arguments can be turned on the sociology of knowledge. One, which interests me particularly, has to do with the justificationist form of argumentation, and the exploitation of the so-called "hermeneutical circle" which is common in such literature. (For this see my "Rationality, Criticism and Logic", op. cit., *The Retreat to Commitment,* and Part II of this volume.) Another is its dependence on reductionism and determinism. For a critique of the last two ideas, see K. R. Popper, *The Open Universe,* and *Quantum Theory and the Schism in Physics.*

Name Index

Ackermann, Robert, 71, 73 & n
Agassi, Joseph, 10n, 71 & n, 225n,
    228n, 229n, 243n, 244n, 272 & n,
    273, 314, 329n
Albert, Hans, 1, 174 & n, 285n
Alexander, Samuel, 157–58
Anderson, Alan Ross, 316n
Andersson, Gunnar, 279n, 280n, 287n,
    292n, 318n, 473
Aomi, Junichi, 1
Apel, K.-O., 285, 296–99, 300 & n, 301
Applebury, Meredith L., 128n
Archimedes, 284–85
Aristotle, 185–86, 325n, 337, 369, 378,
    420n, 421
Armstrong, D. M., 47n
Asch, Solomon E., 68n
Ashby, W. Ross, 47n, 56 & n, 57–58,
    65, 76, 92–93, 98, 109n
Atkinson, R. C., 51n
Auger, Pierre, 71
Augustine, Saint, 415n
Aune, Bruce 223 & n, 225, 226 & n,
    228n
Austin, J. L., 70n, 389
Avogadro, Amedeo, 13
Ayala, F. J., 8n, 24n, 41n, 146n, 425n
Ayer, Sir Alfred J., 16, 209–10, 227n,
    270 & n, 285 & n, 295, 300–1,
    308, 317 & n, 396, 424n

Babbitt, Irving, 364–66
Bach, J. S., 350
Bacon, Francis, 51, 53, 56n, 64, 183
Baehr, Wolfgang, 128n
Bain, Alexander, 64 & n, 96–97, 104,
    111
Baldwin, James Mark, 60n, 61 & n, 62,
    66, 68 & n, 73, 77 & n, 82 & n,
    85n, 92, 119
Bandura, A., 68n
Bar-Hillel, Y., 315n
Barber, B., 104
Barnes, Barry, 408–9, 442n
Barr, H. J., 47n, 55n, 83
Barringer, H. R., 70n
Barth, Karl, 285, 294–95, 302, 308,
    317 & n

Bartley, W. W., III, 1, 2, 28n, 121n,
    133 & n, 144n, 157, 159 & n, 205,
    219–20, 223, 225 & n, 226n, 229n,
    242 & n, 243 & n, 244, 247n,
    253n, 254 & n, 258 & n, 259n,
    260 & n, 261n, 262, 264, 265 & n,
    266 & n, 269–70, 271 & n,
    272 & n, 273, 275 & n, 276–77,
    279n, 280–81, 282 & n, 284n,
    285 & n, 289 & n, 293 & n,
    295 & n, 296n, 298–300, 301 & n,
    302–4, 305 & n, 307 & n, 308 & n,
    309, 313 & n, 314n, 366n,
    423 & n, 473
Bass, B. M., 68n
Bateson, Gregory, 9 & n, 10, 39n, 47n
Bekerman, Gerard, 426n
Bellarmino, Robert, Cardinal, 10
Benedict, Ruth, 386
Benjamin, Walter, 426
Bennett, Jonathan, 218, 225n, 325n
Bennett, Neville, 404, 405 & n
Beres, D., 352n
Berg, Charles, 406 & n, 407
Berg, I. A., 68n
Bergmann, Gustav, 158, 160
Bergson, Henri, 74 & n, 75, 157
Berkeley, George, Bishop, 9, 10 & n, 11,
    17n, 36, 52, 207, 340, 419–20
Bernays, Paul, 139, 307, 316n
Bernstein, Richard, 223n
Bertalanffy, Ludwig von, 21, 37n, 83, 86
Besso, M., 16n
Betti, Emilio, 368
Birmingham, John, 47n
Black, Max, 418n
Blackburn, R., 410n
Blackmore, John T., 9n, 10 & n, 11n,
    12n, 15 & n, 16n, 17n, 26n, 40n,
    42
Blackwell, K., 363n
Blanksten, G. I., 70n
Bloch, Ernst, 426
Bloor, David, 407 & n, 408 & n, 442n
Blount, Joseph, 246n
Blum, Alan, 410–11
Bocke, I., 363n
Bogomolni, R.A., 131n

Subject Index

Adaptation, evolutionary,
  active nature of, 137–38,
  sensation as means of, 35
Agency. *See* Free will or Agency.
Alienation, 425, 428–32, 435–41, 451
Alpbach conferences, 1, 2
Analytic-synthetic distinction, 248,
  323–24, 335–36, 341, and Part II,
  passim.
Animal knowledge and learning,
  no induction in, 50,
  self-programmed, 151,
  as a subject of epistemology, 52,
  88–89, 116
A priori knowledge, 79, 119–20
Aristotelian logic, 337
Arrow of time, 193–94
Atomic theory,
  as explanation of thermodynamics, 13,
  problem of entropy and, 13–14
Atoms, alleged non-existence of, 12–13

"Bandwagon/underdog" effect, 180–81
Behavioral programs. *See* Instinct.
Biology, philosophies of,
  acceptance of philosophy of physics
  within, 8n, 40
Bisexuality, 93
Bees, language of, 68–69, 120
Blind variation, 56–72, 91, 92–93,
  and vision, 95–96
Blind variation and selective retention,
  91, 93,
  of creative thought, 96–111, 288n,
  not random, 56–57, 66–67, 100,
  105–8, 117–18.
  See also Blind variation; Selective
  retention; Trial-and-error learning.
"Bootstrap mechanism", 181
"Breakouts" from available wisdom, 92,
  111
Brownian movement,
  as evidence for atomic theory, 14–15

Carotene, 30, 130–32
Categories, Kantian, 79–85, 119–20
Causality, problem of, 193, 207, 318
Causation,
  downward, 146–47, 152–53,

of human actions, 412
Choice, human, 412–21
Chlorella, 30, 129–30, 154–55
Chloroplasts,
  as original cell nuclei, 126
Circle, Hermeneutic, 180, 297, 369,
  451n
Cognitive structures,
  alleged incorrigibility of, 39, 74,
  of animals, 27–32, 86,
  comparative examination of, 34–35,
  differences among, 36–39,
  evolution of, 20, 372,
  and limitations of, 372. *See also*
  Sensations, unreliability of,
  as objective, 20–21, 189–90
Cognitive structures, vicariousness of,
  32–34, 38, 54–72, 73, 89, 94,
  language, 33, 68–70,
  vision, 57, 59–60, 67–68
Commitment, subjective, arbitrary,
  irrational, or ultimate, 3, 208–280,
  301–2, 317, 326, and Part II,
  passim.
Complexity,
  as argument against presentationalism,
  34
Complexity, problem of,
  and epistemology, 170–73
Computers, 66–67, 106–7, 111, 151
Comprehensively Critical Rationalism.
  See Rationality, comprehensively
  critical.
Conjectures and refutation, process, 50,
  179, 214. *See also* Trial-and-error
  learning.
Conventionalism, 85, 88, 188, 447
Creation,
  novelty of, 150. *See also* Emergentism;
  supernatural vs. natural, 140–43,
  special, theory of, 141–42
Creative thought, 91–111, 288n, 292n,
  blindness of, 96–101,
  and genius, 103–5, 111,
  not random, 105–8,
  as substitute for exploration, 96
Critical theory, 296
Criticism, 415–16, 449, and Part II,
  passim,

Contributors

Gerard Radnitzky (born 1921) is Professor of Philosophy of Science at the University of Trier, West Germany. He is the author of *Contemporary Schools of Metascience, Preconceptions in Research, Epistemologia e politica della ricerca,* and of many papers in the philosophy of science and in political philosophy. He is also the editor or co-editor of numerous volumes including *The Structure and Development of Science, Progress and Rationality in Science* (both also in German, Italian, and Spanish), *Die Selbstgefährdung der offenen Gesellschaft,* and *Die i-Waffen: Information im Kräftespiel der Politik.* Formerly Professor of Philosophy at the Ruhr University of Bochum, West Germany, and associate professor at the University of Gothenburg, Sweden, he has also been a visiting professor at the State University of New York at Stony Brook (1972), Fellow of the Japan Society for the Promotion of Science (1978), and has been Premier Assesseur of the Académie Internationale de Philosophie des Sciences since 1982. (Festschrift for his 60th birthday: Andersson, G. (ed.). 1984. *Rationality in Science and Politics.* Dordrecht: Reidel.)

W. W. Bartley, III (born 1934) is Senior Research Fellow of the Hoover Institution on War, Revolution, and Peace, Stanford University, where he is writing the biographies of F. A. von Hayek and Sir Karl Popper. He is the author of numerous books, including *The Retreat to Commitment; Morality and Religion; Wittgenstein;* and *Werner Erhard,* as well as of many papers in epistemology and the theory of rationality. He has edited *Lewis Carroll's Symbolic Logic,* and Sir Karl Popper's *Postscript to the Logic of Scientific Discovery,* and is now Editor of *The Collected Works of F. A. Hayek.* He was formerly Professor of Philosophy and of History and Philosophy of Science, and Associate Director of the Center for the Philosophy of Science at the University of Pittsburgh, and has been Associate Professor at the University of California, a Lecturer at the University of London (Warburg Institute and The London School of Economics), and a Fellow of Gonville and Caius College, Cambridge University. He is a member of the Mont Pèlerin Society and also of the Ludwig Boltzmann Institute for the Theory of Science in Vienna.

Donald T. Campbell (born 1916) is University Professor of Social Relations and Psychology at Lehigh University, and has previously been the State Board of Regents Albert Schweitzer Professor at Syracuse University, and the Morrison Professor of Psychology at Northwestern University. He has been a Fellow of the Center for Advanced Study in the Behavioral Sciences, Stanford; and a visiting professor at Oxford and at Yale. He holds seven honorary degrees, delivered the William James Lectures at Harvard in 1977, and has been President of the American Psychological Association. The recipient of many prizes, he is the author or co-author of *Experimental and Quasi-Experimental Designs for Research; Unobtrusive*

Measures: Nonreactive Research in the Social Sciences; The Influence of Culture on Visual Perception; Ethnocentrism: Theories of Intergroup Conflict, Ethnic Attitudes and Group Behavior; and of other books and many articles. He is a Fellow of the American Academy of Arts and Sciences.

Rosaria Egidi (born 1932) is Professor of Philosophy of Science (ordinario) at the University of Rome. She is author of many articles and books, including *Studi di Logica e Filosofia della Scienza* and *Il Linguaggio delle Teorie Scientifiche.*

Antony G. N. Flew (born 1923) is Emeritus Professor of Philosophy in the University of Reading, England, and Distinguished Research Fellow at the Social Philosophy and Policy Center, Bowling Green, Ohio. His many books include *Hume's Philosophy of Belief; Crime or Disease?; A Rational Animal and Other Philosophical Essays on the Nature of Man; The Politics of Procrustes; Darwinian Evolution; God and Philosophy; Evolutionary Ethics; The Presumption of Atheism;* and *Sociology, Equality, and Education.* He is also the editor of *Logic and Language* and of many papers. He has previously been Professor of Philosophy at the University of Keele, the University of Calgary, and York University, and has held visiting appointments at many universities.

Peter Munz (born 1921) is Professor of History at the Victoria University of Wellington, New Zealand, and is one of the very few persons to have been students both of Popper and of Wittgenstein. He is the author of many books, including *The Place of Hooker in the History of Thought; Problems of Religious Knowledge; The Origin of the Carolingian Empire; Relationship and Solitude - an Inquiry into the Relationship between Myth, Metaphysics and Ethics; Life in the Age of Charlemagne; Frederick Barbarossa: A Study in Medieval Politics; When the Golden Bough Breaks—Structuralism or Typology?; The Shapes of Time: A New Look at the Philosophy of History;* and *Our Knowledge of the Growth of Knowledge.*

Sir *Karl Popper* (born 1902) is a Fellow of the Royal Society, and in 1982 was named Companion of Honour by Queen Elizabeth II. For many years Professor of Logic and Scientific Method at the University of London (London School of Economics and Political Science), he is now Honorary Professor at the University of Vienna, Head of the Ludwig Boltzmann Institutes for the Theory of Science in Vienna and London, and Senior Research Fellow of the Hoover Institution, Stanford University. He holds fifteen honorary doctorates from American, British, Austrian, New Zealand, and Canadian universities, and is a member or honorary member of twelve academies, among them the three oldest. He is a member of the Order Pour le Mérite (German Federal Republic), and has received many prizes, including the Sonning Prize (University of Copenhagen); the Dr. Leopold Lucas Prize of the University of Tübingen; the Grand Decoration of Honour in Gold (Austria); the Gold Medal for Distinguished Service to Science of the American Museum of Natural History; and the Ehrenzeichen für Wissenschaft und

Kunst (Austria). He is the author of *Die beiden Grundprobleme der Erkenntnistheorie; The Logic of Scientific Discovery; The Open Society and Its Enemies; The Poverty of Historicism; Conjectures and Refutations; Objective Knowledge; The Self and Its Brain* (with Sir John Eccles, FRS); *Realism and the Aim of Science; The Open Universe; Quantum Theory and the Schism in Physics;* and *Auf der Suche nach einer besseren Welt.* He delivered the William James Lectures at Harvard in 1950 and is an honorary member of the Harvard Chapter of Phi Beta Kappa.

John F. Post (born 1936) is Professor of Philosophy at Vanderbilt University, where he has taught since 1965, and has been visiting professor at the University of Notre Dame. Educated at Harvard, the University of Wisconsin, and the University of California, Berkeley, he has held fellowships from the American Council of Learned Societies and the National Endowment for the Humanities. He is the author of many papers on logic, and is Advisory Editor for *The Southern Journal of Philosophy.*

Gerhard Vollmer (born 1943) is Professor of Biophilosophy at the Zentrum für Philosophie und Grundlagen der Wissenschaft in the University of Gießen, West Germany, and previously taught at the University of Hannover. He holds doctorates both in physics and in evolutionary epistemology, and is the author of *Evolutionäre Erkenntnistheorie, Was können wir wissen?: Die Natur der Erkenntnis* and *Die Erkenntnis der Natur;* and *Künstliche Intelligenz,* as well as of many scientific and philosophical papers.

Günter Wächtershäuser (born in 1938) has been working as an international patent lawyer in Munich since 1970 specializing in chemical and biochemical inventions. He has published numerous articles in organic chemistry, genetic engineering and in patent law.

John W. N. Watkins (born 1924) is Professor of Philosophy in the University of London (London School of Economics and Political Science), where he has taught since 1950. Educated at the Royal Naval College, at the London School of Economics, and at Yale, he is the author of *Hobbes's System of Ideas, Freiheit und Entscheidung,* and *Science and Scepticism,* as well as of many papers in philosophy. He is past president of the British Society for the Philosophy of Science, and was co-editor of *The British Journal for the Philosophy of Science* from 1974–79.